Study Guide

Thomas M. Beveridge
Durham Technical Community College

Principles of Macroeconomics

Ninth Edition

Karl E. Case
Ray C. Fair
Sharon Oster

Prentice Hall, Upper Saddle River, NJ 07458

VP/Editorial Director: Natalie Anderson
AVP/Executive Editor: David Alexander
Senior Development: Editor: Lena Buonanno
Editorial Project Manager: Virginia Guariglia
Production Project Manager: Lynn Breitfeller
Buyer: Nick Sklitsis

Pearson Prentice Hall™ **is a trademark of Pearson Education, Inc.**

10   9   8   7   6   5   4   3   2   1

ISBN-13: 978-0-13-605903-5
ISBN-10:   0-13-605903-1

Contents

Preface

This Study Guide has been developed to accompany *Principles of Macroeconomics* by Karl Case, Ray Fair and Sharon Oster. For students using Case, Fair and Oster's *Principles of Economics* (Chapters 1–36), the corresponding chapter and page numbers appear in brackets. When referring to specific pages, the *Macroeconomics* reference is given first. I have devised this Guide to help you as you learn the concepts that are presented in the text; if used consistently throughout your course, this Guide can enable you to master the material in what is likely to be your first economics course. In addition, you'll be given opportunities to learn how to apply these concepts in a variety of situations. Most economists stress the need to develop competence in three major areas—the application of economic concepts to real-world situations, the interpretation of graphs, and the analysis of numerical problems. This Guide gives you practice in developing each of these important skills.

I believe that learning how to apply concepts to our world creates a better and more long-lasting understanding of the material than mere memorization does. A reasonable goal for a noneconomics major is to have absorbed enough insight to understand the economic content of an article in a publication like the *Wall Street Journal* or *Newsweek*.

STUDY GUIDE CONTENTS

The Study Guide contains one chapter for each chapter in the text. In general, each chapter has two large sections and an Answers and Solutions section.

♦   The *Objectives* section tells you what you should be able to accomplish after you've studied the material.

It gives a summary of the chapter's important ideas. Each point is followed by some multiple-choice questions, so that you can monitor how well you're understanding the concepts. You'll find some applications and examples, along with specific learning tips, comments and "helpful hints." Concepts that may prove particularly troublesome are covered here. Many of these "tricks" and memory aids have been suggested to me by students. In most chapters I've also included a "Brain Teaser" related to the concepts to be covered in that chapter—an issue for you to chew over while learning the concepts. Also included are *Economics in Practice* features, extending those presented in the textbook.

♦   The *Practice Test* section contains *Multiple-Choice Questions* and *Application Questions*.

These questions provide opportunities to practice the skills—graphing, numerical analysis, and application of concepts—presented in the text. Go through this section thoroughly.

These exercises give you an opportunity to try your hand at using economic principles and practices—often in fairly complex situations. Do the problem sets in the textbook, too. Many of the *Multiple-Choice Questions* are quite tough. Think of each multiple-choice question as four true-false statements; don't just decide on the one "right" answer—determine why the other three options are wrong.

♦   The *Answers and Solutions* feature numerical and graphical solutions. Be aware, though, that real-world analysis is much more difficult to condense into such a simple form.

The textbook is divided into several parts. I've provided a Comprehensive Review Test for each part of the textbook. If you have problems with any of the questions on the review test, treat it as a red light—go back and review that material before proceeding.

STUDY RECOMMENDATIONS

I recommend the following procedure for using this Guide to improve your effective understanding and use of the key principles and practices from the text.

1.   Read the textbook chapter. There is no substitute for this step! Ideally, you should do this *before* the material is presented in class; in any case, *don't* wait until the day before your professor has scheduled a test! Use the *Objectives* section of the Guide to identify the key issues and to test your knowledge.

2.   Attend class regularly! In study after study, researchers have shown that regularity of class attendance is the single best predictor of performance.

3.   Now that you're acquainted with the material, use the *Learning Tips* to polish your understanding.

4.   Complete the practice sections to test your ability to utilize key concepts. If you fail to complete an exercise correctly, even after having seen the answers, reread the text. If you're still stuck, ask your professor for clarification.

5.   Before a scheduled examination, read the *Objectives* sections for review.

6.   Before a scheduled examination, do the relevant Comprehensive Review Test.

With a conscientious and consistent use of this Guide, you can improve your understanding of economics and your ability to use and apply the concepts contained in this field of study. Learning can be interesting, as well as enjoyable.

This Guide has been written with the hope that, after the final exam, it will have helped you to gain a better understanding of economic issues and analysis and of the exciting and challenging concerns that we must address in our contemporary world.

Best wishes to you with your study of economics. I hope that you will find it to be a rewarding and worthwhile experience, and that this Guide will stimulate you in your endeavors.

Please send any comments, brain teasers, or suggestions about this study guide to me, care of Economics Editor, Prentice Hall, 1 Lake Street, Upper Saddle River, NJ 07458.

Thomas Beveridge
Hillsborough, North Carolina

Acknowledgments:

I am grateful to the many students whose questions, through the years, have given me a better insight into the difficulties that arise when macroeconomics is approached for the first time. The practice material included in this Guide springs largely from such "after class" discussions.

The beneficial influence of Steven Pitts (Houston Community College) continues to be felt in the Graphing Tutorial in Chapter 1 and throughout the text. The efforts of reviewers and other correspondents have added much to the quality of the final product. Virginia Guariglia of Prentice Hall deserves credit for keeping things moving smoothly. Needless to say, any remaining *lapsi calami* are my responsibility.

This Guide is dedicated to Pam (my long-suffering wife of thirty years who drew the diagrams and orchestrated the formatting), to our son Andrew (who believes that the marginal propensity to consume exceeds 1 and who did much to disrupt this Guide's production), to the memory of my parents, and to that of Diana Fuerman Kongable, who would have enjoyed its attempts at humor.

ANOTHER STUDY RESOURCE FOR YOU

Here is another resource you can use in addition to this Study Guide to help you understand economic concepts and build your skills solving problems and exercises.

MyEconLab puts you in control of your learning through a collection of tests, practice, and study tools tied to the online, interactive version of the textbook, and other media resources. At the core of MyEconLab are the following features:

1. Sample Tests, two per chapter
2. Personal Study Plan
3. Tutorial Instruction
4. Graphing Tool

Sample Tests

Two Sample Tests for each chapter are preloaded in MyEconLab, enabling you to practice what you have learned, test your understanding, and identify areas in which you need further work. You can study on your own, or you can complete assignments created by your instructor.

Personal Study Plan

Based on your performance on tests, MyEconLab generates a personal Study Plan that shows where you need further study. The Study Plan consists of a series of additional practice exercises with detailed feedback and guided solutions and keyed to other tutorial resources.

Tutorial Instruction

Launched from many of the exercises in the Study Plan, MyEconLab provides tutorial instruction in the form of step-by-step solutions and other media-based explanations.

Graphing Tool

A graphing tool is integrated into the Tests and Study Plan exercises to enable you to make and manipulate graphs. This feature helps you understand how concepts, numbers, and graphs connect.

Additional MyEconLab Tools

MyEconLab includes the following additional features:

1. Economics in the News—This feature provides weekly updates during the school year of news items with links to sources for further reading and discussion questions.

2. eText—While you are working in the Study Plan or completing homework assignments, part of the tutorial resources available is a direct link to the relevant page of the text so that you can review the appropriate material and complete the exercise.

3. Glossary—This searchable version of the textbook glossary provides additional examples and links to related terms.

4. Glossary Flashcards—Every key term is available as a flashcard, allowing you to quiz yourself on vocabulary from one or more chapters at a time.

5. Ask the Author—You can e-mail economics-related questions to the author.

6. Research Navigator (CourseCompass™ version only)—This feature offers extensive help on the research process and provides four exclusive databases of credible and reliable source material, including *The New York Times*, the *Financial Times*, and peer-reviewed journals.

Part I

Introduction to Economics

1

The Scope and Method of Economics

Chapter objectives:

1. Define economics.
2. State four reasons for studying economics.
3. Distinguish between the concepts of opportunity cost and marginal cost.
4. Define market efficiency in terms of profit opportunities.
5. Make clear the difference between microeconomic and macroeconomic concerns.
6. Distinguish between positive economics and normative economics.
7. Explain the value of the *ceteris paribus* assumption within the context of economic modeling.
8. State the fallacies discussed in the text, give examples, and explain *why* such statements are fallacious.
9. State and explain the four criteria used to assess the outcomes of economic policy.
10. Construct and interpret graphs and linear equations.

Much of this chapter is devoted to setting out the framework of economics. Don't be overwhelmed and don't try to remember it all. Chapter 1 is simply a good place to gather together this information, which will be dealt with more fully as the chapters go by.

BRAIN TEASER: An increasing number of basketball players move directly to the NBA draft without graduating from college. Some, such as LeBron James, even go to the NBA straight from high school. James, the first pick in the NBA draft of 2003, went to the Cleveland Cavaliers with whom he signed a three-year, $12.96 million contract. He also signed a $90 million endorsement deal with Nike. What was the opportunity cost for LeBron James of choosing to go directly to the NBA, given that he was eligible for college?

SOLUTION: The answer to this and subsequent brain teasers will be found after our discussion of the learning objectives and before the Practice Tests.

 OBJECTIVE 1:
Define economics.

Because of conditions imposed by nature and the choices previously made by society, resources are scarce. Economics studies how we choose to use these resources to best satisfy society's unlimited wants. In a sense, economics is the "scientific study of rational choice." (page 1)

 Practice

1.   Which one of the following best describes the study of economics? Economics studies
   (a)   how businesses can make profits.
   (b)   how the government controls the economy and how people earn a living.
   (c)   how society uses its scarce resources to satisfy its unlimited desires.
   (d)   the allocation of income among different sectors of the economy.

   ANSWER: (c) All of the options represent aspects of the study of economics. However, the most general statement is given in Option (c)—economics is the study of choice. ∎

 OBJECTIVE 2:
State four reasons for studying economics.

A study of economics helps one to learn a way of thinking, to understand society, to understand national and global affairs, and to be an informed citizen. Essential to the economic way of thinking is the concept of "opportunity cost"—choices involve forgoing some options. Accordingly, the applicability of the economic way of thinking is very extensive. (page 2)

 OBJECTIVE 3:
Distinguish between the concepts of opportunity cost and marginal cost.

"Marginal" is a frequently used term in economics and it's important to understand it right away. "Marginal" means "additional" or "extra." "Marginal cost," then, means "additional cost."

Suppose you buy a nonreturnable, nontransferable ticket to the zoo for $10. This is not an additional cost. You've paid whether or not you visit the zoo.

Let's change the example a little. Suppose you win a free admission to the zoo and decide to go this Saturday. The trip is not entirely free, however. You still have to bear some costs—travel, for example. There is certainly an additional cost (caused by the trip to the zoo). It is a *marginal cost*. Suppose you always buy lunch on Saturdays. The cost of lunch is not a marginal cost as you'd have had lunch whether or not you went to the zoo. The cost of lunch is not contingent on the trip to the zoo—it's not an extra cost.

If wants exceed the resources to satisfy them, choices must be made and some alternatives must be forgone. You choose to visit the zoo this Saturday. The *opportunity cost* is the value of the activity you would have undertaken instead—that is, the next most-preferred activity. Perhaps it might be playing a round of golf or studying for a big economics test. The opportunity cost of the trip to the zoo is the value you attach to that *one* activity you would otherwise have chosen. (page 2)

Opportunity Cost and Marginalism: The "big concept" in this chapter is *opportunity cost*, with *marginalism* and *efficiency* a close second and third. You'll see all three repeatedly throughout the textbook. For practice on the concept of opportunity cost, try Application Questions 4 and 6 below in this chapter. For practice on marginal thinking, look at Application Question 7 below.

> ▶▶▶   LEARNING TIP: Any time you make a choice where one alternative is chosen over others, remember that an opportunity cost is involved. ◀

────────■────────────────────────── **Practice** ──────────────────────────────

2.   Your opportunity cost of attending college does not include
     (a)   the money you spend on meals while at college.
     (b)   your tuition.
     (c)   the money you spend on traveling between home and college.
     (d)   the income you could have earned if you'd been employed full-time.

     ANSWER: (a) You would have bought food whether or not you were at college. All the other expenses occur solely because of attending college.

3.   _____ may be defined as the extra cost associated with an action.
     (a)   Marginal cost
     (b)   Operational cost
     (c)   Opportunity cost
     (d)   Action cost

     ANSWER: (a) Refer to p. 2. Marginalism is a fundamental tool of economic analysis.

4.   Jean owns a French restaurant—*La Crème*. Simply to operate this week, he must pay rent, taxes, wages, food costs, and so on. This amounts to $1,000 per week. This evening, a diner arrives and orders a bottle of Château Neuf du Pape wine to go with her meal. Jean has none and sends out to Wine World for a bottle. It costs $20, and Jean charges his guest $30. Which of the following is true for Jean?
     (a)   The marginal cost of the wine is $20.
     (b)   The marginal cost of the wine is $30.
     (c)   The efficiency cost of the meal is $1,020.
     (d)   The efficiency cost of the meal is $1,030.

     ANSWER: (a) The up-front expense is $1,000. The extra cost that Jean bears for buying the wine is $20. "Efficiency cost" is not a real term. ■

ECONOMICS IN PRACTICE: Your textbook offers (page 6), as its example of "economics in practice" for this chapter, the case of Apple's iPod. Where is it manufactured? It's a more difficult question to answer than it might at first appear. Our northern neighbor and most important trading partner, Canada, imports 34% of its merchandise. Although the United States imports only 15% of its overall production, most of the goods that you buy do contain "foreign content". Can you think of any goods that are purely domestically produced? Of course, we don't buy only goods? What else do we buy? Are those items more likely to be domestically produced and, if so, why?
ANSWER: Agricultural produce, perhaps bought at a farmers' market, is (almost by definition) "home-grown). Even here, though, the labor used to harvest the crop may be foreign, as may other factors used in production, such as oil or fertilizer. Goods frequently have high levels of foreign content, but this is less true of services. Although your computer support may originate in Banglalore, India, your hairdresser, car mechanic or accountant offers services with a high domestic content. Services are more likely to have a relatively high domestic content because it's usually more difficult to transport services than goods.

OBJECTIVE 4:
Define market efficiency in terms of profit opportunities.

The rapid elimination of profit opportunities is a signal that a market is operating efficiently. The stock market is a good example. If a firm's stock is priced "too low," increased bidding will drive the price higher, eliminating the excess profits. At a farmers' market, Farmer Brown may charge $1.20 for a dozen eggs, although the going rate is $1.00. She might make excess profits for a while, but this will not persist in an efficient market. This means that sustained high profits indicate the presence of an inefficient market. (page 3)

 OBJECTIVE 5:
Make clear the difference between microeconomic and macroeconomic concerns.

Economics is split into two broad parts. *Microeconomics* focuses on the operation of individual markets and the choices of individual economic units (firms and households). *Macroeconomics* deals with broad economic variables such as national production, total consumer spending, and overall price movements. Economics also contains a number of subfields, such as international economics, labor economics, and industrial organization. (page 7)

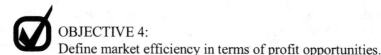 Practice

5.   **Macroeconomics** approaches the study of economics from the viewpoint of
      (a)   individual consumers.
      (b)   the government.
      (c)   the entire economy.
      (d)   the operation of specific markets.
      ANSWER: (c) Macroeconomics looks at the big picture—the entire economy.

6.   **Microeconomics** approaches the study of economics from the viewpoint of
      (a)   the entire economy.
      (b)   the government.
      (c)   the operation of specific markets.
      (d)   the stock market.
      ANSWER: (c) Microeconomics examines what is happening with individual economic units (households and firms) and how they interact in specific markets.

7.   Which of the following is most appropriately a microeconomic issue?
      (a)   The study of the relationship between the unemployment rate and the inflation rate
      (b)   The forces determining the price level in an individual market
      (c)   The determination of total output in the economy
      (d)   The aggregate behavior of all decision-making units in the economy
      ANSWER: (b) Microeconomics examines what is happening with individual economic units (households and firms) and how they interact in specific markets. ■

 OBJECTIVE 6:
Distinguish between positive economics and normative economics.

Economists classify issues as either positive or normative. Positive questions explore the behavior of the economy and its participants without judging whether the behavior is good or bad. *Positive economics* collects data that describe economic phenomena (descriptive economics) and constructs testable (cause-and-effect) theories to explain the phenomena (economic theory). *Normative economic questions* evaluate the results of behavior and explore whether the outcomes might be improved. (page 10)

────■─────────────────────────────── **Practice** ────────────────────────────────

8.   A difference between positive statements and normative statements is that
      (a)   positive statements are true by definition.
      (b)   only positive statements are subject to empirical verification.
      (c)   economists use positive statements and politicians use normative statements when discussing economic matters.
      (d)   positive statements require value judgments.

      ANSWER: (b)   A positive statement is not necessarily true by definition and can be disproved by empirical verification. ■

 OBJECTIVE 7:
Explain the value of the *ceteris paribus* assumption within the context of economic modeling.

Economists (and other scientists) construct models—formal statements of relationships between variables of interest—that simplify and abstract from reality. Graphs, words, or equations can be used to express a model. In testing the relationships between variables within a model it is convenient to assume *ceteris paribus*, that all other variables have been held constant. (page 11)
      Models focus on the most essential elements under examination. Distracting real-world detail is set aside. Many factors may have affected your decision to buy Case, Fair and Oster's textbook—theory attempts to isolate the key factors.

────■─────────────────────────────── **Practice** ────────────────────────────────

9.   "An increase in the price of shampoo will cause less shampoo to be demanded, *ceteris paribus*."
      Ceteris paribus means that
      (a)   there is a negative relationship between the price and quantity demanded of shampoo.
      (b)   the price of shampoo is the only factor that can affect the amount of shampoo demanded.
      (c)   other factors may affect the amount of shampoo demanded but that these are assumed not to change in this analysis.
      (d)   the price of shampoo is equal for all buyers.

      ANSWER: (c)   The price of shampoo is equal for all buyers, and there may be a negative relationship between the price and quantity of shampoo demanded, but *ceteris paribus* means that any other factors that may affect the amount of shampoo demanded are assumed to be constant. ■

OBJECTIVE 8:
State the fallacies discussed in the text, give examples, and explain *why* such statements are fallacious.

Beware false logic! The *fallacy of composition* involves the claim that what is good for one individual remains good when it happens for many. If one farmer gains by having a bumper harvest it *doesn't* mean that all farmers will gain if each has a bumper crop. The *post hoc, ergo propter hoc* fallacy occurs when we assume that an event that happens after another is caused by it. (page 12)

Two examples of the fallacy of composition: One person at a football game who stands up to see a good play derives a benefit—therefore, all will benefit similarly if the entire crowd stands up. Running to the exit when there is a fire in a theater will increase your chances of survival—therefore, in a fire, we should all run for the exit.

 **Practice**

10.   Which of the following is **not** an example of the fallacy of composition?
   (a)   Jane leaves work at 4:00 each day and avoids the rush-hour traffic at 5:00. Therefore, if businesses regularly closed at 4:00, all commuters would avoid the rush-hour traffic.
   (b)   John stands up so that he can see an exciting football play. Therefore, if the entire crowd stands up when there is an exciting play, all spectators will get a better view.
   (c)   Because society benefits from the operation of efficient markets, IBM will benefit if markets become more efficient.
   (d)   Because Mary on her own can escape from a burning building by running outside, individuals in a crowded movie theater are advised to run outside when there is a fire.

   ANSWER: (c) This example is arguing from the general to the specific. The fallacy of composition argues from the specific to the general. ■

 OBJECTIVE 9:
State and explain the four criteria used to assess the outcomes of economic policy.

Economists construct and test models to aid policy making. Policy makers generally judge proposals in terms of efficiency, equity (fairness), growth, and stability. (page 14)

 **Practice**

11.   The nation of Arboc claims to have achieved an equitable distribution of income among its citizens. On visiting Arboc, we would expect to find that
   (a)   each citizen receives the same amount of income.
   (b)   Arbocali residents believe that the distribution of income is fair.
   (c)   Arbocali residents believe that the distribution of income is equal.
   (d)   each citizen receives the amount of income justified by the value of his or her contribution to production.

   ANSWER: (b) Whether or not the distribution of income is equitable depends on what Arbocali citizens believe to be fair.

Use the following information to answer the next two questions. Nicola and Alexander each have some dollars and some apples. Nicola values a pound of apples at $3 whereas Alexander values a pound of apples at $1.

12.   In which of the following cases has an allocatively efficient trade taken place?
   (a)   The market price of apples is $3 per pound. Nicola sells apples to Alexander.
   (b)   The market price of apples is $1 per pound. Nicola sells apples to Alexander.
   (c)   The market price of apples is $2 per pound. Nicola sells apples to Alexander.
   (d)   The market price of apples is $2 per pound. Alexander sells apples to Nicola.

   ANSWER: (d)   When the market price of apples is $2 per pound and Alexander is the seller, he gains $1. Nicola also gains because she receives goods she values at $3 for a payment of only $2.

13.   In which of the following cases has an allocatively efficient trade **not** taken place?
   (a)   The market price of apples is $3 per pound. Alexander sells apples to Nicola.
   (b)   The market price of apples is $1.50 per pound. Alexander sells apples to Nicola.
   (c)   The market price of apples is $1.50 per pound. Nicola sells apples to Alexander.
   (d)   The market price of apples is $2 per pound. Alexander sells apples to Nicola.

   ANSWER: (c)   An efficient trade can occur only when some participant is better off and no participant is worse off (or if the gainer can adequately compensate the loser). In Option (a), Alexander gains $2 and Nicola does not lose. In Option (b), Nicola and Alexander both gain. In Option (d), Alexander and Nicola both gain. In Option (c), Alexander gains 50¢ but Nicola loses $1.50. ■

 OBJECTIVE 10 (APPENDIX):
Construct and interpret graphs and linear equations.

Economic graphs depict the relationship between variables. A curve with a "rising" (positive) slope indicates that as one variable increases, so does the other. A curve with a "falling" (negative) slope indicates that as one variable increases in value, the other decreases in value. Slope is easily measured by "rise over run"—the extent of vertical change divided by the extent of horizontal change. (page 18)

   ▶▶   LEARNING TIP: It is a natural tendency to shy away from graphs—they may seem threatening—but this is a mistake. To work with economic concepts, you must master all the tools in the economist's tool kit. Economists almost automatically begin to scribble diagrams when asked to explain ideas, and you'll need to learn how to use the tools of the trade. In economics, graphs often feature financial variables like "price," "the interest rate," or "income." Usually the dependent variable is placed on the vertical axis and the independent variable on the horizontal axis. In graphing economic variables, it's a pretty safe bet that the *financial* variable will go on the vertical axis every time. Application Questions 9 and 10 and the Graphing Tutorial below offer some graphing practice.◀

   ▶▶   LEARNING TIP: Examine the graphs you see accompanying economics-based articles in the daily newspaper or news magazines. It's common to find examples of deceptive graphs, especially when variables are being compared over time. A graph comparing, say, the difference between government spending and tax revenues can be quite misleading if the vertical axis does not start at zero.◀

———————————————————————— **Practice** ————————————————————————

Use the following diagram to answer the next four questions.

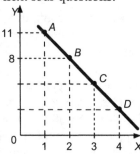

14.   In the diagram, the slope of the line is
(a)   positive and variable.
(b)   positive and constant.
(c)   negative and variable.
(d)   negative and constant.

ANSWER: (d) The diagram shows a straight line—straight lines have a constant slope. Visually, or by using the "rise over run" formula, the relationship is negative because, as one variable increases in value, the other decreases in value.

15.   The slope of line between Point A and Point B is
(a)   3.
(b)   1/3.
(c)   –3.
(d)   –1/3.

ANSWER: (c) Use the "rise over run" formula. The rise is –3 (from 11 to 8) and the run is +1 (from 1 to 2).

16.   At Point D, the value of Y is
(a)   –3.
(b)   3.
(c)   5.
(d)   2.

ANSWER: (d) As X "steps up" in value by 1, Y "steps down" in value by 3. At Point B, X has a value of 2 and Y has a value of 8. Moving to Point D, X increases by 2 and Y decreases by 6, from 8 to 2.

17.   In the diagram, when the line reaches the vertical (Y) axis the value of Y will be
(a)   3.
(b)   8.
(c)   11.
(d)   14.

ANSWER: (d) As X "steps down" in value by 1, Y "steps up" in value by 3. At Point A, X has a value of 1 and Y has a value of 11. X decreases by 1 and Y increases by 3, from 11 to 14. ■

BRAIN TEASER SOLUTION: James's opportunity cost was the value of the next most-preferred alternative to going to the NBA. We might assume that that choice would be college. Was it a sensible choice for him? In fact, it's a no-brainer. Taking only the three-year contract amount of $12.96 million, and dividing by 40 (earning years), James would have to have averaged $324,000 per year from his college degree to match his earnings. You should note that the present discounted value of those earnings decades into the future will be significantly less than $324,000. Also, we are ignoring any earnings James might have made in addition to the sum from the player's contract, for example, the Nike endorsement or income from future contracts. So, not only was LeBron James a talented basketball player, but he had a solid grasp of economics!

PRACTICE TEST

I.   MULTIPLE-CHOICE QUESTIONS

Select the option that provides the single best answer.

_____ 1.   Local farmers reduce the price of their tomatoes at the farmers' market. The price of corn is 30¢ per ear. A passing economist theorizes that, *ceteris paribus*, buyers will purchase more tomatoes than before. Which of the following is TRUE? The economist is
(a)   implying that the price of tomatoes will fall even further.
(b)   assuming that the price of corn will remain at 30¢ per ear.
(c)   assuming that tomatoes are of a better quality than before.
(d)   implying that corn is of a poorer quality than before.

_____ 2.   Which of the following is **not** given in the textbook as a criterion for judging the results of economic policy?
(a)   Economic stability
(b)   Employment
(c)   Efficiency
(d)   Equity

_____ 3.   Economic growth may occur if
(a)   more machines become available.
(b)   more workers become available.
(c)   workers become more efficient.
(d)   All of the above

_____ 4.   Economics is the study of how
(a)   scarce resources are used to satisfy unlimited wants.
(b)   we choose to use unlimited resources.
(c)   limitless resources are used to satisfy scarce wants.
(d)   society has no choices.

_____ 5.   The opportunity cost of Choice *X* can be defined as
(a)   the cheapest alternative to Choice *X*.
(b)   the most highly valued alternative to Choice *X*.
(c)   the price paid to obtain *X*.
(d)   the most highly priced alternative to Choice *X*.

_____ 6.   In economics, efficiency means that
(a)   income is distributed equally among all citizens.
(b)   there is a low level of inflation and full unemployment of economic resources.
(c)   total productivity is increasing at a constant and equal rate within each sector of the economy.
(d)   the economy is producing those goods and services that citizens desire and is doing so at the least possible cost.

_____ 7.   Which of the following statements is true?
(a)   Microeconomics studies consumer behavior, whereas macroeconomics studies producer behavior.
(b)   Microeconomics studies producer behavior, whereas macroeconomics studies consumer behavior.
(c)   Microeconomics studies behavior of individual households and firms, whereas macroeconomics studies national aggregates.
(d)   Microeconomics studies inflation and opportunity costs, whereas macro-economics studies unemployment and marginal costs.

_____ 8.   Which of the following statements is true?
(a)   There is a positive relationship between the price of a product and the quantity demanded.
(b)   There is a positive relationship between the number of umbrellas bought and the amount of rainfall.
(c)   There is a negative relationship between height and weight.
(d)   There is a negative relationship between sales of ice cream and noon temperature.

_____ 9.   Oliver Sudden discovers that if he cuts the price of his tomatoes at the farmers' market, his sales revenue increases. Expecting similar results, all the other tomato sellers follow his example. They are guilty of committing
(a)   the fallacy of composition.
(b)   the fallacy of *post hoc, ergo propter hoc*.
(c)   the fallacy of correlation.
(d)   *ceteris paribus*.

_____ 10.   The quantity of six-packs of Quite Lite beer demanded per week (Qd) in Hometown is described by the following equation:

$$Qd = 400 - 100P,$$

where P (in dollars) is the price of a six-pack. This equation predicts that
(a)   300 six-packs will be bought this week.
(b)   a $1 rise in price will cause 100 more six-packs to be bought this week.
(c)   300 six-packs will be bought per $100 this week.
(d)   a 50¢ rise in price will cause 50 fewer six-packs to be bought this week.

_____ 11.   The *ceteris paribus* assumption is used to
(a)   make economic theory more realistic.
(b)   make economic analysis more realistic.
(c)   avoid the fallacy of composition.
(d)   focus the analysis on the effect of a single factor.

Use the following diagram below to answer the next four questions.

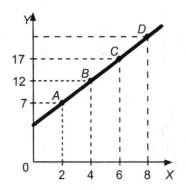

_____ 12. In the preceding diagram, the slope of the line is
   (a)   positive and variable.
   (b)   positive and constant.
   (c)   negative and variable.
   (d)   negative and constant.

_____ 13. In the preceding diagram, the slope of the line between Point *A* and Point *B* is
   (a)   5/2.
   (b)   2/5.
   (c)   –2/5.
   (d)   –5/2.

_____ 14. In the preceding diagram, at Point *D*, the value of *Y* is
   (a)   5.
   (b)   8.
   (c)   19.5.
   (d)   22.

_____ 15. In the preceding diagram, when the line reaches the vertical (*Y*) axis the value of *Y* will be
   (a)   2.
   (b)   5/2.
   (c)   7.
   (d)   12.

Use the following diagrams to answer the next four questions.

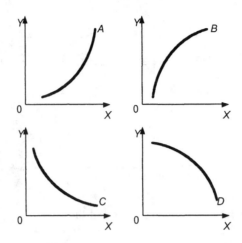

_____   16.   Of the four curves, which curve has a slope that is negative and decreasing?
(a)   A
(b)   B
(c)   C
(d)   D

_____   17.   Of the four curves, which curve has a slope that is positive and increasing?
(a)   A
(b)   B
(c)   C
(d)   D

_____   18.   Of the four curves, which curve has a slope that is positive and decreasing?
(a)   A
(b)   B
(c)   C
(d)   D

_____   19.   Of the four curves, which curve appears to be described by the equation $y = x^2$?
(a)   A
(b)   B
(c)   C
(d)   D

_____   20.   During the debate about balancing the federal government's budget, it was proposed that Medicaid benefits be reduced. This proposal was criticized because low-income families (who receive Medicaid) would spend a higher percentage of their income on medical services than high-income families would spend. This argument was based on concerns about
(a)   economic growth.
(b)   efficiency.
(c)   economic stability.
(d)   equity.

_____ 21.   The Channel Tunnel, linking the United Kingdom and France, was originally planned to cost $100 million. After work had begun and the two excavators were under the English Channel, with $70 million already spent, the estimate of the total bill was revised to $150 million. At this point the marginal cost of completion was best estimated as
   (a) $30 million.
   (b) $50 million.
   (c) $70 million.
   (d) $80 million.

II.   APPLICATION QUESTIONS

1.   The small nation of Smogland is unhappily situated in a valley surrounded by mountains. Smogland's Secretary of the Environment has determined that there are 4,000 cars in operation, each of which pollutes the air. In fact, Smogland's air is so unhealthy that it is rated as "hazardous." If emission controls, costing $50 per car, are introduced, the air quality will improve to a rating of "fair." A survey has revealed that of the 40,000 inhabitants, 10,000 would value the air quality improvement at $5 each, and the other 30,000 would value it at $7 each. The Secretary of the Environment has asked you to analyze the issue and make a recommendation. Should emission controls be introduced?

2.   Refer to the following diagram, which plots inflation rate and unemployment rate.

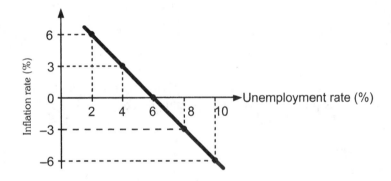

   (a)   Construct a table from the data presented in the diagram.
   (b)   Calculate the slope of the line.
   (c)   What is the inflation rate when the unemployment rate is 9%?
   (d)   What is the inflation rate when the unemployment rate is 5%?

3.   What are some elements of the opportunity cost of "clean" air? In total, the "cost" of cleaner air increases as we remove more and more pollution. Do you think, however, that the extra (marginal) cost of cleaner air increases as we progressively remove pollution? Graph the behavior of "extra cost" (vertical axis) and "cleanness of air" (horizontal axis).

4.   Suppose that the opportunity cost of attending today's economics class is study time for a math test. By not studying you will lose 15 points on your test. Attending the econ. class will increase your future econ. test score by no more than three points. Was your choice—to attend the econ. class—rational?

5.   You have a summer internship in a bank just before your senior year. You are "noticed" and are offered a full-time position in the bank, with a salary of $35,000 a year. A rival bank, keen to attract you, offers you $37,000 for a similar position. After much thought, you decide to return to college to complete your economics degree. Based on the information given, what was the opportunity cost of your decision?

If you had chosen one of the banking jobs instead of resuming your studies, how could you have explained your decision to your parents, who would have pointed out that you would have "wasted" three years of college?

6.   Choose a local natural resource with which you are familiar, e.g., an acre of farmland or a nearby lake.
(a)   List three alternative uses for your chosen raw material.
(b)   Choose one of the three uses. What is the opportunity cost of this use? Should you include the cost of clean-up (if this is appropriate) following use?
(c)   Is the resource renewable or not? If not, should this be factored into your calculations?
(d)   Describe how your community has chosen to use the resource so far, if at all. Who and what have determined that choice?

7.   You're offered three deals, each of which will give you $11 in return for $8. Your profit will be $3 in each case. *Deal A* is a straight swap—$11 for $8.
Deal B involves four steps and you can quit at any point.
Step 1. $5 in exchange for $2
Step 2. $3 for $2
Step 3. $2 for $2
Step 4. $1 for $2
What would you do? Go all the way through the four steps and collect a total of $3 profit? A better solution, stopping after two steps, would yield $4.
Deal C also involves four steps.
Step 1. $4 in exchange for $1
Step 2. $4 for $2
Step 3. $2 for $2
Step 4. $1 for $3
Would you collect your $3 profit or stop after two steps and gain $5?
Moral: If you assess the effects of extra (marginal) steps, you can raise your profits above $3. Without examining each step, the chance of greater profits would have been missed.

8.   Using your intuition, graph each of the following relationships in the space below.
       (a)   Height and weight of adult females.
       (b)   Height and weight of adult males (on the same graph).

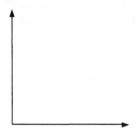

       (c)   Do these lines have a positive slope or negative slope?
       (d)   Have you drawn the relationships differently? If so, why? By referring to your own observations, you have constructed a model!
       (e)   Which factors have you "held constant"?
       (f)   (i)   In the space following, sketch the relationship between the price of California wine and the consumption of California wine. Use your intuition.
              (ii)   According to your theory and your diagram, is there any point, even if wine is free, at which consumers will not wish to buy any more wine?
              (iii) Will the total number of dollars spent on wine remain the same at every price level?

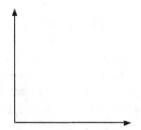

       (g)   (i)   In the space following, sketch the relationship between the interest rate and house purchases. Use your intuition.
              (ii)   According to your theory and your graph, is there any interest rate that will completely deter house purchases?

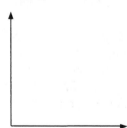

9.   Suppose there is a relationship between two variables, X (on the horizontal axis) and Y (on the vertical axis), and that you have collected the following data.

X	2	4	6	8	10
Y	5	6	7	8	9

(a)   Do we have a positive or a negative relationship?
(b)   Describe (in words) what these data would look like graphically.
(c)   Calculate the slope (rise over run) of the line.
(d)   Graph the relationship here.

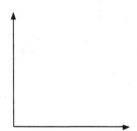

10.   You have a new brand of low-alcohol, reduced-calorie beer, "Quite Lite," that you intend to market. What variables do you think will be important in determining the amount of Quite Lite that people will want to buy? You should be able to develop a fairly long list of variables. You have begun to construct an economic model of consumption behavior. Now prune down your list to include, say, the five most important variables.

Now work out in which way each variable will impact the consumption of Quite Lite. You should be able to work out a specific cause-and-effect pattern in each case. A higher price for Quite Lite should cause less to be bought. A price hike for competing beers should increase the demand for Quite Lite. Note that not all variables have been included in the model; an all-inclusive list would (1) be cumbersome and (2) distract from the major elements in the model. You have wielded Ockham's razor!

The variables that you have compiled in your list will be continually changing their values. To isolate the effect of any one on the consumption of Quite Lite, you must invoke the *ceteris paribus* assumption. You might think of this as being the economic equivalent of the "standard temperature and pressure" conditions applied in the natural sciences.

Use the model that you developed for Quite Lite beer. Putting "quantity demanded" on the horizontal axis, graph each of the relationships in the model.

11.   Which of the following statements are positive and which are normative?
(a)   The moon is made of green cheese.
(b)   States to the west of the Mississippi have lower state income tax rates than states to the east have.
(c)   The federal government should be made to balance its budget.
(d)   The most serious economic problem confronting the nation is unemployment.
(e)   We should abolish the minimum wage.
(f)   We should index-link the minimum wage to the rate of price inflation.
(g)   If the federal budget deficit is reduced, then interest rates will decrease.

12.   Which of the following—your campus bookstore or Amazon.com—is more likely to be efficient and why?

13.   Opportunity cost may well be the biggest concept in all of economics—it's everywhere. Any time you make a choice, you choose to get something and you necessarily choose to give up the next-best alternative. Consider your Economics course. What is the opportunity cost of your course?

14. Some time ago, you bought a ticket for a concert by a local group, Saxon Violins, for $40. However, more recently, a friend invited you to a party that you'd much prefer to attend. All your efforts to sell your concert ticket have been unsuccessful. Should you go to the concert, which you've paid for, or to the party?

PRACTICE TEST SOLUTIONS

I. *Solutions to Multiple-Choice Questions*

1. (b) If the price of corn fell, perhaps very sharply, buyers might buy more corn and fewer tomatoes. Therefore, the economist is assuming that the price of corn is not going to change. That's what *ceteris paribus* implies.

2. (b) Unemployment is certainly an important economic variable, but it is not one of the criteria for evaluating the results of economic policy. Refer to p. 14.

3. (d) Growth will occur if resources become more plentiful or more productive.

4. (a) Economics is about choice—how we ration scarce resources to meet limitless wants.

5. (b) Price is not necessarily a reliable guide to value for a particular individual. Opportunity cost is the measure of the value placed on the next most-preferred item forgone as a result of Choice X.

6. (d) Efficiency means that producers are using the least costly method of production to supply those goods that are desired by consumers.

7. (c) To review the micro/macro distinction, refer to p. 8.

8. (b) There is a *negative* relationship between price and quantity demanded, so A is incorrect. The greater the rainfall, the larger the number of umbrellas bought.

9. (a) Just because an action done by one individual produces a given outcome, the same action done by many need not.

10. (d) Put in numbers. If $P = \$2$, then Qd will equal $400 - 100(2)$, or 200. If the price rises by 50¢, then Qd will equal $400 - 100(2.5)$, or 150—a fall of 50.

11. (d) The *ceteris paribus* assumption freezes the effect of all but one change so that the effects of that change may be examined.

12. (b) The diagram shows a straight line—straight lines have a constant slope. Visually, or by using the "rise over run" formula, the relationship is positive because, as one variable increases in value, the other also increases in value.

13. (a) Use the "rise over run" formula. The rise is +5 (Y goes from 7 to 12) and the run is +2 (X goes from 2 to 4).

14. (d) As X "steps up" in value by 2, Y "steps up" in value by 5. At Point C, X has a value of 6 and Y has a value of 17. Moving to Point D, X rises by 2 and Y rises by 5, from 17 to 22.

15.   (a)   As X "steps down" in value by 2, Y "steps down" in value by 5. At Point A, X has a value of 2 and Y has a value of 7. X decreases by 2 and Y decreases by 5, from 7 to 2.

16.   (c)   The relationship shows that as the X variable increases in value, the Y variable decreases in value—a negative relationship. The slope is decreasing because, as X increases in value, the decrease in the value of Y becomes smaller and smaller.

17.   (a)   The relationship shows that as the X variable increases in value, the Y variable also increases in value—a positive relationship. The slope is increasing because, as X increases in value, the increase in the value of Y becomes larger and larger.

18.   (b)   The relationship shows that as the X variable increases in value, the Y variable also increases in value—a positive relationship. The slope is decreasing because, as X increases in value, the increase in the value of Y becomes smaller and smaller.

19.   (a)   As X assumes higher values, the values of Y will increase more rapidly.

20.   (d)   For equity, read "fairness." Critics of the proposal argue that it is unfair to make poor families spend a larger part of their lower income on medical services.

21.   (d)   To complete the project would cost $80 million more than had already been spent.

II.   *Solutions to Application Questions*

1.   The (marginal) cost of the air quality improvement is valued at $50 × 4,000, or $200,000. The benefit derived from the improvement is valued at ($5 × 10,000) + ($7 × 30,000), or $260,000. Smogland should proceed with the implementation of emission controls.

2.   (a)

Unemployment Rate (%)	Inflation Rate (%)
2.0	6.0
4.0	3.0
6.0	0.0
8.0	−3.0
10.0	−6.0

       (b)   Slope is −1.5.
       (c)   −4.5%.
       (d)   1.5%.

3.   To have cleaner (if not clean) air, we might wish to reduce emissions of cars, homes, and factories. The next most-preferred use of the resources used to achieve this would be included in the opportunity cost. An initial 5% improvement in the quality of the air might be accomplished quite simply—perhaps by requiring more frequent car tune-ups—but, progressively, the "cost" of achieving more stringent air cleanliness standards will rise. The marginal cost will increase. This will graph as an upward-sloping line that rises progressively more steeply.

4.   The answer cannot be determined given the information. This choice may well have been rational. Perhaps the three extra points will save you from flunking the course whereas, in the math class, you are confident of making an easy "A."

5.   The opportunity cost is the salary forgone—$37,000 if you had chosen the first bank. Presumably, the offer of the job at the bank was based on your abilities—some of which would have been developed while at college. That time, then, was not wasted. You could have taken the bank job and explained that the three years of college got you the internship and sufficient skills to be noticed in the first place. Also, the three college years cannot be relived—decisions should be based on the future, not the past.

6.   This is an open question. The natural resource might be a river, a seam of coal, deer, a piece of waste land used as a dump, prime agricultural land, or downtown lots. The main point is that using the resource one way means that it is not available for other uses. The final part of the question may lead you into a consideration of private property rights, social pressure, and the role of the government.

7.   The answer to Question 7 is included in the question.

8.   (a, b)   Refer to the diagram below.

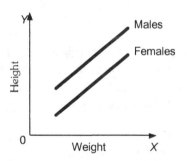

(c)   Both positive—as height increases, so does weight.
(d)   Probably the lines will be different. Perhaps, at any given height, males may weigh more than females, for example.
(e)   Race, geographical location, and age are factors that have been ignored.
(f)   (i)   Refer to the following diagram.
       (ii)   Even if wine is free, consumers are likely to reach a point of satiation. This is shown on the diagram as the quantity at which the line reaches the horizontal axis.
       (iii) It depends on your demand for wine, of course, but probably not. We take up this issue in Chapter 5, when we consider elasticity of demand. In general, we'll find that total spending declines at high prices.

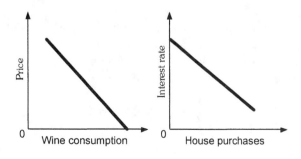

(g)   (i)   Refer to the preceding diagram.
       (ii)   It depends on the demand for houses, of course, and is shown as the point at which the line reaches the vertical axis.

9.   (a)   It's a positive relationship.
      (b)   The line would be "rising" to the right.
      (c)   Rise over run: *Y* rises by one unit every time *X* rises by two units, so the slope is +1/2.
      (d)   Refer to the following diagram.

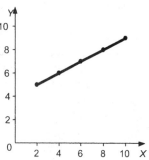

10.   Your short list of variables probably will include the price of Quite Lite, the prices of its competitors, advertising, the time of year, health attitudes, the income of potential buyers (launching a new product during an economic downturn might be difficult, for instance), and so on.

       The negative relationship you will have modeled (if not, why not?) between price and quantity demanded is called the demand curve. A movement along this curve indicates that price has changed causing a change in the amount of beer demanded, with all other variables held constant (*ceteris paribus*). (Keep this conclusion in mind when you read Chapter 3.)

11.   Positive statements are testable; normative statements are opinions.
       (a)   Positive. A statement need not be correct to be positive.
       (b)   Positive. Data can be gathered and analysis undertaken.
       (c)   Normative, as signaled by the use of *should*.
       (d)   Normative. This is an opinion, even during the Great Depression.
       (e)   Normative. This is an opinion, as signaled by the use of *should*.
       (f)   Normative. This is an opinion, as signaled by the use of *should*.
       (g)   Positive. This statement can be tested.

12.   With all due respect to your campus bookstore, it is less likely to be as efficient than Amazon. Amazon is open to competition from other internet firms and it's fairly easy to make comparisons between offers from different sellers. High prices at Amazon will be penalized as customers go elsewhere. Your campus bookstore, on the other hand, may have no local competition and, with "captive" customers, can afford to sustain high prices.

13.   Your opportunity cost is the value of the next most-preferred alternative you gave up in order to take the course. Perhaps you would have taken another course in the same time-slot. Or worked. Or used the time to study. Whatever. The most-valued alternative you couldn't pursue is the opportunity cost of your Economics course.

14.   Go to the party! The $40 you paid should be irrelevant to your decision. In either case, the $40 has been spent.

APPENDIX

Introduction: Why a Special Section on Graphing?

You may be surprised by the amount of mathematics—geometry in particular—that you encounter in economics. The professor introduces a new concept and quickly draws a graph to illustrate the idea—economic theory and graphs are inseparable. This union of a social science course and mathematical techniques can baffle some students. You could struggle so much with the techniques that you miss the powerful insights that economics has to offer. This section is designed to help you gain a working understanding of graphing techniques and to help you apply this knowledge to economics.

Why Are Graphs Important?

Graphs are important for several reasons. First, graphs are a compact way of conveying a large amount of information. An old adage says that "one picture is worth one thousand words." This is particularly true in economics, as the movement of an economic variable over time or the relationship between two economic variables can be quickly grasped through the use of graphs. Second, as Case, Fair and Oster mention in the Appendix to Chapter 1, economics uses quantitative (mathematical) techniques more than any other social science. Every academic discipline possesses its own "tool kit," which must be mastered in order to truly appreciate the content of the course. In an economic principles class, the primary "tool" is graphs. Third, there is a clear relationship between student success in economics and skill with graphs. Research on student performance indicates that of the skills that lead to success (verbal, quantitative reasoning, graphing) graphing ability is vital. Fourth, an important component of a vibrant democratic society is *economic literacy*: a basic understanding of certain central economic concepts. Citizens who follow current events constantly encounter graphs, as print and television journalists use the visual medium to communicate with its audience.

Why Graphs Trouble Many Students

Several factors may cause you to have difficulty with graphs. Several years may have elapsed since you completed a high school geometry course. Consequently, many graphing skills that were developed have been forgotten. More fundamentally, you read every day; however, you do not practice math every day. Therefore, most students enter an economic principles class with a stronger reading ability than a mathematical ability. Because of this, you must remember that the graphs in your textbook are not photographs worthy of only a glance; *graphs must be studied*.

General Tips for Studying Graphs

Here are some general tips that should assist you in developing graphing skills:

1.   *Relax*! Remember that math is simply another language; therefore, graphs are just a specific form of communication.
2.   When studying a graph, first identify the labels that are on the graph axes and curves. These labels are like road signs, which inform the reader.
3.   Once the labels are recognized, try to understand what economic intuition lies behind the curve (e.g., the demand curve indicates that as the product price falls, the amount that consumers wish to buy increases).
4.   Get into the habit of tracing the graphs that are in the text and copying the graphs as reading notes are taken.
5.   *Draw, draw, draw*!!! The process of learning economics must be an active process. Graphing skills can be enhanced only by repeated attempts to graph economic concepts.

What Are Graphs?

Graphs are visual expressions of quantitative information. Economic theory attempts to establish relationships between important concepts. If the value of a concept changes, the concept is considered a *variable*. Graphs illustrate the relationship between two variables. If two variables have a *direct* (positive) relationship the value of one variable increases as the value of the other variable increases. If two variables have an *inverse* (negative) relationship, the value of one variable decreases as the value of the other variable increases.

 EXAMPLE 1

As children get older, they grow taller. There exists a direct relationship between a child's age and its height.

Age	6	7	8	9	10
Height	48"	50"	52"	54"	56"

This relationship can be graphed:

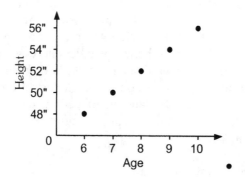

 EXAMPLE 2

After attending class, sleeping, eating, and working at a part-time job, a student has seven hours that can be used for studying or socializing. There exists an inverse relationship between time spent studying and time spent socializing.

Studying	7	5	3	1	0
Socializing	0	2	4	6	7

A graph of this relationship is shown below:

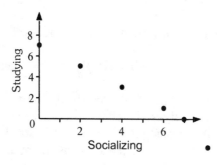

Types of Graphs

There are two types of graphs. *Descriptive* graphs relate the observed association of two variables. The graphs in Examples 1 and 2 are descriptive graphs. Newspapers often express monthly unemployment data in descriptive graphs. *Analytical* graphs convey the hypothetical relationship between two variables. The existence of association is derived from economic theory, and its accuracy is the object of economic research.

 EXAMPLE 3

An understanding of a firm's goals and its constraints leads to the development of a hypothesis, which states that as wages rises, a firm would hire fewer workers. Graphically, this relationship is expressed as:

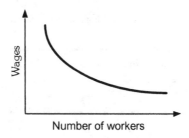

Often, the value of one variable determines the value of the other variable. In these cases, the former variable is called the *independent* variable; the latter variable is called the *dependent* variable. The independent variable is the cause; the dependent variable is the effect. Normally (but not always), the independent variable is placed on the horizontal axis and the dependent variable is placed on the vertical axis.
•

Drawing Graphs

Earlier, we examined the direct relationship between a child's age and its height. One would expect another direct relationship between a child's age and its weight.

 EXAMPLE 4

Age	6	7	8	9	10
Weight	70 lbs	75 lbs	80 lbs	85 lbs	90 lbs

Graph this relationship on the axes below.

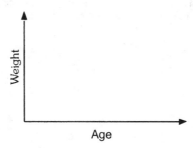

Combining the two series of data yields the following table:

Age	6	7	8	9	10
Height	48"	50"	52"	54"	56"
Weight	70 lbs	75 lbs	80 lbs	85 lbs	90 lbs

EXAMPLE 5

Graph the height-weight combination for each age on the axes below.

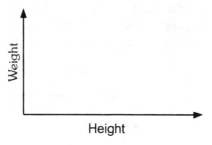

Is the relationship between height and weight direct or inverse? _____ •

EXAMPLE 6

Graph the relationship between the annual U.S. unemployment rate ($U\%$) and the years 1986–1999.

Year	1986	1987	1988	1989	1990	1991	1992	1993	1994	1995	1996	1997	1998	1999
$U\%$	7.0	6.2	5.4	5.3	5.5	6.7	7.4	6.8	6.1	5.6	5.4	4.9	4.5	4.2

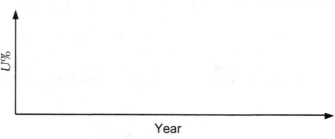

This graph, depicting the movement of one variable over time, it is called a *time-series* graph. Between which years is there a direct relationship? _____
Between which years is there an inverse relationship? _____ •

Reading Graphs

In addition to graphing economic relationships, students must develop the skill of reading graphs.

EXAMPLE 7

Following are a time-series graph of the movement of the poverty rates for U.S. families between 1986 and 1998 and a scatter diagram indicating the association between poverty rates and unemployment rates. Study both graphs and answer the following questions:

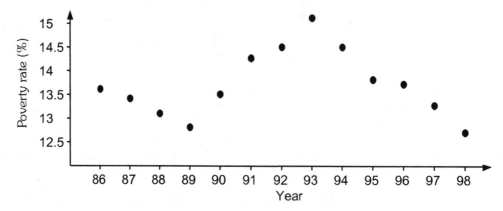

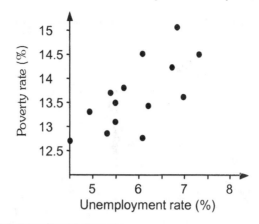

Year	1986	1987	1988	1989	1990	1991	1992	1993	1994	1995	1996	1997	1998
$U\%$	7.0	6.2	5.5	5.3	5.5	6.7	7.4	6.8	6.1	5.6	5.4	4.9	4.5
Poverty Rate %	13.6	13.4	13.1	12.8	13.5	14.2	14.5	15.1	14.5	13.8	13.7	13.3	12.7

1.   What are the poverty rates in:
      (a)   1987 _____
      (b)   1990 _____
      (c)   1995 _____
2.   What are the poverty rate/unemployment rate combinations in:
      (a)   1988 _____ _____
      (b)   1992 _____ _____
      (c)   1996 _____ _____
3.   When is there a direct relationship between poverty rate and unemployment rate?
4.   Is there ever an inverse relationship between poverty rate and unemployment rate?●

Understanding and Calculating Slopes

The *slope* of a curve is one measure of the relationship between two variables. It indicates both the type of relationship (direct or inverse) and the rate of change of one variable as the other variable changes. For a straight line, the slope is constant. For a curve, the slope changes from one point along the curve to another. At any particular point, the slope of the curve is identical to the slope of the straight line that is tangent to that point. The slope of a line is calculated by identifying two points on the line and computing the ratio of the change in the variable on the vertical axis and the change in the variable on the horizontal axis. (In high school geometry, this was referred to as "the 'rise' over the 'run'"; more formally, slope is the "change in Y divided by the change in X.")

 EXAMPLE 8 ━━━━━━━━━━━━━━━━━━━

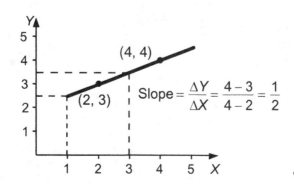

EXAMPLE 9

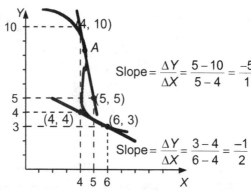

In Example 8, any two points alone that line will show a slope of 1/2. In Example 9, the slope varies: at point A, the slope is $-5/1$; at point B the slope is $-(1/2)$. These slope numbers can be interpreted indicating the unit change in the value of Y in response to a one unit change in X. For Example 8, Y will increase by 1/2 in response to a one unit change in X. At Point A in Example 9, Y decreases by 1 and, at Point B, Y decreases by 1/2. The fact that the slope is positive in Example 8 means that there is a direct relationship between Y and X. The negative slope in Example 9 illustrates an inverse relationship between Y and X.

Solving Equations

Often, the economic relationship between two concepts can be expressed in algebra with an equation. The advantage of this approach is that we can calculate the specific impact that a change in one variable has upon another variable.

 EXAMPLE 10

It is a reasonable assumption that as the price of a good rises, more of that good will be supplied. This positive relationship can be expressed with an equation. Let P represent price and Qs represent quantity supplied. For our purposes, let $Q_S = -10 + 80P$. Thus, if $P = 1$, then $Q_S = 70$. The table below captures this relationship:

Price	1	2	3	4	5
Quantity supplied	70	150	230	310	390

1.   What is Qs if $P = 7$? _____
2.   What is Qs if $P = 10$? _____

The table can be graphed. The line is a supply curve, as you will see in Chapter 3—it is usually labeled "S."

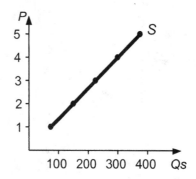

3.   What is the slope of the line? _____

If the equation is $Qs = -10 + 50P$, the slope of the line will change. Below is the new table.

Price	1	2	3	4	5
Quantity supplied	40	90	140	190	240

4.   Draw this new line on the graph below. Label it S_1.

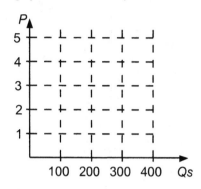

5.   What is the slope of this line? _____

If the equation for the supply curve is $Qs = -20 + 75P$, answer the following question.

6.   Complete the following table.

Price	1	2	3	4	5
Quantity supplied					

7.   Graph the line shown in the table on the following graph. Label it S_2.

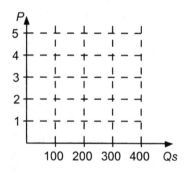

8.   What is the slope of the line? _____
9.   What is Qs if $P = 8$? _____
10.   What is Qs if $P = 20$? _____ ●

SOLUTIONS TO APPENDIX PROBLEMS

Example 4:
Refer to the following diagram.

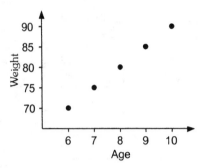

Example 5:
Refer to the following diagram.

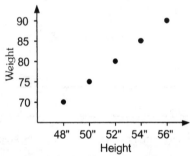

The relationship between height and weight is direct (positive).

Example 6:
Refer to the following diagram.

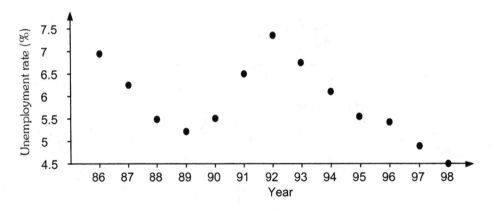

Between 1989 and 1992, there is a direct (positive) relationship.
Between 1986 and 1989, there is an inverse (negative) relationship. There is also an inverse relationship between 1992 and 1999.

Example 7:
1.   (a)   13.4%
      (b)   13.5%
      (c)   13.8%
2.   (a)   1988   5.5%   13.1%
      (b)   1992   7.4%   14.5%
      (c)   1996   5.4%   13.7%
3.   There is a direct relationship between poverty rate and unemployment rate in all years except 1993.
4.   There is an inverse relationship between poverty rate and unemployment rate only in 1993.

Example 10:
1. $Qs = -10 + 80P = -10 + 80(7) = 550$.
2. $Qs = -10 + 80P = -10 + 80(10) = 790$.
3.   Slope = rise/run = 1/80. A 1-unit increase in P leads to an 80-unit increase in Qs.
4.   Refer to the following diagram.

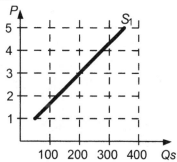

5.   Slope = rise/run = 1/50. A 1-unit increase in P leads to a 50-unit increase in Qs.

6.
Price	1	2	3	4	5
Quantity supplied	55	130	205	280	355

7.   Refer to the following diagram.

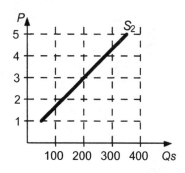

8.   Slope = rise/run = 1/75. A 1-unit increase in P leads to a 75-unit increase in Qs.
9. $Qs = -20 + 75P = -20 + 75(8) = 580$.
10. $Qs = -20 + 75P = -20 + 75(20) = 1480$.

2

The Economic Problem: Scarcity and Choice

Chapter objectives:

1. Identify the three basic economic questions.
2. Distinguish between absolute advantage and comparative advantage. Relate comparative advantage to the theory that individuals can gain from specialization and exchange.
3. Explain why a production possibility frontier has a negative slope and why the slope depicts the concept of opportunity cost.
4. Interpret what is depicted by a production possibility frontier.
5. Explain why increasing opportunity costs occur and how this is shown in the production possibility frontier diagram.
6. Identify ways in which economic growth may occur.
7. Identify and distinguish how economic systems differ in their solutions to the three basic questions. State the "mistakes" to which an unregulated market system is prone.

BRAIN TEASER: You graduate from college and are offered three jobs (Job A, Job B, and Job C). Assume that they are identical in all respects (duties, benefits, promotion prospects, and so on) except that the salaries differ, as shown below:

Job A	$150,000
Job B	$120,000
Job C	$100,000

First, which of the three jobs would you choose? (No, you can't have all three!) Because you have made a choice, you have incurred an opportunity cost. What is the opportunity cost of your job choice? Comparing benefits and costs, have you made a rational choice? Why or why not?

Suppose, for a moment, that you select Job B. What is the cost of that choice? Comparing benefits and costs, have you made a rational choice? Why or why not?

Now suppose that you select Job C. What is the cost of that choice? Again, is Job C a rational choice? Why or why not?

SOLUTION: The answer to this and subsequent brain teasers will be found after our discussion of the learning objectives and before the Practice Tests.

ECONOMICS IN PRACTICE: This chapter's textbook example of economics in action in the real world centers on opportunity costs, in particular, the value we place on time. Refer to page 28 in the textbook. First, think about the costs of preparing a meal. To be sure, the price of the ingredients is one factor, but time is another. The textbook makes the point that we are often willing to trade dollars (and perhaps taste) for convenience. Can you think of two or three other examples of the same sort of trade-off in your own life? What do you consider in your decision-making process?

ANSWER: Answers will vary, of course, but fast food is an obvious example. How much more convenient it is to go through the drive-through that spend time shopping and cooking. If you use paper plates on a picnic, you're making the same sort of calculation. A trip to a (typically high-price) convenience store is another example. Many students who sign up for online classes cite "convenience" as the main reason for preferring this form of learning experience. Finally, how much more convenient is it to "google" a subject rather than visit your campus library's book stacks?

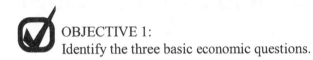 OBJECTIVE 1:
Identify the three basic economic questions.

Economics studies the production and consumption choices that are made by society and the outcomes that occur. Solutions must be found to three "basic questions": What goods should be produced? How should the goods be produced? and Who gets what is produced? Every economy must transform its scarce natural, capital, and human resources into usable production. In a complex society the opportunity to cooperate and specialize offers great scope for increased production—but decisions must be made regarding the extent of cooperation, who specializes in what, and how goods are distributed. Even Robinson Crusoe and Friday on their island must come up with answers to these questions. Wants are limitless, but resources are scarce. We are compelled to make choices. (page 26)

Opportunity Cost: Economics has to do with making choices when constraints (scarcity) are present. Constrained choice occurs, for example, when you go to the grocery store with only a $20 bill in your pocket—you have to make choices based on this limitation. Unconstrained choice would be if you were allowed to take as many groceries home as you wanted, free of charge. Sadly, though, we know there's "no such thing as a free lunch."

Practical examples of the consequences and costs of choice include: present vs. future benefits (for example, do you study hard now so that, at exam time, reviewing is easier, or do you take it easy now and sweat it before the exam?), and capital vs. consumer production (for example, should we produce taxicabs or sports cars?).

▶▶ LEARNING TIP: Everyone has been confronted with some version of the following scene: A favorite grandmother lets you choose one item from two or more items (ice cream sundaes, for example) on a menu. From your viewpoint, is your chosen ice cream sundae free? Or is there an opportunity cost? If you have a range of sundaes from which to choose, what is the cost? The dollar amount of the chosen sundae? All the other sundaes you could have had? The opportunity cost is the value you place on the next most-favorite sundae.

▶▶ LEARNING TIP: To calculate opportunity cost, use the "give up to get" approach. If you can determine what (next-best) choice was forgone to get your preferred selection, you have determined opportunity cost. This is most clearly seen as a movement along a production possibility frontier.

—————————————————————— **Practice** ——————————————————————

1.   Which of the following statements about the operation of an economy is false? Each economy has a mechanism to determine
        (a)   what is produced.
        (b)   how to satisfy all of the desires of its citizens.
        (c)   how much is produced.
        (d)   how goods and services are distributed among its citizens.

        ANSWER: (b) Because resources are limited, the economy cannot satisfy all the desires of its
                    citizens.

 OBJECTIVE 2:
        Distinguish between absolute advantage and comparative advantage. Relate comparative advantage to the theory that individuals can gain from specialization and exchange.

A producer has an *absolute advantage* in the production of Good A if, compared with another producer, she can produce Good A more efficiently. A producer has a *comparative advantage* in the production of Good A if, compared with another producer, she can produce Good A at a lower opportunity cost.
        The *theory of comparative advantage* provides the rationale for free trade. In a two-country, two-good world, Ricardo showed that trading partners can benefit from specialization in the production of the good in which they have a comparative advantage. (page 27)
        Specialization and trade based on comparative advantage lets each participant achieve a higher consumption level than otherwise would be possible. As shown in the graphical representation, each participant can live outside the constraints of his own production opportunities. (page 30)

        ▶▶   LEARNING TIP: If you're like most individuals, you'll need several numerical examples to strengthen your
              grasp of comparative advantage. The following questions take you through all the steps included in the text.
              Problem 5 in the textbook is recommended.

        Comparative advantage hinges on the concept of opportunity cost. The producer (person, firm, or country) with the lowest opportunity cost holds the comparative advantage in that product. Don't be misled—it is irrelevant to comparative advantage whether or not the producer can produce *more* of the good. The issue revolves around the relative opportunity costs. The increased production could be traded. In terms of a *production possibility* diagram, trade will be advantageous if the diagrams have differing slopes because differing slopes indicate differing opportunity costs.

PRACTICE: Think back to when you used to trade baseball cards or Pokemon cards in the schoolyard. Why did you trade? Did you and your trading partner necessarily benefit equally? Should that matter?
ANSWER: If you voluntarily entered into trade, presumably you did so because you thought it would be beneficial for you. Perhaps you traded a duplicate card for one you didn't have. Presumably your partner approached the deal in the same way. Just because you got a good deal didn't mean that s/he got a bad deal—both traders could gain, although there's no requirement that the traders will gain equally.

—————————————————————— **Practice** ——————————————————————

Use the following information to answer the next seven questions. George and Laura live on an island in the Caribbean. Their diet is fishes and biscuits. George can bake 20 biscuits or spear 10 fishes each day, while Laura can bake 48 biscuits or spear 12 fishes each day. For each person, costs remain constant.

2.   Which of the following statements is false?
  (a)   For George, the opportunity cost of 1 fish is 2 biscuits forgone.
  (b)   For Laura, the opportunity cost of 1 fish is 4 biscuits forgone.
  (c)   The opportunity cost of 1 fish is greater for Laura than for George.
  (d)   An increase in George's production of fish requires a decrease in Laura's production of biscuits.

  ANSWER: (d) An increase in George's production of fish requires a decrease in *George's* production of biscuits. In fact, both George and Laura might choose independently to increase fish production.

3.   Which of the following statements is true?
  (a)   For George, the opportunity cost of 1 biscuit is 2 fish forgone.
  (b)   For Laura, the opportunity cost of 1 biscuit is 4 fish forgone.
  (c)   The opportunity cost of 1 biscuit is greater for Laura than for George.
  (d)   The opportunity cost of 1 biscuit is greater for George than for Laura.

  ANSWER: (d) For George, the opportunity cost of a biscuit is 1/2 of a fish forgone, and for Laura, the opportunity cost of a biscuit is 1/4 of a fish forgone.

4.   For _____ , the opportunity cost of 1 fish is _____ biscuits forgone, which is less than the opportunity cost of 1 fish for _____ .
  (a)   George, 1/2, Laura
  (b)   George, 2, Laura
  (c)   Laura, 4, George
  (d)   Laura, 1/4, George

  ANSWER: (b) For George, each fish "costs" 2 biscuits forgone. For Laura, each fish "costs" 4 biscuits forgone. Fish cost less for George to produce.

5.   For _____ , the opportunity cost of 1 biscuit is _____ fish forgone, which is less than the opportunity cost of 1 biscuit for _____ .
  (a)   George, 1/2, Laura
  (b)   George, 2, Laura
  (c)   Laura, 4, George
  (d)   Laura, 1/4, George

  ANSWER: (d) For George, each biscuit "costs" 1/2 of a fish forgone. For Laura, each biscuit "costs" 1/4 of a fish forgone. Biscuits cost less for Laura to produce.

6.   According to the preceding information,
  (a)   George has a comparative advantage in the production of both goods.
  (b)   George has a comparative advantage in producing fish, and Laura has a comparative advantage in producing biscuits.
  (c)   George has a comparative advantage in producing biscuits, and Laura has a comparative advantage in producing fish.
  (d)   Laura has a comparative advantage in the production of both goods.

  ANSWER: (b) George has a comparative advantage in the production of fish (1 fish costs 2 biscuits forgone), and Laura has a comparative advantage in the production of biscuits (1 biscuit costs 1/4 of a fish forgone). Note: Neither person can be relatively better at producing both goods!

7.   Which of the following statements is false?
    (a)   If George spent half his time fishing and the other half baking, he could produce 10 biscuits and 5 fishes each day.
    (b)   If Laura spent half her time fishing and the other half baking, she could produce 24 biscuits and 6 fishes each day.
    (c)   If George and Laura specialized according to comparative advantage, they could produce 34 biscuits and 11 fishes each day.
    (d)   If George and Laura specialized according to comparative advantage, they could produce 48 biscuits and 10 fishes each day.
    ANSWER: (c)   George should produce fish, and he can spear 10 each day. Laura should produce biscuits, and she can bake 48 each day. Option (c) is incorrect because it fails to take account of the effects of comparative advantage.

8.   George and Laura specialize according to comparative advantage and trade at a rate of 1 fish for 3 biscuits. George sells Laura 5 fish. Which of the following statements is true?
    (a)   George gains from trade but Laura does not, because George's opportunity cost for producing fish is greater than 3 biscuits per fish.
    (b)   George gains from trade but Laura does not, because George's opportunity cost for producing fish is less than 3 biscuits per fish.
    (c)   Both George and Laura gain from trade, because each attains a consumption level impossible without trade.
    (d)   Both George and Laura gain from trade, because each is able to use their resources to the maximum.
    ANSWER: (c)   George's opportunity cost for producing fish is less than 3 biscuits per fish, so he gains from trade. However, Laura also gains, because her opportunity cost of producing biscuits is less than 1/3 of a fish. George ends up with 5 fish and 15 biscuits and Laura ends up with 5 fish and 33 biscuits.

 OBJECTIVE 3:
Explain why a production possibility frontier has a negative slope and why the slope depicts the concept of opportunity cost.

A production possibility frontier depicts the boundary between possible and impossible (unattainable) levels of production. Employing resources for one use prevents them from being employed for other uses—there is an *opportunity cost* involved in the choice. The *production possibility frontier* portrays graphically the opportunity cost of transferring resources from one activity to another in a two-good environment. If all resources are fully employed, as more of Good A is produced, fewer resources are available to produce Good B. (page 33)
    Why Does the Production Possibility Frontier Slope Downward?: The production possibility frontier is the key piece of economic analysis in this chapter. It's always presented as having only two goods or bundles of goods. It slopes downward because "the more you get of one thing the less you get of the other." The more you study economics, the less time you have for other activities. The opportunity cost of an extra hour of studying economics is the value of an hour of other activities.
    Graphing Pointer: Draw a graph with "study time per day" on the horizontal (X) axis and "time for all other activities per day" on the vertical (Y) axis. As you increase "study time" you must reduce "other time." Graphically, the cost of one hour of study time (the lost time for other activities) is the (negative) change in Y divided by the (positive) change in X. The slope of the ppf is the geometric representation of the opportunity cost of transferring resources from one productive activity to another.

Graphing Pointer: When drawing a production possibility frontier, remember that the frontier extends all the way from the vertical axis to the horizontal axis. It is a mistake to leave the frontier unconnected to the axes. If the frontier is not connected, it implies that an infinitely large quantity of either good could be produced, which is exactly opposite to the message that the diagram is intended to give.

———■——————————————————————— **Practice** ————————————————————————

9.   Along the production possibility frontier, trade-offs exist because
   (a)   buyers will want to buy less when price goes up, but producers will want to sell more.
   (b)   even on the frontier itself, not all production levels are efficient.
   (c)   at some levels, unemployment or inefficiency exists.
   (d)   the economy has only a limited quantity of resources to allocate between competing uses.

   ANSWER: (d) Along the production possibility frontier, resources are fully and efficiently employed. However, because resources are scarce, an increase in the production of Good A requires that resources be taken from the production of Good B. ■

 OBJECTIVE 4:
Interpret what is depicted by a production possibility frontier.

The ppf shows all the combinations of two goods that can be produced when all resources are employed efficiently. Points inside the ppf represent unemployment and/or inefficiency whereas points outside are currently unattainable. An outward movement of the ppf represents growth. Growth occurs if more resources become available or if existing resources become more productive (e.g., through better education, more efficient techniques of production, or technological innovations). (page 36)

Production Efficiency and Output Efficiency: The vision of a great volume of production, with all resources employed, is an attractive one. For this reason, it's often difficult to understand that, in serving the needs of consumers, producing the *right* goods is more important than mere quantity. This distinction lies at the heart of most confusion about production efficiency and output efficiency. Consider a remote Inuit economy that is fully employed producing refrigerators. Would it be "better" (more efficient) for the Inuits to have some unemployment but be producing warm clothing? Turning out (unwanted) refrigerators is productively efficient, whereas making warm clothing is efficient (in terms of output). Ideally, you'd want to be on the production possibility frontier (output efficiency) and also producing the most desired mix of output.

▶▶   LEARNING TIP: Think of the production possibility frontier as a way to depict opportunity cost and constrained choice. In general, you want to be somewhere on the curve because otherwise you're losing production, which is inefficient. Production on the curve means that resources are being used to the maximum (no unemployment). However, the inefficiency of a mismatch between an "efficient" production mix and society's needs is easily explained—just because we're producing "on the line" doesn't mean we're meeting society's needs as effectively as possible. Employing all our resources to produce taxicabs, for example, is unlikely to be desirable!

▶▶   LEARNING TIP: Suppose that, at one point on the ppf, we can produce 16 cars and 5 pickups, and at another point, we can produce 12 cars and 7 pickups. Note that the opportunity cost is calculated by looking at the *change* in production levels—the 2 extra trucks cost 4 cars.

▶▶   LEARNING TIP: Reducing unemployment does not shift the ppf. Remember the underlying assumptions! The ppf is drawn *given* a set of resources (whether or not those resources are being used). Unemployment represents a situation where the resources are not fully utilized. If unemployment is reduced, the economy moves closer to the ppf.

──■────────────────────────── **Practice** ──────────────────────────

10. Which of the following is **not** an assumption underlying the production possibility frontier?
    (a) Technological knowledge is fixed.
    (b) Resources are fully employed.
    (c) Resources are efficiently employed.
    (d) The quantity of labor resources is variable.

    ANSWER: (d) When drawing a ppf, the quantity of all resources is assumed to be fixed.

11. The production possibility frontier represents
    (a) the maximum amount of goods and services that can be produced with a given quantity of resources and technology.
    (b) those combinations of goods and services that will be demanded as price changes.
    (c) the maximum amount of resources that are available as the wage level changes.
    (d) those combinations of goods and services that will be produced as the price level changes.

    ANSWER: (a) The production possibility frontier represents what it is "possible to produce" given the available resources and technology.

12. The Arbezani economy is operating at a point inside its production possibility frontier. This may be because
    (a) the economy has very poor technological know-how.
    (b) Arbez is a very small nation and can't produce much.
    (c) poor management practices have led to an inefficient use of resources.
    (d) Arbez has only a small resource base.

    ANSWER: (c) Very poor technological know-how or a small resource base will result in a production possibility frontier that is close to the origin. Fully and efficiently employed resources would still be on the production possibility frontier.

 OBJECTIVE 5:
Explain why increasing opportunity costs occur and how this is shown in the production possibility frontier diagram.

Increasing opportunity costs are present when the production possibility frontier bulges outwards from the origin. Increasing costs occur if resources are not equally well suited to the production of Good A and Good B. (page 35)

▶▶▶ LEARNING TIP: Why is the production possibility frontier bowed out? The geometry of the ppf flows from its economics. A bowed-out production possibility frontier indicates that the opportunity cost (marginal rate of transformation) is increasing as resources become more heavily allocated to the production of one good. That bowed-out shape occurs because of the imperfect adaptability of resources to different uses. A farmer wishing to produce dairy products, for example, will select the most-suited resources first, and production will increase sharply. Further increases will be less easy to achieve and more expensive in terms of lost production of other goods as resources more suited to other endeavors are pressed into dairy service. If all resources were identical in their productive abilities, the opportunity cost of reallocation would be constant, and the ppf would be a straight line (a constant slope).

━━━━━ ■ ━━━━━━━━━━━━━━━━━━━━━━━━━━━━ **Practice** ━━━━━

13.   There are increasing costs in the economy of Arbez. To portray this fact in a production
possibility diagram, we should
(a)   move the ppf outwards (up and to the right).
(b)   draw the ppf bulging outwards.
(c)   shift the ppf's endpoint on the horizontal axis to the right.
(d)   shift the ppf's endpoint on the vertical axis upwards.

ANSWER: (b)   The slope of the ppf represents the behavior of opportunity cost as production
level changes. A straight ppf represents constant costs. To show increasing costs,
the ppf is bowed outwards from the origin.

 OBJECTIVE 6:
Identify ways in which economic growth may occur.

If an economy increases the quantity or quality of its resources, or if technological change or innovation
increase productivity, economic growth can occur—the production possibility frontier shifts
outward. (page 37)

   Investment and Capital: "Investment" and "capital" are two terms with very specific meanings
in economics. Beware! Investing doesn't just mean buying something. To an economist, investing means
only the creation of capital. What, then, is capital? Capital refers to manufactured resources usable in
production. A hammer is capital; a share of GM stock is not. A nail is capital; a dollar bill is not. Buying
a hammer is capital investment; buying GM stock is not!

   If this capital/noncapital distinction gives you problems, ask yourself if the purchase of the item
in question increases the economy's ability to produce. If it does, it's an investment in capital.

━━━━━ ■ ━━━━━━━━━━━━━━━━━━━━━━━━━━━━ **Practice** ━━━━━

14.   France experiences an improvement in productivity due to the introduction of improved
technology. In terms of France's production possibility frontier, we would show this change as
(a)   a movement along the frontier.
(b)   a shift from a point inside the frontier to a point on the frontier.
(c)   a shift from a point on the frontier to a point outside the frontier.
(d)   a shift outwards by the entire frontier.

ANSWER: (d) France's resource base has improved in quality, so it is possible for it to produce
more than it could previously.

 OBJECTIVE 7:
Identify and distinguish how economic systems differ in their solutions to the three basic
questions. State the "mistakes" to which an unregulated market system is prone.

The two "pure" types of economic system are the command economy and the laissez-faire economy. A
command (planned) economy has a central agency that sets production targets, income, and prices and
finds answers for the three basic questions. In a *laissez-faire (market) economy*, the three basic questions
are answered through the operation of individual buyers and sellers following their own self-interest in
markets.

   All economies are driven by a mixture of market forces, government intervention, and regulation.
Government intervention is felt to be necessary to correct laissez-faire "mistakes" such as an excessive
inequality in the distribution of income and periodic spells of unemployment or inflation. (page 38)

———■——————————————————— **Practice** ————————

15.   The basic mechanism that coordinates activities in a laissez-faire economy is
        (a)   how much customers wish to buy.
        (b)   how much producers wish to sell.
        (c)   price.
        (d)   how much producers are able to sell.
ANSWER: (c) Price regulates market activities, reflecting the desires of both buyers and sellers.

16.   Advocates comparing the performance of a pure laissez-faire system with that of a command
        economy would claim that a pure laissez-faire system would do all of the following EXCEPT
        (a)   promote efficiency,
        (b)   stimulate innovation.
        (c)   achieve an equal income distribution.
        (d)   be directed by the decisions of individual buyers and sellers.

        ANSWER: (c) A pure laissez-faire system, which rewards those who contribute most, would
                have an unequal income distribution.

BRAIN TEASER SOLUTION: Presumably, you would choose Job A. The opportunity cost is the next-best
alternative given up (Job B), which is valued at $120,000. You have made a rational choice because the
benefits ($150,000) outweigh the costs ($120,000).

        If you select Job B, the opportunity cost is the next-best alternative given up (Job A), which is
valued at $150,000. This isn't a rational choice, because you receive a benefit of $120,000 at a cost of
$150,000.

        If you select Job C, once again the opportunity cost is the value of Job A, which you could have
chosen instead. Job C isn't a rational choice, because you receive a benefit of $100,000 at a cost of
$150,000.

PRACTICE TEST

I.   MULTIPLE-CHOICE QUESTIONS

Select the option that provides the single best answer.

_____   1.   Because the nation of Arboc is operating at a point inside its production possibility
                frontier, it
                (a)   has full employment.
                (b)   has unemployed or inefficiently employed resources.
                (c)   must cut output of one good to increase production of another.
                (d)   will be unable to experience economic growth.
_____   2.   Arboc commits more of its resources to capital production than does Arbez. _____
                should experience a(n) _____ rapid rate of economic growth.
                (a)   Arboc; more
                (b)   Arbez; more
                (c)   Arboc; less
                (d)   Both; equally

_____ 3.   Which of the following does not count as a productive resource?
       (a)   Capital resources, such as a tractor
       (b)   Natural resources, such as a piece of farmland
       (c)   Financial resources, such as a $20 bill
       (d)   Human resources, such as a hairdresser

Use the following diagram to answer the next four questions.

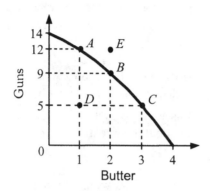

_____ 4.   Point E might become attainable if this economy
       (a)   reduces prices.
       (b)   reduces wages.
       (c)   improves the quality of its workforce.
       (d)   encourages emigration.

_____ 5.   A movement from A to B and then to C indicates that
       (a)   the cost of additional butter is decreasing.
       (b)   the cost of additional guns is increasing.
       (c)   the economy is becoming more efficient.
       (d)   the cost of additional butter is increasing.

_____ 6.   To move from D to A indicates that
       (a)   the opportunity cost would be zero.
       (b)   some butter would have to be given up.
       (c)   there would have to be an increase in the quantity of resources.
       (d)   the opportunity cost would be 7 guns forgone.

_____ 7.   The opportunity cost of producing another unit of butter is
       (a)   higher at B than at C.
       (b)   lower at D than at C.
       (c)   higher at A than at B.
       (d)   equal at D and at C.

_____ 8.   A production possibility frontier diagram illustrates all of the following concepts
             EXCEPT
       (a)   scarcity.
       (b)   unlimited wants.
       (c)   constrained choice.
       (d)   the marginal rate of transformation.

_____ 9.   Of the following, the least serious problem for laissez-faire economies is
   (a)   unemployment.
   (b)   income inequality.
   (c)   inflation.
   (d)   satisfaction of consumer sovereignty.

Use the following production possibility table to answer the next three questions. Suppose that wheat is on the *y*-axis.

Alternative	A	B	C	D	E	F
Wheat	0	1	2	3	4	5
Tobacco	15	14	12	9	5	0

_____ 10.   The marginal rate of transformation of a unit of wheat as the economy moves from *C* to *D* is
   (a)   1/3 unit of tobacco production forgone.
   (b)   3 units of tobacco production forgone.
   (c)   9 units of tobacco production forgone.
   (d)   12 units of tobacco production forgone.

_____ 11.   The marginal rate of transformation of a unit of tobacco as the economy moves from *C* to *B* is
   (a)   1/2 unit of wheat production forgone.
   (b)   1 unit of wheat production forgone.
   (c)   2 units of wheat production forgone.
   (d)   12 units of wheat production forgone.

_____ 12.   An output of 3 units of wheat and 7 units of tobacco indicates that
   (a)   this economy has poor technology.
   (b)   resources are being used inefficiently.
   (c)   tobacco is preferred to wheat.
   (d)   it is not possible for this economy to produce at a point on the production possibility frontier.

_____ 13.   Which of the following is most likely to shift the production possibility frontier outward?
   (a)   A sudden expansion in the labor force
   (b)   An increase in stock prices
   (c)   A shift of productive resources from capital goods to consumer goods
   (d)   A general increase in the public's demand for goods

_____ 14.   Which of the following is not one of the basic economic questions?
   (a)   What will be produced?
   (b)   How will it be priced?
   (c)   How will it be produced?
   (d)   Who will get what is produced?

_____ 15.   Private markets work best when
    (a)   they are competitive.
    (b)   they are regulated by a government agency.
    (c)   a monopolist is present.
    (d)   consumer sovereignty is restricted.

_____ 16.   Arboc has an increasing-cost production possibility frontier. Its slope must be
    (a)   positive and increasing.
    (b)   positive and decreasing.
    (c)   negative and increasing.
    (d)   negative and decreasing.

_____ 17.   For Jill to have a comparative advantage in the production of pins means that, relative to Jack, with the same resources
    (a)   Jill is relatively better at producing pins than at producing needles.
    (b)   Jill is relatively better at producing both pins and needles.
    (c)   Jill can produce fewer needles than Jack can produce.
    (d)   Jill can produce more pins than Jack can produce.

_____ 18.   Each of the following is a basic concern of any economic system EXCEPT
    (a)   the allocation of scarce resources among producers.
    (b)   the mix of different types of output.
    (c)   the distribution of output among consumers.
    (d)   the quality of resources allocated among consumers.

The following table shows the maximum output of each good in each country, e.g. maximum Arbezani production of goat milk is 6 units.

	Arboc	Arbez
Goat milk	3	6
Bananas	5	2

_____ 19.   According to the preceding table,
    (a)   Arboc has a comparative advantage in producing both goods.
    (b)   Arboc has a comparative advantage in the production of bananas, and Arbez has a comparative advantage in the production of goat milk.
    (c)   Arboc has a comparative advantage in the production of goat milk, and Arbez has a comparative advantage in the production of bananas.
    (d)   Arbez has a comparative advantage in the production of both goods.

_____ 20.   The nation of Regit has a bowed-out production possibility frontier with potatoes on the vertical axis and steel on the horizontal axis. A movement down along the ppf will incur _____ opportunity costs in the production of steel; a movement up along the ppf will incur _____ opportunity costs in the production of potatoes.
    (a)   increasing; increasing
    (b)   increasing; decreasing
    (c)   decreasing; increasing
    (d)   decreasing; decreasing

II.   APPLICATION QUESTIONS

1.   Farmer Brown has four fields that can produce corn or tobacco. Assume that the marginal rate of transformation between corn and tobacco *within* each field is constant. The maximum yields for each field are given in the following table. Field A, for instance, can produce 40 units of corn and no tobacco or, as another alternative, no corn and 10 units of tobacco.

Field	A	B	C	D
Corn	40	30	20	10
Tobacco	10	20	30	40

(a)   Draw Farmer Brown's production possibility frontier.
(b)   To be on the production possibility frontier, what conditions must hold true?
(c)   Brown is currently producing only corn: If he wants to produce some tobacco, in what order would he switch his fields from corn to tobacco production?
(d)   Explain your answer to (c).

2.   Two countries, Arboc and Arbez, produce wine and cheese, and each has constant costs of production. The maximum amounts of the two goods for each country are given in the following table.

Arboc	Arbez	Goods
40	120	Wine
20	30	Cheese

(a)   Draw the production possibility frontier for each country.

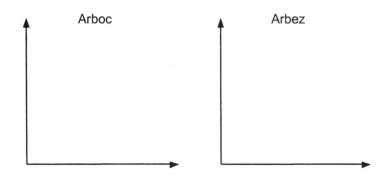

(b)   Calculate the opportunity cost of wine in Arboc and in Arbez.
(c)   In which country, then, is wine production cheaper?
(d)   Answer questions (b) and (c) for cheese production—remember that the opportunity costs are reciprocals of one another.
        Note that Arbez has an advantage in both goods in terms of total production, but a comparative advantage only in wine production.
        Now assume that Arboc becomes more efficient and can double its output of both wine and cheese.
(e)   Graph the new production possibility frontier on the preceding diagram.
(f)   Which good should Arboc now produce?
        Suppose, instead, that Arbez has a specific technological advance that permits it to increase cheese production to a maximum of 90.
(g)   Now which nation should produce wine?

3.   In a national contest, the first prize is a town. The winner receives a furnished house, a general store and gasoline station, a pick-up truck, and 100 acres of land. The store comes fully stocked with everything you might find in a country general store. The town is located 100 miles from a small city. It is the shopping center for about a thousand families who live in the countryside. In addition, the road through the town is fairly well traveled. Suppose you win the contest and decide to try running the town as a business for at least a year.

(a)   Describe the resources available to the economy of your town. What is the potential labor force? What are the natural resources?

(b)   Describe the capital stock of your town.

(c)   List some of the factors that are beyond your control that will affect your income.

(d)   List some of the decisions you must make that could affect your income, and explain what their effects might be.

(e)   At the end of the year, you must decide whether to stay or go back to college. How will you decide? What factors will you weigh in making your decision? What role do your expectations play?

4.   The following data give the production possibilities of an economy that produces two types of goods, guns (horizontal axis) and butter (vertical axis).

Production Possibilities	Guns	Butter
A	0	105
B	10	100
C	20	90
D	30	75
E	40	55
F	50	30
G	60	0

(a)   Graph the production possibility frontier.

(b)   Explain why Point D is efficient, but Point H (30 guns and 45 units of butter) is not.

(c)   Calculate the per-unit opportunity cost of an increase in the production of guns in each of the following cases.

(i)   From Point A to Point B?

(ii)   From Point B to Point C?

(iii)   From Point E to Point F?

(iv)   From Point F to Point G?

(d)   Calculate the per-unit opportunity cost of an increase in the production of butter in each of the following cases.

(i)   From Point G to Point F?

(ii)   From Point D to Point C?

(iii)   From Point C to Point B?

(iv)   From Point B to Point A?

(e)   Using the production possibility frontier concept, explain what will happen if this nation declares war on one of its neighbors.

5.   Draw a production possibility frontier with farm goods (*X*-axis) and manufacturing goods (*Y*-axis) on the axes. In each of the following cases, explain what will happen to the production possibility frontier.

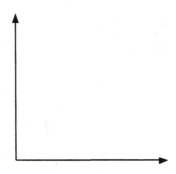

(a)   There is an increase in the unemployment rate.
(b)   There is an improvement in farming techniques.
(c)   There is a decrease in quantity of physical capital.
(d)   The productivity of workers doubles.
(e)   The government requires farmers to slaughter a portion of their dairy herds.

6.   Consider the following production possibility frontier diagram.

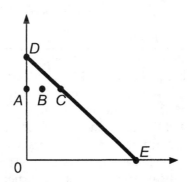

(a)   Which point is "best" and which is "worst"?
(b)   Now suppose that you're told that the axes measure food (horizontal) and moonshine whisky (vertical). Would your answer be different?
(c)   Point *B* may be preferable to Point *D*, although Point *B* in terms of production Point *B* is less efficient. Why might it be preferable?

7.   The nation of Arbez can produce two goods—corn and steel. The table shows some points on the Arbezani production possibility frontier.

Alternative	A	B	C	D	E	F
Corn	0	1	2	3	4	5
Steel	20	16	12	8	4	0

(a)   Draw the production possibility frontier in the space below.

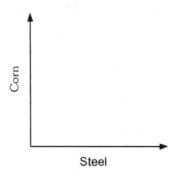

(b)   Moving from Alternative *A* to *B*, *B* to *C*, and so on, calculate the opportunity cost of each additional unit of corn. Going from *F* to *E*, *E* to *D*, and so on, calculate the opportunity cost *per unit* of steel. Confirm that the pairs of values are reciprocals of each other. (This must always be true.)

Production Alternative	Opportunity Cost of 1 Unit of:	
	Corn	**Steel**
A – B		
B – C		
C – D		
D – E		
E – F		

(c)   Consider each of the following situations.
Situation *X*: Arbez is producing 4 units of corn and no steel. What is the opportunity cost of the next unit of corn? The next unit of steel?
Situation *Y*: Arbez is producing 4 units of corn and 4 units of steel. What is the opportunity cost of the next unit of corn? The next unit of steel?

(d)   Why do you find a different set of answers in Situation *X* and Situation *Y*?

(e)   Now consider a new situation, Situation *Z*: Arbez is producing 3 units of corn and 5 units of steel. What is the opportunity cost of the next unit of corn? The next unit of steel?

(f)   Which situation (*X*, *Y*, or *Z*) is the most productively efficient and which the least productively efficient?

(g)   On the Arbezani production possibility frontier, what is the cost of each unit of corn and what is the cost of each unit of steel?
The nation of Arboc also produces corn and steel. The following table shows some points on the Arbocali production possibility frontier.

Alternative	*A*	*B*	*C*	*D*	*E*	*F*
Corn	0	1	2	3	4	5
Steel	10	8	6	4	2	0

(h)   On the Arbocali production possibility frontier, what is the cost of each unit of corn and what is the cost of each unit of steel?

(i)   Point to ponder: Because steel is relatively cheaper to produce in one country (which?) and corn is relatively cheaper to produce in the other country (which?), might mutually beneficial trade be possible?

8.   Refer to the following diagram.

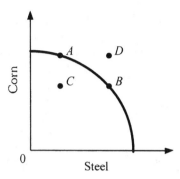

(a)   Which point is unattainable?
(b)   To achieve this currently unattainable production combination, what must happen (two possible answers)?
(c)   Which point represents unemployment or inefficiency?
(d)   Will a movement from *B* to *A* increase corn production or steel production?
(e)   What is the opportunity cost of moving from *C* to *B*?

9.   Draw the axes of a production possibility frontier. Use corn (on the vertical axis) and steel (on the horizontal axis) as the two goods.

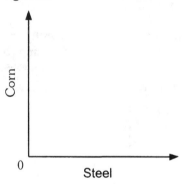

Choose a point, *A*, that represents some corn and some steel production. Suppose that this point is on the ppf—it's a maximum point. Split the diagram up into quarters, with Point *A* in the center.
(a)   Is a production mix to the southwest possible?
(b)   Would such a mix be efficient in terms of production efficiency?
(c)   Would such a mix be efficient in terms of output efficiency?
(d)   Is a move to the northeast quadrant possible? What do you know about it? Only the northwest and southeast quadrants are possible locations in which productively efficient output alternatives can occur.
(e)   What would happen if the present level of corn production (at Point *A*) was reduced?
        If steel production does not change, unemployment occurs. The unemployed resources can be absorbed by the steel industry and more steel can be produced. A parallel case can be made given cutbacks in steel production. Can you see how the production possibility frontier *must* have a negative slope and that it portrays the concept of opportunity cost?

10.   Use the diagrams below to answer this question.

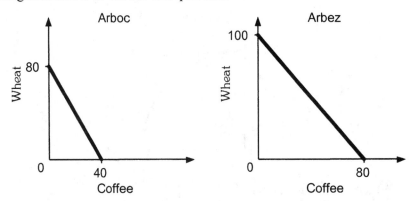

(a)   What is the opportunity cost of one unit of coffee in Arboc?
(b)   What is the opportunity cost of one unit of coffee in Arbez?
(c)   Which country has a comparative advantage in the production of coffee?
(d)   What is the opportunity cost of one unit of wheat in Arboc?
(e)   What is the opportunity cost of one unit of wheat in Arbez?
(f)   Which country has a comparative advantage in the production of wheat?
(g)   *Ceteris paribus*, ignoring other issues, which good should Arboc produce and which good should Arbez produce?

11.   Draw a production possibility curve. Put guns on the vertical axis and butter on the horizontal axis. Suppose that the technology for producing butter improves but the technology for producing guns does not. Describe how your diagram would change. In general, how will this technological advance affect the opportunity cost of producing guns?

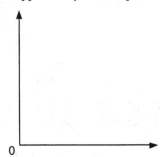

12.   Kara has a total of 12 hours to work on two projects. She must study for an economics test and "polish" an English composition paper. She believes that, with no studying at all, she would score 30 points on the economics test whereas, if she turned in her English paper with no extra work, it would earn 40 points. Suppose that, for each hour studying economics, she can raise her econ. score by 10 points, and that, for each hour of work on her composition, she can raise her English score by 6 points.
    (a)   Draw a production possibility frontier graph, showing all the points (combinations of time) that are feasible if Kara has 12 hours to allocate between economics and English. Put "hours of study for economics" on the vertical axis and "hours of study for English" on the horizontal axis.

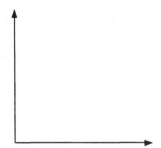

(b)   Show Point *A*, where Kara is studying 6 hours for economics and 6 hours for English.

(c)   Show Point *B*, where Kara is studying 12 hours for economics and 0 hours for English.

(d)   True or false? It is possible for Kara to score 100 on the economics test and at least 70 on the English paper.

(e)   True or false? It is possible for Kara to score 80 on the economics test and at least 80 on the English paper.

(f)   Kara decides to spend 4 hours studying for the economics test. What's the highest score she can expect to get on the English paper?

(g)   If Kara is satisfied with 70 in both subjects, how many hours would she need to study in total this weekend?

(h)   True or false? If Kara scored 70 on the economics test, she could have made at least 90 on the English paper.

(i)   The opportunity cost of scoring 6 points higher on the English paper is a score of _____ points LOWER/HIGHER on the economics test.

(j)   Draw a line (labelled EE) showing all the points that have exactly 2 hours of study time for the English paper.

13.   (a)   Consider the three fundamental economic questions in the context of a restaurant you're planning to open. Someone (you!) must decide what will be on the menu. Will it be Chinese, Mexican, or Italian cuisine? This is the "what to produce" question. You must also determine how your meals will be prepared and served. Will it be fast food or cordon bleu? The "for whom" question involved determining who your clientele will be. How do you advertise? Which demographic is important for you?

(b)   Now consider the case of Jonah Staw. Jonah, a 29-year old advertising executive earning $140,000 annually quit his job to found Little MissMatched, a company that produces "mismatched" gloves and socks for children. What was his opportunity cost? Now do some research—you can Google Staw's name. How did he answer the three economic questions?

PRACTICE TEST SOLUTIONS

I.   Solutions to Multiple-Choice Questions

1.   (b)   To be on the production possibility frontier, Arboc must have all of its resources fully and efficiently employed. Because it is operating inside the ppf, at least one of these conditions must have been violated.

2.   (a)   If Arboc produces relatively more capital, then it is expanding its resource base more rapidly and, *ceteris paribus*, it will grow more rapidly.

3.   (c)   Financial resources may be used to purchase real productive resources, but are not themselves productive. Note that, to an economist, "investment" is the creation of real productive capacity, not merely the purchase of stock in a company.

4.   (c)   To reach Point E the economy must grow, shifting out its production possibility frontier. This could occur if the labor force became more efficient.

5.   (d)   This is an increasing-cost production possibility frontier. As we increase the production of one good (butter), the cost in terms of the other good increases. In this case, a one-unit increase in butter (A to B) costs 3 guns; the move from B to C costs more (4 guns).

6.   (a)   Opportunity cost is defined (loosely) as the quantity of Good B given up to increase production of Good A. The quantity of butter remains at 1 unit, and gun production is increased.

7.   (b)   Refer to the answer to Question 6. Opportunity cost of one unit of butter is 0 at Point D. The opportunity cost of one unit of butter at Point C is 5 guns.

8.   (b)   The production possibility frontier depicts what it is possible to produce but nothing about what is wanted.

9.   (d)   Laissez-faire economies generally respond well to the needs of private consumers.

10.   (b)   A one-unit increase in wheat results in a three-unit decrease in tobacco production.

11.   (a)   A two-unit increase in tobacco results in a one-unit decrease in wheat.

12.   (b)   This point is inside the production possibility frontier. (We could be producing two more units of tobacco with the same amount of wheat production, for example.) This indicates that our resources are unemployed and/or inefficiently employed.

13.   (a)   The labor-force expansion represents an increase in productive resources. Note that the ppf depicts what can be supplied—demand is not reflected in the diagram.

14.   (b)   Refer to p. 25 for a discussion of the three basic questions.

15.   (a)   A general theme in economics is that private competition is highly efficient in providing most goods.

16.   (c)   With scarce resources, the production possibility frontier will *always* have a negative slope. With an increasing-cost production possibility frontier, the cost of producing one good in terms of the other accelerates as production level increases.

17.   (a)   Comparative advantage is a relative concept. If, relative to Jack, Jill is better at producing pins, then she has a comparative advantage in this.

18.   (d)   The first three answers are statements of the three "basic" questions. In any case, resources are allocated among producers, not consumers.

19.   (b)   The cost of one unit of goat milk in Arboc is 5/3 units of bananas whereas the cost of one unit of goat milk in Arbez is 1/3 unit of bananas. Arbez has the advantage in goat milk. One unit of bananas in Arboc costs 3/5 unit of goat milk whereas one unit of bananas in Arbez costs 3 units of goat milk. Arboc has the advantage in bananas.

20.   (a)   A bowed-out ppf indicates increasing costs; the costs increase whether the movement is down along the ppf or up along the ppf.

II.   Solutions to Application Questions

1.   (a)   Your ppf should include the following points:

Corn	100	90	70	40	0
Tobacco	0	40	70	90	100

There will be a straight line between each of the points.

   (b)   Resources are fully employed and employed in the more efficient activity. For example, Field *A* may be producing its maximum output of tobacco, but (because the opportunity cost of tobacco production in that field is high) it should be used to produce tobacco only after the other fields have been switched over to tobacco production. If it is switched before Field *B*, for instance, Brown will be producing inefficiently and inside his ppf.

   (c)   *D, C, B, A.*

   (d)   Refer to the explanation for (b).

2.   (a)   Refer to the following diagrams.

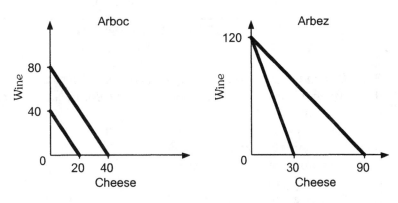

   (b)   1 wine = 1/2 cheese, 1 wine = 1/4 cheese.

   (c)   Arbez

   (d)   1 cheese = 2 wine (Arboc), 1 cheese = 4 wine (Arbez). Arboc can produce cheese more cheaply than Arbez can.

   (e)   Refer to the diagrams above.

   (f)   Arboc should still produce cheese, as the comparative costs have not changed.

   (g)   Arboc. Recompute the opportunity costs. Note that the relative steepness of the ppfs has changed.

3.   (a, b)   This question is intended to get you to think about all of the decisions that must be made in an economic system. The owner has land, labor, and capital at his/her disposal. The capital stock includes the store, the gas station, inventories, trucks, the house, and so forth. The road is also capital even though it was produced by the government. We are not told much about the natural resources of the town. These would include the fertility of the land. The potential labor force includes some fraction of those who live nearby.

   (c)   The people who travel the road, the general economic circumstances of the people who live nearby, the weather, gasoline prices, the potential for competition from other stores, and so forth.

   (d)   What to sell, whether to advertise, what prices to change, whether to fix up the town, how many people to hire, and so forth.

   (e)   I will add up all the future income I will earn, net of costs. I must consider all the alternatives and my expectations about them. How much will I earn here? How much will college cost? What am I likely to earn when I have graduated from college? I also need to consider carefully the personal pleasure I will derive from the two situations.

4.   (a)   Refer to the following diagram.

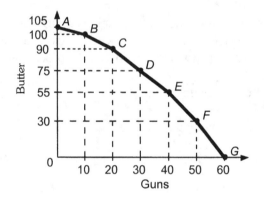

   (b)   Point D is on the ppf, indicating full employment of resources whereas Point H is inside the curve, indicating underproduction and an underutilization of scarce resources.

   (c)   (i)   1/2 unit of butter
         (ii)   1 unit of butter
         (iii) 2 1/2 units of butter
         (iv)   3 units of butter

   (d)   (i)   1/3 of a gun
         (ii)   2/3 of a gun
         (iii) 1 gun
         (iv)   2 guns

   (e)   The ppf will not shift position! We would expect the balance of production to shift in favor of guns. If unemployment exists, indicated by a bundle of goods inside the ppf, war production will shift the economy towards the ppf.

5.   (a)   No change in the position of the ppf.
     (b)   The end of the ppf on the X-axis will shift out. The end on the Y-axis will not move.
     (c)   The ppf would shift inwards.
     (d)   The ppf would shift outwards.
     (e)   The end of the ppf on the X-axis will shift in. The end on the Y-axis will not move.

6.   (a)   You might think C and A are "best" and "worst," respectively—but the question is a trap! What do we mean by "best"? Perhaps a particular point inside the ppf is better than a particular point on it. There's not enough information to give a complete answer.

(b)   Clearly, all points on the production possibility frontier are not created equal, and Point E might be the "best" choice of those depicted.

(c)   The "best" output mix depends on what best meets society's wants. If you think about it, what society *wants* isn't shown on a ppf diagram—only what can be *produced*.

7.   (a)   Refer to the following diagram.

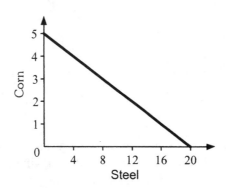

(b)

Production	Opportunity Cost of 1 Unit of:	
Alternative	Corn	Steel
$A - B$	4 steel	1/4 corn
$B - C$	4 steel	1/4 corn
$C - D$	4 steel	1/4 corn
$D - E$	4 steel	1/4 corn
$E - F$	4 steel	1/4 corn

(c)   Situation X: 0 steel; 0 corn
Situation Y: 4 steel; 1/4 corn

(d)   In Situation X there are still some unemployed (inefficiently used) resources. In Situation Y, Arbez is already utilizing all of its resources, and a trade-off is necessary. (Plot the points on the diagram to see the difference.)

(e)   Situation Z: 1 steel; 0 corn

(f)   Situation Y is the most productively efficient. Either X or Z is the least productively efficient—we don't have enough information.

(g)   Each unit of corn costs 4 units of steel; each unit of steel costs 1/4 unit of corn.

(h)   Each unit of corn costs 2 units of steel. Each unit of steel costs 1/2 unit of corn.

(i)   Arbez; Arboc. Yes, trade can be mutually beneficial.

8.   (a) D

(b)   The economy must either grow (more resources) or experience a technological improvement.

(c) C

(d)   Corn

(e)   There is no opportunity cost; more steel is produced without any reduction in corn production. Note that there are "free lunches" if the economy is operating at an inefficient point.

9.   (a)   Yes
      (b)   No, because it is possible to produce more of each good. Also some resources are unemployed.
      (c)   No, not relative to Point *A*, where consumers would have more of each good available to them.
      (d)   It is beyond the maximum level of production, given current resources and technology.
      (e)   Resources would be released and transferred to steel production.

10.   (a)   2 units of wheat
      (b)   5/4 units of wheat
      (c)   Arbez
      (d)   1/2 unit of coffee
      (e)   8/10 unit of coffee
      (f)   Arboc
      (g)   Arboc should specialize in wheat production, and Arbez should specialize in coffee production.

11.   The production possibility frontier would pivot at its "guns" endpoint and become flatter, which indicates that it is possible to produce a greater maximum quantity of butter than before, while still producing the same maximum quantity of guns. The slope of the ppf represents opportunity cost. Producing only guns means that we surrender a larger quantity of butter than before—the opportunity cost of guns has increased (and the opportunity cost of butter has decreased).

12.   (a)   Refer to the following diagram.

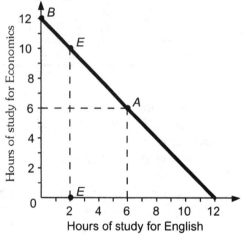

      (b)   Refer to the diagram above.
      (c)   Refer to the diagram above.
      (d)   True. Economics: $30 + (10 \times 7) = 100$. English: $40 + (6 \times 5) = 70$.
      (e)   True. Economics: $30 + (10 \times 5) = 80$. English: $40 + (6 \times 7) = 82$. If she gets 80 on the economics test, 82 is the maximum she can get on the English paper.
      (f)   She has 8 hours for the English paper. English: $40 + (6 \times 8) = 88$.
      (g)   Economics: $30 + (10 \times 4) = 70$. English: $40 + (6 \times 5) = 70$. This totals 9 hours.
      (h)   False. Economics: $30 + (10 \times 4) = 70$. English: $40 + (6 \times 8) = 88$.
      (i)   Ten points lower—an extra hour of work on the English paper will cut Kara's economics score by 10 points.
      (j)   Refer to the preceding diagram.

13.   (a)   Clearly, there are no definitive answers for the restaurant—that's why entrepreneurs are an unusual breed.

       (b)   Staw's opportunity cost of founding his company would include the salary he gave up (and his promotion prospects). He opted to produce deliberately mismatched products, made to his specifications by overseas textiles producers. He set up marketing deals with large retail chains such as Sears.

3

Demand, Supply, and Market Equilibrium

Chapter objectives:

1. Define and apply quantity demanded and quantity supplied, and state the law of demand and the law of supply.
2. Draw and interpret demand and supply graphs.
3. Identify the determinants of demand and supply and indicate how each must change for demand and supply to increase or decrease.
4. Derive market demand and market supply curves from individual demand and supply schedules.
5. Differentiate between a shift of a demand curve or supply curve and a movement along a curve, and depict these cases correctly on a graph.
6. Provide explanations for the slope of a typical demand curve.
7. Distinguish the relationship that exists between two goods that are substitutes and the relationship that exists between two goods that are complements.
8. Distinguish between a good that is normal and a good that is inferior.
9. Determine equilibrium price and quantity and detail the process by which the market moves from one equilibrium situation to another when demand or supply shifts.
10. Define excess demand (shortage) and excess supply (surplus) and predict their effects on the existing price level.

The single best piece of advice, particularly for this essential chapter, is "practice, practice, practice." A second piece of advice must be "draw, draw, draw." Don't be put off by the graphs—develop a solid intuitive feel for demand and supply by talking your way through how the market should behave.

In most of the multiple-choice questions in this chapter, the *first* thing to do is to sketch a demand and supply picture. Graphs are an effective and timesaving tool for organizing your analysis.

Cultivate the habit of asking "What should happen to demand?" and "Will this make supply increase or decrease?" Predict whether price should rise or fall in a given circumstance (common sense should carry you a long way here). Don't try to avoid graphs—they'll make your course a lot easier *and* more rewarding. If you have some initial problems, check the Appendix to Chapter 1 and the "Learning Tips" in this Guide.

BRAIN TEASER I: During the past ten years, the price of cell phones has fallen, while the numbers sold have increased. Is this a contradiction of the law of supply? How could you best explain this phenomenon, in words and graphically?

SOLUTION: The answer to this and subsequent brain teasers will be found after our discussion of the learning objectives and before the Practice Tests.

BRAIN TEASER II: Many large firms (McDonald's, for example) perform research in order to determine where best to locate new branches. Suppose you're responsible for choosing your burger company's next location. Which factors would be important in your deliberations?

OBJECTIVE 1:
Define and apply quantity demanded and quantity supplied, and state the law of demand and the law of supply.

Quantity demanded is the amount of a product that a household would buy, in a given period, if it could buy all it wanted at the current price. *Quantity supplied* is the amount of a product that a firm would be willing and able to offer for sale at a particular price during a given time period. The *law of demand* states that there is a negative relationship between the price and the quantity demanded of a product. When the price of McDonald's fries increases, we buy less. The *law of supply* states that there is a positive relationship between the price and the quantity supplied of a product. When McDonald's raises its hourly wage, it attracts more job applicants. (pages 48/57)

OBJECTIVE 2:
Draw and interpret demand and supply graphs.

A *demand schedule* is a table showing how much of a given product households would be willing and able to buy at different prices in a given time period; a *demand curve* shows this relationship graphically. Demand curves slope downward. (page 49)

A *supply schedule* is a table listing how much of a product a firm will supply at alternative prices in a given time period; a *supply curve*, shows this relationship graphically. Supply curves slope upward. (page 57)

Note: Demand and supply graphs *always* have price on the vertical axis and quantity (demanded or supplied, as appropriate) on the horizontal axis. It is a bad, though common, mistake to reverse the variables. Learn to draw the demand and supply graphs quickly! A demand curve slopes down; a supply curve slopes up. Practice to increase your speed. Label each curve as you go. In diagrams where there are several curves, clear, consistent labeling is critical.

━━━━━━━━━━━━━━━━━━━━━━━ **Practice** ━━━━━━━━━━━━━━━━━━━━━━━

1.   At each price shown, estimate how many apples per month you might demand.

Price per Apple	Quantity Demanded
60¢	
50¢	
40¢	
30¢	
20¢	
10¢	

You have constructed a demand schedule. Now draw vertical (price) and horizontal (quantity) axes. Plot your monthly demand curve for apples. Label the curve D_1.

ANSWER: Although this line is unlikely to be smooth like those in the textbook, but it should have a general downward slope—the lower the price, the more apples you're likely to buy. You should have the horizontal axis labeled "quantity demanded per month" and the vertical axis labeled "price."

2.   In the following diagrams, match each of the numbers with the appropriate term to produce a correct demand or supply diagram for apples.
(a)   Price of apples
(b)   Price of apples
(c)   Quantity of apples supplied per month
(d)   Quantity of apples demanded per month
(e)   Demand curve
(f)   Supply curve

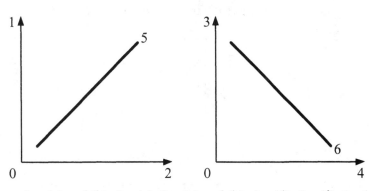

ANSWER: 1 = (a) and (b); 2 = (c); 3 = (a) and (b); 4 = (d); 5 = (f); 6 = (e) ■

 OBJECTIVE 3:
Identify the determinants of demand and supply and indicate how each must change for demand and supply to increase or decrease.

The willingness and ability of a household to buy units of a good (quantity demanded) are likely to depend principally on the price of the good itself. Other factors—including the household's income and wealth, the prices of other products, tastes and preferences, and expectations about price, income, and wealth—will influence demand.

Comment: This section of the textbook may be your most frustrating section. Be patient—time spent understanding demand/supply analysis will serve you well in future chapters.

▶▶   LEARNING TIP: When analyzing the impact of change in a determinant on demand and supply curves, a golden rule to remember is that each curve shifts no more than once for any such change. The market price is changed by shifts in the demand and supply curves, but the demand and supply curves are not changed by shifts in the market price.

Again: a change in price does not cause the demand curve or the supply curve to shift position! Analyze the following sequence of events for errors. "Demand goes up. That makes price go up, which encourages sellers to supply more. But, when more is supplied, price goes down. When price goes down, demand goes up again, and so on."

Answer: A demand increase from D_1 to D_2 will make price rise from P_1 to P_2. Sellers will supply more from Q_1 to Q_2—an increase in *quantity supplied*, not an increase in supply, as the statement claims. Price, therefore, will *not* go back down. The remainder of the statement is incorrect. Draw this example.

When you constructed your demand schedule and demand curve with varying price levels in Practice Question 1, you made assumptions about your income level, wealth, prices of other goods, and so on. Change the assumptions and you will change the diagram. The curve shifts position—a *change in demand*.

Factors that can cause a change in demand are:
(a)   Income
(b)   Wealth
(c)   Prices of related products
(d)   Tastes or preferences of the household
(e)   Expectations (page 51)

Increases in income and wealth, improved preferences, or expectations of a higher price, income, or wealth will increase demand for normal goods. An increase in the price of a substitute product or a decrease in the price of a complementary product will also increase demand, i.e., the entire demand curve shifts to the right. Graphically, an increase in demand (D_1 to D_2) appears as shown in the following diagram:

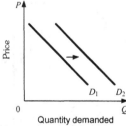

▶▶   LEARNING TIP: When shifting the demand curve, you might naturally associate "rise" and "fall" with a vertical shift. This causes no problems in the case of demand, and you'd expect to be correct in using the same approach in the case of supply—but you'd be wrong! A vertical shift up in supply is a *decrease* in supply. When shifting the demand or supply curve, think in terms of the curve sliding *left* for a decrease (demand less or supply less) and *right* for an increase (demand more or supply more), *not* up and down.

The decision to supply is affected by the ability to earn profits (the difference between revenues and costs). The willingness and ability of a firm to offer units of a good for sale (quantity supplied) are likely to depend mainly on the price of the good itself. If other factors important to producers change, then the supply curve diagram will change. The supply curve shifts position—a *change in supply*.

Factors that can cause a change in supply are:

(a)   Changes in costs of production (input prices)
(b)   New costs and market opportunities
(c)   Changes in prices of related products (page 59)

Improvements in technology, decreases in the costs of inputs and other costs of production, or increases in the price of complementary products will increase supply. Decreases in the price of substitute products will also increase supply, i.e., the entire supply curve will shift to the right. Graphically, an increase in supply (D_1 to D_2) appears as shown in the following diagram:

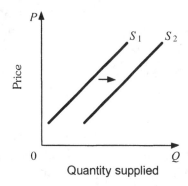

▶▶   LEARNING TIP: When considering if a given factor will cause supply to increase or decrease, ask "Will this change increase or decrease profits?" Producers will want to supply more if their profits are rising—so, if the answer to the question is "increase profits," you should predict an increase (rightward shift) in supply.
        Keep these lists of factors that can change demand or supply in a place very close to your heart! Write them on an index card and review them frequently.

Demand: Do "thought experiments." Pick a good that you buy frequently (preferably a name brand), such as Exxon gasoline. How would you react if Exxon hiked the price of its gas? If your income fell? If the price of engine oil (a complement) increased? If the price of Texaco gas (a substitute) decreased?

Supply: Perhaps you have a part-time job—you supply labor. Which factors affect how many hours you would work per week? The wage (price) you earn affects the quantity of labor you supply. What other factors would make you more or less willing and able to work?

Supply will be analyzed in greater detail in Chapters 7, 8, and 9. Note the reference to the *short run* and the *long run* on page 58. These are important economic concepts that you'll meet later on. Essentially, suppliers will be more responsive to demand-side changes in a longer time period than they will be in a shorter time period.

▶▶   LEARNING TIP: When you are told to imagine that income or some other variable has changed, imagine an *enormous* change—this will help you work out the effects. If a can of Pepsi has risen in price—suppose that it has tripled in price—it's easier to see what will happen to the quantity demanded or supplied of Pepsi and to the demand for Coke.

—■————————————————— **Practice** —————————————————————

3.   A decrease in the supply of American cars might be caused by
    (a)   an increase in the price of imported Japanese cars.
    (b)   an increase in the wages of U.S. car workers.
    (c)   an increase in demand that causes car prices to rise.
    (d)   a reduction in the cost of steel.

    ANSWER: (b) The supply of American cars will decrease if input prices, such as the wages of
        U.S. car workers, increase. Refer to p. 59.

4.   Energizer batteries and Duracell's Coppertop batteries are substitutes. The Energizer Bunny cuts
    supply and increases the price of its batteries. Equilibrium price will _____ and quantity
    exchanged will _____ in the market for Duracell.
    (a)   rise; rise
    (b)   fall; rise
    (c)   fall; fall
    (d)   rise; fall

    ANSWER: (a) If Energizer increases the price of its batteries, consumers will switch over to
        substitutes such as Duracell, increasing the demand for Duracell. This will raise
        both equilibrium price and quantity.

5.   Barney's Bowling Balls and Fred's Bowling Shoes are complements. Fred notices a decrease in
    the quantity demanded of bowling shoes (a movement along his demand curve). This could have
    been caused by
    (a)   a decrease in the income of Fred's customers.
    (b)   an increase in the price of Fred's Bowling Shoes.
    (c)   an increase in the price of Barney's Bowling Balls.
    (d)   an increased expectation that Fred will reduce the price of his bowling balls in the near
        future.

    ANSWER: (b) This is a change in quantity demanded, not a change in demand! The only thing
        that can cause a change in quantity demanded is a change in price. Refer to p. 53.

6.   As the price of oranges increases, orange growers will
    (a)   use more-expensive methods of growing oranges.
    (b)   use less-expensive methods of growing oranges.
    (c)   increase the supply of oranges.
    (d)   decrease the supply of oranges.

    ANSWER: (a) An increase in price results in an increase in quantity supplied. Suppliers are
        able to produce more because, at the higher price, they can afford to hire more-
        expensive resources. Refer to p. 59.

7.   The supply of oranges to households will shift to the right if
    (a)   the price of oranges increases.
    (b)   oranges are rumored to have been treated with an insecticide that causes heart disease.
    (c)   the Florida government requires that all orange workers be given more substantial health
        benefits by employers.
    (d)   citrus growers see the price of grapefruits decreasing permanently.

    ANSWER: (d) As the price of grapefruits falls, citrus farmers will switch over to another
        production option—oranges. Refer to p. 59.

OBJECTIVE 4:
Derive market demand and market supply curves from individual demand and supply schedules.

Market demand is the sum of all the quantities of a good or service demanded per period by all the households buying in the market for that good or service. The *market demand curve* is a summing of all the individual demand curves. At a given price level, the quantity demanded by each household is determined and the total quantity demanded is calculated. (pages 55/61)

The *market supply curve* is a horizontal summing of all the supply curves for the product.

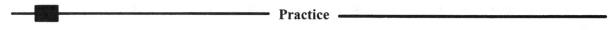 **Practice**

8.   If the firms producing fuzzy dice for cars must obtain a higher price than they did previously to produce the same level of output as before, then we can say that there has been
(a)   an increase in quantity supplied.
(b)   an increase in supply.
(c)   a decrease in supply.
(d)   a decrease in quantity supplied.
ANSWER: (c) Draw the supply curve. At the same output level and at a higher price, the supply curve has shifted to the left—a decrease in supply. Refer to p. 59.

9.   The market supply curve for wheat depends on each of the following EXCEPT
(a)   the price of wheat-producing land.
(b)   the price of production alternatives for wheat.
(c)   the tastes and preferences of wheat consumers.
(d)   the number of wheat farmers in the market.
ANSWER: (c) Tastes and preferences are determinants of demand, not supply. Refer to p. 59.

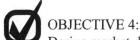 OBJECTIVE 5:
Differentiate between a shift of a demand curve or supply curve and a movement along a curve, and depict these cases correctly on a graph.

When important factors other than the price of the product change, such as tastes or income, the entire demand curve shifts position. This is called a *change in demand* to distinguish it from a movement along the demand curve, which represents a *change in quantity demanded* and can be caused *only* by a change in the price of the commodity. (page 53)

Similarly, when important factors other than price change for a producer, the amount of a given product offered for sale will change, even if the price level is unchanged. This is a *change in supply*. If *only* the price of the product itself changes, there will be a movement along the original supply curve—a *change in quantity supplied*. (page 59)

Graphing Pointer: Changes in Quantity Demanded (Supplied) vs. Changes in Demand (Supply). Most students experience confusion regarding the distinction between a "change in quantity demanded" and a "change in demand." The distinction is rather artificial; the six factors (listed on page 48) that affect demand include the price of the product. However, we regard the price-quantity demanded relationship as the most important and draw the demand curve with these two variables on the axes, assuming that all other factors are fixed at a "given" level. This is the *ceteris paribus* assumption.

Look at a demand curve; price and quantity demanded can have a range of values whereas all other factors (income, other prices, etc.) are fixed at a particular level. If price changes, we move along the curve; if another factor changes, our *ceteris paribus* assumption is broken, and we must redraw the price-quantity demanded relationship.

The *only* thing that can cause a "change in the quantity demanded" of Pepsi is a change in the price of Pepsi—a movement from one point on the demand curve to another point on the same demand curve.

If any other factor on the list changes, we will have to redraw the entire diagram—a "change in demand"—because the "all else being equal" assumption has been broken.

Similarly, a "change in the quantity supplied" of chicken can only be caused by a change in the price of chicken. A change in any other factor on the list on page 59 of the text causes a "change in supply."

▶▶   LEARNING TIP: Here is an example that points up the difference between a "change in quantity demanded" and a "change in demand." In the following diagram, we have a demand curve for Ford Rangers on the left and a demand curve for Dodge Rams on the right.

Initially, the price of the Ranger is $27,000, and 2,000 are demanded per week. The Ram sells for $26,000 and has 2,500 demanders at that price. (Note: It's irrelevant whether the Ram's price is above, below, or equal to that of the Ranger—at any realistic prices, each truck will have some enthusiasts.)

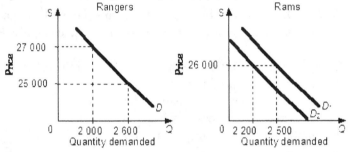

Suppose that the price of Rangers decreases to $25,000. More truck buyers will order Rangers—an increase in quantity demanded, as there is a movement along the demand curve. Some of those new Ford customers would have bought the Dodge Ram, but now will not. At the same price ($26,000) as before, demand for Rams has decreased, perhaps to 2,200. The entire demand curve for Rams has shifted.

■━━━━━━━━━━━━━━━━━━━━━━━━━━ **Practice** ━━━━━━━━━━━━━━━━━━━━━━━━━━━

10.   Return to Practice Question 1. Suppose that the prices of other fruits you might buy increase. What would happen to the number of apples you demand per month? Sketch this change on your diagram. Label the demand curve D_2. What is likely to happen to the price of apples?

ANSWER: Refer to your diagram for Practice Question 1. Presumably you'd demand more apples at each price. The demand curve shifts right, to D_2. Because apples are more popular now, the price of apples will likely rise.

11.   A "change in demand" means
   (a)   the quantity demanded changes as price changes.
   (b)   a movement along a given demand curve or schedule.
   (c)   a shift in the position of the demand curve.
   (d)   a change in the shape of a demand curve.

ANSWER: (c) A "change in demand" means that, at every price level, more or less is being demanded. This is represented as a shift in the position of the demand curve. Refer to p. 53.

12.   Which of the following will cause a decrease in the demand for tennis racquets?
    (a)   A rise in the price of squash racquets
    (b)   A rise in the price of tennis racquets
    (c)   A rise in the price of tennis balls
    (d)   A fall in the price of tennis shoes
    ANSWER: (c)   A decrease in the demand for tennis racquets will occur if a complement (tennis balls) increases in price because fewer tennis balls will be bought. ■

 OBJECTIVE 6:
Provide explanations for the slope of a typical demand curve.

Demand curves slope down—as price rises, quantity demanded falls. We know this intuitively, but economists have explored this important "social law" more analytically. The higher the price of a good, lowfat milk, for instance, the higher the opportunity cost of buying it (i.e., the more of other goods we will give up, and the less willing we are to buy lowfat milk).

    Utility is a conceptual measure of satisfaction. Successive units of a good bestow satisfaction, but typically at a decreasing rate—the second cup of coffee may be less enjoyable than the first. Accordingly, the price we are willing to pay will decrease. (page 50)

■————————————————————— **Practice** —————————————————————

13.   The demand curve diagram has
    (a)   "price" on the vertical axis, "quantity demanded per time period" on the horizontal axis, and an upward sloping demand curve.
    (b)   "price" on the horizontal axis, "quantity demanded per time period" on the vertical axis, and an upward sloping demand curve.
    (c)   "price" on the vertical axis, "quantity demanded per time period" on the horizontal axis, and a downward sloping demand curve.
    (d)   "price" on the horizontal axis, "quantity demanded per time period" on the vertical axis, and a downward sloping demand curve.
    ANSWER: (c)   Refer to p. 49.

14.   We are trying to explain the law of demand. When the price of pretzels rises,
    (a)   the opportunity cost of pretzels increases along the demand curve.
    (b)   sellers switch production and increase the quantity supplied of pretzels.
    (c)   income rises for producers of pretzels.
    (d)   the opportunity cost of other goods increases.
    ANSWER: (a)   Refer to p. 50 for a full explanation of the negative relationship between price and quantity demanded.

 OBJECTIVE 7:
Distinguish the relationship that exists between two goods that are substitutes and the relationship that exists between two goods that are complements.

If, when the price of Good *A* rises, the demand for Good *B* also rises, then *A* and *B* are *substitutes*; however, if the demand for *B* falls when the price of *A* rises, then *A* and *B* are *complements*. Substitutes are used in place of each other: complements are used together. (page 51)

▶▶▶   LEARNING TIP: Think of several ready-made examples of substitute goods and complementary goods from your own life. Using with your own examples (during an exam) makes it easier to do the analysis correctly. Here are a few examples.
Substitutes: Coke and Pepsi, Exxon gasoline and Texaco gasoline, phone calls and e-mail.
Complements: peanut butter and jelly, CDs and CD players, cars and gasoline, cameras and film, left and right shoes.

━━━━■━━━━━━━━━━━━━━━━━━━━━━ **Practice** ━━━━━━━━━━━━━━━━━━━━

15.   The demand for JIF peanut butter will decrease if there is an increase in
    (a)   the price of JIF peanut butter.
    (b)   the price of Peter Pan peanut butter (a substitute).
    (c)   the demand for jelly (a complement).
    (d)   the price of bread (a complement).

    ANSWER: (d) Bread and peanut butter are complements. An increase in the price of bread will result in less bread being bought and a lower demand for JIF to spread on it. Refer to p. 52.

16.   Good *A* and Good *B* are substitutes for one another. An increase in the price of *A* will
    (a)   increase the demand for *B*.
    (b)   reduce the quantity demanded of *B*.
    (c)   increase the quantity demanded of *B*.
    (d)   reduce the demand for *B*.

    ANSWER: (a) Suppose *A* is Coke and *B* is Pepsi. If Coke rises in price, we would buy less Coke (a fall in quantity demanded of Coke) and more of Pepsi (an increase in the demand for Pepsi). Refer to p. 52.

 OBJECTIVE 8:
Distinguish between a good that is normal and a good that is inferior.

When income increases, demand increases for *normal* goods. If demand for a good decreases when income increases, then the good is *inferior*. (page 51)

▶▶▶   LEARNING TIP: Think of several ready-made examples of both normal goods and inferior goods from your own life. Slotting in your own examples (during an exam) makes it easier to do the analysis correctly. Here are some examples:
Normal goods: movie tickets, steak, restaurant meals, imported beers.
Inferior goods: second-hand clothes, store-brand (versus name-brand) foods, generic medicines, rice, beans, bus rides.

━━━━■━━━━━━━━━━━━━━━━━━━━━━ **Practice** ━━━━━━━━━━━━━━━━━━━━

17.   If the economy's income rises by 10% then, *ceteris paribus*, we would predict
    (a)   a decrease in demand for a normal good.
    (b)   an increase in quantity demanded for a normal good.
    (c)   an increase in quantity demanded for an inferior good.
    (d)   a decrease in demand for an inferior good.

    ANSWER: (d) Refer to p. 51. Remember that a change in "quantity demanded" can only be due to a change in the price of the good.

18.   The demand for Good *A* has been increasing over the past year. Having examined the following facts, you conclude that Good *A* is an inferior good. Which fact led you to that conclusion?
        (a)   The price of Good *A* has been increasing over the past year.
        (b)   An economic slowdown has reduced the income of the traditional buyers of Good *A*.
        (c)   Good *B*, a substitute for Good *A*, has cut its price over the last 12 months.
        (d)   Household wealth has increased among the traditional buyers of Good *A*.

        ANSWER: (b) Inferior goods experience increasing popularity as income levels fall.
                Refer to p. 52.

19.   Turnips are available in both the United States and in Mexico. During the past year, incomes have grown by 10% in each country. The demand for turnips has grown by 12% in the United States and by 3% in Mexico. We can conclude that turnips are
        (a)   normal goods in the United States and normal goods in Mexico.
        (b)   normal goods in the United States and inferior goods in Mexico.
        (c)   inferior goods in the United States and normal goods in Mexico.
        (d)   inferior goods in the United States and inferior goods in Mexico.

        ANSWER: (a) In each case, demand has increased as income has increased. Refer to p. 51.

 OBJECTIVE 9:
Determine equilibrium price and quantity and detail the process by which the market moves from one equilibrium situation to another when demand or supply shifts.

In the market for a particular good or service, quantity demanded may be greater than, less than, or equal to quantity supplied. *Equilibrium* occurs when quantity demanded equals quantity supplied. There is no tendency for the price to change because, at that price, there is a perfect match between the quantity of the good demanded and the quantity supplied. (page 62)

▶▶▶   LEARNING TIP: **Equilibrium.** The notion of equilibrium is important throughout the remainder of the course. The simple, less analytical, way to think about this concept is as "the point where the lines cross." It will help your understanding if you remember that equilibrium is the "balance" situation in which there is no tendency for change—unless some outside factor intervenes.
            Changes in Equilibrium Price and Quantity. Demand and supply may change position simultaneously. If the magnitudes of the shifts are unknown, then either the effect on equilibrium price or on equilibrium quantity *must* be uncertain. It's easy to forget this important fact. If demand and supply change position simultaneously, break down the situation into two separate graphs, one for the "demand shift" and the other for the "supply shift." In each case, decide the direction of change in price and quantity, and then add them together.
            Example: Demand decreases and supply increases.

	Price Change	Quantity Change
Demand-side effect	Decrease	Decrease
Supply-side effect	Decrease	Increase
Total effect	Decrease	Uncertain

            In this case, where demand decreases and supply increases, we predict a certain decrease in price and an uncertain change in equilibrium quantity.

ECONOMICS IN PRACTICE: On page 67, the textbook looks at the effects of demand and supply on the market for orange juice. What about other markets? In 2002, the *Economist* magazine reported record low levels of wool production in Australia following a severe drought. Wool prices surged to a 15-year peak. What do you think was the effect on the market for cotton, a substitute fiber?

ANSWER: Initially, cotton prices had been languishing at a 30-year low. However, as garment producers switched from wool to cotton, they caused the demand for cotton to increase, resulting in a 50% boost in the price of cotton. For "extra credit,' can you draw a demand and supply diagram (one for wool and another for cotton) depicting what happened?

ECONOMICS IN PRACTICE (CONTINUED): During the spring and summer of 2008, the corn-growing states of the mid-west suffered from extreme wet weather. Corn planting declined by 10 percent while, simultaneously, the use of corn for ethanol was increasing. The Chicago Board of Trade has a futures market where dealers can bid for future deliveries of corn and other goods, such as soy beans. This market is largely driven by predictions about future market conditions. What do you think happened to the price of corn and soy beans on the futures market as a result of the storms?

ANSWER: The price of corn tripled to about $7.00 per bushel. Soy beans, (a production substitute of corn) also experienced price increases.

ECONOMICS IN PRACTICE: Your textbook examines the opinions of three analysts on page 69. Essentially, the issue of rising prices boils down to whether it is triggered by changes in demand or changes in supply. The market for corn offers another example. During the first few months of 2008, corn prices rose throughout the world. Was this caused by cutbacks in supply or increases in demand? Background: Over the two previous years, major corn-growing regions had experienced poor weather conditions, the Chinese economy was experiencing increased affluence, and there had been a push by environmental-conscious governments to produce more ethanol (an oil substitute that uses corn). Given these facts, how would you analyze the changes in the corn market?

ANSWER: There were changes in both supply and demand. The poor growing conditions reduced supply while increasing affluence expanded the demand for corn (a normal good). At the same time, the demand for corn to be used to produce ethanol increased, which reduced the amount available for food production.

PRACTICE: In the summer of 2008, President Bush appealed to Saudi Arabia to increase the supply of oil in order to reduce pressure on gas prices at the pumps. His point was that restricted supply was forcing up prices. The Saudi response, in summary, was "There is no shortage of oil. World oil prices are responding as they should to the increase in demand." However, the Law of Demand states that rising prices should reduce the amount of a good demanded. First, is there some inconsistency here in the Law of Demand? Following this, can you analyze who was correct about the oil market in 2008, President Bush or the Saudi Oil Ministry?

ANSWER: There's no contradiction of the Law of Demand. In fact, as prices rose in the United States, oil consumption fell, as we should expect. On the second point, both parties are correct. An increase in supply would have slowed or, perhaps, reversed the rise in oil prices, as President Bush argued. However, the main cause of rising oil prices was the worldwide increase in demand. The Saudis were correct—the market was seeking to compete away excess demand by raising prices. If a market is in equilibrium there is no shortage.

——————————————————————————— **Practice** ———————————————————————————

20.   Equilibrium quantity will certainly decrease if
   (a)   demand and supply both increase.
   (b)   demand and supply both decrease.
   (c)   demand decreases and supply increases.
   (d)   demand increases and supply decreases.

   ANSWER: (b) A decrease in demand will decrease equilibrium quantity. Similarly, a decrease in supply will decrease equilibrium quantity.

21.   The market for canned dog food is in equilibrium when
        (a)   the quantity demanded is less than the quantity supplied.
        (b)   the demand curve is downward-sloping and the supply curve is upward-sloping.
        (c)   the quantity demanded and the quantity supplied are equal.
        (d)   all inputs producing canned dog food are employed.

        ANSWER: (c) A market is in equilibrium when price has adjusted to make the quantity demanded and the quantity supplied equal. Refer to p. 62.

22.   In the market for broccoli, the price of broccoli will certainly increase if the supply of broccoli
        (a)   increases and the demand for broccoli increases.
        (b)   increases and the demand for broccoli decreases.
        (c)   decreases and the demand for broccoli increases.
        (d)   decreases and the demand for broccoli decreases.

        ANSWER: (c) An increase in demand will increase equilibrium price. Similarly, a decrease in supply will increase equilibrium price.

23.   In the market for mushrooms, the price of mushrooms will certainly increase if the supply curve shifts
        (a)   right and the demand curve shifts right.
        (b)   right and the demand curve shifts left.
        (c)   left and the demand curve shifts right.
        (d)   left and the demand curve shifts left.

        ANSWER: (c) When demand increases and supply decreases, both shifts are prompting a price increase.

24.   In the market for broccoli, the equilibrium quantity of broccoli will certainly increase if the supply of broccoli _____ and the demand for broccoli _____ .
        (a)   increases; increases
        (b)   increases; decreases
        (c)   decreases; increases
        (d)   decreases; decreases

        ANSWER: (a) An increase in supply will increase the quantity traded; similarly, an increase in demand will increase the quantity traded. ∎

 OBJECTIVE 10:
Define excess demand (shortage) and excess supply (surplus) and predict their effects on the existing price level.

If the quantity demanded is greater than the quantity supplied of a good, there is *excess demand* (shortage). We would expect the price of the good to rise. If quantity supplied is greater than the quantity demanded of a good, there is an *excess supply* (surplus), and we would expect the price of the good to fall. (pages 62/63)

━━━ **Practice** ━━━

25. When there is a surplus, quantity supplied _____ quantity demanded. Price will _____ .
    (a) exceeds; rise
    (b) is less than; fall
    (c) is less than; rise
    (d) exceeds; fall

    ANSWER: (d) A surplus (excess supply) occurs when quantity supplied exceeds quantity demanded. This surplus will force price down. Refer to p. 63.

26. The equilibrium price of a gallon of unleaded gas is $4.50. At a price of $3.00
    (a) quantity supplied will be less than quantity demanded, causing a shortage of unleaded gas.
    (b) quantity supplied will be greater than quantity demanded, causing a surplus of unleaded gas.
    (c) quantity supplied will be greater than quantity demanded, causing a shortage of unleaded gas.
    (d) quantity supplied will be less than quantity demanded, causing a surplus of unleaded gas.

    ANSWER: (a) If the current price is less than the equilibrium price, a shortage will occur (quantity supplied will be less than quantity demanded). This shortage will force price to increase. ■

BRAIN TEASER I SOLUTION: Behavior in the cell phone market did not contradict the law of supply. Market behavior depends on both supply and demand. Demand increased (the demand curve shifted to the right from D_1 to D_2) as more consumers were attracted to the benefits of cell phones—particularly their convenience, and supply increased (the supply curve shifted to the right from S_1 to S_2) due to technological improvements. Increasing supply and vigorous competition drove down the price (from P_1 to P_2) even as the market grew (from Q_1 to Q_2).

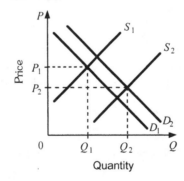

BRAIN TEASER II SOLUTION: The presence of competitors, income and wealth of the neighborhood, the percentage of families with young children, expected growth, and volume of traffic should all be important considerations. It is rumored that McDonald's also figures in the direction of after-work traffic.

PRACTICE TEST

I.   MULTIPLE-CHOICE QUESTIONS

Select the option that provides the single best answer.

_____   1.   Households are
                (a)   suppliers in the input market.
                (b)   demanders in the labor market.
                (c)   suppliers in the product market.
                (d)   demanders in the input market.

_____   2.   Following a decrease in supply, Good *C* increases its price. The demand for Good *D* increases. The goods are
                (a)   complements.
                (b)   substitutes.
                (c)   normal.
                (d)   inferior.

_____   3.   The demand for prerecorded CDs is downsloping. Suddenly the price of CDs rises from $12 to $20. This will cause
                (a)   demand to shift to the left.
                (b)   demand to shift to the right.
                (c)   quantity demanded to increase.
                (d)   quantity demanded to decrease.

_____   4.   All of the following will shift the supply curve of yo-yos to the right EXCEPT
                (a)   an increase in price of yo-yos.
                (b)   an improvement in the production processes used to manufacture yo-yos.
                (c)   a reduction in the price of plastic from which yo-yos are made.
                (d)   an improvement in storage resulting in fewer defective yo-yos.

_____   5.   Along a given supply curve for eggs,
                (a)   supply increases as price increases.
                (b)   supply increases as technology improves.
                (c)   quantity supplied increases as price increases.
                (d)   quantity supplied increases as technology improves.

_____   6.   Price is currently below equilibrium. There is a situation of excess _____ . We would expect price to _____ .
                (a)   demand; rise
                (b)   demand; fall
                (c)   supply; rise
                (d)   supply; fall

_____ 7. Consumers expect their income to rise. For a normal good, this would result in an increase in
   (a) quantity demanded and a fall in price.
   (b) demand and a fall in price.
   (c) quantity demanded and a rise in price.
   (d) demand and a rise in price.

_____ 8. The price of Frisbees (a normal good) will definitely increase if
   (a) there is an improvement in the technology of making Frisbees and Frisbees become more popular.
   (b) the cost of plastic used to produce Frisbees increases and people have more leisure time to throw Frisbees.
   (c) Frisbee workers negotiate a wage increase and boomerangs (a Frisbee substitute) decrease in price.
   (d) a sales tax is imposed on Frisbees and (because of widespread unemployment) incomes fall.

_____ 9. A rightward shift in the supply of U.S. cars might be due to
   (a) an increase in the price of steel.
   (b) a reduction in foreign competition.
   (c) the introduction of cost-saving robots.
   (d) increased popularity of foreign cars.

_____ 10. If the market is initially in equilibrium, a technological improvement will cause price to _____ and quantity demanded to _____ .
   (a) fall; fall
   (b) rise; rise
   (c) fall; rise
   (d) rise; fall

_____ 11. The price of beans rises sharply. Which of the following cannot be true?
   (a) The supply of beans may have decreased with no change in the demand for beans.
   (b) The demand for beans may have increased with no change in the supply of beans.
   (c) The demand for beans may have increased with an increase in the quantity supplied of beans.
   (d) The supply of beans may have increased with an increase in the quantity demanded of beans.

_____ 12. The market for peas is experiencing a surplus. You should predict that price will
   (a) increase, quantity demanded will fall, and the quantity supplied will rise.
   (b) increase, quantity demanded will rise, and the quantity supplied will fall.
   (c) decrease, quantity demanded will rise, and the quantity supplied will fall.
   (d) decrease, quantity demanded will fall, and the quantity supplied will rise.

_____ 13.   Today, you change your expectations about your future income. In fact, you now believe that your future income will be significantly higher than you had previously expected. For a normal good, this would result in an increase in
(a)   quantity demanded today.
(b)   demand today.
(c)   quantity demanded but only in the future.
(d)   demand, but only in the future.

_____ 14.   If less is demanded of a product at each possible price, then there has been
(a)   a decrease in the quantity demanded.
(b)   a decrease in demand.
(c)   an increase in demand.
(d)   an increase in the quantity demanded.

_____ 15.   Chuck's Chips and Debi's Dip are complements. Costs of chip production fall. At the same time a government health report alleges that dip consumption causes bone cancer. For Debi's Dip, the equilibrium price will _____ and the equilibrium quantity will _____.
(a)   fall; be indeterminate
(b)   be indeterminate; rise
(c)   be indeterminate; fall
(d)   be indeterminate; be indeterminate

_____ 16.   The market for legal secretaries is in equilibrium. Now there is a simultaneous increase in the demand for legal secretaries and a decrease in the supply of legal secretaries. If there is no change in the wage paid to legal secretaries,
(a)   there will be a shortage of legal secretaries.
(b)   there will be a surplus of legal secretaries.
(c)   law firms will have no difficulty in hiring the desired number of legal secretaries at the current wage.
(d)   the supply of legal secretaries will decrease even more.

Use the following diagram to answer the next six questions. The diagram refers to the demand for and supply of hot dogs. The hot dog market is initially in equilibrium at Point *A*. Assume that hot dogs are a normal good.

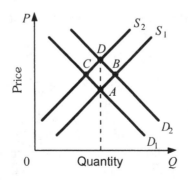

_____ 17.   The hot dog market moves from Point *A* to a new equilibrium at Point *B*. There has been an increase in
(a)   demand and an increase in supply.
(b)   demand and an increase in quantity supplied.
(c)   quantity demanded and an increase in quantity supplied.
(d)   quantity demanded and an increase in supply.

_____ 18.   The movement from Point *A* to Point *B* might have been caused by
(a)   an increase in the price of hamburgers (a substitute for hot dogs).
(b)   an increase in the price of fries (a complement for hot dogs).
(c)   a new widespread belief that meat products are bad for the heart.
(d)   a decrease in the price of ketchup (an ingredient used in making hot dogs).

_____ 19.   The hot dog market moves from Point *A* to a new equilibrium at Point *C*. There has been a decrease in
(a)   demand and a decrease in supply.
(b)   demand and a decrease in quantity supplied.
(c)   quantity demanded and a decrease in quantity supplied.
(d)   quantity demanded and a decrease in supply.

_____ 20.   The movement from Point *A* to Point *C* might have been caused by a
(a)   decrease in the price of hamburgers (a substitute for hot dogs).
(b)   tightening of sanitary regulations required for the preparation of hot dogs.
(c)   decrease in the wages of workers in the hot dog industry.
(d)   decrease in the price of hot dog buns.

_____ 21.   The hot dog market moves from Point *A* to a new equilibrium at Point *D*. There has been a(n)
(a)   increase in demand and an increase in supply.
(b)   increase in demand and a decrease in supply.
(c)   decrease in demand and an increase in supply.
(d)   decrease in demand and a decrease in supply.

_____ 22.   The movement from Point *A* to Point *D* might have been caused by a(n)
(a)   increase in the price of hot dogs and no change in the equilibrium quantity of hot dogs.
(b)   expected increase in the income of hot dog consumers and a hike in the wages of hot dog preparers.
(c)   expected decrease in the price of hot dogs and an increase in the cost of making hot dogs.
(d)   decrease in the income of hot dog consumers and a reduction in the cost of making hot dogs.

_____ 23.   Generic aspirin is an inferior good. As Jorge's income decreases we would expect a(n)
(a)   decrease in Jorge's demand for generic aspirin.
(b)   increase in Jorge's quantity demanded of generic aspirin.
(c)   increase in Jorge's demand for generic aspirin.
(d)   decrease in Jorge's quantity demanded of generic aspirin.

_____ 24.   The supply of computer software packages increases. As a result, the demand for personal computers rises. These two goods are _____ . The price of microchips, used to produce personal computers, will _____ .
    (a)   substitutes; increase
    (b)   substitutes; decrease
    (c)   complements; increase
    (d)   complements; decrease

_____ 25.   Along a given demand curve for corn, which of the following is not held constant?
    (a)   The price of corn
    (b)   The income of corn farmers
    (c)   The income of corn demanders
    (d)   The price of wheat

_____ 26.   The law of demand is best illustrated by
    (a)   the price of Pepsi rising, leading consumers to buy more Coke.
    (b)   increased purchases of Coke as the price of Coke decreases.
    (c)   an increase in income, which results in reduced purchases of store-brand soft drinks.
    (d)   an increase in income, which results in increased purchases of Coke.

Use the following table to answer the next three questions. The table refers to the demand for and supply of cans of tuna.

Price of Tuna	Quantity Demanded	Quantity Supplied
90¢	30	80
80¢	45	70
70¢	60	60
60¢	75	50
50¢	90	40
40¢	105	30

_____ 27.   The equilibrium price is _____ and the equilibrium quantity is _____ ¨cans.
    (a)   70¢; 60
    (b)   60¢; 75
    (c)   60¢; 50
    (d)   70¢; 70

_____ 28.   There would be an excess demand for tuna if the price were at
    (a)   90¢.
    (b)   80¢.
    (c)   70¢.
    (d)   60¢.

_____ 29.   If the price were 80¢, there would be
    (a)   an excess demand of 70 cans.
    (b)   an excess demand of 25 cans.
    (c)   an excess supply of 25 cans.
    (d)   an excess supply of 70 cans.

_____ 30.   New costly regulations to protect workers are introduced in the production of tuna. We would expect the equilibrium price of tuna to _____ and the equilibrium quantity of tuna to _____ .
   (a)   increase; increase
   (b)   increase; decrease
   (c)   decrease; increase
   (d)   decrease; decrease

II.   APPLICATION QUESTIONS

1.   Consider the following information regarding the quantity of corn demanded and supplied per month at a number of prices.

Price per Bushel	Quantity Demanded	Quantity Supplied
80¢	39,000	83,000
70¢	48,000	78,000
60¢	58,000	74,000
50¢	67,000	67,000
40¢	75,000	62,000
30¢	81,000	59,000

   (a)   What is the equilibrium price? What is the equilibrium quantity?
   (b)   Describe the situation when the price is at 80¢ per bushel and predict what will happen.
   (c)   Describe the situation when the price is at 30¢ per bushel and predict what will happen.
   (d)   Explain what would happen if a serious transport strike reduced corn output (at each price) by 30,000 bushels.

2.   DoughCrust Bread is a normal good produced by the DoughCrust Bakery. What will happen to the equilibrium price and quantity of DoughCrust Bread in each of the following situations?
   (a)   Due to a recession, households that buy DoughCrust experience a decrease in income.
   (b)   The cost of wheat used in DoughCrust increases significantly.
   (c)   DoughCrust buys improved ovens that reduce the costs of DoughCrust bread.
   (d)   Luvly Loaf, a rival, cuts the price of its bread.
   (e)   Consumers become health conscious and switch to low-calorie breads.

3.   How will each of the following changes affect the supply of hamburgers?
   (a)   There is an increase in the price of hamburger buns (used in the production of burgers).
   (b)   There is an increase in the price of hamburgers.
   (c)   Producers discover that the price of cheeseburgers is increasing.

4.   Pietro Cavalini sells ice cream at the beach. He is in competition with numerous other vendors. How will each of the following changes affect the demand for Pietro's ice cream?
   (a)   Hot dog vendors reduce the price of hot dogs. Hot dogs are consumption substitutes for ice cream.
   (b)   The cost of refrigeration decreases.
   (c)   Fine weather attracts record crowds to the beach.

5.   The market for DVDs has demand and supply curves given by $Qd = 60 - 2P$ and $Qs = 3P$, respectively. DVDs are a normal good.

(a)   Complete the following table.

Price	Quantity Demanded	Quantity Supplied
$30		
$25		
$20		
$15		
$10		
$5		
$0		

(b)   Calculate the equilibrium price and quantity. You can do this either by graphing the curves or algebraically.

(c)   Suppose that the current market price of a DVD is $20. Calculate the number of units that will be traded.

(d)   Suppose that the demand equation changed to $Qd = 80 - 2P$. Is this an increase or a decrease in demand? Suggest what might have caused such a change.

(e)   Calculate the new equilibrium price and quantity.

6.   Here is a demand and supply schedule for loaves of bread in East Yeastville, Colorado.

Price ($)	Quantity Demanded	Quantity Supplied
5.00	1,000	6,000
4.50	1,300	4,500
4.00	1,600	4,000
3.50	2,000	3,500
3.00	3,000	3,000
2.50	3,200	2,700
2.00	4,000	2,200
1.50	4,500	1,800
1.00	5,400	1,400
0.50	7,000	1,200

(a)   Find equilibrium price and equilibrium quantity.

(b)   Graph the demand (D_1) and supply (S_1) schedules in the space below and confirm the equilibrium values.

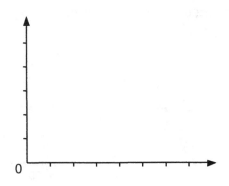

(c)   At a price of $1, is there an excess demand or supply? How great is the excess?

Suppose supply increases by 1,800 loaves at each price level.
(d)   Draw the new supply curve (S_2) on the graph in (b).
(e)   At the original equilibrium price level, is there an excess demand or an excess supply?
(f)   What will now happen to price, quantity demanded, and quantity supplied?

7.   The diagram following shows the labor market. D is the demand for labor and S is the supply. The minimum wage is $6.00 and unemployment is 150 workers. Can you verify that 150 workers are unemployed?

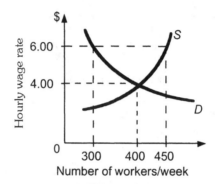

If the minimum wage law was revoked, the wage would fall to an equilibrium level of $4.00, and there would be no unemployment because quantity demanded would be equal to quantity supplied. However, the number of workers demanded would rise by only 100, not 150. Reconcile this apparent contradiction.

8.   Here are the demand schedules for orange juice for three buyers in the orange juice market and the supply schedules for three sellers in the orange juice market.

Price/Gallon	Quantity Demanded By:			Quantity Supplied By:		
	Blue	**Black**	**Brown**	**Gray**	**Green**	**Scarlett**
$5	1	0	0	5	10	14
$4	3	2	0	4	7	9
$3	7	5	4	3	6	7
$2	9	9	5	0	4	5
$1	11	12	7	0	0	1

(a)   Graph market demand (D_1) and market supply (S_1).

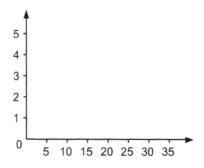

(b)   Show equilibrium price (P^*) and quantity (Q^*).

(c)   Now suppose the farm workers who pick oranges are given a higher wage rate. Show on your graph the changes that will occur in the orange juice market. Label any new demand curve D_2 and supply curve S_2. Discuss why curves shift, why price changes, and the significance of any shortage or surplus. Note that you don't have the data to draw precise curves.

(d)   Suppose now that, in addition to the orange pickers' higher wage rate, All-Cola, a substitute for orange juice, reduces its price. Sketch in the new demand curve for orange juice (D_3), and explain the reason why you moved the curve as you did.

9.   (a)   Draw a demand and supply graph for milk, and establish the equilibrium price (P^*).

(b)   There is an increase in the demand for milk (from D_1 to D_2). How will this change affect the equilibrium price?

(c)   In terms of the diagram you just sketched, what is the only way that the equilibrium price can increase, if the supply curve doesn't shift?

(d)   Draw in the new demand curve. Now trace through the process by which a new equilibrium is established.

10.   Mooville is a small town in Texas. Assume that beef is a normal good. What happens to the amount of beef demanded or supplied in each of the following cases? Draw a separate demand and supply graph for each part of this question, label the axes, and show how the change will shift the demand and/or the supply curve. Explain any curve shifts in each case. Show initial and final equilibrium price (P^* and P^{**}) and initial and final equilibrium quantity (Q^* and Q^{**}) for beef.

(a)   A subsidy that reduces production costs for beef producers.

(b)   A reduced supply of fish (consumers view beef and fish as substitutes).

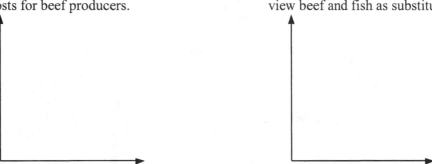

(c)   A rise in the wage rate in the beef industry.

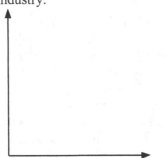

(d)   A rise in income.

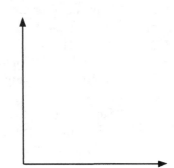

(e)   An improvement in the productivity of producing beef.

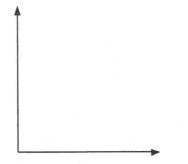

(f)   A bad tomato crop (beef and ketchup are complements and tomatoes are used to produce ketchup).

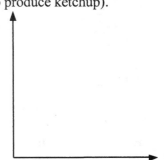

11.   Think of some commodity that you like. Try to avoid "lumpy" things, like cars or houses, and pick something like coffee, movies, CDs, or long-distance phone calls.

(a)   Sketch your demand curve for this good. Does it intersect the price axis? Where? How much of this commodity would you buy at a zero price?

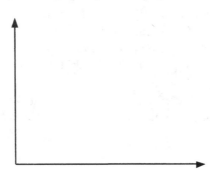

(b)   Are there substitutes for this commodity? How does the availability of substitutes affect the shape of your curve?

(c)   How would your demand curve change in response to an increase in the price of a substitute?

(d)   How would your demand curve change if you won the lottery and were to receive $2,000 per week for life?

12.   During the last few years, home prices in the northeastern United States have soared. The result was a significant increase in new home construction and a large increase in the demand for labor in the region. At the same time, though, high home prices caused a drop in the supply of labor, as people found it too expensive to live in the region. Draw a diagram of the labor market and discuss the impact of these events on wages and thus on the costs of doing business in the Northeast.

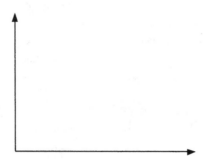

13.   In London, cabbies must be able to demonstrate a knowledge of at least 400 streets in order to obtain a license. This is quite difficult, so the number of cabbies is rather limited.
       (a)   Draw a demand and supply diagram for taxi service in London. How has this diagram been affected by the presence of the test?

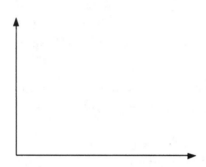

       (b)   How has the presence of the test affected usage of other forms of public transport—for example, the red buses and the "tube" (subway)? How have these prices responded?
       (c)   If the effect of restricting the numbers of cabbies is to reduce the number of customers, why might cabdrivers favor the restriction?

14.   Indicate in each case whether demand for steak (a normal good) will increase (I), decrease (D), or remain unchanged (U) in the following cases.
       (a)   ____   Pork, a substitute for steak, decreases in price.
       (b)   ____   High levels of unemployment sweep the nation.
       (c)   ____   The price of steak falls.
       (d)   ____   The price of steak sauce increases dramatically.
       (e)   ____   A government report establishes a conclusive link between the consumption of steak and cancer.
       (f)   ____   New refrigeration techniques reduce spoilage of steaks before they reach the market.
       (g)   ____   It is expected that the price of steak will skyrocket within two months.

15.   Indicate in each case whether the supply of beer will increase (I), decrease (D), or remain unchanged (U) in the following cases.
   (a)   ____   Wine coolers become more popular with consumers.
   (b)   ____   Beer decreases in price.
   (c)   ____   States impose a new tax on beer producers.
   (d)   ____   Beer workers' wages increase.
   (e)   ____   The price of hops, an important ingredient in brewing, decreases.
   (f)   ____   Costs of transportation decrease.
   (g)   ____   Improved technology results in less waste of beer.
   (h)   ____   The economy enters a downturn, and many beer drinkers become unemployed.
   (i)   ____   Fuel costs rise at the brewery.

16.   Indicate in each case whether the market price and quantity of popcorn will increase (I), decrease (D), or be uncertain (U) in the following cases. Assume that popcorn and lemonade are normal goods.

	Price	*Quantity*	
(a)	____	____	The price of lemonade, a complement of popcorn, rises while the harvest of popping corn is unusually poor this year.
(b)	____	____	Consumers' income falls; low-cost migrant workers cause the cost of popping corn to decline.
(c)	____	____	Oil, used in popcorn production, falls in price; consumers expect an imminent rise in the price of popcorn.
(d)	____	____	Eating popcorn is shown to be healthy; new hybrid corn is less expensive to produce and provides higher yields.

17.   Kornville is a small town in rural Virginia. Work out what will happen to the amount of corn supplied in each of the following cases and explain your answer.

   Result *A* = increase in the supply of corn
   Result *B* = decrease in the supply of corn
   Result *C* = increase in the quantity supplied of corn
   Result *D* = decrease in the quantity supplied of corn

   (a)   ____   A new government tax is imposed on corn.
   (b)   ____   Landlords raise the rent on land used for growing corn.
   (c)   ____   A new spray, effective in controlling insects harmful to corn plants, is made available.
   (d)   ____   The local senator campaigns effectively for an increase in the price of corn, which can be grown in Kornville.
   (e)   ____   The local senator campaigns effectively for a rise in the price of tobacco.
   (f)   ____   Many corn-growing farmers suffer bankruptcy.
   (g)   ____   The cost of diesel fuel, used in farm machinery, falls.
   (h)   ____   Red McPinkie unionizes agricultural workers and raises their wages.
   (i)   ____   Tougher laws stop foreign workers from working at harvest time.
   (j)   ____   Cornflakes (which are made from corn) become much more popular. (Careful!)

PRACTICE TEST SOLUTIONS

I.   *Solutions to Multiple-Choice Questions*

1.   (a)   In the input market, firms demand inputs and household supply inputs.

2.   (b)   To check your answer, put in a pair of substitutes, such as Pepsi and Coke. If Pepsi increases in price, we will buy less Pepsi and the demand for Coke will increase.

3.   (d)   A change in price leads to a movement along the demand curve. This is a "change in quantity demanded." An increase in price causes a decrease in quantity demanded.

4.   (a)   A change in price leads to a movement along the supply curve. Refer to p. 59.

5.   (c)   A movement along a supply curve (a change in quantity supplied) can only be caused by a change in the price of the good itself. Refer to p. 59.

6.   (a)   Draw the demand and supply diagram. In equilibrium, quantity demanded equals quantity supplied. At lower prices, quantity demanded exceeds quantity supplied.

7.   (d)   For a normal good, higher income will stimulate additional demand. Higher demand will cause the equilibrium price to increase. Refer to p. 51.

8.   (b)   If the cost of plastic increases, supply will decrease. If buyers have more leisure time, demand for leisure goods (like Frisbees) will increase. A decrease in supply, coupled with an increase in demand, will push up the price.

9.   (c)   A rightward shift—an increase in supply—will occur if costs are reduced.

10.   (c)   A technological improvement will increase supply. This will drive down the equilibrium price. As the price decreases, quantity demanded will increase.

11.   (d)   If the price of beans rises, then it cannot have been caused by an increase in the supply of beans.

12.   (c)   A surplus means that quantity supplied is greater than the quantity demanded. To reduce the surplus, sellers will accept lower prices. As price falls, quantity demanded will increase and quantity supplied will decrease.

13.   (b)   For a normal good, expected higher income will increase demand now and in the future.

14.   (b)   Try drawing this. At each price level the demand curve will be further to the left.

15.   (d)   Chip supply increases because costs have fallen. Consumers will buy more chips (and the demand for dip will increase). The health report will reduce demand for dip. Because we don't know which has the stronger effect on the demand for dip, the change in both equilibrium price and quantity is indeterminate.

16.   (a)   Higher demand and less supply will lead to a shortage if the wage level doesn't increase.

17.   (b)   The demand curve has shifted right from D_1 to D_2. As the price increased, quantity supplied increased.

18.   (a)   There has been an increase in demand. This could have been due to an increase in the price of hamburgers because consumers would wish to buy fewer hamburgers and would switch over to demanding hot dogs.

19.   (d)   The supply curve has shifted left, from S_1 to S_2. As the price increased, quantity demanded decreased.

20.   (b)   There has been a decrease in supply. This could have been due to a tightening of the sanitary regulations required for the preparation of hot dogs (which would have increased costs and/or reduced the number of sellers).

21.   (b)   The demand curve has shifted right, from D_1 to D_2, and the supply curve has shifted left, from S_1 to S_2.

22.   (b)   An expected increase in the income of hot dog consumers will increase demand for a normal good, and a hike in the wages of hot dog preparers will increase costs and reduce supply. Option *A* is incorrect—it describes the effect rather than the cause.

23.   (c)   As income changes, it changes the *demand* for a good. A decrease in income results in a decrease in the demand for a normal good. A decrease in income results in an increase in the demand for an inferior good.

24.   (c)   If the supply of software increases, the price will fall. As one might expect, software and computers are complements—the evidence in the question bears this out. As the quantity of computers traded increases, the demand for microchips will increase, which pushes up their price. Refer to p. 52.

25.   (a)   A movement along a demand curve is a change in quantity demanded. The only factor that can cause such a change is a change in the price of the good. Refer to p. 49.

26.   (b)   The law of demand relates the relationship between the price of a good and the quantity demanded. Refer to p. 50.

27.   (a)   Equilibrium occurs where quantity demanded equals quantity supplied. Refer to p. 62.

28.   (d)   At 60¢, quantity demanded is 25 units greater than quantity supplied.

29.   (c)   At 80¢, quantity supplied is 25 units greater than quantity demanded.

30.   (b)   The new regulations will decrease the supply of tuna which, in turn, will increase the equilibrium price and decrease the equilibrium quantity.

II.   *Solutions to Application Questions*

1.   (a)   50¢. 67,000 bushels.
      (b)   There is a surplus of 44,000 bushels at a price of 80¢ per bushel. Pressure is present to force price down.
      (c)   There is a shortage of 22,000 bushels at a price of 30¢ per bushel. Pressure is present to force price up.
      (d)   Supply would shift to the left by 30,000 bushels. Equilibrium price would increase to 70¢ per bushel, and the equilibrium quantity would be 48,000 bushels.

2.   (a)   A decrease in income will reduce demand. Equilibrium price will fall and equilibrium quantity will fall.
      (b)   An increase in the cost of wheat will decrease supply. Equilibrium price will rise and equilibrium quantity will fall.
      (c)   A decrease in the cost of wheat will increase supply. Equilibrium price will fall and equilibrium quantity will rise.
      (d)   A fall in the price of a substitute will reduce the demand for DoughCrust. Equilibrium price will fall and equilibrium quantity will fall.
      (e)   There will be a decrease in demand. Equilibrium price will fall and equilibrium quantity will fall.

3.   (a)   Supply will decrease—cost of inputs has increased.
      (b)   Supply will not change. A change in the price of a good results in a change in quantity supplied.
      (c)   Supply of hamburgers will decrease—producers will switch resources to cheeseburger production.

4.   (a)   Hot dogs are substitutes for ice cream. Demand for ice cream will decrease.
      (b)   No effect on demand. Changes in the cost of refrigeration will affect supply.
      (c)   Demand will increase as the number of buyers increases.

5.   (a)

Price	Quantity Demanded	Quantity Supplied
$30	0	90
$25	10	75
$20	20	60
$15	30	45
$10	40	30
$5	50	15
$0	60	0

      (b)   Equilibrium price is $12 and equilibrium quantity is 36. In equilibrium, $Qd = Qs$, therefore,

$$60 - 2P = 3P$$
$$60 = 5P \text{ and } P = 12$$

If $P = 12$, then $Q = 60 - 2(12) = 36$.

      (c)   At $20, there is an excess supply of 40 units. It's a buyers market—only 20 units will be traded.

(d)   This is an increase in demand. Tastes might have changed, consumer incomes may have risen (if DVDs are a normal good), and so on.

(e)   Equilibrium price is $16 and equilibrium quantity is 48. In equilibrium, $Qd = Qs$, therefore,

$$80 - 2P = 3P$$
$$80 = 5P \text{ and } P = 16$$

If $P = 16$, then $Q = 80 - 2(16) = 48$.

6.   (a) $3; 3,000 loaves
      (b)   Refer to the following diagram.

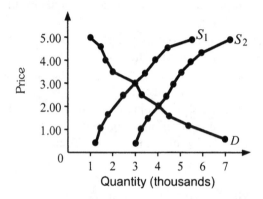

(c)   There is an excess demand (shortage) equal to 4,000 units (5,400 – 1,400).
(d)   Refer to the diagram above ($2, 4,000).
(e)   There will be an excess supply (surplus) of 1,800 loaves.
(f)   Price will fall to $2; quantity demanded and supplied will move to 4,000 loaves.

7.   The unemployment was removed because 100 extra jobs were created (increase in quantity demanded), and because the wage had become too low, 50 workers decided to cease offering themselves for employment (decrease in quantity supplied).

8.   (a)   Refer to the following diagram.

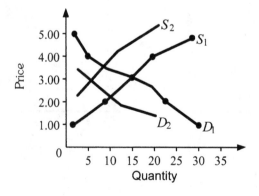

(b) $P^* = \$3; Q^* = 16$.
(c)   Refer to the preceding diagram. There will be no change in demand! Costs have risen, reducing profits, so supply will shift to the left (although we can't say how far). At $3, a shortage now exists, which will push prices higher.

(d)   Refer to the preceding diagram. Demand for orange juice will fall (although we can't say by how much). Consumption of All-Cola will rise, and some consumers of orange juice will substitute the relatively cheap All-Cola.

9.   (a)   Refer to the following diagram.

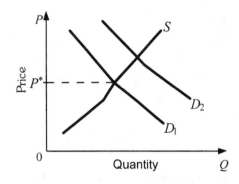

(b)   Increase
(c)   The demand curve must shift to the right.
(d)   Excess demand, leading to pressure for price to rise, will cause a reduction in the quantity demanded and an increase in the quantity supplied. This will continue until a new equilibrium is established.

10.   (a)   The subsidy will increase supply. Price will fall and output will rise.

(b)   The price of fish will increase and consumers will switch to beef. The demand for beef will increase. Price will rise and output will rise.

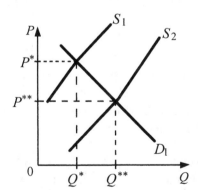

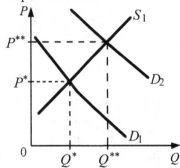

(c)   Costs of production have risen. This will decrease supply. Price will rise and output will fall.

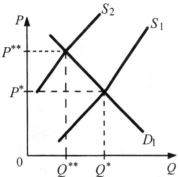

(d)   Beef is a normal good. Higher in-comes will cause the demand curve to shift right. Price will rise and output will rise.

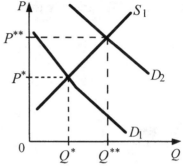

(e)   Costs of production will fall. Supply will shift to the right. Price will fall and output will rise.

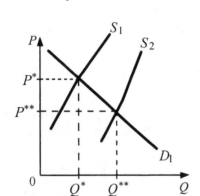

(f)   A poor tomato crop will drive up the price of tomatoes (and ketchup). Less ketchup will be used, so less beef will be demanded. Price and output will fall.

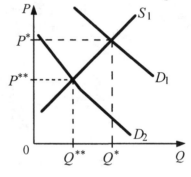

11.   (a)   Presumably, your demand curve is downsloping and intersects the price axis at some point.

       (b)   With a greater number of substitutes, you will be more sensitive to changes in the price of your good. The curve will tend to be flatter. This refers to elasticity of demand, which we will discuss in Chapter 5.

       (c)   The demand curve would shift to the right.

       (d)   If this is a normal good, demand would increase. If it is an inferior good, demand would decrease.

12.   Demand for labor would increase and, as workers moved away from the region, supply of labor would decrease. Wages, then, would increase, and the costs of doing business in the Northeast would rise.

13.   (a)   The test has reduced the supply of cabbies. This has forced up the price of taxi rides in London.

        (b)   Given the raised price of cab rides, the demand for substitutes will have increased. Other forms of public transportation will have been able to increase their prices.

        (c)   Cabbies who have passed the test and earned their license like the scheme because it reduces competition. This is especially true if the degree of substitutability with other types of public transportation is slight.

14.	(a)	D	(b)	D	(c)	U	(d)	D
	(e)	D	(f)	I or U	(g)	I		

15.	(a)	U	(b)	U	(c)	D	(d)	D
	(e)	I	(f)	I	(g)	I	(h)	U
	(i)	D						

16.	(a)	U and D	(b)	D and U	(c)	U and I	(d)	U and I

17.	(a)	*B*	(b)	*B*	(c)	*A*	(d)	*C*
	(e)	*B*	(f)	*B*	(g)	*A*	(h)	*B*
	(i)	*B*	(j)	*C*				

4

Demand and Supply Applications

Chapter objectives:

1. Explain and demonstrate how the market uses the price-rationing mechanism to allocate resources and distribute output.
2. List nonprice rationing policies designed to supplant the price rationing mechanism, identify the rationale behind these, and analyze their effects.
3. Explain, using words and/or diagrams, how an oil import fee would affect the domestic production and total consumption of oil.
4. Define consumer surplus and producer surplus and explain how these concepts relate to market efficiency.

BRAIN TEASER I: The textbook discusses the effects of a price floor such as the minimum wage in this chapter.

First, draw a demand and supply diagram to depict the effect of an effective price floor in the labor market.

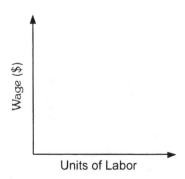

Why might economists oppose the minimum wage? Based on your diagram, what will happen to the number of jobs available if there is a minimum wage increase?

Suppose you own a fast-food restaurant—with many of your staff being paid minimum wage. Why might you oppose a hike in the minimum wage?

BRAIN TEASER II: Over the years, the U.S. government has developed two distinct strategies regarding illegal drugs. One strategy ("the war on drugs") has been to cooperate with the governments of countries where drugs are grown in order to destroy the supply at source. The other strategy (the "Just say no" campaign) has been aimed at discouraging drug consumption. Assume the two strategies have the same effect on the equilibrium quantity of drugs traded. Which strategy would you prefer, if you were a drug dealer?

OBJECTIVE 1:
Explain and demonstrate how the market uses the price-rationing mechanism to allocate resources and distribute output.

The price system has two important functions—it allocates productive resources and rations scarce output. Because of scarcity, rationing always occurs. Price rationing distinguishes those who are "willing and able" to buy from those who are only able but no longer willing, i.e., it allocates according to the willingness and ability of consumers to pay—those who are willing and able to pay as the price increases will get the good. Demand is constrained by income and wealth but, within those limits, individual preferences will prevail. If demand increases, price rises, signaling producers that profits may be made. More of the good will be produced, with resources being switched from other lines of production. (page 73)

▶▶▶   LEARNING TIP: Note the lobster example in the textbook, which describes the allocative and rationing roles that prices play in the marketplace.
                Note, too, that the profit motive is highly durable. Limitations (such as price ceilings or rationing) placed on the operation of the market can lead to black markets so that demand can be serviced.◀

PRACTICE: In fact, the Maine lobster market is changing. In recent years, catches of lobsters and the average size of the lobsters caught have been increasing. This may be due to global warming—lobsters may be moving away from the warmer waters in the south. What effect will this change have on the Maine market for lobsters?
ANSWER: With larger catches, the supply of lobsters will shift to the right. More resources will be allocated to the lobster industry and the price of lobsters will decrease.

──────■──────────────────────────────────── **Practice** ────

1.   In a market, either price must increase or nonprice rationing must occur when _____ exists.
        (a)   a shortage
        (b)   a surplus
        (c)   a horizontal demand curve
        (d)   a vertical supply curve

        ANSWER: (a) Given a shortage, either price will increase (price rationing) or nonprice rationing must be enforced.

2.   In a free market, the rationing mechanism is
        (a)   price.
        (b)   quantity.
        (c)   demand.
        (d)   supply.

        ANSWER: (a) Given an imbalance between quantity demanded and quantity supplied, a free market will adjust price to achieve equilibrium.

Use the following diagram to answer the next five questions. Assume that the demand curve and the supply curve each must be in one the three possible positions shown. The initial market demand and market supply curves for Sam's Supreme Submarine Sandwiches are D_1 and S_1.

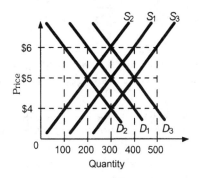

3.   There is an increase in the cost of ingredients. If the price is held at the initial equilibrium level, there will be an excess
(a)   demand of 100 units.
(b)   demand of 200 units.
(c)   supply of 100 units.
(d)   supply of 200 units.

ANSWER: (a) Supply has fallen to S_2. Demand is unchanged. At a price of $5, quantity demanded is 300 units and quantity supplied is 200 units.

4.   There is a simultaneous increase in demand and decrease in supply. At the initial equilibrium price, there will be an excess
(a)   demand of 200 units.
(b)   demand of 400 units.
(c)   supply of 200 units.
(d)   supply of 400 units.

ANSWER: (a) Supply has decreased to S_2. Demand has increased to D_3. At a price of $5, quantity demanded is 400 units and quantity supplied is 200 units.

5.   There is a simultaneous decrease in demand and decrease in supply. At the initial equilibrium price there will be
(a)   an excess demand of 200 units.
(b)   an excess demand of 100 units.
(c)   an excess supply of 200 units.
(d)   equilibrium.

ANSWER: (d) Supply has decreased to S_2. Demand has decreased to D_2. At a price of $5, quantity demanded is 200 units and quantity supplied is 200 units. Equilibrium prevails.

6.   Herman reduces the price of his Humongous Hoagie (a substitute for the Supreme Submarine). At the Supreme Submarine's initial equilibrium price, there will be an excess
     (a)   demand of 100 units.
     (b)   demand of 200 units.
     (c)   supply of 100 units.
     (d)   supply of 200 units.

     ANSWER: (c) Demand has decreased to D_2. Supply has not changed. At a price of $5, quantity demanded is 200 units and quantity supplied is 300 units.

7.   Herman reduces the price of his Humongous Hoagie (a substitute for the Supreme Submarine). *Following* any shifts in the curves, we would expect a(n) _____ in the Supreme Submarine market.
     (a)   increase in quantity demanded and an increase in quantity supplied.
     (b)   increase in quantity demanded and a decrease in quantity supplied.
     (c)   decrease in quantity demanded and an increase in quantity supplied.
     (d)   decrease in quantity demanded and a decrease in quantity supplied.

     ANSWER: (b) Demand has decreased to D_2. Supply has not changed. There is an excess supply which will cause Sam's price to fall. A fall in price will increase quantity demanded and decrease quantity supplied. ■

OBJECTIVE 2:
List nonprice rationing policies designed to supplant the price-rationing mechanism, identify the rationale behind these, and analyze their effects.

Rationing by price may be considered "unfair"—poor people might be priced out of the market for some essentials—so other nonprice rationing methods, including queuing, ration coupons, favored customers, and lotteries, are applied. Such schemes usually involve hidden costs (queuing costs time, for example) that may make them inefficient. Note that different types of rationing benefit different groups of people. (page 75)

At many colleges, basketball tickets are distributed on a first-come first-served basis—meaning that students must queue, perhaps for days, to get tickets to the big game. Not-so-hidden costs include the inconvenience, loss of study time, and possible health effects. As an example of a lottery, colleges may allocate dorm rooms, not by price or need, but by random number selection.

▶▶   LEARNING TIP: It may seem confusing to have a ceiling below the equilibrium price. Remember that a price ceiling stops the price going higher (just like a ceiling in a room), whereas a price floor is a lower limit. To have an effect on equilibrium price, a ceiling must be set *below* the equilibrium price and a floor must be set *above* the equilibrium price.◀

A price ceiling sets a maximum price; a price floor sets a minimum price. The minimum wage is a price floor. An effective price ceiling creates a shortage; an effective price floor creates a surplus.

A price ceiling need not be established below the equilibrium price, although a ceiling set *above* the equilibrium has no effect. Similarly, the imposition of a minimum wage of $2.00 per hour will have no effect on the labor market. Verify that this is true. If demand and/or supply conditions change however, a price ceiling or floor may become effective. For instance, adjustable rate mortgages have "caps" on how high the interest rate can move in response to market conditions—this is a price ceiling.

ECONOMICS IN PRACTICE: There's an old saying that "time is money". Have you noticed how many of the textbook examples of "economics in practice" in this and previous chapters hinge on the trade-off between time and money? The same applies to the Shakespeare example in this chapter. Typically, those for whom time is less valuable are more inclined to queue to get lower prices. But what about situations where price is not explicitly involved? Duke University's Cameron Indoor Stadium (at a pinch) can accommodate 11,000 spectators for basketball games. Students receive tickets for these popular games on a "first come, first served" basis. Students set up "Krzyzewskiville," a tent village, in order to get tickets. Can you think of other similar examples where time and money are traded off?

ANSWER: There are numerous examples. If you've ever clipped coupons or sent off for a rebate, used the services of a ticket scalper, or queued to sign up for a popular class, you've traveled beyond the conventional pricing system.

ECONOMICS IN PRACTICE: In 2009, the minimum wage will increase to $7.25 per hour. Who gains and who loses from this wage? How do teenagers fit into your answer?

ANSWER: There is a transfer of income from employers to minimum-wage employees with jobs. There is a reduction in the quantity of labor demanded—fewer workers are hired than would otherwise be the case. Workers who cannot find jobs (or who lose jobs) as a result of the wage floor are losers. The level of unemployment increases amongst the poor and unskilled—those least able to afford a reduction in job opportunities. Teenagers are amongst the least experienced workers, and evidence suggests that they suffer as a result of the minimum wage. Indeed, to redress the balance, an "opportunity wage" (a sub-minimum wage) was proposed for teenagers in the 1990s.

━━━ **Practice** ━━━

8.   A price ceiling is set below the equilibrium price. We can predict that
   (a)   quantity demanded will decrease.
   (b)   quantity supplied will be greater than quantity demanded.
   (c)   demand will be less than supply.
   (d)   quantity supplied will decrease.

   ANSWER: (d) Price will be reduced by the price ceiling. A decrease in price causes quantity supplied to decrease (not a shift in the supply curve).

9.   A price ceiling is set below the equilibrium price. We can predict that
   (a)   there will be a leftward shift in the demand curve.
   (b)   there will be a leftward shift in the supply curve.
   (c)   quantity demanded will be greater than quantity supplied.
   (d)   quantity supplied will be reduced to equal quantity demanded.

   ANSWER: (c) A change in price does not cause the demand and/or supply curve to shift position! If price is "too low," a shortage (quantity demanded greater than quantity supplied) will occur.

10.   A price floor is set below the current equilibrium price. If supply increases, price would
   (a)   increase.
   (b)   decrease.
   (c)   not change.
   (d)   be indeterminate.

   ANSWER: (b) Initially, the price floor will have no effect. As supply increases, there will be a pressure for the market price to fall. If the price falls enough, then the price floor will become effective.

11.   Ticket scalping will be successful if
    (a)   the demand curve is fairly steep.
    (b)   the demand curve is fairly flat.
    (c)   the official price is below the equilibrium price.
    (d)   the official price is above the equilibrium price.

    ANSWER: (c) The slope of the demand curve is irrelevant in this case. The important issue is that a shortage of tickets exists because the official price has been set too low. ■

OBJECTIVE 3:
Explain, using words and/or diagrams, how an oil import fee would affect the domestic production and total consumption of oil.

The text offers the imposition of a tax on imported oil (an oil import fee) as an example of the usefulness of demand and supply analysis. A new tax will raise the domestic price of oil, cutting quantity demanded and encouraging domestic production. The size of these changes depends on the slopes of the demand and supply curves or, more accurately, the *responsiveness* of demand and supply. Although the imposition of this tax would raise government revenues, reduce dependence on foreign oil, and stimulate domestic production of oil, inefficient domestic producers may be sheltered from lower-priced foreign competition. (page 80)

    Which consumers are most likely to be penalized by an oil import fee? Within the market, some buyers will have a demand that is relatively unresponsive to price changes, whereas others will be more able to trim demand if price rises. Would a price hike discriminate more against the poor (who may have little choice in their fuel consumption) than against those who are better off (who can afford to buy other kinds of heating)?

 Practice

Refer to the following diagram for the next four questions. The world price of oil is $160 per barrel.

World

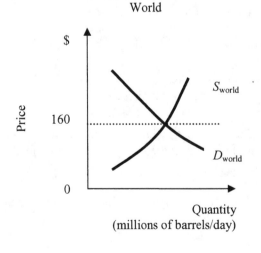

Quantity
(millions of barrels/day)

United States

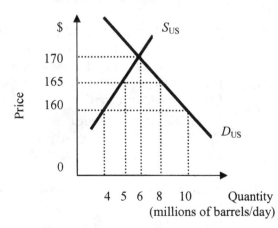

Quantity
(millions of barrels/day)

12.   If the world price is the market price in the United States, then there will be a _____ million barrels per day.
        (a)   surplus of 10
        (b)   surplus of 6
        (c)   shortage of 10
        (d)   shortage of 6

        ANSWER: (d) At $160 per barrel, quantity supplied is 4 million and quantity demanded is 10 million.

13.   Suppose that the United States imposes a $5 per barrel import fee. This will result in each of the following EXCEPT
        (a)   a decrease in imports to 3 million barrels per day.
        (b)   an increase in the quantity supplied of oil in the United States to 5 million barrels per day.
        (c)   a decrease in the quantity demanded of oil in the United States to 8 million barrels per day.
        (d)   a decrease in United States imports of oil by 2 million barrels per day.

        ANSWER: (d) Oil imports had been 6 million barrels per day. After the imposition of the fee, oil imports are 3 million barrels per day. Imports decreased by 3 million barrels per day.

14.   Suppose that the United States imposes a $5 per barrel import fee. This will generate a tax revenue of
        (a) $3 million per day.
        (b) $5 million per day.
        (c) $8 million per day.
        (d) $15 million per day.
        ANSWER: (d) Imports are 3 million barrels per day. Each barrel yields a tax revenue of $5.

15.   Suppose that the United States wishes to become self-sufficient in oil. This could be done by
        (a)   establishing a price ceiling (maximum price) of $15 per barrel of oil.
        (b)   establishing a price ceiling (maximum price) of $30 per barrel of oil.
        (c)   imposing a fee of $10 per barrel on foreign oil.
        (d)   imposing a fee of $30 per barrel on foreign oil.

        ANSWER: (c) A fee of $10 per barrel on foreign oil will result in equilibrium in the U.S. market. ∎

OBJECTIVE 4:
Define consumer surplus and producer surplus and explain how these concepts relate to market efficiency.

For the final unit of a good purchased, the price should equal the value derived by the purchaser. Previous units should be valued more highly, but the same price charged. *Consumer surplus* is the difference between the value the purchaser places on purchases of a product and the price paid. Graphically, the consumer surplus is the area bounded by the demand curve, the vertical axis, and the product price. Changes in the size of the area reflect changes in consumer well-being. Can you see that, if the consumer's demand for steak increases, *ceteris paribus*, then the consumer surplus will increase if price is unchanged? (page 81)

▶▶▶   LEARNING TIP: Put simply, consumer surplus is "the difference between the price you do pay and the price you would pay." If you win an eBay auction at a lower price than you would have paid, the difference is your consumer surplus.◀

Producer surplus is a similar concept but from the point of view of the seller. The difference between the market price and the lowest price a seller would accept is the producer surplus. If you auction a CD on eBay and would take $5 for it but you end up selling it for $12, your producer surplus is $7. (page 82)

▶▶▶   LEARNING TIP: Graphically, consumer surplus is the triangular area between the demand curve and the market price; producer surplus is the triangular area between the supply curve and the market price.◀

By driving buyers and sellers to the intersection of demand and supply, market forces maximize the total surplus derived by participants. Any action that moves production away from the equilibrium level will reduce society's surplus and will result in a deadweight loss to society. (page 83)

─────────■──────────────── **Practice** ────────────────

16.   Given your demand curve for bananas, as the price of bananas decreases, your consumer surplus will
   (a)   increase, because the gap between the price you would pay and the price you do pay is greater than before.
   (b)   decrease, because marginal utility diminishes as more of a good is bought.
   (c)   remain constant, because the demand curve has not changed position.
   (d)   remain constant, because the maximum price you would pay has not changed.
   ANSWER: (a)   Refer to the definition of consumer surplus on p. 82.

Use the following diagram to answer the following question.

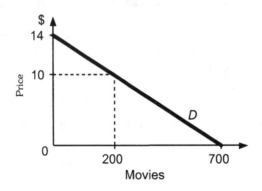

17.   When the price of a movie is $10, the consumer surplus is
   (a) $4.
   (b) $200.
   (c) $400.
   (d) $800.
   [Hint: the area of a triangle is 1/2(base × height).]
   ANSWER: (c)   Consumer surplus is the area between the demand curve and the price. With a straight-line demand curve it is $1/2(P_{max} - P) Q_d$. In this case, consumer surplus is 1/2($14 – $10)200, or $400.

18.   The market for baseballs is in equilibrium. Now there is a decrease in the supply of baseball. Assuming normally sloped curves, consumer surplus will _____ and producer surplus will _____.
    (a)   increase; increase
    (b)   increase; decrease
    (c)   decrease; increase
    (d)   decrease; decrease
    ANSWER: (d) As the supply curve shifts to the left the area above the supply curve and below the demand curve becomes smaller. ∎

BRAIN TEASER I SOLUTION:

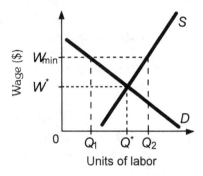

The minimum wage is an effective price floor. Both price floors and price ceilings restrict the free operation of the market. With an effective price floor, quantity supplied of labor will exceed quantity demanded, creating a surplus of job seekers—unemployment. There may be job loss, too, resulting in lower production. With rising labor costs, the economy's ability to compete with low-wage foreign imports is reduced, although this is not a strong argument—minimum wage earners (only about 5% of the labor force) tend to cluster in service industries, and services are not exported or imported.

As the owner of a fast-food restaurant, your bottom line will be hurt. Workers earning above the minimum wage (perhaps with more experience) would expect wage increases (the "ripple effect"). Small businesses on thin profit margins might have to trim back on employment by firing or by reducing hours. Alternatively, prices might have to rise, again reducing business.

BRAIN TEASER II SOLUTION: The first ("the war on drugs") strategy reduces supply and will increase the price. The second ("Just say no") strategy reduces demand and will decrease the price. As a dealer, you should prefer the first strategy because the price you can charge, and the revenue you can earn, would be greater.

PRACTICE TEST

I.   MULTIPLE-CHOICE QUESTIONS

Select the option that provides the single best answer.

_____   1.   The government has decided that the free market price for baby formula is "too high."
              Which of the following rationing proposals will result in the **least** misallocation of baby
              formula resources?
              (a)   Proposal A: establish an official price ceiling, then let sellers decide how to
                     allocate baby formula among customers.
              (b)   Proposal B: issue coupons for baby formula that cannot be resold.
              (c)   Proposal C: issue coupons for baby formula that can be resold.
              (d)   Proposal D: establish a price ceiling and require purchasers to queue.

_____   2.   A government-imposed **ceiling** on apartment rents, if set above the equilibrium rent level,
              would
              (a)   have no effect on the housing market.
              (b)   lead to a persistent shortage of apartments.
              (c)   lead to a persistent surplus of apartments.
              (d)   shift the supply curve for apartments to the right.

_____   3.   A ticket to a concert by the Skreeming Habdabs costs you $35. However, your roommate
              offers you the "scalping" rate of $100 for your ticket. Your opportunity cost of refusing
              the offer and attending the concert is
              (a) $35.
              (b) $65.
              (c) $100.
              (d) $135.

_____   4.   Joe would pay $2.00 for his first cup of soda during the NCAA basketball championship
              game. He would pay $1.20 for his second, $1.00 for his third, and 80¢ for his fourth. If
              the price is
              (a) $1.00 per cup, Joe will buy 3 cups and have a consumer surplus of $4.20.
              (b) $1.00 per cup, Joe will buy 3 cups and have a consumer surplus of $3.20.
              (c) $1.10 per cup, Joe will buy 2 cups and have a consumer surplus of $1.00.
              (d) $1.10 per cup, Joe will buy 2 cups and have a consumer surplus of $2.10.

_____   5.   The market demand curve for pizza is given by $Q_d = 400 - 25P$ where P is the price of
              pizza in dollars. If the price of pizza is $10, the consumer surplus is
              (a) $150.
              (b) $225.
              (c) $450.
              (d) $800.
              [Hint: the area of a triangle is 1/2(base × height).]

Use the following graph to answer the next question.

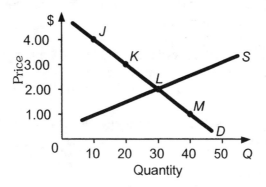

_____   6.   Suppose a price ceiling of $1.00 is set. This will cause a
            (a)   surplus of 50 units.
            (b)   shortage of 50 units.
            (c)   shortage of 30 units.
            (d)   surplus of 30 units.

Use the following diagram showing the oil market in the United States to answer the next two questions. The world price for gasoline is $4.50 per gallon. The equilibrium price in the U.S. market is $5.50 per gallon. Units on the horizontal axis are millions of gallons.

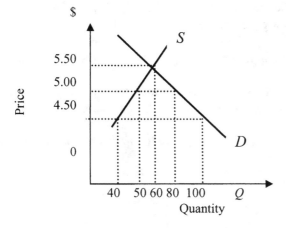

_____   7.   Assume that the United States neither imports nor exports gasoline. At the world price for gasoline, there is a _____ of gas in the United States market of _____ units.
            (a)   surplus; 60
            (b)   surplus; 100
            (c)   shortage; 60
            (d)   shortage; 100

_____ 8.   The government imposes an import tax that raises the domestic price of gas to $5.00 per gallon. If, because of discoveries of new oilfields, the domestic supply of gas increases by 30 million gallons per day
(a)   the domestic shortage of gas would be eliminated.
(b)   government tax revenues would be 30 million times 50¢.
(c)   quantity demanded would increase.
(d)   the equilibrium price would remain at $5.50.

_____ 9.   In a market economy the rationing mechanism operates through adjustments in
(a)   price
(b)   quantity
(c)   expectations
(d)   queuing

_____ 10.   Jill's consumer surplus for Good A will
(a)   increase if the price of A increases.
(b)   increase if the price of B, a substitute for A, decreases.
(c)   decrease if Jill's income decreases and A is a normal good.
(d)   decrease if the price of C, a complement for A, decreases.

_____ 11.   The supply curve of bottled water on an island is completely vertical. The market for bottled water is in equilibrium. A ferryload of thirsty holidaymakers arrives and the demand for bottled water increases. Which of the following statements is true?
(a)   Price will serve as a rationing device.
(b)   Price will not serve as a rationing device because the quantity supplied cannot change.
(c)   Price will not serve as a rationing device because the equilibrium quantity demanded cannot change.
(d)   Price will not serve as a rationing device because neither the equilibrium quantity demanded nor the equilibrium quantity supplied can change.

_____ 12.   A price ceiling is set above current equilibrium price. If supply decreases, price would
(a)   increase.
(b)   decrease.
(c)   not change.
(d)   be indeterminate.

Use the following graph to answer the next three questions. Suppose a price ceiling of $1.00 is set in this market.

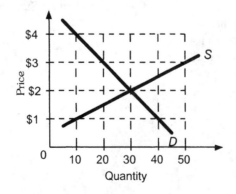

_____ 13. The price ceiling will cause a
- (a) surplus of 50 units.
- (b) shortage of 50 units.
- (c) shortage of 30 units.
- (d) surplus of 30 units.

_____ 14. If the price ceiling is left in place, we would predict that, eventually,
- (a) demand would decrease until quantity demanded and quantity supplied were equal at a price of $1.
- (b) supply would increase until quantity demanded and quantity supplied were equal at a price of $1.
- (c) the market participants will be convinced that $1 is the equilibrium price.
- (d) a persistent excess demand would lead to the emergence of nonprice rationing practices such as queuing.

_____ 15. Relative to equilibrium, what is the value of the deadweight loss if the price ceiling is left in place?
- (a) $30
- (b) $40
- (c) $45
- (d) $60

[Hint: the area of a triangle is 1/2(base × height).]

_____ 16. An effective minimum wage is imposed. In the market for unskilled labor we would expect
- (a) a surplus and an increase in employment.
- (b) a surplus and a decrease in employment.
- (c) a shortage and an increase in employment.
- (d) a shortage and a decrease in employment.

Use the following diagram to answer the next five questions.

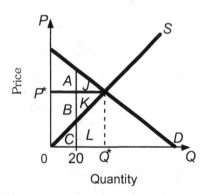

_____ 17. When the market is in equilibrium, area(s) _____ represent consumer surplus.
- (a) J and K
- (b) A and B
- (c) A and J
- (d) B and K

_____ 18.   When the market is in equilibrium, area(s) _____ represent producer surplus.
            (a)   J and K
            (b)   A and B
            (c)   A and J
            (d)   B and K

_____ 19.   When the market is in equilibrium, area(s) _____ represent deadweight loss.
            (a)   J and K
            (b)   C and L
            (c)   J, K and L
            (d)   None of the above.

_____ 20.   If output is restricted to 20 units, area(s) _____ represent consumer surplus and area(s)
            _____ represents producer surplus.
            (a)   B and K; A and J
            (b)   A and J; B and K
            (c)   B; A
            (d)   A; B

_____ 21.   If output is restricted to 20 units, area(s) _____ represent the deadweight loss.
            (a)   J and K
            (b)   C and L
            (c)   J, K and L
            (d)   A, B and C

II.   APPLICATION QUESTIONS

1.   Consider the following diagram, which shows the market for fluid milk. Quantity is in thousands
       of gallons.

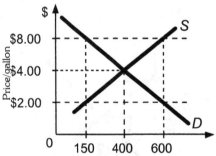

(a)   Calculate total income for dairy farmers.
(b)   Suppose that this income level is felt to be inadequate and that a political decision is
       made to boost farm income to $3,600,000. The government establishes a price floor at
       $6.00, with the government buying the surplus. How much milk will be supplied?
(c)   Who gets the milk?
(d)   The plan achieves the income objective, but what else has it done? There are costs
       involved with tampering with the price mechanism. What are they?

Now suppose the government establishes a price ceiling of $2.00 per gallon.
(e)   How much milk do consumers actually receive?
(f)   Which plan is better for a milk consumer who pays no state tax? Why?
(g)   Calculate the deadweight loss if a price ceiling of $2.00 is imposed.

2.   In Application Question 5 of Chapter 3, we examined the market for DVDs where the supply and demand curves are given by $Q_s = 3P$ and $Q_d = 60 - 2P$, respectively. Refer to the following diagram.

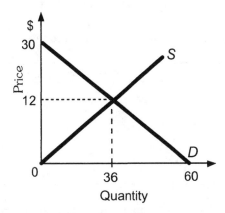

(a)   If the government imposes a price ceiling of $5 in this market, what will happen to the positions of the demand and supply curves?
(b)   Calculate the consumer surplus at the equilibrium price.
(c)   Calculate the producer surplus at the equilibrium price.

Now suppose that a $6 per unit maximum price is imposed in this market. The diagram shows the impact on quantity demanded and quantity supplied.
(d)   Calculate the consumer surplus. (Careful!)
(e)   Calculate the producer surplus.
(f)   Calculate the deadweight loss.

3.   In many Eastern European cities, there is a thriving market in farm produce.
(a)   Draw a demand and supply diagram below for the Warsaw egg market. Label the curves D_1 and S_1 respectively. Show the equilibrium price (P_1) and quantity (Q_1).

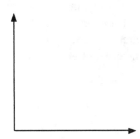

(b)   In August, the price of eggs triples because of a decrease in supply caused by very hot weather. Show how the market changed in August. Label the new supply curve S_2. Show the new equilibrium price (P_2) and quantity (Q_2).
(c)   Is the Warsaw egg market operating efficiently?

(d)   Suppose the government decided to maintain the initial price (P_1). Should it impose a price ceiling or a price floor? Explain whether an excess demand or an excess supply will result.

(e)   Is the Warsaw egg market now operating efficiently?

(f)   How do you think suppliers might react to the price ceiling?

(g)   Which nonprice methods might develop to circumvent the imbalance in this market?

4.   A freeze destroys much of the South American coffee crop. This causes an increase in the price of tea. Explain why, using supply and demand diagrams.

5.   Use the following demand and supply schedule to answer the questions.

Price	Quantity Demanded	Quantity Supplied
$6	10	70
$5	20	60
$4	30	50
$3	40	40
$2	50	30
$1	60	20

(a)   Calculate the equilibrium price and the equilibrium quantity.

(b)   Now the government establishes a price ceiling of $2. Will this cause an excess supply or an excess demand? An excess of how many units?

6.   Several members of a college faculty were standing in a rather long line at the campus cafeteria. One was heard to remark that she wished the cafeteria would increase prices. Can you explain why?

7.   Who gained and who lost from government intervention in the market in the following case? In 1993, Congress scrapped subsidies for honey producers. Until 1988, a price floor was in place, with the government purchasing surpluses of honey. From 1980 to 1988, $525 million was spent on the program.

8.   The auction site, eBay, offers an opportunity to observe consumer surplus and the demand curve. Choose an auction where many bidders have participated. Presumably, each bidder has bid up to the maximum value he or she places on the good for sale. These maximum bids (with the exception of the winner's) are revealed after the auction ends. Can you construct the demand curve for your chosen auction? Suppose the actual price was lower than the winning price— determine the extent of the consumer surplus.

PRACTICE TEST SOLUTIONS

I.   Solutions to Multiple-Choice Questions

1.   (c)   Issuing coupons that can be resold will lead to a market for coupons with those willing and able to pay the most receiving the right to buy baby formula.

2.   (a)   To be effective, a price ceiling must be set below the equilibrium price.

3. (c) The opportunity cost is the value of the next best alternative given up, i.e., in monetary terms, whatever the $100 offered price would buy. The $35 has already been spent—it is a sunk cost.

4. (c) Consumer surplus is the difference between the price and the demand curve. Joe would buy two sodas because the value of the third and subsequent sodas is less than the price. His consumer surplus is ($2.00 – $1.10) + ($1.20 – $1.10).

5. (b) Given Q_d = 400 –25P, the maximum value for P is $16 (i.e., 400/25). When P = $10, Q_d = 150. Consumer surplus is 1/2(P_{max} – P)Q_d. so 1/2($16 – $10)150 = $450.   Refer to p. 82.

6. (c) An effective price ceiling (set below the equilibrium price) will create a shortage. Quantity demanded is 40, but quantity supplied is only 10.

7. (c) The price is below the equilibrium price, with quantity demanded being 100 and quantity supplied being only 40. A shortage of 60 exists.

8. (a) The increase in supply would eliminate the shortage and eliminate government tax revenues. Recall that an "increase in supply" will shift the position of the supply curve to the right.

9. (a) When there is a market imbalance, price adjusts to allocate production.

10. (c) A decrease in income will reduce the demand for a normal good and, given the market price, consumer surplus will decrease.

11. (a) Demand has increased causing an excess demand. Price will rise to remove the imbalance.

12. (a) A price ceiling above the equilibrium price will have no effect. A decrease in supply, therefore, will result in a higher price.

13. (c) An effective price ceiling (set below the equilibrium price) will create a shortage. Quantity demanded is 40, but quantity supplied is only 10, so a shortage of 30 exists.

14. (d) Demand and supply curves do not shift in response to changes in price!

15. (a) The deadweight loss is the area between the demand curve and the supply curve from the restricted output level (10) to the equilibrium output level (30). 1/2($4 – $1)(30 – 10) = $30..

16. (b) The minimum wage is a price floor. To be effective it is set above the equilibrium wage. As the wage increases, more workers will seek jobs but employers will demand fewer workers (a decrease in employment).

17. (c) Consumer surplus is the area between the price and the demand curve.

18. (d) Producer surplus is the area between the price and the supply curve.

19. (d) There is no deadweight loss when the market is in equilibrium.

20.   (d)   Consumer surplus is the area between the price and the demand curve from zero to 20 units of output. Similarly, producer surplus is the area between the price and the supply curve from zero to 20 units of output.

21.   (a)   The deadweight loss is the area between the demand curve and the supply curve from the restricted output level to the equilibrium output level.

II.   *Solutions to Application Questions*

1.   (a) $1,600,000
   (b)   600,000 gallons
   (c)   150,000 gallons are bought by consumers, and the rest (450,000 gallons) is taken by the government.
   (d)   Milk is now more expensive and less plentiful for consumers. Taxpayers—who needn't be milk consumers—will have to pick up the subsidy tab. There will be storage and administrative costs, too. Also, there is an overallocation of resources toward milk production.
   (e)   At $2.00 per gallon, consumers receive 150,000 gallons. In this case there is a shortage of 450,000 gallons.
   (f)   The second plan is better in that the price of milk is lower for milk consumers.
   (g)   Deadweight loss equals $1/2(\$6 - \$2)(400 - 150)$, or $500,000

2.   (a)   Nothing! A change in price leads to movements along the given demand and supply curves.
   (b)   The consumer surplus equals $(\$30 - \$12)(36)/2$, or $324.
   (c)   The producer surplus equals $(\$12 - 0)(36)/2$ or $216.
   (d)   The consumer surplus equals $(\$30 - \$21)(18)/2 + (\$21 - \$6)(18)$ or $351.
   (e)   The producer surplus equals $(\$6 - 0)(18)/2$, or $54.
   (f)   The deadweight loss equals $(\$21 - \$6)(36 - 18)/2$ or $135.

3.   (a)   Refer to the following diagram.

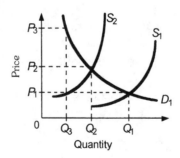

   (b)   Refer to the preceding diagram.
   (c)   The market is efficient, in that it is reflecting the change in supply and equalizing quantity demanded and quantity supplied.
   (d)   The government should impose a price ceiling to place an upper limit on price. Quantity demanded will exceed quantity supplied—there will be an excess demand.
   (e)   This is now a seller's market. Output is restricted to Q_3. At that output, an excess demand exists.

(f)   Suppliers may withdraw eggs from the controlled Warsaw market—selling them either outside Warsaw or on the black market within the city. Substandard (small or damaged) eggs may be offered for sale. Egg quality may be sacrificed.

(g)   Other rationing methods, such as queuing or preferred customers, might be used. Black markets with higher prices are likely to develop. Eggs may be sold as part of a "package" of commodities.

4.   Higher coffee prices increased the demand for tea (a substitute). Refer to the following diagrams.

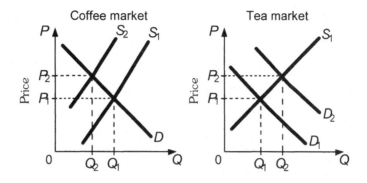

5.   (a) $3; 40
       (b)   Excess demand; 20

6.   Higher prices would reduce quantity demanded and cut down on waiting time. If you value your time highly, you would probably be willing to pay higher prices to avoid waiting in line.

7.   There was a transfer of wealth from taxpayers in general to the nation's 2,000 commercial beekeepers. Honey consumers also lost because the market price was kept higher than it should have been. There was an overallocation of resources to honey production. Note that honey consumption was less than its most efficient level despite the excess supply.

8.   Answers, of course, will vary with the auction chosen. Consumer surplus will be the value of total differences between your supposed actual price and the maximum bid of each participant.

Comprehensive Review Test

The following questions provide a wide-ranging review of the material covered in Part 1 (Chapters 1–4) of the textbook. Each question deals with a topic or technique important for your understanding of economic principles. If you miss a question you should return to the relevant section of the chapter in the textbook and fine-tune your understanding.

I.   MULTIPLE-CHOICE QUESTIONS

Select the option that provides the single best answer.

_____ 1.   The Arbezani economy is operating at a point inside its ppf. This may be because
       (a)   the economy has very poor technological know-how.
       (b)   Arbez is a very small nation and can't produce much.
       (c)   Arbez has specialized in producing a good in which it has a comparative disadvantage.
       (d)   Arbez has some unemployment.

_____ 2.   Movements along the production possibility frontier illustrate
       (a)   the concept of opportunity cost.
       (b)   the operation of market forces.
       (c)   improvements in technology.
       (d)   changes in the resource mix.

_____ 3.   The Arbezani economy can produce consumer goods and capital goods. There is a technological improvement in the production of consumer goods. Along the production possibility frontier, the opportunity cost of consumer goods will
       (a)   increase.
       (b)   decrease.
       (c)   remain unchanged.
       (d)   be indeterminate.

Use the diagram for the next five questions. It illustrates the production possibility frontier for Arbez.

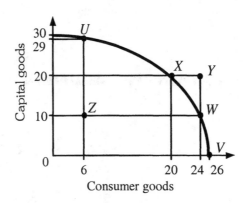

_____ 4.   Which point implies the existence of unemployment?
(a)   Z
(b)   V
(c)   U
(d)   Y

_____ 5.   Of those shown, with which combination of goods would the Arbezani economy grow most rapidly?
(a)   Z
(b)   V
(c)   U
(d)   Y

_____ 6.   Which statement is true? Along the production possibility frontier
(a)   the opportunity cost of capital goods is decreasing.
(b)   the opportunity cost of consumer goods is constant.
(c)   producing at Point V can never be economically efficient.
(d)   the opportunity cost of consumer goods is increasing.

_____ 7.   Arbez is at Point W. The opportunity cost of increasing capital goods production by 10 is
(a)   24 consumer goods given up.
(b)   20 consumer goods given up.
(c)   14 consumer goods given up.
(d)   4 consumer goods given up.

_____ 8.   Arbez is at Point Z. The opportunity cost of increasing capital goods production by 20 is
(a)   24 consumer goods given up.
(b)   14 consumer goods given up.
(c)   6 consumer goods given up.
(d)   0 consumer goods given up.

_____ 9.   Pepsi and Coke are consumption substitutes. The supply of Pepsi increases. This will cause
(a)   an increase in the demand for Pepsi.
(b)   an increase in the demand for Coke.
(c)   a decrease in the demand for Pepsi.
(d)   a decrease in the demand for Coke.

Each week, Jack and Jill can each produce vinegar and brown paper in the quantities shown in the following table. Constant costs apply for each individual.

	Jack	Jill
Vinegar	8	12
Brown paper	10	24

_____ 10.   According to the table,
(a)   Jack has a comparative advantage in the production of both goods.
(b)   Jack has a comparative advantage in the production of vinegar, and Jill has a comparative advantage in the production of brown paper.
(c)   Jack has a comparative advantage in the production of brown paper, and Jill has a comparative advantage in the production of vinegar.
(d)   Jill has a comparative advantage in the production of both goods.

_____ 11.   If producers must obtain a higher price than previously in order to produce the same level of output as before, then we can say that there has been
(a)   an increase in quantity supplied.
(b)   an increase in supply.
(c)   a decrease in supply.
(d)   a decrease in quantity supplied.

_____ 12.   The widget market is in equilibrium at a price where
(a)   there is no shortage of the good.
(b)   the demand curve is downsloping and the supply curve is upsloping.
(c)   the quantity demanded and the quantity supplied are equal.
(d)   there is no surplus of the good.

_____ 13.   The market for peas is experiencing a shortage. You should predict that
(a)   quantity demanded will decrease and quantity supplied will increase.
(b)   demand will increase and supply will decrease.
(c)   quantity demanded will increase and quantity supplied will decrease.
(d)   demand will decrease and supply will increase.

_____ 14.   Californian wine and Italian wine are consumption substitutes. The Italian wine industry decreases wine production following a drought. The equilibrium price will _____ and quantity traded will _____ for Californian wine.
(a)   increase; increase
(b)   decrease; increase
(c)   decrease; decrease
(d)   increase; decrease

_____ 15. Initially, the market for peas is in equilibrium. Suddenly, at the same price, there is a surplus. This might have been caused by an increase in
(a) quantity demanded.
(b) quantity supplied.
(c) demand.
(d) supply.

_____ 16. Costs of production decrease for Debi's Dip. At the same time a government health report alleges that dip consumption causes bone cancer. For Debi's Dip, the equilibrium price will _____ and the equilibrium quantity will _____ .
(a) increase; be indeterminate
(b) decrease; be indeterminate
(c) be indeterminate; increase
(d) be indeterminate; decrease

_____ 17. The Board of Aldermen of Polka, West Virginia, implement a rent control—a ceiling on the maximum rent that can be charged for an apartment. As a result we would expect to see
(a) an increase in the number of apartments supplied in order to meet the increased demand.
(b) lower prices for single-family homes, which will become less popular.
(c) renters renting more expensive or poorer quality apartments outside Polka.
(d) renters now able to find an adequate number of low-rent apartments.

_____ 18. An oil spill reduces lobster fishing off the Maine coast and, simultaneously, a recession reduces consumers' incomes. Compared to the equilibrium price and quantity in the market for lobsters (a normal good) before these events, in the new equilibrium,
(a) the price will be lower and the quantity will be lower.
(b) the price will be higher and the quantity will be lower.
(c) the price will be lower; the effect of the events on quantity cannot be determined without further information.
(d) the effect of the events on price cannot be determined without further information; the quantity will be lower.

_____ 19. The law of demand is best illustrated by
(a) the fact that, as the price of Pepsi rises, consumers buy more Coke.
(b) increased purchases of Coke as the price of Coke decreases.
(c) an increase in income that results in reduced purchases of store-brand soft drinks.
(d) an increase in income that results in increased purchases of Coke.

_____ 20. Each of the following will cause an increase in the demand for tennis racquets (a normal good) except
(a) a decrease in the price of tennis racquets.
(b) an increase in income.
(c) a decrease in the price of tennis balls.
(d) an increase in the number of persons playing tennis.

_____ 21. In the lettuce industry, an increase in the wage of lettuce harvesters will
(a)   increase the supply of lettuce, as workers will work harder than before.
(b)   increase the supply of lettuce, as more workers will be employed.
(c)   decrease the supply of lettuce, as workers will not need to work as hard as before.
(d)   decrease the supply of lettuce, as fewer workers will be employed.

_____ 22. The demand for Good A has been decreasing over the past year. Having examined the following facts, you conclude that Good A is a normal good. Which fact led you to that conclusion?
(a)   The price of Good A has been decreasing over the past year.
(b)   An economic slowdown has reduced the income of the traditional buyers of Good A.
(c)   Good B, a substitute for Good A, has increased its price over the last twelve months.
(d)   Household wealth has decreased among the traditional buyers of Good A.

Use the following diagram to answer the next three questions. The diagram refers to the market for Vito's Vitamins (a normal good). Vito's Vitamins is a substitute for Vinnie's Vitamins.

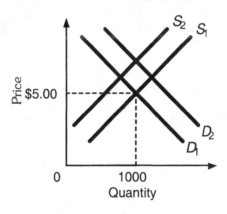

_____ 23. Given demand curve D_1, if supply moves from S_1 to S_2,
(a)   supply has increased.
(b)   demand has decreased.
(c)   price has decreased.
(d)   quantity demanded has decreased.

_____ 24. A change in supply from S_1 to S_2 might have been caused by
(a)   an increase in the price of Vinnie's Vitamins.
(b)   an increase in the demand for Vito's Vitamins.
(c)   an improvement in the technology of manufacturing Vito's Vitamins.
(d)   an increase in the production costs of Vito's Vitamins.

_____ 25. Demand moves from D_1 to D_2 whereas supply moves from S_1 to S_2. At the initial price level of $5.00 a _____ exists. Price will _____ .
(a)   shortage; increase
(b)   shortage; decrease
(c)   surplus; increase
(d)   surplus; decrease

II.   APPLICATION QUESTIONS

The market for fish oil has supply and demand curves given by $Q_s = -4 + P$ and $Q_d = 28 - P$, respectively. Units are millions of barrels of fish oil per day.

1.   Complete the following table.

Price (P)	Quantity Demanded (Qd)	Quantity Supplied (Qs)
$20	_____	_____
$18	_____	_____
$16	_____	_____
$14	_____	_____
$12	_____	_____
$10	_____	_____
$8	_____	_____
$6	_____	_____

2.   Determine the equilibrium price and quantity traded.

3.   If the government imposes a price ceiling of $12 in this market, what will happen to the positions of the demand and supply curves?

4.   If the government imposes a price ceiling of $12 in this market, what effect will this have on the market?

5.   If the world price of fish oil is $10 per barrel, how many barrels will the United States import each day?

6.   If the United States imposed a $4 per barrel tax on imported fish oil, how many barrels will the United States import each day?

7.   If the United States imposed a $4 per barrel tax on imported fish oil, calculate the tax revenue that would be generated.

REVIEW TEST SOLUTIONS

I.   Solutions to Multiple-Choice Questions

1.   (d)   If the economy is producing inside its frontier, there is an underuse of available resources.

2.   (a)   At full capacity, an increase in the production of one good requires a reallocation of resources and a reduction in the production of the second good.

3.   (b)   One way to look at this is to note that it now takes fewer resources to produce a given quantity of consumer goods—the amount of capital goods forgone is less than before. Recall that the slope of the ppf (which has changed) depicts opportunity cost.

4.   (a)   See the answer to Question 1.

5.   (c)   The more heavily Arbez indulges in capital formation (rather than consumption) the more quickly will its resource base expand.

6.   (d)   This ppf is bowed outwards: it is an increasing-cost ppf. As more of a good is produced the cost, in terms of the other good forgone, will increase.

7.   (d)   Currently the economy is producing 10 capital goods and 24 consumer goods. To increase capital goods production by 10, the economy would have to be at Point X, where 20 consumer goods are produced—a loss of 4 consumer goods.

8.   (c)   Currently the economy is producing 10 capital goods and 6 consumer goods. To increase capital goods production by 20, the economy would have to be on the vertical axis, where no consumer goods are produced—a loss of 6 consumer goods.

9.   (d)   If the price of Pepsi decreases, the quantity demanded of Pepsi will increase and the demand for the substitute good will decrease.

10.   (b)   For Jack, the opportunity cost of a unit of vinegar is 1.25 units of brown paper. For Jill, the opportunity cost of a unit of vinegar is 2 units of brown paper. Jack has the comparative advantage in vinegar. For Jack, the opportunity cost of a unit of brown paper is .8 of a unit of vinegar. For Jill, the opportunity cost of a unit of brown paper is .5 of a unit of vinegar. Jill has the comparative advantage in brown paper.

11.   (c)   Draw this if you got it wrong! Begin with a supply curve. At any given output the price will be higher than before. The entire price/quantity relationship has shifted.

12.   (c)   Equilibrium occurs only at the price level at which all active buyers and sellers can have their needs satisfied.

13.   (a)   To restore equilibrium, price must increase. As price increases, quantity demanded decreases (movement along the demand curve) and quantity supplied increases (movement along the supply curve).

14.   (a)   The decrease in the supply of Italian wine will force up its price. Quantity demanded will fall. The demand for the substitute will increase.

15.   (d)   Draw the diagram if you missed this one! Remember the distinction between a change in supply (the supply curve shifts) and a change in quantity supplied (there is a movement along a given supply curve).

16.   (b)   The decrease in production costs will increase profitability and increase supply. The report will reduce demand. Each factor decreases price but, whereas the increase in supply increases output the decrease in demand will reduce output. The net effect on output is uncertain.

17.   (c)   The rent control is a price ceiling. Assuming that it is set below the equilibrium price, a shortage of rent-controlled housing will occur, forcing renters to take apartments that are not subject to rent control.

18.   (d)   The oil spill will decrease supply (it is now more costly to catch lobsters). The recession will reduce demand for a normal good. Each factor decreases output but, whereas the decrease in supply increases price, the decrease in demand will decrease price. The net effect on price is uncertain.

19.   (b)   Each of the other answers will shift the demand curve for Coke. Recall that the law of demand is depicted as a movement along a given demand curve.

20.   (a)   A decrease in the price of tennis racquets will cause a movement along the demand curve.

21.   (d)   Higher costs reduce profitability and reduce supply.

22.   (b)   If a good is a normal good, a decrease in income will reduce demand.

23.   (d)   As supply decreases, price rises and there is a movement along the demand curve.

24.   (d)   If production costs increase, profitability will decrease, prompting a decrease in supply.

25.   (a)   Quantity demanded exceeds quantity supplied. Price will increase in this seller's market.

II.   *Solutions to Application Questions*

1.   See the following table.

Price (P)	Quantity Demanded (Qd)	Quantity Supplied (Qs)
$20	8	16
$18	10	14
$16	12	12
$14	14	10
$12	16	8
$10	18	6
$8	20	4
$6	22	2

2.   Equilibrium price is $16 and equilibrium quantity is 12. You can derive this by inspecting the demand and supply schedules, careful graphing, or algebra. In equilibrium, $Q_d = Q_s$, therefore, $28 - P = -4 + P$. Given that, $32 = 2P$ and $P = 16$. If $P = 16$, then $Q = 28 - 1(16) = 12$.

3.   The curves will not change position. A change in price leads to movements along the given demand and supply curves. If you missed this, return to Chapter 3 and review the distinction between a "change in demand" and a "change in quantity demanded."

4.   Quantity demanded will increase to 16, and quantity supplied will shrink to 8. There will be a shortage. Black markets may occur. Queuing is likely.

5.   If the price is $10, U.S. suppliers will offer 6 (million) barrels, but buyers will demand 18 (million) barrels. 12 (million) barrels will be imported.

6.   If the price is $14, U.S. suppliers will offer 10 (million) barrels, but buyers will demand 14 (million) barrels. 4 (million) barrels will be imported.

7. $16 million—4 (million) barrels will be imported, yielding $4 each.

Part II

Concepts and Problems in Macroeconomics

5 [20]

Introduction to Macroeconomics

Chapter objectives:

1. Describe the three main concerns of macroeconomics and provide simple definitions of inflation and unemployment.
2. Describe the behavior of the business cycle.
3. List the four economic sectors and describe how they interact through the three market arenas.
4. Explain how macroeconomic issues relate to the government's policy decisions. List three policies that the government may use to influence the economy. Indicate the principal tools of each policy.
5. Briefly describe the development of Keynesian macroeconomic theory and place it within the context of then-current economic events.

The material skimmed over in this introductory chapter will be explored more completely in subsequent chapters. Think of this chapter as a road map showing major points of interest.

▶▶ LEARNING TIP: Different economists support different interpretations of how the economy fits together. If you're grade oriented (or even if you're not) , it might be a good idea to identify the preferences of your own instructor, even if it's for no other reason than that it will help you to identify the areas of controversy.◀

OBJECTIVE 1:
Describe the three main concerns of macroeconomics and provide simple definitions of inflation and unemployment.

Major topics of concern in macroeconomics are: growth in aggregate output (and the business cycle); the unemployment rate (the percentage of labor force that is unemployed); and the inflation rate (a general increase in the aggregate price level). In the sputtering economy of the early 2000s, deflation (a general decrease in the aggregate price level) became a plausible threat. (page 98 [410])

Whereas microeconomics concerns itself with the functioning of individual industries, households and firms and particular prices, macroeconomics focuses on the determinants of national income, the overall price level, and aggregate employment. Macroeconomists attempt to measure aggregate output and to detect business cycles, which feature recessions (when aggregate output is shrinking) and expansions.

The unemployment rate is a key and widely-reported measure of the economy's health. The persistence of unemployment seems to imply that the labor market is not in equilibrium. Macroeconomics examines why this might be so.

Macroeconomics are also concerned with how the overall price level is changing. If the level increases, there is inflation; if it decreases, there is deflation.

Macroeconomics, then, is concerned with aggregate measures whereas microeconomics is concerned with individual measures.

▶▶▶   LEARNING TIP: Refer to Chapter 1 to refresh your memory on the distinction between microeconomics and macroeconomics. ◀

━━━■━━━━━━━━━━━━━━━━━━━ **Practice** ━━━━━━━━━━━━━━━━━━━━━━━

1.   _____ is when there are extremely rapid increases in the overall price level.
   (a)   Inflation
   (b)   Stagflation
   (c)   Hyperinflation
   (d)   Superflation

   ANSWER: (c)   Refer to p. 92 [404] for the definition.

2.   Aggregation refers to
   (a)   the behavior of all individuals in a group taken together.
   (b)   the calculation of average values by adding together and dividing.
   (c)   forecasting future values, based on past data.
   (d)   the development of the microeconomic foundations of macroeconomics.

   ANSWER: (a)   Refer to p. 96 [408] for more on this.

3.   A recession occurs when aggregate output declines for _____ consecutive _____ .
   (a)   two; months
   (b)   two; quarters
   (c)   three; months
   (d)   three; quarters

   ANSWER: (b)   Refer to p. 90 [402] for the definition of recession.

4.   At the beginning of 2009, the Lifeguards' Union negotiates a wage contract of $8 per hour for lifeguards. The summer of 2009 is especially bleak, with little beach activity. Although the demand for lifeguards decreases, their hourly wage rate does not. This is an example of a
   (a)   macroeconomic price.
   (b)   price control.
   (c)   sticky price.
   (d)   price ceiling.

   ANSWER: (c) If the price of lifeguard services were influenced by changes in market conditions, the price (wage) should have fallen. The contractual agreement made the price "sticky." ■

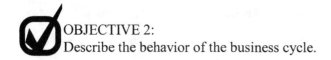OBJECTIVE 2:
Describe the behavior of the business cycle.

The U.S. economic record since 1900 has shown a long-term underlying expansion (growth trend), but with fluctuations around this trend. Economists call these fluctuations "business cycles"—the Great Depression being the most grave example. Each cycle consists of four phases—peak, recession, trough, and expansion. One goal of government economic policy has been to smooth out business cycles and have the economy stay on a more even keel. (page 90 [402])

▶▶▶   LEARNING TIP: Do a little simple macroeconomic research. Find out the inflation rate and the unemployment rate. The numbers are reported monthly. How is your state doing, in terms of unemployment, relative to the national economy? Why?◀

━━━━ ■ ━━━━━━━━━━━━━━━━━━ **Practice** ━━━━━━━━━━━━━━━━━━━

5.   In a recession we expect to see unemployment _____ and output _____ .
        (a)   increasing; increasing
        (b)   increasing; decreasing
        (c)   decreasing; increasing
        (d)   decreasing; decreasing
        ANSWER: (b) In Question 3 we defined a recession as a period of decreasing output. As output
                     decreases (usually because of falling aggregate demand), the unemployment
                     lines lengthen

Use the following diagram of a business cycle to answer the next two questions.

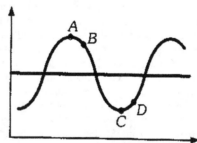

6.   In the diagram of a business cycle, _____ is on the vertical axis; _____ is on the horizontal axis.
        (a)   inflation; unemployment
        (b)   unemployment; inflation
        (c)   gross domestic product; time
        (d)   time; gross domestic product
        ANSWER: (c) The diagram plots output level over time. Add this information to the preceding
                     diagram. Refer to the diagram on p. 91 [403].

7.   In the preceding diagram, the expansion of the business cycle occurs at Point _____ and the recession occurs at Point _____.

(a)   *A; B*

(b)   *A; C*

(c)   *B; C*

(d)   *D; B*

ANSWER: (d) The peak is at Point *A*, the recession at Point *B*, the trough at Point *C*, and the expansion at Point *D*. ■

 OBJECTIVE 3:
List the four economic sectors and describe how they interact through the three market arenas.

The circular flow model (Figure 5.3 [20.3]) represents the linkages among the four different sectors of the economy—households, firms, the government, and the rest of the world. There are three major markets—goods-and-services, labor, and money—and the four sectors interact in each of these. (page 92 [404])

▶▶   LEARNING TIP: The circularity makes an important point—each dollar spent is also a dollar earned as income by producers. You will see this concept again in Chapter 6 (21).◀

There are numerous markets within each "market arena"—the goods-and-services market contains the market for cars, coffee, corn flakes, and cotton swabs, for example. Each "market arena" is a macroeconomic aggregation. (page 93 [405])

▶▶   LEARNING TIP: Learn the model! The macro model begun in this chapter will be built upon through successive chapters, but the logic within it will remain the same. You'll find the going easier if you master each step as it is presented, rather than waiting and trying to make sense of it all at once in its completed form or before a test. The circular flow diagram (p. 93 [405]) is the place to start. Throughout the remainder of your macro course the fourfold division— consumers/businesses/government/international—will be present, and the three market arenas will be at, or close to, center stage.

▶▶   LEARNING TIP: As Case, Fair and Oster advise, you'll find macroeconomics easier if you think in terms of the "typical" consumer or firm. Macroeconomists don't claim that all individuals respond in the same way in each circumstance, but they do try to draw out the general tendency, and you should strive to do the same. Macroeconomics is interested in the forest, not the trees, so ignore exceptions. Inflation, for example, occurs when the general (aggregate) price level is rising. Some prices (DVDs, CDs, calculators) may be falling—but the general price trend is upward. Similarly, although you have a friend who has just found a job, the general unemployment rate can still be rising.◀

━━━━ ■ ━━━━━━━━━━━━━━━━━━━━━ **Practice** ━━━━━━━━━━━━━━━━━━━━━

8.   Households are

(a)   only demanders in the money market.

(b)   only suppliers in the money market.

(c)   both demanders and suppliers in the money market.

(d)   neither demanders nor suppliers in the money market—banks are.

ANSWER: (c) Households deposit (supply) funds and borrow (demand) funds. Refer to p. 93 [405].

9.   The main point to draw from the circular flow diagram is that
    (a)   saving will always equal investment.
    (b)   every dollar of expenditure is also a dollar of income.
    (c)   exports equal imports.
    (d)   wages equal income.

    ANSWER: (b) Option (d) is incorrect—other payments (rent and dividends, for example) are part of income. Because we typically run a trade deficit in the United States, we know that exports and imports are not necessarily equal. Saving and investment are not mentioned explicitly in the diagram—more about them later.

10.   In the money market, all of the following are true EXCEPT that
    (a)   households supply funds and demand funds.
    (b)   the government borrows by issuing bonds.
    (c)   businesses borrow by issuing bonds.
    (d)   businesses borrow by issuing dividends.

    ANSWER: (d) A dividend is a payment received from a firm by its shareholders.

11.   In our model of the macroeconomy, each of the following is a market arena in which households, firms, the government, and the rest of the world interact EXCEPT
    (a)   the goods-and-services market.
    (b)   the foreign trade market.
    (c)   the labor market.
    (d)   the money market.

    ANSWER: (b) Modeling in economics, as in other sciences, involves selection. Our model chooses to exclude the foreign trade market as a separate arena. Refer to p. 93 [405]. ■

OBJECTIVE 4:
Explain how macroeconomic issues relate to the government's policy decisions. List two policies that the government may use to influence the economy. Indicate the principal tools of each policy.

Macro problems may be attacked through the use of fiscal policy actions or monetary policy actions. *Fiscal policy* involves manipulating the amount of taxation and government spending; *monetary policy* involves adjusting the quantity of money available. An expansionary policy is designed to encourage economic growth; a contractionary policy is designed to slow expansion. An expansionary fiscal policy might reduce taxes and/or increase government spending. An expansionary monetary policy will increase the money supply and reduce interest rates. (page 95 [407])

———— ■ ———————————————————— **Practice** ————————————————————

12. The economy is in a recession. Using fiscal policy tools, the government might _____ government spending and _____ taxes.
    (a)   increase; increase
    (b)   increase; decrease
    (c)   decrease; increase
    (d)   decrease; decrease

    ANSWER: (b) Raising government spending will increase overall spending (aggregate demand). Cutting taxes will also increase overall spending. This is an expansionary fiscal policy.

13. A contractionary fiscal policy is likely to be enacted during a(n) _____ ; a contractionary monetary policy is likely to be enacted during a(n) _____ .
    (a)   expansion; expansion
    (b)   expansion; contraction
    (c)   contraction; expansion
    (d)   contraction; contraction

    ANSWER: (d) Contractionary policies are intended to stimulate a faltering economy.

14. In 2007, working-class parents received a child tax credit rebate of $500 per child. This is best classified as a
    (a)   fiscal policy because it used taxes to stabilize the economy.
    (b)   fiscal policy because taxes were used as incentives to work, save, and invest.
    (c)   monetary policy because it was designed to stabilize the economy.
    (d)   monetary policy because taxes were used as incentives to work, save, and invest.

    ANSWER: (a) This payment had little impact on the decision to work, save, and invest. The check was meant to be spent while the economy was faltering. ■

OBJECTIVE 5:
Briefly describe the development of Keynesian macroeconomic theory and place it within the context of then-current economic events.

Macroeconomics was born out of the dark days of the Great Depression in the 1930s when the labor market didn't clear in the way that the classical model predicted it should—wages and prices were "sticky" and unemployment persisted for years. John Maynard Keynes performed a theoretical rethink and argued that employment is not determined by prices and wages but by the level of aggregate demand for goods and services. Macroeconomics remains a controversial area of study. (page 96 [408])

Evolution: Macroeconomics evolves in light of new information and phenomena. Keynes's economic theory was a product of, and response to, his own (unemployment-ridden) era. Existing theory couldn't analyze the conditions that he observed. Later developments have followed the same pattern— an orthodox view; some fresh, "awkward" real-world facts; a revision of the theory.

The 1960s had high levels of demand, a booming war-time economy, and a quest for the Great Society. It was believed that the government should act to stabilize the macroeconomy. Employment levels and job opportunities were high, but so was the inflation rate. This environment differed from the one that prompted Keynes to rethink economic analysis. Inflation, which became a serious issue in the 1970s, hadn't been a critical factor for him. A new controversy arose—between Keynesians and "monetarists." More on this in Chapter 18 (33).

Next came the soaring oil prices in the 1970s and the phenomenon of stagflation—supply-side economics was born. Refer to Chapter 18 (33).

The long strong economy of the 1990s bred a feeling of consensus, but macroeconomics remains riddled with controversy and debate.

ECONOMICS IN PRACTICE: On page 97 [409], the textbook invites you to compare passages from two novels, "The Great Gatsby" and "The Grapes of Wrath." The former was written and based on a time before the Great Depression, the latter during it. For a change of medium, visit Blockbuster and rent "Gold Diggers of 1933." "Gold Diggers" opens with "We're in the Money" (a Broadway production number that is interrupted as local deputies close the theater for nonpayment of bills) and climaxes with a harrowing staging of "Remember My Forgotten Man" (a song which features hundreds of extras and is about unemployed doughboys consigned to the breadline and the soup kitchen). Why did the Hollywood studios choose to make such extravagant movies during the depths of the Great Depression?

ANSWER: During the Depression, with high unemployment, labor was cheap, and studios were able to afford large casts in front of, and behind, the camera. On the demand side, with shrinking incomes, audiences discovered that movies were a cheap form of entertainment and, often, a temporary escape from one's troubles. Movies were an inferior good—refer to Chapter 3. Movie theaters were warm in the winter and cool in the summer. Popcorn (a complement) was a luxury that families could afford—popcorn sales increased during the Depression.

ECONOMICS IN PRACTICE: On page 98 [410], the textbook offers a brief biography of John Maynard Keynes, the father of modern macroeconomics. Keynes began as a so-called "classical' economist and broke away during the Great Depression when orthodox theory seemed to be failing. His "General Theory" appeared in 1936. However, in 1930, between the Wall Street collapse of 1929 and the publication of his ground-breaking book, Keynes published a non-technical piece entitled "Economic Possibilities for our Grandchildren," an article speculating on the economy of the future. It begins, "We are suffering just now from a bad attack of economic pessimism." Read Keynes's article (it's available on the Internet or in collections of his writings) and compare his predictions with what has happened since 1930.

ANSWER: Some of Keynes's predictions are remarkably accurate although some are not. Keynes clearly believed that the Great Depression was only a temporary setback. He argued that the subsistence needs of society would be satisfied and that future generations would be enjoying "an age of leisure and of abundance" and 15-hour workweeks. There is an old joke in economics that forecasters have correctly predicted nine of the last six recessions—even our best models have limitations! Your reading of this article by one of the most eminent of economists should convince you to take the predictions of present-day economic and political pundits with a generous grain of salt.

—— **Practice** ——

15. The notion that the government can stabilize the economy is known as
   (a) classical macroeconomics.
   (b) growth economics.
   (c) proactive business cycle management.
   (d) fine-tuning.

   ANSWER: (d) "Fine-tuning" suggests that the government can adjust macroeconomic variables (inflation and unemployment) very precisely through carefully selected policy actions.

16.   Before the Great Depression, the "classical" economists assumed that wages were _____ upward and _____ downward.
(a)   flexible; flexible
(b)   flexible; not flexible
(c)   not flexible; flexible
(d)   not flexible; not flexible

ANSWER: (a) The classical economists believed that the wage would respond to shifts in the demand for, and supply of, labor. Refer to p. 96 [408].

17.   Before the Great Depression, the "classical" economists predicted that, if the demand for labor fell, then
(a)   the wage would increase, the supply of labor would increase, and unemployment would occur.
(b)   the wage would decrease, the supply of labor would decrease, and unemployment would occur.
(c)   the wage rate would fall to clear the market, resulting in higher unemployment.
(d)   the wage rate would fall to clear the market, reducing the quantity of labor supplied and eliminating unemployment.

ANSWER: (d) Try drawing the labor market using demand and supply curves. The classical economists used microeconomic tools. Unfortunately, they failed to take into account contracts, minimum wages, and the possibility that the wage level could become stuck.

18.   In general, over the past 25 years, the inflation rate has been _____ and the unemployment rate has been _____ .
(a)   increasing; increasing
(b)   increasing; decreasing
(c)   decreasing; increasing
(d)   decreasing; decreasing

ANSWER: (d) Refer to Figures 5.5 (20.5) and 5.6 (20.6). While there has been some variability, there has been a general downward trend.

19.   In 2008, there was some concern about "stagflation" in the economy. If stagflation was present, we should expect
(a)   high inflation and low stock market prices.
(b)   high inflation and high unemployment.
(c)   low interest rates and falling stock market prices.
(d)   a declining overall price level and high unemployment.

ANSWER: (b) Stagflation means high inflation and high unemployment with negative growth.

20.   Keynes believed that the level of employment is determined by
(a)   the wage level.
(b)   the aggregate (overall) price level.
(c)   aggregate demand.
(d)   stock prices.

ANSWER: (c) Keynes's macroeconomic model is driven by aggregate demand (refer to p. 96 [408]). When there is an increase in the demand for goods and services, there is an increase in employment. ∎

PRACTICE TEST

I.   MULTIPLE-CHOICE QUESTIONS

Select the option that provides the single best answer.

_____ 1.   Which of the following is not a macroeconomic variable?
   (a)   The interest rate
   (b)   The general price level
   (c)   The price of beer
   (d)   Gross domestic product

_____ 2.   Keynes argued that the primary determinant of the level of economic activity is
   (a)   the amount of money there is to spend.
   (b)   the aggregate demand for goods and services.
   (c)   the aggregate price level.
   (d)   the demand for labor.

_____ 3.   In the financial market, each of the following is traded EXCEPT
   (a)   Treasury notes.
   (b)   corporate bonds.
   (c)   capital gains.
   (d)   shares of stock.

_____ 4.   A Keynesian fiscal policy intended to pull the economy out of a recession might include cutting
   (a)   interest rates.
   (b)   taxes.
   (c)   government spending.
   (d)   the unemployment rate.

_____ 5.   Which of the following is not a phase of a typical business cycle?
   (a)   Recession
   (b)   Trough
   (c)   Peak
   (d)   Inflation

_____ 6.   One objective of expansionary policies is to increase aggregate _____ by _____ personal taxes.
   (a)   output; increasing
   (b)   output; decreasing
   (c)   price level; increasing
   (d)   price level; decreasing

_____ 7.   Employment typically rises during
   (a)   a period of stagflation.
   (b)   a period of inflation.
   (c)   a recession.
   (d)   the period from the peak to a trough in a business cycle.

_____ 8.   Each of the following is an example of a transfer payment EXCEPT
(a)   a welfare check.
(b)   Social Security benefits.
(c)   interest on a Treasury bond.
(d)   veterans' benefits.

_____ 9.   In the labor market, suppliers are
(a)   households.
(b)   households and firms.
(c)   firms and government.
(d)   firms.

_____ 10.   In the circular flow model
(a)   households purchase resources.
(b)   firms and the government purchase resources.
(c)   government sells resources.
(d)   households produce goods and services.

_____ 11.   As the economy moves into a recession, we typically see inflation _____ and unemployment _____ .
(a)   increasing; increasing
(b)   increasing; decreasing
(c)   decreasing; increasing
(d)   decreasing; decreasing

_____ 12.   In 2008, President Bush cut taxes for individuals by sending them a rebate. This is best described as an example of
(a)   fiscal policy.
(b)   monetary policy.
(c)   fine-tuning policy.
(d)   cyclical policy.

_____ 13.   Stagflation is characterized by _____ unemployment and a _____ price level.
(a)   high; rising
(b)   high; falling
(c)   low; rising
(d)   low; falling

_____ 14.   To know where the economy is in the business cycle, one must know
(a)   the unemployment rate.
(b)   the rate of change in the level of economic activity.
(c)   the rate of change in the price level.
(d)   the rate of change in the unemployment rate.

_____ 15.   "Sticky" prices in a given market suggest that excess demand _____ be sustained and excess supply _____ be sustained.
(a)   can; can
(b)   can; cannot
(c)   cannot; can
(d)   cannot; cannot

_____ 16. Which of the following statements is true?
- (a) During a period of hyperinflation, we would expect an increase in the value of savings, because everyone needs to have more money.
- (b) During a period of high inflation, fine-tuning would call for an increase in the money supply.
- (c) Stagflation is defined as a rapid increase in the overall price level.
- (d) During a period of high inflation, fine-tuning would call for a decrease in the money supply.

_____ 17. In sequence, the four phases of a business cycle are
- (a) the trough, the expansion, the peak, and the recession.
- (b) the recession, the peak, the expansion, and the trough.
- (c) the trough, the expansion, the recession, and the peak.
- (d) the trough, the recession, the expansion, and the peak.

_____ 18. Each of the following is one of the major concerns of macroeconomics EXCEPT
- (a) growth in aggregate output.
- (b) the national debt.
- (c) unemployment,
- (d) inflation and deflation.

_____ 19. Dissaving occurs when
- (a) households receive more income than they spend.
- (b) households receive less income than they spend.
- (c) businesses issue a share of stock or a corporate bond.
- (d) the government issues a Treasury bond

_____ 20. The circular flow diagram shows us that household income is allocated to each of the following EXCEPT
- (a) purchases of exports.
- (b) purchases of imports.
- (c) purchases of domestically produced goods and services.
- (d) payment of taxes.

II. APPLICATION QUESTIONS

1. Devise a hypothesis about the link between household income and household spending. As one increases, does the other increase or decrease? Which variable is the "cause" and which the "effect"? Why is your theory an abstraction? Is your theory invalidated if one household behaves differently?

2. How do you personally participate in the markets for goods and services, labor, and finance?

3.   Identify the following topics as either predominantly macroeconomic (MAC) or microeconomic (MIC).

(a)   _____   gross domestic product
(b)   _____   the demand for beer
(c)   _____   inflation
(d)   _____   the price of gold relative to the price of silver
(e)   _____   unemployment among economics professors
(f)   _____   wages in regulated public utilities
(g)   _____   economic growth
(h)   _____   stagflation
(i)   _____   price of medical care
(j)   _____   job discrimination
(k)   _____   recession
(l)   _____   apartment rents
(m)   _____   total employment
(n)   _____   a household's income
(o)   _____   national income
(p)   _____   business cycles
(q)   _____   the government budget deficit
(r)   _____   the money supply

4.   A circular flow diagram is presented in the text. After going over the section in the text, draw it from your memory and understanding.

5.   Our macroeconomic analysis is not yet theoretically rigorous, but use your existing knowledge of the business cycle to help you interpret current affairs. Suppose that our economy slips into a recession.

(a)   What is happening to the overall level of production in the economy?
(b)   Predict what is likely to be happening to the unemployment rate.
(c)   Predict what is likely to be happening to household income.
(d)   Predict what is likely to be happening to the level of household spending.
(e)   What is likely to be happening to the inflation rate?
(f)   Now suppose the government reduces income taxes on households. What effect is this likely to have on household spending, the overall output level, employment, unemployment, and the aggregate price level?

PRACTICE TEST SOLUTIONS

I.   *Solutions to Multiple-Choice Questions*

1.   (c)   The price of a single good (like beer) is microeconomic in nature.

2.   (b)   Keynes believed that aggregate demand is the driving force in determining macroeconomic activity. Refer to p. 96 [408].

3.   (c)   Capital gains occur when an asset is sold at a higher price than its purchase price. Refer to p. 95 [407].

4.   (b)   To move the economy out of a slump, the government could cut taxes. This would give taxpayers more income to spend. Interest rates are connected to monetary policy.

5.	(d)	A business cycle reflects changes in production level. The missing phase is the expansion. Refer to the diagram on p. 91 [403].

6.	(b)	Expansionary policies are intended to stimulate production. A side effect of this might be an increase in the aggregate price level. A tax cut is an expansionary fiscal policy.

7.	(b)	Refer to the discussion of U.S. business cycles beginning on p. 90 [402]. Note that if aggregate supply decreases, the economy can experience both inflation and increasing unemployment—i.e., stagflation.

8.	(c)	Transfers are payments that require no good or service in return. Interest on a bond is a fee (reward) for lending the government money.

9.	(a)	Refer to the circular flow diagram on p. 93 [405].

10.	(b)	Refer to the circular flow diagram on p. 93 [405].

11.	(c)	When the economy is slowing down, it is harder to sell goods (harder to raise prices) and harder to find a job. Note that if a decrease in aggregate supply has caused the recession, inflation will increase—i.e., stagflation.

12.	(a)	Tax changes are elements of a fiscal policy.

13.	(a)	Stagflation combines stagnation (high unemployment) with inflation (rising aggregate price level). Refer to p. 96 [408].

14.	(b)	If the rate of change is positive, the economy is expanding; at the peak and at the trough, the rate of change is zero; in a recession, the rate of change is negative. Refer to p. 90 [402].

15.	(a)	When prices are sticky (not very responsive to demand or supply changes), a situation of excess demand or excess supply can persist because, in either case, price does not move to eliminate the market imbalance. Refer to p. 96 [408].

16.	(d)	Inflation, we shall see, has more than one cause, but increasing the money supply will aggravate the problem. Fine-tuning refers to the supposed ability of the government to make quite precise adjustments in inflation and unemployment. During hyperinflation, the value of currency is decreasing rapidly. The worst thing to do is hold money—it is better to spend it before it falls further in value. Stagflation is more than just inflation.

17.	(a)	Refer to the diagram on p. 91 [403].

18.	(b)	Refer to p. 90 [402].

19.	(b)	Dissaving occurs when households spend more than they receive as income. Refer to p. 93 [405].

20.	(a)	Exports are bought by foreigners.

II.   Solutions to Application Questions

1.   There is a positive relationship between household income (independent variable) and household spending (dependent variable). The theory is an abstraction because it excludes all other factors that might affect household spending. If, in general, households behave as predicted by the theory, it is supported, exceptions notwithstanding.

2.   In the market for goods and services, you are probably a buyer (e.g., groceries), in the market for labor you are probably a seller, and in the money market you are a seller if you save and a buyer if you borrow (e.g., student loans).

3.
(a)	MAC	(b)	MIC	(c)	MAC	(d)	MIC
(e)	MIC	(f)	MIC	(g)	MAC	(h)	MAC
(i)	MIC	(j)	MIC	(k)	MAC	(l)	MIC
(m)	MAC	(n)	MIC	(o)	MAC	(p)	MAC
(q)	MAC	(r)	MAC				

4.   Refer to the text for the solution to this exercise.

5.   (a)   A recession means that the economy's overall output level is shrinking.
      (b)   With less production, employers will cut back on employment. (Usually this is not an immediate effect,)
      (c)   With fewer jobs, households will start to cut back on spending.
      (d)   With less income, households will spend less.
      (e)   Inflation is likely to lessen and, possibly, become deflation.
      (f)   If the government reduces income taxes on households, after-tax income would increase, and household spending would increase. Output level and employment would increase, unemployment would decrease, and the aggregate price level would increase.

6 [21]

Measuring National Output and National Income

Chapter objectives:

1. Define gross domestic product (GDP) and its components. Detail those transactions that are excluded from GDP calculations. Distinguish between GDP and GNP.

2. Use the expenditure approach to calculate GDP. Distinguish between gross investment and net investment. Discuss the meaning of depreciation and the problems of measuring it. Define the three categories of personal consumption expenditures.

3. Outline the procedure and rationale for determining GDP through the income approach. Distinguish the various national income accounts.

4. Distinguish between real GDP and nominal GDP and explain why real GDP is the preferred measure of production. Discuss the weaknesses of a fixed-weight index to measure real GDP. Discuss how the GDP deflator is constructed.

5. Outline the shortcomings of GDP and per capita GDP as a measure of social well-being.

Most students find this chapter a bit of a chore. Memorize the important definitions: GDP, the components of the expenditure approach, depreciation, saving (nonconsumption), and disposable personal income.

BRAIN TEASER: This chapter explores how economists measure an economy's production, using gross domestic product (GDP), gross national product (GNP), and other aggregates. Usually, the difference between GDP and GNP (net factor payments to the rest of the world) are minimal—for the United States, about one-fifth of 1% of GDP. Consider though, Lesotho, a tiny nation with a poor domestic economy, which is entirely surrounded by wealthy South Africa. Most Lesothans work in South Africa's mines and industries. Which is larger, Lesotho's GDP or its GNP?

OBJECTIVE 1:

Define gross domestic product (GDP) and its components. Detail those transactions that are excluded from GDP calculations. Distinguish between GDP and GNP.

There is a family of national income accounts, but the key measure of current domestic economic activity is *gross domestic product*. GDP is the market value of all final goods and services produced within the economy. Second-hand sales, sales of intermediate goods, public and private transfers payments, and the value of financial transactions are all excluded. (page 105 [417])

> ▶▶▶   LEARNING TIP: There's no substitute for learning the rationale behind the concept of GDP. Productive economic activity within the economy results in new final goods and services. Sales of final goods plus (or minus) change in inventories will capture this. Compare this idea of new productive activity with the items that are excluded from GDP.
>
> Consider the logic behind the exclusion of some items from GDP calculations, such as transfer payments (public and private), intermediate goods, second-hand sales, and financial transactions. We're measuring *current* production of goods and services. Why are these categories excluded?
>
> Moonlighting, "do it yourself" activities, barter, and illegal activities don't show up either, although current goods and services are provided through these activities. How much would GDP change if, for example, the sale of drugs were decriminalized?◀

GNP is the market value of all final goods and services produced by an economy's resources (wherever located). The distinguishing feature between GDP and GNP, which is location of production, can be seen in the case of Georgia peaches harvested by Mexican migrant workers. The value of these services adds to U.S. production and, therefore, is counted in U.S. GDP. U.S. GNP focuses on ownership of resources and ignores location. U.S. GNP should exclude the services of the migrant workers because they are not performed by U.S. citizens.

ECONOMICS IN PRACTICE: On page 109 [421], the textbook considered how eBay transactions are figured into the national income accounts. The basic principle is quite simple (although the application might be difficult)—new final goods and services should be counted, others should not. Applications 1 and 10 following give you some practice in this area. Here are some more cases—what *should* count in GDP, what *does* count, and what *doesn't*?

1.   You hire a stockbroker to buy $1,000 of stock in Toyota.
2.   You look after the neighbor's child for the afternoon for $20.
3.   You arrange to paint your neighbor's house in exchange for her building you a rock garden.
4.   You sell this Study Guide on eBay for $10.

ANSWER: None of these transactions will be counted as part of GDP. The fee charged by the stockbroker (1) will be included, however, because s/he has provided a service and has charged you for it. Your childcare services (2), and the house painting and gardening (3), *should* be included in GDP—a new final good or service has been provided in each case—but will not be counted, because no transaction has been reported. The sale of the Study Guide (4) will not be included—its value was counted when it was purchased new. The fee charged by eBay will be counted, because eBay has provided a marketing service.

─────■──────────────────────────── **Practice** ─────────────────────────

1.   U.S. gross domestic product for 2009 is defined as the total market value of all
      (a)   final goods and services sold in 2009.
      (b)   goods and services produced in 2009 by productive resources owned by U.S. citizens.
      (c)   final goods and services produced in 2009 within U.S. boundaries by productive resources owned by U.S. citizens.
      (d)   final goods and services produced in 2009 within U.S. boundaries.

      ANSWER: (d) Ownership of resources is irrelevant in GDP calculations; the location of production is—it must be within U.S. boundaries. Refer to p. 105 [417].

2.   _____ goods are goods that are not resold to someone else.
      (a)   Intermediate
      (b)   Final
      (c)   Transfer
      (d)   Consumer durable

      ANSWER: (b) Consumer durables may not be resold (except as second-hand goods)—they are final goods. Goods that are resold are intermediate goods or second-hand goods. Refer to p. 106 [418].

3.   Jean, an avid gardener, buys a packet of carrot seeds. The packet of seeds _____ counted in GDP as a final product; the carrots Jean grows and consumes _____ counted in GDP as a final product.
      (a)   is; are
      (b)   is; are not
      (c)   is not; are
      (d)   is not; are not

      ANSWER: (b) The seeds are sold to the final user. Because Jean grows and eats the carrots, they never reach a market and will not be counted (although they do represent production). This is a limitation of the GDP concept.

4.   Many Arbezani workers cross the border to work in Arboc although few Arbocalis work in Arbez. We should expect that Arbezani GDP will be _____ than its GNP and that Arbocali GDP will be _____ than its GNP.
      (a)   greater; greater
      (b)   greater; smaller
      (c)   smaller; greater
      (d)   smaller; smaller

      ANSWER: (c) GDP measures production by location. More resources are producing in Arboc. GNP measures production by ownership. Refer to p. 107 [419]. ■

✓OBJECTIVE 2:
Use the expenditure approach to calculate GDP. Distinguish between gross investment and net investment. Discuss the meaning of depreciation and the problems of measuring it. Define the three categories of personal consumption expenditures.

Two methods, the *expenditure approach* and the *income approach*, are used to calculate GDP. The two methods should produce the same result, because a dollar spent is also a dollar received as income. The expenditure approach is summed up by:

$$GDP = C + I + G + (EX - IM)$$

where

C = personal consumption expenditures
I = gross private domestic investment
G = government consumption and gross investment
$(EX - IM)$ = net exports

▶▶▶ LEARNING TIP: To organize your thoughts, think of a demand and supply diagram for peaches (the only good the economy produces). The market value of production is the equivalent of price times quantity and can be visualized in two ways. We can measure the market value by focusing on the demand side (expenditure on peaches) or by focusing on the supply side (income of producers of peaches). We'll see later that (aggregate) demand is made up of $C + I + G + (EX - IM)$.◀

Gross private domestic investment (I) includes residential investment, nonresidential investment, and *changes* in the level of business inventories—not financial transactions, or putting money in your savings account. Depreciation is the allowance made by businesses for the deterioration of capital as time passes. This is certainly a cost of production. Net investment is gross investment minus depreciation. (page 110 [422])

▶▶▶ LEARNING TIP: "Change in inventories" is an important part of our upcoming theoretical analysis. What would happen to (total) inventories if (total) demand in the economy exceeded (total) supply? Inventories would fall. Unexpected inventory change is an important part of the economy's signaling mechanism. Falling inventories tell producers to increase production; unpleasantly high inventory levels tell producers to cut back production. Watch for this point in Chapter 8 (23).◀

Personal consumption expenditures (C) are divided among spending on durable goods (e.g., a car), nondurable goods (e.g., gasoline), and services (e.g., an oil change).

Government consumption and gross investment (G) includes expenditures by all levels of government on final goods and services. The salary of your Senator or the purchase of a new school bus would be included.

Net exports ($EX - IM$) is the difference between exports (domestically-produced goods and services that are sold to foreigners) and imports (foreign-produced goods and services that are sold in the United States).

—■———————————————————————— **Practice** ————————————————————

5. The expenditure approach equation is
    (a) $C + I + G + (EX + IM)$.
    (b) $C + I + G - (EX + IM)$.
    (c) $C + I + G + (EX - IM)$.
    (d) $C + I + G - (EX - IM)$.

    ANSWER: (c) Net exports $(EX - IM)$ are added to the total. Refer to p. 108 [420].

6. Peter Rachman builds some apartment buildings. This expenditure is
    (a)   residential consumption.
    (b)   residential investment.
    (c)   durable consumption.
    (d)   inventory investment.

    ANSWER: (b) All new residential construction is classified as investment. Refer to p. 109 [421].

7. Gross private domestic investment has three components:
    (a)   nonresidential investment, residential investment, and inventory investment.
    (b)   business investment in plant and equipment, residential construction, and net exports of machinery.
    (c)   stocks, bonds, and real estate.
    (d)   purchases of new firms, purchases of existing firms, and purchases of residential housing stock.

    ANSWER: (a) Refer to p. 109 [421] for a breakdown of gross private domestic investment.

8. GDP is 1,200, consumption (personal consumption expenditures) is 900, gross private domestic investment is 150, exports are 50, and imports are 125. Depreciation is 40. Government spending (government consumption and gross investment) is
    (a)   15.
    (b)   75.
    (c)   225.
    (d)   265.

    ANSWER: (c) $GDP = C + I + G + (EX - IM)$. $1,200 = 900 + 150 + G + (50 - 125)$. Depreciation is not relevant in this calculation.

9. The capital stock at the end of the year is equal to the capital stock at the beginning of the year
    (a)   plus depreciation.
    (b)   minus depreciation.
    (c)   plus net investment.
    (d)   plus gross investment.

    ANSWER: (c) The change in the capital stock is net investment. It can be negative. Refer to p. 110 [422]. ■

OBJECTIVE 3:

Outline the procedure and rationale for determining GDP through the income approach. Distinguish the various national income accounts.

The *income approach* begins by totaling the *national income*—the income earned by the productive resources owned by a country's citizens. This includes compensation of employees (wages and salaries, mostly), proprietors' income, rental income, corporate profits, net interest, indirect taxes minus subsidies, net business transfer payments, and surplus of government enterprises. (page 111 [423])

The difference between national income and *net national product* is any (usually slight) statistical discrepancy caused by measurement problems. In contrast to gross national product, gross national product adds in payments to foreign factors and subtracts payments earned abroad by U.S. citizens. GNP does not count either of these factor payments and, to get to GNP from GDP, we must *subtract* payments to foreign factors and *add* payments earned abroad by U.S. citizens (i.e., net factor payments to the rest of the world).

Personal income (the total income of households before the payment of personal income taxes) is national income less the earnings that are not distributed to households, such as the retained earnings of corporations. *Disposable personal income* is found by subtracting personal income taxes from personal income.

▶▶▶   LEARNING TIP: Think of saving as "nonconsumption." The income left over after you've bought what you want doesn't have to be put into a bank for an economist to consider as "saved" Bury it in the back yard, keep it in your wallet—if you don't spend it, it's saved.

Keep in mind that investment involves purchases of real productive plant and equipment (and changes in inventory), but *not* financial investments. The buying and selling of stocks and bonds does not, in itself, constitute investment.◀

━━━━━━━━━━━━━━━━━━━━━━━━━━━ **Practice** ━━━━━━━━━━━━━━━━━━━━━

10.   The best measure of the total income received by households is
   (a)   GDP.
   (b)   GNP.
   (c)   national income.
   (d)   personal income.

   ANSWER: (d) National income measures the income earned by a nation's productive resources. Some income though, doesn't reach households—retained earnings, social insurance payments. Some income received by households is unearned—transfer payments such as welfare. Personal income records the income received by all households after these adjustments have been made.

11.   In Arboc, personal income is $680 billion, personal income taxes are $170 billion, and personal saving is $20 billion. The personal saving rate is
   (a)   2.9%.
   (b)   3.9%.
   (c)   11.8%.
   (d)   27.9%.

   ANSWER: (b) The personal saving rate is the percentage of disposable personal income that is saved. Disposable personal income is personal income minus personal income taxes ($680 billion – $170 billion). The saving rate is $20 billion/$510 billion = 0.039, or 3.9%.

12.   Arboc is a simple economy in which all income is either compensation of employees or profits.
       Also, there are no indirect taxes. Using the income approach, GDP is made up of
       (a)   compensation of employees + profits + depreciation
       (b)   compensation of employees + profits – depreciation
       (c)   compensation of employees – profits + depreciation
       (d)   compensation of employees – profits – depreciation

       ANSWER: (a) Given the assumptions about Arboc, all other differences between national
                income and GDP disappear.

13.   GDP minus _____ the rest of the world and minus _____ equals NNP.
       (a)   net factor payments to; depreciation
       (b)   net factor payments to; indirect taxes minus subsidies
       (c)   net factor receipts from; depreciation
       (d)   net factor receipts from; indirect taxes minus subsidies

       ANSWER: (a) GDP includes net factor payments to the rest of the world. GNP subtracts these
                payments. NNP subtracts depreciation from GNP. ∎

OBJECTIVE 4:
Distinguish between real GDP and nominal GDP and explain why real GDP is the preferred
measure of production. Discuss the weaknesses of a fixed-weight index to measure real GDP.
Discuss how the GDP deflator is constructed.

Nominal GDP measures production in current dollars, whereas *real GDP* is a measure of output that
controls for price changes. The Bureau of Economic Analysis (BEA) used to use fixed price weights
when determining real GDP. That method was flawed—real GDP growth rates depended on the year
chosen, prices may not have reflected supply changes, and the chosen base year was likely to become less
typical as time went by. The current method of estimating real GDP uses a sequence of pairs of base
years.

       The GDP deflator, which measures how the overall price level is changing, previously was
calculated by the fixed-weights method. That method overestimates the increase in the price level
because it ignores substitution away from goods whose prices are rising and toward goods whose prices
are increasing less rapidly, or decreasing. The BEA introduced its new approach to calculating the GDP
deflator, avoiding the selection of a single base year and fixed weights. (page 114 [426])

▶▶▶   LEARNING TIP: In a previous learning tip, nominal GDP was likened to price times quantity. If price
       changes, so does the value of nominal GDP. To derive the real quantity produced, we can divide ($P \times Q$) by
       P—at the macro level, this is the GDP deflator.
           A common mistake in macroeconomics is failing to distinguish between real and nominal values, as
       in the case of GDP. *Real* values correct for the effect of price changes, *nominal* values don't. Example: Your
       nominal wage is simply the number of dollars in your paycheck; your real wage (spending power) also
       depends on prices in the grocery store. When your grandmother tells you how wonderfully cheap things were
       back in the good old days, she's comparing nominal values that shouldn't be compared. Ask her about hourly
       wage levels back in those same good old days.
▶▶▶   LEARNING TIP: Note that the formula

                    GDP deflator = (Nominal GDP ÷ real GDP) × 100

       can be rearranged to get

                    Real GDP = (Nominal GDP ÷ GDP deflator) × 100. ◀

— ■ ————————————————————— **Practice** ——————

14.   If real GDP decreases from Year 1 to Year 2, we can conclude that
    (a)   production levels are lower in Year 2 than in Year 1.
    (b)   price levels are lower in Year 2 than in Year 1.
    (c)   there is less unemployment in Year 2 than in Year 1.
    (d)   we need more information before commenting.

    ANSWER: (a) Real GDP measures the level of real production.

Use the fixed-weights method and following information about prices of goods in Arboc to calculate the economy's production for the next three questions.

| | Production | | | Prices | | |
Good	Year 1	Year 2	Year 3	Year 1	Year 2	Year 3
Goat milk	200	180	160	2.00	2.40	2.50
Bananas	80	90	100	3.00	3.20	3.10

15.   Nominal GDP in Year 1 is _____ and nominal GDP in Year 2 is _____ .
    (a)   640; 720
    (b)   640; 736
    (c)   630; 720
    (d)   630; 736

    ANSWER: (a) Nominal GDP for Year 1 = $(200 \times 2.00) + (80 \times 3.00) = 640$. Nominal GDP for Year 2 = $(180 \times 2.40) + (90 \times 3.20) = 720$.

16.   In Year 1 prices, real GDP in Year 2 is _____ and real GDP in Year 3 is _____ .
    (a)   640; 620
    (b)   640; 630
    (c)   630; 640
    (d)   630; 620

    ANSWER: (d) Real GDP for Year 2 = $(180 \times 2.00) + (90 \times 3.00) = 630$. Real GDP for Year 3 = $(160 \times 2.00) + (100 \times 3.00) = 620$.

17.   Using Year 1's prices to get real GDP, the GDP fixed-weight deflator for Year 3 is about
    (a)   82.9.
    (b)   87.3.
    (c)   114.5.
    (d)   120.6.

    ANSWER: (c) Nominal GDP for Year 3 = $(160 \times 2.50) + (100 \times 3.10) = 710$. Real GDP for Year 3 = $(160 \times 2.00) + (100 \times 3.00) = 620$. GDP deflator = (nominal GDP/real GDP) $\times 100 = (710/620) \times 100 = 114.5$.

18.   In Arboc, nominal GDP is 4,000 opeks and real GDP is 3,000 opeks. The GDP deflator is
    (a)   25.
    (b)   33.33.
    (c)   75.
    (d)   133.33.

    ANSWER: (d) To find the GDP deflator, divide nominal GDP by real GDP and then multiply by 100. In this case, $(4,000/3,000) \times 100 = 133.33$.

Use the new BEA annual weights method and the following information about prices of goods in Arboc to calculate the economy's production for the next two questions.

	Production		Prices	
Good	Year 1	Year 2	Year 1	Year 2
Goat milk	200	180	2.00	2.40
Bananas	80	90	3.00	3.20

19.   The real GDP in Year 1 is _____ . The real GDP in Year 2 is _____ . Use Year 1 as the base year.
(a)   600; 720
(b)   600; 630
(c)   640; 720
(d)   640; 630

ANSWER: (d) Real GDP for Year 1 = (200 × 2.00) + (80 × 3.00) = 640. Real GDP for Year 2 = (180 × 2.00) + (90 × 3.00) = 630.

20.   The real GDP in Year 1 is _____ . The real GDP in Year 2 is _____ . Use Year 2 as the base year.
(a)   736; 780
(b)   736; 720
(c)   640; 780
(d)   640; 720

ANSWER: (b) Real GDP for Year 1 = (200 × 2.40) + (80 × 3.20) = 736. Real GDP for Year 2 = (180 × 2.40) + (90 × 3.20) = 720. ■

OBJECTIVE 5:
Outline the shortcomings of GDP and per capita GDP as a measure of social well-being.

It's tempting to equate a rising GDP, or even a rising per capita GDP, with greater well-being, but the limitations of the national income measure disallow this. GDP measures the "market value" of production; but not all goods and services affecting our well-being reach a market—the "underground economy" is a significant area of economic activity that is not counted. Nor does GDP count "bads" such as pollution, and changes in GDP simply might be due to activities, such as childcare or housework, being recorded in the market when they previously weren't. GDP ignores the quality of our leisure time, the distribution of spending power, and what kinds of goods are being produced—all of these factors can affect the well-being of individuals in society. (page 117 [429])

The World Bank now uses *gross national income* (*GNI*) to make international comparisons. A nation's GDP (valued in the domestic currency) is converted into a dollar amount using an average of currency exchange rates.

ECONOMICS IN PRACTICE: On page 113 [425], the textbook pays homage to the development of national income accounting. However, GDP is an imperfect measure of social well-being, or even of production. Can you think of examples of production that our national income accounts might fail to capture?

ANSWER: Activities in the underground economy (also known as the informal sector) are missed by GDP. In particular, in countries with high tax rates, there is a strong incentive to do work "off the books." In the U.S. economy, this may represent 10% of reported GDP. Ticket scalping is a service that is unlikely to be included, nor is criminal activity, such as drug dealing or prostitution. Household production is another potentially large area that is not counted—home preparation of meals, for instance.

—■——————————————————— **Practice** ———————————————

21.   GDP includes
   (a)   the market value of goods and services produced in the underground economy.
   (b)   the value of satisfaction derived from amusement parks.
   (c)   the expenditures involved in changing aerosol production away from the use of CFCs (chlorofluorocarbons).
   (d)   purchases of illegal substances that are produced in the United States.

   ANSWER: (c) The expenditures needed to change production of aerosols would be represented in investment expenditures. ■

THE FAMILY OF ACCOUNTS

Collected below is the entire family of national income and production accounts, showing how to move from one account to another. Applications 4 and 6 give you practice in calculating the different values.

Gross Domestic Product	$C + I + G + (EX - IM)$
	OR
	National income + depreciation – statistical discrepancy + net factor payments to the rest of the world
Gross National Product	GDP – net factor payments to the rest of the world
Net National Product	GNP – depreciation
National Income	NNP – statistical discrepancy
Personal Income	National income – amount of national income not going to households
Disposable Personal Income	Personal income – personal income taxes

BRAIN TEASER SOLUTION: Lesotho's workers earn income in South Africa that is not included in Lesotho's GDP. Lesotho's GDP is the total market value of all final goods and services produced within Lesotho, whereas its GNP is the total market value of all final goods and services produced by its resources anywhere. In fact, in 2008, GNP was about 30% higher than GDP.

PRACTICE TEST

I.   MULTIPLE-CHOICE QUESTIONS

Select the option that provides the single best answer.

_____ 1.   The value of GDP can be found by adding together
    (a)   government consumption and gross investment, private consumption, net exports, and gross private domestic investment.
    (b)   wages, private consumption, gross private domestic investment, and imports.
    (c)   private consumption, government consumption and gross investment, transfer payments, and net exports.
    (d)   wages, investment, government consumption and gross investment, and depreciation.

_____ 2.   For national accounting purposes, which of the following is not investment?
    (a)   Accumulation of inventories on a grocery shelf
    (b)   Construction of a residential housing scheme
    (c)   Purchase of 100 shares of Microsoft stock by Prof. Oster from Prof. Case
    (d)   Purchase of a new machine by the Case and Fair Manufacturing Corp.

_____ 3.   Which of the following would be included in this year's GDP?
    (a)   The purchase this year of a car produced last year
    (b)   The purchase this year of a share of GM common stock
    (c)   The purchase next year of a car produced this year
    (d)   The construction last year of a car factory that will begin production this year

_____ 4.   Nominal GDP is higher this year than last. We can conclude that
    (a)   production levels are higher this year.
    (b)   price levels are higher this year.
    (c)   there is less unemployment this year.
    (d)   we need more information before commenting.

_____ 5.   GDP minus _____ and minus _____ equals national income.
    (a)   investment; depreciation
    (b)   net factor payments to the rest of the world; depreciation
    (c)   net factor payments from the rest of the world; net investment
    (d)   depreciation; net investment

_____ 6.   Which one of the following most accurately reflects the amount of income actually received by households after taxes?
    (a)   Gross domestic product
    (b)   Net national product
    (c)   Disposable personal income
    (d)   Personal income

_____ 7.   Real gross domestic product
    (a)   refers only to manufacturing production.
    (b)   includes government transfers.
    (c)   excludes services.
    (d)   eliminates the effect of price changes on GDP.

_____ 8.   Which of the following items would be included in gross domestic product?
    (a)   The value of a German camera brought back to the United States by a G.I.
    (b)   The output of a U.S.-owned family farm in Kansas
    (c)   The value of clean air
    (d)   The value of imports into the United States

_____ 9.   One problem of incorporating the government sector into GDP is that
    (a)   we must include transfer payments, so double counting occurs.
    (b)   some government production, such as national defense, is not sold.
    (c)   taxes reduce consumption and investment expenditures.
    (d)   the government adds nothing to the value of production.

_____ 10.   The value of imports is subtracted in the expenditure approach, because
    (a)   imports are included when the value of consumption and the other components of expenditure are calculated.
    (b)   imports take away from domestic production.
    (c)   imports are bought by foreigners.
    (d)   imports must be bought with foreign currency.

_____ 11.   The most likely immediate response to an unforeseen surge in demand for a firm's product would be to
    (a)   cut the price of the final product.
    (b)   reduce inventory levels.
    (c)   build up inventory levels.
    (d)   reduce depreciation.

_____ 12.   Cambium and Xylem Timber Company of Ontario, Canada, produce and sell wooden furniture in the United States. The profits of this foreign-owned company are included in
    (a)   U.S. GDP and U.S. GNP.
    (b)   U.S. GDP but not U.S. GNP.
    (c)   U.S. GNP but not in U.S. GDP.
    (d)   neither U.S. GDP nor U.S. GNP.

_____ 13.   Net investment is
    (a)   depreciation plus inventory levels.
    (b)   depreciation minus inventory levels.
    (c)   gross investment plus depreciation.
    (d)   gross investment minus depreciation.

_____   14.   The personal saving rate is the percentage of _____ that is saved.
        (a)   GDP
        (b)   personal income
        (c)   national income
        (d)   disposable personal income

_____   15.   Assuming no measurement problems, GDP (gross domestic product) equals
        (a)   National income + Depreciation + Net factor payments to the rest of the world.
        (b)   National income + Depreciation – Net factor payments to the rest of the world.
        (c)   National income – Depreciation – Net factor payments to the rest of the world.
        (d)   National income – Depreciation + Net factor payments to the rest of the world.

_____   16.   In Arboc, nominal GDP is 12,000 million opeks and the GDP deflator is 80. Real GDP is
        (a)   150 million opeks.
        (b)   1,500 million opeks.
        (c)   9,600 million opeks.
        (d)   15,000 million opeks.

_____   17.   Which of the following would not be counted in GDP?
        (a) $10 million worth of newly produced IBM PCs that IBM can't sell
        (b)   A $1,000 fee charged by a lawyer to plead a court case that she does not win
        (c)   The salary of a foreign basketball player playing in the NBA
        (d)   The purchase of IBM stock just before its price increases

_____   18.   Which of the following would be included in U.S. GNP but not in U.S. GDP?
        (a)   Profit earned in the United States by Honda Corporation, a Japanese-owned company
        (b)   Wages paid to Mexican migrant workers harvesting peaches for a U.S.-owned company
        (c)   Rent paid to Sean Thornton, the American owner of a piece of property in Ireland
        (d)   Dividends paid to Japanese owners of stock in Honda Corporation, a Japanese-owned company that sells cars in the United States

_____   19.   Which of the following statements about net investment is true?
        (a)   Net investment equals gross investment plus depreciation.
        (b)   When net investment is negative, the stock of capital has decreased.
        (c)   When net investment is negative, inventory levels are decreasing.
        (d)   When net investment is negative, inventory levels are increasing.

_____   20.   In Arbez, nominal GDP is one billion opeks in both 2005 and 2010. The GDP deflator is 50 in 2005 and 120 in 2010. We can conclude that,
        (a)   prices and real GDP have both risen from 2005 to 2010.
        (b)   prices have risen and real GDP has fallen from 2005 to 2010.
        (c)   prices have fallen and real GDP has risen from 2005 to 2010.
        (d)   prices and real GDP have both fallen from 2005 to 2010.

II.   APPLICATION QUESTIONS

1.   Examine the following list of goods and services. Which goods and services should be included in Freedonian GDP in 2009, which should be excluded, and why?

2,500 quarter-pounder hamburgers produced in 2009
100 tons of coal from the mines in the Freedonian mountains
2 Freedonian Drof automobiles, sold in 2009, produced in 2008
3 Freedonian Drof automobiles, sold in 2010, produced in 2009
3 American-built Fords produced in 2009 and sold in 2009
Welfare benefits for Freedonian citizens
625 pounds of beef used in hamburgers
Wages of hamburger employees

2.   Following are some nominal GDP figures for the nation of Regit.

Year	Nominal GDP	Percentage Change	GDP Deflator	Real GDP	Percentage Change
2005	4,268.6	—	0.9700	_____	—
2006	4,539.9	_____	1.0000	_____	_____
2007	4,900.4	_____	1.0390	_____	_____
2008	5,244.0	_____	1.0840	_____	_____
2009	5,513.8	_____	1.1310	_____	_____
2010	5,672.6	_____	1.1760	_____	_____

(a)   Calculate the percentage change in nominal GDP from one year to the next, i.e., divide the difference in GDP by the GDP in the first year.
(b)   Use the GDP deflator to calculate real GDP for each year.
(c)   Use the real GDP figures to calculate the percentage change in real GDP from one year to the next.
(d)   Write a brief report on the similarities and differences between the "percentage change" columns.

3.   In Macrovia, the only two goods produced are bread and wine. In 1999 bread cost 90¢ a loaf and wine cost $4.00 a bottle; 800 loaves of bread and 180 bottles of wine were produced. In 2004, bread cost $1.00 a loaf and wine cost $5.00 a bottle. 1,000 loaves and 200 bottles of wine were produced. In 2009, bread cost $1.20 a loaf and wine cost $5.50 a bottle. 1,200 loaves and 220 bottles of wine were produced.
(a)   Calculate the nominal GDP for each of the three years.
(b)   Calculate the real GDP for each of the three years. Use the fixed-weight method and 2004's prices.
(c)   Calculate the GDP fixed-weight deflator for each of the three years. Use the fixed-weight method and 2004's prices.
(d)   Calculate the real GDP for 1999 and 2004. Use the fixed-weight method and 1999's prices.
(e)   Determine the percentage change in the real GDP from 1999 to 2004, using 1999's prices.
(f)   Calculate the real GDP for 1999 and 2004 using 2004's prices.
(g)   Determine the percentage change in the quantity index from 1999 to 2004.
(h)   How much has real GDP changed from 1999 to 2004?

4.   You are given the following information by a colleague who is doing research on the Freedonian economy. Because she has never taken an economics course, she has turned to you for help using the information she has found. (Assume any unreported values are zero.)

Compensation of employees	1175.2
Corporate profits minus dividends	90.8
Freedonian exports of goods and services	94.4
Depreciation	283.2
Personal income taxes	150.5
Personal consumption expenditures	878.2
Government consumption and gross investment	400.4
Indirect taxes minus subsidies	122.4
Gross private domestic investment	322.7
Freedonian imports of goods and services	70.5

Use the information above to calculate

(a)   GDP   _____
(b)   National income   _____
(c)   Personal income   _____
(d)   Disposable personal income   _____
(e)   Net exports   _____
(f)   Personal saving rate   _____

5.   (a)   A Macrovian farmer produces 2,005 bushels of wheat, which he sells to a miller for 20¢ a bushel. The farmer receives a payment of $_____ from the miller. The value added by the farmer is $_____ .

(b)   The miller grinds the wheat into flour. She makes 1,200 pounds of flour that she sells to a baker for 40¢ per pound. The miller receives a payment of $_____ from the baker. The value added by the miller is $_____ .

(c)   The baker bakes the flour into 1,000 loaves, which he sells for 50¢ apiece to a food distributor. The baker receives a payment of $_____ from the distributor. The value added by the baker is $_____ .

(d)   The distributor sells 200 loaves to a local restaurant (Loafers) for $1.00 each. The remainder is sold to grocery stores at 80¢ each. The distributor receives payments totaling $_____ . The value added by the distributor is $_____ .

(e)   At the retail level, Loafers sells 180 loaves at $1.50 each. 20 loaves are unsold and must be discarded. The grocery stores sell all of their consignment for $1.00 each. Retailers receive payments totaling $_____ . The value added by the retailers is $_____ .

(f)   The total value added by all participants in the production process is $_____ .

6.   Given the following national income and product accounts data, compute:
      (a)   Gross private domestic investment _____
      (b)   Net exports _____
      (c)   National income _____
      (d)   Personal income _____
      (e)   Disposable personal income _____
      (f)   Net national product _____
      (g)   Gross national product _____
      (h)   Gross domestic product _____

Depreciation	105
Amount of national income not going to households	51
Compensation of employees	1,407
Corporate profits	161
Dividends	49
Exports	133
Government consumption and gross investment	433
Imports	147
Indirect taxes minus subsidies	371
Net business transfer payments	12
Net interest	42
Net private domestic investment	490
Personal consumption expenditures	1,377
Receipts of factor income from the rest of the world	22
Personal income taxes	392
Proprietors' income	168
Payments of factor income to the rest of the world	43
Rental income	21
Statistical discrepancy	15
Surplus of government enterprises	98

7.   Arboc and Arbez are two neighboring nations. Each produces only corn. In each case, net factor income from the rest of the world is zero. Last year, sales of corn in each country was 500 units. Inventory rose by 50 in Arboc and fell by 25 in Arbez. Assume no statistical discrepancy. Calculate GDP for:
      (a)   Arboc _____
      (b)   Arbez _____
      Suppose depreciation runs at 10% of GDP in each country. Calculate NNP for:
      (c)   Arboc _____
      (d)   Arbez _____
      Undistributed earnings are a greater percentage of GDP in Arboc (12%) than in Arbez (5%). Calculate personal income for:
      (e)   Arboc _____
      (f)   Arbez _____

8.   Use the following table to answer the following questions.

Year	Nominal GDP	Nominal GDP (% change)	GDP Deflator	Real GDP	Real GDP (% change)
1995	1,212.8	—	46.5		—
2000	1,990.5		67.3		
2005	3,166.0		100.0		
2010	4,486.2		117.3		

(a)   Calculate the percentage increase in nominal GDP from one year to the next.
(b)   Use the GDP deflator to derive real GDP.
(c)   Calculate the percentage increase in real GDP from one year to the next.

9.   The nation of Arboc produces pencils and notepads. Using the following information, calculate:

	Pencils	Notepads
Year 1	2,000 at 10¢ each	75 at $1.00 each
Year 2	2,400 at 15¢ each	60 at $1.10 each

(a)   Nominal GDP for Year 1   _____
(b)   Nominal GDP for Year 2   _____
(c)   Real GDP for Year 1 (Year 1 as base)   _____
(d)   Real GDP for Year 2 (Year 1 as base)   _____

10.   Should each of the following enter into a measure of "the market value of all currently produced final goods and services"? Write "Yes" or "No."

1. _____ the purchase of a new camera by Joe Blow
2. _____ the gift of the same camera from Joe to Flo Blow
3. _____ the purchase of the same camera by F. Stop Fitzgerald at a yard sale
4. _____ the purchase of a new camera by the CIA
5. _____ the services of a photographer hired by the CIA
6. _____ the services of a photographer hired by Joe and Flo Blow on the occasion of their wedding
7. _____ the services of Cousin Bo Blow (amateur photographer extraordinaire) to photograph the wedding
8. _____ the production of a camera that remains unsold at the factory
9. _____ the purchase of a Japanese camera by Joe Blow
10. _____ the use of welfare money by Moe Blow to buy a new camera
11. _____ the provision of welfare money to Moe Blow
12. _____ the use of welfare money to buy a second-hand camera
13. _____ the use of welfare money to open a bank account
14. _____ the use of welfare money to buy Kodak stock on the stock exchange
15. _____ the purchase of in-store surveillance equipment for "The Camera Cabin"
16. _____ the purchase of a camera for display in "The Camera Cabin"
17. _____ the purchase of film by Joe Blow
18. _____ the purchase of a U.S. camera by Josef von Blau (a German tourist)
19. _____ the purchase, in Germany, of a U.S. camera, by Josef von Blau
20. _____ the payment for the services of a camera repairman hired by Joe Blow, who fails to repair the broken camera
21. _____ the payment for the services of the trashman, who takes the broken camera to the city dump

PRACTICE TEST SOLUTIONS

I.   Solutions to Multiple-Choice Questions

1.   (a)   This is the expenditure approach. Refer to the equation on p. 108 [420].

2.   (c)   The stock transfer does not represent the production of any additional goods or services.

3.   (c)   We are interested in measuring how much has been produced this year (whether or not it is sold this year). The stock purchase adds no production, so it is not counted.

4.   (d)   Nominal GDP measures the current value of production. This value might have increased because more goods and services were produced this year than last (with correspondingly lower unemployment), or because prices are higher this year than last. In short, we must be wary of reading too much into the change in this single figure. Refer to p. 114 [426].

5.   (b)   Refer to Table 6.4 (21.4) for the relationships between the measures.

6.   (c)   This is the after-tax income of all households. Refer to p. 114 [426].

7.   (d)   Real GDP certainly includes manufacturing production, but it includes other forms of production too, including services. "Real" variables are variables that have had the effects of price changes removed. Refer to p. 114 [426].

8.   (b)   The German camera is not U.S. production. The value of clean air is intangible. Imports are included in the value of consumption purchases, etc., and then subtracted from GDP.

9.   (b)   GDP measures the market value of production—this is difficult when there is not an explicit market. Note that transfer payments are not included in GDP.

10.   (a)   Refer to p. 111 [423] for more on net exports.

11.   (b)   If the demand for orange juice surges at the Food Tiger grocery store, the shelves begin to empty even before the management decides to raise the price.

12.   (b)   The profits of a foreign-owned company are included in U.S. GDP (which is concerned with the location of production) but not in U.S. GNP (which is concerned with ownership of resources).

13.   (d)   Refer to p. 110 [422] for more on net investment.

14.   (d)   Refer to p. 114 [426] for the definition of the personal saving rate.

15.   (b)   The value of production equals the costs of domestic resources plus other production costs (depreciation) and net income earned outside the country. Refer to p. 111 [423].

16.   (d)   Real GDP = (nominal GDP divided by the GDP deflator) × 100 = (12,000/80) × 100 = 15,000 million opeks.

17.   (d)   The purchase of stock is a financial transaction that does not reflect productive activity. Note that goods that are produced but not sold are included in inventory.

18.   (c)   GNP measures production by resources owned by U.S. citizens, regardless of where that output is produced.

19.   (b)   Net investment will be negative if gross investment is less than depreciation. In that case, the addition to the capital stock is less than the reduction due to wear and tear. Note that net investment is gross investment *minus* depreciation. Refer to the equation on p. 110 [422].

20.   (b)   Rising prices are indicated by the higher GDP deflator in 2010. Real GDP = nominal GDP/GDP deflator, therefore the real GDP is lower in 2010 than in 2005, (833,333,333 opeks instead of 2 billion opeks).

II.   *Solutions to Application Questions*

1.   There were 2,500 quarter-pounder hamburgers produced in 2009, 100 tons of coal from the mines in the Freedonian mountains, and 3 Freedonian Drof automobiles sold in 2010 but produced in 2009 are final items that would qualify for inclusion in 2009's GDP.

       The 2 Freedonian Drof automobiles produced in 2008 were not produced in 2009. The 3 American-built Fords were not produced in Freedonia. Welfare benefits for Freedonian citizens are transfer payments. The beef used in hamburgers and the wages of hamburger employees are costs of intermediate goods and services that are captured in the price of the hamburgers.

2.   (a)   Refer to the following table. Percentage change in nominal GDP = (GDP in Year 2 – GDP in Year 1) ÷ GDP in Year 1.
              Example, using 2006 and 2007: (4,900.4 – 4,539.9) ÷ 4,539.9 = 7.94. Note: other formulas could also be used giving somewhat different results, for example

              (GDP in Year 2 – GDP in Year 1) ÷ (GDP in Year 2 + GDP in Year 1)/2.

Year	Nominal GDP	Percentage Change	GDP Deflator	Real GDP	Percentage Change
2005	4,268.6	—	0.9700	4,400.6	—
2006	4,539.9	6.36	1.0000	4,539.9	3.17
2007	4,900.4	7.94	1.0390	4,716.5	3.89
2008	5,244.0	7.02	1.0840	4,837.6	2.57
2009	5,513.8	5.14	1.1310	4,875.2	0.77
2010	5,672.6	2.88	1.1760	4,823.6	−1.06

       (b), (c) Refer to the preceding table. Real GDP = nominal GDP × 100/GDP deflator. Example: 2007's real GDP = 4,900.4 × 100/103.9 = 4,716.5.

       (d)   The "percentage change" figures display similarities, e.g., 2007 is the best year and 2010 the worst in each case. Notably, the real values are consistently lower than the nominal values because of rising prices. The nominal result for 2010 is the most misleading— recording 2.88% growth while the economy in fact shrank in size.

3.   (a)   Refer to the following table.

	1999	2004	2009
Bread	800 × 0.9 = $720	1,000 × $1.00 = $1,000	1,200 × $1.20 = $1,440
Wine	180 × $4.00 = $720	200 × $5.00 = $1,000	220 × $5.50 = $1,210
Nominal GDP	$1,440	$2,000	$2,650
Bread	800 × $1.00 = $800	1,000 × $1.00 = $1,000	1,200 × $1.00 = $1,200
Wine	180 × $5.00 = $900	200 × $5.00 = $1,000	220 × $5.00 = $1,100
Real GDP	$1,700	$2,000	$2,300
GDP deflator	0.8471	1.0000	1.1522

(b), (c) Refer to the preceding table.

(d)   Refer to the following table.

	1999	**2004**
Bread	800 × 0.90 = $720	1000 × 0.90 = $900
Wine	180 × $4.00 = $720	200 × $4.00 = $800
Real GDP (1999 prices)	$1,440	$1,700

(e)   Percentage change from 1999 to 2004 = [(1,700 − 1,440)/1,440] × 100 = 18.0556.

(f)   Refer to the following table.

	1999	**2004**
Bread	800 × $1.00 = $800	1,000 × $1.00 = $1,000
Wine	180 × $5.00 = $900	200 × $5.00 = $1,000
Real GDP (2004 prices)	$1,700	$2,000

(g)   Percentage change from 1999 to 2004 = [(2,000 − 1,700)/1,700] × 100 = 17.6471.

(h)   Real GDP has grown by 17.85% from 1999 to 2004, because 117.85 = (118.0556 × 117.6471).

4.   (a)   GDP = $C + I + G + (EX − IM)$ = 878.2 + 322.7 + 400.4 + (94.4 − 70.5) = 1,625.2.

(b)   National income = GDP − depreciation = 1342.0.

(c)   Personal income = national income − retained earnings = 1,251.2.

(d)   Disposable personal income = personal income − personal income taxes = 1,100.7

(e)   Net exports = exports − imports = 94.4 − 70.5 = 23.9

(f)   Personal saving rate = (national income − personal consumption expenditures)/ national income = (1,100.7 − 878.2)/ 1,100.7 = 222.5/ 1,100.7 = 20.2%.

5.   (a) $400; $400   (b) $480; $80   (c) $500; $20   (d) $840; $340

(e) $1,070; $230   (f) $1,070

6.   (a)   Gross private domestic investment = net private domestic investment + depreciation = 490 + 105 = 595

(b)   Net exports = exports − imports = 133 − 147 = −14

(c)   National income = compensation of employees + proprietors' income + rental income + corporate profits + net interest + indirect taxes minus subsidies + net business transfer payments + surplus of government enterprises = 1,407 + 168 + 21 +161 + 42 + 371 + 12 + 98 = 2,280

(d)   Personal income = NI − amount of national income not going to households = 2,280 − 51 = 2,229

(e)   Disposable personal income = PI − personal income taxes = 2,229 − 392 = 1,837

(f)   Net national product = NI − statistical discrepancy = 2,280 − 15 = 2,265

(g)   Gross national product = NNP + depreciation = 2,265 + 105 = 2,370

(h)   Gross domestic product = GNP − receipts of factor income from the rest of the world + payments of factor income to the rest of the world = 2,370 − 22 + 43 = 2,391
Check using expenditure approach. GDP = personal consumption expenditures + gross private domestic investment + government consumption and gross investment + net exports = 1,377 + (490 + 105) + 433 + (133 − 147) = 2,391

7.   (a)   GDP = GNP (because net factor payments are zero) = sales + inventory change = 500 + 50 = 550 units

(b)   GDP = GNP (because net factor payments are zero) = sales + inventory change = 500 − 25 = 475 units

(c)   Depreciation = 10% of GDP = 55;
NNP = GNP − depreciation = 550 − 55 = 495 units

(d)   Depreciation = 10% of GDP = 47.5;
NNP = GNP − depreciation = 475 − 47.5 = 427.5 units

(e)   Personal income = GDP − depreciation − (undistributed earnings) − net factor payments
= 550 − 55 − 550(0.12) − 0 = 429 units

(f)   Personal income = GDP − depreciation − (undistributed earnings) − net factor payments
= 475 − 47.5 − 475(0.05) − 0 = 403.75 units

8.   Refer to the following table.

Year	Nominal GDP	Nominal GDP (% change)	GDP Deflator	Real GDP	Real GDP (% change)
1995	1,212.8	—	46.5	2,608.2	—
2000	1,990.5	+64.1	67.3	2,957.7	+13.4
2005	3,166.0	+59.1	100.0	3,166.0	+7.0
2010	4,486.2	+41.7	117.3	3,824.6	+20.8

Note: Rearrange the formula GDP deflator = (Nominal GDP ÷ real GDP) × 100 to get: Real GDP = (Nominal GDP ÷ GDP deflator) ×100

9.   (a)   Nominal GDP for Year 1 $275
(b)   Nominal GDP for Year 2 $426
(c)   Real GDP for Year 1 (Year 1 as base) $275
(d)   Real GDP for Year 2 (Year 1 as base) $300

10.   1. Yes   2. No   3. No   4. Yes   5. Yes   6. Yes
7. No   8. Yes   9. No   10. Yes   11. No   12. No
13. No   14. No   15. Yes   16. Yes   17. Yes   18. Yes

7 [22]

Unemployment, Inflation, and Long-Run Growth

Chapter objectives:

1. Define the labor force and the unemployment rate and give the official definition of employment. Describe the limitations of the unemployment rate statistic, outlining the effects of "discouraged workers" on official unemployment statistics.
2. Distinguish among, and give examples of, frictional, structural, and cyclical unemployment. Define the natural rate of unemployment and describe the economic and social costs of unemployment.
3. Define inflation. Outline the problems of price indexes such as the Consumer Price Index.
4. Indicate who gains and who loses from inflation. Distinguish between anticipated and unanticipated inflation and indicate how their impacts on the economy differ. Describe the concept of the real interest rate and outline the effect of anticipated inflation on it.
5. Detail the factors influencing output growth.

This chapter concludes the sequence of three largely definitional chapters, looking at two short-run concepts (unemployment and inflation) and two long-run concepts (output growth and productivity growth). A working knowledge of these concepts is essential when you study policy formulation in subsequent chapters.

BRAIN TEASER: Probably, you don't habitually play your car audio at maximum volume—there's an ideal level that holds some additional capacity in reserve. The same principle is true for the economy. A normally functioning economy has some excess capacity and some rate of unemployment. This rate of unemployment is the natural rate of unemployment. In 1950, this natural rate was estimated to be 4%. Since then, the natural rate of unemployment has risen, with the President's Council of Economic Advisers placing it at 6.5% in 1986. The expectation was that it would continue to increase. Why did the natural rate of unemployment increase in the latter part of the twentieth century? Is it still increasing?

OBJECTIVE 1:

Define the labor force and the unemployment rate and give the official definition of employment. Describe the limitations of the unemployment rate statistic, outlining the effects of "discouraged workers" on official unemployment statistics.

The *labor force* totals the employed and unemployed. The *employed* include any person 16 years of age or older who:

a.   works one hour or more per week for pay, or
b.   works fifteen or more hours a week without pay in a family enterprise, or
c.   has a job but is temporarily absent from work, with or without pay.

The *unemployed* person must be available and looking for work during the previous four weeks. Otherwise, s/he is considered to be out of the labor force. Some workers, *discouraged* by their inability to find jobs, stop looking for work and drop out of the labor force. (page 123 [435])

The *unemployment rate* is the ratio of unemployed persons (who have no job and are actively seeking employment) to the labor force. An analysis of unemployment reveals large ethnic, gender, and regional differences in unemployment rates. (page 124 [436])

▶▶▶   LEARNING TIP: Remember that to be officially "unemployed," a member of the labor force must not have a job or recently have had a job, and must be looking actively for work. Behind this distinction is the concept of the "discouraged" worker. Memorize the definitions of unemployment rate, participation rate, inflation, and the three types of unemployment and their causes. ◀

━━━━━━■━━━━━━━━━━━━━━━━━ **Practice** ━━━━━━━━━━━━━━━━━━━━

The population of Arbez is 150,000, of which 100,000 are aged 16 or older. Of this 100,000, 60,000 have jobs and 40,000 do not. 20,000 are unemployed but actively seeking jobs, and there are 20,000 who have given up the job search in frustration.

1.   What is the unemployment rate? _____

ANSWER: The unemployment rate is 25%; the labor-force participation rate is 80%. Of the 150,000 Arbezanis, only 100,000 are of an age that qualifies them to be in the labor force. Of the 100,000, 60,000 are employed, and an additional 20,000 are unemployed (without jobs, seeking work). The remaining 20,000 discouraged workers have dropped out of the labor force. There are, then, 80,000 workers in the labor force. Unemployment rate = unemployed/labor force = 20,000/80,000 = 25%.

2.   What is the labor-force participation rate? _____

ANSWER: Labor-force participation rate = labor force/population (over 16) = 80,000/100,000 = 80%.

3.   During a recession, we expect to see output _____ and unemployment _____ .
    (a)   increasing; increasing
    (b)   increasing; decreasing
    (c)   decreasing; increasing
    (d)   decreasing; decreasing

    ANSWER: (c) By definition, a recession occurs when real GDP falls for two or more quarters. As output falls, more workers are laid off. Refer to p. 125 [437].

4.   Typically, workers in a fishing-gutting factory have a high rate of absenteeism. Phyllis the Filleter has been "off sick" this week. She is correctly classified as
    (a)   employed.
    (b)   unemployed.
    (c)   a discouraged worker.
    (d)   not in the labor force.

    ANSWER: (a) If Phyllis is temporarily absent, with or without pay, she is considered employed. Refer to p. 124 [436].

5.   The labor force is comprised of
    (a)   the employed plus the unemployed.
    (b)   the employed minus the unemployed.
    (c)   the employed, the unemployed, and discouraged workers who could work.
    (d)   the employed plus the unemployed minus discouraged workers who could work.

    ANSWER: (a) Discouraged workers are not counted as part of the labor force.

6.   In Arbez, there are 80,000 persons in the labor force, and the unemployment rate is 25%. As the economy moves out of a long recession and job openings increase, 5,000 discouraged workers become "encouraged" and begin searching for a job. The unemployment rate will become
    (a)   18.75%.
    (b)   23.5294%.
    (c)   29.4118%.
    (d)   31.25%.

    ANSWER: (c) Initial unemployment rate = 25% = unemployed/80,000. The number unemployed is 20,000. When 5,000 new (unemployed) workers enter the labor force, the unemployment rate = 25,000/85,000 = 29.4118%.

7.   The nation of Regit has a population of 1 million citizens. The labor-force participation rate is 80%. The number of Regitanis with jobs is 728,000. The unemployment rate is
    (a)   7.20%.
    (b)   8.00%.
    (c)   9.00%.
    (d)   9.89%.

    ANSWER: (c) The unemployment rate = unemployed ÷ labor force = 72,000/800,000 = 0.09. Labor force = participation rate × population = 0.8 × 1,000,000 = 800,000. Unemployed = 800,000 − 728,000 = 72,000.

8.   The nation of Noil has a population of 1 million citizens. The labor-force participation rate is 80%. 50,000 persons are unemployed in March. By June, 10,000 persons have given up seeking employment. This is the only change over the quarter. We can conclude that the unemployment rate was

(a)   6.25% in March and 7.50% in June.
(b)   6.25% in March and 6.25% in June.
(c)   6.25% in March and 5.06% in June.
(d)   5.00% in March and 6.25% in June.

ANSWER: (c)   In March, the unemployment rate = unemployed ÷ labor force = 50,000/800,000 = 0.0625. In June, the unemployment rate = unemployed ÷ labor force = 40,000/790,000 = 0.05063, or 5.06%. ■

OBJECTIVE 2:
Distinguish among, and give examples of, frictional, structural, and cyclical unemployment. Define the natural rate of unemployment and describe the economic and social costs of unemployment.

The three types of unemployment are:

♦   *Frictional*—short-run unemployment due to the movement of individuals between jobs, while seeking a better match for their skills.

♦   *Structural*—longer-term unemployment, caused by changing tastes or changing technology that make some job skills less desirable. Automation or change in public preferences (foreign cars instead of U.S. cars) might cause structural unemployment.

♦   *Cyclical*—caused by recessions and depressions. (page 129 [441])

The first two types of unemployment are inevitable in a healthy, dynamic economy. Together, they comprise the rather imprecise concept of the *natural rate of unemployment*—the rate of unemployment that occurs during the normal operation of the economy. Full employment doesn't imply zero percent unemployment. (page 129 [441])

Recessions and cyclical unemployment result in lost output and adverse social consequences (broken homes, alcoholism, and suicide), and lower investment and economic growth. (page 129 [441])

▶▶   LEARNING TIP: Think of **full employment** as being 100% employment minus the natural rate of unemployment. The economy may have a lower or higher rate of employment than 94 to 96%, but such a divergence will be *temporary*. Note that, even when unemployment is greater than zero, society can still be at a point on (not inside) its production possibilities frontier.◀

ECONOMICS IN PRACTICE: On page 127 [439], the textbook looks at the increasing role of women in the labor market, with the female labor force participation rate expanding from 36% in 1955 to 60% in 1996. The male rate declined from 85% to 75% during the same time period. What might have caused the male participation rate to decrease? Also, by examining Table 7.2 (22.2), we can see that female unemployment rates are consistently lower than the rates for comparable males. Can you suggest why?

ANSWER: The male labor force participation rate may have decreased as married couples swapped roles, with more men staying home as women went out to work. This is, at best, a partial explanation because participation rates for single males have also declined. Many non-participating single males live with parents or others who provide support for them. In addition, a growing number of males receive disability payments.

Unemployment rates for females may be lower than those for males because female workers are "better" in some way—more reliable, quicker to learn, or willing to accept lower wages. An alternative (but not mutually exclusive) explanation is that some females remain in the role of the secondary wage-earner. If this type of marginal worker loses her job she may be more likely to become "discouraged," drop out of the labor force, and no longer be counted as unemployed.

────────────────■──────────────────── **Practice** ────────────────────

9.   Unemployment caused by short-run job/skill matching problems is
      (a)   frictional unemployment.
      (b)   structural unemployment.
      (c)   cyclical unemployment.
      (d)   natural unemployment.

      ANSWER: (a) Refer to p. 129 [441] for the definition of frictional unemployment.

10.   Recessions have all of the following beneficial effects EXCEPT
      (a)   inflation is reduced.
      (b)   efficiency is improved.
      (c)   the crime rate is decreased.
      (d)   the balance of payments improves because imports decrease.

      ANSWER: (c) Typically, the crime rate rises during a recession.

11.   During the Great Depression of the 1930s, many laborers found great difficulty finding a job. They were
      (a)   frictionally unemployed.
      (b)   structurally unemployed.
      (c)   cyclically unemployed.
      (d)   discouraged workers.

      ANSWER: (c) In the 1930s, demand was low throughout the economy.

12.   The unemployment rate that occurs as a normal consequence of the efficient functioning of the economy is the
      (a)   frictional rate of unemployment.
      (b)   structural rate of unemployment.
      (c)   cyclical rate of unemployment.
      (d)   natural rate of unemployment.

      ANSWER: (d) Refer to p. 129 [441]. This rate includes both frictional and structural unemployment.

13.   For many years, Noil was a traditional agrarian economy, specializing in rice production. In the past few years, however, due to loans from the World Bank, Noil has developed a thriving industrial sector, and farming (although increasingly mechanized) has declined. We would conclude that, over the past few years, frictional unemployment has _____ and structural unemployment has _____ .

    (a)   increased; increased
    (b)   increased; decreased
    (c)   decreased; increased
    (d)   decreased; decreased

ANSWER: (a) As the economy's structure is changing, new skills are being required and old skills are becoming obsolete—structural unemployment is increasing. As skills become more specific and more complex, the search time to find a suitable job increases—frictional unemployment increases. ■

OBJECTIVE 3:
Define inflation. Outline the problems of price indexes such as the Consumer Price Index.

Inflation is a rise in the overall price level. It can be measured by a price index (such as the Consumer Price Index). The CPI and most other price indexes are based on a typical "basket" of commodities and measure how the price of the basket changes over time. Clearly, the effectiveness of a fixed-weight price index like the CPI depends on how well its basket of commodities reflects the economy as time passes and prices change. Research has suggested that the CPI overstates the increases in the cost of living. The Chained Consumer Price Index, which uses charging weights, attempts to correct for the bias introduced as consumers shift away from high-priced goods. (page 130 [442])

   ▶▶   LEARNING TIP: The Consumer Price Index has a base year that is assigned an index value of 100. Use the following formula to calculate the price index for a given year:

$$\frac{\text{price of bundle in given year}}{\text{price of bundle in base year}} \times 100 = \text{price index}$$

In the base year itself, the index is 1.00×100, or 100. An index of more than (less than) 100 in a given year indicates that prices are more than (less than) those in the base year.

   ▶▶   LEARNING TIP: Be careful! If the CPI rises from 120 to 132, the rate of inflation is *not* 12%, but 10% [(132 − 120)/120]. Don't just subtract one value from the other—be sure to divide by the value of the first year's price index. ◀

━━━━━━━━━━━━━━━━━━━━━━━━━━ **Practice** ━━━━━━━━━━━━━━━━━━━━━━━

14.   If the CPI is 120 in Year 1 and 135 in Year 2, what is the percentage change in the price level from Year 1 to Year 2?

    (a)   12.5%
    (b)   15%
    (c)   20%
    (d)   35%

ANSWER: (a) The price index changes by 15 relative to the initial price level of 120 so $(15/120) \times 100 = 12.5\%$. ■

OBJECTIVE 4:
Indicate who gains and who loses from inflation. Distinguish between anticipated and unanticipated inflation and indicate how their impacts on the economy differ. Describe the concept of the real interest rate and outline the effect of anticipated inflation on it.

Costs of inflation are difficult to measure. Inefficiencies occur, and administrative costs increase. Also, capital investment may decrease, affecting the economy's long-term growth rate. Losers include those on fixed incomes and lenders (creditors), whereas winners include borrowers (debtors). Indexation, adjustable rate mortgages, and cost of living adjustments (COLAs) reduce the impact of inflation—in fact, such corrective devices were introduced specifically because inflation had been causing adverse redistributional effects. Unanticipated inflation is more troublesome than anticipated inflation when we consider the distribution of income. By definition, if inflation is anticipated, its presence can be incorporated into contracts and agreements. Unanticipated inflation, on the other hand, is a surprise that will injure some and benefit others. Lenders, for instance, tend to lose when inflation is unexpectedly high. (page 132 [444])

> ▶▶▶   LEARNING TIP: Common sense should help you work out who wins and who loses during inflation; if it doesn't, memorize this part of the chapter! Note that the difference between the market interest rate and the real interest rate is defined in the textbook as the inflation rate, but the associated example refers to the anticipated inflation rate. The market interest rate is determined by the anticipated inflation rate.
>
> ▶▶▶   LEARNING TIP: Despite some "menu costs" (the costs of changing price tags, printing new catalogs, etc.), **fully anticipated** inflation is not much of a problem. Rational economic behavior can continue. However, when the rate of inflation is variable and unpredictable, persons run the risk of making "bad" deals and try to compensate by overestimating wage claims and price increases. Adding this safety margin fuels the fires of inflation.◀

──────■───────────────────────── **Practice** ─────────────────────────────

15.   Inflation is expected to run at 10% this year. Instead, it slows to 3%. This change will hurt
    (a)   creditors.
    (b)   debtors.
    (c)   creditors and debtors equally, because it's the same for both parties.
    (d)   neither, because inflation is lower.

    ANSWER: (b) If inflation is higher than expected, creditors lose because they will fail to compensate themselves through a higher interest rate. When inflation is lower than expected, debtors lose because they are paying an interest rate that is "too high."

16.   Inflation is expected to run at 10% this year. Instead, it slows to 3%. This year, there has been
    (a)   an anticipated deflation.
    (b)   an unanticipated deflation.
    (c)   an anticipated reduction in inflation.
    (d)   an unanticipated reduction in inflation.

    ANSWER: (d) The change was not expected. This is not a deflation—the price level is still rising at 3% a year. A deflation occurs when the price level (not the rate of increase in the price level) falls.

17.   Inflation is expected to run at 10% this year. The real interest rate is 4%. This year, the market interest rate is _____ . If, during the year, the actual inflation rate is 4%, _____ lose.
    (a)   6%; lenders

(b)   6%; borrowers
(c)   14%; lenders
(d)   14%; borrowers

ANSWER: (d) The interest rate = inflation rate + real interest rate = 10% + 4% = 14%. Unanticipated deflation hurts borrowers.

18.   Which of the following statements is false?
(a)   When interest rates are high, the opportunity cost of holding cash is high.
(b)   The more difficult it becomes to predict the rate of inflation, the more the level of investment decreases.
(c)   Individuals on fixed incomes gain during periods of deflation.
(d)   In the mid-1970s, prices were lower than in the 1990s, and, therefore, inflation was lower too.

ANSWER: (d) Historically, Option (d) is false; inflation rates were higher in the mid-1970s than in the 1990s. Refer to Table 7.5 (22.5) in the textbook. Option (d) is false theoretically, too. The fact that the price level is low doesn't imply that the rate of increase will also be low.

19.   The difference between the interest rate a bank charges on a loan and the inflation rate is
(a)   the profit margin.
(b)   the real interest rate.
(c)   the anticipation markup.
(d)   the nominal interest rate.

ANSWER: (b) Refer to p. 133 [445] for this definition. ∎

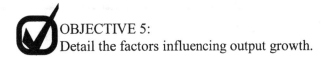

OBJECTIVE 5:
Detail the factors influencing output growth.

Output requires inputs. The two major inputs are capital and labor. The nation's rate of growth depends on the rate of increase in the quantity of capital and labor and on improvements in the productivity of these resources. Positive net investment increases the stock of capital whereas the labor force can be increased by either an increase in population or the labor-force participation rate. The productivity of a resource can be increased by providing a greater quantity and quality of complementary resources—labor productivity will increase if workers have better machines. In addition, the productivity of a resource will rise through greater efficiency and, in the case of labor, through improvements in human capital. (page 134 [446])

——————————————————————————————— Practice ———————————————————————————————

20.   Output growth depends on each of the following EXCEPT
(a)   positive net investment.
(b)   an increasing consumer price index.
(c)   the growth rate of human capital per worker.
(d)   an increase in the labor-force participation rate.

ANSWER: (b) Refer to p. 134 [446]. Output depends on availability and usage of resources.

21.   Each of the following will increase labor productivity EXCEPT
       (a)   an increase in the amount of capital being used.
       (b)   an increase in the efficiency of the capital being used.
       (c)   an increase in human capital.
       (d)   an increase in the number of workers.

       ANSWER: (d) Labor productivity is output per worker hour. If we increase the number of
               workers, total output should increase, but there is no guarantee that average
               output will increase. ■

BRAIN TEASER SOLUTION: Demographic changes, government policy, and structural change have affected the natural rate of unemployment. As the 1950s turned into the 1960s and 1970s, greater numbers of teenagers, minorities, and women entered the labor market. These groups typically face poorer employment opportunities. Unemployment insurance reduced the pressure to get another job immediately—workers waited longer to find the "right" job. Two income families similarly reduced the need for the "breadwinner" to be employed. In addition, the increasing pace of technological change reduced the likelihood that an employee would stay with the same firm, or even in the same industry, throughout his working life. New job skills would need to be learned.
By the end of the century the trend had reversed somewhat. The baby-boomers (still a large fraction of the labor market) are embedded in stable jobs, looking toward retirement.

PRACTICE TEST

I.   MULTIPLE-CHOICE QUESTIONS

Select the option that provides the single best answer.

_____   1.   A newly qualified dental school graduate, Phil McCafferty, is looking for a place to set
               up practice. He is _____ unemployed.
               (a)   frictionally
               (b)   structurally
               (c)   cyclically
               (d)   residually

_____   2.   The unemployment rate will fall if
               (a)   there is an increase in the number of discouraged workers.
               (b)   there is a recession.
               (c)   the number in the labor force decreases.
               (d)   there is a decrease in the population.

_____   3.   Francine loses her job because of the introduction of labor-saving machinery. Because
               she has few marketable skills, she stops looking for work. We would consider her to be
               _____ unemployed.
               (a)   cyclically
               (b)   frictionally
               (c)   structurally
               (d)   None of the above

_____ 4.   Labor-saving robots are introduced into a car assembly line. The resulting unemployment is
(a)   frictional.
(b)   structural.
(c)   mechanical.
(d)   cyclical.

_____ 5.   Arbez is producing at the full-employment level of production. There is
(a)   no unemployment.
(b)   some frictional and structural unemployment.
(c)   some cyclical unemployment.
(d)   a maximum participation rate.

_____ 6.   Recently, a flood of cheap computer chips has poured over the border from Arboc to Arbez. Thousands of workers in the Arbezani computer chip industry have lost their jobs. This unemployment is best described as
(a)   frictional.
(b)   structural.
(c)   competitive.
(d)   cyclical.

_____ 7.   Oliver Sudden has been jobless for the last six weeks, and he is still looking for the right job. He has job offers that are appropriate for his skills and that pay well. He is
(a)   frictionally unemployed.
(b)   structurally unemployed.
(c)   cyclically unemployed.
(d)   a discouraged worker.

_____ 8.   A fully anticipated increase in the inflation rate can lead to
(a)   increased efficiency.
(b)   greater speculative activity.
(c)   higher market interest rates.
(d)   a decrease in barter.

_____ 9.   Unanticipated inflation erodes the purchasing power of money. _____ is hurt least by unanticipated inflation.
(a)   A person on a fixed income
(b)   A lender
(c)   A creditor
(d)   A borrower

_____ 10.   The Consumer Price Index has risen from 110 to 121 during the last year. We should estimate the annual inflation rate for the last year at about
(a)   9.1%.
(b)   10%.
(c)   11%.
(d)   12%.

_____ 11. With unanticipated inflation, there will be all of the following EXCEPT
- (a)   greater risks involved in long-term contracts.
- (b)   less investment.
- (c)   more rapid growth in the economy.
- (d)   falling real rewards for lenders.

_____ 12. Your real wage has risen by 3% whereas the inflation rate has risen by 7%. Your nominal wage must have
- (a)   risen by 4%.
- (b)   risen by 10%.
- (c)   fallen by 4%.
- (d)   fallen by 10%.

_____ 13. As the economy moves out of a recession, the discouraged-worker effect will tend to _____ the unemployment rate.
- (a)   increase
- (b)   decrease
- (c)   leave unaffected
- (d)   have no influence on

_____ 14. Which of the following statements about the labor market is true?
- (a)   Discouraged workers are those workers who have voluntarily chosen to become unemployed.
- (b)   The labor force includes everyone over the age of 16, including those who are unemployed.
- (c)   The labor-force participation rate is the ratio of employed persons to the total labor force.
- (d)   The natural rate of unemployment is usually taken to be the sum of frictional and structural unemployment.

_____ 15. Which of the following statements about inflation is false?
- (a)   The real interest rate is equal to the nominal interest rate plus the anticipated inflation rate.
- (b)   Changes in the CPI tend to overstate changes in the cost of living.
- (c)   During periods of unanticipated inflation, debtors benefit at the expense of creditors.
- (d)   "Inflation" is an increase in the overall level of prices; when the overall level of prices decreases, it's called "deflation."

_____ 16. As a result of greater access to the Internet, there is an increase in the speed with which unemployed workers are matched with suitable jobs. This will
- (a)   increase the natural rate of unemployment.
- (b)   decrease the natural rate of unemployment.
- (c)   not affect the natural rate of unemployment but reduce structural unemployment.
- (d)   not affect the natural rate of unemployment but reduce frictional unemployment.

Use the following information to answer the next two questions. The Arbocali Bureau of Labor Statistics provides you with the following information.

Employed	360,000
Unemployed	40,000
Not in the labor force	100,000
Population (aged 16 +)	500,000

_____ 17. The Arbocali unemployment rate is
    (a)   8%.
    (b)   10%.
    (c)   11.11%.
    (d)   40%.

_____ 18. The labor-force participation rate is
    (a)   36%.
    (b)   40%.
    (c)   72%.
    (d)   80%.

_____ 19. We would expect to see each of the following during a recession EXCEPT
    (a)   decreased production.
    (b)   a worsening balance of payments.
    (c)   an increased incidence of psychological disorder and stress.
    (d)   decreased capacity utilization rates.

_____ 20. In an economy where inflation is usually unpredictable, the degree of risk associated with investment
    (a)   increases.
    (b)   decreases.
    (c)   depends on the nominal interest rate.
    (d)   is not affected.

II.   APPLICATION QUESTIONS

1.   Can you think of any adaptations that have been made in our economy to alleviate the redistributional effects of inflation?

2.   (a)   The market interest rate on a savings account is 5%. The inflation rate is 2%. Calculate the real interest rate that savings account depositors will earn.
    (b)   Suppose that the nominal interest rate that banks charge on loans is subject to a price ceiling of 7%. To be worthwhile, banks require a real interest rate of 4% or more. The inflation rate is currently 5%. Describe what will happen in this market.

3.   The following table provides information on inflation rates and unemployment rates for Arboc over a seven-year period.

Year	Inflation Rate (%)	Unemployment Rate (%)
Year 1	0.0	7.5
Year 2	–2.0	9.0
Year 3	4.0	5.0
Year 4	6.0	4.0
Year 5	10.0	2.5
Year 6	2.0	6.0
Year 7	–4.0	10.5

Arboc has a population of 1,000,000 over the age of 16. The labor-force participation rate is 90%.
(a)   Calculate the number of workers unemployed in Year 1.
(b)   Calculate the number of workers employed in Year 7.

Assume that the citizens of Arboc, when trying to determine the inflation rate for the next 12 months, base their calculations solely on the current inflation rate.
(c)   During the period from Year 2 to Year 5, will borrowers be gaining or losing?
(d)   In Year 5, the market interest rate was 12%. Calculate the real interest rate.

4.   Gilligan is a small island economy containing 10 individuals. In each of the following cases, determine if the individual is employed, unemployed, or not in the labor force. Explain your classification.
(a)   Krystal Krazy, Ph.D., 32, works 20 hours per week and is looking for a full-time job.
(b)   Lisa Looney, 20, is a student who is not working.
(c)   Maggie Madd, 84, works 10 hours a week doing cleaning services for her son, Norman Neurotic. He pays her minimum wage.
(d)   Norman Neurotic, 50, works full-time but hates his job and really wants a new job.
(e)   Olivia Opprest, a housewife, does not work outside the home and isn't looking for other employment.
(f)   Pete Paranoid, 40, used to work as a fisherman but believed that everyone hated him and has given up in disgust.
(g)   During the entire week containing the 12th of the month, Rosie the Riveter misses work simply because she didn't feel like going in to work.
(h)   BiBi Bratt, a hugely successful film star, aged 12, has earned over $10,000,000 each year for the past five years. Currently, BiBi is filming a new movie on location on Gilligan.
(i)   Maxwell Edison, a full-time Ph.D. student, is involved in ground-breaking research into fiber optics. His dissertation advisor has already claimed that Maxwell's work will revolutionize telecommunications.
(j)   Jenny Wren is a volunteer 10 hours a week on a Rape Crisis telephone hotline. She feels she makes an important contribution to society and would not accept a paid job if one were offered to her.
(k)   Calculate Gilligan's labor-force participation rate.
(l)   Calculate Gilligan's unemployment rate.

5.   Using the following figures, calculate the economic quantities for each year.

	2005	2010
Total population (16+)	200 million	210 million
Labor force	130 million	144 million
Employed	120 million	125 million

		2005	2010
(a)	the labor-force participation rate	_____	_____
(b)	the number unemployed	_____	_____
(c)	the unemployment rate	_____	_____

(d)   There is more likely to have been a recession in which year?

(e)   The President, denying that unemployment is growing, claims that:
   (i)   "We've created more jobs" and
   (ii)   "Some of the unemployed in the statistics have stopped seeking work."
   How would you respond to these points?

6.   Answer the questions, based on the following information.

Year	Nominal GDP (bill.)	Price Index	Real GDP (bill.)	Nominal Wage	Real Wage
Year 1	$4,486.0	108	_____	$40,000	_____
Year 2	$4,710.3	112	_____	$40,800	_____

(a)   Between Year 1 and Year 2, nominal GDP has _____ by _____%.

(b)   Between Year 1 and Year 2, the price level has _____ by _____%.

(c)   Frank loaned Freda $500 in Year 1 to be paid back in Year 2. He guessed inflation would run at 5% and accordingly increased the interest rate on the loan. In the circumstances, who won?

(d)   Calculate the real GDP figures.

(e)   Now calculate the real wage of the typical worker in each year.

(f)   To have maintained her/his Year 1 standard of living, the typical worker would need to have received a nominal wage of _____ in Year 2.

7.   Calculate the annual rates of inflation and complete the following table.

Year	Price Index	Rate of Inflation
Year 1	100.00	—
Year 2	113.00	_____
Year 3	121.50	_____
Year 4	126.70	_____
Year 5	125.10	_____

8.   The following table shows the market value of a given basket of goods in a number of selected years. The hourly nominal wage is also given.

Year	Value of Market Basket	Price Index	Rate of Increase	Nominal Wage/Hour	Rate of Increase	Real Wage/Hour
Year 1	$887.00	_____	—	$4.55	—	_____
Year 2	$993.44	_____	_____	$5.01	_____	_____
Year 3	$1,132.52	_____	_____	$5.61	_____	_____
Year 4	$1,245.78	_____	_____	$6.40	_____	_____
Year 5	$1,320.52	_____	_____	$6.98	_____	_____

(a)   Use the preceding table to calculate the price index values, with Year 1 as the base year.

(b)   Using the price index values, calculate the real hourly wage.

(c)   Work out the rate of increase in the price index (what does it measure?) _____ , and the rate of increase in nominal wage/hour _____ .

(d)   Compare the two "rates of increase" and the behavior of real wage/hour. Make up a rule of thumb linking these variables.

9.   (a)   Distinguish between frictional, structural, and cyclical unemployment. Give an example of each. Suggest ways in which each of these types of unemployment might be reduced.

        (b)   Suppose you've just become unemployed because of company cutbacks. Are you frictionally unemployed? Is it a good idea to accept the first job offer that comes along? Can you see any disadvantages to doing so?

PRACTICE TEST SOLUTIONS

I.   *Solutions to Multiple-Choice Questions*

1.   (a)   Job openings exist for Phil. It's merely a case of tracking down a position. Refer to p. 129 [441] for a discussion of the types of unemployment.

2.   (a)   If there are more discouraged workers, the numbers on the unemployment rolls will decrease because workers who have ceased looking for a job (discouraged workers) no longer meet the definition of being "unemployed." Refer to p. 127 [439].

3.   (d)   Francine has stopped seeking work—she is not classified as unemployed. Refer to p. 127 [439] on discouraged workers.

4.   (b)   The skills of a group of workers have become obsolete, either through a change in demand or, as in this case, through a technological change. Refer to p. 129 [441].

5.   (b)   The concept of full employment assumes that some (frictional and structural) unemployment will be present. Refer to p. 129 [441].

6.   (b)   The new Arbocali computer chip industry represents a structural change. U.S. car and steel workers have experienced similar unemployment.

7.   (a)   We don't know why Oliver became unemployed in the first place, but we do know that he can accept several suitable jobs—he has desirable job skills.

8.   (c)   The nominal (or market) interest rate is the real interest rate plus the anticipated inflation rate. Refer to p. 133 [445].

9.   (d)   A borrower pays a lower rate of interest than s/he should have if inflation had been fully anticipated. In fact, if inflation is very high, the cost of a loan may be zero or negative. Refer to p. 133 [445].

10.   (b)   The inflation rate = (change in CPI/initial CPI) × 100 = (11/110) × 100% = 10%.

11.   (c)   If investment falls (as it will because unanticipated inflation hurts lenders), the economy will grow less rapidly because fewer capital resources are being created.

12.   (b)   If the nominal wage rose by 7% and the inflation rate rose by 7%, the real wage would not have changed. For the real wage to have risen by 3%, the nominal wage must have risen by more than 7%—10%, in fact.

13.   (a)   Discouraged workers, seeing an improving economy, will begin to look for jobs—and will be counted as unemployed whereas, previously, they were not.

14.   (d)   Refer to p. 127 [439]. Discouraged workers aren't classified as unemployed. The labor force includes those over the age of 16 who are, or who wish to be, employed. The labor-force participation rate is the number in the labor force divided by the population.

15.   (a)   The real interest rate is equal to the nominal interest rate minus the anticipated inflation rate.

16.   (b)   Structural and frictional unemployment should both be reduced, as will the natural rate (the sum of structural and frictional unemployment).

17.   (b)   The labor force is the population minus those not in the labor force (500,000 – 100,000). The unemployment rate equals the number unemployed divided by the labor force. In this case, the unemployment rate equals 40,000/400,000, or 10%.

18.   (d)   The labor-force participation rate equals the number in the labor force (400,000) divided by the population (500,000). Refer to p. 124 [436].

19.   (b)   As the economy slows down, fewer imports are bought.

20.   (a)   The more unpredictable a situation is, the riskier it is. Refer to p. 133 [445].

II.   Solutions to Application Questions

1.   Adjustable-rate mortgages, indexation of the tax system, and indexation of pension benefits are a few of the changes.

2.   (a)   The real interest rate (3%) equals the market interest rate (5%) minus the inflation rate (2%).

      (b)   There will be an excess demand for loans. In fact, loans will dry up. The maximum nominal interest rate is 7%; with inflation, the maximum real interest rate is 2%, which is insufficient to induce banks to lend.

3.   (a) $900,000 \times 0.075 = 67,500$
      (b) $900,000 \times 0.895 = 805,500$
      (c)   Inflation is increasing—borrowers gain and creditors lose.
      (d)   The market interest rate is based on the real interest rate plus the expected inflation rate. In Year 5, the market interest rate was 12% and the expected inflation rate was 10% (based on the current inflation rate). The real interest rate was 2%.

4.   (a)   Krystal is employed.
      (b)   Lisa is not in labor force.
      (c)   Employed—Maggie is paid and employed.
      (d)   Norman is employed.
      (e)   Olivia is not in labor force.
      (f)   Pete is not in labor force.
      (g)   If Rosie is temporarily absent, with or without pay, she is considered employed.
      (h)   BiBi is not in the labor force. She is less than 16 years old.
      (i)   Maxwell is not in the labor force. He is a full-time student.
      (j)   Jenny is not in the labor force. She is not seeking a job nor does she meet the criteria required to be classified as employed.
      (k) $4/9 = 0.44$, or 44%. Bratt is neither in the population over 16 years of age nor in the labor force.
      (l)   No one is unemployed in this economy.

5.   (a)   The labor-force participation rate is labor force/population. In 2005, $130/200 = 65\%$; in 2010, $144/210 = 68.57\%$.

      (b)   Labor force equals the number employed plus the number unemployed. In 2005, the number unemployed = 130 million – 120 million = 10 million; in 2010, the number unemployed = 144 million – 125 million = 19 million.

      (c)   The unemployment rate = number unemployed/labor force. In 2005, number unemployed/labor force = $10/130 = 7.69\%$; in 2010, number unemployed/labor force = $19/144 = 13.9\%$.

      (d)   2010x, because the unemployment rate is higher in 2005.

      (e)   (i)   It is possible for a growing economy to experience rising employment and rising unemployment but, if the increase in the participation rate outstrips the increase in job openings, the unemployment rate will rise.

             (ii)   If, indeed, some individuals have stopped seeking work, then they would have dropped off the unemployment rolls. Admitting the presence of discouraged workers, on top of the listed unemployed, actually makes the President's performance worse!

6. (a) risen; 5%; percentage change = (change in nominal GDP/initial GDP) × 100 = (224.3/4,486) × 100 = 5%
    (b) risen; 3.7%; percentage change = (change in price index/initial price index) × 100 = (4/108) × 100 = 3.7%
    (c) Frank as creditor, because anticipated inflation was greater than the actual inflation rate.
    (d) Refer to the following table. Real GDP = (nominal GDP/price index) × 100
         Example: Real GDP for Year 1 = (4,486/108) × 100 = 4,153.7.

Year	Nominal GDP (bill.)	Price Index	Real GDP (bill.)	Nominal Wage	Real Wage
Year 1	$4,486.0	108	$4,153.7	$40,000	$37,037.04
Year 2	$4,710.3	112	$4,205.6	$40,800	$36,428.57

    (e) Refer to the preceding table. Real wage = (nominal wage/price index) × 100.
         Example: Real wage for Year 1 = ($40,000/108) × 100 = $37,037.04
    (f) Real wage in Year 1 was $37,037.04 ($40,000/1.08). To maintain the same value in Year 2, (x/1.12) = $37,037.04. Therefore, x = $37,037.04(1.12) = $41,481.48.

7. Refer to the following table.
    Example: rate of inflation for Year 3 = [(121.5 − 113)/113] × 100 = 7.52%.

Year	Price Index	Rate of Inflation
Year 1	100.00	—
Year 2	113.00	13.00%
Year 3	121.50	7.52%
Year 4	126.70	4.28%
Year 5	125.10	−1.26%

8. (a) Refer to the following table.
         Example: price index for Year 2 = (nominal value in Year 2/nominal value in base year) × 100 = (993.44/1,132.52) × 100 = 87.72.

Year	Value of Market Basket	Price Index	Rate of Increase	Nominal Wage/Hour	Rate of Increase	Real Wage/Hour
Year 1	$887.00	78.32	—	$4.55	—	$5.81
Year 2	$993.44	87.72	12.0%	$5.01	10.1%	$5.71
Year 3	$1,132.52	100.00	14.0%	$5.61	12.0%	$5.61
Year 4	$1,245.78	110.00	10.0%	$6.40	14.1%	$5.82
Year 5	$1,320.52	116.60	6.0%	$6.98	9.1%	$5.98

    (b) Refer to the preceding table. Example: real hourly wage for Year 2 = (nominal wage in Year 2/price index) × 100 = ($5.01/0.8772) × 100 = $5.71.
    (c) Inflation. Refer to the preceding table. Example: rate of increase in nominal wage for Year 2 = [(nominal wage in Year 2 − nominal wage in Year 1)/nominal wage in Year 1] × 100 = ($0.46/$4.55) × 100 = 10.1%.
    (d) When inflation is rising faster than the rate of increase in the nominal wage, the real wage will fall.

9.   (a)   Refer to the definitions on p. 129 [441]. A graduate in economics or business entering the job market is frictionally unemployed. The graduate has desirable qualifications; it's only a matter of tracking down an acceptable job. Defense industry workers and military personnel are becoming structurally unemployed as a result of the end of the Cold War. "Restructuring" at IBM is another example. Cyclical unemployment occurred during the recession of 1991 as consumer confidence plummeted and demand declined and, more recently, during the mild recession of 2001.

       (b)   If the company cutbacks are due to a fall in demand that is being felt nationwide, you are cyclically unemployed. If this one industry is affected, perhaps due to aggressive foreign competition, you are structurally unemployed. Whether you should accept the first job that is offered depends on the costs and benefits of staying unemployed. If you think it unlikely that a sufficiently better job offer will materialize that will cover the costs of a continued search, you should accept.

Comprehensive Review Test

The following questions provide a wide-ranging review of the material covered in Part II (IV)—Chapters 5–7 (20–22) of the textbook. Each question deals with a topic or technique important for your understanding of economic principles. If you miss a question you should return to the relevant section of the chapter in the textbook and fine-tune your understanding.

I.   MULTIPLE-CHOICE QUESTIONS

Select the option that provides the single best answer.

_____ 1.   Policies designed to control the amount of money in circulation are known as
            (a)   fiscal policies.
            (b)   monetary policies.
            (c)   growth policies.
            (d)   supply-side policies.

_____ 2.   A new type of mortgage is introduced into Macrovia—the adjustable rate mortgage (ARM). In contrast to a fixed-rate mortgage (where the interest rate does not change during the life of the loan), an ARM changes its interest rate as market interest rates change. Given unanticipated inflation, we would predict that this innovation will
            (a)   increase the losses for borrowers.
            (b)   increase the losses for lenders.
            (c)   decrease redistributional effects.
            (d)   increase uncertainty.

_____ 3.   Each of the following is a source of economic growth EXCEPT
            (a)   improvements in human capital.
            (b)   increases in physical capital.
            (c)   import tariffs against foreign competition.
            (d)   research and development.

_____ 4.   A measure of the overall rate of inflation is provided by
            (a)   the level of the GDP deflator.
            (b)   the percentage change in the level of the GDP deflator.
            (c)   the level of the GDP deflator divided by 12.
            (d)   the level of the GDP deflator multiplied by 12.

_____ 5.   A(n) _____ in government spending is an expansionary fiscal policy; a(n) _____ in taxes is an expansionary fiscal policy.
(a)   increase; increase
(b)   increase; decrease
(c)   decrease; increase
(d)   decrease; decrease

_____ 6.   There is an increase in government spending. We predict that aggregate output will _____ and that unemployment will _____ .
(a)   increase; increase
(b)   increase; decrease
(c)   decrease; increase
(d)   decrease; decrease

_____ 7.   Stagflation is a situation where the overall price level _____ and unemployment is _____ .
(a)   rising rapidly; rising rapidly
(b)   rising rapidly; high and persistent
(c)   declining; rising rapidly
(d)   declining; high and persistent

_____ 8.   Using your knowledge of demand and supply, which of the following situations is most likely to permit stagflation to occur?
(a)   An increase in overall demand
(b)   A decrease in overall demand
(c)   An increase in overall production (supply)
(d)   A decrease in overall production (supply)

_____ 9.   Wheat is used in the production of bread. Wheat is a(n) _____ good; bread is a(n) _____ good.
(a)   final; final
(b)   final; intermediate
(c)   intermediate; final
(d)   intermediate; intermediate

_____ 10.   Having totaled the other components of GDP, Arbez finds that (i) business inventories have fallen during the last year while (ii) imports have exceeded exports. (i) will _____ GDP; (ii) will _____ GDP. Use the expenditure approach to GDP.
(a)   increase; increase
(b)   increase; decrease
(c)   decrease; increase
(d)   decrease; decrease

_____ 11.   Disposable personal income can be used for each of the following purposes EXCEPT
(a)   personal consumption expenditures.
(b)   personal income tax payments.
(c)   personal transfer payments to foreigners.
(d)   personal saving.

_____   12.   In the nation of Arbez, between Year 1 and Year 2, nominal GDP rose by 3.9% whereas real GDP fell by 1.3%. We can conclude that the overall price level
(a)   rose by about 5.2% between Year 1 and Year 2.
(b)   rose by about 2.6% between Year 1 and Year 2.
(c)   fell by about 2.6% between Year 1 and Year 2.
(d)   fell by about 5.2% between Year 1 and Year 2.

_____   13.   Hester Investor wishes to earn a 6% real return on a $500 loan that she is planning to make to Buck Poor. Last year the inflation rate was 2%, but Hester expects the inflation rate to rise to 4%. She should charge an interest rate of
(a)   3%.
(b)   4%.
(c)   10%.
(d)   12%.

_____   14.   The nation of Arboc has recently been at the trough of a business cycle and is moving through the next phase. The unemployment rate is rising. Which of the following is a plausible explanation?
(a)   After the trough, Arboc will move into the recession phase, and unemployment rises during recessions.
(b)   After the trough, different sectors of the Arbocali economy will recover at different rates, so the average unemployment rate may increase.
(c)   Firms will not hire extra workers until the recovery is assured, therefore the numbers of workers employed will be artificially reduced.
(d)   The expansion phase will encourage previously discouraged workers to reenter the labor force, leading to an initial increase in the number without jobs.

_____   15.   Country singer Johnny Paycheck sang the song "Take This Job and Shove It." Following this advice the jobless worker is best considered to be
(a)   a discouraged worker.
(b)   frictionally unemployed.
(c)   structurally unemployed.
(d)   cyclically unemployed.

_____   16.   The "classical" economists believed that
(a)   recessions were self-correcting.
(b)   wage adjustments would prevent the persistence of surplus labor.
(c)   the economy would deviate from full employment only temporarily,
(d)   All of the above

_____   17.   The economy is in a recession. Each of the following policy proposals _could_ restore full employment EXCEPT
(a)   increasing government spending and increasing tax collections.
(b)   increasing government spending and decreasing tax collections.
(c)   decreasing government spending and increasing tax collections.
(d)   decreasing government spending and decreasing tax collections.

_____ 18.   You are told that net investment is positive this year. You can conclude that
   (a)   depreciation has been negative.
   (b)   gross investment has exceeded depreciation.
   (c)   interest rates have fallen this year.
   (d)   interest rates have risen this year.

_____ 19.   In Arboc, the personal saving rate is 10%. Personal saving is 1,000,000 opeks. Disposable personal income is _____ . Personal consumption expenditures are _____ .
   (a)   10,000,000 opeks; 1,000,000 opeks
   (b)   10,000,000 opeks; 9,000,000 opeks
   (c)   11,000,000 opeks; 10,000,000 opeks
   (d)   11,000,000 opeks; 12,000,000 opeks

_____ 20.   Typically, during a recession the personal saving rate
   (a)   increases because consumers become worried about their future.
   (b)   increases because interest rates decrease during recessions.
   (c)   decreases because households earn less disposable personal income.
   (d)   decreases because unemployed workers have less money available.

II.   APPLICATION QUESTIONS

In 2010, the population of the nation of Macrovia is 3,700,000 persons, of which 1,600,000 are aged 16 or older. Of these 1,600,000 persons, 1,184,000 have jobs, and 416,000 do not. 296,000 are unemployed but actively seeking jobs, and there are 120,000 who have given up the job search in frustration.

1.   Calculate the number of unemployed workers in Macrovia.

2.   Calculate the number of discouraged workers in Macrovia.

3.   Calculate the number of workers in the Macrovian labor force.

4.   Calculate the Macrovian unemployment rate.

5.   Calculate the Macrovian labor-force participation rate.

Use the following information on the 2010 Macrovian economy. Quantities are given in millions of Macrovian dollars (M$). Assume that any unreported values are zero.

Non-residential investment	586.1
Change in business inventories	−30.9
Compensation of employees	5178.6
Personal interest income	215.9
Depreciation	1133.5
Amount of National Income not going to Households	366.2
Macrovian exports of goods and services	380.8
Personal income taxes	600.0
Personal consumption expenditures	3514.8
Government consumption and gross investment	1589.7
Net factor payments to the rest of the world	0.0
Residential investment	453.7
National Income	5,075.7
Statistical Discrepancy	490.0
Macrovian imports of goods and services	285.0

6.   Calculate Macrovia's gross private domestic investment.

7.   Calculate Macrovia's net exports.

8.   Calculate Macrovian Gross Domestic Product for 2010.

9.   Calculate Macrovia's Gross National Product.

10.   Calculate Macrovia's Net National Product.

11.   Calculate Macrovia's Personal Income.

12.   Calculate Macrovia's Disposable Personal Income.

13.   Calculate personal saving in Macrovia.

14.   Use the information above to calculate Macrovia's personal saving rate.

15.   By how much has Macrovia's private capital stock changed from 2009 to 2010?

16.   Use the preceding information to calculate Macrovia's per capita GDP.

Macrovian economists have constructed a production index to monitor output per quarter.

Quarter:	2008				2009				2010			
	I	II	III	IV	I	II	III	IV	I	II	III	IV
Output	100	98	96	93	90	88	87	86	90	95	99	103

17.   In terms of the business cycle, describe what was happening to the Macrovian economy from 2008 to 2009.

18.   Using the preceding table, predict what is likely to be happening to the unemployment rate during 2008 and 2009.

19.   If the government wished to restore the economy's production level to 100 using fiscal policy, should it use an expansionary fiscal policy or a contractionary fiscal policy? Why?

Assume that the citizens of Macrovia, when trying to determine the inflation rate for the next 12 months, base their calculations solely on the current inflation rate. The following table provides information on the Consumer Price Index (CPI) and unemployment rate for Macrovia over a five-year period.

Year	CPI	Unemployment Rate	Inflation Rate
Year 1	100.00	4.2	—
Year 2	100.00	4.2	
Year 3	110.00	6.7	
Year 4	115.50	9.8	
Year 5	117.81	12.3	

20.   Based on this information, calculate the inflation rate for Year 2, Year 3, Year 4, and Year 5.

21.   Based on this information, during the period from Year 2 to Year 5, will borrowers gain or lose?

22.   In Year 3, the market interest rate was 12%. Based on the information, calculate the real interest rate.

23.   Betty loaned Wilma $1,000 in Year 2 to be paid back in Year 3. She guessed inflation would run at 0% and adjusted the interest rate on the loan accordingly. Based on the preceding information, who wins and who loses?

24.   Fred loaned Barney $1,000 in Year 3 to be paid back in Year 4. He guessed inflation would run at 10% and adjusted the interest rate on the loan accordingly. Based on the preceding information, who wins and who loses?

25.   In Year 4, Fred and Barney negotiate a new wage contract with their employer. The contract locks in an annual 5% wage increase. In Year 5, were Fred and Barney gainers or losers as a result of the contract? Explain, based on the preceding information.

REVIEW TEST SOLUTIONS

I.   *Solutions to Multiple-Choice Questions*

1.   (b)   Refer to p. 95 [407].

2.   (c)   Redistributional effects should be reduced. The market interest rate will adjust to changes in the inflation rate, making fluctuations in the real interest rate smaller. Refer to p. 133 [445].

3.   (c)   Although it may be a bitter pill, foreign competition promotes increased efficiency.

4.   (b)   The rate of inflation is the rate of change in the overall price level. Refer to p. 92 [404].

5.   (b)   The adjective "expansionary" refers to the impact on the output level for the economy—not whether government spending or taxes are expanding or not.

6.   (b)   An increase in government spending increases the economy's demand for goods. As demand increases, we should expect output to increase and, with more production, unemployment to decrease.

7.   (b)   Stagflation is a situation where the overall price level rising rapidly and unemployment is high and persistent. Refer to p. 96 [408].

8.   (d)   If overall production decreases (supply shifts left), then total output level will fall, causing unemployment to increase and the overall price level to increase, stimulating inflation.

9.   (c)   The wheat is used in producing the bread. To count both it and the bread as final products would be double counting. Refer to p. 106 [418].

10.   (b)   A decrease in inventories means that, on balance, sales have exceeded production. If imports have exceeded exports, net exports are negative.

11.   (b)   Personal income tax payments have been taken into account before disposable personal income is calculated. Note that another use of disposable personal income is as interest paid by consumers to businesses.

12.   (a)   If real GDP had been unchanged, the increase in nominal GDP would tell us that prices had risen by 3.9%. Because real GDP did fall, the increase in price level must have been even greater.

13.   (c)   The nominal interest rate is the real interest rate (6%) plus the expected inflation rate (4%).

14.   (d)   Refer to p. 90 [402] for more on business cycles.

15.   (b)   A worker is most likely to quit if he believes he has desirable job skills and another job is easy to come by.

16.   (d)   Refer to p. 96 [408] for a summary of the beliefs of the classical economists.

17.   (c)   The policy should attempt to boost overall demand in the economy. Both parts of Option (b) would do this. Options (a) and (d) each contain expansionary and contractionary elements—they might work. Option (c)'s elements both depress the economy's demand for goods and services.

18.   (b)   Interest rates may have changed, but this is uncertain. Gross investment minus depreciation equals net investment.

19.   (b)   Personal saving rate = personal saving/disposable personal income. Disposable personal income is divided between saving and consumption.

20.   (a)   Refer to p. 114 [426] for more on the personal saving rate.

II.   Solutions to Application Questions

1.   296,000 are unemployed and actively seeking jobs.

2.   120,000 workers

3.   1,480,000 workers

4.   Unemployment rate = unemployed/labor force = 296,000/1,480,000 = 20%

5.   Labor-force participation rate = labor force/population = 1,480,000/3,700,000 = 40%

6.   Gross private domestic investment = non-residential construction + residential construction + changes in business inventories = 586.1 + 453.7 – 30.9 = 1008.9

7.   Net exports = Exports – Imports 380.4 – 285.0 = 95.4

8.   GDP = C + I + G + (EX – IM) = 3,514.8 + (586.1 + 453.7 – 30.9) + 1,589.7 + (380.8 – 285.0) = 6,209.2 (millions of Macrovian dollars)

9.   GNP = GDP – Net Factor Payments to the Rest of the World = 6,208.8 – 0.0 = 6,209.2

10.   NNP = GNP – Depreciation = 6,209.2 – 643.5 = 5,565.7

11.   Personal Income = National Income – Amount of National Income not going to Households = 5,075.7 – 366.2 = 4,709.5

12.   Disposable Personal Income = Personal Income – Personal Income Taxes = 4,709.5 – 600.0 = 4,109.5

13.   Personal Saving = Disposable Personal Income – Personal Consumption Expenditures 4,109.5 – 3,920.6 = 188.9

14.   Personal Saving Rate = (Personal Saving /Disposable Personal Income) × 100% = (206.2/4,126.8) × 100% = 4.9966%

15.   Change in capital stock = Gross private domestic investment – depreciation = 1,008.9 – 643.5 = 365.4

16.   Per capita *GDP* = *GDP/population* = 6,208,800,000/3,700,00 = 1,678.05M$

17.   There is a recession. In fact, because output has declined for at least two years, this may be classified as a depression.

18.   The unemployment rate will be increasing as output level shrinks.

19. An expansionary policy would be called for. The government would wish aggregate output to expand.

20. The inflation rate = (change in CPI/initial CPI) × 100. Year 2—0%; Year 3—10%; Year 4—5%; Year 5—2%

21. Inflation is decreasing—creditors gain and borrowers lose.

22. The market interest rate is based on the real interest rate plus the expected inflation rate. In Year 3, the market interest rate was 12% and the expected inflation rate was 10%. The real interest rate was 2%.

23. Wilma gains as borrower and Betty loses as lender, because the anticipated inflation rate is lower than the actual inflation rate.

24. Fred gains as a lender and Barney loses as borrower, because the anticipated inflation rate is higher than the actual inflation rate.

25. Fred and Barney gain—the inflation rate in Year 5 is 2%, but their wages increase by 5%.

Part III

The Core of
Macroeconomic Theory

8 [23]

Aggregate Expenditure and Equilibrium Output

Chapter objectives:

1. Describe the relationship between consumption and income. Define the marginal propensity to consume (*MPC*) and the marginal propensity to save (*MPS*).

2. Explain how actual investment and intended investment differ. Describe the role of inventory change in establishing equilibrium in the economy.

3. Derive and graph the planned aggregate expenditure (*AE*) function. State why its slope has a value of less than one. Describe the adjustment process when planned aggregate expenditure differs from aggregate output. Use the expenditure and output approach and the saving/investment (leakages/injections) approach to specify the meaning of equilibrium in the model.

4. Analyze the effects on the macroeconomy of a change in planned investment or consumption. Describe the role of the multiplier in the inventory-adjustment process and, given *MPC*, derive the numerical value of the multiplier.

5. Describe the reasoning behind the paradox of thrift and explain what is paradoxical.

Give yourself plenty of time to understand the model developed in this chapter—it's the basis for what comes later. Can you prove that aggregate output does equal aggregate income? Can you confirm that income must equal consumption plus saving? Given the consumption function diagram, can you draw the related saving function diagram? Can you derive the consumption and saving equations? Can you see how unplanned inventory changes "balance" expenditures and output? Can you see why a $100 change in investment is "multiplied"? If not, work through this chapter again.

▶▶▶ LEARNING TIP: Don't skip over the introductory material on pp. 139-140 [451-452]. This easily-missed little section sets the scene and establishes the structure of the macroeconomy (goods-and-services and money markets leading to aggregate demand and the labor market leading to aggregate supply) analyzed in Chapters 8-14 (23-29). The figure on page 139 [451] will be referenced throughout. ◀

BRAIN TEASER: Do a thought experiment. Suppose your after-tax monthly income rose by $100. What would you do with the extra money? How much would you spend; how much would you save? Calculate your marginal propensity to consume and your marginal propensity to save. Calculate the expenditure multiplier. Case, Fair and Oster observe that the actual expenditure multiplier for the American economy is about 1.4. Can you explain the apparent discrepancy?

OBJECTIVE 1:
Describe the relationship between consumption and income. Define the marginal propensity to consume (*MPC*) and the marginal propensity to save (*MPS*).

In the complete model of the economy, aggregate expenditure (*AE*) is found by adding: $C + I + G + (EX - IM)$. That formula now simplifies to $AE = C + I$ because the model in this chapter has only two sectors (household and business) and only one market (goods-and-services). (page 142 [454])

For households, income (*Y*) is split between consumption (*C*) and saving (*S*). Determinants of aggregate *consumption* include

i.   Household income
ii.   Household wealth
iii.   Interest rates
iv.   Household expectations about the future

The Index of Consumer Confidence is a closely watched variable—as confidence sags about our future income, so does consumer spending, especially on durable goods. (page 145 [457])

If your monthly salary increases by $100, your consumption rises too, but by something less than $100. How much of the extra $100 you choose to spend depends on your *marginal propensity to consume (MPC)*. If you spend $80, *MPC* is 80/100 = 0.8. *Marginal propensity to save (MPS)* is 20/100 = 0.2 because any income not spent is saved ($20 out of $100). Clearly, *MPC + MPS* must sum to one (100% of any extra income must be spent or saved). (page 143 [455])

▶▶▶   LEARNING TIP: Keep in mind that we are considering "real" variables, not nominal ones. Although it is convenient to talk in terms of dollar amounts of consumption, income or output, ultimately real quantities prevail rather than prices. ◀

▶▶▶   LEARNING TIP: In Chapter 9 (24), we introduce taxes. This affects the calculation of *MPC* and *MPS*. You'll find the transition easier if you read the denominator term, "change in income," as "change in disposable (after-tax) income." In this chapter, the former term is identical with the latter (with no taxes, all income is disposable income); in Chapter 9 (24), *MPC* and *MPS* will be based on the change in disposable income. ◀

The Keynesian consumption function shows the relationship between consumption spending and income; its slope ("rise" over "run") is the value of *MPC* ("change in consumption" over "change in income" or $\Delta C/\Delta Y$). For simplicity, Keynes assumed a straight-line relationship. Algebraically, the consumption function is:

$$C = a + bY \quad \text{(page 144 [456])}$$

A similar function, the saving function, can be developed because consumption and saving are related activities. Given income, the amount consumed determines the amount saved and *vice versa*.

Note: You can calculate *MPS* (and, therefore, *MPC*) quickly if you have the intercept value (a) and the income value (*Y*) where the consumption function intersects the 45° line. *MPS = a/Y*. Use this "trick" in Practice Question 6 to confirm your answer.

Graphing Pointer: The 45° line is a reference line that helps you to read the graph. Use the 45° line to determine when saving is zero (or positive or negative) when the consumption function is drawn. Saving is zero when consumption crosses the 45° line. In this and subsequent chapters, the 45° line will help you to determine equilibrium aggregate output. Check your understanding of this in Practice Question 5.

──■────────────────── **Practice** ──────────────────

1. Aggregate consumption will certainly increase if
    (a)   income increases and wealth decreases.
    (b)   income increases and interest rates decrease.
    (c)   interest rates increase and household wealth increases.
    (d)   interest rates increase and consumer confidence about the future strengthens.

    ANSWER: (b) Lower interest rates reduce the cost of borrowing. Refer to p. 145 [457].

2. Given the income level, saving is directly (positively) related to
    (a)   interest rates and wealth, and inversely (negatively) related to households' expectations about the future.
    (b)   interest rates, and inversely (negatively) related to wealth and households' expectations about the future.
    (c)   households' expectations about the future, and inversely (negatively) related to interest rates and wealth.
    (d)   wealth, and inversely (negatively) related to interest rates and households' expectations about the future.

    ANSWER: (b) Higher interest rates encourage saving. As wealth increases and households become richer, and/or as households' expectations about the future improve, consumption increases. Given the income level, though, saving must decrease if consumption increases. Refer to p. 145 [457].

3. When *MPC* is 0.75, *MPS* is
    (a)   0.25.
    (b)   0.75.
    (c)   3.00.
    (d)   4.00.

    ANSWER: (a) *MPC + MPS* = 1. Refer to p. 143 [455].

4. The consumption function is $C = 200 + 0.9Y$. The saving function is
    (a) $S = 200 - 0.1Y$.
    (b) $S = -200 - 0.1Y$.
    (c) $S = 200 - 0.9Y$.
    (d) $S = -200 + 0.1Y$.

    ANSWER: (d) Recall that $Y = C + S$. The equations must sum to *Y*. The first term must be negative because consumption is positive. Also, recall that saving increases as income increases—the second term must be positive.

Use the following diagram to answer the next three questions.

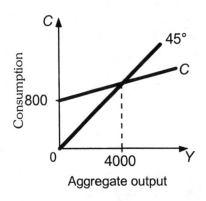

5.   When income equals 4,000, consumption equals _____ and saving equals _____ .
   (a)   4,000; 0
   (b)   3,200; 800
   (c)   4,000; 4,000
   (d)   2,000; 2,000

   ANSWER: (a) The 45° line shows all the points at which the variable on the vertical axis
          equals the variable on the horizontal axis, in this case, where $C = Y$. If $Y =$
          4,000, $C = 4,000$. If all income is being spent, saving must be zero.

6.   The equation for this consumption function is
   (a) $C = 800 + 0.75Y$.
   (b) $C = 800 + 0.8Y$.
   (c) $C = 4,000 + 0.75Y$.
   (d) $C = 4,000 + 0.8Y$.

   ANSWER: (b) The intercept term (a) is 800. As income increases from 0 to 4,000,
          consumption increases from 800 to 4,000, an increase of 3,200. MPC
          = change in consumption/change in income = $\Delta C/\Delta Y$ = 3,200/4,000 = 0.8.

   Note: When the consumption (saving) function intercepts the vertical axis, the associated
value indicates the level of consumption (saving), which is independent of income. If income = 0,
this level of spending (saving) would still exist.

7.   If income is 6,000, consumption is _____ and saving is _____ .
   (a)   4,800; 1,200
   (b)   5,600; 400
   (c)   5,200; 1,000
   (d)   6,000; 0

   ANSWER: (b) When $Y = 4,000$, $C = 4,000$ and $S = 0$. $MPC = 0.8$. As income increases by
          2,000 (from 4,000 to 6,000), consumption will increase by 2,000 × 0.8, or
          1,600. Consumption will total 5,600 (4,000 + 1,600). We know that $Y = C +$
          S, therefore $S = Y - C$. $S = 6,000 - 5,600 = 400$. Option (c) cannot be
          correct because $C + S$ must equal income (Y), and 5,200 + 1,000 does not
          equal 6,000. ∎

ECONOMICS IN PRACTICE: On page 147 [459], the textbook looks at saving behavior. Saving is rather like exercise or studying for exams—we know it's a good thing to do, but we still might not wish to do it. Essentially, it's a trade-off between current enjoyment and future enjoyment. Keynes famously remarked, "In the long run we're all dead." If our focus is purely short run, we're unlikely to save. In order to increase the likelihood of saving, either the benefit from current consumption must be reduced or the gain from future consumption must be increased. Can you think of some ways that the trade-off could be adjusted to encourage additional saving? Include government policies if you wish.

ANSWER: Higher interest rates encourage additional saving. Reduced taxes on interest income or schemes to defer taxes, such as IRAs (Individual Retirement Accounts) are government policy options. Higher taxes on consumption may also stimulate saving. Simply having funds automatically contributed to saving reduces the conscious effort ("cost") involved in saving and is a successful way to accumulate wealth. In addition, saving for a particular short-term or long-term goal makes it easier to forgo current consumption. Reductions in the risk involved in saving (less fear of bank default or loss of the value of investments because of oversight of the financial system) will prompt more households to surrender current consumption. Finally, a society in which saving is emphasized as a virtue is likely to produce thrifty behavior.

OBJECTIVE 2:
Explain how actual investment and intended investment differ. Describe the role of inventory change in establishing equilibrium in the economy.

Planned investment (*I*) is assumed to remain constant as output level changes—investment graphs as a horizontal line. However, *actual investment* can differ from *planned investment* because of unplanned changes in the level of inventories. (page 146 [458])

> ▶▶▶   LEARNING TIP: Investment is one of the most difficult concepts to learn. Economists use the word differently from others. Investment does *not* mean saving, not even financial investment although, in this model, saving and investment are equal when the system is in equilibrium. Investment is the purchase of new machinery and buildings (productive capacity) and changes in inventory levels. In contrast, if you save you are *not* purchasing. ◀

Note that firms buy more than investment goods. They hire workers, for example. To count this expenditure would be double counting—the wages are used by households for consumption and saving.

> ▶▶▶   LEARNING TIP: In this model, actual investment will *always* equal saving but that, *only in equilibrium*, will planned investment equal saving. In equilibrium, unplanned inventory investment will be zero. ◀

If aggregate output exceeds (is less than) consumption and planned investment, there will be an unplanned increase (decrease) in inventory investment. (For an example, refer to Application 3.) (page 148 [460])

> **Unplanned Inventory Change and Equilibrium:** Unplanned inventory changes draw the economy into equilibrium. Call expenditures "demand" and output "supply" for the moment. When "demand" is more than current "supply," firms must sell their previously accumulated inventory. Emptying shelves are the signal to increase production.
>
> When "demand" is less than "supply," unsold production piles up—the signal to cut output.
>
> Firms feel no pressure to adjust production levels (i.e., there is equilibrium) only when "demand" equals "supply."
>
> Also, when unplanned inventory change is not zero (either positive or negative), the actual level of investment differs from the level managers wish to have. If, for example, actual investment is "too low," managers will boost production to compensate.

▶▶▶   LEARNING TIP: An economic system requires some mechanism to drive it towards equilibrium. In the market for coffee, the equilibrating mechanism is price. In our model, price is fixed and the equilibrating mechanism is unplanned inventory change. When unplanned inventory change occurs, it is a signal to adjust output. ◀

—————■——————————————————————— **Practice** ———————————————————————————

8.   Investment refers to
   (a)   the purchase of new stock in a company.
   (b)   the purchase of new or existing stock in a company.
   (c)   the creation of capital stock.
   (d)   the stock of accumulated saving.

   ANSWER: (c) Investment is the addition to the capital stock. Financial transactions are excluded from GDP—review Chapter 6 (21).

9.   The change in inventories is
   (a)   production minus sales.
   (b)   sales minus production.
   (c)   a value equal to or greater than zero, but cannot be negative.
   (d)   consumption minus saving.

   ANSWER: (a) Refer to p. 146 [458]. ■

OBJECTIVE 3:
Derive and graph the planned aggregate expenditure (*AE*) function. State why its slope has a value of less than one. Describe the adjustment process when planned aggregate expenditure differs from aggregate output. Use the expenditure and output approach and the saving/investment (leakages/injections) approach to specify the meaning of equilibrium in the model.

Planned aggregate expenditure is the sum of consumption and planned investment at each income level. Because planned investment is assumed to be constant at each income level, the *AE* function is an upward sloping line whose slope equals *MPC*. (page 147 [459])

▶▶▶   LEARNING TIP: Sometimes you'll find understanding easier if you think about "output," and
sometimes about "income." For example, "When unplanned inventory reductions occur, output level
will rise" is more obvious than "When unplanned inventory reductions occur, income level will rise."
However, "Output is split between consumption and saving" is much less intuitive than "Income is
split between consumption and saving."◀

Equilibrium occurs when planned aggregate expenditure equals aggregate output
(income)—i.e., when $C + I = C + S$. Only then does planned investment equal actual investment—
there is no unplanned inventory change.

Getting to Equilibrium: If output is less than planned expenditures ($Y < C + I$), inventory
levels unexpectedly decrease below the desired level. Firms respond by increasing production.
Higher production results in higher income and, given MPC, greater consumption spending.
Spending increases, but at a slower rate than output increases. Eventually, the two will be equal.

If output exceeds planned expenditures ($Y > C + I$), inventory levels are unexpectedly added
to. Firms respond rising levels of unsold output by decreasing production. Lower production results
in lower income and, given MPC, less consumption spending. Spending falls, but at a slower rate
than output falls. Eventually, the two will be equal.

In each case, how big a change in output level is needed to achieve equilibrium depends on
the value of the multiplier. (page 151 [463])

The conditions necessary for equilibrium can be stated in different ways.

(a)   If actual and planned investment differ, the economy is not in equilibrium.
       Equilibrium condition: planned investment must equal actual investment.
(b)   Aggregate planned expenditure must equal aggregate output (income).
       Therefore, $C + I = C + S$.
       Equilibrium condition: planned investment must equal planned saving.
(c)   Because, in equilibrium, planned investment must equal actual investment
       Equilibrium condition: unplanned investment must equal zero.

There's no requirement that the equilibrium level of production will be enough to provide
full employment to the economy's workers.

Note: Unlike most other curves you have seen, the consumption, investment, saving, and AE
functions are all shown to increase by moving vertically upward (not to the right).

Graphically, equilibrium must occur where the AE function crosses the 45° line. The 45°
line plots all the points where spending equals output—i.e., all the points where equilibrium might
occur.

 ──────── Practice ────────

Use the following table to answer the next six questions.

Output	Consumption	Investment	Planned Aggregate Expenditure	Unplanned Change in Inventory
2,000	2,100	400	_____	_____
3,000	2,850	400	_____	_____
4,000	3,600	400	_____	_____
5,000	4,350	400	_____	_____
6,000	5,100	400	_____	_____
7,000	5,850	400	_____	_____

10.   Complete the planned aggregate expenditure column in the preceding table.

ANSWER: Refer to the following table.

Output	Consumption	Investment	Planned Aggregate Expenditure	Unplanned Change in Inventory
2,000	2,100	400	2,500	−500
3,000	2,850	400	3,250	−250
4,000	3,600	400	4,000	0
5,000	4,350	400	4,750	+250
6,000	5,100	400	5,500	+500
7,000	5,850	400	6,250	+750

11.   Equilibrium output level is
(a)   3,000.
(b)   4,000.
(c)   5,000.
(d)   6,000.

ANSWER: (b) Equilibrium occurs where output equals planned aggregate expenditure.

12.   Complete the unplanned change in inventory column in the preceding table.

ANSWER: Refer to Question 10 for the completed table. Unplanned change in inventory is the difference between output and planned aggregate expenditure.

13.   In the preceding table, *MPC* is
(a)   0.6.
(b)   0.75.
(c)   0.8.
(d)   0.9.

ANSWER: (b) $MPC = \Delta C/\Delta Y$. Every time income rises by 1,000, consumption rises by 750.

14.   When income level is 0, consumption is
(a)   0.
(b)   250.
(c)   600.
(d)   1,000.

ANSWER: (c) When income is 2,000, consumption is 2,100. If income decreases by 2,000 and *MPC* is 0.75, consumption will decrease by 1,500.

15.   When output is 6,000, firms will
(a)   increase production.
(b)   decrease production.
(c)   increase planned investment.
(d)   decrease planned investment.

ANSWER: (b) Output exceeds planned aggregate expenditure and inventories are too high. Firms would cut production. ∎

OBJECTIVE 4:

Analyze the effects on the macroeconomy of a change in planned investment or consumption. Describe the role of the multiplier in the inventory-adjustment process and, given *MPC*, derive the numerical value of the multiplier.

The *multiplier* measures the extent to which the output level will change given a particular initial change in the level of spending. It's calculated by the formula: $1/(1 - MPC)$ or $1/MPS$. (p. 153 [465])

> ▶▶ LEARNING TIP: You might find the subsequent material easier if you focus more on the $1/MPS$ formula. The strength of the multiplier depends on how rapidly spending power leaks out of the circular flow diagram. This is even more obvious when leakages other than saving (taxes, imports) make their appearance. ◀

One way to visualize the multiplier is to use the following circular flow diagram.

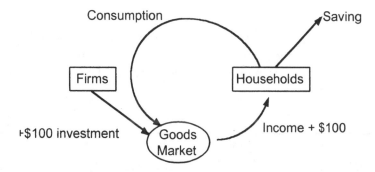

Households split their income into consumption expenditures and saving. Some investment also takes place. Suppose *MPC* is 0.9 and *MPS* is 0.1. If, for example, firms indulge in an extra $100 of investment spending, then income rises by $100. Trace through the circular flow—consumption rises by $90, $81, $72.90, and so on. Where is the rest going? It's leaking away into saving (nonspending).

The same $100 increase in investment, with a lower *MPC*, such as 0.5, gives a *less*-substantial expansion in spending because the extra income drains away more quickly. The multiplier is smaller, right?

The expansion is less if spending power drains away more rapidly—if *MPS* is relatively high. The multiplier value is linked negatively to *MPS* and positively to *MPC*.

An increase in investment (or consumption) generates extra income. Extra income, however, stimulates consumption and saving—*MPC* and *MPS* determine how much consumption and saving will rise. Extra consumption generates more new income. The process of "spend-earn income-spend" runs out of steam as progressively more of the extra dollars leak away into saving. (page 151 [463])

> ▶▶ LEARNING TIP: As shown in the textbook, the multiplier model works given a change in investment, but it is more general than that. The analysis works for any component of planned aggregate expenditure—in this chapter, consumption and investment and, in Ch. 9 (24), government spending. ◀

Example: If planned investment increases, the *AE* line shifts upwards. At the initial output level, inventories unexpectedly fall. As firms boost production to restore desired inventory levels, income and consumption rise, and the economy moves to the point where the new (higher) *AE* function crosses the 45° line. Now tell the same story using the saving/investment (leakages/injections) approach.

▶▶▶   LEARNING TIP: Memorize the two multiplier formulas given on p. 153 [465]. Also, memorize the likely values for the multiplier that might show up on a test. These are:

MPC	MPS	Multiplier
0.50	_____	2.0
0.60	_____	2.5
0.75	_____	4.0
0.80	_____	5.0
0.90	_____	10.0

For practice, fill in the MPS values and confirm the multiplier values using both formulas. ◀

Practice

By comparing the two cases that follow, you should get a good idea about how the multiplier operates.

CASE 1: ARBOC. In Arboc, MPC is 0.9. The economy is in equilibrium. Suddenly, there is a 100-opek increase in investment spending, which creates 100 opeks of extra income. The income is split 90:10 between new consumption and new saving. The new consumption spending generates additional income.

New Expenditure	New Income	=	New Consumption	+	New Saving
100.00	100.00	=	90.00	+	10.00
90.00	90.00	=	81.00	+	9.00
81.00	81.00	=	72.90	+	8.10
72.90	72.90	=	65.61	+	7.29
65.61	65.61	=	59.05	+	6.56
.	.		.		.
.	.		.		.
.	.		.		.
1,000.00	1,000.00	=	900.00	+	100.00

This process goes through many "rounds," only the first five of which are given. The final row gives the total results.

Notes
1.   The initial "injection" of spending is 100; ultimately this will all become new saving. Indeed, the opeks must continue to circulate (generating more income and expenditure) until all of the "extra" 100 opeks have leaked into saving (non-consumption). *The leakage must equal the injection.* The multiplier's strength depends on how rapidly the injection of extra spending leaks away.
2.   We know that income equals consumption plus investment. Income increased by 1,000, consumption increased by 900, and investment increased by 100.

CASE 2: ARBEZ. In Arbez, MPC is 0.8. The economy is in equilibrium. Suddenly, there is a 100 bandu increase in investment spending, which creates 100 bandu of extra income. Income is split 80:20 between new consumption and new saving.

16.   Complete the following table.

New Expenditure	New Income	=	New Consumption	+	New Saving
100.00	___	=	___	+	___
___	___	=	___	+	___
___	___	=	___	+	___
___	___	=	___	+	___
___	___	=	___	+	___
.	.		.		.
.	.		.		.
.	.		.		.
500.00	500.00	=	400.00	+	100.00

ANSWER: Refer to the following table.

New Expenditure	New Income	=	New Consumption	+	New Saving
100.00	100.00	=	80.00	+	20.00
80.00	80.00	=	64.00	+	16.00
64.00	64.00	=	51.20	+	12.80
51.20	51.20	=	40.96	+	10.24
40.96	40.96	=	32.77	+	8.19
.	.		.		.
.	.		.		.
.	.		.		.
500.00	500.00	=	400.00	+	100.00

Notes
1.   As in Case 1, the initial "injection" of spending leaks away to saving; ultimately all of this injection of spending ends up as new saving.
2.   Income increases by 500, consumption increases by 400, and investment increases by 100.
3.   The expansion in income is less in Case 2 (the multiplier is smaller) because *MPC* is smaller (*MPS* is greater). The extra 100 units of spending leak away into saving more slowly in Case 1 and are recycled more frequently.

Remember: The steeper the *AE* curve, the higher the value of the multiplier. Can you figure out why?

17.   The formula for the multiplier is
       (a) $1/MPC$.
       (b) $1/MPS$.
       (c) $1/(1 - MPS)$.
       (d) $1/(1 + MPS)$.

       ANSWER: (b) Refer to p. 153 [465] for the two versions of the multiplier formula.

Use the following diagram, which builds on the previous diagram, to answer the next five questions.

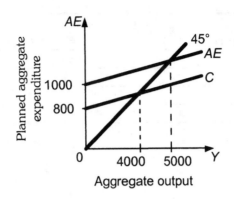

18.   The level of investment in this economy is
(a)   200.
(b)   800.
(c)   1,000.
(d)   5,000

ANSWER: (a) $AE = C + I$. When $Y = 0$, $AE = 1,000$, and $C = 800$.

19.   The slope of the *AE* function is
(a)   0.6.
(b)   0.75.
(c)   0.8.
(d)   0.9.

ANSWER: (c) The slope of the *AE* function depends on *MPC*. Question 6 determined that *MPC* is 0.8. If we refer to the *AE* function by itself, we get the same result. Spending increases by 4,000 (from 1,000 to 5,000) as income increases from 0 to 5,000.

20.   The multiplier has a value of
(a)   4.
(b)   5.
(c)   8.
(d)   10.

ANSWER: (b) The multiplier formula is $1/(1 - MPC)$. *MPC* is 0.8.

21.   If planned investment increases by 100, equilibrium output level will increase by _____ . In equilibrium, saving will equal _____ .
(a)   100; 200
(b)   100; 300
(c)   500; 200
(d)   500; 300

ANSWER: (d) The multiplier is 5. Equilibrium output will increase by 500 (100 × 5). In equilibrium, saving equals investment. Recall that investment was 200 and rose further by a 100. Alternatively, because *MPS* is 0.2 (can you see why?), an increase in income of 500 will cause a 100 increase in saving.

22.   When the output level is 4,000, unplanned inventories will
         (a)   increase by 1,000.
         (b)   increase by200.
         (c)   decrease by1,000.
         (d)   decrease by 200.
         ANSWER: (d) At an output level of 5,000, planned aggregate expenditure is 5,000. If
                  income falls by 1,000, consumption falls only by 800 because *MPC* is 0.8.
                  Therefore, we know that, at an output level of 4,000, planned aggregate
                  expenditure is 4,200. Planned aggregate expenditure is 200 more than
                  output and inventories will decrease accordingly.

23.   If the slope of the *AE* function became steeper, *MPC* would become _____ and the
         multiplier would become _____ .
         (a)   larger; larger
         (b)   larger; smaller
         (c)   smaller; larger
         (d)   smaller; smaller
         ANSWER: (a) Refer to Case A and Case B above. ∎

OBJECTIVE 5:
Describe the reasoning behind the paradox of thrift and explain what is paradoxical.

The *paradox of thrift* shows that attempts to increase saving (an upward shift in the saving function
and a downward shift in the consumption function) will be fruitless. Total saving won't change, but
the economy will suffer a decrease in output (income) level. (page 154 [466])
         Note: The paradox of thrift is inevitable, given our model. Investment is constant and, when
equilibrium is achieved, saving *must* equal that value. As long as investment behavior does not
change, saving can neither increase nor decrease.

ECONOMICS IN PRACTICE: On page 154 [466], the textbook raises the issue of the "paradox of
thrift." At first sight, this result may seem enough to persuade you that Keynes must have got it
wrong somewhere! After all, as children we are taught that it is wise to save (if not fun).
Economists show that there is a clear link between saving and economic growth. There are, in fact,
two components to the paradox of thrift—one involving the level of income (production) and the
other involving the level of saving in the economy. Assuming that households decide to save more,
what does our model predict will happen to (i) income and (ii) saving?
ANSWER: Given more saving initially, consumption will decrease, pulling down the level of income
as the economy adjusts to its new equilibrium—thriftiness seems to reduce our standard of living.
Saving will remain unchanged (although the distribution of saving may change)—trying to save
more appears impossible.
ECONOMICS IN PRACTICE (CONTINUED): In part, the result is due to the assumption that planned
investment is constant. If saving and investment must be equal in equilibrium, and investment is
constant, then the level of saving *can't* change. However, do you think that the level of planned
investment is fixed, or do you think that, as production increases, investment will also increase? If
so, does the paradoxical result disappear?

ANSWER: Evidence shows that planned investment does increase as the economy grows. That means that planned investment must decrease as the economy shrinks. An increase in saving (decrease in spending) will make the economy (and investment) shrink. The final equilibrium level of saving, therefore, will be *lower* than the initial level. Injecting some realism into the model makes the paradoxical result more intense!

ECONOMICS IN PRACTICE (CONTINUED): At this point, it is a natural reaction to give up on Keynes. However, during the Great Depression, households did cut consumption and the economy did contract. As the textbook indicates, there is a resolution, and it comes through financial markets. How might increased saving stimulate increased investment?

ANSWER: Higher supplies of funds (saving) in financial markets should reduce the price (interest rate) of those funds. Cheaper loans should encourage more borrowing by businesses for investment purposes. More on this in Chapter 12 (27). Finally, as you'll discover in Chapter 13 (28), as demand in the economy declines, the aggregate price level will decrease, encouraging additional expenditures.

───■──────────────────────── **Practice** ────────────────────────

24. Refer to the table used in Practice Question 10. The economy is in equilibrium. If saving increases by 100, equilibrium output will decrease by _____ and consumption will decrease by _____ .
    (a)   100; 100
    (b)   100, 400
    (c)   400; 100
    (d)   400; 400

    ANSWER: (d) *MPC* is 0.75 (Question 13); the multiplier is 4. If saving increases by 100, consumption decreases by 100 and output decreases by 400 (100×4). When output (income) decreases by 400, consumption is reduced by an additional 300. The total decrease in consumption is 400.

25. If households increase saving, the paradox of thrift indicates that, in equilibrium, consumption will _____ and output will _____ .
    (a)   decrease; increase
    (b)   decrease; decrease
    (c)   not increase; increase
    (d)   not increase; decrease

    ANSWER: (b) The increase in saving causes consumption to decrease. The decrease in consumption spending will make equilibrium output decrease. As income falls, consumption falls even more. ■

SUMMARY: EQUILIBRIUM CONDITIONS

Equilibrium can be described in several ways. Learn them all!

$$
\begin{aligned}
\text{Planned aggregate expenditure} &= \text{aggregate output (income)} \\
C + S &= C + I \\
S &= I \\
\text{Planned investment} &= \text{actual investment} \\
\text{Unplanned inventory change} &= 0
\end{aligned}
$$

Note: As the model is extended in later chapters, all but the first of these conditions will be modified.

BRAIN TEASER SOLUTION: If you're like most people, you'd end up spending most of the extra dollars. Often, households save about 5% of the additional income received and spend the rest. *MPS* is 0.05, *MPC* is 0.95, and the multiplier is 20. Clearly, the multiplier model in the present chapter has omitted some ingredients. Taxes, which increase as income increases, drain some dollars from the "spend-earn income-spend" process. As demand increases, rising prices and higher interest rates choke off spending. Some dollars are spent overseas.

PRACTICE TEST

I.   MULTIPLE-CHOICE QUESTIONS

Select the option that provides the single best answer.

_____   1.   *MPC* is _____ divided by _____
(a)   consumption, income.
(b)   change in consumption, income.
(c)   change in consumption, change in income.
(d)   consumption, change in income.

_____   2.   The larger the value of *MPC*, the
(a)   larger the value of the multiplier.
(b)   steeper the slope of the saving function.
(c)   smaller the value of the multiplier.
(d)   flatter the slope of the consumption function.

Use the following table to answer the next three questions.

Income	Consumption	Investment
2,000	1,800	1,000
3,000	2,600	1,000
4,000	3,400	1,000
5,000	4,200	1,000
6,000	5,000	1,000
7,000	5,800	1,000

_____ 3.   The equilibrium income level is _____ and the equilibrium saving level is _____ .
    (a)   7,000; 200
    (b)   greater than 7,000; 1,000
    (c)   6,000; 1,000
    (d)   1,000; 100

_____ 4.   The *MPS* is _____ and the multiplier is _____ .
    (a)   0.1; 10
    (b)   0.2; 5
    (c)   0.2; 10
    (d)   0.1; 5

_____ 5.   If planned saving suddenly rises by 100, then, at the new equilibrium, income will _____ . Eventually, saving will _____ .
    (a)   fall by 100; fall by 100
    (b)   fall by 500; not change
    (c)   fall by 500; fall by 100
    (d)   fall by 100; not change

Use the following table to answer the next three questions.

Income	Consumption
0	100
100	180
200	260
300	340
1,000	900
2,000	1,700

_____ 6.   Referring to the equation $C = a + bY$, the value of "a" is _____ .
    (a)   0
    (b)   20
    (c)   80
    (d)   100

_____ 7.   Marginal propensity to consume is _____ .
    (a)   80
    (b)   0.2
    (c)   0.8
    (d)   0.9

_____ 8.   An increase in investment of $100 would _____ income by _____ .
    (a)   raise; 500
    (b)   raise; 100
    (c)   lower; 500
    (d)   lower; 100

_____ 9. The economy is in equilibrium at an output level of 2,000. Now planned investment increases. At the initial output level, all of the following are true EXCEPT
(a)   aggregate expenditure is greater than aggregate output.
(b)   saving is less than planned investment.
(c)   inventory levels are rising unexpectedly.
(d)   consumption level has remained unchanged.

_____ 10. A decrease in *MPS* would
(a)   cause the consumption function to shift upwards, all along its length.
(b)   cause the consumption function to shift downwards, all along its length.
(c)   cause the consumption function to rotate upwards, pivoting where it meets the vertical axis.
(d)   have no effect on the consumption function.

_____ 11. In our model, *MPC* must be less than _____ and *MPS* must exceed _____ .
(a)   one; one
(b)   one; zero
(c)   zero; one
(d)   zero; zero

_____ 12. If planned investment suddenly decreases, the *AE* line will shift _____ and equilibrium saving will _____ .
(a)   upward; increase
(b)   upward; decrease
(c)   downward; increase
(d)   downward; decrease

_____ 13. Equilibrium occurs when aggregate output is equal to planned _____ plus planned _____ .
(a)   consumption; saving
(b)   consumption; investment
(c)   investment; saving
(d)   inventories; investment

_____ 14. Aggregate output is currently less than planned aggregate expenditure. We can predict that inventory levels are unexpectedly _____ and saving is _____ than planned investment.
(a)   increasing; greater
(b)   increasing; less
(c)   decreasing; greater
(d)   decreasing; less

_____ 15. Which of the following statements is true?
(a)   Savings is the difference between current income and current consumption.
(b)   When expenditures are high, saving is less than actual investment.
(c)   Saving is a flow variable: savings is a stock variable.
(d)   When the interest rate falls, saving increases and consumption decreases.

_____ 16.   If income is zero, consumption will be
      (a)   positive.
      (b)   zero, because you can't spend what you don't have.
      (c)   zero, because consumption and saving must sum to equal income.
      (d)   unknown—it depends on the slope of the consumption function.

_____ 17.   As consumer uncertainty in the future increases, consumption will _____ and saving will _____ .
      (a)   increase; increase
      (b)   increase; decrease
      (c)   decrease; increase
      (d)   decrease; decrease

_____ 18.   Firms have the least control over
      (a)   inventory levels.
      (b)   production levels.
      (c)   planned investment.
      (d)   purchases of new equipment.

_____ 19.   *MPC* equals 0.9. Consumers receive an extra $100 of income. We can say that
      (a)   the consumption function has moved upwards.
      (b)   the consumption function has moved downwards.
      (c)   consumption spending increases by $100.
      (d)   saving increases by $10.

_____ 20.   *MPC* equals 0.9. Planned investment is 100 and equilibrium income level is 1,000. If income were at 800, what would be the level of **saving**?
      (a)   100
      (b)   90
      (c)   80
      (d)   70

Use the following diagram to answer the next five questions.

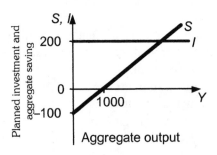

_____ 21.   The equation for this consumption function is
      (a) $C = 100 + 0.8Y$.
      (b) $C = 100 + 0.9Y$.
      (c) $C = 200 + 0.8Y$.
      (d) $C = 200 + 0.9Y$.

_____ 22.   The multiplier value is
              (a)   0.9.
              (b)   8.
              (c)   9.
              (d)   10.

_____ 23.   The equilibrium output level is
              (a)   200.
              (b)   1,000.
              (c)   3,000.
              (d)   4,000.

_____ 24.   If investment decreases by 50, equilibrium output will decrease by _____ and
              consumption will decrease by _____ .
              (a)   200, 450
              (b)   200, 500
              (c)   500, 450
              (d)   500, 500

_____ 25.   The equation for this saving function is
              (a) $S = 100 + 0.1Y$.
              (b) $S = 100 + 0.9Y$.
              (c) $S = -100 + 0.1Y$.
              (d) $S = -100 + 0.9Y$.

II.   APPLICATION QUESTIONS

1.   The Arbezani Minister of Macroeconomics gives you the following data about Arbez.

$$
\begin{aligned}
C &= 300 + 0.75Y &&(1) \\
I &= 200 &&(2) \\
AE &= C + I &&(3) \\
AE &= Y &&(4)
\end{aligned}
$$

(a)   Calculate the marginal propensity to consume and the marginal propensity to save.
(b)   Derive the algebraic formula for the saving function.
(c)   What are the four conditions necessary for the economy to be in equilibrium?
(d)   Using your knowledge of the model, confirm that each equilibrium condition is
       consistent with the others.
(e)   Solve for equilibrium income. Calculate equilibrium income.
(f)   Graph equations (3) and (4) in the following diagram.

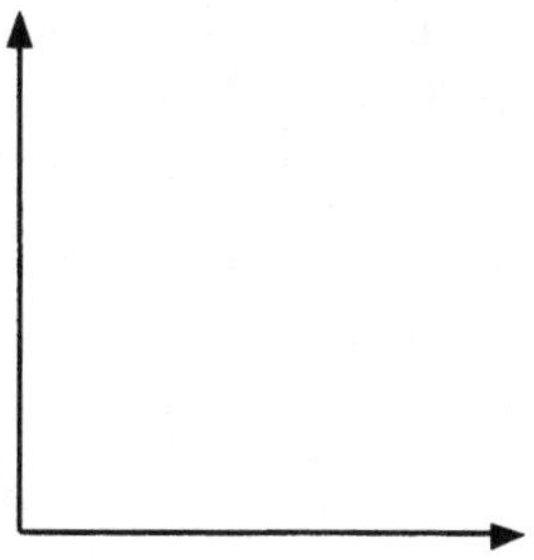

(g)   If GDP were 1,200, unplanned inventory accumulation would be how much?

(h)   If GDP were 2,200, unplanned inventory accumulation would be how much?

(i)   Based on these results, make up a rule relating the direction of unplanned inventory change, the 45° line, and the expenditure function.

(j)   How much saving will occur if GDP is 1,200?

(k)   How much saving will occur if GDP is 2,200?

(l)   Calculate the value of the multiplier.

When the economy is at the natural rate of unemployment, the output level is 2,800.

(m)   How much would investment have to change to create full employment?

The economy is at its original equilibrium income level. Now, because of a surge in consumer optimism, consumption increases by 100 at each income level.

(n)   Inventories are changing by how much? Are they rising or falling?

(o)   Calculate the new equilibrium income level.

(p)   Calculate the new equilibrium consumption level.

(q)   Calculate the new equilibrium saving level.

(r)   Calculate the new equilibrium investment level.

(s)   Explain the result that has emerged regarding the net amount of change in the level of saving.

2.   Most of the ideas associated with the consumption function are quite intuitive. Try to prove to yourself that the theory reflects common sense. The following questions cover many of the main points about consumption and saving that are dealt with in this chapter.

(a)   Suppose you have received a $100 per week wage increase (after tax). Would you spend:

(i)   All of the extra $100?

(ii)   Some of the extra $100?

(iii)   None of the extra $100?

(b)   Would you save:

(i)   All of the extra $100?

(ii)   Some of the extra $100?

(iii)   None of the extra $100?

(c)   The level of disposable income affects the amount spent and saved. Do you agree or disagree with the following statements?

(i)   Other things, as well as income, affect how much I spend and save.

(ii)   If I increase my personal consumption expenditures, I will have less available to save.

(iii)   If I had no current income, I'd still try to buy food and other necessities.

(iv)   Poor households spend a bigger proportion of their income than rich households do.

(d)   Given my income level, if I increase my personal spending by $1, my saving will _____ (increase/decrease) by _____ (more than/less than/exactly) a dollar.

In most other cases you should find yourself agreeing with the textbook's theory of consumption and saving.

3.   Ask (or pretend to ask) five persons the following question:

> "You are a typical consumer with an after-tax income of $100 per week. How much of your income will you set aside as saving?"

Now ask yourself (the owner of a small business):

> How much of your expected value of production (which you forecast to be $500 per week) will you plan to plow back into the firm? (Remember you have employees and other bills to pay!)

Enter the results of the two questions in the following table.

Saving	Investment

There's no single "right" answer—it depends on preferences, wealth, and so on. It's unlikely saving and planned investment will be equal. Suppose saving totals $15 and planned investment equals $20.

(a)   Which is greater: $C + I$ or $C + S$?
(b)   Which is greater: planned aggregate expenditure or aggregate output?
(c)   Will firms be able to meet the planned demand for output, given their current level of production?
(d)   What will happen?
(e)   Write the formula for actual investment.
(f)   Calculate actual investment.

So actual investment is forced to the saving level!

4.   "Investment is equal to 100. Consumption is equal to income. *MPC* equals 0.9."
(a)   Saving is equal to _____ .
(b)   "Currently, the marginal propensity to save equals zero." (True/False)
(c)   Currently, the economy _____ (is/is not) in equilibrium. Aggregate expenditure is _____ (greater than/less than) aggregate output.
(d)   Calculate the value of the multiplier.
(e)   Unplanned inventory change is _____ (positive/negative).
(f)   To establish equilibrium, output level will have to _____ (rise/fall) by _____ , in which case consumption will _____ (rise/fall) by _____ and saving will _____ (rise/fall) by _____ .

Now suppose that the income level (where consumption equals income) is 1,000.

(g)   When income equals zero, consumption will equal _____ and saving will equal _____ .
(h)   Calculate the formula for the consumption function.

(i)   Algebraically, confirm your results from (f) above, and calculate the equilibrium income level.

(j)   Sketch the saving-investment diagram, showing the slope of the saving function, the present income level (1,000) and the equilibrium income level.

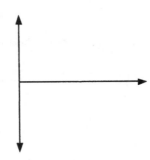

5.   (a)   Fill in the blanks in the following table, based on the model given in the text.

Income	Consumption	Saving	Investment	Expenditures
0				
100	180			
200	260			
300			20	
400				
500				
600				
700				

$MPC =$ _____ $MPS =$ _____   multiplier = _____

(b)   The equilibrium output level is _____ .

(c)   Algebraically, determine the consumption function.

(d)   Confirm your answer to (b) algebraically.

(e)   When income level is 300, there will be unplanned inventory _____ (accumulation/decumulation) while, at an income level of 700, inventories will unexpectedly _____ (increase/decrease).

(f)   Graph the AE function on the following 45° line diagram. Show the income range in which inventories will be rising unexpectedly and the income range in which they will be falling.

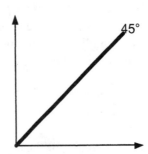

(g)   If investment increases by 50, by how much would equilibrium output level increase?

(h)   Consumption and saving would increase by _____ and _____ respectively.

(i)   The final value of saving would be _____ and investment would be _____ .

(j)   Confirm your results for (g), (h), and (i) algebraically.

(k)   The economy's equilibrium income level is 850. Suppose that 1,000 is the level of production that would provide full employment. How much more would investment have to rise in order to achieve full employment? _____

6.   Suppose that the consumption function does *not* graph as a straight line, but rather increases at a decreasing rate (flattening off). Given your knowledge of the relationships between consumption, saving, and income, could you now draw the saving function? What sort of slope would it have? What would be happening to the value of the multiplier as income level increased?

7.   We have modeled investment as remaining constant as output level increases. Suppose, more realistically, that investment increases as income level rises. What would happen to the slope of the *AE* curve? What would happen to the value of the multiplier?

PRACTICE TEST SOLUTIONS

I.   Solutions to Multiple-Choice Questions

1.   (c)   Refer to p. 143 [455] for the definition.

2.   (a)   The multiplier formula is $1/(1 - MPC)$. Refer to p. 153 [465].

3.   (c)   Equilibrium occurs where income equals consumption plus investment, at 6,000. In equilibrium, $S = I$, so saving must equal 1,000. Alternatively, when income is 6,000 and consumption is 5,000, saving must be 1,000.

4.   (b)   When the income level changes by 1,000 (from 3,000 to 4,000, for example), consumption increases by 800 (from 2,600 to 3,400). The additional 200 is saved. $MPS =$ change in saving/change in income $= \Delta S/\Delta Y = 200/1,000 = 0.2$. The multiplier $= 1/MPS = 1/0.2 = 5$.

5.   (b)   If saving rises by 100, consumption must fall initially by 100, given the income level. The multiplier is 5. The final change in equilibrium income is 500 (i.e., 100 × 5). If income falls by 500 and the *MPC* is 0.8, consumption will fall by an additional 400. The total decrease in consumption is 500.

6.   (d)   In the equation, "*bY*" is the portion of consumption that responds to changes in income. When income is zero, consumption is 100.

7.   (c)   When the income level changes by 100 (from 200 to 300, for example), consumption increases by 80 (from 180 to 260). $MPC =$ change in consumption/change in income $= \Delta C/\Delta Y = 80/100 = 0.8$.

8.   (a)   If expenditure increases, then equilibrium income will increase. The multiplier is 5 because MPC is 0.8. The multiplier equals $1/(1 - MPC)$. Income, then, will increase by 500 (i.e., 100×5).

9.   (c)   Because the demand for goods has risen, inventory levels will be drawn down.

10.   (c) MPS is the slope of the saving function. A decrease in MPS requires an increase in MPC. An increase in MPC will cause the slope of the consumption function to become steeper.

11.   (b)   If income increases by 100, our theory assumes that we consume some quantity less than 100 and save some positive quantity.

12.   (d)   Investment is a part of aggregate expenditure. A decrease in investment will decrease AE, shifting the line downward. In equilibrium, $S = I$. If investment falls, saving must fall too.

13.   (b)   In equilibrium, $Y = C + I$. Refer to p. 148 [460].

14.   (d)   If aggregate output is less than planned aggregate expenditure, then demand is high. Inventory levels will be falling. Because spending is high, saving is low and will be less than planned investment.

15.   (c)   *Savings* is the accumulation of saving from past periods; it is a stock, while saving is a process (a flow). Saving *always* equals actual investment. When the interest rate falls, saving decreases and consumption increases.

16.   (a)   The slope of the consumption function is irrelevant in this question. Consumption is positive even when income is zero because it is necessary to buy food, housing, and other staples of life. Without income, this is financed by "dissaving."

17.   (c)   When future prospects are less clear, households tend to hold back on purchases, saving more of their current income.

18.   (a)   Firms choose output levels and set up investment programs, but their inventory levels are affected by sales which are dependent on the whims of their customers.

19.   (d)   An increase in income will not shift the consumption function—there will be a movement along it. If MPC is 0.6, MPS is 0.1. A \$100 increase in income will generate a \$10 increase (\$100 $\times$ 0.1) in saving.

20.   (c)   Equilibrium income level is 1,000 and planned investment is 100. In equilibrium, consumption must be 900 and saving must be 100. If income falls by 200, consumption falls by 180 (200×0.9) and saving falls by 20 (200×0.1). Saving will be 80.

21.   (b)   The intercept term (a) is 100 because income is zero and $C + S$ must equal this. As income increases from zero to 1,000, saving increases from −100 to 0, an increase

of 100. MPS = change in saving/change in income = $\Delta S/\Delta Y$ = 100/1,000 = 0.1. MPC = 1 − MPS.

22.　(d)　The multiplier equals $1/(1 - MPC)$.

23.　(c)　In equilibrium, saving must equal investment and, therefore, must equal 200. For saving to increase by 300 (from −100 to 200), income must increase by 3,000 (from zero) if MPS is 0.1.

24.　(c)　Expenditure decreases by 50. The multiplier is 10. Equilibrium output will decrease by 500 (50 × 10). Because MPC is 0.9, consumption will decrease by 450 (500 × 0.9). Saving will fall by 50 (500 × MPS), causing saving to be 150 and to be equal to investment.

25.　(c)　$S = Y - C = Y - (100 + 0.9Y) = -100 + 0.1Y$.

II.　*Solutions to Application Questions*

1.　(a)　MPC = 0.75. Equation 1 tells us that, as income (Y) increases by 100, consumption increases by 75. MPS = 0.25. Recall that $MPC + MPS = 1$. Alternatively, as income (Y) increases by 100 and consumption increases by 75, the remaining 25 must be saved.

　　(b)　$S = -300 + 0.25Y$.

　　(c)　The equilibrium conditions are:

Planned aggregate expenditure	=	aggregate output (income)	(1)
$C + S$	=	$C + I$	
PLANNED SAVING	=	PLANNED INVESTMENT	(2)
S	=	I	
Planned investment	=	actual investment	(3)
Unplanned inventory change	=	0	(4)

　　(d)　If, in equilibrium, equation (1) holds, then (2) must also hold because AE is defined as consumption plus investment and Y is defined as consumption plus saving. Similarly, canceling the "consumptions," we can derive (3).

　　　　We know that actual investment always equals planned investment plus unplanned inventory change. In equilibrium, unplanned inventory change is zero (5), therefore equation (4) is consistent. If actual investment equals planned investment plus zero, then actual investment equals planned investment.

　　(e)　$Y = C + I$ (in equilibrium)

$$Y = 300 + 0.75Y + 200 = 500 + 0.75Y$$
$$Y - 0.75Y = 500$$
$$0.25Y = 500$$
$$Y = 2,000$$

(f)   Refer to the diagram following.

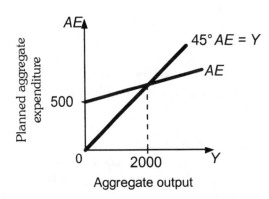

(g)   200 decrease in inventories. Demand (1,400) exceeds production (1,200).

(h)   50 increase in inventories. Production (2,200) exceeds demand (2,150).

(i)   At income levels where the *AE* line is above the 45° line, unplanned inventory change will be negative (e.g., when $Y = 1,200$); at income levels where the *AE* line is below the 45° line, unplanned inventory change will be positive (e.g., when $Y = 2,200$).

(j) $C = 300 + 0.75Y$. $Y = 1,200$. $C = 300 + 0.75(1,200) = 1,200$. $S = Y - C = 0$.

(k) $C = 300 + 0.75Y$. $Y = 2,200$. $C = 300 + 0.75(2,200) = 1,950$. $S = Y - C = 250$.

(l)   An autonomous 100-unit increase in expenditure causes a 400 increase in equilibrium income. The multiplier is 4.00.

Check: Multiplier $= 1/(1 - MPC) = 1/0.25 = 4.00$

(m) $\Delta Y = m \times \Delta I$. $m = 4$ and $\Delta Y = 800$, therefore $\Delta I = 200$.

(n)   Inventories are falling by 100 as producers use previously produced output to meet the unexpected demand.

(o) $Y = C + I$ (in equilibrium)

$$
\begin{aligned}
Y &= 400 + 0.75Y + 200 = 600 + 0.75Y \\
Y - 0.75Y &= 600 \\
0.25Y &= 600 \\
Y &= 2,400
\end{aligned}
$$

(p)   When $Y = 2,400$, $C = 400 + 0.75(2,400) = 2,200$

(q)   When $Y = 2,400$, $S = -400 + 0.25(2,400) = 200$

Check: $Y = C + S$; $2,400 = 2,200 + 200$

(r) I is unchanged at 200. Note that, in equilibrium, $S = I$.

(s)   Saving has remained unchanged. In equilibrium, $S = I$, and I has remained unchanged.

2.   (a)   some (probably most, in fact)

(b)   some

If you answered "all" for (i) you should have answered "none" for (ii). Such answers indicate you're not "typical"—most folks try to set some saving aside. Groups who don't are the young (who may have high initial expenses and low incomes) and the retired (who don't earn much).

(c)   You probably "agree" with all of these statements.

The "other things" in (i) and the logic behind (iv) will be developed in Chapter 12 (27).

(d)   If I increase my personal spending by $1, my saving will *decrease* by *exactly* $1.

If you missed this one, reread the first few pages of the chapter!

3. (a) $C + I$ exceeds $C + S$ because I exceeds S.
    (b) aggregate expenditure
    (c) No
    (d) Firms will have to reduce their inventories unexpectedly.
    (e) Actual investment = planned investment + unplanned inventory change.
    (f) $15 = 20 + -5$.

4. (a) Zero. If consumption equals income, no income can be saved.
    (b) False. Because MPC equals 0.9, we can say that MPS equals 0.1.
    (c) is not; greater than.
    (d) 10. Multiplier = $1/(1 - MPC) = 1/0.1 = 10$.
    (e) negative. Planned aggregate expenditure exceeds aggregate output.
    (f) rise; 1,000; rise; 900; rise; 100. The "gap" between planned aggregate expenditure and aggregate output is 100. The multiplier is 10. Equilibrium income will fall by 1,000. MPC is 0.9. Given the increase in income, consumption will increase by $1,000 \times 0.9$. MPS is 0.1. Given the increase in income, saving will increase by $1,000 \times 0.1$.
    (g) 100; –100. If income changes from zero to 1,000, consumption increases by 900 to 1,000 (because MPC is 0.9). We know, therefore, that consumption is (1,000 – 900) when income level is zero. Because income equals consumption plus saving, saving must equal –100.
    (h) $C = 100 + 0.9Y$.
    (i)
$$Y = C + I$$
$$= 100 + .9Y + 100$$
$$= 200 + .9Y$$
$$Y - .9Y = 200$$
$$.1Y = 200$$
$$Y = 2,000$$

    (j) Refer to the diagram following.

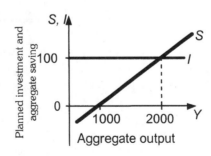

5.　　(a)　Refer to the following table. When income rises by 100 (from 100 to 200), consumption rises by 80 (from 180 to 260). *MPC*, therefore, is 0.8. *MPC* + *MPS* = 1, therefore *MPS* = 0.2. Given *MPC*, the consumption column can be filled in. Given income and consumption, saving can be derived by subtraction. Investment is assumed to be constant at 20. The expenditure column is derived by adding consumption and investment.

Income	Consumption	Saving	Investment	Expenditures
0	100	−100	20	120
100	180	−80	20	200
200	260	−60	20	280
300	340	−40	20	360
400	420	−20	20	440
500	500	0	20	520
600	580	20	20	600
700	660	40	20	680

$$MPC = 0.8 \qquad MPS = 0.2 \qquad \text{multiplier} = 5$$

　　(b)　600. Equilibrium occurs where planned expenditure equals income (and where saving equals investment).

　　(c)　$C = 100 + 0.8Y$

　　(d)　$Y = 100 + .8Y + 20$

$$.2Y = 120$$

$$Y = 600$$

　　(e)　decumulation; increase

　　(f)　Refer to the following diagram.

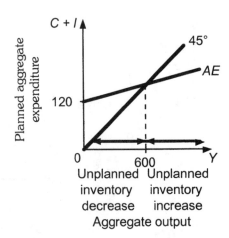

(g)   250. The multiplier is 5.

(h)   200; 50. Consumption increases by $0.8 \times \Delta Y$. Saving increases by $0.2 \times \Delta Y$.

(i)   70; 70. In equilibrium these two values must be equal.

$Y = 100 + 0.8Y + 70$

(j) $0.2Y = 170$

$Y = 850$

$C = 100 + 0.8Y$

$\quad = 100 + 0.8(850) = 780$

At $Y = 600$, C was 580 (Refer to the preceding table.)

$S = Y - C = 850 - 780 = 70$.

At $Y = 600$, S was 20 (Refer to the preceding table.)

(k)   30. The economy's equilibrium income level is 850, 150 short of the goal. The multiplier is 5, so an autonomous 30-unit increase, multiplied by 5, will hit the target.

6.   The slope of the consumption function is *MPC* and the slope of the saving function is *MPS*. We know that *MPC* + *MPS* equals one. *MPC* decreases as the slope of the consumption function becomes flatter, so *MPS* must increase and the slope of the saving function must become progressively steeper. The value of the multiplier is given by the formula: 1/*MPS*. As *MPS* increases, the size of the multiplier will decrease as income level increases. In fact, the effect of this weakened multiplier can be shown graphically. The same vertical increase in aggregate spending will push the economy's equilibrium income level less far when the slope of the *AE* curve is decreasing.

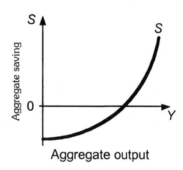

7.   The *AE* function is the total of the consumption function and the investment function. In the original model, the slope of *AE* is determined solely by the slope of the consumption function—i.e., *MPC*. However, the slope of the *AE* curve is properly interpreted as the change in spending (from both sources) that occurs as income changes. If investment also increases, as income increases, the *AE* curve will become steeper. The value of the multiplier will increase too; in the more complex model we'll be developing in later chapters, the multiplier formulas we have devised are incomplete. In fact, the effect of this strengthened multiplier can be shown graphically. The same vertical increase in aggregate spending will push the economy's equilibrium income level farther as the *AE* curve becomes steeper.

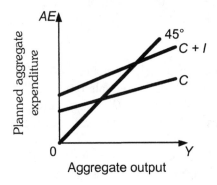

9 [24]

The Government and Fiscal Policy

$\mathbf{C}$hapter objectives:

1. Identify the tools of fiscal policy.
2. Describe how the inclusion of the government sector affects the aggregate expenditure model.
3. Derive and explain the difference between the government spending multiplier and the tax multiplier. Explain how the balanced-budget multiplier result occurs.
4. Analyze the effects on output and unemployment of a change in government spending and/or a change in taxes.
5. Define the deficit (surplus) and explain how it relates to and differs from the federal debt. Describe how the federal government's expenditures and revenues move with the economy. Distinguish between and explain the effects of fiscal drag and automatic stabilizers.
6. Define the full-employment budget, the structural deficit, and the cyclical deficit.
7. Explain how the incorporation of tax rates will influence the spending multiplier.

The basic logic in this chapter is the same as in Chapter 8 (23). Even the Appendices contain little that is very new. If you're confused in this chapter, it's a sure sign that you need to go back *now* and work on Chapter 8 (23) some more.

BRAIN TEASER: In our current model, we assume that net taxes are lump-sum, that is, that they don't change as the level of economic activity changes. However, automatic stabilizers (such as the federal income tax system) do, in fact, change with the level of economic activity. How do automatic stabilizers affect the size of the expenditure multiplier and why?

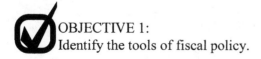
OBJECTIVE 1:
Identify the tools of fiscal policy.

Fiscal policy has three basic tools: government purchases (G), taxation, and transfer payments. To simplify matters, our model uses *lump-sum taxes* (which are not related to income). Collectively, taxes and transfers are termed net taxes (T). For simplification, the text (except in Appendix 9B (24B)) assumes that net taxes are unrelated to income. (page 159 [471])

————————◼—————————— **Practice** ——————————

1.   Each of the following might be a specific fiscal policy action EXCEPT
      (a)   reducing interest rates to stimulate consumer demand.
      (b)   increasing government spending on military hardware.
      (c)   easing the eligibility requirements for welfare recipients.
      (d)   imposing a national sales tax.

      ANSWER: (a)   Interest rate changes come under the category of monetary policy. ◼

OBJECTIVE 2:
Describe how the inclusion of the government sector affects the aggregate expenditure model.

When the government sector is added to the aggregate expenditure model, government spending is included in aggregate expenditure alongside consumption and investment. Consumption and saving are based on disposable (after-tax) personal income and the equilibrium condition is:

$$Y = C + I + G$$

or

$$S + T = I + G \quad \text{(page 161 [473])}$$

Increasing government spending or reducing net taxes increases aggregate expenditure and the equilibrium level of production.
      Note: When taxes are "lump-sum," the marginal propensity to consume is not affected. If a tax rate is included in the model, as in Appendix B of this chapter, the *MPC* value must be modified.

————————◼—————————— **Practice** ——————————

2.   Disposable income is total income
      (a)   plus transfer payments.
      (b)   plus net taxes.
      (c)   minus net taxes.
      (d)   minus taxes.

      ANSWER: (c)   Be careful with the concept of net taxes. This term includes taxes and transfer payments. Refer to p. 160 [472].

3.   When taxes are lump-sum, tax revenues _____ as income increases.
      (a)   will increase
      (b)   will decrease
      (c)   may either increase or decrease depending on the tax rate
      (d)   will not change

      ANSWER: (d)   Lump-sum taxes are not related to income. Refer to p. 160 [472].

4.   When taxes are lump-sum, disposable income _____ as income increases by $100.
      (a)   will increase by $100
      (b)   will increase, but by less than $100
      (c)   may increase but by how much depends on the tax rate
      (d)   will not change

      ANSWER: (a) If taxes are lump-sum, no additional taxes will be collected from the additional
               income. All of the additional income will be disposable income.

5.   When the government sector is added to the model, the consumption function formula is
      (a) $C = a + b(Y + T)$.
      (b) $C = a + b(Y - T)$.
      (c) $C = a - b(Y + T)$.
      (d) $C = a - b(Y - T)$.

      ANSWER: (b) Refer to p. 162 [474]. $(Y - T)$ is disposable income.

6.   When the government sector is added to the model, it must be true that in equilibrium
      (a) $G = T$.
      (b) $S = I$.
      (c) $S + I = G + T$.
      (d) $S + T = I + G$.

      ANSWER: (d) Saving and net taxes are drains on spending (i.e., leakages). Investment and
               government spending add to spending. In equilibrium, the two forces are equal.
               Note that "$S = I$" is no longer an equilibrium condition in this expanded model.
               Refer to p. 164 [476].

Use the following table to answer the next four questions. The abbreviations are those used in the
textbook.

Y	T	Y_d	C	S	I	G	AE
1,000	200	_____	1,060	_____	340	400	1,800
2,000	200	_____	1,860	_____	340	_____	_____
3,000	200	_____	2,660	_____	_____	_____	_____
4,000	_____	_____	_____	_____	_____	_____	_____
5,000	_____	_____	_____	_____	_____	_____	_____
6,000	_____	5,800	5,060	_____	340	400	5,800

7.   Complete the table.
      ANSWER: Refer to the following table.

Y	T	Y_d	C	S	I	G	AE
1,000	200	800	1,060	−260	340	400	1,800
2,000	200	1,800	1,860	−60	340	400	2,600
3,000	200	2,800	2,660	140	340	400	3,400
4,000	200	3,800	3,460	340	340	400	4,200
5,000	200	4,800	4,260	540	340	400	5,000
6,000	200	5,800	5,060	740	340	400	5,800

8.   The marginal propensity to consume is

(a)   0.6.

(b)   0.75.

(c)   0.8.

(d)   0.85.

ANSWER: (c)   As disposable income changes by 1,000 (e.g., from 1,800 to 2,800), consumption changes by 800 (from 1,860 to 2,660).

9.   Equilibrium income level is

(a)   3,000.

(b)   4,000.

(c)   5,000.

(d)   6,000.

ANSWER: (c)   This is where $AE = Y$, and where $S + T = I + G = 740$.

10.   In equilibrium, the government has a

(a)   deficit of 200.

(b)   deficit of 240.

(c)   surplus of 200.

(d)   surplus of 240.

ANSWER: (a)   The government's deficit is 200 because net tax revenues (T) are 200 and government expenditure (G) is 400. ∎

OBJECTIVE 3:
Derive and explain the difference between the government spending multiplier and the tax multiplier. Explain how the balanced-budget multiplier result occurs.

The *government spending multiplier* is identical to the expenditure multiplier developed in the previous chapter—if *MPC* is 0.75, a one dollar increase in government spending will cause the equilibrium income level to expand by $4. The multiplier is 4. The formula is 1/*MPS*. (page 164 [476])

The *tax multiplier* is absolutely smaller than the government spending multiplier because, with a tax cut, not all of the resulting increase in disposable income will be spent—some will leak away into saving. The tax multiplier is always negative—an *increase* in taxes will *decrease* in production. If *MPC* is 0.75, a one dollar increase in tax collections will cause the equilibrium income level to decrease by $3. The tax multiplier is –3. The formula is –*MPC/MPS*. (page 167 [479])

The value of the *balanced-budget multiplier* is *always* equal to one in our model. An equal increase in government spending and net taxes will have a dollar-for-dollar expansionary effect on equilibrium income. The formula is *MPS/MPS*. (page 168 [480])

▶▶▶   LEARNING TIP: In our model, with lump-sum taxes, the (government) spending multiplier and the tax multiplier have a simple numerical relationship. Here are a few common values.

MPC	MPS	Spending Multiplier	Tax Multiplier
0.50	0.50	2.0	–1.0
0.60	0.40	2.5	–1.5
0.75	0.25	4.0	–3.0
0.80	0.20	5.0	–4.0
0.90	0.10	10.0	–9.0

Given *MPC* or *MPS*, if you can work out the regular multiplier, subtract one to get the (negative) tax multiplier. If the spending multiplier is 3, then the tax multiplier is –2. Confirm these results using the tax multiplier formula. ◀

———————————————————————————— **Practice** ————————————————————————————

Use the table you completed for Practice Question 7 to answer the next question.

11.   In the table, the government spending multiplier is _____ and the tax multiplier is _____ .
        (a)   4; –3
        (b)   4; 3
        (c)   5; –4
        (d)   5; 4

        ANSWER: (c) As disposable income changes by 1,000 (e.g., from 1,700 to 2,700), saving
                changes by 200 (from –60 to 140). *MPS* is 0.2. The formula for the government
                spending multiplier is 1/*MPS*, and the formula for the tax multiplier is –
                MPC/MPS.

12.   In the nation of Arbez, which has a government sector, an increase in investment spending of 100
        will cause equilibrium income level to increase by 1,000. The government spending multiplier is
        _____ and the tax multiplier is _____ .
        (a)   5; –5
        (b)   5; –4
        (c)   10; –10
        (d)   10; –9

        ANSWER: (d) If an increase in investment can be "multiplied" tenfold, then the multiplier must
                be 10. If so, *MPC* is 0.9 and *MPS* is 0.1. Note that, with taxes that do not depend
                on income, the *MPC* formulas in Chapter 8 (23) and Chapter 9 (24) are
                equivalent. The formula for the government spending multiplier is 1/*MPS*, so, in
                this case, the multiplier is 10. The formula for the tax multiplier is –*MPC/MPS*;
                the tax multiplier in this case is –9 (–0.9/0.1). ∎

OBJECTIVE 4:
Analyze the effects on output and unemployment of a change in government spending and/or a
change in taxes.

An increase (decrease) in government spending will increase (decrease) planned aggregate expenditure,
dollar for dollar. A decrease (increase) in net taxes will also increase (decrease) planned aggregate
expenditure—but *not* dollar for dollar. The impacts of the two policy actions are different—the "tax
multiplier" is smaller. (page 164 [476])

        In a Congressional "deficit reduction" debate, Republicans called for substantial reductions in
government spending programs. Democrats favored hiking taxes. The Republican option would have had
the more powerful (negative) economic effect because the government spending multiplier is more
powerful.

        Caution: When working out the effects of policy actions, make sure the result looks sensible. It's
easy to forget a negative sign or mess up the arithmetic. Have confidence in your intuition. If your results
don't look right, they probably aren't!

━━━━━━━━━━━━━━━━━━━━━━━━━━━━ **Practice** ━━━━━━━━━━━━━━━━━━━━━━━━━━━━

Use the table you completed for Practice Question 7 to answer the next four questions.

13.   The equilibrium income level would be 6,000 if government spending
   (a)   increased by 200.
   (b)   increased by 1,000.
   (c)   decreased by 200.
   (d)   decreased by 1,000.

   ANSWER: (a)   The multiplier is 5. The increase in equilibrium income
         $(\Delta Y) = 1,000 = \Delta G \times 1/MPS = 200 \times 5$. Refer to p. 165 [477].

14.   The equilibrium income level would be 4,000 if net taxes
   (a)   increased by 200.
   (b)   increased by 250.
   (c)   decreased by 200.
   (d)   decreased by 250.

   ANSWER: (b)   The tax multiplier is –4. Decrease in equilibrium income
         $(\Delta Y) = 1,000 = \Delta T \times -MPC/MPS = 250 \times -4$. Refer to p. 165 [477].

15.   If government purchases increased by 100 and taxes decreased by 100, equilibrium income level
   would
   (a)   increase by 100.
   (b)   increase by 900.
   (c)   decrease by 100.
   (d)   not change.

   ANSWER: (b)   Split this question into two parts—the effect of the spending change and the
         effect of the tax change.
   Spending change: $\Delta Y = \Delta G \times 1/MPS = 100 \times 5 = +500$.
   Tax change: $\Delta Y = \Delta T \times (-MPC/MPS) = -100 \times -4 = +400$.

16.   If government purchases decreased by 100 and taxes decreased by 100, equilibrium income level
   would
   (a)   increase by 100.
   (b)   decrease by 900.
   (c)   decrease by 100.
   (d)   not change.

   ANSWER: (c)   This is a "balanced-budget" change (i.e., $\Delta G = \Delta T$).

Refer to the following diagram to answer the next five questions.

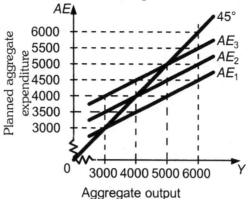

17.   If expenditures are as shown by AE_2, the equilibrium income level is
       (a)   3,000.
       (b)   4,000.
       (c)   5,000.
       (d)   6,000.

       ANSWER: (b) AE_2 crosses the 45° line at this income level.

18.   Given AE_2, if the income level is at 3,000, we know that
       (a)   government spending is greater than net taxes.
       (b)   government spending is less than net taxes.
       (c)   unplanned inventory investment is positive.
       (d)   unplanned inventory investment is negative.

       ANSWER: (d) Expenditure exceeds production; inventory level will be decreasing.

19.   The government spending multiplier is _____ and the tax multiplier is _____ .
       (a)   2; –1
       (b)   2; –3
       (c)   4; –3
       (d)   4; –5

       ANSWER: (a) As income level rises by 1,000 (from 3,000 to 4,000), planned expenditure rises
                    by 500 (from 3,500 to 4,000). MPC is 0.5 and MPS is 0.5.

20.   To shift the AE curve from AE_2 to AE_3, we could
       (a)   increase government spending by 500.
       (b)   increase government spending by 1,000.
       (c)   increase net taxes by 500.
       (d)   increase net taxes by 1,000.

       ANSWER: (a) Increasing taxes will reduce aggregate expenditure—consumers would have less
                    after-tax income to spend. Increasing government spending by 500 will work.
                    Note that the vertical distance between AE_2 and AE_3 is 500.

21.   Given AE_2, each of the following policies except _____ would reduce the equilibrium output level to 3,000.

   (a)   decreasing government spending by 1,000 and decreasing taxes by 1,000
   (b)   decreasing government spending by 1,000
   (c)   increasing government spending by 500 and increasing taxes by 2,000
   (d)   increasing taxes by 1,000

   ANSWER: (b) The government spending multiplier is 2. $\Delta G \times 1/MPS = -1,000 \times 2 = 2,000$. Option (a) is the balanced-budget case. Option (c) is quite complex but works as follows:

   Government spending change = $\Delta G \times 1/MPS = 500 \times 2 = 1,000$.
   Tax change = $\Delta T \times -MPC/MPS = 2,000 \times -1 = -2,000$.

22.   Given AE_3, when income is 4,000,

   (a)   injections exceed leakages by 500.
   (b)   injections exceed leakages by 1,000.
   (c)   leakages exceed injections by 500.
   (d)   leakages exceed injections by 1,000.

   ANSWER: (a) Demand exceeds production. ∎

OBJECTIVE 5:

Define the deficit (surplus) and explain how it relates to and differs from the federal debt. Describe how the federal government's expenditures and revenues move with the economy. Distinguish between and explain the effects of fiscal drag and automatic stabilizers.

This year's *deficit* (or surplus) is the difference between government receipts this year and outlays this year, i.e., $G - T$. If receipts are less than outlays there is a deficit. The *federal debt* is the total amount owed by the federal government to the public (because of this year's deficit, if any, and those of previous years). A surplus reduces the size of the debt. (page 169 [481])

   The major sources of government income are personal and corporate income taxes and social security contributions; the major types of expenditures are transfer payments, government consumption expenditures, and grants-in-aid to state and local governments. As a percentage of GDP, transfers and consumption expenditures generally declined during the years of the Clinton Administration and increased during the years of the Bush Administration. Similarly, the deficit was steadily transformed into a surplus during the Clinton Administration through increasing tax rates and declining expenditures; the trend was reversed during the Bush Administration because of cut in the average tax rate and ongoing war-related expenses.

   Automatic stabilizers (revenue or expenditure items in the federal budget that adjust in magnitude as the level of economic activity changes) reduce the change in GDP as the economy moves through the business cycle. During a recession, for instance, when incomes are low, transfer payments increase and partly replace the lost income—spending doesn't fall as much as it otherwise would have. Tax liabilities decrease, too, in such a situation. Automatic stabilizers reduce the severity of fluctuations in the business cycle. (page 175 [487])

   Fiscal drag occurs because, as the economy expands, incomes rise, pushing taxpayers into higher tax brackets and increasing the average tax rate. Out of each dollar, less is available to spend or save than otherwise would have been the case. The tax structure slows the rate of economic expansion. (page 175 [489])

———■————————————————— Practice ————————————————————

23.   During the last ten years, the Arbocali federal budget deficit expanded sharply. Which of the following is not a likely cause of this expansion?
        (a)   Government spending (as a percentage of GDP) rose during the last ten years.
        (b)   Interest payments on the Arbocali federal debt (as a percentage of GDP) rose during the last ten years.
        (c)   Personal income tax rates were reduced eight years ago.
        (d)   Transfer payments (as a percentage of GDP) fell during the last ten years.
        ANSWER: (d)   A reduction in transfer payments reduces the size of the deficit.

24.   In general, the average tax rate _____ during the Clinton Administration and _____ during the Bush Administration.
        (a)   increased; increased
        (b)   increased; decreased
        (c)   decreased; increased
        (d)   decreased; decreased
        ANSWER: (b)   Refer to p. 171 [483] for details.

25.   In general, as a percentage of GDP, government consumption expenditures _____ during the Clinton Administration and _____ during the Bush Administration.
        (a)   increased; increased
        (b)   increased; decreased
        (c)   decreased; increased
        (d)   decreased; decreased
        ANSWER: (c)   Refer to Figure 9.5 (22.5) for details.

26.   Automatic stabilizers make the federal deficit _____ during recessions and _____ during expansions.
        (a)   larger; larger
        (b)   larger; smaller
        (c)   smaller; larger
        (d)   smaller; smaller
        ANSWER: (b)   Refer to p. 175 [487] to review the effects of automatic stabilizers. ■

OBJECTIVE 6:
Define the full-employment budget, the structural deficit, and the cyclical deficit.

Some components of the government's budget depend on the state of the economy and beyond the government's direct control. A recession will reduce tax revenues and increase transfer payments. Inflation may drive up the expense of government purchases and, if interest rates increase, the cost of servicing the debt will increase. The *full-employment budget* calculates what the deficit would be, given the structure of current spending and tax programs, if the economy were at full employment. At full employment, the effects on the deficit of cyclical changes should be zero—any remaining deficit is called the *structural deficit*. The *cyclical deficit* is that part of the actual deficit that is caused by cyclical unemployment. At full employment, the actual deficit might be $50 million—this is the structural deficit. If, however, unemployment is currently running at 8%, this indicates the presence of some cyclical unemployment. The deficit is $200 million. The cyclical deficit is $150 million ($200 million – $50 million). (page 175 [487])

ECONOMICS IN PRACTICE: On page 174 [486], the textbook describes the fiscal stimulus package passed by Congress and signed by President Bush in 2008 as a response to an economic slowdown that many feared would precede a recession. At the beginning of the Great Depression, the Hoover Administration chose a different path, adopting a "balanced budget" policy that attempted to equalize government outlays and receipts. What impact would this policy have had on the intensity of the Great Depression?

ANSWER: At the outset of the Depression, workers lost their jobs and profits declined, leading to a decrease in government receipts. Given the "balanced budget" policy and the prevailing "classical" school of thought, the Hoover Administration decided against using active fiscal policy to stimulate the economy. In fact, even in 1932, President Hoover was requesting broader taxes and a drastic reduction in government expenditures because "nothing is more necessary at this time than balancing the budget." The consensus of modern economists is that Hoover was mistaken! The balanced-budget policy cost millions of jobs and drove the economy even deeper into the doldrums.

ECONOMICS IN PRACTICE (CONTINUED): During the 1980s, there was a strong movement to "balance the budget" and, in 1995, a balanced-budget amendment to the Constitution was approved by the House of Representatives and failed in the Senate by only one vote. Had Congress forgotten the lessons of President Hoover and the Great Depression? Or had experience taught them caution in the application of the balanced-budget doctrine? Do some research to determine how Congress has approached this issue.

ANSWER: Congress did learn from history when crafting their balanced-budget amendment. Although requiring that the budget be balanced annually, exceptions were allowed during times of war or national emergency. Also, Congress could overrule the provision by voting it down. Presumably, the threat of a severe recession would foster such a vote. Balanced-budget proposals continue to surface.

———■——————————————————— **Practice** ————————————————————————

27.   Arboc's deficit this year is $300 million. If Arboc were fully employed, the deficit would be $60 million. Arboc's structural deficit is
   (a) $60 million
   (b) $240 million
   (c) $300 million
   (d) $360 million

   ANSWER: (a) The structural deficit is the deficit that remains when the economy is at full employment.

28.   At full employment, the federal deficit would be $20 billion. Last year, unemployment was 6.5% and the deficit was $40 billion. This year, however, unemployment is 7.8% and the deficit is $82 billion. This year, the
   (a)   structural deficit is $42 billion.
   (b)   structural deficit is $62 billion.
   (c)   cyclical deficit is $42 billion.
   (d)   cyclical deficit is $62 billion.

   ANSWER: (d) The structural deficit is $20 billion. The remainder of this year's $82 billion deficit is cyclical. Refer to p. 175 [487]. ■

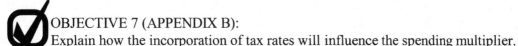

OBJECTIVE 7 (APPENDIX B):
Explain how the incorporation of tax rates will influence the spending multiplier.

When a tax rate is introduced into the model, the formula for the expenditure multiplier must be adjusted—the multiplier's value is reduced (because the leakage of additional spending power is greater than before). Graphically, the consumption function and the *AE* function become flatter. As income increases, consumption still increases, but at a slower rate, because less income is available as disposable income. (page 179 [491])

——■———————————————— **Practice** ————————————————

29.   In Arboc, the income tax rate is 20% and the *MPC* is 0.75. The government spending multiplier is
       (a)   2.5.
       (b)   3.0.
       (c)   3.75.
       (d)   4.0.

       ANSWER: (a)   The multiplier's formula is $1/(1 - b + bt)$, where b is *MPC* and t is the tax rate. In this case, the value is $1/(1 - 0.75 + 0.75(0.2))$, or $1/0.4$, which gives a value of 2.5.

30.   In Arboc, the income tax rate is 20% and the *MPC* is 0.75. The tax multiplier is
       (a)   –1.5.
       (b)   –1.875.
       (c)   –3.75.
       (d)   –2.75.

       ANSWER: (b)   The multiplier's formula is $-b/(1 - b + bt)$, where b is *MPC* and t is the tax rate. In this case, the value is $-0.75/(1 - 0.75 + 0.75(0.2))$, or $-0.75/0.4$, which gives a value of –1.875.

31.   In Arboc, the income tax rate is 20% and the *MPC* is 0.75. An equal increase of 1,000 in government spending and taxes would cause equilibrium income to
       (a)   increase by 625.
       (b)   increase by 1,000.
       (c)   decrease by 625.
       (d)   increase by 1,000.

       ANSWER: (a)   The government spending multiplier is 2.5 and the tax multiplier is –1.875. The balanced-budget multiplier is 0.625 (2.5 – 1.875).

32.   In Arbez, the income tax rate is 50% and the *MPC* is 0.80. To increase equilibrium income by 400, taxes should be
       (a)   increased by 80.
       (b)   increased by 300.
       (c)   decreased by 80.
       (d)   decreased by 300.

       ANSWER: (d)   The tax multiplier's formula is $-b/(1 - b + bt)$, where b is *MPC* and t is the tax rate. In this case, the value is $-0.80/[1 - 0.80 + 0.80(0.50)]$, or $-0.80/0.60$, which gives a value of –1.333. To increase output, taxes should decrease. $\Delta T \times 1.333 = 400$; $\Delta T = -300$. ■

BRAIN TEASER SOLUTION: Automatic stabilizers reduce the size of the expenditure multiplier. Considering the federal income tax system will show how. As the economy begins to expand, individuals move into higher tax brackets and pay a higher proportion of their income in taxes. This chokes off some of the consumption spending that would otherwise be taking place. If the economy is sliding into a recession and income levels are falling, tax liabilities decrease at a more rapid rate than the rate of decrease in income. Therefore, the fall in income is made less severe.

PRACTICE TEST

I.   MULTIPLE-CHOICE QUESTIONS

Select the option that provides the single best answer.

_____   1.   *MPS* is 0.1. If, at each income level, taxes are increased by 100 this will
    (a)   shift the *AE* function up by 100.
    (b)   shift the *AE* function down by 100.
    (c)   shift the *AE* function down by 90.
    (d)   shift the *AE* curve up by 10.

_____   2.   If *MPS* is 0.2, a decrease in government spending of 100 will
    (a)   increase income by 500.
    (b)   increase output by 500.
    (c)   decrease saving by 100.
    (d)   decrease output by 400.

_____   3.   An increase in government spending of 100 causes the level of output to rise by 250. *MPS* is
    (a)   0.25.
    (b)   0.4.
    (c)   0.6.
    (d)   2.5.

_____   4.   The President wants output to increase by 300. Also, he wants the change in the deficit caused by any policy action to be minimized, and government spending to rise by no more than 75. *MPC* is 0.75. Of the following, you would recommend
    (a)   increasing government spending by 75.
    (b)   reducing net taxes by 100.
    (c)   a balanced-budget increase of 300.
    (d)   a balanced-budget increase of 75.

_____   5.   Government spending rises by a dollar. If taxes were _____ , equilibrium production level could remain unchanged.
    (a)   raised by more than a dollar
    (b)   raised by less than a dollar
    (c)   cut by more than a dollar
    (d)   cut by less than a dollar

_____ 6. Saving rises from $150 to $190 as income rises from $600 to $800. The marginal propensity to
(a)   consume is 0.8 and the government spending multiplier is 5.
(b)   save is 0.4 and the government spending multiplier is 2.5.
(c)   save is 0.25 and the balanced-budget multiplier is 1.0.
(d)   save is 0.2 and the tax multiplier is –6.

_____ 7. Automatic stabilizers stabilize
(a)   government tax receipts.
(b)   the government deficit.
(c)   income.
(d)   investment.

_____ 8. The economy is experiencing widespread unemployment. An economist might suggest that the government
(a)   decrease taxes.
(b)   decrease government spending.
(c)   decrease the government deficit.
(d)   increase investment spending.

_____ 9. There is a sharp fall in investment spending. The administration could maintain the economy at its current output level by using any of the following measures except _____ government spending and _____ taxes.
(a)   raising; lowering
(b)   lowering; raising
(c)   raising; raising
(d)   lowering; lowering
        (Be careful with this one! There is only one correct answer.)

_____ 10. _MPC_ = 0.8. The Administration wants to raise output by $100 million. It could achieve that goal by doing any of the following EXCEPT
(a)   simultaneously raising government spending by $40 million and cutting taxes by $50 million.
(b)   cutting taxes by $25 million.
(c)   simultaneously raising government spending by $100 million and raising taxes by $100 million.
(d)   raising government spending by $20 million.

_____ 11. All of the following are true EXCEPT
(a)   during a recession, there is a cyclical deficit.
(b)   during a recession, there will be a structural deficit.
(c)   at full employment, there may be a structural deficit.
(d)   at full employment, there is no cyclical deficit.

_____ 12. A Federal budget deficit occurs when
(a)   Federal tax receipts exceed Federal government expenditures.
(b)   total Federal tax receipts exceed total government debt.
(c)   Federal transfer payments exceed Federal government expenditures.
(d)   Federal government expenditures exceed net Federal tax collections.

Use the following diagram for the next five questions. The economy is in initial equilibrium at an output level of 5,000. Government purchases are fixed at 500 and investment is fixed at 300. Net taxes are constant at 200.

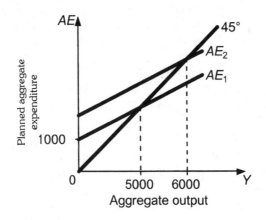

_____ 13.   Calculate the marginal propensity to consume.
    (a)   0.60
    (b)   0.75
    (c)   0.80
    (d)   0.85

_____ 14.   Derive the formula for the saving function.
    (a) $S = -360 + 0.20(Y - T)$
    (b) $S = -360 - 0.20(Y - T)$
    (c) $S = -200 + 0.20(Y - T)$
    (d) $S = -200 - 0.20(Y - T)$

_____ 15.   Calculate the tax multiplier.
    (a)   4
    (b)   5
    (c)   -4
    (d)   -5

_____ 16.   The government wishes to shift the AE_1 function to AE_2 by changing the level of taxes. Taxes should
    (a)   increase by 200.
    (b)   increase by 250.
    (c)   decrease by 200.
    (d)   decrease by 250.

_____ 17.   Given the tax change in the previous question, calculate how much consumption and saving, respectively, will change to attain the new equilibrium.
    (a)   Consumption increases by 800, saving increases by 200.
    (b)   Consumption increases by 1,000, saving increases by 250.
    (c)   Consumption increases by 1,000, saving increases by zero.
    (d)   Consumption increases by 1,200, saving decreases by 200.

_____ 18.   A tax decrease of $15 billion results in a $60 billion increase in equilibrium income. The government spending multiplier is
(a)   –5.
(b)   –4.
(c)   4.
(d)   5.

_____ 19.   When the government sector is added to the model, the economy can be in equilibrium only when
(a)   the government balances its budget.
(b)   saving equals investment.
(c)   unplanned inventory change is zero.
(d)   disposable income is equal to consumption plus saving.

_____ 20.   Automatic stabilizers _____ income taxes and _____ government spending during a recession.
(a)   increase; increase
(b)   increase; decrease
(c)   decrease; increase
(d)   decrease; decrease

II.   APPLICATION QUESTIONS

1.   (a)   Use the following information to fill in the gaps in the table. *MPC* is constant, and investment and government spending are determined autonomously. Net taxes are constant at a level of 200.

Real GDP Income	Consump -tion	Planned Invest- ment	Govern- ment Spending	Net Taxes	Aggregate Planned Expenditures
0					
1,000	1,200		500		
2,000	2,000				
3,000		300			3,600
4,000	3,600			200	
5,000	4,400				
6,000					
7,000		300			

(b)   Calculate *MPC* and *MPS*.
(c)   Determine the equilibrium income level for this economy.
(d)   If real GDP is 3,000, is unplanned inventory investment positive or negative? Predict how businesses will respond.
(e)   If real GDP is 7,000, is unplanned inventory investment positive or negative?
(f)   At which output level is saving zero?
(g)   At which output level is saving equal to investment?
(h)   At which output level is saving equal to nonconsumption spending?

(i)   Given your preceding answers, formulate a rule regarding the level of saving at the equilibrium output level.

(j)   If government spending falls by 200, would the equilibrium output level fall by more than 200, by less than 200, or by exactly 200? Use the table to confirm your answer. Describe the pressure that would cause the equilibrium output level to change.

2.   You have been called in by the Arbocali Minister of Finance. The full-employment level of output is 124,000 opeks. She tells you that an econometrician has provided the following model of the Arbocali economy. The currency is opeks.

Consumption function: $C = 6,000 + 0.75Y_d$

Investment function: $I = 11,000$

Government spending: $G = 20,000$

Net taxes: $T = 16,000$

Disposable income: $Y_d = Y - T$

Equilibrium: $Y = C + I + G$

(a)   Calculate the current equilibrium income level.

(b)   Determine the value of the government spending multiplier and the tax multiplier.

The Minister, who is extremely concerned about the level of the national debt, is considering two proposals.

Proposal I: Maintain the current level of government spending and increase taxes until the budget is balanced.

Proposal II: Maintain taxes at their present level and decrease federal spending until the budget is balanced.

(c)   Both policies will be contractionary. Which proposal will have the smaller impact on output and employment?

(d)   Write a brief to the Minister so that she can answer questions about the relative effects of the two proposals during Ministers' Question Time in Parliament.

Due to rising protests about the level of unemployment, the Minister scraps both of the proposals above and turns her attention to expansionary policies.

(e)   She is presented with several possible courses of action, listed below, and asks you to evaluate them. In each case, does the proposal restore full employment?

Proposal III: Increase government spending on defense by 8,000 opeks.

Proposal IV: Increase welfare payments by 8,000 opeks.

Proposal V: Increase taxes by a lump-sum of 4,000 opeks and increase spending on defense by 9,000 opeks.

Proposal VI: Increase welfare payments by 6,000 opeks and reduce taxes by a lump-sum of 2,000 opeks.

(f)   Of the proposals that achieve the goal of establishing output at the full-employment level, which is preferred in terms of helping to balance the budget?

(g)   Of the proposals that achieve the goal of establishing output at the full-employment level, which is preferred in terms of boosting consumption?

3.   Use the following information to calculate the multipliers. Assume that taxes are lump-sum.
   (a) $MPS = 0.20$. The government spending multiplier is _____ .
   (b) $MPC = 0.95$. The government spending multiplier is _____ .
   (c) $MPS = 0.40$. The government spending multiplier is _____ .
   (d) $MPC = 0.90$. The tax multiplier is _____ .
   (e) $MPS = 0.20$. The tax multiplier is _____ .
   (f)   If the government spending multiplier is 8, then the tax multiplier is _____ .
   (g)   If the tax multiplier is –5, then the government spending multiplier is _____ .
   (h) $MPS = 0.20$. The government spending multiplier is _____ and the tax multiplier is

         _____

         Using the information from (h) we know that a simultaneous decrease in G and T of $200
         each would cause the following total changes in:
   (i) Y _____
   (j) C _____
   (k) S _____
   (l) G _____
   (m) T _____

4.   Use the information in the table to answer the following questions.

Output (Income)	Saving	Planned Investment	Government Spending	Net Taxes	Consumption
1,300	150	200	100	50	_____
1,500	200	200	100	50	_____
1,700	250	200	100	50	_____
1,900	300	200	100	50	_____

   (a)   Fill in the "consumption" column.
   (b)   Calculate MPC _____ and equilibrium level of income _____ .
   (c)   Calculate the level of unplanned inventory investment when Y is 1,300.
   (d)   Will the equilibrium level of output (income) increase or decrease if the government
          were required to balance its budget?
   (e)   What action could the government have taken to achieve the full employment level of
          production (2,000)?
   (f)   Calculate the new equilibrium level of output (income) if G increases by 50 and T
          increases by 50.

5.   At the equilibrium output (income) level of 720, the following values occur.

$$C = 300 \qquad MPC = 0.75$$
$$I = 120$$
$$G = 300$$
$$T = 250$$

   (a)   Calculate the equilibrium value of saving. _____
   (b)   Calculate the marginal propensity to save. _____
   (c)   Calculate the value of the expenditure multiplier. _____

(d)   The government surplus/deficit now has a value of _____ .
       Pessimism occurs in the business community. Planned investment falls by 15. How much of an effect does this have on equilibrium GDP?
(e)   GDP will _____ (rise/fall) by _____ .
(f)   At the original GDP level, unplanned inventories are now _____ (rising/falling).
       The Administration attempts to restore the original production level by changing the tax level.
(g)   Taxes should be _____ (raised/lowered) by _____ .
(h)   When the economy reaches its final equilibrium, the surplus/deficit is _____ .
(i)   The final value for consumption is _____ .

6.   (a)   Fill in the blanks in the table.

Y	T	Y_d	C	S	I	G	AE
0	20	_____	_____	_____	_____	_____	_____
100	20	_____	_____	_____	30	10	_____
200	20	_____	_____	_____	_____	10	_____
300	20	_____	_____	0	_____	10	_____
400	20	_____	_____	20	30	_____	_____

(b)   Find MPC _____ , MPS _____ , the government spending multiplier _____ , and the tax multiplier _____ .
(c)   Express the consumption function algebraically. _____
(d)   What is the equilibrium income level? _____

7.   Assume the following data for the economy, which is in equilibrium at an output level of 480. This example uses the information in the textbook's Appendix B.

$$C = 280 \qquad b = MPC = 5/7$$
$$S = 80 \qquad MPS = 2/7$$
$$G = 150 \qquad I = 50$$
$$T = 120 \qquad t = 0.3$$

(a)   Calculate the value of the government spending multiplier. _____ Currently the economy is in a recession. You, as Chairperson of the Council of Economic Advisors, have been asked by how much government spending must be raised to increase equilibrium Y to 550.
(b)   Calculate the change in output necessary to achieve equilibrium at 550.
(c)   Use the multiplier to deduce the change in G needed to bring about the above change in equilibrium income.
(d)   Draw a 45° line picture representing the problem you've just solved.

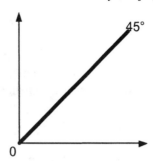

Now government spending has risen, as have taxes. The new level of government spending is the old level plus the policy recommendation you've calculated. The change in taxes can be derived using the tax rate.

(e)   What was the surplus/deficit originally? _____

(f)   How much have tax collections changed? _____

(g)   The new surplus/deficit is _____ .

8.   The economy has full employment and a balanced budget. Suddenly, because of a drop in planned investment, there is a recession.

(a)   What will happen to the surplus/deficit? Explain why.

(b)   Has the structural deficit changed, or has the cyclical deficit changed?

(c)   Suppose the government responds by increasing government spending and taxes by an equal amount. What will happen to the structural deficit and to the full-employment budget?

(d)   If the government is committed to balancing the budget, what will be the consequences of maintaining a balanced budget if automatic stabilizers are present in the economy?

PRACTICE TEST SOLUTIONS

I.   Solutions to Multiple Choice Questions

1.   (c)   An increase in lump-sum taxes will decrease consumption and, therefore, shift the *AE* function downward. If taxes rise by 100, disposable income will fall by 100. If *MPC* is 0.9, consumption (and *AE*) will decrease by 90.

2.   (c)   If *MPS* is 0.2, the government spending multiplier is 5. Income will decrease by 500 (100 × 5). If income decreases by 500 and *MPS* is 0.2, saving will decrease by 100.

3.   (b)   For an increase in government spending to make output rise by 250, the multiplier must be 2.5. If *MPS* is 0.4, the government spending multiplier is 2.5.

4.   (a)   If *MPC* is 0.75, the government spending multiplier is 4 and the tax multiplier is –3. If government spending increases by 75, output would increase by 300. The deficit would rise by 75. Reducing taxes by 100 would achieve the required expansion in output, but the increase in the deficit is 100 (greater than with option (a)). Option (c) cannot be considered because the maximum increase in government spending allowable is 75. Option (d) will not work because output would expand by only 75.

5.   (a)   Expenditure rises by a dollar. To neutralize this change, taxes would have to be increased. If taxes are raised by a dollar, consumption would fall, but by less than a

dollar. To neutralize the increase in expenditures, taxes will have to increase by more than a dollar.

6.   (a)   If saving increases by 40 as income increases by 200, *MPS* is 0.2. *MPC*, therefore, is 0.8. When *MPS* is 0.2, the government spending multiplier (1/*MPS*) is 5.

7.   (c)   Refer to p. 175 [487] for a discussion of automatic stabilizers.

8.   (a)   If expenditure increases, equilibrium output will increase. The government can increase government spending and/or cut taxes. Either action will increase the deficit. Investment decisions are made by the private sector.

9.   (b)   To neutralize the effect on *AE* of the investment decrease, the government wants an action that will make *AE* increase. Cutting government spending and increasing taxes will certainly not achieve this result. Note that Options (c) and (d) may make *AE* increase—it depends on the relative changes in *G* and *T*. Refer to the answer to Question 5 above.

10.   (a)   When *MPC* is 0.8, the government spending multiplier is 5 and the tax multiplier is –4. If government spending increases by 20, output will increase by 100 (20 × 5). If taxes are cut by 25, output will increase by 100 (–25 × 4). Similarly, the balanced-budget change will achieve the objective. Option (a) won't. The government spending increase will raise output by 200 (40 × 5), whereas the tax cut will raise output by a further 200 (–50 × 4).

11.   (b)   The presence or absence of a structural deficit depends on government policy.

12.   (d)   Refer to p. 169 [481] for a discussion of the federal deficit.

13.   (c)   As income rises by 5,000 (from zero to 5,000), spending rises by 4,000 (from 1,000 to 5,000).

14.   (a)   First, find the consumption function, which is in the form $C = a + bY_d$. From Question 13, $b = 0.80$. To find (autonomous) consumption, find consumption when $Y = 0$. Aggregate expenditures ($C + I + G$) are 1,000 when $Y = 0$, so $C = 200$ (1,000 – 300 – 500). $200 = a + 0.8(Y – 200)$, so $a = 360$. $C = 360 + 0.8 Y_d$. $Y_d = C + S$, therefore $S = Y_d – C = Y_d – (360 – 0.8 Y_d)$. The saving function is $S = –360 + 0.2 Y_d$.

15.   (c)   If *MPC* = 0.80, the tax multiplier is –4.

16.   (d)   If *MPC* = 0.80, the tax multiplier is –4. The desired change in income is +1,000.

17.   (b)   The tax cut will hike consumption autonomously by 250 × 0.80, or 200. The tax multiplier is –4, so income will increase by 1,000. After income has risen by 1,000, consumption will increase by an additional 800 because *MPC* = 0.80. The tax cut will hike saving autonomously by 250 × 0.20, or 50. After income has risen by 1,000, saving will increase by an additional 200 because *MPS* = 0.20.

18.   (d)   If a tax decrease of $15 billion results in a $60 billion increase in equilibrium income, the tax multiplier is –4. The tax multiplier formula is $-MPC/MPS$. $MPC = 0.80$ and $MPS = 0.20$. The government multiplier formula is $1/MPS$, so the value in this case is 5.

19.   (c)   Option (d) is not an equilibrium condition—this identity holds whether or not equilibrium is established. Option (b) was an equilibrium condition in the previous chapter, but is no longer. In equilibrium, leakages ($S + T$) must equal injections ($I + G$).

20.   (c)   Refer to p. 175 [487] for a discussion of automatic stabilizers.

II.   Solutions to Application Questions

1.   (a)   Refer to the following table.

Real GDP Income	Consumption	Planned Investment	Government Spending	Net Taxes	Aggregate Planned Expenditures
0	400	300	500	200	1,200
1,000	1,200	300	500	200	2,000
2,000	2,000	300	500	200	2,800
3,000	2,800	300	500	200	3,600
4,000	3,600	300	500	200	4,400
5,000	4,400	300	500	200	5,200
6,000	5,200	300	500	200	6,000
7,000	6,000	300	500	200	6,800

(b) $MPC = 0.8$ and $MPS = 0.2$

(c)   Aggregate planned expenditures equal real GDP at 6,000

(d)   When real $GDP = 3,000$, aggregate planned expenditures exceed 3,000 (3,800), causing unplanned inventory decumulation. Businesses will respond by hiring more resources and increasing output.

(e)   When real $GDP = 7,000$, aggregate planned expenditures are less than 7,000 (6,800), causing unplanned inventory accumulation.

(f)   Saving is zero when income is 3,000. $C + S + T = 2,800 + 0 + 200 = 3,000$.

(g)   Saving equals investment (which is constant at 300) when income is 4,500.

(h)   Saving equals planned nonconsumption spending ($I + G$, which is constant at 800) when income equals 7,000.

(i)   When saving (plus taxes) equals planned nonconsumption spending, output will be at its equilibrium level. Leakages must equal injections in equilibrium.

(j)   Equilibrium output would fall by 1,000 to 5,000. At an income level of 5,000, $C + I + G$ equals 4,400 plus 600. The decrease in expenditures will result in unplanned inventory accumulation. Firms will cut production, forcing the equilibrium output level to fall.

2.   (a) $Y = C + I + G = 6,000 + 0.75(Y – T) + 11,000 + 20,000 = 37,000 + 0.75Y – 0.75T$. But $T = 16,000$, therefore, $Y – 0.75Y = 37,000 – 0.75(16,000)$, therefore, $Y = 100,000$.

(b) $MPC = 0.75$, therefore the government spending multiplier is 4.0 and the tax multiplier is –3.0.

(c)   Proposal I is less contractionary.

(d)   Proposal I: The deficit is currently 16,000 − 20,000, or 4,000 opeks. A 4,000-opek increase in taxes will initially reduce consumption by 3,000 opeks. Spending will fall by 3,000 opeks.

Proposal II: A 4,000-opek decrease in government spending will reduce aggregate expenditures by 4,000 opeks—a larger initial spending reduction than in Proposal I.

Note: The economy will not contract by only 3,000 opeks. With Proposal I, the economy will contract by 3,000 × 4, or 12,000 opeks. With Proposal II, the economy will contract by 4,000 × 4, or 16,000 opeks.

(e)   Proposal III is overkill! The multiplier is 4, therefore an autonomous increase in government spending of 8,000 will push the economy past the full-employment output level.

Proposal IV will work. The tax multiplier is −3 and an increase in welfare payments operates in the same way as a reduction in taxes.

Proposal V will work. $\Delta T(4,000) \times -3 = -12,000$. $\Delta G(9,000) \times 4 = 36,000$. The net change in income is +24,000, which is the amount required.

Proposal VI will work. Welfare is a form of negative tax. $\Delta T(-2,000) \times -3 = 6,000$. Δwelfare$(-6,000) \times -3 = 18,000$. The total change in income is +24,000, which is the amount required.

(f) $G - T =$ a deficit of 4,000.

Proposal IV will reduce net taxes by 8,000 and widen the deficit to 12,000.

Proposal V will increase net taxes by 4,000 but increase government spending by 9,000. The deficit will increase by 5,000 opeks.

Proposal VI will reduce net taxes by 6,000 + 2,000, or 8,000 opeks. The deficit will increase by 8,000 opeks.

Proposal IV and VI are equivalent, but Proposal V is better than either.

(g)   Proposal IV will reduce net taxes by 8,000 and increase consumption autonomously by 6,000 opeks. As income increases by 24,000, consumption will be induced to increase by an additional 18,000. Total increase in consumption is 24,000 opeks.

Proposal V will increase net taxes by 4,000 and reduce consumption autonomously by 3,000 opeks. As income increases by 24,000, consumption will be induced to increase by an additional 18,000. Total increase in consumption is 15,000 opeks.

Proposal VI will increase welfare payments by 6,000 opeks and increase consumption autonomously by 4,500 opeks. The reduction taxes by a lump-sum will increase consumption autonomously by 1,500 opeks. As income increases by 24,000, consumption will be induced to increase by an additional 18,000. Total increase in consumption is 24,000 opeks.

Proposal IV and VI have identical effects on consumption.

3.   (a)   5.   (b)   20.   (c)   2.5.   (d)   −9.
       (e)   −4.   (f)   −7.   (g)   6.   (h)   5; −4.
       (i)   −200.   (j)   −160.   (k)   −40.   (l)   −200.
       (m)   −200.

4.   (a)   Refer to the following table.

Output (Income)	Saving	Planned Investment	Government Spending	Net Taxes	Consumption
1,300	150	200	100	50	1,100
1,500	200	200	100	50	1,250
1,700	250	200	100	50	1,400
1,900	300	200	100	50	1,550

(b)   MPS is 0.25, so MPC is 0.75; $Y = C + I + G$ at an income level of 1,700.

(c) $AE = C + I + G = 1,400$. If output is only 1,300, inventory is falling by 100.

(d)   You can't give a precise numerical answer—it depends on the level at which G and T are equalized—although, in any case, output will decrease because either taxes must increase or government spending must decrease.
Suppose the budget is balanced at 50. G must fall by 50, and output will fall by 200.
If G and T are made equal at 100, taxes would have to rise by 50. Output would fall by 150.

(e)   Increase government spending by 75 (with a multiplier of 4), decrease net taxes by 100 (with a tax multiplier of –3), or undertake a balanced-budget increase of 300.

(f)   This is a balanced-budget change and the balanced-budget multiplier is 1. Income level will increase by 50 to 1,750.

5.   (a)   In equilibrium, $S + T = I + G$.
Substituting in numerical values, we get $S + 250 = 120 + 300$.
$S = 420 - 250 = 170$.

(b) $MPS = 1 - MPC = 1 - 0.75 = 0.25$.

(c)   Multiplier $= 1/MPS = 1/0.25 = 4$.

(d) $G - T = 300 - 250 =$ deficit of 50.

(e)   Spending change: $\Delta Y = \Delta I \times 1/MPS = -15 \times 4 = -60$.

(f)   Unplanned inventories are rising. Expenditure has fallen, so unsold stock is accumulating.

(g)   lowered by 20. We want income to rise by 60.
Tax change: $\Delta Y = 60 = \Delta T \times -MPC/MPS = -20 \times -3$.

(h) $G - T = 300 - 230 =$ deficit of 70. Taxes were 250, then they were cut by 20.

(i)   The equilibrium income level is unchanged, but disposable income has risen by 20 because of the tax cut. As MPC is 0.75, consumption will increase by 15 (20×0.75) to 315.

6.   (a)   Refer to the following table.
Saving rises by 20 as income rises by 100. $MPS = 0.2$, $MPC = 0.8$. This is enough information to complete the saving and consumption columns. Investment is constant at 30, and government spending is constant at 10. Disposable income is $Y - T$.

Y	T	Y_d	C	S	I	G	AE
0	20	–20	40	–60	30	10	80
100	20	80	120	–40	30	10	160
200	20	180	200	–20	30	10	240
300	20	280	280	0	30	10	320
400	20	380	360	20	30	10	400

(b) $MPC = 0.8$; $MPS = 0.2$ (refer to Answer (a) above); the government spending multiplier is $1/MPS = 5$; the tax multiplier is $-MPC/MPS = -4$.

(c) $C = 40 + 0.8(Y - T)$.

(d)   Equilibrium occurs at 400, where $S + T = I + G$.

7.   (a)   The government spending multiplier is $1/(1 - b + bt)$, where $b = MPC = 5/7$ and $t = 0.3$. The multiplier value is 2.

(b)   Given that the economy is in equilibrium at 480, the President wishes output to increase by 70 (550 − 480).

(c)   Spending change: $\Delta Y = 70 = \Delta G \times 1/MPS = 35 \times 2.0$. G must increase by 35.

(d)   Refer to the following diagram.

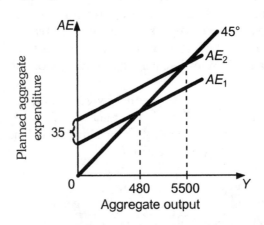

(e)   Originally, $(G - T) = 150 - 120 = $ a deficit of 30.

(f)   Income has risen by 70. The tax rate is 0.3. Increase in tax collections $= 0.3 \times 70 = 21$.

(g)   Now, $(G - T) = (150 + 35) - (120 + 21) = 185 - 141 = $ a deficit of 44.

8.   (a)   A decrease in investment or consumption will reduce aggregate expenditure and output. As output falls, transfer payments will increase and tax revenues will decrease, opening up a deficit without any explicit government action.

(b)   This change has occurred because of the recession—it is a cyclical deficit.

(c)   A balanced-budget increase will increase the government's role but leave the size of the structural deficit unchanged. (Note: In the presence of tax rates and other automatic stabilizers, the structural deficit will, in fact, decrease.)

(d)   If the government wishes to balance the budget, taxes will have to increase (decrease) more (less) than government spending. Increasing taxes, for example, will depress the economy still further. In this case, there is an incompatibility between balancing the budget and fighting the recession.

10 [25]

The Money Supply and the Federal Reserve System

Chapter objectives:

1. Identify the three functions of money. List the various types of money and the differences among them.
2. Identify two different measures of the U.S. money supply.
3. Determine which items are assets and which are liabilities on a bank's balance sheet. Distinguish among total, excess, and required reserves. Describe the process of deposit creation. Derive and explain the importance of the money multiplier.
4. Outline the functions of the Federal Reserve (the Fed). Identify the three monetary policy tools of the Fed and how they are adjusted to increase (decrease) the money supply.
5. Analyze the Fed's ability to expand or contract reserves and the money supply.

This chapter begins to build a model of the financial market that continues in Chapter 11 (26), where the factors that determine the demand for money holdings and the establishment of money market equilibrium are considered. This model will then be combined with the aggregate expenditure model in Chapter 12 (27). It is important that you develop a good understanding of financial markets at this point.

BRAIN TEASER: In 2000 the United States introduced its eighth dollar coin—the Sacagawea golden dollar. Over one billion of the coins were minted during 2000. About half remained in the vaults of Federal Reserve Banks and the U.S. Mint and the other half were in circulation. However, a large proportion of the "circulating" dollars were being hoarded. Are the Sacagawea dollars "money"? In practice, do they perform the functions of money?

OBJECTIVE 1:
Identify the three functions of money. List the various types of money and the differences among them.

Money fulfils three functions in the economy. The three functions of money are:

(a)   a medium of exchange (or means of payment)
(b)   a store of value
(c)   a unit of account (page 181 [493])

Before money, there was barter. But because trading goods for goods relies on a double coincidence of wants (where each trader must be willing to trade something that the other trader is willing to accept), barter was inefficient. *Commodity money* (a good that has some value over and above its value as money) was an intermediate stage between barter and the *fiat money* of the modern economy. Gold and cigarettes are examples of commodity money. Dollar bills (Federal Reserve notes) are fiat money—they derive their value from the willingness of individuals to accept them as payment. That willingness, in turn, derives from the government's declaration that its notes are legal tender—an acceptable means of settling all debts, private and public. To ensure compliance, the government must protect its currency from being debased, either through forgery or by printing too much of it. (page 182 [494])

▶▶   LEARNING TIP: In this section, liberate yourself from equating "money" with dollar bills. Try a thought experiment: If dollars (and checks, etc.) disappeared overnight, how would the U.S. economy adapt? What might be used instead of dollars? Which features favor some commodities, such as gold, silver or tobacco, over others, such as fish, cows, or iron? Would credit cards (or debit cards) take over?◀

ECONOMICS IN PRACTICE: On page 183 [495], the textbook describes how dolphin's teeth are used as money in the Solomon Islands. Is this commodity money or fiat money? How well does it fulfill the functions of money?
ANSWER: Dolphin's teeth are a form of commodity money—they have some value (as jewelry) beyond their role as money. Clearly, this money is acceptable as a medium of exchange and, since it is durable, (unlike cows, for example, which can die), seems to perform well as a store of value.
ECONOMICS IN PRACTICE (CONTINUED): Douglas Adams, in his *Hitchhiker's Guide to the Galaxy*, describes the efforts of the Golgafrinchams to devise their own money. They choose the leaf. The problem is that, because leaves are so available, inflation becomes rife, provoking a program of forest burn-down. The leaf is not a good choice as money. So what, in fact, are the characteristics of a "good" money? Compile a list of desirable qualities. How well do dolphin's teeth (and dollar bills) meet your characteristics? And why are leaves such a poor choice?
ANSWER: To be a good candidate as "money," an item must exhibit particular qualities including durability, portability, divisibility, comparability, and a limited supply. Dollars are fairly long-lived and portable. We can sub-divide a dollar into one hundred smaller units (cents) and one dollar is essentially the same as any other. Finally, it is illegal to forge dollars. Dolphin's teeth similarly are portable and durable (although the article mentions the problem of decay) and are limited in supply (despite bat-tooth counterfeiters). Also, presumably, one tooth is quite similar to another. Leaves, in contrast, are not limited in supply, durable or comparable. A better choice for the Golgafrinchams would have been one particular type of leaf that is durable, difficult to substitute or counterfeit, and valuable in its own right—tobacco, for instance.

─────────■────────────────────────── **Practice** ──────────────────────

1. Money's prime function is as
   (a)   the standard for credit transactions.
   (b)   the medium of exchange.
   (c)   a store of value.
   (d)   a unit of account.

   ANSWER: (b) The main reason for having money is because it eases the process of exchange. Refer to p. 182 [494].

2. In a barter economy,
   (a)   money functions only as a medium of exchange.
   (b)   multiple "exchange rates" are likely.
   (c)   money functions are a medium of exchange and as a store of value.
   (d)   saving can not occur.

   ANSWER: (b) In a barter economy, there is no money, so Options (a) and (c) are incorrect. Saving can occur; saving, recall, is non-consumption. In a barter economy, there will be an exchange rate between apples and corn, another between corn and tobacco, another between tobacco and tomatoes, and so on.

Use the following information to answer the next two questions. At a flea market, Mary spots some valuable Depression glassware valued at the ridiculously low price of 25¢. She hands over the quarter to secure the item.

3. The price tag on the glassware used money in its role as a
   (a)   medium of exchange.
   (b)   store of value.
   (c)   unit of account.
   (d)   means of payment.

   ANSWER: (c) Money establishes a consistent way of quoting prices. Money is functioning well in this case—Mary can see that the glassware is undervalued.

4. As Mary hands over the quarter, she is using money in its role as a
   (a)   medium of exchange.
   (b)   store of value.
   (c)   unit of account.
   (d)   form of credit.

   ANSWER: (a) The quarter, by being acceptable to the seller, permits the exchange to occur. Refer to p. 182 [494].

5. Jack is saving money to buy a new DVD. Money is functioning as a
   (a)   medium of exchange.
   (b)   store of value.
   (c)   unit of account.
   (d)   standard of deferred payment.

   ANSWER: (b) An asset that carries purchasing power from one time period to another is functioning as a store of value. Refer to p. 182 [494].

6.   Each of the following is an example of commodity money EXCEPT
      (a)   dollar bills.
      (b)   gold.
      (c)   cigarettes.
      (d)   salt.
      ANSWER: (a) Dollar bills have value only as dollar bills—they are fiat money. The three
                   commodities have all been used as money. Salt, in fact, is the source of the term
                   "salary." ■

 OBJECTIVE 2:
Identify two different measures of the U.S. money supply.

At the heart of the various measures of the money supply is the concept of *liquidity*. The more easily and
cheaply an asset can be converted into spending power, the more liquid it is. The most liquid assets are
included in M1, the narrowest definition of money. M1, or transactions money, includes currency held
outside banks, demand deposits and other checkable deposits, and the value of traveler's checks. Other
assets, such as savings accounts, are called *near monies*. M2 (broad money) includes everything in M1
and near monies such as savings accounts and money market accounts. (page 185 [497])

> ▶▶ LEARNING TIP: The definition of M1—currency held outside banks, demand deposits, the value of
>   traveler's checks, and various checkable accounts—prevents "double-counting." When you deposit a dollar
>   bill into your checking account, the money supply doesn't change. "Demand deposits" increase by a dollar,
>   but "currency *held outside banks*" decreases by a dollar, because the dollar bill is now held by the banking
>   system, *not* by the public.
> ▶▶ LEARNING TIP: From this point on, when the textbook refers to "money," it is referring to our MI
>   definition of money—transaction money. In fact, it's being even more restrictive than that; from now on, for
>   simplicity's sake, "money" will mean "currency in circulation" and "deposits". ◀

—————————————————————————————————— **Practice** ——————————————————————————————————

7.   Which of the following financial items is not included in M2?
      (a)   Money market accounts
      (b)   Excess reserves
      (c)   Demand deposits
      (d)   Savings accounts
      ANSWER: (b) Excess reserves are not found in any definition of the money supply. Note that
                   demand deposits are included in M2 because they are included in M1. Refer to
                   p. 185 [497].

8.   Near monies are
      (a)   included in the M1.
      (b)   liquid assets that are close substitutes for transactions money.
      (c)   stocks, bonds, and collectible artwork.
      (d)   Federal Reserve notes.
      ANSWER: (b) Refer to p. 185 [497] for a discussion of near monies. ■

OBJECTIVE 3:
Determine which items are assets and which are liabilities on a bank's balance sheet. Distinguish among total, excess, and required reserves. Describe the process of deposit creation. Derive and explain the importance of the money multiplier.

▶▶▶   LEARNING TIP: Balance sheets, often called T-accounts because the lines form a big "T," are used extensively in this chapter. You may never have seen them before. A basic rule to memorize is that "assets go on the left and liabilities go on the right" in a balance sheet.◀

Bankers have discovered that, because they need keep only a fraction of their total reserves available for withdrawal by depositors (*required reserves*), the rest (*excess reserves*) can be loaned out at a profit. Banks create money through these lending activities. When loaned out, the funds advanced to the borrower increase her/his spending power and count as an addition to the money supply. Each bank, therefore, can expand the money supply by the value of its excess reserves. As a whole, the banking system, by recirculating deposits, can expand the money supply by a multiple (the *money multiplier*) of its total reserves, the multiple being determined by the fraction of funds that is held as required reserves. In practice, the Federal Reserve establishes a *required reserve ratio*, and that determines the maximum size of the money multiplier. The money multiplier is equal to 1/(required reserve ratio). (page 187 [499])

▶▶▶   LEARNING TIP: The balance sheet is looked at from the viewpoint of the bank—not that of the customers or the Fed. Go through the process described in the text, but using different numbers. Explain each step to yourself as you go. The best way to practice the case of money "destruction," which can effectively challenge your understanding, is by increasing the required reserve ratio. Initially, banks will have inadequate funds to meet their reserve requirements. They will have to reduce their lending activities and add to their reserves instead.◀

The following table will help to organize your thoughts on the money creation process. Suppose Alice deposits $1,000 in her bank (Bank A). The required reserve ratio is 20%. Bank A's reserves increase by $1,000 (of which $200 are required reserves, which can't be loaned out) and $800 are excess reserves (which can be loaned out). A loan to Peter is made and $800 worth of spending power is released. Peter writes an $800 check to Brenda, who deposits it in her bank (Bank B). Bank A's excess reserves fall to zero when the check is cleared, but it still has the $1,000 deposit, $200 in required reserves, and $800 in loans.

Bank B has $800 in deposits, $160 in required reserves, and $640 in excess reserves. Now Bank B lends $640 to Eric, who writes a check to Chris. Chris deposits the check in Bank C. When Eric's check is cleared, Bank B's excess reserves fall to zero, but it still has the $800 deposit, $160 in required reserves, and $640 in loans. And so on.

Bank	New Demand Deposits =	Change in Reserves =	Change in Required Reserves +	Change in Excess Reserves	Change in Loans
A.	1,000.00	1,000.00	200.00	800.00 /0	800.00
B.	800.00	800.00	160.00	640.00 /0	640.00
C.	640.00	640.00	128.00	512.00 /0	512.00
D.	512.00	512.00	102.40	409.60 /0	409.60
etc.	…	…	…	…	…
Total	5,000.00	5,000.00	1,000.00	0	4,000.00

Points to note:

(a)   The "change in excess reserves" column contains two steps, the first indicating how much excess reserves increase, the second assuming that all excess reserves have been loaned out and the borrower's check has been honored.

(b)   It becomes clear, using the table, that the expansion process will continue until all of the original injection of new reserves ($1,000) has been converted into required reserves. At that point the process must stop.

(c)   The $5,000 expansion in demand deposit liabilities is balanced on the asset side of the balance sheet by $1,000 of required reserves and $4,000 of loans.

A Circular Flow Diagram: This "leakage" process is similar to that described for the expenditure multiplier in Practice Question 16 of Chapter 8 (23). To get an intuitive feel for the money expansion process, you can use a diagram similar to the one presented there. In this case, the "household" sector is split into two parts, borrowers and depositors, but otherwise the argument is similar. In the money creation situation, the leakage occurs when banks retain funds as required reserves. Over and above the leakage of reserves into required reserves, other "leakages," such as holding funds as currency, (either by the borrower or other members of the public) or holdings of excess reserves by the banks, will diminish the strength of the circular flow.

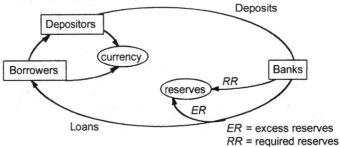

▶▶   LEARNING TIP: The formula relating commercial bank reserves (RR) and deposits (D) via the required reserve ratio (g) is $D = RR/g$. Memorize it!◀

A small point. Note that the money multiplier refers to the multiple change in *deposits* (which is not quite the same thing as the money supply). M1 is comprised of deposits and also of currency held outside banks. A 10% increase in reserves doesn't necessarily translate into a 10% increase in the money supply. If bank reserves increase because Alice deposits $100 into her checking account, the decrease in currency will partly offset the multiple expansion in deposits.

———■——————————————— **Practice** ———————————————

9.   The basic equation for a bank's balance sheet is
   (a)   Liabilities = Assets + Net Worth.
   (b)   Net Worth = Liabilities + Assets.
   (c)   Assets = Liabilities + Net Worth.
   (d)   Assets = Liabilities − Net Worth.

   ANSWER: (c)   Refer to p. 187 [499].

10.   Assets are things that are _____ ; on a balance sheet they are entered on the _____ .
    (a)   owned; right
    (b)   owned; left
    (c)   owed; right
    (d)   owed; left

ANSWER: (b) Refer to p. 187 [499].

Use the following balance sheet for First Union National Bank to answer the next three questions. First Union has a reserve ratio of 20%.

Assets		Liabilities	
Reserves	$2,500,000	Checking deposits	6,000,000
Loans outstanding	5,500,000		
Other assets	1,000,000	Net Worth	3,000,000
Total	$9,000,000	Total	$9,000,000

11.   First Union has $2,500,000 in reserves, checking deposits of $6,000,000, and a reserve ratio of 20%. First Union has _____ of required reserves and _____ of excess reserves.
    (a) $500,000; $2,000,000
    (b) $500,000; $5,500,000
    (c) $1,200,000; $1,300,000
    (d) $1,200,000; $4,800,000

ANSWER: (c) The required reserves are calculated relative to the bank's liabilities, therefore $6,000,000 × 0.20. Total reserves = required reserves + excess reserves.

12.   Assuming prudent management, First Union can increase its loans by up to
    (a) $1,300,000.
    (b) $1,500,000.
    (c) $2,000,000.
    (d) $3,000,000.

ANSWER: (a) First Union can increase its loans by the extent of its excess reserves.

13.   Assuming all banks have a reserve ratio of 20%, and that the other banks were loaned up initially, the nation's money supply could expand by
    (a) $1,300,000.
    (b) $6,500,000.
    (c) $12,500,000.
    (d) $10,000,000.

ANSWER: (b) The money supply can expand by the extent of the excess reserves ($1,300,000) times the money multiplier, which is 1/0.20 = 5.

Use the following balance sheet for First Federal Bank to answer the next two questions.

Assets		Liabilities	
Reserves	$400,000	Checking deposits	$1,000,000
Loans	$600,000		
Total	$1,000,000	Total	$1,000,000

14.   First Federal is fully loaned up. The reserve requirement is
   (a)   2.5%.
   (b)   40%.
   (c)   60%.
   (d)   250%.

   ANSWER: (b) If all reserves are required reserves, the requirement is to hold 40% of deposit
              liabilities.

15.   Assume that First Federal is the only bank in the economy and the banking system is closed to
       foreign banks. The reserve requirement is 40%. Now an additional $100,000 is deposited. The
       bank can expand its loans up to the point where its total deposits are
   (a) $1,100,000.
   (b) $1,250,000.
   (c) $1,400,000.
   (d) $2,000,000.

   ANSWER: (b) Total (required) reserves will be $500,000. The money multiplier is 2.5. ■

OBJECTIVE 4:
Outline the functions of the Federal Reserve (the Fed). Identify the three monetary policy tools of
the Fed and how they are adjusted to increase (decrease) the money supply.

The main macroeconomic role of the Fed is to control the money supply and interest rates, but it also
oversees the banking system and gives check-clearing and other services. As well as functioning as the
bankers' bank, it is the government's bank, the lender of last resort to commercial banks, and a major
player in international currency transactions. (page 192 [504])

The primary method used by the Federal Open Market Committee (FOMC) to control the money
supply is the manipulation of commercial bank reserves. (Recall that the commercial banks can create
deposits only if they have the excess reserves available to support such an expansion.)

The three major tools of monetary policy are:

(a)   the required reserve ratio
(b)   the discount rate (which largely have the effect of announcing policy changes)
(c)   open market operations, which are the most frequently used and the most precise (page 195
       [507])

To expand the money supply, the Fed can buy government securities (which increases the
reserves of the banking system), cut the reserve requirement (which results in the commercial banks
having more excess reserves, and thus, greater lending capacity), or cut the discount rate (which reduces
the "price" of borrowing funds from the Fed). In each case, the effect is to make more reserves available
to the commercial banking system. When these reserves are loaned out, the money supply increases.

▶▶▶   LEARNING TIP: This section includes material crucial to the following chapters and will handsomely
       reward your study time. Take each of the policy tools (required reserve ratio, discount rate, and open market
       operations) in turn, and see how it would affect your ability to lend if you were a banker. If you become
       more able to lend, the money supply will increase.

▶▶▶   LEARNING TIP: In recent years, the Fed has been fairly active in attempting to manipulate the economy—
       stay alert to what's happening in the news. Often, Fed policy changes are signaled by a change in the
       "federal funds rate," which is the interest rate at which banks can borrow from each other and one which is
       closely linked to the discount rate.

▶▶ LEARNING TIP: The following "trick" will help you to sort out the operation of the monetary policy tools. The discount rate and reserve ratio move in the same direction (both down for an expansionary policy, for example) while, with open market operations, the Fed (**B**)uys securities to make the money supply (**B**)igger, and (**S**)ells them to make it (**S**)maller.◀

──────────■────────────────────────── **Practice** ──────────────────────────

16.   Which of the following instruments is not used by the Fed to change the money supply?
      (a)   Open market operations
      (b)   The discount rate
      (c)   The tax rate on interest earnings
      (d)   The required reserve ratio

      ANSWER: (c) Changes in tax rates are undertaken by Congress as part of fiscal policy.

17.   U.S. government securities owned by the Fed are a(n) _____ of the Fed; Federal Reserve notes are a(n) _____ of the Fed.
      (a)   asset; asset
      (b)   asset; liability
      (c)   liability; asset
      (d)   liability; liability

      ANSWER: (b) The securities are claims against the government and owned by the Fed. Federal
                   Reserve notes are issued by the Fed and must be honored by it.

18.   Which of the following is not a responsibility of the Fed?
      (a)   Regulating the banking system
      (b)   Clearing interbank payments
      (c)   Managing exchange rates
      (d)   Issuing new bonds to finance the federal deficit

      ANSWER: (d) New bonds to finance the deficit are issued by the Treasury.

19.   The preferred instrument of monetary policy is
      (a)   the discount rate.
      (b)   the required reserve ratio.
      (c)   open market operations.
      (d)   the exchange rate.

      ANSWER: (c) Refer to p. 197 [509]. Open market operations seldom make headlines, but are
                   the policy tool of choice because of convenience and precision.

20.   *Ceteris paribus,* an open market sale of government securities to First Union National Bank will _____ First Union's assets and _____ First Union's liabilities.
      (a)   increase; increase
      (b)   increase; not change
      (c)   not change; increase
      (d)   not change; not change

      ANSWER: (d) The composition, but not the level, of First Union's assets will change.

21.   The Fed decreases the required reserve ratio. The excess reserves of banks will _____ and the money supply will _____.

    (a)   increase; increase

    (b)   increase; decrease

    (c)   remain constant; increase

    (d)   decrease; increase

ANSWER: (a) Lower reserve requirements mean that banks have more excess reserves available to lend.

22.   First Union National Bank is fully loaned up. Ultimately, an open market sale of government securities to First Union will _____ First Union's reserves and _____ First Union's deposit liabilities.

    (a)   increase; increase

    (b)   increase; decrease

    (c)   decrease; increase

    (d)   decrease; decrease

ANSWER: (d) To buy the securities, First Union must transfer some of its reserves to the Fed. Because reserves have fallen, First Union will be unable to support its original level of demand deposit liabilities. ■

 OBJECTIVE 5:
Analyze the Fed's ability to expand or contract reserves and the money supply.

The Fed changes the required reserve ratio infrequently because it is a crude instrument of monetary control. When changes do occur, they tend to exert a powerful, if imprecise, impact on the private banks. (page 195 [507])

    Discount rate adjustments help the Fed to "signal" changes in policy, but this policy tool also has some problems. First, the effect of a discount rate change is imprecise. Second, movements in other interest rates may counteract the hoped-for effect of the discount rate change. Moral suasion (threats!) may be used to discourage banks from borrowing heavily from the Fed and then re-lending the reserves. (page 196 [508])

    Open market operations are a quick, precise, and flexible method of manipulating reserves. (page 197 [509])

    The Fed, by its policy actions, clearly can influence the economy's money supply. Is the supply of money affected by the interest rate? At this point, Case, Fair and Oster assume that it is not—the money supply curve graphs as a vertical line. This simplifying assumption will be relaxed in Chapter 13 (28).

—■——————————————————— **Practice** ———

23.   Which of the following is false? Open market operations

    (a)   are fast and flexible.

    (b)   are fairly predictable in their impact on the money supply.

    (c)   are an effective instrument of monetary policy because they are used infrequently.

    (d)   involve the purchase and sale of preexisting U.S. government securities.

ANSWER: (c) Open market operations are the most frequently used tool of monetary policy.

24. Although the required reserve ratio is a tool of monetary policy, it is used infrequently because
    (a) only banks that are members of the Federal Reserve System must comply with the requirement, and this discriminates in favor of the many banks that are not members of the Fed.
    (b) when the Fed reduces the required reserve ratio, banks will have to "call" some of their loans.
    (c) a change in the requirement will take two weeks to have an impact on banks due to lags in bank reporting.
    (d) it may take a long time to get Congressional permission to proceed with a change in the ratio.

    ANSWER: (c) Refer to p. 195 [507]. All depository institutions are members of the Fed. Congressional approval of Fed decisions is not required—the Fed is separate from Congress. *Raising* the ratio might result in called loans.

25. Each of the following is a problem associated with the use of the discount rate EXCEPT that
    (a) the discount rate cannot be adjusted quickly.
    (b) the impact of a change in the discount rate is imprecise.
    (c) the impact of a change in the discount rate can be offset by changes in other interest rates.
    (d) the effect of a change in the discount rate on banks' demand for reserves is uncertain.

    ANSWER: (a) This rate is established, and can be changed at will, by the Fed. ■

BRAIN TEASER SOLUTION: Certainly, the unissued dollars are not money because, to be counted, currency must be held outside banks. However, what of the dollars held by the public? The prime role for currency is to serve as a medium of exchange and, in 2000 at least, many of the Sacagawea dollars that could have been used in this way were not being used. Presumably, the keepsake value of the coins exceeded one dollar and so they were hoarded—more a collectible than currency. Paper dollars were used in their stead. Certainly, though, the Sacagawea dollars fulfilled the store-of-value and unit-of-account functions of money.

PRACTICE TEST

I.   MULTIPLE-CHOICE QUESTIONS

Select the option that provides the single best answer.

_____ 1.   Each of the following is included in M1 EXCEPT
    (a) Federal Reserve notes.
    (b) cash held by the public.
    (c) demand deposit accounts.
    (d) credit card balances.

_____ 2.   Which of the following is not a function of money?
    (a) A form of speculation
    (b) A medium of exchange
    (c) A unit of account
    (d) A store of value

_____ 3.   Robin Hood borrows $100 in dollar bills from Friar Tuck and deposits it at Bank of America. The required reserve ratio is 25%. What is the maximum amount by which the banking system can expand checking accounts?
(a) $500
(b) $100
(c) $300
(d) $400

_____ 4.   Excess reserves equal
(a)   demand deposits plus required reserves.
(b)   actual reserves minus required reserves.
(c)   total reserves minus actual reserves.
(d)   demand deposits minus required reserves.

_____ 5.   It is assumed that the money supply curve is _____ ; it _____ affected by changes in the interest rate.
(a)   horizontal; is
(b)   vertical; is
(c)   vertical; is not
(d)   horizontal; is not

_____ 6.   Checking account deposits at Centura Bank are Centura _____ ; money market accounts at Centura Bank are Centura _____ .
(a)   assets; assets
(b)   assets; liabilities
(c)   liabilities; assets
(d)   liabilities; liabilities

_____ 7.   In a T-account, liabilities go on the _____ side and net worth goes on the _____ side.
(a)   left; left
(b)   left; right
(c)   right; left
(d)   right; right

_____ 8.   An increase in the required reserve ratio will
(a)   increase the demand for money balances.
(b)   reduce the money supply.
(c)   increase the value of the money multiplier.
(d)   increase the amount of excess reserves.

_____ 9.   The required reserve ratio is 20%. $200 is deposited into a demand deposit account in the banking system.
(a)   Initially, the money supply has changed its composition but not its size.
(b)   Eventually, the money supply will increase by $1,000.
(c)   Initially, the money supply will increase by $200.
(d)   Initially, the money supply will increase by $40.
(Be careful on this one! There is only one correct answer.)

Use the following information to answer the next two questions.
The commercial banks are loaned up and have reserves of $500 billion. Now the required reserve ratio is changed from 25% to 10%.

_____ 10.   Initially, excess reserves will
  (a)   increase by 15%.
  (b)   decrease by $300 billion.
  (c)   increase by $300 billion.
  (d)   increase by $3,000 billion.

_____ 11.   Eventually, the money supply can
  (a)   increase by 15%.
  (b)   increase by a multiple of 10.
  (c)   increase by $1,250 billion.
  (d)   increase by $3,000 billion.

_____ 12.   The Board of Governors is responsible for all of the following EXCEPT
  (a)   setting the discount rate for lending to commercial banks.
  (b)   establishing and changing the required reserve ratio of the commercial banks.
  (c)   clearing interbank payments.
  (d)   deciding whether to buy or to sell U.S. government securities.

_____ 13.   Which one of the following pairs of policy actions would definitely *not* increase the money supply?
  (a)   Open market sales of securities, increasing the discount rate
  (b)   Open market sales of securities, reducing the discount rate
  (c)   Open market purchases of securities, increasing the discount rate
  (d)   Open market purchases of securities, reducing the discount rate

_____ 14.   The required reserve ratio is 25%. First Union National Bank makes an additional loan of $500,000 to the public. If the banking system holds no excess reserves (it is fully loaned up), then the eventual increase in the money supply will be
  (a)   zero.
  (b) $500,000.
  (c) $1,500,000.
  (d) $2,000,000.

_____ 15.   If Kristin deposits $5,000 cash into her savings account, then
  (a)   M1 goes down and M2 goes up.
  (b)   M1 goes up and M2 goes down.
  (c)   M1 goes down and M2 stays the same.
  (d)   M1 stays the same and M2 goes down.

_____ 16.   The value of the money multiplier will be reduced when
  (a)   recipients of bank loans redeposit the proceeds of their loans into another bank.
  (b)   each bank holds zero excess reserves.
  (c)   recipients of bank loans do not keep any of the loan as cash.
  (d)   the required reserves of the banking system are less than its total reserves.

_____   17.   The pressure exerted by the Fed on bankers to discourage them from borrowing from the Fed is called
  (a)   open market operations.
  (b)   closed market operations.
  (c)   closing the discount window.
  (d)   moral suasion.

_____   18.   The discount rate is the interest rate paid by
  (a)   the Fed to banks who deposit funds with it.
  (b)   banks when they borrow from the Fed.
  (c)   banks when they borrow from each other.
  (d)   the Fed to the Treasury to buy U.S. government securities.

_____   19.   Most of the Fed's liabilities are
  (a)   Federal Reserve notes.
  (b)   loans made to the private banks.
  (c)   U.S. government securities.
  (d)   bank reserves deposited by depository institutions.

_____   20.   The required reserve ratio is 25% and all banks, whose total reserves are valued at $200 million, are fully loaned up. If the Fed reduces the required reserve ratio to 20%, the banking system could support an additional
  (a) $100 million in deposits.
  (b) $200 million in deposits.
  (c) $400 million in deposits.
  (d) $500 million in deposits.

II.   APPLICATION QUESTIONS

1.   In the nation of Arboc, the required reserve ratio is 20%. 30% of cash assets end up in foreign accounts. Arbobank (the central bank) buys 500 million opeks of government securities. Calculate how much the money supply will increase. How does the movement of funds to foreign accounts affect the size of the money multiplier?

2.   The required reserve ratio is 20%. All banks are "loaned up." Assume that banks lend their excess reserves.
  (a)   Now First Union discovers an additional $1,000 in excess reserves. Make the final entries on the T-account of each of the following banks after deposits have been received, loans made, spending undertaken, and checks cleared. Assume that a borrower from First Union deposits at Second Union, and so on.

First Union

Assets		Liabilities	
Reserves	_____	Deposits	_____
Loans	_____		

Second Union

Assets		Liabilities	
Reserves	_____	Deposits	_____
Loans	_____		

Third Union

Assets		Liabilities	
Reserves	_____	Deposits	_____
Loans	_____		

Fourth Union

Assets		Liabilities	
Reserves	_____	Deposits	_____
Loans	_____		

(b)   Calculate the extent of overall expansion in the money supply once this process is complete.

3.   ArbeFed (the central bank of Arbez) has assets of 1,000 bandu (in the form of government securities). ArbeFed's liabilities are 800 bandu of currency and 200 bandu of deposits by banks in the central bank. All banks are "loaned up" and all currency is held by the public. Assume that no leakages from the banking system occur.

(a)   Draw a T-account showing ArbeFed's financial position.

(b)   The required reserve ratio is 20%. Determine the size of the Arbezani money supply, M1 (currency plus demand deposits).

(c)   ArbeFed wishes to increase the money supply to 2,000 bandu by adjusting the reserve requirement.

   (i)   Would the reserve requirement have to increase or decrease?

   (ii)   What should the new reserve requirement be?

(d)   ArbeFed decides to reduce the money supply by 300, opting for an open market operation.

   (i)   Should ArbeFed buy bonds or sell bonds on the open market?

   (ii)   How big should this transaction be if ArbeFed sells to the banking system?

   (iii)   How big should this transaction be if ArbeFed sells to the public, which pays by check?

4.   How would each of the following, *ceteris paribus*, affect the M1 and M2 measures of the money supply?

(a)   Households move $10 billion of their liquid wealth from demand deposits to money market accounts.

(b)   Households buy $10 billion worth of traveler's checks and pay with checks drawn on their checking accounts.

(c)   Households cash in $10 billion in savings accounts and keep the proceeds as cash.

5.   List the following assets in terms of their liquidity—i.e., ease and cheapness of conversion into spending power. Put the most liquid first, the least liquid last.

A house; a dollar bill; a car; some IBM stock; a passbook savings account; an individual retirement account.

1. _____   4. _____

2. _____   5. _____

3. _____   6. _____

6.   Use the following information to calculate the total value of M1 (transactions money) and M2 (broad money) as defined in the text.

Money market accounts	50
Credit cards	403
Stock market holdings	1,009
Demand deposits	140
Federal reserve notes held by public	146
Other near monies	196
Treasury bills	708
Traveler's checks	20
Other checkable deposits	80
Savings accounts	300
Treasury bonds	513
Currency held outside banks	10
Gold	73

(a)   M1 _____

(b)   M2 _____

7.   The following table gives several possible required reserve ratios.

Required Reserve Ratio	Money Multiplier	Max. Expansion (Single Bank)	Max. Expansion (Banking System)
10%	_____	_____	_____
12.5%	_____	_____	_____
20%	_____	_____	_____
25%	_____	_____	_____

(a)   Calculate the money multipliers and enter the values in the table.

(b)   Suppose a "loaned up" bank receives a deposit of $100. Given the required reserve ratio, calculate the maximum amount by which the bank could expand its *loans*.

(c)   In each case, calculate the maximum amount by which the banking system will be able to expand its *deposits*.

8.   Suppose that Ace deposits $1,000 into his bank (Bank A), which is fully loaned up. Complete the following table, showing the maximum amount by which deposits, reserves, and loans can increase. Assume that the required reserve ratio is 12.5%.

Bank	New Demand Deposits =	Change in Reserves =	Change in Required Reserves +	Change in Excess Reserves =	Change in Loans
A					
B					
C					
D					
etc.					
Total					

9.   A commercial bank has deposits of $100,000 and total reserves amounting to $31,000. The required reserve ratio is 15%. All other banks are loaned up.
      (a)   What is the largest loan that this bank can make? _____
      (b)   What is the value of the money multiplier? _____
      (c)   If the initial loan is made, what is the maximum expansion that can occur in the money supply if other banks also lend as much as possible? _____

10.   Arboc's central bank (Arbobank) holds 2,000 opeks in government securities. The commercial banks have deposited 200 opeks with Arbobank and hold 100 in vault cash. 700 opeks are held as currency by the public. The required reserve ratio is 20%; banks are loaned up.
      (a)   The money multiplier value is _____.
      (b)   Calculate Arboc's money supply. _____
      It is felt that the money supply should be increased by 900 opeks. Either an open market operation or a change in the reserve ratio is possible.
      (c)   If the reserve ratio is changed, what should be the new ratio? _____
      (d)   If an open market operation is undertaken, it should be a: purchase/sale of _____ opeks.

PRACTICE TEST SOLUTIONS

I.   *Solutions to Multiple-Choice Questions*

1.   (d)   Federal Reserve notes are the official name for dollar bills. Refer to p. 184 [496]. From the economist's point of view, credit cards are a means of obtaining a loan, not a means of payment. Payment comes later, when you send a check to Visa or Mastercard.

2.   (a)   Refer to p. 182 [494] for a discussion of the functions of money.

3.   (d)   The money multiplier is 4 (1/required reserve ratio). Checking accounts (demand deposits) will increase by 400 (100 × 4). Refer to p. 191 [503].

4.   (b)   Refer to p. 189 [501]. Typically, some of a bank's actual reserves will be excess reserves.

5.   (c)   Refer to p. 200 [512] for a discussion of the slope of the money supply curve.

6.   (d)   Centura owes depositors the value of their checking accounts; Centura also owes depositors the value of their money market accounts. Both are liabilities.

7.   (d)   Assets to the left; liabilities to the right. Net worth is the value of the firm (the difference between assets and liabilities).

8.   (b)   Given the reserves of the banking system, if more reserves are required to be held back, the money multiplier (1/required reserve ratio) will decrease and the money supply will decrease. Excess reserves = total reserves − required reserves. As required reserves increase, excess reserves decrease.

9.   (a)   On its own, the deposit has no effect on the money supply. The "currency held outside banks" category decreases by $200; the "demand deposits" category increases by $200. Refer to p. 185 [497]. Eventually, because the money multiplier is 5, deposits will increase by $1,000, but currency held outside banks has decreased by $200. The net change in the money supply is $800.

10.   (c)   When the banking system is loaned up, all reserves are required reserves. Excess reserves are zero. If the required reserve ratio is 25%, the banking system's reserves must be supporting $2,000 billion ($500 billion × 4) in deposits. If the reserve requirement decreases to 10%, only $200 billion will be required, liberating $300 billion as excess reserves.

11.   (d)   If the required reserve ratio is 10%, the banking system's reserves can support $5,000 billion ($500 billion × 10) in deposits—an increase of $3,000 billion.

12.   (c)   The Board of Governors is in charge of monetary policy actions. Clearing checks is not a part of monetary policy. Refer to p. 192 [504].

13.   (a)   An open market sale of securities draws reserves away from the private banking system, reducing the money supply. Increasing the discount rate discourages borrowing. Options (b) and (c) each contain two conflicting policies—if the expansionary element is stronger (open market purchase, discount rate decrease), the money supply would increase.

14.   (d)   The money multiplier is 4. Each dollar loaned out will be multiplied four times by the banking system as a whole.

15.   (c)   M2 includes all components of M1, so the transfer has no effect on the total value of M2. M1 is reduced because savings accounts are not included in M1.

16.   (d)   When the required reserves of the banking system are less than its total reserves, some excess reserves exist. Excess reserves represent a leakage from the money creation process.

17.   (d)   Refer to p. 197 [509] for a reference to moral suasion.

18. (b) Refer to p. 196 [508]. For your information, the rate charged when banks borrow from each other is the federal funds rate.

19. (a) Refer to p. 194 [506].

20. (b) If the banking system is fully loaned up, all reserves are required reserves. With a required reserve ratio of 25%, total deposits must be $800 million ($200 million × 4). If the Fed reduces the required reserve ratio to 20%, the money multiplier will increase to 5, and the banking system will be able to support $1,000 million of deposits ($200 million × 5)—an increase of $200 million.

II.   *Solutions to Application Questions*

1.   Although it should be clear that the leakage of currency to foreign accounts reduces the money multiplier, the exact calculation is more complex than for the case in which there is no such leakage. The individuals who sold the 500 million opeks worth of securities to the government deposit 30% of their receipts abroad, so only 70% (350 million opeks) are deposited in Arbocali accounts. Of the 350 million opeks deposited, 70 million opeks (20%) are retained by private banks as reserves and 280 million opeks are loaned out. Of the 280 million opeks, 30% (84 million) are held in foreign accounts and 70% (196 million) are redeposited domestically. At each stage in the money multiplier process, 20% of each opek is held as reserves and a further 24% (0.8 × 0.3) leaks to foreign accounts, a total of 44%. The money multiplier, then, is 1/0.44, or 2.2727. The total increase in the money supply is 350 million × 2.2727, or 795.4545 million opeks.

2.   (a) Refer to the following T-accounts.

First Union

Assets		Liabilities	
Reserves	−1,000	Deposits	_____
Loans	+1,000		

Second Union

Assets		Liabilities	
Reserves	+200	Deposits	+1,000
Loans	+800		

Third Union

Assets		Liabilities	
Reserves	+160	Deposits	+800
Loans	+640		

Fourth Union

Assets		Liabilities	
Reserves	+128	Deposits	+640
Loans	+512		

(b) The money supply can expand by $5,000.

3.   (a)   Refer to the following T-account.

ArbeFed			
Assets		Liabilities	
Securities	1,000	Currency	800
		Deposits of Banks	200

(b)   Currency = 800. Because the banking system is fully loaned up and the money multiplier is 5.00, demand deposits are 200 × 5, or 1,000. M1 is 1,800 bandu.

(c)   (i)   The reserve requirement must be decreased to 16.67%.

(ii)   The money multiplier is 1/0.1667, or 6. Bank reserves are 200, therefore demand deposits will be 1,200 bandu. Currency remains at 800 bandu.

(d)   (i)   ArbeFed should sell bonds.

(ii)   If the central bank sells bonds worth 60 bandu to the banking system and the money multiplier is 5, the money supply will decrease by 300 bandu.

(iii)   If the central bank sells bonds worth 60 bandu to the public and the public uses demand deposits from the banking system, banking system reserves will fall by 60. The banking system's reserves are 48 bandu too low (i.e., 60 × 0.80). Deposits will shrink by an additional 240 bandu (i.e., 48 × 5). Total decrease is 300 bandu.

4.   (a)   Moving funds from demand deposits to money market deposits: M1, which includes demand deposits but not money market deposits, would decrease by $10 billion; M2 would remain unchanged.

(b)   Moving funds from demand deposits to traveler's checks: M1 and M2 both include both demand deposits and traveler's checks, so each would remain unchanged.

(c)   Moving funds from savings accounts to cash: M1, which includes cash held outside banks but not savings accounts, would increase by $10 billion. M2 wouldn't change.

5.   A dollar bill; a passbook savings account; some IBM stock; an individual retirement account; a car; a house.

6.   (a)   M1 is 396—that is, the total of coins (10) and Federal Reserve Notes (146) held outside banks, traveler's checks (20), demand deposits (140), and other checkable deposits (80).

(b)   M2 is 942—that is, M1 (396) plus savings accounts (300), money market accounts (50), and other near monies (196).

7.   (a)   Refer to the following table.

Required Reserve Ratio	Money Multiplier	Max. Expansion (Single Bank)	Max. Expansion (Banking System)
10%	10	$90.00	$1,000
12.5%	8	$87.50	$800
20%	5	$80.00	$500
25%	4	$75.00	$400

(b)   Refer to the preceding table.
(c)   Refer to the preceding table.

8.   Refer to the following table. "Change in Excess Reserves for Bank A" is $875.00 initially, but will eventually be decreased to zero as Bank A continues to lend.

Bank	New Demand Deposits =	Change in Reserves =	Change in Required Reserves +	Change in Excess Reserves =	Change in Loans
A	$1,000.00	$1,000.00	$125.00	$875.00/0	$875.00
B	$875.00	$875.00	$109.38	$765.62/0	$765.62
C	$765.62	$765.62	$95.70	$669.92/0	$669.92
D	$669.92	$669.38	$83.74	$586.18/0	$586.18
etc.	$4,689.46	$4,689.46	$586.18	$4,103.28/0	$4,103.28
Total	$8,000.00	$8,000.00	$1,000.00	$7,000.00/0	$7,000.00

9.   (a)   Required reserves are $15,000 and excess reserves are $16,000. The bank can lend out all of its excess reserves—that is, $16,000.

(b)   The money multiplier = 1/required reserve ratio = 1/0.15 = 6.667.

(c) $16,000 × 6.667 = $106,666.67

10.   (a)   The money multiplier = 1/required reserve ratio = 1/0.20 = 5.

(b)   Bank reserves are vault cash (100) and deposits at the central bank (200). If the banks are loaned up and the money multiplier is 5, demand deposits must be 1,500 (300 × 5). The money supply includes currency (700) and demand deposits (1,500) = 2,200 opeks.

(c)   To support a money supply of 3,100, with 2,400 opeks of demand deposits (1,500 + 900), using the same quantity of reserves (300), the money multiplier must be 8 (2,400/300). To get a money multiplier of 8, the required reserve ratio must be 12.5%.

(d)   If the money multiplier is 5, a purchase of 180 opeks will increase the money supply by 900.

11 [26]

Money Demand and the Equilibrium Interest Rate

Chapter objectives:

1.   Define the interest rate.
2.   Describe the trade-off facing households when choosing the quantity of money balances to hold for transactions.
3.   Distinguish between the transaction motive and the speculation motive for holding money.
4.   List the variables that influence the demand for money and indicate in which direction the demand for money will be affected by a change in each of them.
5.   Draw a supply and demand diagram of the money market and describe how equilibrium is reached following a demand or supply curve shift.
6.   Discuss the reasoning behind, and the conclusions of, the expectations theory of the term structure of interest rates.

BRAIN TEASER: Can there be too much money supplied—that is, more money in circulation than households and firms wish to hold? What does it mean when the actual interest rate is higher than the equilibrium interest rate? If the stock of money is fixed, how can an excess supply of money be eliminated? How would the behavior of participants in the market cause the market to reach a new equilibrium?

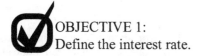
OBJECTIVE 1:
Define the interest rate.

The *interest rate* is the annual interest payment expressed as a percentage of the loan (as opposed to *interest*, which is the charge imposed by a lender on a borrower for the use of funds). (page 203 [515])

For simplicity, the text assumes that there is only one interest rate and that money earns no interest. Historically, the assumption that money earns no interest was accurate—currency doesn't, and, in previous decades, checking accounts earned no interest.

ECONOMICS IN PRACTICE: On page 204 [516], the textbook considers the economic basis of Chekhov's play "Uncle Vanya." Securities yield a return of about 5 percent while Serebryakov's estate yields a return of only 2 percent. Serebryakov proposes to sell his estate and buy securities. Your text asks "If an investor…can earn 5 percent on these securities, why…buy an estate earning only 2 percent?" Can you find an *economic* reason why the low-yielding estate might still be an attractive option? Do you engage in such behavior?

ANSWER: A key principle in investing is diversification, i.e., not putting all of one's eggs in one basket. In investment strategy, variety is often the spice of life. By holding a range of assets (not just bonds; not just real estate), one spreads one's risk. If, personally, you own stock, you most probably own stock in a range of companies, rather than one. Perhaps you've spread the risk by investing in a mutual fund. Some stock will offer higher returns than others but, even if all returns were equal, it is still wise to diversify. Also, you may wish to have a spectrum of assets with differing yields, risks and maturities. Liquidity may also be a consideration.

─────────■──────────────────────────── **Practice** ────────────────────────────

1.   Hansel borrows $50 from Gretel. The loan will last one year. At the end of the year, Hansel will pay Gretel $60. The interest received by Gretel is _____ ; the interest rate is _____ .

    (a) $10; 10%

    (b) $10; 20%

    (c) $60; 10%

    (d) $60; 20%

    ANSWER: (b) Interest is the fee charged for the use of the $50. The interest rate is the annual interest payment ($10) expressed as a percentage of the loan amount ($50). ■

OBJECTIVE 2:

Describe the trade-off facing households when choosing the quantity of money balances to hold for transactions.

The major reason that individuals choose to hold money balances (the *transaction motive*) stems from the need to buy goods and services. Households face an ever-present problem—the *nonsynchronization of income and spending*—i.e., the mismatch in timing between the receipt of income and the need for expenditures. Income may be a single payment per period whereas expenditures are ongoing throughout the period. In a two-asset world, an optimal balance can be achieved by transferring some portion of money balances into interest-bearing assets (bonds). If interest rates are high, the opportunity cost of holding (non-interest-bearing) money is high—less money will be demanded and more interest-bearing assets well be held. (page 205 [517])

   ▶▶   LEARNING TIP: The simple way to remember the reason why there is a negative relationship between the interest rate and the demand for money is in terms of *opportunity cost*. Money earns no interest. If the interest rate rises, the cost of keeping funds in the form of money increases and individuals will transfer their dollars from money to bonds (interest-bearing assets).

           The interest rate is the opportunity cost of holding money—a higher interest rate means less money is demanded and more bonds are demanded. Transaction fees are the opportunity cost of holding bonds—the higher these fees are, the less the demand for bonds and the higher the demand for money.

   ▶▶   LEARNING TIP: Note that the definition of "money" has been restricted to deposits in checking accounts." Cash (which was part of our narrow definition of money in Chapter 10 (25)) has been excluded.◀

As a student with (presumably) limited means, you face the problem described above. Having amassed a bankroll from summer work, how do you allocate your assets? Typically, funds that are less liquid earn higher interest rates, but there may be a "penalty for early withdrawal." Holding all your funds as cash or in a checking account results in an opportunity cost (the interest earnings not obtained). If you could visit the bank only once a month, you would be obliged to hold a fair portion of your assets in readily spendable form (cash, checkbook). With the convenience of the neighborhood 24-hour ATM, you can cut back on idle cash or assets earning lower interest rates. The higher the interest rate, the greater is the incentive to reduce holdings in your checking account.

--- **Practice** ---

2. In economics, when discussing Tessa's "demand for money," we mean
   (a)   how much cash Tessa would like to have.
   (b)   the income that Tessa would need, per time period, to satisfy her minimum living requirements.
   (c)   how much wealth Tessa would like to have.
   (d)   the quantity of Tessa's financial assets that she wishes to hold in non-interest-bearing form.

   ANSWER: (d) The meaning of this phrase is quite specific in economics. Refer to p. 205 [517].

3. The mismatch between income inflows and spending outflows is known as
   (a)   the double coincidence of wants.
   (b)   the want of double coincidence
   (c)   the nonsynchronization problem.
   (d)   cash-flow independence.

   ANSWER: (c) Refer to p. 205 [517]. The mismatch allows us to hold some assets in nonmoney (interest-earning) form.

4. Peter earns $3,000 a month. He deposits $300 in an interest-bearing savings account, and buys $200 worth of government securities. The rest he holds in his checking account. What is Peter's money demand?
   (a) $3,000
   (b) $2,800
   (c) $2,700
   (d) $2,500

   ANSWER: (d) Peter's money demand is the part of his income he does not convert into an interest-bearing asset.

5. Thelma receives a $120 check from home each month. This is just enough to meet her spending needs. She deposits the check in her savings account and regularly draws out enough cash to last her 6 days. In a 30-day month, Thelma's average money balance is
   (a) $4.
   (b) $6.
   (c) $12.
   (d) $24.

   ANSWER: (c) Thelma makes 5 withdrawals of $24 (120/5) each. If she spends her cash evenly, her average holding will be $12 (24/2).

6.   Bill's average monthly balance is $600. He spends the same amount each day and ends the (30-day) month with a balance of $0. Bill's monthly starting balance is _____ and he spends his money at a rate of _____ per day.
    (a) $600; $20
    (b) $1,200; $20
    (c) $600; $40
    (d) $1,200; $40
    ANSWER: (d)   An average of $600 gives an initial balance of $1,200. $1,200/30 = $40.

7.   The optimal money balance will certainly increase if the interest earned on bonds _____ and the costs of switching between bonds and money _____ .
    (a)   increases; increase
    (b)   increases; decrease
    (c)   decreases; increase
    (d)   decreases; decrease
    ANSWER: (c)   The lower the interest rate, the lower the opportunity cost of holding money. The higher the transaction cost, the fewer (but bigger) switches would be undertaken. Refer to p. 207 [519]. ∎

OBJECTIVE 3:
Distinguish between the transaction motive and the speculation motive for holding money.

The *speculation motive* for holding money focuses on the negative relationship between bond prices and the interest rate. In a two-asset world, expectations about future bond prices and the interest rate affect money demand. When market interest rates rise, bond prices fall: when interest rates are expected to rise, bond prices are expected to fall. Low market interest rates foster an expectation of rising rates (and falling bond prices). If a bond is expected to fall in price, its owner will try to sell it—s/he will wish to hold more money at a lower interest rate than at a higher one. (page 208 [520])

━━━━━ Practice ━━━━━

8.   Which statement is false? When the market interest rate is higher than normal,
    (a)   households will expect the interest rate to decrease.
    (b)   households will expect bond prices to increase.
    (c)   the opportunity cost of holding money is lower than normal.
    (d)   households will wish to buy more (interest-bearing) bonds.
    ANSWER: (c)   The opportunity cost of holding money is the interest rate.

9.   When market interest rates are lower than normal,
    (a)   bond prices are expected to increase.
    (b)   bond prices are expected to decrease.
    (c)   the demand for bonds is higher than normal.
    (d)   the yield on bonds is higher than normal.
    ANSWER: (b)   If market interest rates are lower than normal, we expect them to increase. Because there is a negative relationship between the interest rate and bond prices, we expect bond prices to decrease. With low interest rates (and yield), the quantity of bonds demanded will be low.

10.   There is a temporary excess supply in the money market. Eric will
   (a)   hold bonds instead of cash. Interest rates should increase in the future, bringing about an increase in the price of bonds.
   (b)   hold bonds instead of cash Interest rates should decrease in the future, bringing about an increase in the price of bonds.
   (c)   hold cash instead of bonds. Interest rates should increase in the future, bringing about an increase in the price of bonds.
   (d)   hold cash instead of bonds. Interest rates should decrease in the future, bringing about an increase in the price of bonds.

   ANSWER: (b)   An excess supply in the money market leads Eric to expect a decrease in interest rates. A decrease in interest rates causes an increase in the price of bonds. If Eric expects bond prices to rise, he should buy bonds now and sell them after the price increase. ■

OBJECTIVE 4:
List the variables that influence the demand for money and indicate in which direction the demand for money will be affected by a change in each of them.

The *transaction motive* shows that money is demanded to finance transactions, and that the demand for money increases when the dollar value of transactions increases. This may happen if prices rise, or it may happen if there is a greater amount of economic activity, i.e., more transactions. An increase in aggregate output or an increase in the price level will shift the money demand curve to the right. The *speculation motive* reinforces the negative relationship between the interest rate and the quantity of money demanded. With a higher than normal interest rate, the expectation is that the rate will fall and that bond prices will rise. If so, we should hold more of our wealth in the form of bonds (because we think they will become more valuable) and less in the form of money. (page 208 [520])

ECONOMICS IN PRACTICE: On page 209 [521], the textbook examines the effect on the demand for money of more widely available automated teller machines (ATMs). With ATMs more accessible, average cash holdings decrease. Note that the study cited recasts the analysis with interest-earning checking deposits in the role of "bonds" and cash in the role of "non-interest-earning checking deposits". Any factor that decreases the cost of converting deposits to cash should decrease the optimal amount of cash held. Towards the end of 1999, there were concerns over the so-called "Y2K" problem. The rumor was spread that the calendar shift at midnight, Jan. 1, 2000 would cause computer systems (including ATMs) to fail. If this rumor was believed, how should citizens have reacted? Thinking ahead, how might the Fed have changed the money supply as the Y2K deadline approached?
ANSWER: Citizens should have withdrawn a larger-than-average quantity of funds from their bank accounts to be held as cash. Anticipating this, the Fed increased the money supply in the three months leading up to the deadline at an annualized rate of over 70% in order to ensure that there was sufficient liquidity in the system. The Fed estimated that each household would draw out an additional $450 to tide it over the crisis.
ECONOMICS IN PRACTICE (CONTINUED): Although most households do not actively trade bonds, most of us are influenced by interest-earning opportunities (money market accounts, certificates of deposits, and so on) and do not hold all of our funds as cash or in a checking account. What has the development of debit cards done to the demand for cash? Some banks now charge fees when cash is withdrawn from an ATM—what will this do to the optimal amount of cash held?

ANSWER: With the growth in popularity of debit cards, the need for currency has been reduced and there has been increased talk of a "cashless" society. Fees for the withdrawal of funds should result in larger, but less frequent, withdrawals—increasing the optimal amount of cash held.

———————————————————— **Practice** ————————————————————

11.   An increase in the interest rate will _____ the quantity of money demanded for transactions and _____ the quantity of money demanded for speculation.
       (a)   increase; increase
       (b)   increase; decrease
       (c)   decrease; increase
       (d)   decrease; decrease

       ANSWER: (d) The change in the interest rate has a negative effect in each case.

12.   The demand for money curve will shift to the left when
       (a)   the interest rate increases.
       (b)   the price level increases.
       (c)   aggregate output decreases.
       (d)   the price of bonds is expected to decrease.

       ANSWER: (c) Less money will be demanded if the dollar volume of transactions decreases because of a price level decrease or an output level decrease. Changes (Option (a)) or expected changes (Option (d)) in the interest rate don't cause a shift in the position of the demand curve.

13.   The demand for money curve will shift to the right except when there is an increase in
       (a)   aggregate output.
       (b)   the price level.
       (c)   the transactions cost of switching between money and bonds.
       (d)   the money supply.

       ANSWER: (d) An increase in the money supply hikes the interest rate and the quantity of money demanded but will not affect the position of the money demand curve. Option (c) will increase money demand—at each interest rate, more idle cash balances will be held.

14.   If the price level falls, the money demand curve will
       (a)   shift to the right.
       (b)   shift to the left.
       (c)   become steeper.
       (d)   become flatter.

       ANSWER: (b) Refer to p. 210 [522]. ■

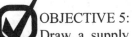OBJECTIVE 5:
       Draw a supply and demand diagram of the money market and describe how equilibrium is reached following a demand or supply curve shift.

The money market is modeled quite simply. The money demand curve shows the negative relationship between the quantity of money demanded and the interest rate. Money supply is fixed at a particular level at any point in time—the curve is vertical. The interaction of money supply and money demand establishes an equilibrium interest rate (r_1^*), where quantity demanded equals quantity supplied. Suppose the market is initially in equilibrium at r_1^*. If, for example, the demand for money increases (from $M^d{}_1$ to $M^d{}_2$), the interest rate will rise (from r_1^* to r_2^*) because, at the original interest rate (r_1^*), an excess demand for money is now present. To dissuade individuals from holding cash and to encourage bond purchases, the interest rate must increase. (page 211 [523])

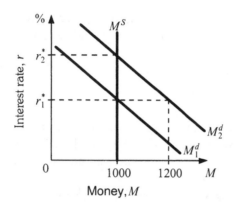

One key player in the money market is the Fed, of course, because Fed actions can increase or decrease the money supply. The Fed, for instance, may decide to buy bonds (an open market purchase). This will shift the money supply curve to the right and, at the original equilibrium interest rate, an excess supply of money will be created. The Fed action (an easy monetary policy) will cause the market interest rate to decrease. As we see in the following chapter, a lower interest will stimulate aggregate output.

▶▶▶   LEARNING TIP: Review the material in Chapter 10 (25) referring to the Fed's three monetary policy instruments. Keep in mind the factors that can shift the money demand curve—aggregate income level and the price level. An increase in either will shift the money demand curve to the right. Changes in the interest rate will cause a *movement along the curve*. If you are a little rusty on demand and supply analysis, e.g., the difference between a "change in demand" and a "change in quantity demanded," review Chapter 3 now.

Because its actions can increase or decrease the money supply, it plays a key role in the money market. Review the material in Chapter 10 (25) referring to the Fed's three main monetary policy instruments.

───────■─────────────────────── **Practice** ───────────────────────────

15.   If the supply of money increases as a result of an open market _____ of securities by the Fed, the interest rate will _____ .

(a)   purchase; increase
(b)   purchase; decrease
(c)   sale; increase
(d)   sale; decrease

ANSWER: (b) The Fed buys bonds to increase the money supply. An increase in the money supply decreases the equilibrium interest rate.

16. If the demand for money decreases as a result of a(n) _____ in the price level, the interest rate will _____ .
    (a)   increase; increase
    (b)   increase; decrease
    (c)   decrease; increase
    (d)   decrease; decrease

    ANSWER: (d) As the price level falls, less cash is needed to finance a given level of transactions.

17. If the demand for money increases as a result of an increase in the price level, the money supply will _____ and, ultimately, the size of money balances will _____ .
    (a)   increase; increase
    (b)   increase; not change
    (c)   not change; increase
    (d)   not change; not change

    ANSWER: (d) A change in demand does not cause the supply curve to shift. In equilibrium, demand must equal supply, so the quantity of money demanded will return to its original level (as the interest rate increases).

Use the following diagram to answer the next four questions.

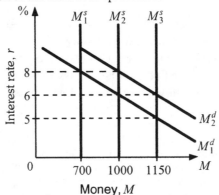

18. The money demand curve is M^d_1 and the money supply curve is M^s_1. At an interest rate of 5%, there is an excess
    (a)   demand of 150.
    (b)   demand of 300.
    (c)   supply of 150.
    (d)   supply of 300.

    ANSWER: (a) At 5%, quantity demanded (1,150) exceeds quantity supplied (1,000).

19. The money demand curve might shift from M^d_1 to M^d_2 if
    (a)   the money supply increased.
    (b)   the interest rate decreased.
    (c)   the Fed bought bonds in the open market.
    (d)   the real output level increased.

    ANSWER: (d) The real output level is a determinant of money demand. Refer to p. 210 [522].

20.   The money supply curve might shift from M^s_2 to M^s_3 if
   (a)   the Fed undertook an easy monetary policy such as an open market purchase of securities.
   (b)   the Fed undertook an easy monetary policy such as an open market sale of securities.
   (c)   the Fed undertook a tight monetary policy such as an open market purchase of securities.
   (d)   the Fed undertook a tight monetary policy such as an open market sale of securities.

   ANSWER: (a) The shift from M^s_2 to M^s_3 is an expansion, caused by an easy money policy. An open market purchase of securities could cause this.

21.   The equilibrium interest rate will definitely increase if the money demand curve shifts from _____ and the money supply curve shifts from _____ .
   (a) M^d_1 to M^d_2; M^s_1 to M^s_2
   (b) M^d_1 to M^d_2; M^s_2 to M^s_1
   (c) M^d_2 to M^d_1; M^s_1 to M^s_2
   (d) M^d_2 to M^d_1; M^s_2 to M^s_1

   ANSWER: (b) Refer to the diagram.

22.   Which of the following pairs of events will definitely result in an increase in the equilibrium interest rate? A(n) _____ in the price level and an open market _____ of securities.
   (a)   increase; purchase
   (b)   increase; sale
   (c)   decrease; purchase
   (d)   decrease; sale

   ANSWER: (b) An increase in money demand will accompany an increase in the price level. An open market sale of securities is a tight monetary policy. ■

OBJECTIVE 6 (APPENDIX A):
Discuss the reasoning behind, and the conclusions of, the expectations theory of the term structure of interest rates.

Appendix A: There is not one "interest rate" but rather a whole family of rates. The *expectations theory of the term structure of interest rates* links the behavior of long-term rates to current short-term rates and expected short-term rates. Essentially, long-term rates are based on current short-term rates and expectations about how short-term rates will change in the future. The Fed can influence long-term rates (such as 30-year mortgage rates) as well as short-term rates, although it has less control over long-term rates. (page 216 [528])

■——————————————— Practice ———————————————

23.   Government securities that take longer than one year to mature are called
   (a)   Treasury bills.
   (b)   government bonds.
   (c)   Federal bonds.
   (d)   Federal Fund bills.

   ANSWER: (b) Refer to p. 216 [528]. Bills mature in less than a year, bonds in one or more years.

24.   The current interest rate on a one-year bond is 4%. On a similar bond next year the rate is expected to be 6%. According to the expectations theory of the term structure of interest rates, the current rate on a two-year bond is
(a)   2%.
(b)   4%.
(c)   5%.
(d)   10%.

ANSWER: (c)   The two-year rate is the average of the current one-year rate and the one-year rate expected in the future—i.e., $(6 + 4)/2$.

25.   The current interest rate on a one-year bond is 4%. The current rate on a two-year bond is 7%. According to the expectations theory of the term structure of interest rates, the expected rate on a similar one-year bond next year is
(a)   3%.
(b)   5.5%.
(c)   7%.
(d)   10%.

ANSWER: (d)   The two-year rate (7%) is the average of the current one-year rate (4%) and the one-year rate expected in the future (10%).

26.   The Fed reduces the interest rate on Treasury bills by 1%. According to the expectations theory of the term structure of interest rates, the interest rate on 30-year government bonds will
(a)   increase by more than 1%.
(b)   increase by less than 1%.
(c)   decrease by more than 1%.
(d)   decrease by less than 1%.

ANSWER: (d)   Rates move together but long-term rates tend to be more stable. Refer to p. 216 [528]. The difficulty that the Fed experienced in the early 2000s in moving down 30-year mortgage rates is an example of such sluggishness. ∎

BRAIN TEASER SOLUTION: The money demand and money supply diagram will help answer this question.

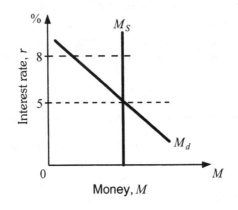

At 8%, the actual interest rate exceeds the equilibrium value, the quantity of money supplied exceeds quantity demanded. If the money supply doesn't change, market forces will bid down the interest rate. At 8%, individuals are unwilling to hold money, preferring bonds because of the attractive interest rate. As the demand for bonds increases, the price of bonds will increase. There is an inverse relationship between the interest rate and the price of bonds—the interest rate will decrease. Put differently, because bonds are attractive, bond sellers will not need to offer as high an interest rate to attract business. As the interest rate (the opportunity cost of holding money) declines, the quantity of money demanded increases. This process will continue until equilibrium is achieved, at 5%.

A WORD TO THE WISE

Obviously, Chapters 10 (25) and 11 (26) go together. In Chapter 12 (27), this material will be combined with the earlier macroeconomic model of the goods market. To understand the more complex model, take some time *now* to make sure that you understand the reasoning behind supply and demand in the money market. Why does the money demand curve slope downward? What can shift it? Why is the money supply curve vertical? How will changes in each of the three policy tools affect its position? What is the reasoning behind the move from one equilibrium interest rate to the next? The following Practice Test should help you locate and correct any remaining weak points in your understanding.

PRACTICE TEST

I.   MULTIPLE-CHOICE QUESTIONS

Select the option that provides the single best answer.

_____   1.   A Fed sale of securities to the banks will cause all of the following EXCEPT
(a)   a fall in bank reserves.
(b)   an increase in the interest rate.
(c)   a fall in the money supply.
(d)   a rise in the value of the money multiplier.

_____   2.   In the demand for money model developed in the text, all of the following are assumed to be true EXCEPT that
(a)   money—checking account balances—earns no interest.
(b)   income is received at a completely uniform rate throughout the month.
(c)   bonds represent interest-bearing assets of all kinds.
(d)   the timing of money inflow and money outflow for household expenses is mismatched.

_____   3.   The money market is in equilibrium. Now the Fed buys securities. There will be an excess _____ money. This will cause the interest rate to _____ .
(a)   demand for; fall
(b)   supply of; rise
(c)   demand for; rise
(d)   supply of; fall

_____   4.   The quantity of money demanded is _____ related to the dollar volume of transactions and _____ related to the interest rate.
(a)   positively; positively
(b)   positively; negatively
(c)   negatively; positively
(d)   negatively; negatively

_____ 5.   A fall in the price level will _____ the demand for money, and a rise in the number of transactions will _____ the demand for money.
   (a)   increase; increase
   (b)   increase; decrease
   (c)   decrease; increase
   (d)   decrease; decrease

_____ 6.   Each of the following will make the public wish to hold more money balances EXCEPT
   (a)   an increase in the price level.
   (b)   a decrease in the interest rate.
   (c)   an increase in the opportunity cost of holding money.
   (d)   an increase in the dollar volume of transactions.

_____ 7.   The money market is in equilibrium. Now there is an *expansion* in the money supply. This will cause the interest rate to _____ and the quantity of money demanded to _____ .
   (a)   increase; increase
   (b)   decrease; increase
   (c)   decrease; decrease
   (d)   increase; decrease

_____ 8.   The demand for money is a _____ measure, and the supply of money is a _____ measure.
   (a)   flow; flow
   (b)   flow; stock
   (c)   stock; flow
   (d)   stock; stock

_____ 9.   When the interest rate rises,
   (a)   the opportunity cost of holding money increases.
   (b)   the transactions cost of holding money increases.
   (c)   the transactions cost of holding money decreases.
   (d)   the opportunity cost of holding money decreases.

_____ 10.   The Fed's ability to control the money supply is due to its ability to
   (a)   encourage banks not to borrow too heavily.
   (b)   affect banking system reserves.
   (c)   sell Treasury bonds at a profit.
   (d)   buy Treasury bonds at a profit.

_____ 11.   The current interest rate on a one-year bond is 8%. On a similar bond next year the rate is expected to rise to 10%, and the year after a similar bond is expected to earn 15%. According to the expectations theory of the term structure of interest rates, the current rate on a three-year bond is around
   (a)   8%.
   (b)   10%.
   (c)   11%.
   (d)   15%.

_____ 12. Each of the following will cause an increase in the money supply EXCEPT
       (a)   a reduction in the required reserve ratio.
       (b)   an increase in the demand for money.
       (c)   a purchase of securities by the Fed from the public.
       (d)   a purchase of securities by the Fed from the commercial banks.

_____ 13. Given an interest rate increase,
       (a)   optimal money balances will increase.
       (b)   optimal money balances will decrease.
       (c)   the equilibrium supply of money will increase.
       (d)   the equilibrium supply of money will decrease.

_____ 14. The slope of the money demand curve illustrates the idea that there is
       (a)   a positive relationship between the interest rate and the quantity of money demanded.
       (b)   a positive relationship between the price level and the quantity of money demanded.
       (c)   a negative relationship between the interest rate and the quantity of money demanded.
       (d)   a negative relationship between the value of transactions and the quantity of money demanded.

_____ 15. The money demand curve will shift right in each of the following cases EXCEPT when
       (a)   the price level increases.
       (b)   the interest rate increases.
       (c)   the nominal output level increases.
       (d)   the real output level increases.

_____ 16. Which of the following pairs of events will most likely result in an increase in the equilibrium interest rate? A(n) _____ in the level of aggregate output and a(n) _____ in the required reserve ratio.
       (a)   increase; increase
       (b)   increase; decrease
       (c)   decrease; increase
       (d)   decrease; decrease

_____ 17. As the number of economic transactions increases,
       (a)   more money will be demanded.
       (b)   less money will be demanded.
       (c)   more money will be supplied.
       (d)   less money will be supplied.

_____ 18. The Fed conducts an open market sale. We would predict each of the following EXCEPT
       (a)   a decrease in the money supply.
       (b)   an increase in the interest rate.
       (c)   an increase in the price of bonds.
       (d)   a decrease in the quantity of money demanded.

_____ 19.   If the Fed were to announce that it would follow an "easy" monetary policy over the next few months, we would expect to see each of the following EXCEPT
(a)   an increasing money supply.
(b)   open market purchases of securities by the Fed.
(c)   falling interest rates.
(d)   a rising required reserve ratio.

_____ 20.   When the Fed undertakes open market operations, the interest rate that it controls most closely is the
(a)   prime rate.
(b)   discount rate.
(c)   federal funds rate.
(d)   government bond rate.

II.   APPLICATION QUESTIONS

1.   The money market and the bond market are closely intertwined. Explain what will happen to the price of bonds and to money holdings if the Fed changes the interest rate as a result of a decrease in the money supply.

2.   Cupro the copper miner earns $1,200 per month and his expenditures (which equal $1,200) proceed at a constant daily rate. Given transactions costs and interest he can earn on savings, he makes 4 trips to the bank each month.
(a)   Calculate his average money demand (M^d).
(b)   Now suppose that the interest rate on Cupro's savings account increases. Predict what will happen to his average money demand.
(c)   Now suppose that the bank announces that the withdrawal forms for savings accounts must be notarized (an expensive and time-consuming business). Predict what will happen to Cupro's average money demand.

3.   Suppose you are lucky enough to get a monthly paycheck of $3,500 which is automatically deposited at the beginning of each month into a checking account. You will spend the entire $3,500 each month, but you can transfer funds into bonds that earn 1% interest each month. Transferring between bonds and money requires you to pay a $1.50-per-transfer charge. Use the following table (based on those in Appendix B in the textbook) to calculate each of the following:
(a)   Your optimal money demand.
(b)   The optimal amount of money to transfer each time you go to the automatic teller machine (ATM).
(c)   The optimal number of trips to take to the automatic teller machine (ATM).
(d)   Your optimal total cost of holding money over the month.

Number of Switches	Average Money Holdings	Average Bond Holdings	Interest Earned	Cost of Switching	Net Profit
0					
1					
2					
3					
4					
5					
6					
7					
8					

(e)   Your income is $4,000 per month, the brokerage fee is $2.50, and the interest rate rises to 1%. Predict what will happen to your money demand.

(f)   Your income is $3,500, the brokerage fee is $2.50, and the interest rate rises to 5%. Predict what will happen to your money demand.

(g)   Your income is $3,500, the interest rate is 1%, and the brokerage fee falls to $1.00. Predict what will happen to your money demand.

4.   Maureen buys a $1,000 fixed rate perpetual bond at the going market interest rate of 10%. Note: A perpetual bond (or "consol") is a bond with no maturity date. The payment received on the bond is constant at $100 per year. To calculate the yield on the bond, use the formula:

(payment on bond × 100%)/Price of Bond

Initially, the yield on the bond is competitive with the interest rate to be earned elsewhere in the financial market. Suppose now that the market interest rate decreases to 5% (Situation A).

	Price of Bond	Payment on Bond	Yield on Bond	Market Interest Rate
Initial purchase	$1,000	$100	10%	10%
Situation A		$100		5%
Situation B		$100		20%

(a)   What yield must Maureen's bond have to be competitive with other financial assets?
(b)   In Situation A, is Maureen's bond attractive or unattractive to potential buyers?
(c)   If Maureen decides to sell the bond, which price is fair, relative to the rest of the market?
Suppose the interest rate increases from 10% to 20% (Situation B).
(d)   In Situation B, is Maureen's bond attractive or unattractive to potential buyers?
(e)   If Maureen decides to sell the bond, which price is fair, relative to the rest of the market?

5.   The Arbezani money demand curve is given by the following equation:

$$M^d = 5,000 - 10,000r + 5Y$$

M^d is money demand, r is the real interest rate, and Y is aggregate income.

(a)   Suppose that aggregate income is 3,000. Graph the money demand curve ($M^{d}{}_{1}$) following. (It's a straight line.)

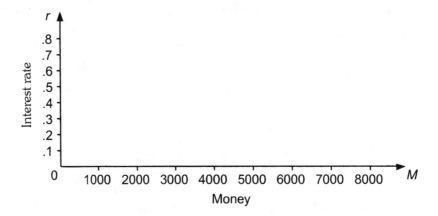

(b)   Why does the equation have a negative value for the second term and a positive value for the third term?

(c)   At an interest rate of 10% ($r = 0.1$), calculate money demand.

(d)   At an interest rate of 20% ($r = 0.2$), calculate money demand.

(e)   Suppose that the equilibrium interest rate is 30% ($r = 0.3$). Draw the money supply curve (M^{s}) on the diagram.

(f)   Income rises from $Y = 3,000$ to $Y = 5,000$. Draw the new money demand curve ($M^{d}{}_{2}$) on the diagram.

(g)   At the existing interest rate, there is an excess _____ (demand/supply) of money.

(h)   The new equilibrium interest rate will be _____ .

(i)   How much must the money supply increase to restore the original interest rate?

(j)   The required reserve ratio in Arbez is 10%. How great an open market purchase or sale of securities should ArbeFed (the central bank) undertake to restore the original interest rate? Purchase/sale of $_____ .

6.   Arlene, Charlene, and Darlene each earn and spend $24,000 each year. What is the average money holding in each case?
(a)   Arlene is paid yearly. _____
(b)   Charlene is paid quarterly. _____
(c)   Darlene is paid monthly. _____

7.   Will money demand increase (I) or decrease (D) in each of the following cases?
(a)   ____   The price level rises.
(b)   ____   New technology makes access to the stock market instantaneous using a home computer.
(c)   ____   More credit cards are accepted.
(d)   ____   It is arranged nationally that all bills and income will be received on the first day of each month.
(e)   ____   The nominal GDP level increases.
(f)   ____   Weakening of strict regulation of the financial sector makes buying bonds more risky.
(g)   ____   Banks begin to require a $1,000 minimum balance to be kept in checking accounts at all times.

8.   The required reserve ratio is 20%. The Fed wants to reduce the money supply by $60 million. Describe an open market operation that will achieve this goal.
Open market _____ (purchase/sale) in the amount of $_____ .

9.   Graphically, the supply curve for money is _____ . The money supply does not depend on the _____ _____ or the level of _____ _____ (both factors that influence the demand for money). In the money market, the equilibrium interest rate is established where the quantity of money supplied equals the quantity demanded. If the interest rate is "too high," the quantity supplied will be _____ (greater/less) than the quantity demanded. To reach equilibrium, the interest rate must _____ (rise/fall). This will happen because, with an _____ (excess demand for/excess supply of) money, households will try to _____ (increase/decrease) their money holdings by _____ (buying/selling) bonds. Those selling bonds will be able to do so at a _____ interest rate.
      If the interest rate is "too low," the quantity supplied will be _____ (greater/less) than the quantity demanded. To reach equilibrium, the interest rate must _____ (rise/fall). This will happen because, with an _____ (excess demand for/excess supply of) money, households will try to _____ (increase/decrease) their money holdings by _____ (buying/selling) bonds. Bond issuers will have to offer _____ (higher/lower) interest rates to attract buyers.

10.   What happens to the amount of money demanded or supplied in each of the following cases? Draw a separate money demand and money supply graph for each part of this question, label the axes, and show how the change will shift the money demand and/or the money supply curve. Explain any curve shifts in each case. Show initial and final equilibrium interest rate and quantity of money.

(a)   The Fed sells securities in the open market while the economy is experiencing high inflation.

(b)   The Fed decreases the required reserve ratio during a recession.

(c)   During a deep recession, the Fed moves to hold the interest rate constant.

(d)   A rise in nominal GDP is accompanied by an increase in the discount rate.

(e)   The Fed conducts an open market purchase of securities, and banks begin imposing a $50 charge on all returned checks.

(f)   The economy moves into a downturn, and the commercial banks become more cautious in their lending policies.

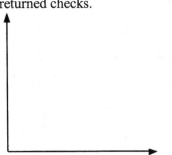

PRACTICE TEST SOLUTIONS

I.   Solutions to Multiple-Choice Questions

1.   (d)   When the Fed sells securities to the commercial banks, the banks pay for them with reserves (Option (a)). As the reserves supporting the money supply fall, the money supply itself will decrease (Option (b)). As the money supply curve shifts to the left, the interest rate will increase (Option (c)). The money multiplier is determined by the size of the required reserve ratio, which has not changed.

2.   (b)   Income is assumed to be "bunched up." Refer to p. 205 [517].

3.   (d)   When the Fed buys securities, the money supply increases. There will be an excess supply of money at the initial interest rate, causing the interest rate to decrease.

4.   (b)   Individuals need more spending power as their level of transactions increases. The amount of money demanded decreases when the interest rate increases because the interest rate is the opportunity cost of holding money. Refer to p. 208 [520].

5.   (c)   When goods can be bought for less, fewer dollars are needed. Refer to p. 210 [522].

6.   (c)   An increase in the opportunity cost of holding money is another way of describing an increase in the interest rate.

7.   (b)   As the money supply increases, the interest rate will decrease, causing a movement down along the money demand curve (an increase in quantity demanded).

8.   (d)   Both the demand for and the supply of money are measured at a point in time—clear evidence that they are stock variables. A flow is measured over a period of time.

9.   (a)   Transactions cost includes the time and inconvenience involved in making a transaction and possible explicit costs such as handling fees. The opportunity cost of holding money is the interest rate.

10.   (b)   Refer to p. 212 [524].

11.   (c)   The current rate on a three-year bond is approximately the average of the interest rates on the three one-year bonds [(8 + 10 + 15)/3]. Refer to Appendix A.

12.   (b)   A change in money demand will not affect the money supply. A reduction in the required reserve ratio will increase the money multiplier, increasing the money supply. A Fed purchase of securities will expand the money supply.

13.   (b)   As the interest rate increases, the opportunity cost of holding money increases and, on average, less money will be held. The money supply is vertical—it is unaffected by changes in the interest rate.

14.   (c)   The downward slope shows that the quantity of money demanded decreases as the interest rate increases. Note that it is true that an increase in the price level will increase the demand for money, but this is depicted as a rightward shift of the money demand curve.

15.   (b)   A change in the interest rate causes a movement along the demand curve. Note that nominal output is the price level times real output and that one or the other must have risen for nominal output to increase.

16.   (a)   An increase in the level of aggregate output will increase the demand for money, while an increase in the required reserve ratio will decrease money supply.

17.   (a)   The dollar volume of transactions has a positive relationship with money demand.

18.   (c)   An open market sale will reduce the money supply—refer to Chapter 10 (25). A decrease in the money supply will drive up the interest rate. When the interest rate increases, the price of bonds decreases.

19.   (d)   Increases in the required reserve ratio are intended to tighten up the money supply.

20.   (c)   Refer to p. 216 [528] for more about the role of this key interest rate.

II.   Solutions to Application Questions

1.   If the Fed decreases the money supply, perhaps through an open market sale of securities, the equilibrium interest rate will increase. At the initial equilibrium interest rate, say 5%, the quantity of money demanded will now exceed quantity supplied—individuals do not have enough funds available to finance their necessary transactions. As a result, individuals will attempt to increase their money holdings by selling off bonds. As the demand for bonds dwindles, bond sellers must increase the reward for holding bonds (the interest rate) to attract customers. This interest rate is the opportunity cost of holding money. As the interest rate rises, the quantity of money demanded falls. The process continues until equilibrium is achieved.

2.   (a) $M^d = \dfrac{1}{2}[1,200/4] = 150$

      (b)   Cupro's average money demand will fall because he has more incentive to leave idle balances in the form of savings deposits rather than cash.

(c)   With notarization of withdrawal forms, the cost involved in converting deposits into cash has increased. Cupro will reduce the number of withdrawals he makes. His average money balance will increase.

3.   (a)   Refer to the following table.

Number of Switches	Average Money Holdings	Average Bond Holdings	Interest Earned	Cost of Switching	Net Profit
0	$1,750.00	$0.00	$0.00	$0.00	$0.00
1	$875.00	$875.00	$8.75	$1.50	$7.25
2	$583.33	$1,166.67	$11.67	$3.00	$8.67
3	$437.50	$1,312.50	$13.12	$4.50	$8.62
4	$350.00	$1,400.00	$14.00	$6.00	$8.00
5	$291.67	$1,458.33	$14.58	$7.50	$7.08
6	$250.00	$1,500.00	$15.00	$9.00	$6.00

(b)   Refer to the preceding table.
(c)   Refer to the preceding table.
(d)   Refer to the preceding table.
(e)   Your money demand should rise. Refer to p. 210 [522] for a review.
(f)   Your money demand should fall. Refer to p. 210 [522] for a review.
(g)   Your money demand should fall. Refer to p. 210 [522] for a review.

4.   (a)   5%.
(b)   Attractive. At the moment, it is yielding 10%, which is better than the marketwide 5%.
(c)   The yield should be comparable with the market interest rate, otherwise Maureen is selling too cheaply. Yield = Payment on bond × 100%/Price of Bond
$100 × 100%/Price of Bond = 5%. The market price of the bond is $2,000.
(d)   Unattractive. At the moment, Maureen's bond is yielding 10%, which is less good than the marketwide 20%.
(e)   The yield should be comparable with the market interest rate, otherwise Maureen is asking too high a price. Yield = Payment on bond × 100%/Price of Bond
$100 × 100%/Price of Bond = 20%. The market price of the bond is $500.
     As shown by the table, there is an inverse relationship between the market interest rate and the price of bonds.

	Price of Bond	Payment on Bond	Yield on Bond	Market Interest Rate
Initial Purchase	$1,000	$100	10%	10%
Situation A	$2,000	$100	10%	5%
Situation B	$500	$100	10%	20%

5.   (a)   Refer to the following diagram. When the interest rate is zero, money demand is 6,500. When money demand is zero, $10,000r = 5,000 + 1,500r$. $r = 0.65$, i.e., 65%.

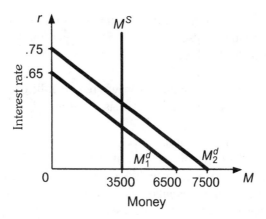

(b)   All this means is that there is a negative relationship between the demand for money and the interest rate and a positive relationship between the demand for money and the level of spending in the economy.

(c)   Money demand = 5,000 – 10,000 (0.1) + 1,500 = 5,500.

(d)   Money demand = 5,000 – 10,000 (0.2) + 1,500 = 4,500.

(e)   Money demand = 5,000 – 10,000 (0.3) + 1,500 = 3,500. In equilibrium, the money supply, which graphs as a vertical line, must also be 3,500. Refer to the preceding diagram.

(f)   Refer to the preceding diagram. When the interest rate is zero, money demand is 7,500. When money demand is zero, $10,000r = 7,000$. $r = 0.75$, i.e., 75%.

(g)   excess demand. In fact, we can be precise. Money supply = 3,500. Money demand = 5,000 – 10,000(0.3) + 2,500 = 4,500. There is an excess demand of 1,000.

(h)   Money supply = 3,500. To restore equilibrium, money demand must be 3,500. Money demand = 5,000 – 10,000(x) + 2,500 = 3,500. $x = 0.40$. The equilibrium interest rate is 40%.

(i) $1,000. Refer to the answer to Part (g).

(j)   The money multiplier = 1/required reserve ratio = 10. An open market purchase of $100 would expand the money supply by $1,000.

6.   (a)   Arlene holds an average of $12,000. Average holding = $24,000/2.
                Maximum withdrawal = $24,000/1 = $24,000.

        (b)   Charlene holds an average of $3,000. Average holding = $6,000/2.
                Maximum withdrawal = $24,000/4 = $6,000.

        (c)   Darlene holds an average of $1,000. Average holding = $2,000/2.
                Maximum withdrawal = $24,000/12 = $2,000.

7.   (a)   I.   Volume of transactions has a positive effect on money demand.

        (b)   D.   The transactions cost of transferring funds has become less, so withdrawals of money will be more frequent but less sizable. Refer to p. 207 [519].

        (c)   D.   As credit cards are used more, cash will be used less.

        (d)   D.   This new national arrangement reduces the problem of nonsynchronization. Money holdings needed to pay the flow of bills will be reduced.

        (e)   I.   Volume of transactions has a positive effect on money demand. Refer to p. 210 [522].

        (f)   I.   There will be more reluctance to hold bonds and less reluctance to hold money.

        (g)   I.   This is a transactions cost.

8.   The Fed wants the money supply to contract, so an open market sale is called for. The money multiplier = 1/required reserve ratio = 5. An open market sale of $12 million would reduce the money supply by $60 million.

9.   vertical; interest rate; economic activity; greater; fall; excess supply of; decrease; buying; lower; less; increase; excess demand for; increase; selling; higher

10.   Refer to the following solutions.

(a)   The Fed sale reduces the money supply; the rising price level will increase money demand. The two changes will drive the interest rate higher.

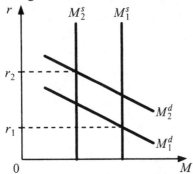

(b)   The decrease in the required reserve ratio will increase the money supply. Money demand will decrease during the recession. Together, the changes will lower the interest rate.

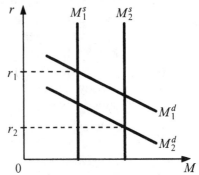

(c)   During a deep recession, money demand will shift left (decrease). This will decrease the interest rate. The Fed must reduce the money supply to hold the interest rate constant.

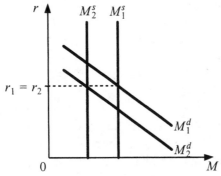

(d)   A rise in nominal GDP will increase the demand for money. An increase in the discount rate will decrease the money supply. Together, the changes will increase the interest rate.

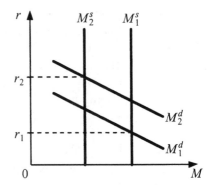

(e)   The open market purchase of securities will increase the money supply. The $50 bank charge will either encourage individuals to use cash more or to keep more funds in their (M1) checking accounts. The effect on the interest rate is ambiguous.

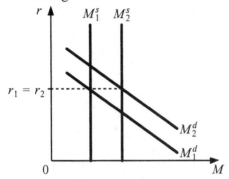

(f)   The downturn in the economy will decrease the demand for money; the new caution in lending will increase excess reserves, decrease the money multiplier, and reduce the money supply. The effect on the interest rate is ambiguous.

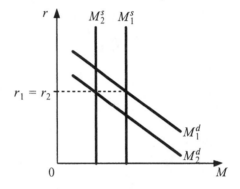

12 [27]

Aggregate Demand in the Goods and Money Markets

Chapter objectives:

1. Identify the two links between the money market and the goods market. Outline the reasons for the inverse relationship between planned investment and the interest rate.
2. Distinguish between fiscal policy and monetary policy. Distinguish between a contractionary and an expansionary policy, specifying the tools used in each case.
3. Explain when and how the crowding-out effect occurs. Explain the impact of the interest sensitivity of investment demand on the effectiveness of monetary policy.
4. Outline the issues involved in determining the optimal policy mix.
5. Derive and explain the slope of the aggregate demand curve. Explain what the curve represents.
6. Identify how aggregate demand is affected by monetary and fiscal policy actions.
7. Explain what is depicted by the *IS* curve and the *LM* curve.

Although there is some important new material in this chapter (aggregate demand), much is not new—it combines material that has been built up independently. The best study tip is to review your notes before beginning this material. If you lose track of the discussion, refer to the earlier chapters.

The most common mistake is to *not* recognize how the goods and money markets influence each other. Think of it this way: If the demand for goods and services is to be met, then output in the goods market must match demand, and this affects the dollar volume of transactions in the economy. Money demand must adjust to this circumstance. The money market must respond by matching the demand and supply of money. Changes in the money market affect the interest rate, which impacts on investment decisions in the goods market. And so on.

▶▶▶ LEARNING TIP: The *Practice Test Solutions* section in this guide carefully traces through the detail of the relationships between the goods market and money market. Think of the "Answers" as additional practice—verify each step and verify *why* each incorrect option is incorrect.

The text contains some "economic shorthand." It's useful for you in note taking, it shows the logical sequence of events, and it summarizes all the steps neatly. For some extra practice, work through each case in the textbook's Table 12.1 (27.1).

Caution! It is easy to forget that an economic notation like "→" represents underlying behavioral relationships that you must understand (rather than just memorize). Take the time to think about each step in these very condensed sequences.◀

BRAIN TEASER: By July 2003 the Fed had cut interest rates to a 40-year low to help stimulate the economy. The federal funds rate was hovering around 1%. Can nominal (market) interest rates be less than zero? This would mean that you would be willing to deposit $100 today with a promise of receiving only $95 a year from now. The alternative is simply holding the $100 in cash. Why might you be willing to accept a negative interest rate?

 OBJECTIVE 1:
Identify the two links between the money market and the goods market. Outline the reasons for the inverse relationship between planned investment and the interest rate.

There are two links between the goods market and the money market.

(a)   Money market to goods market link: If the interest rate rises, planned investment falls—higher borrowing costs make fewer investment projects profitable—and equilibrium output level falls. Because the level of planned aggregate expenditure (which includes planned investment) depends on the interest rate, equilibrium in the goods market depends on circumstances in the money market. (page 220 [532])
A change in the money market that causes a change in the interest rate will also cause a change in the equilibrium level of production in the goods market. Other factors—such as expected future sales, optimism or pessimism ("animal spirits")—will also affect the desired level of investment. These factors will be discussed in Chapter 16 (31).

(b)   Goods market to money market link: Money demand is affected by the level of income. If planned expenditure increases (decreases) in the goods market, the demand for money will increase (decrease), pushing up (down) the equilibrium interest rate. Because the demand for money depends on the level of economic activity, equilibrium in the money market depends on circumstances in the goods market. (page 222 [534])

▶▶▶   LEARNING TIP: If you're unsure about the second link, you should review Chapter 11 (26) where the connection between the demand for money (for transactions purposes) and the level of economic activity is discussed. Simply put, as the level of economic activity expands, so too does the demand for purchasing power.◀

There must be a unique combination of output level and interest rate that will give simultaneous equilibrium in both markets.

Comment: There is only one unique combination of r and Y that will equilibrate both markets simultaneously. Don't get this wrong! As "given" variables—G, T, or M^S for example—change, so will the specific r and Y values that will ensure equilibrium.

▶▶▶   LEARNING TIP: There are two main points to note here. First, the two markets are linked—the movement to equilibrium in one market affects equilibrium in the other. Second, it's a two-way street—changes in the goods market affect the money market, and changes in the money market affect the goods market.
▶▶▶   LEARNING TIP: Make sure you understand Figure 12.2 (27.2). Graphically, it gives you the complete story of the links between the goods market and the money market.
▶▶▶   LEARNING TIP: Follow through the *feedback effects* between the two markets, and you will see that neither the *AE* nor the money demand curve achieves its final equilibrium immediately. As each adjusts, so the other will adjust a little more. Eventually, they reach final equilibrium. The diagrams have been drawn to depict the final equilibrium.◀

ECONOMICS IN PRACTICE: On page 221 [533], the textbook reports on the strength of the negative relationship between the interest rate and investment spending by firms. But what about consumption? So far, our assumption has been that consumption is unaffected by changes in the interest rate. First, do you think that there is a relationship and, if so, is it positive or negative? Why?

ANSWER: As we shall see, (in Chapter 16 (31)), there is a negative relationship between the interest rate and household consumption. As interest rates increase, the cost of borrowing increases, discouraging household spending (or the use of credit cards) and encouraging saving.

ECONOMICS IN PRACTICE (CONTINUED): Given that investment is "highly sensitive" to changes in the interest rate, does this make monetary policy a more powerful tool? Keeping in mind the crowding-out effect, how does this result affect you view of the effectiveness of fiscal policy?

ANSWER: The more interest-sensitive investment spending, the more powerful monetary policy. However, considering the crowding-out effect, the weaker fiscal policy will be. As expansionary fiscal policy drives up interest rates, private sector spending (investment and consumption) will be reduced more vigorously than otherwise.

ECONOMICS IN PRACTICE (CONTINUED): Considering only fiscal policy, what impact will there be on the size of the expenditure multiplier if investment and/or consumption become more sensitive to changes in interest rates?

ANSWER: As the crowding-out effect becomes stronger, the size of the expenditure multiplier will lessen.

─────■───────────────────────── **Practice** ─────────────────────────

1.   The equilibrium interest rate is determined in the _____ market and the equilibrium output level is determined in the _____ market.
    (a)   goods; goods
    (b)   goods; money
    (c)   money; goods
    (d)   money; money

    ANSWER: (c) Refer to p. 220 [532]. In this chapter, we discover that the two markets do not operate in isolation.

2.   Which of the following statements is false? *Ceteris paribus*,
    (a)   an increase in income will reduce the equilibrium interest rate.
    (b)   an increase in the interest rate will reduce planned investment.
    (c)   a decrease in money supply will decrease equilibrium output.
    (d)   when the economy slips into a recession, the interest rate will decrease.

    ANSWER: (a) An increase in income will increase the demand for money, and this will increase the equilibrium interest rate.

3.   When the interest rate decreases, the cost of financing investments _____ and _____ investments projects will be undertaken.
    (a)   increases; more
    (b)   increases; fewer
    (c)   decreases; more
    (d)   decreases; fewer

    ANSWER: (c) Lower interest rates mean lower borrowing costs for firms. As costs decrease, more projects become viable.

4.   A decrease in the interest rate will cause
      (a)   the money supply curve to shift left.
      (b)   the money supply curve to shift right.
      (c)   the planned aggregate expenditure curve to shift up.
      (d)   the planned aggregate expenditure curve to shift down.

      ANSWER: (c)   A decrease in the interest rate will stimulate investment. As investment rises, the
             AE curve will shift up.

5.   Which of the following statements is true? *Ceteris paribus*,
      (a) r (up) $\rightarrow Y$ (up) $\rightarrow I$ (up) $\rightarrow AE$ (up).
      (b) r (up) $\rightarrow Y$ (down) $\rightarrow I$ (down) $\rightarrow AE$ (down).
      (c) r (up) $\rightarrow AE$ (down) $\rightarrow Y$ (down) $\rightarrow I$ (down).
      (d) r (up) $\rightarrow I$ (down) $\rightarrow AE$ (down) $\rightarrow Y$ (down).

      ANSWER: (d)   Refer to p. 225 [537].

6.   Which of the following statements is true? *Ceteris paribus*,
      (a) Y (up) $\rightarrow M^S$ (up) $\rightarrow r$ (up).
      (b) Y (up) $\rightarrow M^S$ (down) $\rightarrow r$ (up).
      (c) Y (up) $\rightarrow M^d$ (up) $\rightarrow r$ (up).
      (d) Y (up) $\rightarrow M^d$ (down) $\rightarrow r$ (up).

      ANSWER: (c)   Refer to p. 222 [534]. ■

 OBJECTIVE 2:
Distinguish between fiscal policy and monetary policy. Distinguish between a contractionary and
an expansionary policy, specifying the tools used in each case.

Expansionary (contractionary) policy is intended to expand (reduce) the equilibrium output level.
Expansionary fiscal policy manipulates the economy through increases in the level of government
spending and/or decreases in net taxes—contractionary fiscal policy reverses these changes.
Expansionary monetary policy manipulates the economy through increases in the money supply and,
from there, decreases in the interest rate. Tools of expansionary monetary policy include open market
purchases, a decrease in the discount rate, and a decrease in the required reserve ratio. (page 223 [535])

———————————————————— **Practice** ————————————————————

7.   The main goal of an expansionary fiscal policy is to _____ ; the main goal of an expansionary
      monetary policy is to _____ .
      (a)   increase output level; increase output level.
      (b)   increase output level; decrease the interest rate
      (c)   decrease the interest rate; increase output level
      (d)   decrease the interest rate; decrease the interest rate

      ANSWER: (a)   Any expansionary policy is designed to make the economy grow. As a stepping-
             stone to achieving this goal, the interest rate may be decreased.

8.   A decrease in net taxes intended to change output level in a particular direction is best described as a(n)
    (a)   expansionary fiscal policy.
    (b)   contractionary fiscal policy.
    (c)   expansionary monetary policy.
    (d)   contractionary monetary policy.

    ANSWER: (a) A reduction in taxes will increase disposable income, consumption, and spending.

Use the diagram to answer the next two questions. AE_1 is the initial planned expenditure level, AE_2 is an intermediate level, and AE_3 is the final planned expenditure level. r_1 is the initial interest rate.

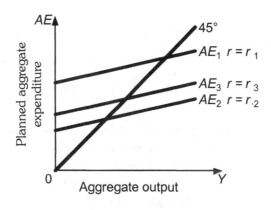

9.   Which policy action would produce the changes seen in the diagram?
    (a)   An open market purchase
    (b)   A decrease in net taxes
    (c)   A decrease in the required reserve ratio
    (d)   A decrease in government spending

    ANSWER: (d) Cutting government spending will cut AE, given the interest rate. As output falls, money demand will fall, the interest rate will decrease, and investment spending will increase.

10.   Which of the following sequences best summarizes the events that occurred in the previous question?
    (a) G (down) $\rightarrow M^d$ (down) $\rightarrow r$ (down) $\rightarrow I$ (up) $\rightarrow Y$ (up)
    (b) G (down) $\rightarrow M^s$ (up) $\rightarrow r$ (down) $\rightarrow I$ (up) $\rightarrow Y$ (up)
    (c) G (down) $\rightarrow Y$ (down) $\rightarrow M^d$ (up) $\rightarrow r$ (down) $\rightarrow I$ (up) $\rightarrow Y$ (up)
    (d) G (down) $\rightarrow Y$ (down) $\rightarrow M^d$ (down) $\rightarrow r$ (down) $\rightarrow I$ (up) $\rightarrow Y$ (up)

    ANSWER: (d) The decrease in spending causes a fall in money demand and a consequent decrease in the interest rate (r_1 to r_2). The lowered cost of borrowing stimulates investment, increasing aggregate expenditures, money demand, and the interest rate (r_2 to r_3). ∎

OBJECTIVE 3:
Explain when and how the crowding-out effect occurs. Explain the impact of the interest sensitivity of investment demand on the effectiveness of monetary policy.

Expansionary fiscal policy, whereas raising expenditures, also raises money demand and, consequently, the interest rate—and the higher interest rate (the cost of borrowing funds) *discourages* planned investment. The policy *crowds out* private sector spending. The more sensitive investment plans are to changes in the interest rate, the greater the crowding out. The presence of the crowding-out effect reduces the potency of fiscal policy and the size of the government spending multiplier. The Fed can restore the potency of fiscal policy by increasing the money supply to prevent the interest rate increase—i.e., by "accommodating." (page 223 [535])

> ▶▶▶   LEARNING TIP: The crowding-out effect occurs whether it's government spending or some other variable that's boosting the interest rate. If households suddenly decide to increase consumption, for example, the extra aggregate expenditure would increase money demand and the interest rate, and investment would be reduced. In the real world, the crowding-out effect reduces not only the government spending multiplier, but the other expenditure multipliers too, even the balanced-budget multiplier. ◀

—————————————■————————————————— **Practice** —————————

11.   Which of the following statements best describes the operation of the crowding-out effect?
   (a) G (up) $\rightarrow Y$ (up) $\rightarrow r$ (up) $\rightarrow I$ (down)
   (b) G (up) $\rightarrow Y$ (up) $\rightarrow M^d$ (up) $\rightarrow r$ (up) $\rightarrow I$ (down)
   (c) G (up) $\rightarrow Y$ (up) $\rightarrow M^d$ (down) $\rightarrow r$ (up) $\rightarrow I$ (down)
   (d) G (up) $\rightarrow r$ (up) $\rightarrow I$ (up)

   ANSWER: (b) Refer to p. 223 [535].

12.   An increase in government spending will lead to a(n) _____ in planned aggregate expenditure and a(n) _____ in planned investment.
   (a)   increase; increase
   (b)   increase; decrease
   (c)   decrease; increase
   (d)   decrease; decrease

   ANSWER: (b) The government spending increase crowds out investment spending because of a higher interest rate, but, despite this, the expansionary fiscal policy will still cause planned expenditure to increase.

13.   An open market sale of securities will be more _____ , the _____ the interest sensitivity of investment.
   (a)   expansionary; greater
   (b)   expansionary; less
   (c)   contractionary; greater
   (d)   contractionary; less

   ANSWER: (c) An open market sale is a contractionary policy that will increase the interest rate. The effect on planned investment (and aggregate expenditure) will be greater the more interest-sensitive investors are. ■

 OBJECTIVE 4:
Outline the issues involved in determining the optimal policy mix.

Because fiscal and monetary policies work through different channels, the effectiveness of policy can be enhanced if a complementary blend of fiscal and monetary policy can be achieved. For example, a mix such as an increase in government spending (expansionary fiscal policy) and open market purchases (expansionary monetary policy) could increase equilibrium output without changing the interest rate. (page 226 [538])

Good examples of effective combinations of policies are mentioned on pp. 223–227 [535–539]. Note that the crowding-out effect of expansionary fiscal policy can be forestalled by accommodating expansionary monetary policy.

▶▶   LEARNING TIP: Fiscal and monetary policies may be coordinated. If the magnitudes of the policy changes are unknown, then either the effect on equilibrium output or on equilibrium interest rate *must* be uncertain. Break down the problem into two separate analyses, one for the "fiscal policy change" and the other for the "monetary policy change." In each case, decide the direction of change in output and interest rate, and then add them together.

Example: a net tax decrease and an open market purchase.

	Output Change	Interest Change
Fiscal policy effect	increase	increase
Monetary policy effect	increase	decrease
Total effect	increase	uncertain

In this case, where net taxes decrease and the money supply increases, we would predict a definite increase in output and an uncertain change in interest.

Note that output and the interest rate will always move in the *same* direction for a given fiscal policy change, but will always move in *opposite* directions for a given monetary policy.

▶▶   LEARNING TIP: Table 12.1 (27.1) is an excellent summary of the entire chapter and you shouldn't overlook it! Your goal should be to trace through each policy mix and verify the results. In particular, focus on variables that exhibit an ambiguous result. ◀

— Practice —

14.   The more sensitive investment demand is to the interest rate, the _____ effective fiscal policy is and the _____ effective monetary policy is.

(a)   more; more
(b)   more; less
(c)   less; more
(d)   less; less

ANSWER: (c)   If investment is very sensitive to interest-rate changes, fiscal policy effectiveness is reduced because of the crowding-out effect. Monetary policy, whose influence on spending is through changes in the interest rate, is rendered more powerful.

Use the following diagrams to answer the next question.

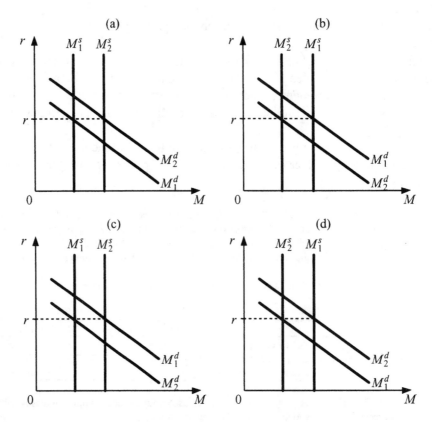

15.   An expansionary policy mix which causes no change in interest rates is best depicted in money market diagram
(a)   A.
(b)   B.
(c)   C.
(d)   D.

ANSWER: (a) An expansionary fiscal policy increases money demand and an accommodating expansionary monetary policy increases money supply to prevent an interest rate increase.

16.   Arboc is in a deep recession, with 35% of its capital not being used. A(n) _____ _____ policy is most likely to be effective in increasing output.
(a)   expansionary fiscal
(b)   expansionary monetary
(c)   contractionary fiscal
(d)   contractionary monetary

ANSWER: (a) This economy needs an expansionary policy. Investment, with such high underutilization of capital, is unlikely to be responsive to interest rate reductions—the crowding-out effect will be slight. Also, if investment is not responsive to interest rate changes, monetary policy is unlikely to have much effect. ∎

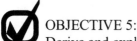 OBJECTIVE 5:
Derive and explain the slope of the aggregate demand curve. Explain what the curve represents.

The *aggregate demand* (*AD*) curve depicts the negative relationship between the price level and aggregate output. Each point on the curve is a point of equilibrium in both the money market and the goods market. If the overall price level increases, it will raise the interest rate because there will be an increase in the demand for money. This will affect the goods market. A higher interest rate will cause cuts in planned investment and consumption as the cost of borrowing increases. Also, as the aggregate price level rises, household wealth is reduced in value, causing a further decline in consumption—the real wealth effect. Equilibrium output falls. (page 227 [539])

▶▶▶   LEARNING TIP: Learn the variables of the model! The *AS/AD* model you are in the process of assembling is quite complex, with many relationships between variables. No variable is determined in isolation—a change in consumption spending will affect the goods market, the money market, wage rates, the interest rate, and the price level. The wisest approach is to list and *learn* the determinants of each major variable. Don't forget the factors that affect money demand. Money demand is a key link between the two markets.

▶▶▶   LEARNING TIP: Note that when you draw an aggregate demand curve, all the price/output level combinations traced out by the curve are combinations that achieve simultaneous equilibrium in the goods and money markets. Policy variables (government spending, net taxes, and the money supply) are fixed. A change in any of these policy variables will shift the position of the aggregate demand curve.◀

Nominal vs. Real Values: When the aggregate price level changes, the distinction between real and nominal values takes on some importance. Nominal variables are affected by price level changes; real variables are not. In this chapter, real output, the real money supply, the real interest rate, etc., are used because it is at that level that the goods and money markets interact.

—————————————————————— **Practice** ——————————————————————

17.   The level of aggregate output demanded decreases as the price level increases because
       (a)   higher prices make market interest rate decrease.
       (b)   as prices increase, producers will sell more output.
       (c)   some goods become relatively more expensive.
       (d)   the demand for money increases, making the interest rate increase.

       ANSWER: (d) A higher price level means that more money will be demanded, forcing up the interest rate (the cost of borrowing).

18.   The best description of the operation of the real wealth effect is that as the price level increases,
       (a)   the interest rate decreases, making interest earnings decrease. This makes consumption decrease.
       (b)   the interest rate increases. This makes the cost of investment increase and results in a decrease in planned investment.
       (c)   profitability increases, encouraging investors to increase planned investment.
       (d)   the purchasing power of household assets decreases, discouraging consumption.

       ANSWER: (d) Refer to p. 229 [541].

19.   When the price level decreases, the resulting _____ in the interest rate will _____ investment.
       (a)   increase; increase
       (b)   increase; decrease
       (c)   decrease; increase
       (d)   decrease; decrease

       ANSWER: (c) Lower interest rates mean lower borrowing costs for firms. ■

 OBJECTIVE 6:
Identify how aggregate demand is affected by monetary and fiscal policy actions.

The *AD* curve will shift to the right (increase) if there is an increase in government spending or in the money supply, or a decrease in net taxes. Because of greater optimism, consumption or investment could increase and shift the *AD* curve to the right. One reason why the U.S. economy expanded so quickly during the 1990s was that consumer confidence grew, fed by the burgeoning stock market, swelling aggregate demand. (page 229 [541])

> **Comment:**   When you shift the AD curve, the curve moves right or left, (not up or down). Given the price level, how will the equilibrium level of aggregate output respond to changes in the policy variables (G, T, M^s) or in the determinants of consumption and planned investment? Ask the same question when shifting the short-run aggregate supply curve in Chapter 13 (28): How will these events affect the amount of aggregate output supplied if the price level does not change?

─────────■──────────────────────── **Practice** ────────────────────────────

20.   A cut in government spending will cause a(n) _____ in aggregate demand, and a decrease in the discount rate will cause a(n) _____ in aggregate demand.
   (a)   increase; increase
   (b)   increase; decrease
   (c)   decrease; increase
   (d)   decrease; decrease

   ANSWER: (c) At each price level, a decrease in government spending shifts the *AE* curve downward—*AD* will decrease. A discount rate cut increases the money supply and lowers the interest rate—*AD* will increase.

Refer to the following diagram to answer the next question.

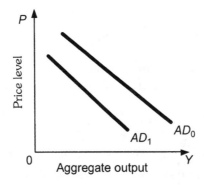

21.   The aggregate demand curve would shift from AD_0 to AD_1 if
   (a)   the government increased welfare payments.
   (b)   the Fed increased the reserve requirement.
   (c)   the government cut taxes.
   (d)   the demand for money decreased.

   ANSWER: (b) A decrease in aggregate demand could be caused by a contractionary monetary policy.

22.   The Arbocali Ministry of Finance increases both government spending and net taxes by one million opeks. Aggregate demand will
  (a)   shift to the right.
  (b)   shift to the left.
  (c)   remain unchanged, but the price level will increase.
  (d)   remain unchanged, but the price level will decrease.

   ANSWER: (a) This is a balanced-budget expansionary policy. At the given price level, *AE* and, therefore, *AD* will increase. ■

 OBJECTIVE 7 (APPENDIX):
Explain what is depicted by the *IS* curve and the *LM* curve.

The *IS/LM* model presents the combinations of output and interest rate that will give equilibrium in the goods market (*IS*) and the money market (*LM*). The *IS curve* depicts combinations of output and the interest rate that give an equilibrium in the goods market, whereas the *LM curve* depicts all combinations of output and the interest rate that give an equilibrium in the money market. The *IS* curve has a negative slope because, in the goods market, a higher interest rate reduces investment spending and cause a lower equilibrium output level. The *LM* curve has a positive slope because higher output levels boosts money demand, causing higher interest rates. Policy variables that cause the *IS* curve to shift are government purchases and net taxes. The policy variable that causes the *LM* curve to shift is the money supply. Changes in income and the interest rate result in movements along the curves. (page 233 [545])

   Comment: The IS and LM curves are not aggregate demand and supply curves. In fact, both curves contribute to our understanding of the demand side of the economy.

   Take each policy variable (*G*, *T*, and *M^s*) in turn. First, ask what you would predict if that variable were to increase. [An increase in *G*, for instance, would cause *Y* to increase in the *goods market* as a first effect.] Now ask what should be happening in the "other market." [Higher levels of economic activity boost money demand, and the interest rate will rise.] Result: The *IS/LM* diagram shifts in such a way that *Y* increases and *r* increases—this must be represented by a shift right in the *IS* (goods market) curve. The "other market" curve does not shift.

   Repeat this procedure for each case. Also do policy mixes using the procedure outlined in the Learning Tip to Objective 4 above.

———————————————— **Practice** ————————————————

Use the following diagram to answer the next four questions. Point A is a point of equilibrium in the goods market, corresponding to AE_1 and an interest rate of 8%.

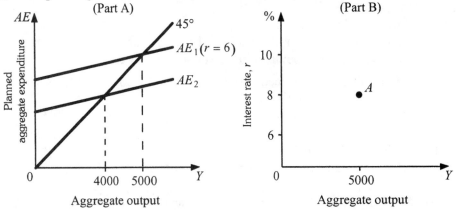

23.   In the goods market, the AE curve might shift from AE_1 to AE_2 if the interest rate _____ . The IS curve has a _____ slope.
(a)   increases; positive
(b)   increases; negative
(c)   decreases; positive
(d)   decreases; negative

ANSWER: (b) The AE curve would decrease because planned investment decreases as the interest rate increases.

24.   Sketch in the IS curve (IS_1) in Part B of the diagram.

ANSWER: Refer to the following diagram.

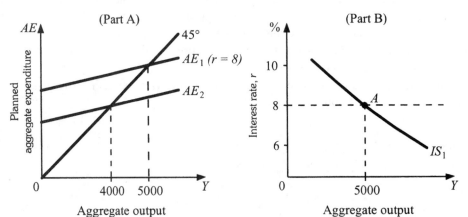

25.   The interest rate is 8% and spending is shown by AE_1. If government spending increases, then, at the same interest rate, the equilibrium output level will _____ . The IS curve will shift to the

_____ .
(a)   increase; right
(b)   increase; left
(c)   decrease; right
(d)   decrease; left

ANSWER: (a) An expansionary fiscal policy will increase planned aggregate expenditure and shift the IS curve to the right.

26.   Sketch in the new *IS* curve (IS_2) in Part B of the diagram.

ANSWER: Refer to the following diagram.

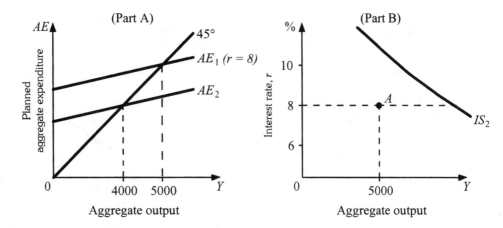

Use the following diagram to answer the next four questions. Point B shows equilibrium in the money market, at an interest rate of 8% and an output level of 5,000.

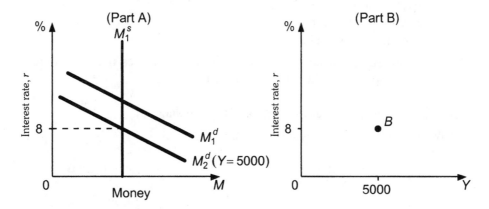

27.   In the money market, the money demand curve might shift from M^d_1 to M^d_2 if the output level _____ . The *LM* curve has a _____ slope.

(a)   increases; positive
(b)   increases; negative
(c)   decreases; positive
(d)   decreases; negative

ANSWER: (c) As output level decreases, money demand decreases. The equilibrium interest rate decreases—*LM* has a positive slope.

28.   Sketch in the *LM* curve (*LM*₁) in Part B of the diagram.

ANSWER: Refer to the following diagram.

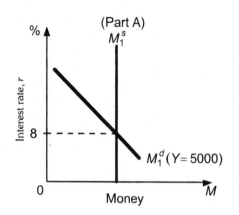
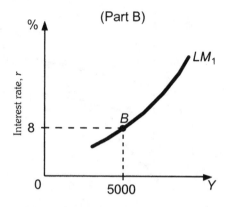

29.   The interest rate is 8% and money demand is $M^d{}_1$. If the money supply increases, then, given the output level, the equilibrium interest rate will _____ . The *LM* curve will shift _____ .
(a)   increase; up and to the right
(b)   increase; down and to the left
(c)   decrease; up and to the right
(d)   decrease; down and to the left

ANSWER: (c) An expansionary monetary policy decreases the interest rate, given the output level, and shifts the *LM* curve to the right.

30.   Sketch in the new *LM* curve (*LM*₂) in Part B of the diagram.

ANSWER: Refer to the following diagram.

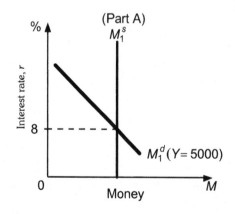
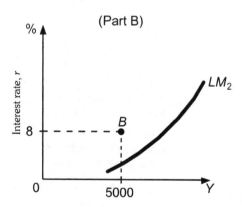

BRAIN TEASER SOLUTION: In the real world, there is a risk involved in holding cash. Cash may be lost, stolen, or destroyed. You may be willing to pay a fee to avoid such risks. There are also costs associated with moving and storing cash, and these costs may not be trivial if large amounts are concerned— deposits at banks, where checking accounts are available may be preferable. The negative interest rate might be looked on as a fee charged by banks for storage, convenience, and risk reduction.

PRACTICE TEST

I.   MULTIPLE-CHOICE QUESTIONS

Select the option that provides the single best answer.

_____ 1.   In each of the following cases we would expect the interest rate to decrease, EXCEPT when
(a)   there is a decrease in the required reserve ratio.
(b)   the government increases tax collections.
(c)   government spending is increased.
(d)   there is a reduction in the level of economic activity.

_____ 2.   The feedback effect between the goods market and money market is best illustrated by the situation when, for example,
(a)   contractionary monetary policy leads to a reduction in the money supply.
(b)   consumption suddenly rises causing a fall in investment due to a rising interest rate.
(c)   contractionary fiscal policy leads to a reduction in the money supply.
(d)   the value of the money multiplier is reduced due to an increasing required reserve ratio.

_____ 3.   If the Fed simultaneously lowered the required reserve ratio and sold government securities, which one of the following could not be a possible consequence?
(a)   An increase in money supply and an increase in money demand
(b)   An increase in money supply and a decrease in money demand
(c)   A decrease in money supply and a decrease in money demand
(d)   A rise in the interest rate
(Be careful on this one!)

_____ 4.   Which of the following would not accompany a fall in the discount rate?
(a)   An expansion in the money supply
(b)   A rise in planned investment
(c)   An unplanned rise in inventories
(d)   An increase in aggregate output (income)

_____ 5.   The money and goods markets are in equilibrium. Now there is an *expansion* in the money supply. This will _____ investment and cause the demand for money to _____ .
(a)   reduce; increase
(b)   stimulate; increase
(c)   stimulate; decrease
(d)   reduce; decrease

_____ 6.   An increase in planned aggregate expenditure will make the interest rate _____ while an increase in the money supply will make planned expenditure _____ .
(a)   increase; increase
(b)   increase; decrease
(c)   decrease; increase
(d)   decrease; decrease

_____ 7.   A decrease in net personal income taxes will cause
    (a)   the *LM* curve to shift to the left.
    (b)   the *IS* curve to shift to the right.
    (c)   the *AE* curve to shift downward.
    (d)   investment to increase.

_____ 8.   An increase in money supply will result in _____ output and a_____ interest rate.
    (a)   higher; lower
    (b)   higher; higher
    (c)   lower; lower
    (d)   lower; higher

_____ 9.   *MPC* is 0.8. Which of the following might achieve the goal of increasing output by $200 billion? Assume that some crowding out occurs.
    (a)   An increase in government spending of $40 billion
    (b)   A decrease in taxes of $50 billion
    (c)   An increase in government spending of $50 billion
    (d)   An increase in government spending and in taxes, each of $50 billion

_____ 10. An open market purchase of securities by the Fed will cause
    (a)   the interest rate to fall.
    (b)   a decrease in the quantity of money demanded.
    (c)   a shortage of money at the original equilibrium interest rate.
    (d)   the *AE* curve to shift down (to the right).

_____ 11. A simultaneous increase in net taxes and open market sale of securities by the Fed will _____ equilibrium output and _____ the interest rate.
    (a)   increase; decrease
    (b)   decrease; have an indeterminate effect on
    (c)   decrease; increase
    (d)   have an indeterminate effect on; increase

_____ 12. The *AD* curve is derived by holding constant all of the following EXCEPT
    (a)   government spending.
    (b)   net taxes.
    (c)   money demand.
    (d)   money supply.

_____ 13. The _____ curve will shift to the _____ if the government cuts taxes.
    (a)   *IS*; right
    (b)   *IS*; left
    (c)   *LM*; right
    (d)   *LM*; left

_____ 14. The _____ curve will shift to the _____ if the Fed buys securities.
    (a)   *IS*; right
    (b)   *IS*; left
    (c)   *LM*; right
    (d)   *LM*; left

_____ 15.   Which of the following statements is false? *Ceteris paribus,*
    (a)   the lower the level of aggregate output, the lower the interest rate.
    (b)   when the interest rate falls, planned aggregate expenditure increases.
    (c)   as real output level increases, money demand increases.
    (d)   as money demand increases, real output level increases.

_____ 16.   An open market sale of government securities is a(n) _____ monetary policy. The *AE* curve will shift _____ .
    (a)   expansionary; up
    (b)   expansionary; down
    (c)   contractionary; up
    (d)   contractionary; down

_____ 17.   The intended goal of an expansionary policy
    (a)   is an increase in the level of aggregate output.
    (b)   is an increase in the interest rate.
    (c)   is a decrease in the interest rate.
    (d)   depends on whether a fiscal policy or a monetary policy is used.

Use the diagram to answer the following question. AE_1 is the initial planned expenditure level, AE_2 is an intermediate level, and AE_3 is the final planned expenditure level. r_1 is the initial interest rate.

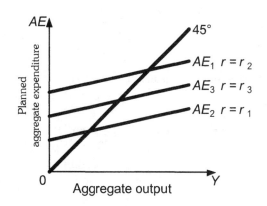

_____ 18.   Which policy action would produce the changes seen in the diagram?
    (a)   An open market purchase
    (b)   A decrease in net taxes
    (c)   An increase in the required reserve ratio
    (d)   An increase in government spending

_____ 19.   An increase in government spending will cause a decrease in planned investment, most directly as a result of an increase in
    (a)   aggregate output.
    (b)   the interest rate.
    (c)   the money supply.
    (d)   the price level.

_____ 20.   Which circumstance will not strengthen the crowding-out effect?
(a)   A higher interest-sensitivity of investment
(b)   A higher money demand as spending increases
(c)   A steeper slope of the AE curve
(d)   A greater money multiplier

_____ 21.   Which of the following statements best describes an expansionary monetary policy?
(a) M^S (up) $\rightarrow r$ (up) $\rightarrow I$ (down) $\rightarrow Y$ (up) $\rightarrow r$ (up) $\rightarrow M^d$ (down)
(b) M^S (up) $\rightarrow r$ (down) $\rightarrow I$ (down) $\rightarrow Y$ (down) $\rightarrow M^d$ (up)
(c) M^S (up) $\rightarrow r$ (down) $\rightarrow I$ (up) $\rightarrow Y$ (up) $\rightarrow M^d$ (up)
(d) M^S (up) $\rightarrow r$ (down) $\rightarrow I$ (up) $\rightarrow M^d$ (up) $\rightarrow Y$ (up)

_____ 22.   In the presence of a crowding-out effect, a contractionary fiscal policy will result in a _____ in output than if there were no crowding-out effect.
(a)   larger increase
(b)   smaller increase
(c)   larger decrease
(d)   smaller decrease

_____ 23.   The IS curve has a _____ slope and depicts equilibrium in the _____ market.
(a)   positive; goods
(b)   positive; money
(c)   negative; goods
(d)   negative; money

_____ 24.   There is a negative relationship between planned investment and the interest rate described by the equation $I = 120 - 10r$. Planned investment will decrease by moving along the curve if
(a)   the Fed buys bonds in the open market.
(b)   the government increases welfare payments.
(c)   entrepreneurs expect sales to decline in the future.
(d)   the government cuts back in government spending.

_____ 25.   If the Fed buys bonds in the open market at the same time as the government increases government spending, the crowding-out effect will be _____ . The _____ interest-sensitive planned investment is, the smaller the crowding-out effect will be.
(a)   heightened; more
(b)   heightened; less
(c)   diminished; more
(d)   diminished; less

II.   APPLICATION QUESTIONS

1.   A businesswoman, Kathleen Williamson, hires you as an economic consultant to assist her in her investment decisions.

(a)   The government has announced a reduction in income taxes and an increase in welfare benefits. Interpret these policy actions.

   (i)   Are they expansionary or contractionary?

   (ii)   How will they affect the interest rate?

   (iii)   Importantly, how will they affect planned business investment?

   (iv)   The following *IS-LM* diagram shows the economy before the policies are initiated. Show how the curve(s) shift(s) in response to the policies.

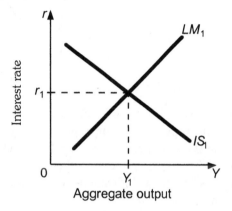

(b)   Ignore the policy actions in Part (a). The Fed announces an immediate increase in the reserve requirement and decrease in the discount rate. Interpret these policy actions.

   (i)   Are they expansionary or contractionary?

   (ii)   How will they affect the interest rate?

   (iii)   Importantly, how will they affect planned business investment?

   (iv)   The following *IS-LM* diagram shows the economy before the policies are initiated. Show how the curve(s) shift(s) in response to the policies.

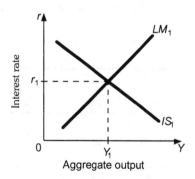

(c)   Ignore the policy actions in Parts (a) and (b). The government initiates an aggressive program of highway construction and inner-city development, effective immediately. Simultaneously, the Fed announces an immediate increase in its purchases of bonds on the open market. Interpret these policy actions.

   (i)   Are they expansionary or contractionary?

   (ii)   Is the Fed action accommodating? Why?

   (iii)   How will the policy actions affect the interest rate?

(iv)   Importantly, how will they affect planned business investment?

(v)   Williamson's business sells to the consumer sector. What other factor(s) ought she to include in determining her investment plans?

(vi)   The following *IS-LM* diagram shows the economy before the policies are initiated. Show how the curve(s) shift in response to the policies.

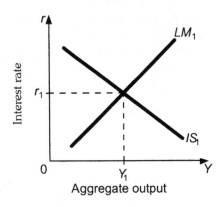

2.   (a)   The Arbocali Minister of Finance (a confirmed believer in the multiplier) notes that the marginal propensity to consume out of income is 0.8. Because Arboc is presently in a recession, he predicts that a 5 million opek increase in government spending will boost output by 25 million opeks. Although a quite junior official in the Ministry, you believe that he is incorrect. Indicate as many assumptions as you can that he had made to arrive at his prediction.

(b)   The Minister (also a confirmed believer in *IS-LM* analysis) suspects that the economy is at some point *above* the *LM* curve but on the *IS* curve. This must be a point of disequilibrium. Explain the situation to him.

3.   Farview, an economic forecasting firm, has hired you as a promising addition to the staff. Your assignment is to predict the effect of a given economic change on a number of variables, where "+" represents increase, "−" represents decrease, "0" represents no change, and "?" represents ambiguous result. Assume that there are progressive federal income taxes and that the initial change in a variable is the dominant one.

(a)   The Fed reduces the discount rate. Predict the effect on:

Y	*r*	*C*	*S*	*I*	M^s	M^d	*federal deficit*

(b)   The government cuts personal income taxes. Predict the effect on:

Y	*r*	*C*	*S*	*I*	M^s	M^d	*federal deficit*

(c)   The capital utilization rate is 70% and firms believe that it should be 85%. Predict the effect on:

Y	r	C	S	I	M^S	M^d	federal deficit

(d)   There is heightened expectation of an interest rate decrease. Predict the effect on:

Y	r	C	S	I	M^S	M^d	federal deficit

4.   Determine the effect of each policy and other actions on the following five given variables. Label it (I) if the variable will increase, (D) if it will decrease, (U) if it will remain unchanged, and (?) if the result is ambiguous.

Policy/Action	r	Y	M^S	M^d	I
Increase M^S					
Increase T					
Increase G					
An increase in optimism by entrepreneurs					
Income and payments become better synchronized					

5.   Refer to the following diagram to answer this question.

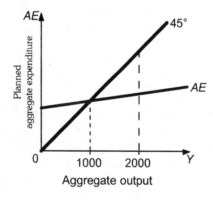

MPC is 0.8 and the full-employment level of production is 2,000.

(a)   Draw the money market in equilibrium. Label the curves $M^d{}_1$ and $M^s{}_1$.

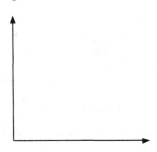

(b)   The government spending multiplier is _____ . Using the *simple* goods market model, by how much would government spending have to change to move the economy to the full-employment equilibrium? Increase/decrease by _____ .

(c)   The tax multiplier is _____ . By how much would the tax level have to change to move the economy to full-employment equilibrium? Increase/decrease by _____ .

(d)   The balanced-budget multiplier is _____ . By how much would government spending and tax levels have to increase (balanced-budget change) to move the economy to full-employment equilibrium? Increase by _____ .

Suppose we adopt the balanced-budget policy.

(e)   How much will the *AE* function shift vertically? Increase/decrease by _____ . Show this on the diagram as *AE'*.

(f)   Unplanned inventory levels will _____ and output will _____ .

(g)   Show the changes that occur in the money market. Label any new curves clearly.

(h)   Depict the new *AE* curve as *AE''* on the diagram. What has caused the change you've drawn?

(i)   Is the balanced-budget multiplier still equal to the value given in (d) above?

(j)   Suppose the Fed acts to prevent the crowding out. Amend your money market picture accordingly.

6.   The text provides several examples of "economic shorthand" while tracing through the effects of given changes. Without referring back to the text, test your knowledge by indicating how each variable will change in the following examples. Write "I" if the variable increases and "D" if the variable decreases as a consequence of the previous step.

(a)   Expansionary fiscal policy involving a $100 change in *G*.
G (I/D) $\rightarrow$ Y (I/D) $\rightarrow$ M^d (I/D) $\rightarrow$ r (I/D) $\rightarrow$ I (I/D) $\rightarrow$ Y (I/D)

(b)   Expansionary fiscal policy involving a $100 change in *T*.
T (I/D) $\rightarrow$ Y (I/D) $\rightarrow$ M^d (I/D) $\rightarrow$ r (I/D) $\rightarrow$ I (I/D) $\rightarrow$ Y (I/D)

(c)   Will the total change in *Y* be greater in (a) than in (b)? Why or why not?

(d)   Expansionary monetary policy.
Begin by selecting the correct option for each monetary policy tool.

Open Market sale/purchase
Discount rate increase/ decrease
Reserve requirement increase/ decrease

M^s (I/D) $\rightarrow$ r (I/D) $\rightarrow$ I (I/D) $\rightarrow$ Y (I/D) $\rightarrow$ M^d (I/D) $\rightarrow$ r (I/D)

Note that the effects go in the opposite direction for contractionary policies.

PRACTICE TEST SOLUTIONS

I.   Solutions to Multiple-Choice Questions

1.   (c)   The increase in government spending is an expansionary policy. Expansionary policies increase money demand and, ultimately, the interest rate.

2.   (b)   Option (b) correctly traces a feedback between markets. Options (a) and (d) are confined to the money market only. Option (c) is just wrong—the money supply is affected only by monetary policy variables.

3.   (b)   Lowering the required reserve ratio is an expansionary monetary policy; selling securities is a contractionary monetary policy. The net effect on the money supply, therefore, is uncertain. If the money supply increases, the interest rate decreases, and the economy expands. This will increase money demand (Option (a)). If the money supply decreases, the interest rate increases (Option (d)), and the economy contracts. This will decrease money demand (Option (c)).

4.   (c)   The discount rate reduction is an expansionary monetary policy, causing the money supply to increase (Option (a)) and the interest rate to decrease. An interest rate decrease will stimulate investment (Option (b)) and aggregate output (Option (d)). As spending increases, there will be an unplanned decrease in inventory levels.

5.   (b)   The increase in the money supply will decrease the interest rate and stimulate investment. Planned aggregate expenditure will increase, prompting an increased transaction demand for money.

6.   (a)   If planned aggregate expenditure increases, the demand for money will increase, as will the interest rate. An expansion in the money supply, which pushes down the interest rate, will stimulate investment and, therefore, planned aggregate expenditure.

7.   (b)   The *IS* curve reports changes in the goods market. If net taxes decrease, aggregate expenditure will increase at each interest rate, shifting the *IS* curve to the right.

8.   (a)   This expansionary monetary policy will reduce the interest rate and raise output.

9.   (c)   If *MPC* is 0.8, the expenditure multiplier is 5, and the tax multiplier is –4. (Check Chapter 9 (24) if you can't verify these values.) As noted on p. 224 [536], the feedback effect from the money market reduces the size of these multipliers. Options (a) and (b) will fall short of $200 billion. The balanced-budget action (Option (d)) has a maximum increase of $50 billion. Option (c) may be overkill (we can't tell), but it has the possibility of hitting the $200 billion target.

10.   (a)   An open market purchase will increase the money supply, causing an excess supply at the original interest rate (not Option (c)) and making the interest rate decrease (Option (a)). The interest rate decrease will increase the quantity of money demanded (not Option (b)). This interest rate decrease will stimulate investment and planned aggregate expenditure (not Option (d)). As planned expenditure increases, there will be an increased transaction demand for money.

11.   (b)   An increase in net taxes is a contractionary policy and a sale of securities is also a contractionary policy. Equilibrium output will decrease. The sale of securities will decrease the money supply, forcing up the interest rate. However, the contraction in output will reduce the transaction demand for money. A decrease in the demand for money will pull down the interest rate. The effect on the interest rate is ambiguous.

12.   (c)   When the price level changes, government spending, net taxes, and the money supply need not change. Money demand, however, will change, causing reductions in planned investment.

13.   (a)   A change in taxes affects the goods market initially. Planned aggregate expenditure will increase, given the interest rate. At each interest rate, then, the equilibrium output level in the goods market will increase. This is shown as a rightward shift of the *IS* curve.

14.   (c)   An open market purchase affects the money market initially by increasing the money supply. At the same output level as before, the interest rate will be lower. This is shown as a rightward shift of the *LM* curve.

15.   (d)   As real output level increases, more money is demanded to finance the increased volume of transactions (Option (c)). However, as money demand increases, the interest rate rises, and this depresses investment and real output level (Option (d)). As output decreases, money demand and the interest rate decrease (Option (a)). Decreases in the interest rate stimulate investment and expenditure (Option (b)).

16.   (d)   An open market sale reduces the money supply, increases the interest rate, discourages investment, and pushes down the *AE* curve.

17.   (a)   All expansionary policies are intended to expand equilibrium output level.

18.   (a)   An open market purchase will reduce the interest rate (from r_1 to r_2) and stimulate planned aggregate expenditure through higher investment. As spending increases, money demand increases, pushing up the interest rate (to r_3). Planned expenditure will decrease. Options (b) and (d) would result in the same shifts in the AE curve, but rate r_2 would be the same as r_1.

19.   (b)   An increase in government spending will increase aggregate output (Option (a)), but the most direct reason for the "crowding out" of investment is the interest rate increase. Refer to p. 223 [535].

20.   (d)   The size of the money multiplier is irrelevant. As government spending increases, the steeper the *AE* curve, the greater the initial expansion in spending. Given the spending increase, the more money demand increases, the more the interest rate will increase. The more sensitive entrepreneurs are to interest-rate increases, the greater the decrease in investment.

21.   (c)   Refer to p. 225 [537]. The higher money supply reduces the interest rate, which stimulates planned investment. As spending increases, money demand increases.

22.   (d)   The crowding-out effect reduces fiscal policy effectiveness.

23.   (c)   As the interest rate increases, investment (and aggregate expenditure) decrease, and the equilibrium output level decreases. Refer to p. 233 [545].

24.   (b)   A movement along the curve is caused by a change in the interest rate. If the interest increases, investment will decrease. Option (a) indicates an increase in the money supply and, therefore, a decrease in the interest rate. Option (c) would shift the curve. Option (d) is a contractionary policy, reducing income. Option (b) will expand spending, increasing the demand for money and the interest rate.

25.   (d)   If the Fed increases the money supply the interest rate will decrease. If the government increases government spending, money demand will increase and the interest rate will increase. The effects counteract each other leading to a lesser crowding-out effect. Given the interest rate change, the impact on planned investment will be lower the less influenced are entrepreneurs by the interest rate.

II.   Solutions to Application Questions

1.   (a)   Both actions will stimulate private sector spending—they are similar to an increase in government spending. As the economy expands, money demand will increase, causing an increase in the interest rate. A higher interest rate will reduce planed investment.

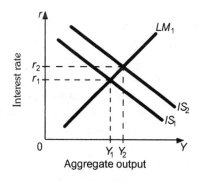

(b)   The first action is contractionary, whereas the second is expansionary. The effect on the interest rate is uncertain, therefore the effect on planned investment is uncertain. The *LM* curve will shift right as a result of the first action and left as a result of the second action. As shown below, the net effect is zero (although, depending on the relative strengths of the policies, the final *LM* curve could end up either to the left of to the right of LM_1.

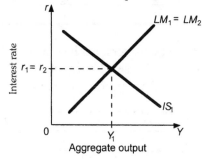

(c)   Both actions are expansionary. The Fed action is accommodating—the spending initiative will drive up interest rates and the Fed action will reduce them. The effect on the interest rate is uncertain, therefore the effect on planned investment is uncertain. As these policies are expansionary, you should predict higher levels of consumer spending. Even if the interest rate is unchanged, Ms. Williamson's planned investment might rise in expectation of increased sales, higher capital utilization rates, and more optimism about the future. The increased government spending will shift the *IS* curve to the right while the purchase of bonds will shift the *LM* curve to the right. Output will increase. The effect on the interest rate depends on the relative strength of the two shifts.

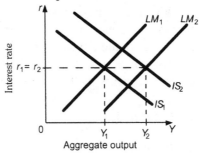

2.   (a)   The Minister has assumed that:
       (i)   The marginal propensity to consume value will remain constant as the economy expands.
       (ii)   The bond-financed expansion in government spending will not provoke an increase in interest rates.
       (iii) Aggregate supply is horizontal, i.e., that, as aggregate demand increases, no price level increases will occur. This is discussed in Chapter 13 (28).

       (b)   Given the level of output, the interest rate is "too high" and should be less, i.e., there is an excess supply in the money market. Because the economy is currently on the *IS* curve, there is equilibrium in the output market.

3.   (a)   If the Fed reduces the discount rate, the money supply will increase and the interest rate will decrease. Investment will be stimulated, and aggregate output will increase. Consumption and saving will rise. Higher spending will provoke a higher money demand (which will partially offset the interest rate decrease). A higher level of activity will increase tax collections, reducing the federal deficit.

Y	r	C	S	I	M^s	M^d	*federal deficit*
+	−	+	+	+	+	+	−

       (b)   If the government cuts personal income taxes, consumption and saving will increase, and aggregate output will rise. Higher spending will increase the demand for money and push up the interest rate. As spending increases, tax collections will rise again somewhat.

Y	r	C	S	I	M^s	M^d	*federal deficit*
+	+	+	+	−	0	+	+

(c)   If the capital utilization rate is too low, firms will reduce investment. As investment falls, output level will decrease. Consumption, saving, and tax collections will fall. The deficit will increase. There is no effect on money supply but money demand will be reduced. This will result in a decrease in the interest rate and a partially offsetting increase in investment.

Y	r	C	S	I	M^s	M^d	federal deficit
−	−	−	−	−	0	−	+

(d)   A heightened expectation of an interest rate decrease implies a heightened expectation of a bond price increase. Asset holders will reduce the demand for money and increase the demand for bonds. As there is no change in the money supply, the interest rate will decrease. A decrease in the interest rate will stimulate additional planned investment and raise aggregate output. As output (income) increases, consumption and saving will rise, as will tax collections. The increase in expenditures will cause a partially offsetting increase in money demand and in the interest rate. Recall that we assume the initial effect dominates subsequent changes.

Y	r	C	S	I	M^s	M^d	federal deficit
+	−	+	+	+	0	−	−

4.   Refer to the following table.

Policy/Action	r	Y	M^s	M^d	I
Increase M^s	D	I	I	I	I
Increase T	D	D	U	D	I*
Increase G	I	I	U	I	D
An increase in optimism by entrepreneurs	I	?**	U	I	?**
Income and payments become better synchronized	D	I	U	D	I

*   Note the unusual result on investment when net taxes are increased.
An increase in optimism will stimulate planned investment, which will lead spending (and output) to increase. As spending increases, money demand increases and, given the unchanged money supply, the interest rate will increase. This will discourage investment.
**   Presumably, the initial increase in investment will be greater than the secondary reduction in investment, although the model is not clear on this.
Better synchronization of income and payments will reduce money demand.

Examples:
An increase in net taxes is a contractionary fiscal policy. Output level (Y) will decrease because consumers' disposable income is reduced. As output decreases, money demand will decrease. Because there is no monetary policy change, money supply is unchanged and the interest rate is decreased. As the interest rate decreases, planned investment is increased.

5.   (a)   Refer to the following money market diagram.

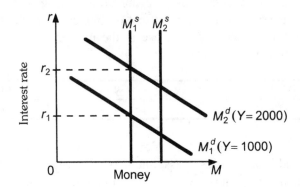

(b)   *MPC* is 0.8, therefore the government expenditure multiplier is 5. To move the economy to the full-employment output level, government spending would have to increase by 200.

(c)   *MPC* is 0.8, therefore the tax multiplier is –4. To move the economy to the full-employment output level, taxes would have to decrease by 250.

(d)   The balanced-budget multiplier is 1. Increase *G* and *T* by 1,000.

(e)   *AE* will increase by 200. Refer to the following diagram.

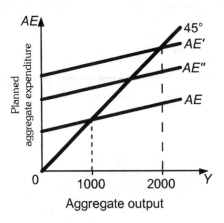

(f)   Inventory levels will fall and output will rise.

(g)   Refer to the preceding money market diagram. The money demand curve will shift to the right.

(h)   Refer to the preceding goods market diagram. Investment, part of *AE*, has been driven down somewhat (presumably not by as much as 200!) because of the higher interest rate, which has discouraged some investment projects.

(i)   No. The investment fall has reduced the power of the balanced budget multiplier. (You would get the same sort of result if you had used a straight increase in *G* or reduction in *T*.)

(j)   The money supply curve will shift to the right, from M^S_1 to M^S_2, in the money market diagram.

6.   (a) $G\,(\text{I}) \to Y\,(\text{I}) \to M^d\,(\text{I}) \to r\,(\text{I}) \to I\,(\text{D}) \to Y\,(\text{D})$

(b) $T\,(\text{D}) \to Y\,(\text{I}) \to M^d\,(\text{I}) \to r\,(\text{I}) \to I\,(\text{D}) \to Y\,(\text{D})$

(c)   The change will be greater in (a) because the government-spending multiplier is greater than the tax multiplier.

Open Market sale/purchase
Discount rate increase/ decrease
Reserve requirement increase/ decrease $\Big\}$

$$M^s \, (\text{I}) \rightarrow r \, (\text{D}) \rightarrow I \, (\text{I}) \rightarrow Y \, (\text{I}) \rightarrow M^d \, (\text{I}) \rightarrow r \, (\text{I})$$

13 [28]

Aggregate Supply and the Equilibrium Price Level

C hapter objectives:

1. Distinguish between the short run and the long run. Explain why the short-run and long-run aggregate supply curves have the slopes they have. Identify the factors that shift the short-run aggregate supply curve.
2. Define potential GDP and relate it to the long-run aggregate supply curve.
3. Define the equilibrium price level.
4. Explain how the economy achieves its long-run equilibrium.
5. Determine the short-run effects of an expansionary or contractionary fiscal or monetary policy on the equilibrium price level and the inflation rate, and link this to the degree of excess capacity in the economy. Determine the long-run effects of expansionary or contractionary policy.
6. Define inflation and identify the major sources of inflation. Explain why sustained inflation is believed to be a purely monetary phenomenon.
7. Explain why the Fed targets the interest rate, rather than the money supply, as a policy variable.
8. State the goals of the Fed since 1970 (as discussed in this chapter) and explain the rationale behind the policy of "leaning against the wind."

BRAIN TEASER: The textbook assumes, for simplicity, that the expenditure multiplier is constant, but is it? A given autonomous increase in, say, consumption will prompt a given rightward shift in the aggregate demand curve and a new equilibrium output level will be reached. Consider two cases: Case A, where there is a relatively large amount of excess capacity in the economy and Case B, where the economy is close to full employment. Does the increase in consumption result in the same expansion in output level? In which case is the multiplier larger? What causes the difference?

OBJECTIVE 1:
Distinguish between the short run and the long run. Explain why the short-run and long-run aggregate supply curves have the slopes they have. Identify the factors that shift the short-run aggregate supply curve.

The *aggregate supply* (*AS*) curve shows how the aggregate output supplied by the economy's productive sector responds to changes in the overall price level. It is *not* merely the sum of the supply curves of all the firms in the economy. In Chapter 3, we assumed that costs were held constant when we constructed a supply curve for a market. However, in the overall economy, the price of one firm's output is often the price of another firm's input. Also, except in a perfectly competitive environment, firms simultaneously determine the price they will charge and the level of output they will produce. The aggregate supply curve may best be thought of as a curve that traces out the price and production decisions of all the firms in the economy under a given set of circumstances—expectations, tax policies, energy prices, and so on. (page 237 [549])

In the long run, all cost and price-level changes have time to work through the economic system. Though wage changes tend to "follow" price changes in the short run, in the long run wages have had enough time to catch up. In the long run, the level of employment (and therefore output) is not influenced by changes in the price level. In the long run, *AS* is vertical. (page 242 [554])

▶▶ LEARNING TIP: The short-run/long-run distinction can be confusing. Focus on the long run first. In the long run, temporary discrepancies (between rates of increase in prices and wages, for example, or between workers' expectations and actual outcomes) disappear. Price changes, then, have no effect on long-run employment or output decisions. In the short run, by contrast, mistakes can be made, with workers in particular failing to read price signals correctly.

▶▶ LEARNING TIP: To get the key point about the shape of the short-run *AS* curve note that, as output increases, the overall price level also increases. Resource costs may also increase (as firms compete for additional inputs) but they increase less rapidly. By having the overall price level increasing more rapidly than production costs, there is a short-run incentive to increase production.◀

In the short run, as prices rise, producers increase output—there is a positive relationship between the price level and production. However, the *short-run AS curve* grows steeper at higher output levels because, as the economy approaches full employment, the additional cost incurred in producing more output increases more rapidly. Eventually, when the economy reaches its full productive capacity, the short-run *AS* curve becomes vertical. (page 238 [550])

Comment: Draw the short-run *AS* curve as a curve whose slope is increasing, not simply as a straight upward-sloping line. The economics of the situation requires this and your ability to analyze the effects of policy actions depends upon it.

The short-run *AS* curve can shift if there are changes in any of the factors affecting the supply decisions of individual firms. These factors include "cost shocks," changes in the quantity or quality of resources, technological changes (usually improvements), shifts in public policy, war, and natural events such as the weather. (page 240 [552])

▶▶ LEARNING TIP: Think of New Orleans as a small nation just before and, then, just after the ravages of Hurricane Katrina in 2005. What must have happened to the position of the city's short-run aggregate supply curve?

▶▶ LEARNING TIP: Think back to the production possibility frontier (ppf) analysis you encountered in Chapter 2. That analysis looks at what it was possible for an economy to produce—so does the aggregate supply curve. The factors that shifted the position of a production possibility frontier are also factors that shift the position of the aggregate supply curve.◀

ECONOMICS IN PRACTICE: On page 243 [555], the textbook introduces the simple Keynesian aggregate supply curve. This curve is horizontal until it reaches its maximum output and then becomes vertical. This suggests that output cannot exceed that maximum output level. Referring to Figure 13.4 (28.4), which shows the short-run aggregate supply exceeding "potential" GDP, do you feel that the simple Keynesian model is plausible? Is it possible to go beyond potential GDP in the short run?

ANSWER: It is highly improbable that all sectors of the economy will experience a binding supply constraint at the same point. In fact, Figure 13.4 (28.4) suggests that, in the short run, the economy can, temporarily, achieve output levels beyond those that are can be sustained in the long run. As a simple example, when demand is high, workers may be willing to work overtime for a limited period, but not indefinitely.

ECONOMICS IN PRACTICE (CONTINUED): What is the implication of the simple Keynesian aggregate supply curve for the size of the expenditure multiplier as, for example, an expansionary fiscal policy is undertaken? What role does the crowding-out effect play?

ANSWER: As aggregate demand expands, the size of the multiplier will remain constant until potential GDP is reached. At that point, when the aggregate supply curve becomes vertical, the expenditure multiplier will become zero. The crowding-out effect will switch from being absent to being total.

───────■─────────────────────────────── **Practice** ───────────────────────────────

1.   The short-run aggregate supply curve plots the relationship between
        (a)   the overall price level and wages—as wages increase, prices increase.
        (b)   output and supply. As supply increases, more output is available.
        (c)   the overall price level and the aggregate quantity of output supplied.
        (d)   equilibrium output and the rate of inflation.

        ANSWER: (c) Refer to p. 238 [550] for a discussion of the short-run aggregate supply curve.

2.   If the economy is in a deep recession, a modest increase in aggregate demand is likely to cause _____ in price and _____ in output level.
        (a)   an increase; an increase
        (b)   an increase; little or no increase
        (c)   little or no change; an increase
        (d)   little or no change; little or no increase

        ANSWER: (c) When the economy is in a recession, the short-run *AS* curve may be horizontal. An increase in demand will increase output with little or no increase in price level. Refer to p. 239 [551].

3.   The economy is operating at full capacity. The short-run *AS* curve is _____ . An increase in the price level will _____ output.
        (a)   horizontal; increase
        (b)   horizontal; not change
        (c)   vertical; increase
        (d)   vertical; not change

        ANSWER: (d) The short-run *AS* curve is vertical at full capacity—additional price inducement can stimulate no further production.

4.   For the short-run aggregate supply curve to have a positive slope,
      (a)   changes in the overall price level must be fully anticipated.
      (b)   input price changes must be fully anticipated.
      (c)   changes in the overall price level must lag behind input price changes.
      (d)   input price changes must lag behind changes in the overall price level.

      ANSWER: (d) Refer to p. 238 [550].

5.   The aggregate supply curve will be positively sloped in each of the following cases except when input prices change _____ output price changes.
      (a)   at the same rate as
      (b)   more slowly than
      (c)   more rapidly than
      (d)   not at all in response to

      ANSWER: (a) Refer to p. 238 [550]. If input prices change at the same rate as output prices, the changes neutralize each other—relatively, inputs become neither more nor less expensive.

Refer to the following diagram to answer the next question.

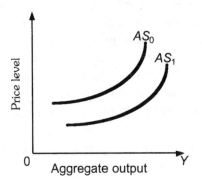

6.   Which of the following would shift the U.S. short-run aggregate supply curve from AS_0 to AS_1?
      (a)   A fall in the number of migrant workers from Mexico
      (b)   An increase in income taxes
      (c)   An increase in welfare benefits
      (d)   An loosening of the restrictions on child labor

      ANSWER: (d) For AS to shift right (an increase in supply), either more resources must be made available or existing resources must become more productive. Option (b) has had some supporters—higher taxes reduce after-tax wages and may encourage more work effort to maintain a given standard of living. This argument, though, is weak and is excluded from our model of the macroeconomy. ∎

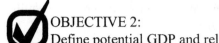

OBJECTIVE 2:
Define potential GDP and relate it to the long-run aggregate supply curve.

Potential GDP (or potential output) is the output level that can be sustained in the long run. Output may be lower (if, for example, there is cyclical unemployment or bad weather) or higher (if resources are being employed overtime), but potential output is that level of production the economy could sustain over the long run with no pressure for inflation to occur. When the economy is on its long-run aggregate supply curve it has achieved its potential GDP level. (page 242 [554])

> ▶▶▶ LEARNING TIP: The concept of potential output is very important. If potential output is the output level that can be sustained in the long run, then any other output level *must* be only *short-run*. If the *AD* curve and short-run *AS* curve intersect at any other level, then economic forces will be exerted to push them to this level.
> ▶▶▶ LEARNING TIP: You can link the concept of potential output to the production possibility frontier diagram from Chapter 2. The economy is at its potential level of output if it is on the production possibility frontier. In any other case, it is not.◀

──────────────────────────── **Practice** ────────────────────────────

7.   The economy may be working at less than its capacity if there is
(a)   cyclical unemployment.
(b)   frictional unemployment.
(c)   natural unemployment.
(d)   structural unemployment.

ANSWER: (a) Some frictional and structural unemployment is considered necessary and healthy. Refer to p. 239 [551].■

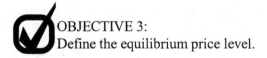

OBJECTIVE 3:
Define the equilibrium price level.

Graphically, the equilibrium price level is the price level at which aggregate demand and aggregate supply intersect.   Each point on the *AD* curve traces out all the price/output combinations that simultaneously achieve equilibrium in both the goods market and the money market. The *AS* curve depicts the price/output choices of the firms in the economy. The intersection is the unique price/output combination where the choices of producers are consistent with those of buyers. (page 241 [553])

──────────────────────────── **Practice** ────────────────────────────

8.   The economy is in equilibrium. There is an increase in government spending. The aggregate _____ curve will shift to the _____ .
(a)   supply; right
(b)   supply; left
(c)   demand; right
(d)   demand; left

ANSWER: (c) Spending, therefore demand, has increased. An increase in aggregate demand will shift the *AD* curve to the right.

9.   The economy is in equilibrium. There is an increase in government spending. The equilibrium price level will _____ and the equilibrium output level will _____ .

(a)   increase; increase

(b)   increase; decrease

(c)   decrease; increase

(d)   decrease; decrease

ANSWER: (a) An increase in aggregate demand will cause both the price level and the output level to increase. ■

OBJECTIVE 4:
Explain how the economy achieves its long-run equilibrium.

If the economy is not at its potential output level, then automatic forces exist in the economy that will push it towards that level in the long run. Figure 13.4 (28.4) shows this process graphically. If the current output level is greater than the potential GDP level, the economy's resources are being stretched and costs will increase. Rising costs shift the short-run aggregate supply curve to the left. This process will continue until the economy's production is no longer greater than its potential level. (page 242 [554])

▶▶   LEARNING TIP: The automatic mechanism that drives the economy towards its potential GDP level is sometimes called "the self-correcting mechanism." Importantly, it operates without explicit government intervention. Figure 13.4 (28.4) is crucial for your understanding of the remainder of your economics course. You need to ensure that you understand *why* the *AD* curve must shift to the left if the economy is currently in short-run equilibrium at an output level exceeding potential GDP. In the long run, as costs catch up the prices, the short-run *AS* curve shifts to the left.

▶▶   LEARNING TIP: The self-correcting mechanism *always* operates through changes in the short-run aggregate *supply* curve. Consider Figure 13.4 (28.4). It is tempting to think that, because the *AD* curve shifts to the right and the short-run *AS* curve then responds by shifting to the left to restore long-run equilibrium that, if the short-run *AS* curve were to shift first, then the *AD* curve would shift to compensate. This, however, is false logic and reveals a lack of understanding of the mechanism involved! Whether the change that shifts the economy away from its initial long-run equilibrium comes from a shift in aggregate demand or in short-run aggregate supply, the automatic forces that impel it back to potential GDP must always spring from the supply side. ◀

Comment: Note that the mechanism depends on adjustments in resource costs. Accordingly, the presence of inflexibilities such as minimum wage may weaken the mechanism so much that the economy may become stuck in a recession and might require policy intervention to push it toward potential GDP. This issue is discussed in Chapter 14 (29).

━━■━━━━━━━━━━━━━━━━━━━━━━━━━ **Practice** ━━━━━━━━━━━━━━━━━━━━━━━━━

Use the following diagram to answer the next three questions. The economy is initially in long-run equilibrium at point *E*.

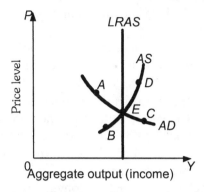

10.   Suppose these is a decrease in consumer confidence. The aggregate _____ curve will shift to the

        _____ .
        (a)   supply; right
        (b)   supply; left
        (c)   demand; right
        (d)   demand; left

        ANSWER: (d) Consumption spending, therefore demand, has decreased.   A decrease in
                aggregate demand will shift the *AD* curve to the left.

11.   In the short run, a decrease in consumer confidence would move the economy to a point such as
        (a)   *A*.
        (b)   *B*.
        (c)   *C*.
        (d)   *D*.

        ANSWER: (b) As the *AD* curve shifts to the left, output and price level will both decrease.

12.   To restore long-run equilibrium, we would expect
        (a)   the short-run aggregate supply curve to shift to the right.
        (b)   the short-run aggregate supply curve to shift to the left.
        (c)   the long-run aggregate supply curve to shift to the right.
        (d)   the long-run aggregate supply curve to shift to the left.

        ANSWER: (a) The "self-correcting mechanism always operates through changes in the short-
                run aggregate supply curve. ■

OBJECTIVE 5:

Determine the short-run effects of an expansionary or contractionary fiscal or monetary policy on the equilibrium price level and the inflation rate, and link this to the degree of excess capacity in the economy. Determine the long-run effects of expansionary or contractionary policy.

Short-run equilibrium occurs where *AD* and short-run *AS* intersect—goods and money markets are in equilibrium and the desires of demanders and suppliers are met. (page 244 [556])

Fiscal (*G*, *T*) or monetary (M^s) policies shift the *AD* curve. When *AS* is relatively flat (the economy has substantial "slack"), an expansionary policy will stimulate much additional output in the short run with a relatively small increase in inflation. When *AS* is relatively steep (the economy is close to full employment), the identical policy will exert a strong upward pressure on the price level with little gain in output. The strength of the multiplier is affected by the slope of the *AS* curve—the multiplier is much smaller in the second case than in the first.

Fiscal policy is more potent if the Fed "accommodates" by issuing more money to stabilize the interest rate—crowding out can be prevented. Put simply, "accommodation" means that the Fed acts to maintain the interest rate. An expansionary fiscal policy would drive up the interest rate—the Fed increases the money supply in response; a contractionary fiscal policy produces the opposite response. In each case, the impact of the fiscal policy action is *intensified*. The Fed might accommodate if its economic objectives coincided with those of the government.

In the long run, neither fiscal nor monetary policy will have any impact on aggregate output because, in the long run, *AS* is vertical. Put differently, in the long run, the economy will reach potential GDP, whether or not policy actions are undertaken. With a vertical long-run aggregate supply curve the government spending multiplier and the tax multiplier are both zero. The issue is "How long does it take to reach the long run?" If the economy can achieve long run equilibrium quickly, then there is little need for active policy. If, on the other hand, the economy's self-correcting mechanism is sluggish, then policy does have a significant role to play. (page 244 [556])

> ▶▶▶   LEARNING TIP: Contractionary policies often seem more difficult to work through. In theory, a reduction in government purchases will simply reverse the effects of an increase. However, working through the effects of contractionary policy actions is a great way for you to test your own knowledge. Draw the diagrams too. Compare your conclusions against those in the textbook examples and you'll quickly find out what you know and what you still have to work on. ◀

Comment: The crowding out of investment by increased government spending was first discussed in the previous chapter. Higher interest rates provoke crowding out. Using the *AS/AD* model, you can think of crowding out occurring a second way—through increases in the aggregate price level. An increase in aggregate demand pushes up the price level, money demand, and the interest rate. Ultimately, investment is reduced.

Comment: The answer to many questions about economic policy is "It depends." Keep in mind that a policy that might be highly successful in one circumstance (a recession, for example) might fail miserably in another. The effectiveness of policy is linked to the multiplier—in our new more realistic model the multiplier's value, and the effectiveness of policy, are variable.

—■————————————————— **Practice** —————————————

13.   Currently, output is substantially less than potential output. Now the Fed buys securities. In the short run we would expect
        (a)   an unanticipated decrease in business inventories.
        (b)   an increase in the interest rate because the demand for money has decreased.
        (c)   a decrease in planned investment because securities are scarcer.
        (d)   a decrease in production as inflation erodes spending power.

        ANSWER: (a) The Fed action is an expansionary policy. Check Chapter 11 (26) if you missed this point. Interest rates fall, planned investment increases, aggregate expenditure and aggregate demand increase, and inventories unexpectedly decrease.

14.   An expansionary fiscal policy is most effective when aggregate demand is _____ initially and when the Fed simultaneously _____ the money supply.
        (a)   high; increases
        (b)   high; decreases
        (c)   low; increases
        (d)   low; decreases

        ANSWER: (c) The flatter the short-run *AS* curve, the smaller the increase in price level that will be caused by the fiscal policy (and the smaller reductions in consumption and investment). An "accommodating" monetary policy would help to keep interest rates low, to prevent the crowding out of investment.

15.   *MPC* is 0.8. In the long run, the most accurate value for the government spending multiplier is _____ , and for the tax multiplier the most accurate value is _____ .
        (a)   5; –4
        (b)   more than 5; less than –4
        (c)   less than 5; more than –4
        (d)   zero; zero

        ANSWER: (d) In the long run, fiscal policy actions have no effect on output level. Refer to p. 246 [558].

Graphically, long-run equilibrium is shown by the intersection of three curves (*AD*, *SRAS*, *LRAS*). Refer to the following diagram. If *AD* or *SRAS* shifts and the economy reaches Points *A*, *B*, *C*, or *D*, those points only represent short-run equilibrium. In the long-run, additional adjustments will have to be made.

        Use the following diagram to answer the next two questions. The economy is initially in long-run equilibrium at point *E*.

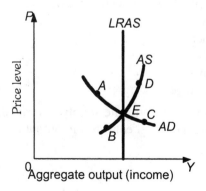

16.   In the short run, an increase in net taxes would move the economy to a point such as
       (a)   *A*.
       (b)   *B*.
       (c)   *C*.
       (d)   *D*.
       ANSWER: (b) This is a contractionary fiscal policy. Aggregate demand would decrease.

17.   In the long run, an increase in money supply would make aggregate demand _____ and later
       cause short-run aggregate supply to _____ .
       (a)   increase; increase
       (b)   increase; decrease
       (c)   decrease; increase
       (d)   decrease; decrease
       ANSWER: (b) A money supply increase is an expansionary monetary policy, designed to shift
                    the aggregate demand curve (to a new equilibrium such as Point *D*). Aggregate
                    supply will shift left, and continue to shift until potential GDP is restored. Refer
                    to p. 242 [554].

Use the following information to answer the next three questions. Arbez is in long-run (and short-run)
equilibrium. Now the central bank (ArbeFed) increases the money supply. Simultaneously, the
government cuts taxes.

18.   We would predict a(n) _____ in the price level and a(n) _____ in the output level in the short
       run.
       (a)   increase; increase
       (b)   increase; decrease
       (c)   decrease; increase
       (d)   decrease; decrease
       ANSWER: (a) Both changes are expansionary. *AD* will shift to the right.

19.   To restore long-run equilibrium, the
       (a)   aggregate demand curve will shift to the right.
       (b)   aggregate demand curve will shift to the left.
       (c)   short-run aggregate supply curve will shift to the right.
       (d)   short-run aggregate supply curve will shift to the left.
       ANSWER: (d) Refer to p. 242 [554].

20.   Relative to the initial situation, we would predict a(n) _____ in the price level and _____ in the
       output level in the long run.
       (a)   increase; an increase
       (b)   increase; no change
       (c)   decrease; an increase
       (d)   decrease; no change
       ANSWER: (b) The long-run aggregate supply is vertical, therefore, although the price level will
                    change, the initial equilibrium output level will be restored. ∎

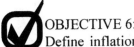

OBJECTIVE 6:
Define inflation and identify the major sources of inflation. Explain why sustained inflation is believed to be a purely monetary phenomenon.

Inflation, a rise in the overall price level, may be caused by a shift to the right in aggregate demand (*demand-pull inflation*) or by a shift to the left in aggregate supply (*cost-push inflation*). Cost-push inflation results in higher prices and lower production—*stagflation*. Inflation may be fueled by inflationary expectations. If higher prices are expected, suppliers may continue to raise prices even if demand is not increasing. If expansionary fiscal policy is "accommodated" by the Fed (that is, if the Fed issues more money to keep the interest rate constant), the rightward shift in the *AD* curve is greater than it would have been with only the expansionary fiscal policy, and higher prices ensue. Sustained inflation cannot occur unless the Fed continues to releases additional money into the economy—long-run inflation is a monetary phenomenon. (page 246 [558])

━━━━■━━━━━━━━━━━━━━━━━━━━━━━━ **Practice** ━━━━━━━━━━━━━━━━━━━━

21.   Demand-pull inflation occurs when the aggregate _____ curve shifts _____ .
       (a)   demand; right
       (b)   demand; left
       (c)   supply; right
       (d)   supply; left

       ANSWER: (a)   An increase in demand will increase the price level. Refer to p. 246 [558].

22.   Which statement is false? An expansionary fiscal policy will be more inflationary
       (a)   in the long run than in the short run.
       (b)   if the Fed accommodates than if it doesn't.
       (c)   in the short run, if the short-run aggregate supply curve simultaneously shifts to the right.
       (d)   the closer the economy is to full employment.

       ANSWER: (c)   If the short-run *AS* curve shifts to the right, the increase in production will absorb some of the increased demand with less of a price-level increase.

23.   In the mainly agricultural economy of Arbez there has been an extremely poor harvest because of heavy rains. The central bank initiates an open market purchase of securities. As a result of the policy, we would expect to see output level _____ and price level _____ .
       (a)   decrease more than otherwise; increase more than otherwise
       (b)   decrease more than otherwise; increase less than otherwise
       (c)   decrease less than otherwise; increase more than otherwise
       (d)   decrease less than otherwise; increase less than otherwise

       ANSWER: (c)   Aggregate supply is decreasing, reducing output and raising the price level (stagflation). The policy increases aggregate demand. This will stimulate output somewhat by increasing the price level still further. ■

OBJECTIVE 7:
Explain why the Fed targets the interest rate, rather than the money supply, as a policy variable.

When the Fed conducts an expansionary monetary policy action, such as buying bonds in the open market, the money supply increases and the interest rate decreases. How much the interest rate decreases depends on how responsive holders of money are to the interest rate. If the money demand curve is steep (unresponsive), a given change in the money supply will have a more powerful an impact on the interest rate than if the money demand curve is relatively flat. Put differently, to achieve a given change in the interest rate, the Fed may have to change the money supply only a little or a great deal. The Fed has chosen to target the interest rate. (page 250 [562])

> ▶▶▶   LEARNING TIP: Study Figure 13.10 (28.10) carefully and keep it in mind as you work through this chapter. It is an excellent summary of the Fed's response to economic conditions. If you can't explain to yourself how each step in the cause-and-effect sequence works, go back to Chapter 12 (27) and review.◀

──────────────■────────────────────────── Practice ──────────────────────────

24.   The Fed sells bonds. This policy will be _____ the steeper the money demand curve.
    (a)   more expansionary
    (b)   less expansionary
    (c)   more contractionary
    (d)   less contractionary

    ANSWER: (c) A Fed purchase of bonds is a contractionary policy action. (Review Chapter 12 (27) if you are unsure about this.) With a relatively steep money demand curve, interest rates will rise more sharply than with a relatively flat curve. ■

OBJECTIVE 8:
State the goals of the Fed since 1970 (as discussed in this chapter) and explain the rationale behind the policy of "leaning against the wind."

The Fed seeks to maintain high output, high employment levels, and low inflation. When aggregate demand is high (low), the Fed will increase (decrease) the interest rate. The Fed may "lean against the wind," which means that it moves interest rates to offset fluctuations in the economy. This practice poses problems during periods of stagflation (both high inflation and high unemployment) because any monetary policy action will reduce one problem but intensify the other.

Figure 13.13 (28.13) shows the relationship between important macroeconomic variables (growth rate, inflation rate) and a key short-term interest rate (the three-month Treasury bill rate). Greater inflation (actual or anticipated) generally provokes higher interest rates, even when output is low. A sluggish economy is likely to prompt interest rate reductions. From early 2001 until 2003, confronted by faltering economic growth, the Fed aggressively trimmed the T-bill rate. (page 253 [565])

Some monetary authorities have based policy decisions more narrowly, striving to maintain inflation within a limited range over time. This is inflation targeting. During a stagflationary period, inflation targeting would call for policies to control inflation.

ECONOMICS IN PRACTICE: On page 255 [567], the textbook highlights a report from May 2008 on global anxieties about rising food prices. There were, for example, food riots in Haiti and restrictions on beef exports in Argentina. In retrospect, was the pressure on prices springing from the demand side or the supply side of the global market? Was there any evidence of recession or stagflation (p. 247 (559)) in the U.S. economy?

ANSWER: With rising oil prices, growing demand for ethanol (which reduced the supply of corn for livestock and humans), and droughts (for instance, in Australia), there was some evidence that the main pressure on prices was coming from the supply side. In the United States, rising consumer prices and rising unemployment (5.7% in August 2008) cast the shadow of stagflation.

ECONOMICS IN PRACTICE (CONTINUED): Using aggregate demand and aggregate supply, how could you model stagflation? What might cause such a shift?

ANSWER: Stagflation (cost-push inflation), which is most simply modeled as a leftward shift of the AS curve, is due to increases in the costs of inputs such as oil.

───■──────────────────────── **Practice** ────────────────────────

25.   The Fed is most likely to increase the money supply when output is _____ and inflation is _____

    (a)   high; high
    (b)   high; low
    (c)   low; high
    (d)   low; low

    ANSWER: (d) An increase in the money supply is an expansionary policy. The Fed is most likely to stimulate the economy when output is low. Given the Fed's concern about inflation, an easy money policy is more likely when inflation is low.

26.   There is a negative demand shock. The Fed "leans against the wind." We would expect the money supply to _____ . The interest rate will decrease _____ than otherwise.
    (a)   increase; more
    (b)   increase; less
    (c)   decrease; more
    (d)   decrease; less

    ANSWER: (a) To compensate for the demand shock, the Fed would undertake an expansionary policy. The initial shock would reduce money demand and the interest rate. The increased money supply will make the interest rate reduction greater.

27.   Stagflation is characterized by
    (a)   high inflation and high unemployment.
    (b)   high inflation and low unemployment.
    (c)   low inflation and high unemployment.
    (d)   low inflation and low unemployment.

    ANSWER: (a) Refer to the definition on p. 247 [559]). Stagflation is caused by a leftward shift of the aggregate supply curve.

28.   The short-run aggregate supply curve shifts to the left. Inflation will _____ . If the Fed decreases the money supply, it indicates that the Fed believes low output to be a _____ problem than high inflation.
    (a)   increase; greater
    (b)   increase; lesser
    (c)   decrease; greater
    (d)   decrease; lesser

    ANSWER: (b) The decrease in aggregate supply will cause stagflation. A contractionary policy is designed to dampen inflation, but it will aggravate the decrease in output. ■

BRAIN TEASER SOLUTION: In Case A, the multiplier will be relatively large because, for a given increase in aggregate demand (from AD_{A1} to AD_{A2}), a comparatively small increase in aggregate price level will occur. Accordingly, the decrease in spending brought about by the price increase (through the real wealth effect, for instance) will be relatively small.

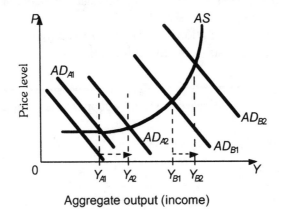

Aggregate output (income)

In Case B, the multiplier will be relatively small because, given the increase in aggregate demand (from AD_{B1} to AD_{B2}), there will be a comparatively large increase in aggregate price level. Accordingly, there will be a sharper decrease in spending due to the price increase.

A LOOK AHEAD

The model that you are learning about has a wide range of applications that will be explored in upcoming chapters. Topics covered in this chapter will be used in a later chapter to explain the similarities and differences among the various schools of economic thought. Also, the closed model developed in this chapter is opened up to include international economic relationships in Chapters 19 (34) and 20 (35).

PRACTICE TEST

I.   MULTIPLE-CHOICE QUESTIONS

Select the option that provides the single best answer.

_____ 1.   One inflation-fighting policy is to shift *AD* to the _____ by _____ .
(a)   right; increasing net taxes
(b)   left; decreasing net taxes
(c)   right; increasing government purchases
(d)   left; decreasing government purchases

_____ 2.   Each of the following will make the *AD* curve shift to the right EXCEPT
(a)   a tax cut.
(b)   an open market sale of securities by the Fed.
(c)   a decrease in the required reserve ratio.
(d)   an increase in government spending.

_____ 3.   *Ceteris paribus*, an increase in the price level will cause
   (a)   the interest rate to fall.
   (b)   an increase in the quantity of money supplied.
   (c)   an excess demand for money at the original equilibrium interest rate.
   (d)   the aggregate demand curve to shift to the left.

_____ 4.   Government spending increases and the price of raw materials falls. In an economy with some "slack," we would predict that, in the short run,
   (a)   price would rise and output would fall.
   (b)   price would fall and output would rise.
   (c)   price would rise but the effect on output would be uncertain.
   (d)   the effect on price would be uncertain but output would increase.

_____ 5.   The president abolishes all subsidies to corporations. In the short run, this will cause the price level to _____ and output to _____ .
   (a)   increase; increase
   (b)   increase; decrease
   (c)   decrease; increase
   (d)   decrease; decrease

_____ 6.   An increase in the price level will certainly cause the *AE* curve to shift _____ as the interest rate _____ .
   (a)   upward; increases
   (b)   upward; decreases
   (c)   downward; increases
   (d)   downward; decreases

_____ 7.   During an expansionary fiscal policy action, the interest rate _____ ; during an expansionary monetary policy action, the interest rate _____ .
   (a)   increases; increases
   (b)   increases; decreases
   (c)   decreases; increases
   (d)   decreases; decreases

_____ 8.   An increase in government spending will cause
   (a)   the aggregate demand curve to shift to the right.
   (b)   the money demand curve to shift to the left.
   (c)   the *AE* curve to shift downward.
   (d)   planned investment to increase.

_____ 9.   The _____ curve will shift to the _____ if the Fed buys securities.
   (a)   *AD*; right
   (b)   *AD*; left
   (c)   *AS*; right
   (d)   *AS*; left

_____ 10.   A decrease in the price level will _____ money demand and _____ the interest rate.
(a)   increase; increase
(b)   increase; decrease
(c)   decrease; increase
(d)   decrease; decrease

Use the following money market diagram to answer the next two questions.

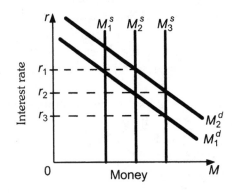

_____ 11.   The government undertakes an expansionary fiscal policy such as a(n) _____ . The Fed accommodates by, for example, _____ .
(a)   increase in net taxes; buying securities
(b)   increase in net taxes; selling securities
(c)   decrease in net taxes; buying securities
(d)   decrease in net taxes; selling securities

_____ 12.   Given the policies described in the previous question, which of the following outcomes is possible? Money demand moves from _____ and money supply moves from _____ .
(a) M^d_1 to M^d_2; M^s_1 to M^s_2
(b) M^d_1 to M^d_2; M^s_2 to M^s_1
(c) M^d_2 to M^d_1; M^s_3 to M^s_2
(d) M^d_2 to M^d_1; M^s_2 to M^s_3

_____ 13.   In the short run,
(a)   input prices are fixed.
(b)   output prices are fixed.
(c)   input prices respond fully to changes in the overall price level.
(d)   input prices do not respond fully to changes in the overall price level.

_____ 14.   In the short run, aggregate supply would decrease in each of the following cases EXCEPT
(a)   an increase in the proportion of high school graduates who go on to college.
(b)   a deterioration in the nation's infrastructure.
(c)   an increase in emigration.
(d)   a decrease in the tax rate on business profits.

_____ 15. The economy is currently at the potential output level. An increase in government spending will result in
(a) no crowding out of investment.
(b) partial crowding out of investment.
(c) complete crowding out of investment.
(d) partial crowding out of the money supply.

_____ 16. The economy is experiencing an expansion. With which policy is the Fed "leaning against the wind."
(a) The Fed increases money growth.
(b) The Fed reduces interest rates.
(c) The Fed decreases the required reserve ratio.
(d) The Fed sells bonds in the open market.

_____ 17. The natural rate of unemployment rate is 6%. The present unemployment rate is 5%. As time passes, we would expect the
(a) long-run aggregate supply curve to shift to the right.
(b) long-run aggregate supply curve to shift to the left.
(c) short-run aggregate supply curve to shift to the right.
(d) short-run aggregate supply curve to shift to the left.

Use the following diagram to answer the next three questions. The economy is in initial long-run equilibrium at point A. AD_1 and AS_1 are the initial positions of the curves.

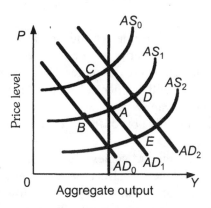

_____ 18. Demand-pull inflation is best represented by the move from
(a) A to B.
(b) A to C.
(c) A to D.
(d) A to E.

_____ 19. The price of oil increases. Initially, this will shift the aggregate
(a) demand curve to AD_0.
(b) demand curve to AD_2.
(c) supply curve to AS_0.
(d) supply curve to AS_2.

_____ 20. The price of oil increases. The government initiates a contractionary fiscal policy to offset the inflationary effects of the rising energy prices. This will shift the aggregate demand curve to

    (a) AD_0 and intensify the decline in output.
    (b) AD_0 and offset the decline in output.
    (c) AD_2 and intensify the decline in output.
    (d) AD_2 and offset the decline in output.

II.   APPLICATION QUESTIONS

1.   The Arbocali economy is initially in long-run equilibrium.

    (a)   Draw the aggregate demand curve (AD_0), short-run aggregate supply curve (AS_0), and the long-run aggregate supply curve ($LRAS$). Label equilibrium output and overall price level Y_0 and P_0, respectively.

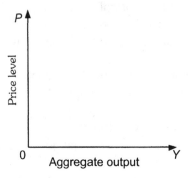

    (b)   There is a slump in consumer confidence and consumption level falls. Show how the diagram will change. Subscript any new curves "1."

    (c)   Now the government decreases taxes by an amount equal to the initial decrease in consumption. What will happen to aggregate demand, output, and the price level? Is there an inflationary gap?

    (d)   Aggregate demand will not shift far enough to the right to restore full employment. Why?

    (e)   Because the tax cut did not achieve full employment, the government hikes spending by an amount equal to the initial decrease in consumption. Show any curve shifts on the diagram and subscript any new curves "2." How will output and the overall price level change? Show these new levels, with "2" subscripts. Is there an inflationary gap?

The following diagram shows the money market in original equilibrium (before the slump in consumer confidence).

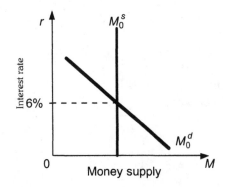

(f)   Given the changes in Parts (a) through (e) above, show how the money market diagram will stand at the end of Part (e). Subscript any new curves "2." Describe what will happen to the interest rate and to bond prices.

(g)   If you've seen *IS-LM* in Chapter 12 (27), you'll know that money market changes can shift the position of the *LM* curve. In this particular situation, how does the *LM* curve shift, if at all?

(h)   The central bank is committed to maintaining the interest rate at 6%. Given the bank's commitment, what policy action should it choose? How might it implement this policy? Show how the money market diagram will stand immediately after the policy action. Subscript any new curves "3."

(i)   What will happen to the *AS/AD* diagram? Subscript any new curves "3." How will output and the overall price level change? Show these new levels, with "3" subscripts.

(j)   Given the changes in the *AS/AD* diagram, will there be any further change in the money market diagram? If so, what? Subscript any new curves "4."

(k)   Given the bank's interest rate commitment, describe the central bank's policy response. Is it accommodating? Is it inflationary?

(l)   If the central bank had undertaken no expansionary monetary policy, i.e., the money supply curve remained at M^s_0, show on the *AS/AD* diagram where the economy will reach equilibrium in the long run (Point *B*).

(m)   Assuming that the central bank makes no further changes to the money supply, i.e., M^s_3 is the final money supply curve, show on the *AS/AD* diagram where the economy will reach equilibrium in the long run (Point *C*).

(n)   "Given an expansionary fiscal policy, an accommodating central bank policy will be more / less inflationary."

2.   For each "event," indicate the specific short-run "result" that will occur.

Result A: increase in aggregate demand.
Result B: decrease in aggregate demand.
Result C: increase in aggregate supply.
Result D: decrease in aggregate supply.

	Result	*Event*
(a)	____	The government cuts personal income taxes.
(b)	____	The price of intermediate goods falls.
(c)	____	The interest rates rises.
(d)	____	Inflationary expectations of firms increase.
(e)	____	New, stringent standards for the construction of residential dwellings are enacted.
(f)	____	Employer contributions to the social security plan are decreased.

3.   The short-run aggregate supply curve suddenly shifts to the left.
(a)   What might have caused this?
(b)   Predict how price and output levels will change.
(c)   What name is used to describe this phenomenon?
(d)   How might the government respond to this supply-side change?
(e)   Describe what will happen to the price level and output level if *AS* shifts to the left and the government pursues an expansionary fiscal policy.

4.   (a)   Draw a goods market diagram and a money market diagram in the space following. Show the equilibrium interest rate (r_0) and output level (Y_0).

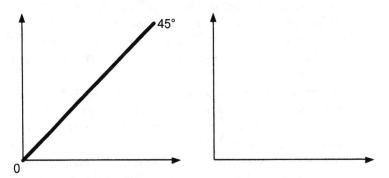

(b)   Suppose the price level falls from P_0 to P_1. Show all the curves that shift.
(c)   On the following diagram, sketch in the aggregate demand curve. Make your labeling consistent!

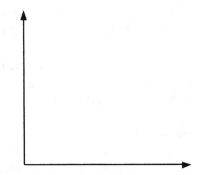

(d)   Explain why the *AD* curve has a negative slope.
(e)   Now suppose that the money supply increases. Show how this will affect all the diagrams.

5.   In each of the following cases, indicate if the variable will increase (I), decrease (D), or remain unchanged (U) in the short run.
(a)   Assume that the Fed is accommodative and Congress undertakes a contractionary fiscal policy (increasing taxes). Predict how each of the following variables will be affected in the short run.
(i)   _____   output
(ii)   _____   the interest rate
(iii)   _____   the price level
(iv)   _____   employment
(v)   _____   the deficit (net taxes minus government spending)
(vi)   _____   the demand for labor (guess on this one!)
(vii)   _____   supply of money

(b)   Assume that the Fed is not accommodative and Congress increases government purchases. Predict how each of the following variables will be affected in the short run.

(i)   ____   output
(ii)   ____   the interest rate
(iii)   ____   the price level
(iv)   ____   employment
(v)   ____   the deficit
(vi)   ____   the demand for labor
(vii)   ____   supply of money

(c)   Assume that the Fed is accommodative and that investment spending suddenly increases because of an upsurge in business optimism. Predict how each of the following variables will be affected in the short run.

(i)   ____   planned expenditure (initial change)
(ii)   ____   demand for money (initial change)
(iii)   ____   the interest rate (initial change)
(iv)   ____   the price level
(v)   ____   the deficit
(vi)   ____   demand for labor
(vii)   ____   supply of money

6.   Explain what will happen as a result of the following events. In each case, draw an aggregate demand and short-run aggregate supply diagram showing the initial equilibrium output level (Y_0) and price level (P_0). Show any changes and indicate the final equilibrium output level and price level.

(a)   The economy is in a recession. Now a reduction in foreign consumption of U.S. products occurs.

(b)   The economy is operating near full capacity. Now environmental pollution standards are tightened substantially.

(c)   The economy is in a recession. An increase in government purchases occurs. The Fed tries to maintain the interest rate.

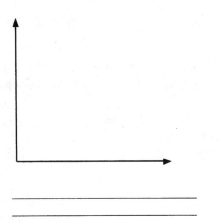

_____
_____
_____

(d)   The economy is operating near full capacity. An import tax (tariff) is imposed on foreign consumer goods, and the Fed tries to maintain the interest rate.

_____
_____
_____

(e)   The economy is in a recession. Household confidence about the future is reduced. Firms expect greater inflation in the future.

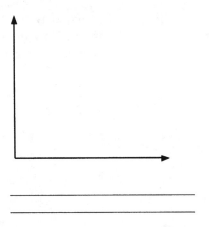

_____
_____
_____

(f)   The economy is operating near full capacity. Now there is an increase in the price of foreign oil. The Fed attempts to maintain the output level.

_____
_____
_____

PRACTICE TEST SOLUTIONS

I.   Solutions to Multiple-Choice Questions

1.   (d)   Shifting the *AD* curve to the left helps to reduce inflation. This may be done by enacting a contractionary policy such as a decrease in government spending or a reduction in the money supply.

2.   (b)   An open market sale of securities is a contractionary policy. A decrease in the money supply will increase the interest rate. This, in turn, will reduce planned investment (and consumption) and cause a lower equilibrium in the goods market.

3.   (c)   As the price level increases, money demand will shift to the right. At the original interest rate, an excess demand will now exist and the interest rate will increase. A change in the price level leads to a movement along the *AD* curve, not a shift.

4.   (d)   The fiscal policy action will increase aggregate demand, which will promote increasing prices and increasing output. The price hike for raw materials will make the short-run aggregate supply curve shift to the right, prompting a decrease in prices and an increase in output. Together, the changes will certainly raise output, but the effect on the price level is ambiguous.

5.   (b)   Removing the subsidies increases production costs—the aggregate supply curve will shift left. As supply contracts, price will increase and output will decrease.

6.   (c)   Higher prices reduce consumption and investment because of a higher interest rate and the real wealth effect. Reductions in consumption and investment shift the *AE* curve downward.

7.   (b)   Higher government spending (or lower net taxes) increase aggregate demand and money demand, and therefore, the interest rate. An increased money supply reduces the interest rate and increases aggregate demand. Note that money demand will increase, partly offsetting the decrease in the interest rate.

8.   (a)   Increased government spending crowds out investment as aggregate demand rises.

9.   (a)   If the Fed buys securities then, *at the same price level*, the money supply will increase and the interest rate will decrease. Planned investment and consumption will increase, shifting the *AD* curve to the right.

10.   (d)   One of the factors affecting money demand is the price level.

11.   (c)   Cutting taxes is an expansionary policy. It will push up the interest rate. To prevent this, the Fed must expand the money supply—the most frequent method is buying securities.

12.   (a)   An expansionary fiscal policy will cause money demand and the interest rate to increase. If the Fed accommodates, it will act to maintain the interest rate at its original level. The Fed must increase the money supply to do this.

13.   (d)   In the long run, input prices have enough time to make a full adjustment to changes in the price level but, in the short run, there is insufficient time.

14.   (d)   The tax rate cut will increase the (self-interested) incentive to produce. Note that an increase in college students will reduce the labor force in the short run; in the long run, because of better *human* capital, aggregate supply would increase.

15.   (c)   The policy action will not be effective. Each additional dollar of government spending will reduce investment spending by a dollar. Refer to p. 246 [558]. Note that some consumption spending, rather than investment spending, may be lost if consumption is interest-sensitive.

16.   (d)   The other options are all expansionary policy actions.

17.   (d)   Production level is higher than the full employment level. To compensate, the short-run aggregate supply curve will shift to the left.

18.   (c)   The moves from *A* to *B* and from *A* to *E* represent decreases in the price level. The move from *A* to *C* is caused by a shift in the position of the short-run aggregate supply curve.

19.   (c)   Oil is an input. Production costs rise, affecting the supply side of the economy.

20.   (a)   A contractionary policy will shift the aggregate demand curve to the left.

II.   *Solutions to Application Questions*

1.   (a)   Refer to the following diagram.

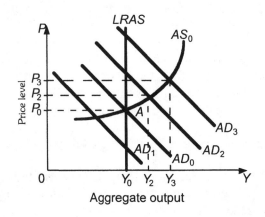

(b)   Refer to the preceding diagram. Aggregate demand will shift to AD_1.
(c)   Aggregate demand will increase as consumer's disposable income increases and therefore, output and the overall price level will increase. Output is less than full-employment output therefore there is no inflationary gap.
(d)   The tax multiplier is less than the multiplier for consumption.
(e)   Refer to the diagram. Aggregate demand will shift to AD_2. Recall that the demand curve shift reflects both the government spending increase and the tax cut. Output and overall price level will both increase. The inflationary gap is the distance $Y_0 Y_2$.

(f)   Money demand, M^d_0, is based on the initial (full-employment) level of expenditures. When the consumption decrease, tax decrease, and government spending increase have taken place, aggregate demand will be at AD_2. Money demand will increase to M^d_2. The interest rate will rise; bond prices will fall. Check Chapter 11 (26) if you're unsure about this.

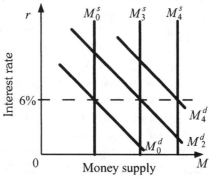

(g)   *LM* doesn't shift! The net effect of the consumption, tax, and government spending changes will be to shift *IS* right. There will be a movement up along the *LM* curve as income level and the interest rate increase.

(h)   The bank should increase the money supply by buying bonds, cutting the discount rate, or cutting the reserve requirement. Money supply will shift to M^s_3. Refer to the diagram.

(i)   *AD* will shift further to the right to AD_3. Refer to the diagram. The price level will increase.

(j)   Higher expenditures will result in higher money demand (M^d_4). Refer to the diagram. The interest rate will increase.

(k)   If the central bank wishes to maintain its target interest rate of 6%, it will be obliged to increase the money supply once more, to M^s_4. Central bank actions are both accommodating and inflationary.

(l)   Refer to the following diagram.

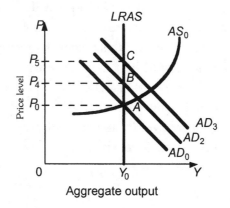

(m)   Refer to the diagram.

(n)   Given an expansionary fiscal policy, an accommodating central bank policy will be more inflationary, as we can see from the diagram above.

2. (a) *A*   (b) *C*   (c) *B*   (d) *D*
    (e) *D*   (f) *C*
    Note: Some of these "shocks" may affect both *AD* and *AS* curves. The above answers are for the single strongest change.

3. (a) Many possible factors could be given. Increases in oil prices have been one major factor. Increased government red tape, poor weather, emigration, and war are other factors.
    (b) As the short-run *AS* curve shifts left, the economy will experience a rising price level and decreasing output.
    (c) Stagflation. Refer to p. 247 [559].
    (d) The traditional response has been to increase demand (through increased government spending, reductions in taxes, or an expansionary monetary policy). A more recent approach, which is discussed in Chapter 18 (33), has been to expand supply (by reducing tax rates to encourage greater work effort).
    (e) The price level will certainly increase, whereas output level might fall, rise, or remain unchanged, depending on the relative strengths of the shifts.

4. (a) Refer to the following diagrams.

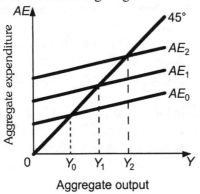 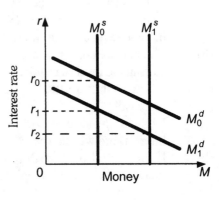

    (b) Refer to the preceding diagrams. Money demand will shift to the left (M^d_1). The interest rate will fall to r_1. The interest rate decrease will boost planned investment, and *AE* will increase to AE_1. Note that this feedback process between the goods and money markets could continue for a while—the money demand curve (M^d_1), for instance, is based on an equilibrium income level that changes as planned investment changes.
    (c) Refer to the following diagram. The *AD* curve is AD_1. At P_0, income level was Y_0. At the new, lower, price level P_1, the level of demand that provides equilibrium in goods and money markets simultaneously is Y_1.

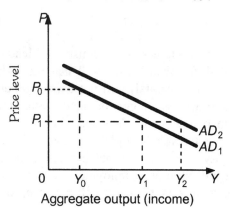

(d)   A fall in price level means that less money will be demanded to purchase planned expenditures. The interest rate will fall from r_0 to r_1. At a lower interest rate more investment will occur, increasing AE from AE_0 to AE_1. The real level of output rises in response to a fall in price level.

(e)   Refer to the preceding diagrams. Money supply moves from M^s_0 to M^s_1. The interest rate falls to r_2. Investment and AE will increase, say to AE_2. At the given price level, P_1, the aggregate demand curve will shift to the right, from AD_1 to AD_2. (There will be further adjustments as money demand increases—in the interests of brevity, these have been ignored.)

5.   In each of the following cases, the strengths of the effects will depend on the point at which the short-run AS curve intersects the AD curve.

(a)   (i)   D   (ii)   U   (iii)   D   (iv) · D
       (v)   D   (vi)   D   (vii)   D
       Explanation: An increase in taxes is a contractionary fiscal policy that will reduce the after-tax income of households. AD will shift to the left. Output and the price level will decrease—both changes will reduce money demand. As money demand decreases, the interest rate will decrease. The Fed's accommodative policy will be to reduce the money supply so that the interest rate will be unchanged. Note that this is an additional contractionary policy. As output decreases, the demand for labor by firms will decrease and there will be cyclical unemployment. Government spending has not changed, but taxes have risen, so the deficit will decrease. Note that if we have tax rates and transfer payments in our economy, rising unemployment will reduce net taxes somewhat.

(b)   (i)   I   (ii)   I   (iii)   I   (iv)   I
       (v)   I   (vi)   I   (vii)   U
       Explanation: An increase in government spending is an expansionary fiscal policy that will make AD shift to the right. Output and the price level will increase—both changes will increase money demand. As money demand increases, the interest rate will increase. The Fed is not accommodative, so the money supply will be unchanged. As output increases, the demand for labor by firms will increase and there will be more employment. Government spending has increased, but taxes have not changed, so the deficit will increase. Note that if we have tax rates in our economy, an expanding economy will increase net taxes somewhat.

(c)   (i)   I   (ii)   I   (iii)   I   (iv)   I

(v)   D   (vi)   I   (vii)   I

Explanation: An increase in optimism will lead to greater planned investment and the *AE* curve will shift upward. This will make *AD* shift to the right. Short-run *AS* (which is based on existing capital) will not shift. Output and the price level will increase—both changes will increase money demand. Initially, as money demand increases, the interest rate will increase. The Fed's accommodative policy will be to increase the money supply so that the interest rate will be unchanged ultimately. Note that this is an additional expansionary policy. As output increases, the demand for labor by firms will increase and there will be more employment. Government spending has not changed, but given automatic stabilizers, net taxes will increase, so the deficit will decrease.

6.   Note: Some of these "shocks" may affect both *AD* and *AS* curves. The following answers are for the single strongest change.

(a)   The decrease in foreign consumption will shift the *AD* curve to the left. In a recession, the fall in price level will be small; the main contraction will be in output.

(b)   The new pollution standards will increase production costs and the *AS* curve will shift to the left, raising price and reducing output. Stagflation results.

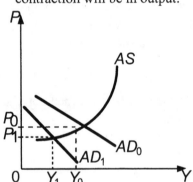

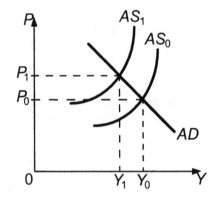

(c)   The increase in government purchases will shift *AD* to the right and raise the interest rate. The Fed will have to increase the money supply, which will increase *AD* even more. In a recession, the price level increase will be small; the main expansion will be in output.

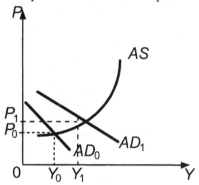

(d)   A tariff makes foreign consumer goods more expensive—demand for domestic goods will rise, moving *AD* rightward and raising the interest rate. The Fed will expand the money supply, which will increase *AD* even more. The main effect will be to raise the price level.

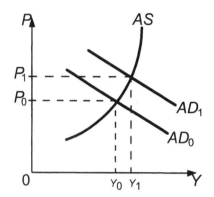

(e)   Low consumer confidence will cause reduced consumption and a decreasing *AD* curve. If firms expect greater inflation, *AS* will shift left. Both effects reduce output; the effect on the price level is ambiguous. Basically, a bad situation has become worse.

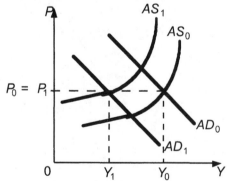

(f)   If foreign oil (which is an input) rises in price, *AS* will shift to the left. To maintain the output level, the Fed would have to expand the money supply and shift the *AD* curve to the right. Both effects are inflationary.

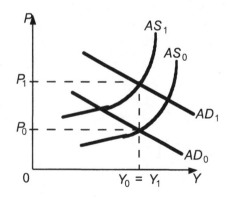

14 [29]

The Labor Market in the Macroeconomy

Chapter objectives:

1. Interpret a diagram representing the classical view of the labor market and explain the beliefs of the classical economists.
2. Distinguish among the theories explaining wage stickiness. Relate wage stickiness to persistent unemployment.
3. Outline the efficiency wage theory, the role of imperfect information in the wage adjustment process, and the possible effects of a minimum wage law.
4. Use the *AS/AD* model to explain the Phillips Curve and the short-run trade-off between the unemployment rate and the inflation rate as it appeared in the 1950s and 1960s and to explain why the relationship collapsed after that.
5. Explain why a vertical *AS* curve implies a vertical (long-run) Phillips Curve. Link the vertical Phillips Curve to the concept of the natural rate of unemployment and comment on the effectiveness of fiscal and monetary policy.
6. Explain what is implied by the non-accelerating inflation rate of unemployment (NAIRU).

The textbook has addressed the issue of unemployment before. This chapter, however, isn't simply a rerun of previous material. Make a list of the theories relevant to unemployment. In most cases, this is new material. Note that theories need not be mutually exclusive.

BRAIN TEASER: On leaving college you will be swamped with job offers (hopefully). How will you choose among them? Will nominal wage be your sole criterion? If not, what else might be important to you? How "perfect" is your information? Will you necessarily accept the job for which you have the least imperfect information? As an entry-level employee, how long do you think you will want to stay in your first job—i.e., how long will you be prepared to "live with" a poor job selection? And lastly, if you consider leaving, aren't you running the risk of entering a similar job market and making another similarly poor selection?

OBJECTIVE 1:

Interpret a diagram representing the classical view of the labor market and explain the beliefs of the classical economists.

Classical economists argued that wages adjust freely to clear the labor market. During economic upswings, workers accept higher wages and, in downturns, accept lower wages. Unemployment shouldn't persist—the wage rate should adjust until equilibrium (full employment) is restored. Price level changes would cause rapid changes in wages, implying a vertical aggregate supply curve. The classical economists saw little role for active fiscal or monetary policy. Persistent (involuntary) unemployment is not possible in such a model; events during the Depression showed that the model was implausible. (page 260 [572])

> ▶▶ LEARNING TIP: The critical assumption of the classical economists is that wages are *perfectly flexible*. Keynesians, however, believe wages are "sticky," especially downward.
>
> ▶▶ LEARNING TIP: The classical economists believe that the aggregate supply curve was vertical, even in the short run. It follows from this that any demand-side (fiscal or monetary) policy changes would be ineffectual in altering output or employment. Increasing aggregate demand would merely cause the price level to increase.
>
> ▶▶ LEARNING TIP: The textbook correctly notes that a decrease in the demand for labor will not necessarily cause an increase in unemployment. This surprising conclusion is due to how we define unemployment. To be unemployed, as we saw in Chapter 7 (22), the individual must have no job and must be actively seeking a job. As the wage decreases, the quantity of labor supplied decreases—workers stop offering their labor services and, therefore, are no longer included in the labor force. ◀

───────────────────────── **Practice** ─────────────────────────

1. _____ unemployment is the type that increases during recessions.
   - (a) Frictional.
   - (b) Structural.
   - (c) Cyclical.
   - (d) Natural.

   ANSWER: (c) Cyclical unemployment varies with the business cycle. Refer to p. 260 [572].

Use the following diagram of the classical labor market to answer the next three questions.

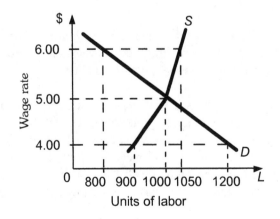

2.   At a wage rate of _____ there is an excess _____ labor of 300.
      (a) $4; demand for
      (b) $4; supply of
      (c) $6; demand for
      (d) $6; supply of

      ANSWER: (a) When the wage rate is low, firms increase quantity demanded and workers
                    reduce quantity supplied. At $4, the excess demand is 300 (1,200 – 900).

3.   If workers increase the value that they place on nonmarket activities, then the labor _____ curve
      will shift to the _____ .
      (a)   demand; right
      (b)   demand; left
      (c)   supply; right
      (d)   supply; left

      ANSWER: (d) Changes in workers' preferences will affect the labor supply curve. In this case,
                    at each wage rate, less labor would be supplied.

4.   In the preceding diagram, the equilibrium wage is _____ . If workers increase the value that they
      place on nonmarket activities, then the equilibrium wage will _____ .
      (a) $4; increase
      (b) $5; increase
      (c) $5; decrease
      (d) $6; decrease

      ANSWER: (b) Equilibrium occurs at the wage rate where quantity demanded equals quantity
                    supplied. The change in preferences will shift the supply curve to the left.

5.   If the price level in the economy decreases, the labor _____ curve will _____ .
      (a)   demand; increase
      (b)   demand; decrease
      (c)   supply; increase
      (d)   supply; decrease

      ANSWER: (b) Because the output of workers is worth less, firms will demand fewer workers at
                    each wage rate.

6.   The government introduces a "guaranteed living standard" program, a plan whereby all citizens,
      whether they work or not, receive a check equal to twice the poverty line. We would predict that
      the
      (a)   labor demand curve will shift right and the wage will increase.
      (b)   labor demand curve will shift left and the wage will decrease.
      (c)   labor supply curve will shift right and the wage will decrease.
      (d)   labor supply curve will shift left and the wage will increase.

      ANSWER: (d) The opportunity cost of leisure has decreased—fewer citizens will seek jobs. ∎

OBJECTIVE 2:
Distinguish among the theories explaining wage stickiness. Relate wage stickiness to persistent unemployment.

▶▶▶   LEARNING TIP: To help yourself organize the material in this and the next objective, note that there are four broad explanations of unemployment:
(a)   Sticky wage theories
(b)   Efficiency wage theories
(c)   Imperfect information
(d)   Minimum wage laws◀

Several theories suggest that wages may be "sticky."

(a)   The *social, or implicit, contract* explanation suggests that workers and employers share an unspoken "understanding" that cutting wages is not one of the rules of the game. (page 263 [575])

(b)   The *relative-wage* theory says that any group of workers will resist wage cuts unless convinced that similar groups are also experiencing them. (page 263 [575])

(c)   *Explicit contracts* attempt to insulate both workers and employers from short-term changes in the economy. Workers may prefer layoffs to wage cuts. Also, layoffs are clear "evidence" that the firm has too much labor. Cuts in wages and prices are far more difficult to monitor. (page 265 [577])

▶▶▶   LEARNING TIP: One fairly obvious reason why workers and employers enter into contracts is so that they can avoid the costs of renegotiation. After all, would you like to haggle over your wage every morning before work?◀

──────────────■────────────── **Practice** ──────────────

7.   The _____ explanation is not included among the "sticky wage" theories of unemployment.
(a)   social contract
(b)   efficiency wage
(c)   relative-wage
(d)   explicit contract
ANSWER: (b) Refer to p. 265 [577] for more on efficiency wage theory.

8.   During a recession, workers in the construction industry are laid off because of an unspoken agreement between employers and workers. This is consistent with the _____ explanation of unemployment.
(a)   social contract
(b)   efficiency wage
(c)   relative-wage
(d)   explicit contract
ANSWER: (a) Refer to p. 263 [575] for more on social contracts.

9.   During a recession, workers in the construction industry in the Northeast are laid off because they are unwilling to accept a wage cut unless they know that similar workers elsewhere are also experiencing such cuts. This is consistent with the _____ explanation of unemployment.
   (a)   social contract
   (b)   efficiency wage
   (c)   relative-wage
   (d)   explicit contract
   ANSWER: (c) Refer to p. 263 [575] for a discussion of the relative-wage explanation of unemployment. ∎

OBJECTIVE 3:
Outline the efficiency wage theory, the role of imperfect information in the wage adjustment process, and the possible effects of a minimum wage law.

The following theories suggest that an above-equilibrium wage may be set. Persistent unemployment is a consequence.

The *efficiency wage theory* argues that worker productivity rises as the wage rate rises. Employers may choose to set the wage rate above the equilibrium wage because higher wages encourage higher productivity. Productivity might increase because of lower labor turnover, improved morale, less shirking, and the retention of an experienced pool of workers. Also, hiring and retraining costs can be reduced. Accordingly, firms have incentives to offer wages higher than the equilibrium wage—generating unemployment. (page 265 [577])

Finally, firms may not have enough information to know what the market-clearing wage is and may choose the wrong wage level. *Imperfect information* about future price behavior can cause wages to be set too high (or too low). Because of the complexity of the wage-setting process and because the economy is continually buffeted by new shocks, it is difficult to correct past mistakes and reach the market-clearing wage. Unemployment may persist if the wage rate is set too high. (page 265 [577])

Minimum wage legislation may cause unemployment for inexperienced or less productive workers whom it isn't profitable to hire at the minimum wage. Simply put, such workers cost too much, produce too little, and won't be hired. (page 266 [578])

▶▶▶   LEARNING TIP: With the profusion of theories, it's easy to miss the point of this section. Economists are trying to explain why unemployment persists in the real world; there may be several contributing factors. ◀

ECONOMICS IN PRACTICE: On page 264 [576], the textbook reports growing fears in 2008 of an economic slowdown and links these to an increase in applications to graduate school by college graduates. First, what are the economic forces underlying the actions of these graduates?
ANSWER: Consider the benefits and costs. There is a benefit to be derived from graduate school. Students are seeking to increase their qualifications in an increasingly competitive labor market. Also, with job prospects stalling, the opportunity to be hired is reduced. Faced with unemployment or a "make-do" job, the opportunity costs of going to grad school are reduced. Note that the report focuses on graduating students who are poised to enter the labor market, i.e., they're unlikely to be already in a career position. As the report notes, after two years in graduate school, the feared recession may be drawing to an end and employers may be hiring again.
ECONOMICS IN PRACTICE (CONTINUED): Is the same phenomenon true at the community college level? Would we expect increasing enrollment when it is feared that job opportunities will decline? Can you apply the preceding analysis in this case? And does it make a difference whether students are enrolling in "credit" or "non-credit" courses?

ANSWER: When we consider non-credit classes, evidence shows that there is a strong *negative* relationship between the unemployment rate and enrollment at community colleges. Non-credit classes often feature personal enrichment without job-related qualifications. Students will apply for such classes during prosperous times and enrollment will decline when times are tough. There is a positive relationship when only credit courses are considered. Credit classes (leading to a degree) will be attractive when the job market is bleak. Also, for those high school graduates considering a four-year degree the cheaper option offered by a community college for the first two years of study may be appealing. These facts fit our theory. Although the payoffs may be different, the economic rationale is the same as for prospective graduate students.

─── **Practice** ───

10.   Marley and Scrooge find that the costs of screening, hiring, and training workers is substantial. To reduce labor turnover, they pay higher-than-average wages. Their behavior is consistent with the _____ explanation of unemployment.
    (a)   minimum wage
    (b)   efficiency wage
    (c)   imperfect information
    (d)   cost effectiveness

    ANSWER: (b) Refer to p. 265 [577] for more on efficiency wage theory.

11.   If, due to imperfect information, firms set the wage above the market-clearing level,
    (a)   wages will decrease rapidly, as unemployed workers seek jobs.
    (b)   wages will not fall, as many workers will be available at that wage.
    (c)   the government will set a minimum wage to prevent unemployment.
    (d)   wages may adjust slowly because of the complexity of the labor market.

    ANSWER: (d) The more complex the labor market and the more changeable the economy, the more difficult it is to determine the "correct" wage rate.

12.   Refer to the diagram used in Question 2 above. If the government imposed a minimum wage of $4,
    (a)   unemployment would be zero
    (b)   unemployment would be 100 (1,000 – 900)
    (c)   unemployment would be 250 (1,050 – 800)
    (d)   unemployment would be 300 (1,200 – 900)

    ANSWER: (a) The equilibrium wage is $5. Setting a minimum wage that is less than $5 will have no impact on the labor market. ∎

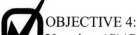

OBJECTIVE 4:
Use the *AS/AD* model to explain the Phillips Curve and the short-run trade-off between the unemployment rate and the inflation rate as it appeared in the 1950s and 1960s and to explain why the relationship collapsed after that.

The *AS/AD* diagram shows that an increase in aggregate demand leads to higher output (and higher employment). The unemployment rate would fall and inflation would occur: This apparent trade-off between unemployment rate and inflation rate is depicted by the *Phillips Curve*. In the 1960s, this negative relationship seemed so stable that many believed that unemployment and inflation were affected by the same single factor—the level of demand. The analysis rested on the fact that the *AS* curve had been fairly stable. In the 1970s and 1980s, supply-side factors (particularly the price of imported oil and inflationary expectations) became more volatile and the stable inflation-unemployment relationship collapsed. Higher prices for imported inputs shifted the *AS* curve to the left; similarly, as the inflationary expectations of workers and producers increased, wages and prices were increased in response, pushing the *AS* curve to the left and disrupting the Phillips Curve relationship. (page 266 [578])

Comment: It's tempting to dismiss the Phillips Curve as irrelevant but, following that logic, one would have to dismiss the demand curve because things other than the price level can change. The Phillips Curve suggests, *ceteris paribus*, that with rising aggregate demand, as the economy approaches full employment, the costs of increasing production increase. Employers will try to pass these cost increases on by raising prices, moving up along the aggregate supply curve. When unemployment is high, the argument is reversed.

Comment: As noted in the text, import prices didn't change much during the 1960s and early 1970s. There is a second point, though, that's worth keeping in mind. The foreign sector of the economy (exports and imports) has become much more significant and a greater source of potential instability. Imports accounted for only about 6% of GDP in 1960; by 2008, the number was almost triple that.

A short-run trade-off between inflation and unemployment does exist but, if factors other than shifts in aggregate demand are involved, they can obscure the relationship. (page 271 [583])

——————————————————————— **Practice** ———————————————————————

13. Which factors led to the breakdown of the Phillips Curve in the 1970s?
    (a) Supply-side policymakers reduced business taxes, which made the aggregate supply curve shift to the left.
    (b) Adverse "supply shocks" such as the oil price increase of 1973–1974 made the aggregate supply curve shift to the left.
    (c) Government spending resulted in large deficits and high inflation.
    (d) The aggregate demand curve shifted to the left following the end of hostilities in Vietnam.

    ANSWER: (b) As the *AS* curve shifted to the left, stagflation (rising inflation and rising unemployment) occurred. Reduced business taxes (Option (a)) would make the aggregate supply curve shift to the right.

14.   If the *AS* curve is stable, there will be a _____ relationship between the inflation rate and the unemployment rate when the *AD* curve shifts to the right and a _____ relationship when the *AD* curve shifts to the left.
(a)   positive; positive
(b)   positive; negative
(c)   negative; positive
(d)   negative; negative

ANSWER: (d) Higher (lower) demand increases (decreases) the inflation rate and decreases (increases) the unemployment rate.

15.   Evidence from 1970 to 2007 suggests that there is _____ relationship between inflation and unemployment.
(a)   no particular
(b)   a weak negative
(c)   a strong negative
(d)   a weak positive

ANSWER: (a) Figure 14.7 (29.7) reveals no detectable relationship between the unemployment rate and the inflation rate.

16.   In the 1970s, increasing inflation became a fact of life. This expectation shifted the *AS* curve to the _____ and shifted the Phillips Curve to the _____ .
(a)   right; right
(b)   right; left
(c)   left; right
(d)   left; left

ANSWER: (c) As we saw in the previous chapter, the short-run *AS* curve will shift to the left as firms expect increased inflation. The Phillips Curve will shift right. Refer to p. 269 [581].

17.   The Fed increases the money supply. Assuming no changes in expectations, this policy would result in a(n) _____ in the unemployment rate and a(n) _____ in the inflation rate.
(a)   increase; increase
(b)   increase; decrease
(c)   decrease; increase
(d)   decrease; decrease

ANSWER: (c) The policy will shift the *AD* curve to the right, increasing output and employment that, in turn, decreases the unemployment rate and increases inflation. ■

OBJECTIVE 5:
Explain why a vertical *AS* curve implies a vertical (long-run) Phillips Curve. Link the vertical Phillips Curve to the concept of the natural rate of unemployment and comment on the effectiveness of fiscal and monetary policy.

If the long-run *AS* curve is vertical, then the long-run Phillips Curve is also vertical. Fiscal or monetary policy will have no long-run impact on output or the unemployment rate. Expansionary fiscal and monetary policies will have no long-run effect except to fuel inflation—in the long run, unemployment will gravitate to the *natural rate of unemployment* (the sum of frictional and structural unemployment) and output will remain at potential GDP level. There is no trade-off between the inflation rate and the unemployment rate in the long run. (page 271 [583])

▶▶▶   LEARNING TIP: Given a deviation from long-run equilibrium, and in the absence of some corrective policy, it is *always* a movement in the short-run aggregate supply curve that pulls the economy back to that equilibrium. Similarly, policy actions intended to shift output to higher or lower levels are doomed to long-run failure because of adjustments by the short-run *AS* curve. The short-run *AS* curve will continue to shift until input prices have "caught up" with output prices.

   In the left panel of the following diagram, aggregate demand has decreased from AD_0 to AD_1. The aggregate price level has fallen to P_1 and aggregate output has fallen to Y_1. [Give reasons for such a shift.] To restore long-run equilibrium at Y_0, the short-run aggregate supply curve will move to AS_1. The price level falls to P_2. For practice, detail the forces that cause the short-run aggregate supply curve to shift to the right.

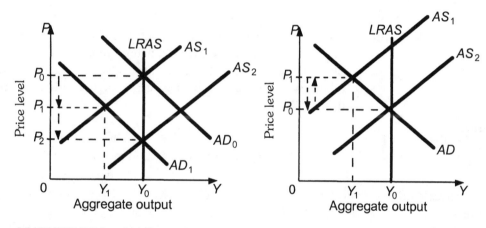

▶▶▶   LEARNING TIP (continued)

   In the right panel of the diagram, the short-run aggregate supply curve has decreased from AS_0 to AS_1. [Give reasons for such a shift.] The aggregate price level has risen to P_1 and aggregate output has fallen to Y_1. Although it's tempting to assume that aggregate demand will shift to restore long-run equilibrium, it doesn't. The short-run aggregate supply curve will shift back to its original position. ◀

——————————————————————————— **Practice** ———————————————————————————

18.   The natural rate of unemployment is the sum of
   (a)   frictional and cyclical unemployment.
   (b)   frictional and structural unemployment.
   (c)   cyclical and structural unemployment.
   (d)   frictional, cyclical, and structural unemployment.

   ANSWER: (b)   Refer to p. 272 [584] for the definition.

19.   If the Phillips Curve is vertical in the long run, then an increase in the money supply from year to year will _____ the unemployment rate and will _____ the inflation rate.
       (a)   increase; increase
       (b)   increase; not change
       (c)   not change; increase
       (d)   not change; not change

       ANSWER: (c) Fiscal or, in this case, monetary policies will not affect the natural rate of employment or the unemployment rate in the long run. However, as we saw in the previous chapter, persistent increases in the money supply fuel inflation.

20.   Currently, the unemployment rate is greater than the natural rate of unemployment. In the long run, the natural rate will be attained if policymakers
       (a)   increase the money supply.
       (b)   decrease the money supply.
       (c)   do nothing.
       (d)   do all of the above.

       ANSWER: (d) This is a trick(y) question! In the long run it doesn't make any difference what policymakers do (or don't do). The natural rate of unemployment will prevail in the long run in any and all circumstances. Note that an argument could be made that doing nothing is preferable because it might shorten the economy's period of adjustment. ■

OBJECTIVE 6:
Explain what is implied by the non-accelerating inflation rate of unemployment (NAIRU).

The nonaccelerating inflation rate of unemployment (NAIRU) is the unemployment rate at which there is no pressure for the inflation rate to change. This does not mean that the inflation rate is zero, however, simply that the rate is not changing. If unemployment is less (greater) than the NAIRU, there will be pressure for inflation to increase (slow). The NAIRU will decrease in the presence of favorable supply shocks. Good weather in an agricultural economy, for instance, may result in reduced unemployment with no increased inflationary tendency. (page 272 [584])

▶▶▶   LEARNING TIP: Revisit Chapter 13 (28) and the factors that shift the *AS* curve. Factors that shift the curve to the right (beneficial supply shocks) will shift the PP curve to the left and reduce the NAIRU. ◀

BRAIN TEASER SOLUTION: Presumably, your job choice will be based on the entire job package offered, including wages, benefits, location, promotion prospects, etc. Will you jump at the first offer? Your information may well be quite restricted—you may not know the benefits in comparable jobs, for instance. If you make a poor first-time job selection, you have to balance the desire to leave against the need to establish a stable work record.

       Comment: In this chapter and the previous one you've been given a number of theories concerning the causes of unemployment and inflation. Notice that the list of causes isn't the same for both. Unemployment and inflation aren't opposite sides of the same problem (as the Phillips Curve might suggest), but rather, different problems. If you need proof, think about stagflation, where both problems occur simultaneously. This new view, that the two problems need to be addressed separately, is an important development in the thinking of economists and policymakers.

PRACTICE TEST

I.   MULTIPLE-CHOICE QUESTIONS

Select the option that provides the single best answer.

_____ 1.   In the classical model, it is always true that there will be full employment
            (no involuntary unemployment) because
            (a)   workers will bid wages downward if necessary.
            (b)   wages are sticky.
            (c)   employers set wages.
            (d)   unions and employers have equal bargaining strength.

_____ 2.   The existence of sticky wages suggests that
            (a)   workers hold most of the bargaining power in wage negotiations.
            (b)   wages will be constant over the business cycle.
            (c)   some unemployment is caused by workers' and firms' unwillingness to negotiate
                   wage cuts.
            (d)   nominal wages are eroded during a period of inflation.

_____ 3.   If firms expect higher prices next quarter, the labor _____ curve will shift to the _____ .
            (a)   supply; right
            (b)   supply; left
            (c)   demand; right
            (d)   demand; left

_____ 4.   Which of the following reasons is given as an explanation why labor markets do not
            always clear?
            (a)   Workers have better price information than employers.
            (b)   The total demand for labor has fallen.
            (c)   Workers are reluctant to accept a lower wage relative to other similar groups of
                   workers.
            (d)   The supply of labor has fallen.

_____ 5.   The relative-wage explanation of sticky wages fails to recognize that
            (a)   the cost of information is virtually zero.
            (b)   firms are not willing to cut wages even when there is a recession.
            (c)   search costs are virtually zero.
            (d)   workers don't have perfect information about wages in similar industries.

_____ 6.   Which of the following will lead to an increase in inflation?
            (a)   A price hike by foreign oil producers.
            (b)   An open market sale of securities by the Fed.
            (c)   A cut in government spending.
            (d)   An increase in the demand for money.

Use the following diagram, showing the demand for and supply of teenage labor, to answer the following question.

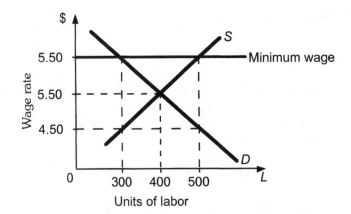

_____ 7.   The government has imposed a minimum wage of $5.50 per hour. Unemployment will be
(a)   500.
(b)   300.
(c)   200.
(d)   400.

_____ 8.   Which of the following is most likely to cause stagflation?
(a)   Falling prices on imported oil
(b)   An increase in the money supply
(c)   A decrease in the money supply
(d)   Rising prices on imported oil

_____ 9.   The Phillips Curve has broken down since the early 1970s for all of the following reasons EXCEPT that
(a)   inflationary expectations became variable.
(b)   rising import prices became a significant feature of the economy.
(c)   aggregate demand was more variable than before.
(d)   the _ceteris paribus_ assumptions, under which the analysis was made, were infringed.

_____ 10.   The Phillips Curve in the 1960s showed that
(a)   the inflation rate and the price level were positively related.
(b)   increases in wages and unemployment were positively related.
(c)   the unemployment rate and the inflation rate were negatively related.
(d)   the money supply and the interest rate were negatively related.

_____ 11.   When the economy is at the natural rate of unemployment there is
(a)   no structural unemployment.
(b)   no frictional unemployment.
(c)   some cyclical unemployment.
(d)   some frictional and structural unemployment.

_____ 12.   The classical economists' model of the labor market is consistent with a
     (a)   horizontal aggregate demand curve.
     (b)   horizontal aggregate supply curve.
     (c)   vertical aggregate demand curve.
     (d)   vertical aggregate supply curve.

_____ 13.   Many economists today believe that the Phillips Curve is _____ in the short run and _____ in the long run.
     (a)   downward sloping; vertical
     (b)   vertical; downward sloping
     (c)   upward sloping; vertical
     (d)   vertical; upward sloping

_____ 14.   If the *AD* curve is stable, there will be a _____ relationship between the inflation rate and the unemployment rate when the *AS* curve shifts to the right, and a _____ relationship when the *AS* curve shifts to the left.
     (a)   positive; positive.
     (b)   positive; negative
     (c)   negative; positive
     (d)   negative; negative

_____ 15.   The large shifts to the left of the *AS* curve in the 1970s were caused mainly by
     (a)   increasing government deficits.
     (b)   substantial increases in the money supply.
     (c)   increases in the price of imported raw materials.
     (d)   aggressive labor union activity during 1973–1977.

Use the following diagram to answer the next five questions. The economy is initially at point *E*. Point *E* represents the rate of unemployment that is the natural rate.

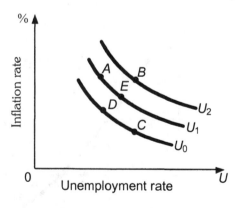

_____ 16.   An increase in government spending would move the economy to Point
     (a)   *A*.
     (b)   *B*.
     (c)   *C*.
     (d)   *D*.

_____ 17.   A move from Point *E* to Point *D* is most likely to be caused by
     (a)   a decrease in the inflationary expectations of firms.
     (b)   a decrease in the money supply.
     (c)   an increase in the price of imported oil.
     (d)   an adverse supply shock, such as bad harvests.

_____ 18.   An increase in the price of imported raw materials would move the economy to Point
     (a)   *A*.
     (b)   *B*.
     (c)   *C*.
     (d)   *D*.

_____ 19.   If point *E* represents the rate of unemployment that is the natural rate, then at Point *A*, actual output _____ potential output, and structural and frictional unemployment rates are _____ .
     (a)   exceeds; positive
     (b)   exceeds; negative
     (c)   is less than; positive
     (d)   is less than; negative

_____ 20.   In the long run, the Phillips Curve will pass through
     (a)   Points *A*, *E*, and *C*.
     (b)   Points *D*, *E*, and *B*.
     (c)   Point *E* only.
     (d)   none of these points because the long-run Phillips Curve is vertical.

II.   APPLICATION QUESTIONS

1.   The small nation of Arboc is at Point *A* on its Phillips Curve. Inflation is expected to be 0%. The natural rate of unemployment is 6.0%.

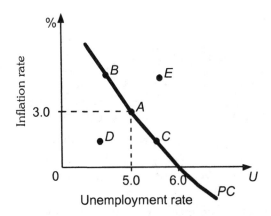

     (a)   If the natural rate of unemployment is 6% and the expected inflation rate is 0%, what sort of macroeconomic action could have moved the economy to Point *A*?

What will happen to the price level and output in each of the following cases? In each case, will the factor in question affect the inflation rate and unemployment rate as a simple Phillips Curve would predict? Using Point *A* as a reference, how would the economy move in the short run?

(b)   A severe hurricane destroys the sugar cane crop, the main agricultural crop in this predominantly rural economy.

(c)   The Arbocali government passes a new environmental protection law that requires producers to decrease emission of atmospheric pollutants.

(d)   In anticipation of a war with neighboring states, the Arbocali government increases its military spending by 50%.

(e)   Legislation is passed making it more difficult to unionize and making union activity such as picketing illegal.

(f)   Consumer confidence in the economy is undermined because of a change in government.

Now suppose that none of the changes above took place. The economy will not remain at point A in the long run.

(g)   Explain why the economy will not remain at Point A.

(h)   Suppose actual inflation remains 3%. Explain how the economy will adjust in the long run.

(i)   Sketch in the long-run Phillips Curve.

2.   Macrovia has a population of 160,000 citizens aged 16 or older. Because of a highly sophisticated computerized job placement program, frictional and structural unemployment runs at a constant 10,000. The nation's labor demand and supply curve are $Q_D = 120 - W$ and $Q_S = 5W$, respectively. Q is the quantity of labor supplied or demanded in thousands of workers, W is the wage in sponduliks, the local currency.

(a)   Calculate the equilibrium wage, the level of employment, and the unemployment rate in Macrovia.

(b)   Calculate the size of the labor force and the participation rate.

(c)   The Secretary of Labor is under pressure to introduce a minimum wage. If the minimum wage is set at 22 sponduliks (a 10% increase), calculate the effect on employment, unemployment, the labor force, the unemployment rate and the participation rate.

3.   Use the following table to answer this question. Columns (1) and (2) give information about the short-run aggregate supply curve for Arboc. Column (3) shows total employment at different output levels. There are 200,000 workers in the total labor force. Normally 10,000 workers are structurally and frictionally unemployed.

(1) Overall Price Level	(2) Aggregate Output	(3) Total Employment	(4) Output Demanded	(5) Output Demanded	(6) Output Demanded	(7) Output Demanded
4.60 opeks	2,550	191,000	100	800	1,400	2,200
4.50 opeks	2,500	190,000	400	1,100	1,700	2,500
4.40 opeks	2,400	189,000	700	1,400	2,000	2,800
4.30 opeks	2,300	188,000	1,000	1,700	2,300	3,100
4.20 opeks	2,000	184,000	1,300	2,000	2,600	3,400
4.10 opeks	1,600	178,000	1,600	2,300	2,900	3,700
4.00 opeks	1,000	168,000	1,900	2,600	3,200	4,000

(a)   Based on the behavior of the aggregate supply curve, potential GDP is _____ and the natural rate of unemployment is _____ %.

(b)   Draw the short-run aggregate supply (*SRAS*) curve below.

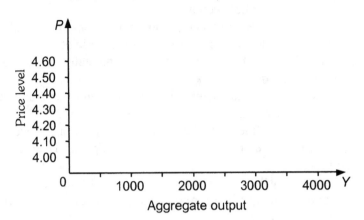

(c)   Currently, aggregate demand is shown by columns (1) and (4). Graph this *AD* curve (*AD*₁). Equilibrium overall price level is _____ and equilibrium output is _____ . The unemployment rate is _____ %.

(d)   The central bank, Arbobank, undertakes an expansionary monetary policy, an open market _____ (purchase/sales) of securities. Aggregate demand curve will shift to the _____ (right/left). The new curve is described by columns (1) and (5). Graph this *AD* curve (*AD*₂). Equilibrium overall price level is _____ and equilibrium output is _____ . Employment has increased by _____ . The unemployment rate is _____ %. Cyclical unemployment is _____ %. The inflation rate is _____ %.

(e)   If the central bank had undertaken a more expansionary monetary policy, *AD* would have shifted further, as described by columns (1) and (6). Graph this *AD* curve (*AD*₃). Equilibrium overall price level is _____ and equilibrium output is _____ . Employment has increased by _____ . The unemployment rate is _____ %. Relative to the original price level, the inflation rate is _____ %.

(f)   If the central bank had undertaken a still more expansionary monetary policy, *AD* would have shifted further, as described by columns (1) and (7). Graph this *AD* curve (*AD*₄). Equilibrium overall price level is _____ and equilibrium output is _____ . Employment has increased by _____ . The unemployment rate is _____ %. Relative to the original price level, the inflation rate is _____ %.

4.   For each "event" affecting equilibrium inflation rate and unemployment rate, indicate the specific short-run "result" that will occur.

Result A: inflation increases, unemployment increases.
Result B: inflation decreases, unemployment decreases.
Result C: inflation decreases, unemployment increases.
Result D: inflation increases, unemployment decreases.

	Result	Event
(a)	____	The government raises personal income taxes.
(b)	____	The price of imported final goods falls.
(c)	____	The interest rate rises.
(d)	____	The price of imported intermediate goods rises.
(e)	____	New, stringent standards for the construction of residential dwellings are enacted.
(f)	____	Environmental pollution standards are tightened substantially.
(g)	____	A reduction in foreign consumption of U.S. products occurs.
(h)	____	Employer contributions to the social security program are decreased.
(i)	____	The imposition of an import tax (tariff) on foreign consumer goods.
(j)	____	An increase in government purchases occurs.
(k)	____	There is an increase in the price of foreign oil.
(l)	____	Households prefer to save more.
(m)	____	An increased demand for new machinery or construction.
(n)	____	Inflationary expectations increase.

5. For each pair of events, work out what will happen to aggregate demand and/or aggregate supply, and then predict the impact on the inflation rate and unemployment rate. Assume that each given change (there are two changes in each case) will affect *only* aggregate demand *or* aggregate supply, but not both curves.

Note: As you saw in Chapter 3, if both demand and supply curves shift, the effect on at least one variable must be uncertain.

Result A: inflation change uncertain, unemployment increases.
Result B: inflation change uncertain, unemployment decreases.
Result C: inflation decreases, unemployment change uncertain.
Result D: inflation increases, unemployment change uncertain.

	Result	Events
(a)	____	The government raises business taxes and the Fed conducts open market purchases of securities.
(b)	____	Inflationary expectations of firms are reduced and government spending is increased.
(c)	____	The Fed raises the discount rate and foreign oil becomes much more expensive.
(d)	____	The government imposes a new sales tax on consumer goods and decreases payroll taxes for employers.
(e)	____	The government trims back on defense spending and gives more generous depreciation allowances for industrial firms.

PRACTICE TEST SOLUTIONS

I.   Solutions to Multiple-Choice Questions

1. (a)   If there is an excess supply of workers—i.e., unemployment—workers will accept lower wages. Refer to p. 260 [572].

2. (c)   Refer to p. 262 [574] for a discussion of sticky wages.

3.   (c)   Employers will demand more labor if it is thought that the value of workers' output will increase.

4.   (c)   This is the relative-wage explanation of unemployment. Refer to p. 263 [575]. With respect to Option (a), it is believed that employers generally have better information about prices.

5.   (d)   Refer to p. 263 [575]. From the discussion in this section of the chapter it is clear that price and wage information is imperfect.

6.   (a)   The oil price hike will affect production costs and push the *AS* curve to the left, raising the price level. Options (b) and (c) are contractionary policies. In Option (d), the demand for money will increase as a consequence of a price increase.

7.   (c)   At the minimum wage level, quantity supplied is 500 and quantity demanded is only 300.

8.   (d)   The classic examples are the oil price increases of the 1970s.

9.   (c)   If aggregate demand became more (or less) variable, the Phillips Curve would not break down. The relationship developed as a result of aggregate demand changes.

10.   (c)   The Phillips Curve revealed a negative relationship between the inflation rate and the unemployment rate.

11.   (d)   The natural rate includes both structural and frictional unemployment.

12.   (d)   Refer to p. 261 [573]. As prices rise, wages rise to keep pace, and the level of employment is stable.

13.   (a)   There is a trade-off between inflation and unemployment in the short run but, as wages adjust to catch up with rising prices, the natural rate of unemployment will be restored.

14.   (a)   Higher (lower) supply decreases (increases) the inflation rate and decreases (increases) the unemployment rate.

15.   (c)   The major raw material to show price increases was oil. Options (a) and (b) would shift aggregate demand. Option (d) is a fiction.

16.   (a)   The spending increase is an expansionary fiscal policy that will shift the *AD* curve to the right. The unemployment rate will decrease and the inflation rate will increase—a move along the Phillips Curve.

17.   (a)   The move from *E* to *D* represents a decrease in inflation and unemployment. This will occur if the *AS* curve shifts to the right, as will happen when firms expect less inflation.

18.   (b)   The rise in the price of raw materials (imported or otherwise) will shift the *AS* curve to the left.

19.   (a)   Point A represents unemployment that is lower than the natural rate, indicating that production is extremely high. Structural and frictional unemployment, although low, can't be negative!

20.   (c)   The long-run Phillips Curve is vertical, to be sure. However, because the unemployment rate shown at Point E is the natural rate, the long-run Phillips Curve will pass through this point.

II.   *Solutions to Application Questions*

1.   (a)   An increase in aggregate demand would decrease unemployment and increase inflation in the short run.

(b)   Aggregate supply will shift left. Price level will increase and output will decrease. The negative relationship between the inflation rate and the unemployment rate will be absent. There would be a move off the existing Phillips Curve to Point E.

(c)   Aggregate supply will shift left. Price level will increase and output will decrease. The negative relationship between the inflation rate and the unemployment rate will be absent. There would be a move off the existing Phillips Curve to Point E.

(d)   Aggregate demand will increase causing the price level to increase and output to increase. There would be a move along the existing Phillips Curve to Point B.

(e)   Aggregate supply will increase causing the price level to decrease and output to increase. The inflation rate will decrease and the unemployment rate will decrease. There would be a move off the existing Phillips Curve to Point D.

(f)   Aggregate demand will decrease causing the price level to decrease and output to decrease. The inflation rate will decrease and the unemployment rate will increase—a movement along the Phillips Curve to Point C.

(g)   There is a mismatch between the actual inflation rate (3%) and the expected inflation rate (0%). The Phillips Curve is based on a particular level of inflationary expectations. In the long run, the actual inflation rate and the expected inflation rate must be equal. Either expectations must increase, which would shift the Phillips Curve to the right, or the actual inflation rate must decrease.

(h)   If actual inflation remains at 3%, the Phillips Curve will shift to the right (as expectations change). This shift will continue until expectations equal reality. When the expected inflation rate exceeds the actual future inflation rate, real wages will rise, unemployment will increase, and output will decrease. The short-run aggregate supply curve will shift to the left.

(i)   The long-run Phillips Curve is vertical at an unemployment rate of 6%.

2.   (a)   In equilibrium, $Q_D = Q_S$ so 120 − W = 5W. 120 = 6W, therefore W = 20. When W = 20, employment is 100, i.e., 100,000. Frictional and structural unemployment run at a constant 10,000. There is no cyclical unemployment. Unemployment rate = 10/110 = 9.09%.

(b)   Labor force = 100,000 employed + 10,000 unemployed = 110,000.
Participation rate = labor force × 100%/population
= 110,000 × 100%/160,000 = 68.75%.

(c)   If $W = 20$, $Q_D = 120 - 1(22) = 98$ and $Q_S = 5(22) = 110$.
Employment will decrease from 100,000 to 98,000.
Frictional and structural unemployment remain at 10,000, but an additional 12,000 individuals will be seeking work. Total unemployed is 22,000.
The labor force has increased by 10,000 to 120,000.
The unemployment rate, which is unemployed $\times$ 100%/labor force, will be 22,000 $\times$ 100%/120,000, or 18.33%.
Participation rate = labor force $\times$ 100%/population
= 120,000 $\times$ 100%/160,000 = 75%.

3.   (a)   Structural and frictional unemployment run at 10,000. The natural rate of unemployment is 10,000/200,000 or 5%. When 190,000 workers are employed, the output level is 2,500. The maximum output level is 2,500. Note that the maximum value of output for the short-run *AS* curve can be greater than the potential output level.

(b)   Refer to the following diagram.

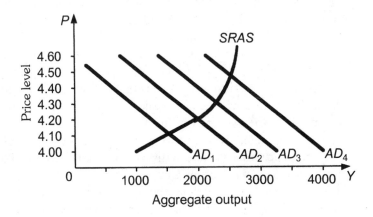

(c)   The equilibrium price level (where $AD = AS$) is 4.10 opeks and equilibrium output is 1,600. The unemployment rate is 11%.

(d)   purchase; right. Price level is 4.20 opeks, and output level is 2,000. Employment has risen by 6,000 workers. 8% of workers remain unemployed. Because structural and frictional unemployment are at 5%, cyclical unemployment must be 3%. The price level has risen from 4.10 opeks to 4.20 opeks, therefore the inflation rate is 2.44%.

(e)   Price level is 4.30 opeks, and output level is 2,300. Employment has risen by 4,000 workers. 6% of workers remain unemployed. The price level has risen from 4.10 opeks to 4.30 opeks, therefore the inflation rate is 4.88%.

(f)   Price level is 4.50 opeks, and output level is 2,500. Employment has risen by 2,000 workers. 5% of workers remain unemployed. The price level has risen from 4.10 opeks to 4.50 opeks, therefore the inflation rate is 9.76%.

4.
(a)	C	(b)	C	(c)	C	(d)	A
(e)	A	(f)	A	(g)	C	(h)	B
(i)	D	(j)	D	(k)	A	(l)	C
(m)	D	(n)	A				

Compare these results with those obtained in Application Questions 2 and 6 in the preceding chapter. *Note:* Some of these "shocks" may affect both aggregate demand and aggregate supply. The above answers are for the single strongest change.

5.   (a)   D. An increase in business taxes will shift the *AS* curve to the left, whereas the open market purchase will increase the money supply and shift the *AD* curve to the right. Both shifts are inflationary, but the effect on output (and on the unemployment rate) is ambiguous.

(b)   B. As firms come to expect less inflation, they will be willing to produce more at any given price level—*AS* will shift to the right. The increase in government spending is expansionary and will shift the *AD* curve to the right. Both shifts will expand output and reduce unemployment, but the effect on the inflation rate is ambiguous.

(c)   A. As oil increases in price, the *AS* curve will shift to the left. The Fed action is contractionary and will shift the *AD* curve to the left. Both shifts will reduce output and increase unemployment, but the effect on the inflation rate is ambiguous.

(d)   C. The sales tax will reduce consumption, and the *AD* curve will shift to the left. The reduction in payroll taxes will reduce the costs of production—*AS* will shift to the right. Both shifts will reduce inflation, but the effect on output (and on the unemployment rate) is ambiguous.

(e)   C. The cutback in defense spending will reduce aggregate demand. The increased depreciation allowances will increase the profitability of firms and encourage more production. In fact, this is a typical "supply-side" policy. Refer to Chapter 18 (33). *AS* will shift to the right. Both shifts will reduce inflation, but the effect on output (and on the unemployment rate) is ambiguous.

Comprehensive Review Test

The following questions provide a wide-ranging review of the material covered in Part III (V)—Chapters 8–14 (23–29) of the textbook. Each question deals with a topic or technique important for your understanding of economic principles. If you miss a question you should return to the relevant section of the chapter in the textbook and fine-tune your understanding.

I.   MULTIPLE-CHOICE QUESTIONS

Select the option that provides the single best answer.

_____   1.   As income increases, consumption will _____ and saving will _____ .
(a)   increase; increase
(b)   increase; decrease
(c)   decrease; increase
(d)   decrease; decrease

_____   2.   Given the income level, as the interest rate increases, consumption will _____ and saving will _____ .
(a)   increase; increase
(b)   increase; decrease
(c)   decrease; increase
(d)   decrease; decrease

_____   3.   Which of the following should reduce consumer spending?
(a)   A decrease in personal income tax rates
(b)   A decrease in disposable personal income
(c)   An expectation that the aggregate price level will increase soon
(d)   An increase in government transfers to individuals

_____   4.   Arbez, an economy with no government or foreign sectors, is in long-run equilibrium. Now consumption decreases autonomously. At the initial output level, all of the following are **false** EXCEPT
(a)   saving is more than planned investment.
(b)   aggregate expenditures are greater than aggregate output.
(c)   inventory levels are falling unexpectedly.
(d)   saving level has remained unchanged.

Use the following information for the next three questions. Marginal propensity to consume is 0.8. The Administration's goal is to increase equilibrium output by 300.

_____ 5.   Equilibrium output could be raised by 300 if the Administration raises government spending by
(a)   300.
(b)   240.
(c)   80.
(d)   60.

_____ 6.   Equilibrium output could be raised by 300 if the Administration cuts taxes by
(a)   300.
(b)   60.
(c)   100.
(d)   75.

_____ 7.   Equilibrium output could be raised by 300 if the Administration raises taxes by 300 and raises government spending by
(a)   300.
(b)   240.
(c)   100.
(d)   75.

_____ 8.   Net exports increase. We would expect to see each of the following EXCEPT
(a)   an increase in spending on domestically produced goods.
(b)   an unplanned decrease in inventories.
(c)   an increase in equilibrium output.
(d)   a larger multiplier.

_____ 9.   An expansionary fiscal policy is intended to expand
(a)   the government deficit.
(b)   government spending.
(c)   output.
(d)   net taxes.

_____ 10.   In Arboc, most workers have labor contracts that lock in the wage rate for a period of three years. In Arbez, however, wages are renegotiated every month. In the short-run, fiscal policy will be more effective in _____ ; monetary policy will be more effective in _____ .
(a)   Arboc; Arboc
(b)   Arboc; Arbez
(c)   Arbez; Arboc
(d)   Arbez; Arbez

_____ 11.   Arboc is an economy with a private sector and a public sector. If private investment increases we could correctly state that
(a)   the aggregate expenditures curve will shift up.
(b)   private saving will increase because investment and saving must be equal.
(c)   private saving will decrease because investment is the opposite of saving.
(d)   the aggregate expenditures curve will shift down.

_____   12.   Which of the following pairs of actions is the most certain to be a tight monetary policy? A(n) _____ in the required reserve ratio and an open market _____ of securities.
(a)   increase; purchase
(b)   increase; sale
(c)   decrease; purchase
(d)   decrease; sale

_____   13.   Which of the following pairs of events will definitely result in a decrease in the equilibrium interest rate? A(n) _____ in the level of aggregate output and a(n) _____ in the discount rate.
(a)   increase; increase
(b)   increase; decrease
(c)   decrease; increase
(d)   decrease; decrease

_____   14.   If the supply of money decreases as a result of a(n) _____ in the required reserve ratio, the size of money balances will _____ .
(a)   increase; increase
(b)   increase; decrease
(c)   decrease; increase
(d)   decrease; decrease

Use the following information for the next two questions. The banking system has deposits of $60 million and is fully loaned up. The required reserve ratio is 25%. Assume no leakages from the banking system occur.

_____   15.   If the required reserve ratio is reduced from 25% to 20%, the banking system could
(a)   increase loans by $3 million.
(b)   increase loans by $12 million.
(c)   increase loans by $15 million.
(d)   increase loans by $20 million.

_____   16.   The Fed wants deposits to increase to $90 million. The Fed would achieve its goal if it changed the reserve ratio from 25% to
(a)   12%.
(b)   15%.
(c)   16.67%.
(d)   67%.

_____   17.   The Fed wishes to increase the money supply. The most likely monetary policy might include the _____ of bonds by the Fed and the _____ of the discount rate.
(a)   purchase; lowering
(b)   purchase; raising
(c)   sale; lowering
(d)   sale; raising

_____ 18.   In the long run, an increase in money supply would make aggregate demand _____ and short-run aggregate supply _____ .
(a)   increase; increase
(b)   increase; decrease
(c)   decrease; increase
(d)   decrease; decrease

_____ 19.   Each of the following will cause the demand for money to increase EXCEPT
(a)   an increase in aggregate output.
(b)   an increase in the average dollar amount of each transaction.
(c)   an increase in the transactions cost of switching between money and bonds.
(d)   an increase in the money supply.

_____ 20.   Maureen's optimal money balance will certainly increase if the costs of switching between bonds and money
(a)   increases and the interest earned on bonds increases.
(b)   decreases and the interest earned on bonds decreases.
(c)   increases and the interest earned on bonds decreases.
(d)   decreases and there is a decrease in the inflation rate.

Use the following table for the next five questions.

Y	T	Y_d	C	S	I	G	AE
2,000	400	_____	2,000	_____	_____	650	_____
3,000	400	_____	2,750	_____	600	_____	4,000
4,000	_____		3,500	_____	_____	_____	_____
5,000	_____	4,600	_____	_____	600	_____	5,500
6,000	_____	_____	_____	_____	_____	_____	_____
7,000	_____	_____	_____	_____	_____	650	_____
8,000	_____	_____	_____	_____	600	_____	7,750

_____ 21.   Refer to the table. The marginal propensity to consume is _____ and the multiplier is _____ .
(a)   0.75; 4
(b)   0.75; 5
(c)   0.8; 4
(d)   0.8; 5

_____ 22.   Refer to the table. Equilibrium income level is
(a)   5,000.
(b)   6,000.
(c)   7,000.
(d)   8,000.

_____ 23.   Refer to the table. In equilibrium, the government has a
(a)   deficit of 50.
(b)   deficit of 250.
(c)   surplus of 50.
(d)   surplus of 250.

_____ 24.   Refer to the table. The equilibrium income level would be 6,000 if government spending
      (a)   increased by 200.
      (b)   increased by 250.
      (c)   decreased by 200.
      (d)   decreased by 250.

_____ 25.   Refer to the table. The equilibrium income level would be 8,200 if net taxes
      (a)   increased by 300.
      (b)   increased by 400.
      (c)   decreased by 300.
      (d)   decreased by 400.

Use the following diagram for the next five questions. The economy has no government sector.

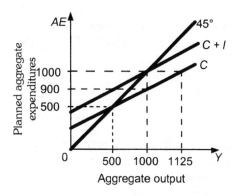

_____ 26.   The equilibrium output level is
      (a)   500.
      (b)   900.
      (c)   1,000.
      (d)   1,125.

_____ 27.   At income level 1,200, planned expenditures are _____ than production and unplanned
 inventory change is _____ .
      (a)   greater; positive
      (b)   greater; negative
      (c)   less; positive
      (d)   less; negative

_____ 28.   Investment is _____ and, in equilibrium, equal to a value of _____ .
      (a)   increasing; 50
      (b)   increasing; 100
      (c)   constant; 50
      (d)   constant; 100

_____ 29. MPC is _____ and the multiplier is _____ .
      (a)   0.75; 4
      (b)   0.75; 5
      (c)   0.8; 4
      (d)   0.8; 5

_____ 30. If, at every income level, saving increases by 50,
     (a)   planned investment will also increase by 50.
     (b)   output level will increase by 50.
     (c)   output will decrease by 250.
     (d)   output will increase by 250.

_____ 31. The price of oil has increased. The government has initiated a contractionary fiscal policy to offset the inflationary effects of the rising energy prices. Given that information, and without further government action, the long-run equilibrium will be restored by
     (a)   aggregate demand curve shifting to the right.
     (b)   aggregate demand curve shifting to the left.
     (c)   short-run aggregate supply curve shifting to the right.
     (d)   short-run aggregate supply curve shifting to the left.

_____ 32. A fiscally-induced increase in aggregate demand will increase prices most sharply when the AS curve is _____ and when the Fed _____ the interest rate constant.
     (a)   flat; holds
     (b)   flat; does not hold
     (c)   steep; holds
     (d)   steep; does not hold

_____ 33. Short-run aggregate supply would increase in each of the following cases EXCEPT
     (a)   an increase in the female labor-participation rate.
     (b)   the imposition of an energy tax.
     (c)   an increase in the stock of capital.
     (d)   an improvement in the health and nutrition of the labor force.

_____ 34. In the long run, an increase in the money supply would make the short-run aggregate supply curve shift left because
     (a)   eventually, all the additional money would be spent.
     (b)   eventually, input prices would increase because the economy would be working beyond its capacity in the short run.
     (c)   interest rates would decrease, discouraging investment in factories and infrastructure.
     (d)   higher prices discourage consumers, and producers cut production when there is a lack of customers.

_____ 35. If the government undertakes an expansionary fiscal policy, the result will be _____ in the long run than in the short run, and it will be _____ if the Fed accommodates.
     (a)   more inflationary; more inflationary
     (b)   more inflationary; less inflationary
     (c)   less inflationary; more inflationary
     (d)   less inflationary; less inflationary

_____ 36. If there is an increase in inflationary expectations by firms that causes them to raise their prices, then we would expect the
     (a)   aggregate demand curve to shift right.
     (b)   aggregate demand curve to shift left.
     (c)   short-run supply curve to shift right.
     (d)   short-run supply curve to shift left.

_____ 37. The Fed increases the money supply in order to expand output and fight unemployment. If this action raises public expectations of higher inflation the Phillips Curve will shift to the _____ and the policy would be _____ effective in fighting unemployment.
    (a)   right; more
    (b)   right; less
    (c)   left; more
    (d)   left; less

_____ 38. Initially the economy is in long-run equilibrium. Now a massive slump in aggregate demand causes a recession and unemployment soars to 10.4%. In the long run we would predict a(n) _____ in market wage levels and a(n) _____ in short-run aggregate supply.
    (a)   increase; increase
    (b)   increase; decrease
    (c)   decrease; increase
    (d)   decrease; decrease

_____ 39. At the initial output level, which of the following would not accompany an open market purchase of bonds by the Fed?
    (a)   An increase in aggregate demand
    (b)   An unplanned rise in inventories
    (c)   A rise in planned investment
    (d)   An expansion in the money supply

_____ 40. The economy is initially in long-run equilibrium. In the long run, an increase in money supply would make the short-run aggregate supply shift left because
    (a)   eventually, all the additional money would be spent.
    (b)   higher prices discourage consumers, and producers cut production when there is a lack of customers.
    (c)   interest rates would decrease, discouraging investment in factories and infrastructure.
    (d)   eventually, input prices would increase because the economy would be working beyond its capacity in the short run.

II.   APPLICATION QUESTIONS

PROBLEM 1: The Arbezani Finance Minister, Count Yamunni, gives you the following national income accounting information for the closed economy of Arbez.

At the equilibrium output (income) level, the following values occur.

$$
\begin{aligned}
C &= 13,000 \quad MPC = 0.75 \\
I &= 1,200 \\
T &= 2,500 \\
G &= 3,000
\end{aligned}
$$

1. Calculate the equilibrium output (income) level.

2. Calculate the equilibrium value of saving.

3. Calculate the marginal propensity to save.

4.   Calculate the value of the expenditure multiplier.

5.   Does the government have a surplus or a deficit? How much is it?

6.   Count Yamunni believes that "In equilibrium, investment must equal personal savings." Is this true? Explain.

Consumer confidence declines dramatically. Consumption spending falls by 60.

7.   How much of an effect does this have on equilibrium GDP?

8.   At the original GDP level, is there unplanned inventories accumulation or decumulation?

The Administration wishes to restore the original production level by changing the tax level.

9.   What is the value of the tax multiplier?

10.   By how much should taxes change? Is it a tax increase or a tax decrease?

11.   After the economy has reached its final equilibrium, what is the size of the surplus or deficit?

12.   After the economy has reached its final equilibrium, what is the final value for consumption?

Go back to the original values you were given for the economy. Forget all about the change in consumption spending and the change in taxes.
    The newly-elected president has pledged to eliminate the deficit. She begins by cutting government spending by 200. Assume no other changes have occurred.

13.   Calculate the increase or decrease in the equilibrium income level.

14.   Calculate the new equilibrium income level.

Now the president responds to the recession by also cutting income taxes by 100. Assume no other new changes.

15.   Calculate the increase or decrease in the equilibrium income level caused only by the tax cut.

16.   Calculate the new equilibrium income level after the spending cut and the tax cut.

Now forget all about the fiscal policy information. Assume that the changes in government spending and taxes did not occur. All values are as they were at the beginning.
    A wave of pessimism sweeps the business community. Planned investment falls by 150.

17.   Calculate the change in the equilibrium value of income.

18.   Calculate the increase or decrease in consumption after the economy has reached its new equilibrium.

19.   Calculate the increase or decrease in saving after the economy has reached its new equilibrium.

PROBLEM 2: You have been hired as a macroeconomic consultant for three small economies—Arbez, Arboc, and Aneyh.

In Arbez, there is concern because the short-run aggregate supply curve has suddenly shifted to the left.

1. The Arbezani Finance Minister asks you which macroeconomic forces determine the shape of the short-run aggregate supply curve. As a Keynesian economist, how would you reply?

2. What might have caused the short-run aggregate supply curve to shift suddenly to the left? Predict how unemployment, and aggregate price and output levels will change. Name this phenomenon.

3. Analyze the adjustments that will occur to re-establish a long-run equilibrium.

4. The Arbezani Finance Minister has heard about the Phillips Curve. Why does the presence of stagflation run counter to the theory presented by the Phillips Curve? What changes in the Arbezani economy have caused traditional Phillips Curve analysis to break down?

5. The government is concerned about unemployment. What policies might the government enact in response to the short-run supply-side change?

6. The central bank (ArbeFed) is also concerned about unemployment. How might ArbeFed respond to the short-run supply-side change? What specific policy options are available?

The economy of Arboc is in a recession caused by a decrease in aggregate demand.

7. You are asked to construct an expansionary policy package, using a fiscal policy and a monetary policy. Explain what will happen to output, the interest rate, and investment. Would it be possible to prevent a change in the interest rate? If so, what would be the magnitude of the crowding-out effect?

Suppose that investment in Arboc becomes more sensitive than before to changes in the interest rate.
8. In terms of monetary policy effectiveness, would this be good news?

9. In terms of fiscal policy effectiveness, would it be good news?

10. Would you predict an adjustment in the policy mix? If so, what change in emphasis would you expect?

In Aneyh, the government is considering an expansionary fiscal policy because the economy is languishing in a deep recession caused by a slump in consumption spending.

11. The Secretary of the Economy wishes to know if the size of the government-spending multiplier is constant. If not, you need to describe how it can be expected to change as the aggregate demand curve moves further to the right.

12. Is the change in the value of the multiplier stabilizing or destabilizing?

REVIEW TEST SOLUTIONS

I.   *Solutions to Multiple-Choice Questions*

1.   (a)   Assuming $MPC > 0$ and $MPS > 0$ higher income will stimulate additional consumption and additional saving.

2.   (c)   Higher interest rates encourage saving. Given the income level, consumption must decrease.

3.   (b)   According to Keynes, the main influence on consumption is income. Note: This is shown as a movement along the consumption function.

4.   (a)   In equilibrium, saving equals investment. If consumption has fallen then, given the income level, saving must have risen, making saving exceed planned investment.

5.   (d)   If $MPC = 0.8$, the government expenditure multiplier is 5.

6.   (d)   If $MPC = 0.8$, the tax multiplier is –4.

7.   (a)   In isolation, the tax increase would reduce equilibrium output by 1,200. To achieve a net increase of 300, government spending would have to increase by 300. Recall that the balanced-budget multiplier is 1.

8.   (d)   If some domestic spending leaks overseas, the multiplier would decrease.

9.   (c)   Ultimately, the goal of any expansionary policy, be it fiscal or monetary, is to stimulate production.

10.   (a)   Policy actions are most effective when the short-run aggregate supply curve is relatively flat. The more responsive input prices are to changes in economic conditions, the less impact policy actions will have.

11.   (a)   The *AE* curve will increase with increased spending. Option (b) is correct if there is no government sector. In the present case however, the equilibrium condition is that $S + T = I + G$.

12.   (b)   Both actions will reduce the money supply.

13.   (d)   A decrease in money demand will accompany a decrease in output, whereas an increase in money supply will accompany a decrease in the discount rate.

14.   (b)   The Fed increases the required reserve ratio to decrease the money supply. A decrease in the money supply increases the equilibrium interest rate and decreases the size of money balances.

15.   (c)   When the ratio is 25%, required reserves are $60 million × 0.25, or $15 million. When the ratio is 20%, required reserves are $60 million × 0.20, or $12 million. Because reserves have not changed, this means that the banking system has excess reserves of $3 million. The multiplier is 1/0.20, or 5.

16.   (c)   When the ratio is 25%, required reserves are $60 million × 0.25, or $15 million. If the reserve ratio is 16.67, the money multiplier is 1/0.1667, or 6.
$15 million × 6 = $90 million.

17.   (a)   Buying securities from the private banks will increase their reserves; cutting the discount rate encourages more borrowing from the Fed.

18.   (b)   An increase in money supply is an expansionary demand-side policy. To restore equilibrium in the long run, the short-run aggregate supply curve will shift to the left.

19.   (d)   An increase in the money supply will affect the interest rate and the quantity of money demanded, but the demand curve will not shift position. Option (c) will increase money demand: At each interest rate, more idle cash balances will be held.

20.   (c)   The opportunity cost of holding money has decreased.

21.   (a)   As disposable income changes by 1,000 (e.g., from 1,600 to 2,600), consumption changes by 750 (from 2,000 to 2,750).

Y	T	Y_d	C	S	I	G	AE
2,000	400	1,600	2,000	−400	600	650	3,250
3,000	400	2,600	2,750	−150	600	650	4,000
4,000	400	3,600	3,500	100	600	650	4,750
5,000	400	4,600	4,250	350	600	650	5,500
6,000	400	5,600	5,000	600	600	650	6,250
7,000	400	6,600	5,750	850	600	650	7,000
8,000	400	7,600	6,500	1,100	600	650	7,750

22.   (c)   This is where $AE = Y$, and where $S + T = I + G = 1,250$.

23.   (b)   The government's deficit is 250 because spending (G) is 650 and net tax revenues (T) are 400.

24.   (b)   The government spending multiplier is 4 and a reduction of 1,000 in equilibrium output is called for.

25.   (d)   The tax multiplier is –3.
Increase in equilibrium income (ΔY) = 1,200 = $\Delta T \times -MPC/MPS$ = –400 × –3.

26.   (c)   This is where $AE(C + I)$ equals Y.

27.   (c)   When planned spending is less than production, unplanned inventory accumulation occurs.

28.   (d)   Equilibrium output level is 1,000, of which consumption accounts for 900. Investment absorbs the remainder. Investment is constant because the gap between the consumption function and the "consumption plus investment" function is constant.

29.   (d)   When income is 500, consumption is also 500. When income is 1,000, consumption is 900. An increase in income of 500 causes an increase in consumption of 400. If MPC, then the multiplier must be 5.

30.   (c)   This is the paradox of thrift result. An increase in saving results in an equivalent decrease in consumption.

31.   (c)   The economy is in short-run equilibrium below potential GDP. Input prices will fall.

32.   (c)   A given expansionary fiscal policy will be augmented if the Fed expands the money supply to hold the interest rate constant. The closer to capacity the economy is (the steeper the *AS* curve), the more inflationary the result.

33.   (b)   An energy tax would raise production costs.

34.   (b)   With high demand, the economy has been pushed past the potential level of output. There is an upward pressure on costs, which causes the short-run *AS* curve to shift left.

35.   (a)   In the long run, output level doesn't change—all demand increases result in higher prices. When the Fed accommodates an expansionary fiscal policy, it increases the money supply.

36.   (d)   At each output level, firms will require higher prices than before.

37.   (b)   Expectations of higher inflation will shift the Phillips Curve up and right. The short-run *AS* curve will shift left. Although *AD* has shifted right, the expansion in output level will be partly offset.

38.   (c)   To restore long-run equilibrium, short-run aggregate supply will increase because input costs will decrease.

39.   (b)   An open market purchase will increase the money supply, reduce interest rates, and stimulate investment and aggregate demand. Inventory levels will decrease in response to the increase in aggregate demand.

40.   (d)   The expansion in the money supply will increase aggregate demand, reducing unemployment. In the long run, wages and other input prices will increase.

II.   Solutions to Application Questions

PROBLEM 1

1.   In equilibrium, $Y = C + I + G = 13,000 + 1,200 + 3,000 = 17,200$.

2.   Saving = 1,700. In equilibrium, $S + T = I + G = 4,200$.

3. $MPS = 0.25$ because $MPC = 0.75$.

4.   If $MPC = 0.75$, the multiplier is 4.

5.   The government has a deficit of 500 $(T - G)$.

6.   Yamunni is wrong! In equilibrium, $S + T = I + G$. There is no requirement that private saving and investment be equal once the economy has a government sector. Yamunni, by the way, is using the wrong term. He should refer to "saving," not to "savings."

7.   GDP will decrease by 60×4, or 240.

8.   Because demand has fallen, inventories will be accumulating if the original output level were sustained.

9.   The tax multiplier is $-MPC/MPS = -0.75/0.25 = -3$.

10.   Taxes should decrease by 80 because $-80 \times -3 = -240$.

11.   The deficit has increased by 80 to $3,000 - 2,420$, or 580.

12.   Consumption remains at 13,000 (its initial value). The tax cut wholly counteracted the decrease in consumption caused by the decline in confidence. That was the point of the tax cut.

13.   −800. The decrease in equilibrium income $(\Delta Y) = \Delta G \times 1/MPS = -200 \times 4$.

14.   Equilibrium income level has fallen by 800, from 17,200 to 16,400.

15.   300. The tax multiplier is -3. $\Delta Y = \Delta T \times -MPC/MPS = -100 \times -3$.

16.   The new equilibrium income level after both fiscal changes is 16,700.

17.   −600. The decrease in equilibrium income $(\Delta Y) = \Delta I \times 1/MPS = -150 \times 4$.

18.   −450. The decrease in consumption $(\Delta C) = \Delta Y \times MPC = -600 \times 0.75$.

19.   −150. The decrease in saving $(\Delta S) = \Delta Y \times MPS = -600 \times 0.25$.

PROBLEM 2

1.   The price/output response curve is positively sloped—as price increases, so does output. At low levels of employment and capacity usage, output can be increased with little additional cost. At higher levels, costs will accumulate more rapidly. The factors that influence slope are the presence of capacity constraints (bottlenecks) and the speed of adjustment of input costs. The greater the capacity constraints and the more rapidly costs adjust to changes in price, the steeper the slope of the short-run *AS* curve will be.

2.   *AS* might shift to the left as a result of higher costs, deterioration of capital, over-regulation or inefficiency by the public sector, or destruction of resources due to war or natural phenomena. As the *AS* curve shifts left, unemployment will increase, the aggregate price level will increase and output will decrease in the short run—stagflation will occur.

3.   Typically, an underutilization of resources occurs as the *AS* curve shifts left; therefore, as time passes, wages will decrease (or, in the real world, rise less rapidly), costs will fall, and the *AS* curve will begin to move to the right.

4.   The Phillips Curve depicts a negative relationship between the inflation rate and the unemployment rate. The inflation rate increases and the unemployment rate decreases as the aggregate demand curve shifts to the right. When stagflation occurs, inflation increases but the unemployment rate increases also. The Phillips Curve relationship breaks down if supply-side factors dominate, as in this case of the short-run aggregate supply curve shifting to the left.

5.   The government, wishing to ease the unemployment caused by the supply shock, could increase government spending or reduce net taxes, to shift *AD* to the right—this would be inflationary, however. A "supply-side" policy would be to reduce government regulation and to increase work incentives, as discussed in Chapter 18 (33).

6.   To help the economy to expand, ArbeFed should enact an expansionary monetary policy—open market bond purchases, reduction of the discount rates, or reduction of the reserve requirement.

7.   There are many packages. An open market purchase of securities and an increase in government spending is one option. Output level will increase, but the effect on the interest rate and investment is ambiguous. The government spending increase, which will increase the interest rate because money demand will be affected, will tend to crowd out investment. The open market purchase, which reduces the interest rate, will encourage investment. The crowding-out effect could be prevented if the expansion in the money supply were such that the interest rate were held constant.

8.   The effectiveness of monetary policy is increased as investment becomes more interest-sensitive to the extent that a given change in the money supply and the interest rate will have a larger impact on investment and planned aggregate expenditure.

9.   The effectiveness of fiscal policy is reduced; the more interest-sensitive investment is, the greater the offsetting crowding-out effect.

10.   To avoid this greater risk of crowding out, the government might have to rely more on monetary policy to accommodate the fiscal policy actions—i.e., changing the money supply to hold the interest rate constant.

11.   The government-spending multiplier decreases as the *AD* curve shifts right, encountering a progressively steeper short-run *AS* curve; in the long run, the multiplier is zero because changes in government spending will have no effect on output level. This result occurs because higher prices reduce investment and consumption spending and this partly offsets the increase in government spending. The offsetting effect increases as the *AD* curve shifts further to the right because the short-run *AS* curve, while getting steeper, drives prices higher.

12.   The multiplier is becoming smaller. This reduces the ability of the economy to move from its current level of activity.

Part IV

Further Macroeconomic Issues

15 [30]

Policy Timing, Deficit Targeting, and Stock Market Effects

C hapter objectives:

1. Distinguish the three types of time lag in stabilization policies. Discuss the problems time lags cause for stabilization policy.

2. Outline the responses of the government to the large federal deficits of the late 1980s and early 1990s. Discuss the objectives and drawbacks of the Gramm-Rudman-Hollings (GRH) Bill and the proposed balanced-budget amendment of 1995.

3. Use the concept of the deficit response index to demonstrate the effects on the deficit of a cut in government spending.

4. Describe the function of bonds in capital investment and explain the relationship between bond prices and the interest rate.

5. Distinguish between stocks and bonds and identify those factors that can influence the price of a stock.

6. Outline the recent behavior of the stock market.

7. Analyze the macroeconomic effects of a change in stock prices.

8. Describe and explain the impact on macroeconomic variables of the stock market's behavior from 1995 to 2000.

This chapter contains an assortment of topics, each of which deepens our understanding of the complexity of conducting macroeconomic stabilization policy and the environment in which it must operate. It gives you a good opportunity to review your understanding of the macroeconomic model that Case, Fair and Oster have constructed and to analyze the economics behind topical issues and your own political beliefs.

BRAIN TEASER I: This chapter notes that the Fed can manipulate the economy by adjusting interest rates. The money supply is adjusted, but only as a way to change interest rates. An issue that has long occupied economists is: "Does money matter?" Does the quantity of money in the economy have an influence on economic conditions or is it merely the handmaiden of interest rates?

BRAIN TEASER II: Your firm is planning to buy additional capital equipment in the near future. Your firm can borrow from a bank, issue bonds, or sell stock. The first two of these options increase the firm's indebtedness, but the third does not. Why is there this difference?

OBJECTIVE 1:

Distinguish the three types of time lag in stabilization policies. Discuss the problems time lags cause for stabilization policy.

Fiscal and monetary *stabilization policies* are intended to smooth out fluctuations in output, employment, and prices, but policy actions do not operate immediately. There are *time lags*. Economists distinguish three:

(a)   The *recognition lag* is the time between the development of a problem and its recognition.

(b)   The *implementation lag* is the time necessary to hammer out and enact a policy following the recognition of the problem. Implementation lags tend to be shorter for monetary policy than for fiscal policy.

(c)   The *response lag* is the time it takes for the economy to react to the policy action. Response lags tend to be longer for monetary policy than for fiscal policy. (page 277 [589])

A case (sometimes referred to as "the fool in the shower") can be made that stabilization policies actually destabilize the economy because, by the time a policy is taking effect, the problem it is designed to address (rising unemployment, for example) may have been replaced by another (inflation, for example) for which the policy is completely inappropriate. (page 278 [590])

The conventional wisdom has been that post-1945 stabilization policy has reduced the size of business cycles (relative to their magnitude in the 1930s and before). Interestingly, more recent studies have found that the size of the business cycle may have been unaffected by stabilization policy.

> **Comment:**   The main differences in terms of time lags between fiscal and monetary policy are at the implementation stage (where monetary policy can be almost instantaneous and fiscal policy lumberingly slow) and the response stage (where fiscal policy tends to work more quickly).
>
> The problems of policy effectiveness have led some economists to call for the complete abandonment of stabilization policy.

> **Comment:**   GDP is measured neither continuously nor with great accuracy. Policymakers may, however, reveal a bias. In fact, in the 25 quarters from the first quarter of 1994 to the first quarter of 2000, the Fed underestimated GDP growth on all but five occasions and overestimated inflation on all but two occasions!

> **Comment:**   Sometimes policymakers can get lucky. In 2000, presidential candidate George W. Bush called for tax cuts during his campaign (because of large federal surpluses). Following his election, and faced with a slowing economy, this policy prescription became appropriate to stimulate the economy and a delay was avoided.

—■——————————————————————— **Practice** ———————————————————————

1. Stabilization policy attempts to
    (a)   stabilize the federal budget.
    (b)   minimize changes in the money supply and interest rates.
    (c)   minimize changes in the levels of output and prices.
    (d)   increase the size of automatic stabilizers.
    ANSWER: (c) Refer to p. 278 [590] for a discussion of stabilization policy.

2. The response lag is shorter for
    (a)   fiscal policy, because changes in, say, government spending have an immediate impact on aggregate demand.
    (b)   fiscal policy, because monetary policy requires approval by a minimum of 75% of the Federal Reserve Board.
    (c)   monetary policy, because open market operations are very easy to perform.
    (d)   monetary policy, because money (currency, demand deposits) must be used in almost all transactions.
    ANSWER: (a) Refer to p. 279 [591].

3. The _____ lag is similar for both monetary policy and fiscal policy.
    (a)   stabilization
    (b)   response
    (c)   recognition
    (d)   implementation
    ANSWER: (b) Monetary and fiscal policymakers take a similar amount of time to recognize the presence of a boom or a slump.

4. Implementation lags tend to be _____ for monetary policy than for fiscal policy; response lags tend to be _____ for monetary policy than for fiscal policy.
    (a)   shorter; shorter
    (b)   shorter; longer
    (c)   longer; shorter
    (d)   longer; longer
    ANSWER: (b) Refer to p. 279 [591].

5. With the "fool in the shower" analogy, critics of stabilization policies argue that
    (a)   we should leave the economy to adjust on its own to cure fluctuations.
    (b)   the government and the Fed should coordinate policy actions throughout the business cycle.
    (c)   policymakers must provide alternating periods of stimulus and restraint to keep the economy from stagnating.
    (d)   given time lags, expansionary policies are required to stabilize the economy.
    ANSWER: (a) Refer to p. 278 [590] for more on this topic. ■

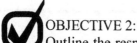

OBJECTIVE 2:
Outline the responses of the government to the large federal deficits of the late 1980s and early 1970s. Discuss the objectives and drawbacks of the Gramm-Rudman-Hollings (GRH) Bill and the proposed balanced-budget amendment of 1995.

Pressure for deficit reduction legislation led to the 1986 *Gramm-Rudman-Hollings (GRH) Bill,* which set targets for the maximum deficit values in successive years. Failure to meet the targets would trigger across-the-board cuts in spending programs. In fact, the targets were "moved" when it became clear that they would not be met! Dissatisfaction with this approach led many politicians to call for a balanced-budget amendment in the early 1990s. (page 281 [593])

Any deficit reduction strategy makes an assumption about the behavior of the Fed. The Fed might move to compensate for cuts in government spending by reducing the interest rate, or it might not. In the former case, the deficit reduction strategy would be more successful because tax collections would not fall.

Deficit targeting is an automatic destabilizer, calling for spending cuts or tax hikes when economic activity decreases through, for example, a negative demand shock. Such contractionary action would further aggravate the recession. Only aggressive expansionary action by the Fed or increased confidence by the private sector could offset this effect. (page 284 [596])

> ▶▶▶   LEARNING TIP: As you approach this section, note that there is an important distinction between the deficit and the (national) debt. In personal finance terms, the deficit is how much your unpaid credit card balance has increased this time period; the debt is the balance itself. If you're still unsure about this distinction, return to Chapter 9 (24) and review.
>
> ▶▶▶   LEARNING TIP: Now is a good time to review the basic Keynesian model developed in Chapter 9 (24). Also, review Figure 9.6 (24.6), which shows the behavior of the deficit (surplus) over time.◀

—————————————————— **Practice** ——————————————————

6.   Congress introduces a deficit-reduction program. If the Fed "leans against the wind," output will be _____ than otherwise and net taxes will be _____ than otherwise.
    (a)   greater; greater
    (b)   greater; smaller
    (c)   smaller; greater
    (d)   smaller; smaller

    ANSWER: (a) "Leaning against the wind" (which was discussed in Chapter 13 (28)) means that the Fed moves to offset other economic changes. The deficit-reduction package is contractionary, so the Fed's policy will be expansionary, causing output to fall less. Net taxes will fall less.

7.   The effectiveness of GRH targets in the 1980s is best summarized by which of the following?
    (a)   GRH succeeded in its objective, because the deficit was reduced.
    (b)   GRH succeeded in its objective, but the deficit remained high.
    (c)   GRH failed in its objective, although the deficit was reduced.
    (d)   GRH failed in its objective, because the deficit remained high.

    ANSWER: (d) GRH did not fix the deficit problem. The size of the deficit remained an important issue until almost the end of the 1990s and re-appeared after 2001.

8.   Each of the following is a partial explanation for the fact that the federal deficit increases during
       a recession EXCEPT
       (a)   a decrease in output results in more government transfer payments to households.
       (b)   a decrease in output causes personal income tax revenues to decrease (because taxable
               income decreases during an economic slowdown).
       (c)   a decrease in output results in expansionary fiscal policy.
       (d)   a decrease in output causes decreases in tax revenues collected from corporations.

       ANSWER: (c) The government may not choose to enact expansionary fiscal policies during a
               recession.

9.   The balanced-budget amendment proposed in the mid-1990s would have been destabilizing
       because, if the economy dips into a recession, the legislation would require _____ in government
       spending and/or _____ in net taxes.
       (a)   increases; increases
       (b)   increases; decreases
       (c)   decreases; increases
       (d)   decreases; decreases

       ANSWER: (c) Refer to p. 282 [594] for more on the balanced-budget amendment.

10.   Deficit targeting is in effect when the economy is hit by a negative demand shock. The deficit
       will _____ . By acting to balance the budget, government policy will make aggregate demand
       decrease _____ .
       (a)   increase; more
       (b)   increase; less
       (c)   decrease; more
       (d)   decrease; less

       ANSWER: (a) Refer to Figure 15.4 (30.4) for a summary of this process. ∎

OBJECTIVE 3:
Use the concept of the deficit response index to demonstrate the effects on the deficit of a cut in
government spending.

GRH was overly simple. To remove a deficit of $20 billion doesn't require a government spending cut of
$20 billion, but rather a greater reduction because spending cuts have a negative impact on tax revenues.
A spending cut reduces aggregate output and, therefore, tax receipts. Lower tax receipts widen the deficit
again. The *deficit response index* measures how much a one dollar cut in income will reduce the
deficit. (page 283 [595])
       Without deficit targeting, expansions and contractions in the deficit operate to stabilize the
economy—feeding it additional spending power during economic recessions and drawing off spending
power during economic expansions. The more negative the deficit response index the more powerful is
the stabilizing impact of the deficit.

▶▶▶   LEARNING TIP: Review Chapter 9 (24) to see that private sector saving must finance investment and public sector borrowing. When deficits increase, there is less left over for private sector investment. (In an open economy, of course, funds can be borrowed from foreigners.)

The *DRI* is a tricky concept. Take the time to work through the textbook's example carefully. Try it again with your own numbers.◀

Comment: The government multiplier approaches zero as the (short-run) aggregate supply curve becomes steeper.

───────■─────────────────────────────── **Practice** ───────────────────────────

11.   The multiplier is 2.5. Investment spending falls by $200 million causing taxes to fall by $100 million. The deficit response index is
(a)   0.5.
(b)   0.2.
(c)   −0.2.
(d)   −0.5.

ANSWER: (c)   Output will decrease by $500 million (200 × 2.5).

DRI = change in deficit/change in income = 100/−500 = −0.2.

12.   In the U.S. economy, the government wishes to cut the deficit by $50 billion. This could be achieved by _____ government spending by _____ $50 billion.
(a)   increasing; more than
(b)   increasing; less than
(c)   decreasing; more than
(d)   decreasing; less than

ANSWER: (c)   A spending cut of exactly $50 billion reduces equilibrium income by some multiple (perhaps 1.4). As income falls, net taxes decrease, partly offsetting the deficit-reducing effect of the spending cut.

13.   Arboc and Arbez are neighboring economies. The deficit response index in each is −0.2. The government spending multiplier in Arboc is 2; the government spending multiplier in Arbez is 4. An equal decrease in government spending of $20 (million) in each economy would result in a
(a)   bigger reduction in the deficit in Arbez.
(b)   smaller reduction in the deficit in Arbez.
(c)   bigger increase in the deficit in Arbez.
(d)   smaller increase in the deficit in Arbez.

ANSWER: (b)   Arboc: $\Delta Y = -\$20 \times 2 = -\$40$.

Change in deficit = $\Delta Y \times DRI = -\$40 \times -0.2 = \$8$. The deficit decreases by $20 − $8, or $12.

Arbez: $\Delta Y = -\$29 \times 4 = -\$80$.

Change in deficit = $\Delta Y \times DRI = -\$80 \times 0.2 = \$16=$. The deficit decreases by $20 − $16, or $4.

14. During the 2000 election campaign, calls were made to replace the current tax system (in which tax rates increase as income increases) with a flat tax system. If implemented, this would have made the deficit response index _____ negative and would have _____ the deficit's power as an automatic stabilizer.
    (a)   more; increased
    (b)   more; decreased
    (c)   less; increased
    (d)   less; decreased
    ANSWER: (d) Suppose the economy expands. Tax collections would increase less with a flat tax than with the current tax system—the deficit response index would be less negative. The more spending power is withdrawn during an expansion the less powerful the expansion will be. ■

OBJECTIVE 4:
Describe the function of bonds in capital investment and explain the relationship between bond prices and the interest rate.

A firm can finance the purchase of capital by
    (1)   self-finance,
    (2)   borrowing from a bank,
    (3)   issuing bonds, or
    (4)   selling stock.
    A bond is a document that promises to pay back a loan under specified conditions. Each bond is issued with a face value, a maturity date, and a fixed interest payment (or coupon). Bonds can be bought and sold in the bond market and the price of a bond can vary. (page 285 [597])
    There is a negative relationship between bond prices and the interest rate. The interest payment on a bond (the coupon) is fixed. Therefore, for an existing bond to remain attractive if the market interest rate increases, the price of acquiring the right to the coupon must decrease, otherwise the "reward" from buying the bond will not be competitive with the going interest rate. If the market interest decreases, bondholders could receive a capital gain by selling their asset at the higher price. As the wealth of bondholders changes, so will their level of consumption spending.

—————————————————————————————— **Practice** ——————————————————————————————
15. The guaranteed payment on a bond is called the
    (a)   maturity.
    (b)   coupon.
    (c)   interest rate.
    (d)   yield.
    ANSWER: (b) See the definition on p. 203 [515] in Chapter 11 (26).

16. Which of the following does not change over the life of a bond?
    (a)   The interest rate.
    (b)   The coupon or guaranteed payment.
    (c)   The market value.
    (d)   The estimated spread.
    ANSWER: (b) A bond's riskiness affects its market value and its spread. The interest rate varies with the market value. The coupon payment is contractually specified for the life of the bond.

Use the following information for the next two questions. The Fed decreases the reserve requirement.

17.   The money supply will _____ and the interest rate will _____.
   (a)   increase; increase
   (b)   increase; decrease
   (c)   decrease; increase
   (d)   decrease; decrease

   ANSWER: (b) A decrease in the reserve requirement is an expansionary monetary policy. The interest rate will decrease.

18.   Bondholders will experience a
   (a)   capital gain and consumption will increase.
   (b)   capital gain and consumption will decrease.
   (c)   capital loss and consumption will increase.
   (d)   capital loss and consumption will decrease.

   ANSWER: (a) An interest rate decrease will result in an increase in bond prices (a capital gain). As wealth increases, bondholders will increase consumption.

19.   A bond pays a fixed payment of $6 per $100 of face value. The current yield on new bonds of similar risk and maturity is 10%. The current price of the bond
   (a)   is certainly higher than its face value.
   (b)   is certainly lower than its face value.
   (c)   may be higher than its face value—it also depends on the extent of capital gains or losses.
   (d)   may be lower than its face value—it also depends on the extent of capital gains or losses.

   ANSWER: (b) If the current yield is greater than 6%, the price of the bond must have fallen to less than $100 (because the payment is fixed contractually). We can conclude this with certainty, without knowing the extent of the capital loss. ■

OBJECTIVE 5:
Distinguish between stocks and bonds and identify those factors that can influence the price of a stock.

A stock is a certificate that certifies ownership of a share of a firm. The stockholder is a part owner of the firm with a right to a share in the firm's profits and to have a voice in the selection of management. A bondholder is a creditor of the firm; a stockholder is an owner of the firm. A bondholder has a right to a guaranteed annual payment (coupon); a stockholder does not. If profits allow, a stockholder may receive a dividend. Additionally, if the stock's price increases, the stockholder may choose to sell and realize a capital gain. (page 285 [597])

      The price of a stock is determined by its expected future dividends, the interest rate, and risk. The stock will be more attractive if the public expects future dividends to increase. This attractiveness, though, will be lessened the further into the future the payments are expected to be made. A dividend of $100 paid in three years' time is less attractive than a dividend of $100 paid in one years' time. The interest rate determines how deeply we discount the value of future payments. As the interest increases, the lower the discounted value of future dividends.

      Risk is another factor used to discount the value of future payments. The riskier the expected dividend, the more heavily it is discounted.

If participants in the stock market believe that the price of the stock will rise in the future it makes sense for stockholders to hold onto their stock at the current (apparently low) price and for buyers to be eager to buy at the current (apparently low) price. This behavior can drive stock prices up in what is known as a "speculative bubble."

■ **Practice**

20.   Other things remaining equal, the price of a stock should increase if the interest rate _____ or if risk _____.
   (a)   increases; increases
   (b)   increases; decreases
   (c)   decreases; increases
   (d)   decreases; decreases

   ANSWER: (d) The interest rate and risk as factors that affect the value of expected future dividends. A lower interest rate and reduced risk both discount future payments less deeply. Higher expected dividends will increase the price of the stock.

21.   The price of a stock should increase if
   (a)   the stock's expected future dividend increases.
   (b)   the economy experiences a recession.
   (c)   the overall price level is decreasing.
   (d)   the interest rate increases.

   ANSWER: (a) If expectations improve regarding future dividends, the stock will become more attractive and command a higher price.

22.   The Fed decreases the reserve requirement. This action will to _____ the interest rate. The discounted value of expected future dividends will _____ .
   (a)   increase; increase
   (b)   increase; decrease
   (c)   decrease; increase
   (d)   decrease; decrease

   ANSWER: (c) A decrease in the reserve requirement is an expansionary monetary policy. The interest rate will decrease. Lower interest rates increase the discounted value of expected future dividends. ■

OBJECTIVE 6:
Outline the recent behavior of the stock market.

The Dow Jones Industrial Average is the most frequently reported measure of stock market performance, but it is based on only 30 large companies. However, the Standard and Poor's 500 index is more broadly based and more representative of overall stock performance. (page 286 [598])

Between 1995 and 2000, the S&P 500 index rose by over 200 percent. The largest boom in U.S. stock market history, the expansion added $14 trillion to the wealth of households, or $2.5 trillion annually. By comparison, GDP in 1998 was $9 trillion. Stock prices are determined by expected future dividends, the interest rate and risk, but interest rates were fairly stable, profitability was not unusually high, and there is little evidence that stockholders felt that riskiness had declined. The stock price hike, then, seems to have been a bubble, brought about by a feeding frenzy of over-exuberant investors. After March 2000, stock prices tumbled—the bubble had burst.

Comment: In 1970, only about 10% of American families owned stock and most stockholders were affluent; by the mid 2000s the number was over 50%, but about half of those were earning less than the average household income. Stock investments comprised 28% of household wealth. Perhaps less well-educated investors were entering the market, bringing with them unreasonably high expectations. Newer investors often borrowed against other assets, such as home equity, to buy more stock. Faced with losses, and scant other assets, it might have seemed sensible to sell.

Although the S&P 500 index is more representative of market conditions, the Dow Jones is more widely reported. For your information, here is a table showing when milestone numbers were reached by the Dow. From the numbers it's easy to see how inexperienced investors could be filled with "irrational exuberance." The Dow peaked at 11,722 in January 2000. After declines, the Dow reached that peak once more in May 2006. At the time of writing (July 2008), the Dow is once again below 11,000, in response to housing market declines, high oil prices, and fears about the financial sector.

Dow Jones Industrial Average	Date Milestone Reached	Months to Reach Milestone
1,000	11/72	
2,000	1/87	170
3,000	4/91	51
4,000	2/95	46
5,000	11/95	9
6,000	10/96	11
7,000	2/97	4
8,000	7/98	5
9,000	4/98	9
10,000	3/99	11
11,000	5/99	2
12,000	10/06	89
13,000	4/07	6
14,000	7/07	3

———————————————————————— **Practice** ————————————————————————

23.   A stock market bubble occurs because
   (a)   most stock prices are rising rapidly.
   (b)   many buyers expect higher stock prices in the future.
   (c)   the discounted value of expected future dividends is rising rapidly.
   (d)   businesses are becoming less risky.

   ANSWER: (b) Although the other options may trigger a rising markets, it is the speculative behavior of those expecting even higher future prices that distinguishes a bubble.

24.   The stock market boom of the late 1990s is best explained by
   (a)   a substantial decrease in interest rates.
   (b)   self-fulfilling expectations of rising stock prices.
   (c)   increased profitability of corporations due to expanding demand in the economy.
   (d)   a diversification of risk due to the expansion in the number of firms issuing stock.

   ANSWER: (b) The stock market boom seems to have been a speculative bubble. ■

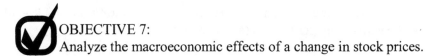

OBJECTIVE 7:
Analyze the macroeconomic effects of a change in stock prices.

Consumer and investor spending increases when stock prices increase. An increase in stock prices makes households wealthier, which encourages them to increase consumption spending. In addition, with higher prices for its stock, a firm can attract more funds per share issued—per share of stock, the cost of an investment decreases. Evidence suggests that a $100 increase in the value of stocks results in a $4 increase in spending. (page 288 [600])

The 1987 stock market crash, which wiped out about $1 trillion of wealth, was expected to generate a recession, with spending falling by about $40 billion ($1 trillion × 0.04). With a multiplier of 1.4, the final decline in GDP would have been $56 billion.

The predicted slump didn't materialize, however, perhaps because of the prompt action of the Fed, which pushed interest rates downward to stimulate spending and to signal that the recession would be resisted and that the loss of wealth was temporary. (page 288 [600]).

The stock market boom of 1995-2000 increased household wealth by $2.5 trillion per year. If the multiplier is 1.4, we could predict a $2.5 trillion × 0.04 × 1.4 (i.e., $140 billion) boost to spending, which is about 1.5% of GDP. Monetary policy "leaned against the wind" and raised interest rates.

The stock market correction of 2000-2002 wiped out about $7 trillion in household wealth, and slowed economic growth, even to the extent that there was a mild recession, despite the presence of expansionary fiscal and monetary policies.

▶▶   LEARNING TIP: Treat this section as one long application on the macroeconomic effects of the stock market. The material is fairly challenging, but the payoff is worthwhile.◀

━━■━━━━━━━━━━━━━━━━━━━━━ **Practice** ━━━━━━━━━━━━━━━━━━━━━━━

25.   From 1995 to 2000, rising stock prices added about $2.5 trillion to household wealth annually. Assuming households spend about 4% of this additional wealth, and the expenditure multiplier is 1.4, aggregate spending should
(a)   increase by about $14 billion.
(b)   decrease by about $14 billion.
(c)   increase by about $140 billion.
(d)   decrease by about $140 billion.

ANSWER: (c) $2,500 billion × 0.04 × 1.4 = $140 billion. See p. 288 [600].

26.   A boom in the stock market affects the economy because
(a)   businesses increase investment as demand increases.
(b)   the stock market results in an increased money supply.
(c)   the saving rate increases because of profit opportunities.
(d)   spending by households decreases as stock assets absorb a larger percentage of after-tax income.

ANSWER: (a)   As stock prices increase, the greater the amount of funds firms can raise for each additional unit of stock.

27.   Compared to a "no boom" scenario, the Fed kept interest rates _____ during the stock market boom of 1995-2000, and the Federal budget surplus (as a percentage of GDP) was _____.
(a)   higher; higher
(b)   higher; lower
(c)   lower; higher
(d)   lower; lower

ANSWER: (a) The Fed "leaned against the wind" and boosted interest rates while, because of the prosperity, net tax collections increases.

28.   If there is a fall in stock prices, consumption will _____ and planned investment will _____ .
(a)   increase; increase
(b)   increase; decrease
(c)   decrease; increase
(d)   decrease; decrease

ANSWER: (d) Planned investment will decrease as firms anticipate reductions in consumption spending and an economic downturn. ■

OBJECTIVE 8:
Describe and explain the impact on macroeconomic variables of the stock market's behavior from 1995 to 2000.

The economic boom from 1995 to 2000 was driven by the stock market boom at the same time—without rising stock prices the extraordinary performance of the U.S. economy would have been unremarkable.

Measures such as the personal saving rate and the unemployment rate were lowered—greater wealth encouraged greater consumption spending (less saving) which was translated into more jobs.

Measures such as investment, the federal deficit (as a percentage of GDP), real growth rate, the inflation rate, and short-term interest rates were all increased because of the stock market boom. (page 289 [601])

ECONOMICS IN PRACTICE: On page 293 [605], the textbook looks at research into the psychology underlying speculative bubbles. Should the Fed attempt to restrain bubbles, or should market forces be allowed to prevail? As we'll see in the next chapter, this debate is broader than control of bubbles— should the authorities intervene in free markets? First, according to the article, what are the two courses of action that the Fed can take in the presence of a bubble?
ANSWER: The Fed can either intervene to restrain bubbles or let them run their course and stand ready to support the financial system when the bubble bursts.
ECONOMICS IN PRACTICE (CONTINUED): In some ways, bubbles are merely the reverse of market "corrections." Can you think of a market where prices are explicitly prevented from falling too precipitously? Why would this be done?
ANSWER: The stock market has "circuit breakers" that are activated if the value of stocks drops too far too fast. These trading curbs were introduced after 1987's "Black Monday," when stock markets crashed worldwide, with the New York Stock Exchange losing 22.6% of its value in one day. The Fed reacted to that crisis by pumping liquidity into the financial system.
In 2008, when the major privately-owned investment bank, Bear Stearns, failed following the sub-prime mortgage crisis, the Fed stepped in to supply loans in order to prevent a decline in confidence. Similarly, the Fed extended credit limits and granted low-interest loans to the privately-owned mortgage corporations, Fannie Mae and Freddie Mac, in order to bolster investor spirits.

Essentially, the Fed is operating as a stabilizer for the economy, reducing the volatility caused by market fluctuations. As we have learned in this chapter, consumption expands as wealth increases and declines as wealth is lost.

—■——————————————— **Practice** ———————————————————

29. During a stock market boom we would expect investment to be relatively _____ and the personal saving rate to be relatively _____.
    (a)   high; high
    (b)   high; low
    (c)   low; high
    (d)   low; low

    ANSWER: (b) With high stock prices, wealth increases, leading to greater consumption (less saving). Because a share of stock is more expensive, firms can raise financial capital with a smaller (cheaper) issue of stock.

30. During a stock market boom we would expect the unemployment rate to be relatively _____ and the inflation rate to be relatively _____ .
    (a)   high; high
    (b)   high; low
    (c)   low; high
    (d)   low; low

    ANSWER: (c) As aggregate demand increases, we would see more job creation and a greater pressure on the aggregate price level to increase.

31. During the stock market boom of 1995-2000 which of the following was not true?
    (a)   The inflation rate was higher than if there had been no boom.
    (b)   The growth rate of real GDP was lower than if there had been no boom.
    (c)   The investment-output ratio was higher than if there had been no boom.
    (d)   The personal saving rate was lower than if there had been no boom.

    ANSWER: (b) Real GDP grew more rapidly with boom than it would have without the boom.

32. During the stock market boom of the late 1990s, the actual federal surplus (as a percentage of GDP)
    (a)   increased more than if there had been no boom.
    (b)   increased less than if there had been no boom
    (c)   decreased more than if there had been no boom
    (d)   decreased less than if there had been no boom

    ANSWER: (a) See Figure 15.9 (30.9). ■

BRAIN TEASER I SOLUTION: Chapter 18 (33) offers an answer to this question. The quantity of money does have a major effect on sustained inflation over the long term. Price level increases are fueled by an increasing supply of dollars. However, the consensus of economists is that short-term economic decisions are influenced more by interest rate variations than money supply variations.

BRAIN TEASER II SOLUTION: Money borrowed from a bank must be repaid (with interest). Similarly, funds received from a bond issue must be repaid, with interest. Both of these transactions are loans from the creditor to the firm. A stockholder owns a portion of the firm but the firm has no contractual obligation to pay the stockholder—there is no claim against the firm in that respect. Of course, dividends are expected, but they need not be paid.

POLICY PROBLEMS

This chapter is excellent in pointing out the problems faced by policymakers. It's easy to think that we should be able to "fine tune" the economy, efficiently curing inflation, unemployment, output, the deficit, and so on. (Economists used to believe so, too.) But time lags, lack of coordination between Congress and the Fed, political considerations, slippages in the economy, and the ticklish problem of expectations conspire to make policy more like a blunt instrument than a surgeon's scalpel.

PRACTICE TEST

I.   MULTIPLE-CHOICE QUESTIONS

Select the option that provides the single best answer.

_____ 1.   The Fed increases the discount rate. The money supply will _____. The wealth of bondholders will _____.
(a)   increase; increase
(b)   increase; decrease
(c)   decrease; increase
(d)   decrease; decrease

_____ 2.   Expansionary monetary policies _____ the deficit and expansionary fiscal policies _____ the deficit.
(a)   increase; increase
(b)   increase; decrease
(c)   decrease; increase
(d)   decrease; decrease

_____ 3.   The multiplier is 2 and the deficit response index is –0.3. The government cuts spending by $100 million. Taxes will
(a)   rise by $200 million.
(b)   fall by $200 million.
(c)   rise by $60 million.
(d)   fall by $60 million.

_____ 4.   The multiplier is 1.6 and the deficit response index is –0.2. The government cuts spending by $50 million. Taxes will fall by _____ and the deficit will fall by _____ .
(a) $80 million; $34 million
(b) $80 million; $16 million
(c) $16 million; $34 million
(d) $34 million; $16 million

_____ 5.   Common stock holdings are
(a)   insured by the Federal Reserve.
(b)   regulated by the Federal Reserve.
(c)   a part of the wealth of households.
(d)   issued to pay for the federal deficit.

_____ 6.   The implementation lag is the length of time between _____ and _____ .
(a)   the recognition of a problem; the resolution of the problem
(b)   the recognition of a problem; the development and enactment of a remedy
(c)   the development of a problem; its ultimate resolution
(d)   the development of a problem; the development and enactment of a remedy

_____ 7.   The multiplier is 2. The government cuts spending by $100 million. Taxes fall by $50 million. The deficit response index is
(a)   0.5.
(b)   –0.5.
(c)   0.25.
(d)   –0.25.

_____ 8.   Because the change occurs directly in aggregate demand, the _____ lag for fiscal policy is _____ than that for monetary policy.
(a)   implementation; shorter
(b)   implementation; longer
(c)   response; shorter
(d)   response; longer

_____ 9.   The multiplier is 1.6. The government cuts spending by $50 million. The deficit falls by $40 million. The deficit response index is
(a)   0.125.
(b)   –0.125.
(c)   0.25.
(d)   –0.25.

_____ 10.   GRH is recognized as an automatic destabilizer because
(a)   during a recession, it required tax cuts if the deficit target had not been met.
(b)   during a boom, it required spending increases if the deficit target had not been met.
(c)   during a recession, it required contractionary fiscal measures if the deficit target had not been met.
(d)   during a recession, it required expansionary fiscal measures if the deficit target had not been met.

_____ 11.   Government bonds have a lower interest rate (yield) than corporate bonds because government bonds
(a)   have a higher risk of default.
(b)   have a lower risk of default.
(c)   are insured by the Federal Reserve.
(d)   mature more quickly.

_____ 12.   In the stock market boom of the late 1990, the S&P 500 index increased by about
(a)   100%.
(b)   200%.
(c)   500%.
(d)   1,000%.

_____ 13.   Arbocorp issues bonds worth 1,000,000 opeks and 600,000 shares of one-opek stock.
(a)   Household wealth increases by 400,000 opeks.
(b)   Household wealth increases by 600,000 opeks.
(c)   Household wealth increases by 1,000,000 opeks.
(d)   Household wealth increases by 1,600,000 opeks.

_____ 14.   During a stock market boom we would expect the personal saving rate to be relatively
(a)   high, because wealthier people save more.
(b)   high, because interest rates are likely to be high.
(c)   low, because wealthier people spend more.
(d)   low, because interest rates are likely to be high.

_____ 15.   It has been estimated that an increase in the value of stocks of $1,000 will cause an initial increase in spending of about
(a) $4.
(b) $40.
(c) $200.
(d) $400.

_____ 16.   During 2000, the value of the technology-laden NASDAQ slumped by 20%. The performance of other sectors of the stock market also were disappointingly poor. We would predict that personal saving rates would begin to _____ and that the Fed might consider an interest rate _____ .
(a)   increase; increase
(b)   increase; decrease
(c)   decrease; increase
(d)   decrease; decrease

_____ 17.   During the stock market boom of the late 1990s, the unemployment rate was relatively low and the inflation rate was relatively high. This would suggest that the effect of the stock market was being felt mainly as
(a)   an increase in aggregate demand.
(b)   an increase in aggregate supply.
(c)   a decrease in aggregate demand.
(d)   a decrease in aggregate supply.

_____ 18.   During the stock market boom of the late 1990s, the real growth rate was relatively _____ and short-term interest rates were relatively _____.
(a)   high; high
(b)   high; low
(c)   low; high
(d)   low; low

_____ 19. Following the bursting of the stock market bubble in 2000, interest rates _____. *Ceteris paribus*, we would predict _____ bond prices.
- (a) increased; higher
- (b) increased; lower
- (c) decreased; higher
- (d) decreased; lower

_____ 20. When stock prices increase, household consumption _____ and household saving _____ .

- (a) increases; increases
- (b) increases; decreases
- (c) decreases; increases
- (d) decreases; decreases

II.   APPLICATION QUESTIONS

1. (a) "The less negative the deficit response index, the more effective a government spending cut will be in reducing the deficit." True or false? Explain.
   (b) "The Gramm-Rudman-Hollings legislation, if applied as originally intended, would have operated as an additional automatic stabilizer." True or false? Explain.
   (c) "If the Fed expands the money supply during a period of substantial excess capacity, the government deficit will be reduced." True or false? Explain.

2. The economy is at the full-employment output level. The budget deficit is currently $240 million. Evidence shows that the government spending multiplier is 1.5 and that, for each $1 decrease in GDP, net tax revenues decrease by 20¢. The Congress decides to balance the budget by cutting government spending by $240 million.
   (a) Calculate the effect on GDP.
   (b) Calculate the effect on net taxes.
   (c) Calculate the effect on the deficit.
   (d) Calculate the size of the deficit following the policy action.
   (e) In terms of the *AS/AD* diagram, describe what the government's policy action has done to the curves, to prices, and to unemployment.
   (f) If policymakers make no other changes, what will happen, qualitatively, to the deficit? Why? Can you give numbers to support your view?
   (g) Policymakers are too impatient to wait for the long run. Can you calculate how much government spending would have to be cut in order to balance the budget immediately. (We know it must be a cut of more than $240 million.)
   Congress returns to its original proposed cut of $240 million. This will be inadequate to balance the budget.
   (h) What sort of policy action could the Fed take to help balance the budget?
   (i) Given the three tools of monetary policy, indicate in which direction each would have to change in order to effect the desired policy?

3.   Suppose the economy is described by the following model.

$$C = 280 + 0.8Yd \qquad (1)$$

$$I = 400 \qquad (2)$$

$$G = 800 \qquad (3)$$

$$T = -400 + 0.2Y \qquad (4)$$

$$Yd = Y - T \qquad (5)$$

(a)   Calculate the equilibrium income level (where $Y = C + I + G$).
(b)   Calculate the government deficit (D) where the deficit = $G - T$.
(c)   The value of the expenditure multiplier is _____ .
(d)   Given the initial model, suppose that, suddenly, investment falls by $50. Calculate the change in the equilibrium income level.
(e)   How will this investment change affect the deficit?
(f)   The deficit response index in this model is _____ .
(g)   Given the initial model, to achieve a balanced budget through a cut in government spending, GDP would have to fall by _____ .
(h)   To achieve this GDP cut with a reduction in government spending, G must fall by _____ .
(i)   Given the initial model, suppose that this year's deficit target is 200. Suddenly, as we saw above, investment falls by $50. To restore the deficit target of 200, government spending would have to _____ (rise/fall) by _____ .
(j)   The investment change and the government spending change together would make income _____ (rise/fall) by _____ .

4.   Suppose that the budget is required by law to be balanced. Now suppose investment spending falls because of business pessimism.
(a)   What will happen to production and output if investment spending falls?
(b)   What will happen to tax receipts?
(c)   What will happen to public transfer payments?
(d)   Bearing these factors in mind, what must now be happening to the budget?
(e)   What would you recommend, given the balanced budget requirement that demands equality between government spending and net tax receipts?
(f)   What would your obligatory policy recommendation do to an economy already experiencing recession and growing unemployment?

5.   Congress cuts government spending by $50 to reduce the deficit. If the spending multiplier has a value of 2, aggregate output will _____ (rise/fall) by $_____ . If the deficit response index is – 0.1, taxes will _____ (rise/fall) by $_____ and the deficit will _____ (increase/decrease) by $_____ . If the multiplier has a value of 1.4, however, aggregate output would _____ (rise/fall) by $_____ . If the deficit response index is still –0.1, taxes will _____ (rise/fall) by $_____ and the deficit will _____ (increase/decrease) by $_____ . We can conclude that a given cut in government spending will be more effective in reducing the deficit the _____ (larger/smaller) the value of the spending multiplier.

6.   Imagine a 30-year bond issued by HAL Corp. It has a face value of $1,000 and a fixed coupon payment of $100.

      (a)   What is the interest rate on this bond? _____ (Suppose that this is the market interest rate too.)

      (b)   Now the market interest rate moves to 5%. Is HAL's bond attractive or unattractive, and why?

      (c)   What is happening to the demand for this bond?

      (d)   What will happen to the supply of this bond flowing onto the market?

      (e)   Predict what will happen to the price of the bond, based on demand and supply behavior.

      (f)   Formulate a rule relating movements in the interest rate and bond prices.

7.   Following 1987's stock market crash, the Fed increased the money supply and cut interest rates somewhat. What effects was the Fed trying to achieve by this action? How might the stock market have been affected? The bond market? (Remember the link between the interest rate and bond prices!) Because all of these actions were financial, why should we have expected changes in the levels of real production and employment in the economy?

8.   We know that a $100 increase in wealth will cause a $5 increase in spending. Also, the spending multiplier has a value of 2, and the deficit response index is –0.1. The value of stocks increases by $150 billion this year.

      (a)   Aggregate output will _____ (increase/decrease) by $_____.

      (b)   The government deficit will _____ (increase/decrease) by $_____.

      (c)   Given the change in stock prices, if the multiplier has a value of 1.4, aggregate output will _____ (increase/decrease) by $_____, and the deficit will _____ (increase/decrease) by $_____.

      (d)   We can conclude that a given change in stock values will be more effective in reducing the deficit the _____ (larger/smaller) the value of the spending multiplier.

      (e)   If the Fed "leans against the wind," we would expect interest rates to be _____ (higher/lower) than if stocks had increased in value. [Refer to Chapter 13 (28) if you're unfamiliar with this term.]

PRACTICE TEST SOLUTIONS

I.   Solutions to Multiple-Choice Questions

1.   (d)   An increase in the discount rate reduces the money supply. The interest rate increases. As the interest rate increases, the price of bonds and, therefore, the wealth of bondholders decrease.

2.   (c)   An expansionary monetary policy increases spending and income—net taxes increase and the deficit decreases. An increase in government spending or a decrease in net taxes results in an immediate increase in the deficit. Unless the *DRI* is more negative than – 1.00, the deficit will increase.

3.   (d)   Output decreases by $200 million (2 × $100 million). As output decreases, net taxes decrease by $60 million (–0.3 × $200 million).

4.   (c)   Output decreases by $80 million (1.6 × $50 million). As output decreases, net taxes decrease by $16 million (–0.2 × $80 million). The net change in the deficit is $34 million (50 – 16).

5.   (c)   Stock is an asset that has some value. As such, it is part of household wealth. The stock market crash of 1987 resulted in the obliteration of billions of dollars of wealth.

6.   (b)   Refer to p. 279 [591] for the definition of the implementation lag.

7.   (d)   Output decreases by $200 million (2 × $100 million). As output decreases, net taxes decrease by $50 million ($DRI$ × $200 million). DRI = –0.25.

8.   (c)   Refer to p. 279 [591] for a discussion of this topic.

9.   (b)   Output decreases by $80 million (1.6x $50 million). The net change in the deficit is $40 million (50 – 10). Net taxes, therefore, decrease by $10 million ($DRI$ × $80 million). DRI = –0.125.

10.   (c)   GRH requires across-the-board spending cuts, even during a recession.

11.   (b)   Government bonds are backed by the "full faith and credit of the United States Government," making them less risky than corporate bonds.

12.   (b)   See Figure 15.5 (30.5) on p. 287 [599].

13.   (d)   Stocks and bonds are both assets that add to the wealth of households.

14.   (c)   Wealthier people spend more of their current income and, therefore, save less. Recall that the personal saving rate is the percentage of disposable income that is saved.

15.   (b) $1,000 × 0.04 = $40. See p. 288 [600].

16.   (b)   Declining wealth reduces consumption. Given income, saving should increase. With decreasing demand the Fed is more likely to lower, rather than raise, interest rates.

17.   (a)   Relatively low unemployment and relatively high inflation is best explained by the aggregate demand curve shifting to the right (as household wealth increases).

18.   (a)   With increased demand, there would be an expansion an production. If the Fed chose to slow the pace of economic growth, to prevent inflation, it would increase interest rates.

19.   (c)   Interest rates decreased in an effort to stimulate the economy. There is a negative relationship between interest rates and bond prices.

20.   (b)   When stock prices increase, household wealth increases, encouraging additional consumption. Because household income has not changed, saving decreases.

II.   Solutions to Application Questions

1.   (a)   True. If output falls by $1 billion, the deficit response index indicates how much the deficit will increase as a result. If the *DRI* were zero, the deficit would not change at all. If, to reduce the deficit, government spending were cut and it was this that prompted the decline in output, and the *DRI* were zero, there would be no offsetting increase in the deficit. Refer to p. 283 [595].

(b)   False. GRH would have been destabilizing, calling, for example, for cuts in government spending during a recession. Refer to p. 281 [593].

(c)   True. An expansionary monetary policy will increase output and employment. Net taxes will be increased, reducing the deficit.

2.   (a) $\Delta GDP = \Delta G \times$ multiplier $= -\$240$ million $\times 1.5 = -\$360$ million.

(b) ΔNet taxes $= \Delta GDP \times 0.2 = -\$360$ million $\times 0.2 = -\$72$ million.

(c) $D = \Delta G - \Delta T = (-\$240 - \$72)$ million $= -\$168$ million.

(d)   The deficit has been reduced by $168 million, from $240 million to $72 million.

(e)   The *AD* curve has shifted to the left. The new intersection of *AD* and the short-run *AS* curve is $360 million below the full-employment output level where the vertical *LRAS* curve is located. The overall price level is lower and, as output has been reduced, unemployment is higher.

(f)   In the long run the economy will move back to the full-employment output level—the short-run aggregate supply curve will shift to the right. As output expands (by $360 million), net taxes will increase by $360 million times 0.2, or $72 million. The budget will be balanced.

(g) $\Delta D = \Delta G - \Delta T = \Delta G - 0.2\Delta GDP$.
$\Delta GDP = 1.5\Delta G$.
$\Delta D = \Delta G - 0.2(1.5)\Delta G = \Delta G - 0.3\Delta G = 0.7G$.
$\Delta D = \$240$ million.
$0.7\Delta G = \$240$ million, therefore $\Delta G = \$342.8571$ million.
Government spending must be cut by $342,857,143.

(h)   The Fed would need to undertake an expansionary monetary policy.

(i)   Open market purchases of bonds, a reduction in the discount rate, or a reduction in the reserve requirement.

3.   (a)
$$\begin{aligned} Y &= C + I + G \\ &= 280 + 0.8(Y - T) + 400 + 800 \\ &= 1{,}480 + 0.8(Y + 400 - 0.2Y) \\ &= 1{,}480 + 0.8Y + 320 - 0.16Y \\ 0.36Y &= 1{,}800 \\ Y &= 5{,}000 \end{aligned}$$

(b) $G - T = 800 + 400 - 0.2(5{,}000) = 200$

(c)   multiplier $= 1/(1 - MPC) = 1/(1 - 0.64) = 2.7778$
Note: A simple way to get *MPC* is to conduct the following "thought experiment." If income (*Y*) increases by 100, taxes will increase by 20 (0.2*Y*). Disposable income will increase by 80. Consumption increases by 64 (0.8*Yd*). As income changes by 100, consumption changes by 64.

(d)   The new equilibrium level of income may be calculated by changing the value of I as follows:

$$
\begin{aligned}
Y &= C + I + G \\
&= 280 + 0.8(Y - T) + 350 + 800 \\
&= 1{,}430 + 0.8(Y + 400 - 0.2Y) \\
&= 1{,}480 + 0.8Y + 320 - 0.16Y \\
0.36Y &= 1{,}750 \\
Y &= 4{,}861.11
\end{aligned}
$$

so income decreases by 138.89.

Alternatively, $\Delta Y = \Delta I \times multiplier = -50 \times 2.7778 = -138.89$.

(e) $G - T = 800 + 400 - 0.2(4{,}8611.11) = 227.78$. The deficit increases by 27.78.

(f) $DRI = \Delta D / \Delta Y = 27.78 / -138.89 = -0.20$.

(g)   GDP must decrease by \$1,250.

Thought experiment: A 100-dollar cut in spending will reduce income by 277.78. Taxes will fall by 55.56 (277.78×0.2). The deficit will be decreased by 44.44. To reduce the deficit by 200, income must decrease by 1,250.

(h)   To achieve this change in income, government spending must decrease by 450.

$\Delta Y = \Delta G \times multiplier = -1{,}250 = -450 \times 2.778$.

Check: $G = 350(800 - 450)$

$T = -400 + 0.2(3{,}750) = 350$.

(i)   When I decreases by 50, Y equals 4,861.11, so income decreases by 138.89. The deficit increases by 27.78.

We want the deficit to decrease by 27.78.

A 100-dollar cut in spending will reduce the deficit by 44.44. A 62.5 decrease in spending will achieve a 27.78 decrease in the deficit.

(j)

$$
\begin{aligned}
Y &= C + I + G \\
&= 280 + 0.8(Y - T) + 350 + 737.5 \\
&= 1{,}367.5 + 0.8(Y + 400 - 0.2Y) \\
&= 1{,}480 + 0.8Y + 320 - 0.16Y \\
0.36Y &= 1{,}687.5 \\
Y &= 4{,}687.5
\end{aligned}
$$

Income will decrease by 312.5.

Check: $G = 737.5(800 - 62.5)$

$T = -400 + 0.2(4{,}687.5) = 537.5$

$G - T = 737.5 - 537.5 = 200$.

4.   (a)   Less demand, rising inventories, cutbacks in production and employment
(b)   Personal and corporate income tax revenues will fall, as will sales tax revenues.
(c)   Welfare payments and unemployment compensation will be rising.
(d)   It will be experiencing a deficit.
(e)   Cut spending or increase taxes.
(f)   Make the situation worse.

5.   fall; 100; fall; 10; decrease; 40; fall; 70; fall; 7; decrease; 43; smaller

6.   (a)   The rate is (coupon $\times$ 100%)/face value = (\$100 $\times$ 100%)/\$1,000 = 10%.

(b)   The bond is attractive because it is paying an interest rate (10%) that is higher than the market rate (5%).

(c)   Demand for this attractive bond will increase.

(d)   Supply will decrease. Why sell such a high-yielding bond? Note the difference between the supply of this bond (a flow) versus the total number in existence at any point in time (a stock).

(e)   The price of the bond should rise to more than $1,000. In fact, if the market interest rate remains at 5% and we recall that the coupon is a fixed value, the price must increase to $2,000 to make the rate on this bond equal to the market interest rate—i.e., 100/2,000 equals 5%.

(f)   As the market rate falls (rises), the price of bonds rises (falls).

7.   The stock market crash reduced the wealth of households. As wealth decreases, consumption decreases. By increasing the money supply, the Fed decreased interest rates and stimulated planned investment. Also, by its prompt action, the Fed may have affected the animal spirits of firms, encouraging them not to scrap investment plans. A second factor was present. By reducing interest rates, the Fed increased the price of bonds—increasing the wealth of bondholders. This helped to sustain consumption. By demonstrating a commitment to bolstering the economy, the slide in stock prices may have been reduced. Although the initial changes were financial, they affected the real spending decisions of individuals within the economy and, so, production and employment.

8.   (a)   Aggregate output will increase by $15 billion ($150 billion × 0.05 × 2).

(b)   The government deficit will decrease by $1.5 billion.

(c)   Aggregate output will increase by $10.5 billion ($150 billion × 0.05 × 1.4) and the deficit will decrease $1.05 billion.

(d)   larger

(e)   higher

16 [31]

Household and Firm Behavior in the Macroeconomy: A Further Look

Chapter objectives:

1. State the reasoning behind the life-cycle hypothesis, explaining how it goes beyond Keynes's theory of consumption.
2. Distinguish between the substitution effect and the income effect. Relate these effects to the factors affecting the decision to supply labor.
3. Outline the factors that affect the decisions to consume and to supply labor.
4. Outline the implications of employment constraints on the consumption and labor-supply decisions of households.
5. Describe the factors that influence the decisions of firms regarding employment and investment in plant and equipment.
6. Discuss the role of inventories in the output decision and describe the trade-off involved in reaching the optimal level of inventories.
7. Describe the relationship between the productivity of labor and the holding of excess labor by firms.
8. State Okun's Law and list the "slippages" that make the "law" unstable.
9. Indicate how changes in each of the factors affecting the multiplier influence the size of the multiplier.

BRAIN TEASER: Consider the following table, which shows labor-force participation rates for male workers in France, Germany, and the United States.

Age	France		Germany		United States	
	1967	**2001**	**1967**	**2001**	**1967**	**2001**
20–24	85.8	52.9	86.2	72.0	85.4	82.0
25–54	95.8	94.5	96.5	93.2	95.5	91.5
60–64	63.0	15.3	77.7	29.9	76.9	55.4

As you can see, the participation rates for prime-age males (those between 25 and 54) have varied only slightly across countries and over time. However, it is equally true that men are entering the labor force later and leaving it earlier, particularly in the European countries. Why? Can you think of government policies that might cause these variations across countries?

☑ OBJECTIVE 1:
State the reasoning behind the life-cycle hypothesis, explaining how it goes beyond Keynes's theory of consumption.

Whereas Keynes argued that households base their consumption and saving decisions on current income, the life-cycle theory argues that current income is not the only determinant of consumption. Permanent income—i.e., current *and* expected future income—is important, as is wealth. The household's long-range goal is to maintain a fairly stable level of consumption over the life cycle. It accomplishes this goal by dissaving in low-income periods of the life cycle (young and old) and accumulating a "nest egg" during the prime earning years. (page 297 [609])

The more permanent a change in income is perceived to be, the more consumption/saving behavior will adjust. Temporary "blips" in income will have little effect on consumption. If it is permanent income that affects consumption, we get a conclusion that, at first glance, seems unusual. If Jill's income unexpectedly increases (she finds $100), the theory suggests that her consumption pattern will not change—she will save the money rather than spend it. (page 298 [600])

Jack and Jill, who have identical current income levels, should have identical consumption levels according to the simple Keynesian view, *ceteris paribus*. But, according to the life-cycle theory, if Jack's permanent income is higher than Jill's, Jack will spend more of his current income, perhaps even borrowing against expected future income.

▶▶▶   LEARNING TIP: Because the life-cycle hypothesis builds on Keynesian consumption theory you should review the Keynesian theory as set out in Chapter 8 (23).

▶▶▶   LEARNING TIP: Remember that your course is macroeconomics! During this chapter, it is easy to end up thinking about the consumption and labor supply decisions of individual households and firms, rather than aggregate behavior. The point of this chapter is to increase your understanding of *aggregate* consumption behavior by investigating the basis for individual decisions. For example, unexpected changes in inventories will affect our macroeconomic model on the supply side, and changes in consumption will have an impact on aggregate demand. Although you might find exceptions to each of the cases mentioned the exceptions do not prove the theory wrong. What is being described are the general relationships that apply most of the time for most households. ◀

■————— Practice —————

1.   According to the life-cycle theory, households tend to
(a)   save the highest proportion of their current during their working years.
(b)   consume more as they approach their retirement years.
(c)   consume less than they earn during their retirement years.
(d)   save the lowest proportion of their current during their working years.
ANSWER: (a) Refer to Figure 16.1 (31.1).

2.   According to the life-cycle theory, households _____ during their early working years and _____ during their retirement years.
      (a)   save; save
      (b)   save; dissave
      (c)   dissave; save
      (d)   dissave; dissave

      ANSWER: (d) Households have relatively low earnings during each of these periods, borrowing during the former period and drawing down wealth during the latter period.

3.   Permanent income is
      (a)   the total income earned during one's lifetime.
      (b)   after-tax income.
      (c)   the income left after all unavoidable bills have been paid.
      (d)   the average level of one's expected future income stream.

      ANSWER: (d) Refer to p. 298 [600] for the definition of permanent income.

4.   The _____ theory states that consumption and saving decisions are based on _____ .
      (a)   simple Keynesian; permanent income only
      (b)   simple Keynesian; current and expected future income
      (c)   life-cycle; current income only
      (d)   life-cycle; current and expected future income

      ANSWER: (d) Keynesian consumption theory singles out current income; the life-cycle theory focuses on income expected throughout the life cycle. ∎

OBJECTIVE 2:
Distinguish between the substitution effect and the income effect. Relate these effects to the factors affecting the decision to supply labor.

Several factors influence the economy's supply of labor—demographics (the birth rate, and the amount of immigration), the wage rate, prices, wealth and nonlabor income. Focusing on the wage rate, there is a trade-off between hours of work and hours of leisure. According to the *substitution effect*, if the real wage rate rises, the opportunity cost of leisure increases, and work will be substituted for leisure. However, at higher real wage rates, more income is earned and households may prefer to reduce work-time to consume leisure—this is the *income effect*. Usually, the substitution effect dominates—higher wages lead to an increase in the quantity of labor supplied. (page 299 [611])

Comment: A curious example of the power of the income effect in determining labor supply was encountered by U.S. managers in North Africa. Local workers seemed loyal and dependable when employed by locally-run businesses but, despite offering somewhat higher wages and better working conditions, turnover rates of local workers were quite high when working for U.S. firms. Even higher wages exacerbated the problem. Investigation revealed that workers worked up to a particular "acceptable" income level and would then quit to enjoy their earnings. By quadrupling wage rates, foreign firms quadrupled the turnover rate.

▶▶▶   LEARNING TIP: You may have completed a microeconomics course and come across the income effect and the substitution effect! Case, Fair and Oster cover this topic in Chapter 6 of their *Microeconomics* textbook if you'd like to review it.◀

The microeconomic model argues that consumption and labor supply decisions are made together. Accordingly, wage rates, prices, and preferences determine both consumption and the amount of labor supplied. The wage rate of importance is the *real wage rate*. (page 300 [612])

Comment: As in previous chapters, the distinction between real and nominal variables is important. Nominal wage is how many dollars you earn; real wage is how much those dollars are worth at the store. The real wage (and income) is what is significant when deciding how much to spend and how much to work.

─────■───────────────────── **Practice** ─────────────────────────

5.   There is a real wage rate decrease. The income effect will lead to a(n) _____ in the quantity of labor supplied, and the substitution effect will lead to a(n) _____ in the quantity of labor supplied.
   (a)   increase; increase
   (b)   increase; decrease
   (c)   decrease; increase
   (d)   decrease; decrease

   ANSWER: (b) Income has decreased, given the number of hours worked. Workers are poorer and, therefore, will work more hours. The opportunity cost of leisure has decreased. Workers will more readily substitute leisure for labor.

6.   There is a real wage rate increase. If the substitution effect dominates the income effect, the quantity of labor supplied will _____ and leisure will _____ .
   (a)   increase; increase
   (b)   increase; decrease
   (c)   decrease; increase
   (d)   decrease; decrease

   ANSWER: (b) Typically, the substitution effect is the stronger effect. Higher real wages typically result in more work time and less leisure.

7.   Between 1997 and 2007, the minimum wage remained at $5.15 but prices in the economy increased. If the substitution effect dominates the income effect, the quantity of labor supplied would _____ and leisure would _____ for workers earning the minimum wage.
   (a)   increase; increase
   (b)   increase; decrease
   (c)   decrease; increase
   (d)   decrease; decrease

   ANSWER: (c) The real wage rate decreased over time. We would expect workers to have taken more leisure time, if the substitution effect dominated the income effect. ■

✓ OBJECTIVE 3:
Outline the factors that affect the decisions to consume and to supply labor.

The decision to consume and the decision to work are related. Other factors that influence household consumption and labor supply decisions are:

(a)   Current and expected future real wage rates
(b)   Initial value of wealth
(c)   Current and expected nonlabor income
(d)   Interest rates
(e)   Current and expected tax rates and transfer payments (page 303 [615])

Greater wealth and nonlabor income discourage labor supply and increase consumption. The same holds true for higher tax rates (assuming that the substitution effect dominates) and more generous transfer payments. A higher interest rate will also discourage current consumption by rewarding saving. (page 300 [612])

> ▶▶▶   LEARNING TIP: Note that a change in wealth or nonlabor income has an income effect on labor supply but that the substitution effect is absent. ◀

When the interest rate rises, the substitution effect discourages consumption—the opportunity cost of spending a dollar (i.e., saving it and earning interest) is higher. If the household owns positive wealth, a higher interest rate translates into higher income—the income effect operates to stimulate consumption. If the household is in debt, a higher interest rate makes it poorer—the income effect operates to depress consumption. Generally, the substitution effect dominates the income effect—higher interest rates reduce consumption. (page 301 [613])

Tax rates and transfer payments affect consumption and the labor-supply decision. To increase labor supply, tax rates and transfers should be reduced, assuming that the substitution effect is dominant. Lower tax rates, which increase disposable income, will increase consumption and stimulate labor supply, while lower transfers will reduce consumption and stimulate labor supply. (page 301 [613])

> **Comment:**   Analysis using income and substitution effects is daunting at the beginning but this method of looking at the household's decision-making process provides rich results—stick with it!

> **Comment:**   Both income and substitution effects are present any time that a wage change occurs, although usually the substitution effect will dominate. Note, too, that income and substitution effects are not limited to influencing only labor supply through wage rates—consumption and saving are also affected. Also, income and substitution effects are felt when there are changes in the interest rate or tax rates.

────■──────────────────────── **Practice** ────────────────────

8.   Complete the following table. Let "I" represent "increase" and "D" represent "decrease". Assume the substitution effect dominates the income effect.

Factor	Consumption	Labor Supply
Current real wage rates increase		
Wealth increases		
Current (or expected) nonlabor income increases		
Current (or expected future) income tax rates increase		
Current (or expected future) transfer payments increase		

ANSWER: Refer to the following table.

Factor	Consumption	Labor Supply
Current real wage rates increase	I	I
Wealth increases	I	D
Current (or expected) nonlabor income increases	I	D
Current (or expected future) income tax rates increase	D	D
Current (or expected future) transfer payments increase	I	D

9.   A household's wealth increases. *Ceteris paribus*, the household will _____ current consumption and _____ future consumption.
      (a)   increase; increase
      (b)   increase; decrease
      (c)   decrease; increase
      (d)   decrease; decrease

      ANSWER: (a) Greater wealth encourages households to spend more in both time periods.

10.   Households have positive wealth. According to the income effect, an increase in the interest rate will _____ nonlabor income and will _____ current consumption.
      (a)   increase; increase
      (b)   increase; decrease
      (c)   decrease; increase
      (d)   decrease; decrease

      ANSWER: (a) Wealth generates additional interest income and, as income increases, consumption increases.

11.   The government cuts welfare benefits. As a result, consumption will _____ and labor supply will _____ .
      (a)   increase; increase
      (b)   increase; decrease
      (c)   decrease; increase
      (d)   decrease; decrease

      ANSWER: (c) Refer to p. 301 [613] for a discussion of this topic.

12.   Increased tax rates reduce after-tax income. If the tax rate increases and the change is thought to be permanent, the effect on current consumption will be _____ . The effect on labor supply will be _____ than if the tax rate increase is thought to be temporary.
      (a)   greater; greater
      (b)   greater; smaller
      (c)   smaller; greater
      (d)   smaller; smaller

      ANSWER: (a) A temporary change in circumstances can be ridden out without changing behavior very much. In the face of a permanent change, behavior will be affected more.

13.   During the late 1990s, household wealth increased substantially through higher stock market prices. We would predict that an interest rate _____ designed to reduce consumption would be _____ effective than if household wealth were low.

(a)   increase; more
(b)   increase; less
(c)   decrease; more
(d)   decrease; less

ANSWER: (b) The greater the wealth held by the household sector, the more the income effect of an interest rate hike (increase consumption) would offset the substitution effect (decrease consumption). ∎

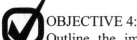

OBJECTIVE 4:
Outline the implications of employment constraints on the consumption and labor-supply decisions of households.

If the economy is fully employed, the supply of labor is not constrained—workers seeking jobs will find them. In an economy suffering from unemployment, workers are restricted in the hours they actually work—they may be on short-time or may have been laid off. The number of hours actually worked depends less on the number of hours that households could supply and more on how many hours they can get. When the number of hours worked is not a variable workers control, it is reasonable to argue that, if current wage income increases, so will current consumption. This was the original Keynesian position. The Keynesian theory is thought to apply well during periods of unemployment. (page 302 [614])

ECONOMICS IN PRACTICE: On page 305 [617], the textbook considers the role of the housing market in the macroeconomy. Fannie Mae (Federal National Mortgage Association) and Freddie Mac (Federal Home Loan Mortgage Corporation) are two big private corporations that are listed on the New York Stock Exchange. They facilitate home mortgages by buying mortgages from savings and loans and banks and then issuing guaranteed, mortgage-backed securities to investors. In the summer of 2008, there were concerns about foreclosures, slumping housing prices and the solvency of Fannie Mae and Freddie Mac. In July 2008, Congress passed "mortgage rescue" legislation that would support the housing market. First, what happened to that legislation? Fannie and Freddie, which own or guarantee over half of the $12 trillion mortgage market, were said to be "too big to fail." Another element of the legislation allowed borrowers to renegotiate loans at more attractive terms (i.e., less attractive terms for lenders), in order to prevent foreclosures. Do you think that the government should have a role in supporting (or even bailing out) private firms or individuals who have entered into contracts that have gone sour?

ANSWER: At the time of writing, the proposed legislation is awaiting the President's signature but is likely to become law. This issue is very much related to the question of whether to control "speculative bubbles" that was discussed in Chapter 15 (30)—regulation of markets is an age-old debate in economics, going back as far as Adam Smith. The failure (or threat of failure) of an important institution, such as Fannie Mae, or sector, such as the housing market, can have significant adverse ripple effects on the rest of the economy. The issue may best be approached by considering the evolution of the institutions concerned. When, for instance, Fannie was a small player, its failure would have had little national impact. With growth, failure becomes a national concern.

—■————————————————————————— **Practice** —————————————————————

Use the following information for the next two questions. The Smith household needs to spend $1,000 a month to maintain an adequate standard of living, but it is severely constrained (by part-time employment) to spending only $600. Expected future income is not an important factor—changes in current income will determine current consumption.

14.   The number of hours that the Smiths would work if they could is the
        (a)   constrained supply of labor.
        (b)   unconstrained supply of labor.
        (c)   actual supply of labor.
        (d)   planned supply of labor.
        ANSWER: (b)   Refer to p. 302 [614] for the definition of the unconstrained labor supply.

15.   The Smiths are limited to a lesser level of employment than they would have chosen. Each of the following will occur EXCEPT that the Smiths'
        (a)   saving will decrease.
        (b)   savings will decrease.
        (c)   income will decrease.
        (d)   will work more hours.
        ANSWER: (b)   As income is reduced, the Smiths will save less, but they may not need to draw
                      down their previously accumulated savings. ■

OBJECTIVE 5:
Describe the factors that influence the decisions of firms regarding employment and investment
        in plant and equipment.

Firms must make decisions about their usage of capital and labor. When it buys new plant and equipment, the firm makes a commitment that may affect its production capacity for many years. The firm must choose whether to increase output by adopting a relatively capital-intensive or labor-intensive method of production. The relative costs of the inputs are clearly an important factor in the choice of technology. (page 306 [618])

Expectations about sales and profits also play a major role in investment choices. Keynes named the entrepreneur's feelings about the firm's prospects "animal spirits." Because expectations are subject to much uncertainty, rapid changes in investment strategy are likely, making investment a particularly volatile component of GDP. The *accelerator effect* is the name given to the tendency to postpone investment during slumps and to expand it rapidly during upturns. As a buffer against fluctuations in production (caused by fluctuations in sales), firms may hold excess labor and/or capital. Sharp shifts in the levels of capital stock and employment cause adjustment costs—in some cases, it may be cheaper to maintain excess inputs. (page 306 [618])

To summarize, factors that influence the investment and employment decisions of firms are:

(a)   Wage rate and cost of capital (including the interest rate)
(b)   Firms' expectations about the future
(c)   Amount of excess labor and excess capital on hand (page 310 [622])

▶▶▶ LEARNING TIP: Underpinning the discussion of the behavior of the firm is the assumption of profit maximization. If you've done the microeconomic course, review your notes. If you've never heard of profit maximization, a very brief outline is given here.

The goal of firms is assumed to be profit maximization. To achieve this goal, firms make decisions at the margin. Will this additional unit of output draw in more revenue than it costs to produce? If not, it shouldn't be produced. Will this extra unit of an input (a machine or worker) pay its way? If not, it shouldn't be hired. By hiring inputs until the final unit of each input just breaks even, and by producing until the final unit of output just pays its way, the firm will maximize profits.

▶▶▶ LEARNING TIP: Think of the two types of investment as different kinds of activities. Firms often use inventory investment in response to short-term fluctuations in demand, as a buffer between production and sales, and to avoid adjustment costs. This may occur almost "accidentally," i.e., without conscious planning. Investment in plant and equipment is different in nature, representing reflections on the long-term trends in the firm's operation.◀

━━━■━━━━━━━━━━━━━━━━━━━ **Practice** ━━━━━━━━━━━━━━━━━━━━━

16. The firm can add to its capital stock by
   (a) purchasing additional raw materials.
   (b) reducing its inventory levels.
   (c) investing in plant and equipment.
   (d) hiring additional labor capacity.

   ANSWER: (c) Investment is the addition to the capital stock. The capital stock can be increased by buying more plant and equipment or by accumulating additional inventory.

17. The accelerator effect argues that, as aggregate output expands, firms _____ investment. This, in turn, _____ the rate of growth of aggregate output.
   (a) increase; increases
   (b) increase; decreases
   (c) decrease; increases
   (d) decrease; decreases

   ANSWER: (a) With an expanding economy, firms become more optimistic about future profit opportunities and invest more vigorously. This increased spending further adds to the expansion.

18. Technology X uses 10 units of capital and 20 units of labor. If Technology Y is relatively more capital-intensive, it might use
   (a) 5 units of capital and 5 units of labor.
   (b) 5 units of capital and 10 units of labor.
   (c) 20 units of capital and 40 units of labor.
   (d) 40 units of capital and 100 units of labor.

   ANSWER: (a) A method of production is relatively more capital-intensive the greater the ratio of capital to labor. Options (b) and (c) have the same level of capital intensity as Technology X (1:2). Option (d) is less capital-intensive.

19.   Technology *Z* is labor-intensive. An expansion in output is likely to _____ the demand for labor and _____ the demand for capital.
       (a)   increase; increase
       (b)   increase; decrease
       (c)   decrease; increase
       (d)   decrease; decrease

       ANSWER: (a) The demand for additional machines for workers should increase, albeit only modestly. ∎

OBJECTIVE 6:
Discuss the role of inventories in the output decision and describe the trade-off involved in reaching the optimal level of inventories.

Inventory is unsold production. Inventory investment occurs when production exceeds sales. Holding inventories involves both a cost and a benefit for the firm. Too low an inventory might mean lost sales, but too high an inventory involves storage costs and the tying up of funds that could be earning interest. The *optimal level of inventories* is at the point of balance between these two concerns. Sales tend to be more variable than production, and inventories can be used to smooth out the mismatch between the two, resulting in lower adjustment costs. (page 309 [621])

       A clear example of the smoothing function of inventories can be seen in fireworks manufacturing. Typically, sales have one peak—just before the Fourth of July—but production may occur for many months before. Inventories accumulate to prevent a rush of production at the last moment. Inventories, though, represent payments to inputs that have already been made, and there are risks and storage costs. These may be high in the case of fireworks.

       Comment: In a way, saving operates for the household in the same way that inventories operate for the firm. Inventories allow the firm to smooth its production in the face of fluctuating sales; saving (and dissaving) permits the household to smooth consumption and maintain a stable standard of living in the face of fluctuating income.

——————————————————————————— **Practice** ———————————————————————————

20.   Stock of inventories (end of period) equals stock of inventories (beginning of period)
       (a)   plus production plus sales.
       (b)   plus production minus sales.
       (c)   minus production plus sales.
       (d)   minus production minus sales.

       ANSWER: (b) Refer to p. 309 [621] for the definition of inventories.

21.   If the sales of the Caledonian Curling Stone Company are less than expected, inventories will be
       (a)   higher than expected and future production will increase.
       (b)   higher than expected and future production will decrease.
       (c)   lower than expected and future production will increase.
       (d)   lower than expected and future production will decrease.

       ANSWER: (b) Unsold production will be greater than expected. This is a signal that the firm's production level is too high.

22.   Plant-and-equipment investment is _____ volatile than housing investment and _____ volatile than inventory investment.

(a)   more; more
(b)   more; less
(c)   less; more
(d)   less; less

ANSWER: (d) While volatile, plant-and-equipment investment is the most stable of the three types of investment.

23.   The desired, or optimal, level of inventories is the level at which the extra cost in lost sales from _____ inventories by a small amount is just equal to the extra gain (in interest revenue and _____ storage costs).

(a)   increasing; increased
(b)   increasing; decreased
(c)   decreasing; increased
(d)   decreasing; decreased

ANSWER: (d) Refer to the discussion on p. 309 [621]. ∎

OBJECTIVE 7:
Describe the relationship between the productivity of labor and the holding of excess labor by firms.

In the short term, labor productivity—total output divided by the number of hours worked—may be a misleading guide to the economy's performance because business cycles affect the measurement. Although workers are still capable of producing just as much as before, productivity falls in an economic slowdown because firms tend to hold excess labor. Output fluctuates much more than employment over the business cycle. Productivity also follows the cycle. In the long run, productivity measures, such as GDP per capita, are less misleading. (page 312 [624])

———■——————————————— **Practice** ———————————————————

24.   Which of the following statements is true?

(a)   Employment fluctuates more than output over the business cycle, causing high productivity during periods of high output and low productivity during periods of low output.

(b)   Employment fluctuates more than output over the business cycle, causing high productivity during periods of low output and low productivity during periods of high output.

(c)   Employment fluctuates less than output over the business cycle, causing high productivity during periods of high output and low productivity during periods of low output.

(d)   Employment fluctuates less than output over the business cycle, causing high productivity during periods of low output and low productivity during periods of high output.

ANSWER: (c) By holding onto excess labor during downturns and by having existing employees work more during upswings, employment remains fairly stable. When output is high, therefore, productivity is high. ∎

✓ OBJECTIVE 8:
State Okun's Law and list the "slippages" that make the "law" unstable.

Simple macroeconomic relationships are seldom reliable—the Phillips Curve is one example. *Okun's Law*—which attempts to link output and the unemployment rate in a stable relationship—is another. Okun's Law is flawed because output depends on more than just the total number of workers who are employed. (page 313 [625])

Three "slippages," all of which vary over the course of the business cycle, occur between a change in output and a change in the unemployment rate. First, as output increases, firms utilize their excess capacity and/or offer overtime rather than increase their labor force. Second, some persons hold more than one job—in general, the number of jobs exceeds the number of employed workers. New jobs (and expanded production) may be filled by currently employed workers—the unemployment rate will not be affected. Finally, with higher production, discouraged workers may be attracted back into the ranks of the officially unemployed, actively seeking work but swelling the unemployment rate.

■———————————— **Practice** ————————————

25.   Okun's Law states that the unemployment rate
       (a)   increases by three percentage points for every 1% increase in GDP.
       (b)   increases by one percentage point for every 3% increase in GDP.
       (c)   decreases by three percentage points for every 1% increase in GDP.
       (d)   decreases by one percentage point for every 3% increase in GDP.

       ANSWER: (d) As production increases, the unemployment rate decreases. Refer to p. 313 [625].

26.   When production increases, discouraged workers may _____ the ranks of the officially unemployed. This will _____ the unemployment rate.
       (a)   enter; increase
       (b)   enter; decrease
       (c)   leave; increase
       (d)   leave; decrease

       ANSWER: (a) Higher production offers the prospect of jobs where none were before.

27.   As output increases by 1%, the number of jobs tends to increase by less than 1%. In part, this is because
       (a)   firms expand output by expanding the number of hours worked by workers who are already on the payroll.
       (b)   discouraged workers enter the labor force.
       (c)   discouraged workers leave the labor force.
       (d)   firms reduce the quantity of excess capital.

       ANSWER: (a) Refer to p. 313 [625]. The presence or absence of discouraged workers (Options (b) and (c)) has no effect on the number of jobs created. ■

OBJECTIVE 9:
Indicate how changes in each of the factors affecting the multiplier influence the size of the multiplier.

The real-world multiplier is smaller (1.4) and less immediate than that suggested by the marginal propensity to consume. Various factors dampen the effect of an increase in, for example, government spending. Automatic stabilizers offset pressures for change. The interest rate may rise, crowding out investment and consumption. Prices, instead of output, may rise, especially if the economy is close to full employment. If output is low initially, firms may be holding excess labor and capital, or a large stock of inventories, which could be used to meet higher demand without much of a rise in employment or investment. The consumption response of households may be lukewarm if the new income is considered temporary, and businesses may not be tempted to launch new investment programs. Finally, if a portion of the extra income "leaks" overseas to buy imports, domestic production will not feel the benefit. (page 314 [626])

—————————————————————— Practice ——————————————————————

28.   _____ is the policy with the greatest multiplier.
    (a)   A permanent increase in government spending when inventory levels are high
    (b)   A permanent increase in government spending when inventory levels are low
    (c)   A temporary increase in government spending when inventory levels are high
    (d)   A temporary increase in government spending when inventory levels are low

    ANSWER: (b) Permanent changes have a greater effect on people's behavior than temporary changes. When inventory levels are low, firms must increase production more vigorously to meet expansions in demand.

29.   Automatic stabilizers _____ the multiplier; the more interest-sensitive planned investment, the _____ the multiplier.
    (a)   increase; larger
    (b)   increase; smaller
    (c)   decrease; larger
    (d)   decrease; smaller

    ANSWER: (d) For the full discussion on this point, refer to p. 314 [626]. ■

BRAIN TEASER SOLUTION: One reason European men may delay entering into the labor force is the high rate of unemployment in this age group and the high educational subsidies available, both of which reduce incentives for students to work while in school. In addition, social programs (health care, for instance) tend to be more generous in Europe—less of a requirement to earn a living. Older European men may choose early retirement—European pension schemes are comparatively generous, while progressive taxes penalize those who continue to work.

PRACTICE TEST

I.   MULTIPLE-CHOICE QUESTIONS

Select the option that provides the single best answer.

_____   1.   According to the life-cycle theory, Jill will save
         (a)   when she is young.
         (b)   when she is in her prime earning years.
         (c)   when she is old.
         (d)   both when she is young and when she is old.

_____   2.   According to the microeconomic model, which of the following certainly will make labor
              supply increase?
         (a)   A decrease in nonlabor income
         (b)   An increase in wealth
         (c)   An increase in tax rates
         (d)   An increase in the nominal wage rate

_____   3.   Three major and interlinked economic decisions of households are
         (a)   how much to work, how much to invest, and how much to save.
         (b)   how much to consume, how much to invest, and how much to work.
         (c)   how much to work, how much to consume, and how much to save.
         (d)   how much to produce, how much to invest, and how much to borrow.

_____   4.   According to the permanent income view, the household's estimate of its permanent
              income will be affected by all of the following EXCEPT
         (a)   a tax hike viewed as temporary.
         (b)   an annual merit raise.
         (c)   institutional changes, for example in the social security system.
         (d)   a tax hike viewed as permanent.

_____   5.   Capacity constraints imply all of the following EXCEPT that
         (a)   firms may be unable to meet unexpected increases in demand.
         (b)   the economy may be unable to raise production levels if it is at full
                employment.
         (c)   increasing output may be increasingly costly.
         (d)   increasing output is possible without increasing prices.

_____   6.   The nominal wage increases and the price level remains constant. The income effect tells
              us that
         (a)   workers' opportunity cost of each hour of leisure has increased.
         (b)   workers' opportunity cost of each hour of leisure has decreased.
         (c)   workers' opportunity cost of each hour of leisure has remained constant.
         (d)   workers can afford to work fewer hours.

_____ 7.   An increase in nonlabor income (such as transfer payments) will _____ consumption and _____ the labor supply.
(a)   increase; increase
(b)   increase; decrease
(c)   decrease; increase
(d)   decrease; decrease

_____ 8.   The labor-force participation rate for prime-age males is _____ , and is _____ than that of prime-age females.
(a)   rising; greater
(b)   rising; smaller
(c)   falling; greater
(d)   falling; smaller

_____ 9.   During an economic expansion, we would expect _____ to expand most rapidly.
(a)   services; such as those of a dentist
(b)   services; such as those of a manicurist
(c)   consumer durables; such as groceries
(d)   consumer durables; such as CD players

_____ 10.   Holding inventory allows the firm to
(a)   reduce storage costs.
(b)   lower its productive capacity.
(c)   increase its ability to meet unexpected demand.
(d)   smooth its sales pattern.

_____ 11.   An increase in expected future sales will have a _____ effect on investment, and an increase in the cost of labor will have a _____ effect.
(a)   positive; positive
(b)   positive; negative
(c)   negative; positive
(d)   negative; negative

_____ 12.   An increase in expected future sales will have a _____ effect on employment, and an increase in the cost of labor will have a _____ effect.
(a)   positive; positive
(b)   positive; negative
(c)   negative; positive
(d)   negative; negative

_____ 13.   The _____ the expected decline in sales and the _____ the adjustment cost, the greater the amount of excess labor that will be held.
(a)   shorter; smaller
(b)   shorter; greater
(c)   longer; greater
(d)   longer; smaller

_____   14.   Investment depends on each of the following EXCEPT
　　　　　(a)   expected future sales.
　　　　　(b)   the accelerator effect.
　　　　　(c)   the cost of capital.
　　　　　(d)   the cost of labor.

_____   15.   According to the life-cycle theory, the main determinants of consumption include all of the following EXCEPT
　　　　　(a)   current disposable income.
　　　　　(b)   expected future income.
　　　　　(c)   nominal wages.
　　　　　(d)   wealth.

_____   16.   The "discouraged worker" effect is most noticeable among _____ during a recession
　　　　　(a)   prime-age males
　　　　　(b)   prime-age females
　　　　　(c)   non-prime-age workers
　　　　　(d)   males aged between 25 and 54

_____   17.   Miss Faversham has a sudden increase in wealth. The substitution effect will _____ her consumption and _____ her labor supply.
　　　　　(a)   increase; increase
　　　　　(b)   increase; have no impact on
　　　　　(c)   have no impact on; increase
　　　　　(d)   have no impact on; have no impact on

Use the following diagram to answer the next two questions. "Income" refers to disposable (after-tax) income.

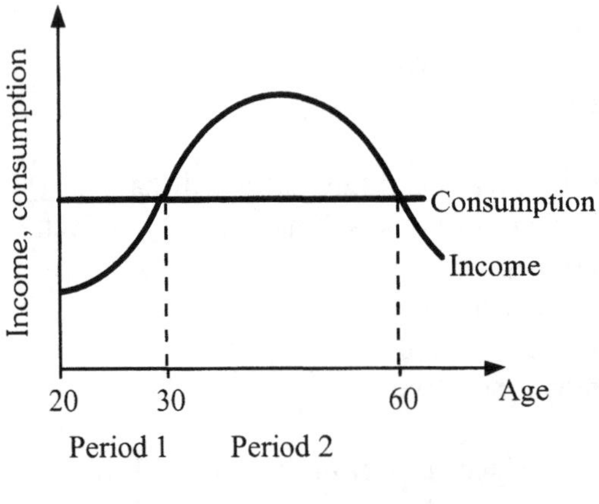

_____   18.   In the preceding diagram, consumption is relatively _____ in Period 1, and the household is _____ .
　　　　　(a)   high; saving
　　　　　(b)   high; borrowing
　　　　　(c)   low; saving
　　　　　(d)   low; borrowing

_____ 19.   In the preceding diagram, consumption _____ income in Period 2, and saving is _____ .
   (a)   exceeds; positive
   (b)   exceeds; negative
   (c)   is less than; positive
   (d)   is less than; negative

_____ 20.   The actual multiplier is smaller than the theoretical multiplier because of all of the following reasons EXCEPT that, as spending increases,
   (a)   the interest rate rises and reduces investment spending.
   (b)   producers may increase prices instead of output.
   (c)   transfer payments tend to increase.
   (d)   excess labor may be pressed into service, with no change in employment.

II.   APPLICATION QUESTIONS

1.   As the "baby boomers" age and retire, what will happen to the national saving rate, according to the life-cycle model?

2.   Suppose that there is an increase in the hourly cost of child care for Jan's toddler, Teddy. How might this affect Jan's labor-supply decision? What are the income and substitution effects? How do they apply to Jan?

3.   Forty-year-old Simon Simple is a life-long resident of the state of South Virginia—he has frequently observed that nothing could induce him to leave his home state. Simon is a highly skilled lathe operator employed in the furniture industry. He has some wealth and no debts. Indicate how each of the following circumstances will affect Simon's current consumption and saving.
   (a)   Simon is told that a long-lost relative has left him a large bequest. The bequest, however, is to be kept in a trust and Simon will not be able to withdraw funds from it until he is 50 years old.
   (b)   Simon's doctor tells him that Simon has an amazingly healthy constitution and should easily expect to live until he is in his nineties. This prediction, which adds an additional 20 years to Simon's expected life span, does not influence Simon's plan to retire at age 60 in order to perfect his fishing skills.
   (c)   Simon, who is a taxpayer, reads a reliable newspaper report that South Virginia's state government's budget deficit is much worse than had previously been thought. A substantial tax increase next year and in subsequent years now seems inevitable.
   (d)   Because of foreign competition, which is thought likely to become increasingly intense in future years, Simon's employer has announced that, after the end of this year, no overtime work will be allowed and that, indeed, workers must anticipate reduced work weeks.

4.   Arbez has the following consumption function: $C = 400 + 0.8Y$.
   (a)   What is the marginal propensity to consume in Arbez? _____
   (b)   Calculate consumption when income is:
       1,000 _____   2,000 _____   3,000 _____
   (c)   At which income level will saving be:
       zero _____   positive _____   negative _____
   (d)   When consumption is greater than current income, suggest two ways that a household might finance its consumption.

5.   Arboc and Arbez are neighboring nations. In each of the following cases, in which economy would we expect to see higher levels of inventory investment? Why?
   (a)   Aggregate demand in Arbez is very stable, but aggregate demand in Arboc is highly variable and unpredictable.
   (b)   The interest rate is historically lower in Arboc than in Arbez.
   (c)   Arboc has begun to move away from manufacturing toward an economy that is more oriented to production of services. Arbez remains based in manufacturing.

6.   Jack and Jill both earn $30,000 this year. Jack expects his income to increase by $2,000 every year over the next five years. Jill expects her income to decrease by $2,000 every year over the same period. Who should have the higher level of consumption? Why?

7.   Bill and Ben have identical current incomes.
   (a)   Bill has more wealth than Ben. Who should have the higher level of consumption? _____ . Who will tend to work more? _____ .
   (b)   Bill receives dividend payments, but Ben doesn't. Who will have the higher level of consumption? _____ . Who will tend to work more? _____ .
   (c)   Personal income tax rates are cut in the state where Bill lives, but not in the state where Ben lives. Who should have the higher level of consumption? _____ . Who will tend to work more? _____ .
   (d)   As a new member of a credit union, Bill is eligible for a lower interest rate on loans. Who should have the higher level of consumption? _____ .
   (e)   The President pledges "no new taxes." Bill believes him; Ben doesn't. Who should have the higher level of consumption? _____ Who will tend to work more? _____ .
   (f)   Bill spends more of his current income than Ben does (but not all of it). Now interest rates increase. Who is more likely to increase his savings? _____ .
   (g)   Bill and Ben return to school. Bill attends a business school, while Ben embarks on a degree in theology. Who should have the higher consumption level today? _____ .

8.   Here are two production functions for the Caledonian Curling Stones Company.

Output	Mix 1		Mix 2	
	K	L	K	L
11	6	1	2	7
12	7	3	3	10
13	9	5	4	14
14	12	7	5	20
15	15	9	6	26
16	21	11	7	32

   (a)   The firm wishes to produce 14 units of output. Capital (K) costs $4/unit and the labor ($L$) costs $2/unit. Which input mix will be chosen?
   (b)   At this output level, will the chosen input mix still be the cheaper method if the input prices change to $2 and $4, respectively?
   (c)   As the rental cost of capital falls from $4 to $2, investment _____ from _____ units to _____ units, and there is a _____ (positive/ negative) effect on employment.

9.   In each of the following cases, predict what will happen to consumption, labor supply, planned investment, the overall price level, output, and employment.

    (a)   While the Arbocali economy is operating at full employment, the Arbocali central bank (Arbobank) increases the discount rate.

    (b)   The Arbezani economy is in a deep recession. The government hikes government spending.

    (c)   The Noilian economy is in a deep recession. The government increases welfare benefits.

10.   In each of the following cases, determine whether the given factor will make the size of the Arbezani government spending multiplier higher or lower than would otherwise be the case. Assume an expansionary fiscal policy.

    (a)   Due to the Arboc-Arbez Free Trade Agreement, trade is liberalized and Arbez buys more Arbocali imports.

    (b)   ArbeFed, the central bank, is committed to a policy of maintaining the interest rate at its current level.

    (c)   The Arbezani economy is in a recession (as opposed to close to full employment).

    (d)   Arbezani firms have low inventory levels.

    (e)   The government's action is viewed as temporary.

    (f)   Costs of inventory storage have decreased.

    (g)   Households become less sensitive to interest rate changes because of a high burden of credit card debt.

PRACTICE TEST SOLUTIONS

I.   Solutions to Multiple-Choice Questions

1.   (b)   During the prime earning years, Jill's earnings will be more than her consumption. Refer to p. 298 [610].

2.   (a)   As workers' nonlabor income decreases, they will wish to work more. Note that an increase in tax rates has an ambiguous result—the income effect will stimulate the supply of labor, but the substitution effect will dampen it.

3.   (c)   Note that, when deciding how much of current income will be consumed, the household is simultaneously determining how much will be saved.

4.   (a)   A temporary change will have no permanent effect. Refer to p. 298 [600].

5.   (d)   At the macroeconomic level, consider the shape of the short-run aggregate supply curve in answering this question.

6.   (a)   If the nominal wage increases with no change in the price level, the real wage has increased. An increase in the real wage will increase labor income. As income increases, the income effect tells us, the demand for leisure time will increase, reducing work time. The substitution effect refers to the opportunity cost of the leisure/labor decision—in this case, the opportunity cost increased.

7.   (b)   As household wealth increases, consumption increases. The desire to work will decrease. Note that there is no substitution effect in this case.

8.   (c)   Refer to Figure 16.4 (31.4) on p. 306 [618]. Note that the female participation rate has increased very little since 1990.

9.   (d)   Groceries are nondurables. Consumer durables, the purchases of which may be postponed during an economic slowdown, are purchased more vigorously during an economic expansion.

10.   (c)   The firm does not have to match production to sales as closely when inventory is present. Production levels can be smoother, therefore.

11.   (a)   If sales are expected to increase, the firm will wish to expand production capacity. As labor costs rise, machinery becomes relatively less expensive (and more attractive).

12.   (b)   If sales are expected to increase, the firm will wish to expand its productive capacity, including its labor force. The more expensive workers are, the fewer the firm will wish to employ.

13.   (b)   If a decline in sales is expected to last a long time, the relative cost involved in laying off workers becomes less. The smaller the cost of hiring and firing workers, the less excess labor will be held.

14.   (b)   The accelerator effect is the consequence, not the cause, of investment.

15.   (c)   The wage is an important part of income, but the nominal wage is less of a consideration than the real wage and is, in any case, included in the more general term "income."

16.   (c)   Nonprime-age workers tend to be more "marginal" members of the labor force. Refer to Figure 16.4 (31.4).

17.   (d)   Changes in nonlabor income and wealth have only income effects. The opportunity cost of leisure (the substitution effect) remains untouched.

18.   (b)   Consumption exceeds current income, therefore this household must be borrowing.

19.   (c)   In Period 2, consumption is less than income; the remaining income is saved.

20.   (c)   Transfers, such as welfare payments, decrease as workers leave the unemployment rolls and are hired.

II.   *Solutions to Application Questions*

1.   Most "baby boomers" are presently in their prime earning years. They should be saving for retirement. Current consumption, therefore, should be low relative to current income and the national saving rate should be comparatively high. As more baby boomers begin to retire, their income will decrease more sharply than their consumption levels—they will be dissaving—and the national saving rate will decrease.

2.   The increase in child-care costs will have an income effect and a substitution effect for Jan. In effect, Jan's hourly wage rate has decreased. The substitution effect indicates that the opportunity cost of not working (staying home and caring for Teddy) has decreased—Jan may supply less labor. The income effect goes in the opposite direction. The increase in the cost of child care (and the effective wage decrease) has made Jan poorer. The poorer one is, the greater the need to work. Jan, therefore, is driven to supply more labor. Whether Jan works longer hours or chooses to stay home more will depend on the relative strengths of the two effects.

3.   (a)   Consumption will increase (saving will decrease). Although he cannot access the funds, Simon's permanent income has increased.

        (b)   Consumption will decrease (saving will increase). Simon must eke out his lifetime earnings over a longer period.

        (c)   Consumption will decrease (saving will increase). Simon's expectation is that his after-tax income will be decreased in future years. This news reduces his lifetime income.

        (d)   Consumption will decrease (saving will increase). Simon's expectation is that his income will be decreased in future years. This news reduces his lifetime income.

4.   (a)   0.8. *MPC* is the rate at which consumption changes as income changes. If income increases by 1,000, consumption will change by 800.

        (b)   Refer to the following table.

Income	Consumption
0	400
1,000	1,200
2,000	2,000
3,000	2,800

        (c)   2,000; 3,000; 1,000. Saving = income – consumption

        (d)   The household could borrow, reduce accumulated savings, or receive wealth transfers (from parents, for example).

5.   (a)   Arboc will hold higher stocks of inventories because the danger of inadequate stock is greater there.

        (b)   Arboc. The interest rate is a major cost of holding inventories.

        (c)   Arbez. It is impossible to hold inventories of services.

6.   Jack should have the higher level of consumption will be higher. It will be higher because his expected future income is greater. Jill will be saving more today, in anticipation of bad times to come.

7.   (a)   Bill; Ben. Bill will be able to finance more consumption out of his wealth. Ben is poorer. The income effect (which discourages work) will be less strong for Ben.

        (b)   Bill; Ben. Dividend payments are nonlabor income. The higher one's income, the less one tends to work.

        (c)   Bill; Bill. Bill's after-tax income has increased; Ben's has not. With more income, Bill will consume more. Assuming that the substitution effect dominates, Bill will work extra hours. Ben has no incentive to work extra hours because his tax rate did not change.

        (d)   Bill. The cost of borrowing has decreased for Bill.

(e)   Bill will have the higher level of consumption. Bill's expectations about his future real income are more optimistic than Ben's. Ben is likely to work more now.

(f)   Bill is more likely to increase savings. The substitution effect is similar for both, but the income effect of the increased interest rate will be greater for Ben. Higher future income will encourage Ben to indulge in greater current consumption. Because the income effect is smaller for Bill, his savings are more likely to increase.

(g)   The business school graduate (Bill) should expect a higher future income stream, and so his current consumption level should be higher than that of the theology student (Ben).

8.   (a)   Mix 2 will be chosen; Mix 2 will cost $60 [(5 × $4) + (20 × $2)] instead of Mix 1's $62 [(12 × $4) + (7 × $2)].

         (b)   Mix 1 will have a total cost of $52 [(12 × $2) + (7 × $4)], whereas Mix 2 will have a total cost of $90 [(5 × $2) + (20 × $4)].

         (c)   As the rental cost of capital falls from $4 to $2, investment increases from 5 units to 12 units, and there is a negative effect on employment (as the firm substitutes away from the relatively expensive input).

9.   (a)   This is a contractionary monetary policy. The interest rate will increase, resulting in lower investment. The effect on consumption is ambiguous—if the income effect dominates, consumption will increase; if the substitution effect dominates, consumption will decrease. The effect on labor supply is similarly ambiguous. As aggregate demand decreases, the overall price level and output will decrease although, because we are operating on the steep part of the Arbocali aggregate supply curve, price will decrease more significantly than output. Employment will decrease.

         (b)   The government spending increase will shift the aggregate demand curve to the right. Because we are operating on the relatively flat portion of the *AS* curve, aggregate output and employment will increase substantially while the overall price level will increase less vigorously. If firms are holding excess labor, the expansion in employment will be less marked. The interest rate will increase, reducing (crowding out) planned investment. The effect on consumption is ambiguous—if the income effect dominates, consumption will increase; if the substitution effect dominates, consumption will decrease.

         (c)   This is an expansionary fiscal policy. Consumption will increase and the labor supply will decrease. The increase in aggregate demand will increase the price level (a little, because we are on the relatively flat portion of the *AS* curve) and increase output (a lot). Employment should increase, unless firms already have excess labor. Higher output levels should prompt greater investment although this increase is likely to be partly offset by the operation of the crowding out effect.

10.   (a)   The multiplier will be lower. A greater portion of any injection of spending power by the government will be removed from the Arbezani economy.

         (b)   The multiplier will be higher. There will be no crowding out effect to offset the government spending change.

         (c)   The multiplier will be higher during a recession. Close to full employment, further expansion is likely to be cramped by supply bottlenecks, i.e., close to full employment the economy is operating on the steep portion of the *AS* curve.

         (d)   The multiplier will be higher. If inventories are high, there is less need to hire extra workers and generate additional spending power.

(e)   The multiplier will be lower. Firms will be less likely to step up investment plans and expand production if the source of the economy's growth is temporary. Households are more likely to save any "bonus" income received as a cushion against hard times in the future.

(f)   The multiplier will be lower. Inventories will be higher than otherwise, so when the government enacts its policy, there is less need to increase production and hire more workers.

(g)   The multiplier will be higher. An expansion in government spending increases the interest rate. If households are less concerned than before about debt repayments, they will reduce their current purchases less vigorously.

17 [32]

Long-Run Growth

Chapter objectives:

1. Define economic growth and identify the sources of economic growth.
2. Explain the information presented by an aggregate production function. Describe the circumstances that cause diminishing returns and relate this concept to the work of Malthus and Ricardo.
3. List the four factors that affect growth.
4. Outline the strategies proposed to increase the growth rate.
5. Summarize the relationship between economic growth and environmental quality.

BRAIN TEASER: How can growth occur in a "Robinson Crusoe" type of economy? Does the arrival of Friday represent economic growth? Compare and contrast economic growth in primitive economies with growth in developed economies.

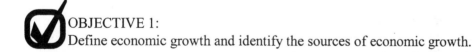OBJECTIVE 1:
Define economic growth and identify the sources of economic growth.

Economic growth is an increase in real per capita GDP resulting in improved standards of living. This chapter is concerned with what causes the upward trend. Production is limited by the resources and technology that the economy possesses. Growth occurs when more resources become available or when current resources are used more efficiently. In terms of the production possibility frontier, the maximum levels of production shift to the right as the resource base expands and/or technology improves. (page 319 [631])

Growth can take place in two ways: either the economy discovers new resources or it uses its given resources more efficiently. Growth occurs, then, through:

(a) An increase in resources
   (i)   Labor supply
   (ii)   Physical capital
   (iii) Human capital

(b)   The discovery of new ways to combine resources more efficiently—to increase their productivity

    (i)   Technological change

    (ii)   Other advances in knowledge

    (iii)   Economies of scale.

Convergence theory suggests that less developed countries may "catch up" with those that are more developed, essentially, by learning from their mistakes and by adopting successful technologies.

    ▶▶▶   LEARNING TIP: Remember the "Rule of 72." This rule of thumb lets us estimate how quickly a quantity will double in size, given a growth rate. The growth rates included in Table 17.1 (32.1) may seem fairly similar but, when we apply the "rule of 72" we see that, if the U.S. growth rate of 2.7% is sustained, the American GDP would double in about 27 years while China's growth rate of 9.6% would make the Chinese economy double in less than 8 years!◀

━━━━■━━━━━━━━━━━━━━━━━━━━ **Practice** ━━━━━━━━━━━━━━━

1.   Economic growth is defined as an increase in

    (a)   real output.

    (b)   consumption per household.

    (c)   economic well-being.

    (d)   the rate at which inventions occur.

ANSWER: (a) Growth is difficult to measure—the accepted yardstick is real GDP (or real GDP per capita).

2.   When we draw a production possibility frontier, we assume that the quantity of

    (a)   capital available increases as we move along the production possibility frontier.

    (b)   capital available increases and the quantity of labor decreases as we move along the production possibility frontier.

    (c)   labor available increases as we move along the production possibility frontier.

    (d)   capital and labor is fixed.

ANSWER: (d) It is assumed that the resource base and technology are fixed. Changes in any one of these constraints will cause the production possibility frontier to shift position.

3.   Graphically, economic growth can be represented by a

    (a)   rightward shift of the aggregate demand curve.

    (b)   leftward shift of the aggregate demand curve.

    (c)   rightward shift of the production possibility frontier.

    (d)   leftward shift of the production possibility frontier.

ANSWER: (c) Economic growth is, indeed, an expansion in an economy's possible levels of production. Refer to p. 320 [632].

4.   A production possibility frontier shows

    (a)   how much of a good will be produced as the price of the good changes.

    (b)   all the combinations of two goods that can be produced when all resources are being used efficiently.

    (c)   all the combinations of two resources that can be produced efficiently.

    (d)   how much of a product can be produced as additional units of input are added to the production mix.

ANSWER: (b) Refer to the diagram on p. 320 [632].

5.   Which of the following is an incorrect statement about the term "capital"?
   (a)   Capital has no effect on the productivity of labor.
   (b)   Capital yields services to people over a period of time.
   (c)   The act of producing capital goods may involve a sacrifice in terms of current consumption.
   (d)   The addition to the stock of capital is called investment.
   ANSWER: (a)   Capital can be combined with labor to make workers more productive.

6.   Colleen and Bill construct a net out of vines so that they can trap fish. Having never done this before, they find that they are "learning by doing." Colleen and Bill are
   (a)   acquiring physical capital only.
   (b)   acquiring human capital only.
   (c)   acquiring physical capital and human capital.
   (d)   acquiring a consumption good.
   ANSWER: (c)   The net is a tool that should increase their ability to catch fish—it is physical capital. By learning as they work, Colleen and Bill are increasing their human capital. ■

OBJECTIVE 2:
Explain the information presented by an aggregate production function. Describe the circumstances that cause diminishing returns and relate this concept to the work of Malthus and Ricardo.

A production function relates combinations of inputs (either graphically or mathematically) to the maximum level of output of a good; an *aggregate production function* does the same thing for national output in the entire economy. Increases in the quantity and quality of resources and increases in productivity cause the output level to rise. (page 322 [634])

      As additional units of a resource (e.g., labor) are added to a fixed quantity of other resources, after some point, their productivity will begin to decline. When capacity constraints begin to make themselves felt, *diminishing returns* result. This phenomenon was the reason for the gloomy predictions of Malthus and Ricardo.

   ▶▶▶   LEARNING TIP: Production functions and diminishing returns are covered more completely in Chapter 7 of Case, Fair and Oster's *Principles of Microeconomics*. The usual assumption made is that diminishing returns go into effect immediately. Each additional unit of a resource will experience diminishing returns when added to a fixed quantity of other resources. Note that diminishing returns apply to any resource, not just labor. To ensure your understanding of diminishing returns, verify that, if you kept adding (equally skilled) employees into, say, a pizzeria, eventually their productivity would start to decline as they ran out of productive things to do.
   ▶▶▶   LEARNING TIP: The production function used throughout this chapter $(Y = 3K^{1/3}L^{2/3})$ is fairly standard in economics and is referred to as a Cobb-Douglas production function. Output is determined by the quantities of capital (K) and labor (L) applied. To familiarize yourself with the production function, verify the total output values given in Table 17.2 (32.2).◀

—◼———————————————————— **Practice** ————————————————————

7.   Malthus and Ricardo were concerned that the fixed supply of _____ would lead to diminishing returns.

        (a)   capital
        (b)   technology
        (c)   labor
        (d)   land

        ANSWER: (d) Refer to p. 322 [634] for more on the thoughts of Malthus and Ricardo.

8.   In Arbez, the capital stock is fixed. Because of immigration, the supply of labor increases. As diminishing returns set in, we should expect output to _____ and average labor productivity to _____ .

        (a)   increase; increase
        (b)   increase; decrease
        (c)   decrease; increase
        (d)   decrease; decrease

        ANSWER: (b) As additional resources are added, output should increase, but more slowly. As diminishing returns set in, average productivity will decline.

9.   An economy experiencing modern economic growth would expect to see
        (a)   a decreasing capital to labor (K/L) ratio.
        (b)   a more rapid growth in labor than in capital.
        (c)   diminishing labor productivity as the capital stock expands.
        (d)   an increasing capital to labor (K/L) ratio.

        ANSWER: (d) Economic growth is typified by increasing quantities of capital for each worker.

10.   Malthus and Ricardo believed that, in order to provide enough food for a rapidly growing population, farmers would have to cultivate _____ productive land _____ intensively.
        (a)   more; more
        (b)   more; less
        (c)   less; more
        (d)   less; less

        ANSWER: (c) Presumably, the best land was already under cultivation, with less good land left unexploited. This land would have to be pressed into service and farmed intensively.

11.   Diminishing returns to labor will occur if
        (a)   capital accumulation takes place, given the supply of labor.
        (b)   there is technological change, given the supply of labor.
        (c)   the labor supply grows more rapidly than the capital stock.
        (d)   the labor supply gains additional skills.

        ANSWER: (c) Refer to p. 322 [634] for more on diminishing returns. ◼

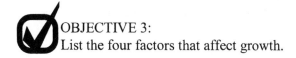OBJECTIVE 3:
List the four factors that affect growth.

There are four factors that lead to growth:

(a)   Increases in the supply of labor, caused by immigration, maturity of the population, and improved health

(b)   Increases in physical capital (plant and equipment) either from domestic savings or foreign direct investment

(c)   Increases in human capital, caused by education, on-the-job training, and improved health

(d)   Increases in productivity due to
        (i)   Technological change (invention and innovation)
        (ii)   Other advances in knowledge
        (iii)   Economies of scale (page 322 [634])

An increasing focus has been on the role of institutions in fostering growth. So-called *fragile countries* have weak financial and governmental institutions, corruption, and inadequate protection for lenders and investors. Similarly with human capital, an economy with a strong educational system and healthy workers will prosper while one with low educational standards and whose workers are less healthy will not.

▶▶▶   LEARNING TIP: You may have met the concept of economies of scale in a microeconomics course. Case, Fair and Oster cover this topic in Chapter 9 of their *Principles of Microeconomics* textbook. A larger scale of operation can reduce unit costs of production through a more effective division of labor and management, or more efficient use of plant and equipment. If a firm can spread its overheads over a greater amount of production, average costs will decrease. Here, however, the text refers to "external" economies of scale. External economies are cost savings experienced by a firm because of the expansion of an industry. An expanding industry may attract a larger pool of more skilled workers, more specialized equipment, and better support services—all of which factors can reduce the costs for the individual firm. Movie studios in Hollywood, software development in Silicon Valley, and computer support services in Bangalore are examples from the past and the present.◀

ECONOMICS IN PRACTICE: On page 329 [641], the textbook looks at the expansion of wellness programs in corporate America. It is often said that "an ounce of prevention is worth a pound of cure". What are some of the benefits, for the firm, of establishing a wellness program or an in-house clinic?

ANSWER: For many years, Japanese firms have adopted the practice of group calisthenics before work, partly for the health benefits and partly because of its morale-building elements. Clearly, there are productivity benefits from having healthy workers—under-par or absent workers are less productive. Firms that are early adopters of wellness programs may receive an additional gain from reduced labor turnover and higher morale, if workers feel that their employer has a commitment to them.

ECONOMICS IN PRACTICE (CONTINUED): The textbook considers the cost-cutting advantages of wellness programs. Can you extend this notion to other benefits that employers might offer their employees?

ANSWER: Many employers offer their workers opportunities to enhance their educational qualifications, including participation in degree programs. Benefits might include financial support from the employer, time off, or educational programs that are available on-site. Flexible hours and working from home are other examples. In such cases, the advantage to the employer is increased worker loyalty and morale, lower turnover rates, and a more educated workforce.

—■——————————————————————— **Practice** ———————————————————————

12.   An increase in human capital will _____ labor productivity and _____ output.
    (a)   increase; increase
    (b)   increase; decrease
    (c)   decrease; increase
    (d)   decrease; decrease

    ANSWER: (a) Refer to p. 325 [637] for more on human capital.

13.   As industries increase in size, they derive cost savings called
    (a)   innovations.
    (b)   inventions.
    (c)   external economies of scale.
    (d)   cost depreciations.

    ANSWER: (c) As industries expand, "overheads" might be reduced—for example, by training
            or educational programs for employees—or the creation of a pool of skilled labor
            in a region.

14.   Arboc has experienced growth, although the quantity of its inputs has remained unchanged. This
    growth must have been caused by
    (a)   random shocks to the economic system.
    (b)   an increase in the productivity of inputs.
    (c)   an increase in imports.
    (d)   a decrease in imports.

    ANSWER: (b) If the quantity of resources is unchanged but more output is produced,
            productivity must have increased. Labor productivity is defined as output/labor.
            Changes in imports are irrelevant. If Arboc had imported extra machinery, for
            example, the quantity of capital in Arboc would have changed.

15.   An industrial consultant enters a car factory and reorganizes the layout of the assembly line.
    Without changing the amount of capital or the number of workers, car production can be
    increased by 10%. This change is
    (a)   both labor saving and capital saving.
    (b)   labor saving but not capital saving.
    (c)   capital saving but not labor saving.
    (d)   neither labor saving nor capital saving.

    ANSWER: (a) Each worker and each unit of capital are more productive than before. ■

OBJECTIVE 4:
Outline the strategies proposed to increase the growth rate.

Although, since the mid-nineteenth century, the United States has achieved a record of growth that would
be the envy of most nations, there was some concern during the 1970s and early 1980s that the growth
rate—and, more particularly, labor productivity—was slowing down. Proposed public policies to correct
sagging growth included policies intended to:

(a)   Improve the quality of education and training
(b)   Increase the saving rate (through changes in tax laws)
(c)   Stimulate investment (through investment tax credit schemes)
(d)   Increase research and development (through subsidization)
(e)   Involve the government in a coordinated *industrial policy* of targeting specific industries for preferential treatment (page 330 [642])

The growth rate and productivity have improved somewhat since the mid 1980s. The focus of discussion now is on how much of this productivity "bounce" is due to the emergence of the Internet and information technology and, if so, whether or not these factors will lead to sustained higher growth.

▶▶   LEARNING TIP: Notice that monetary growth is *not* one of the variables listed as affecting long-term economic growth. The point is that changes in the quantity of money might influence production in the short term, but that monetary expansions, boosting aggregate demand, will ultimately run up against the supply-side constraint. Pumping up the money supply might enhance short-term growth but also might breed inflation. Unanticipated inflation, which heightens risk and lessens the willingness of individuals to make long-term commitments, might have an adverse effect on investment. (Remember, too, that during rapid inflation individuals may prefer to buy goods rather than save a currency that is losing its spending power.)◀

Comment: Society can accumulate capital only through net investment, and investment in future production can occur only if current consumption is given up. Saving then is the basis for growth. This key point can be applied both to the accumulation of physical capital and also to investment in human capital.

ECONOMICS IN PRACTICE: On page 332 [644], the textbook considers the pitfalls of measuring productivity. Productivity of labor is determined by dividing the value of output by the quantity of labor hours applied. Healthier, better-trained workers, or workers with improved equipment should be more productive. First, what causes productivity to be so difficult to measure?
ANSWER: As the textbook notes, it is difficult to measure output, especially when controlling for changing prices. Usually our valuation of output requires the use of market prices, which can change. (Refer to Chapter 6 (21) for more on price indexation.) An additional factor that makes it difficult measuring output accurately is changing technology. Even if we measure output in physical terms, technological improvements would make year-to-year comparisons inaccurate.
ECONOMICS IN PRACTICE (CONTINUED): Can you think of some examples of technological improvements that might be difficult to capture if we measure output in real terms?
ANSWER: Agricultural output should be easy to compare over time but genetic modification makes this less true. Modifications that improve yield (drought- or insect-resistant crops) will be reflected in productivity measures but modifications that improve taste or healthfulness will not be captured.
Similarly, as mentioned in the article, technological change means that a "computer" today is not the equivalent of a "computer" from 20 years ago.
ECONOMICS IN PRACTICE (CONTINUED): Can There are many anecdotes that, back in the days of the Soviet Union, the central planners continually ran into problems when trying to establish targets for production. A glass factory that was required to produce a ton of glass would meet its target in the easiest way—a large single ball of glass that was totally unusable. If the target were changed to specify a certain "surface" area of glass, then very thin, very fragile sheets of glass would be produced, again frustrating the planners.
Now put yourself in the position of such a planner. Choose three goods or services and devise a way to measure how much of each is produced. Let's assume that "market value" is not an option.
ANSWER: Answers will vary, depending on the goods or services you choose. The main point is that it is extremely difficult to come up with a satisfactory measure of output, even for one good. That's why "market value" is still used.

─────────■───────────────────────────── **Practice** ───────────────────────────────────

16.   According to Denison, approximately _____ of U.S. growth in output from 1929 to 1982 was due to increases in factors of production.
       (a)   20%
       (b)   25%
       (c)   50%
       (d)   75%
       ANSWER: (c)   Refer to Table 17.8 (32.8) on p. 327 [639] for a summary of Denison's study.

17.   According to Denison, the contribution of education and training to growth between 1929 and 1982
       (a)   increased steadily.
       (b)   increased at first and then decreased.
       (c)   decreased steadily.
       (d)   remained fairly constant.
       ANSWER: (d)   Refer to Table 17.8 (32.8) on p. 327 [639] for the details.

18.   Which of the following has not been advanced as a way of increasing the rate of growth in the United States?
       (a)   Increasing the rate of consumption spending
       (b)   Stimulating investment
       (c)   Encouraging additional research and development
       (d)   Implementing an industrial policy
       ANSWER: (a)   Increasing the rate of consumption spending requires that the saving rate be decreased. One of the key determinants of growth is the economy's willingness to forego current consumption. ■

OBJECTIVE 5:
Summarize the relationship between economic growth and environmental quality.

The Millennium Development Goals, adopted by the United Nations in 2000, established a set of quantifiable targets for developing countries to meet. The targets included measures of education, mortality, and income growth but also included environmental criteria such as the availability of clean air and clean water. Evidence suggests a complex relationship between growth and the environment, with pollution initially increasing as growth takes place and then declining at higher levels of growth. In the early phases of development it seems that there is a trade-off between the benefits of growth and the costs of pollution. In many cases, pollution is not limited by national boundaries—global warming is an obvious example.

       A further issue is that of sustainability. Because extractive industries require little skilled labor, it is important to use the revenues from such industries to build a strong infrastructure. If growth involves the depletion of nonrenewable resources then, if revenues are not used to establish other alternative types of production, there may be a limit to a country's ability to grow. (page 334 [646])

———■———————————————— **Practice** ————————————————————

19.   The study by Grossman and Krueger suggests that
       (a)   higher GDP per capita leads to more environmental problems.
       (b)   higher GDP per capita leads to less environmental problems.
       (c)   there is no relationship between GDP per capita and environmental quality.
       (d)   there is an inverted U-shaped relationship between GDP per capita and environmental quality.

       ANSWER: (d) Refer to p. 334 [646] for more details of this study.

20.   Typically, the nations of Southeast Asia have fueled their growth through _____; the nations of sub-Saharan Africa have tended to grow through _____ .
       (a)   resource extraction; agriculture
       (b)   resource extraction; export-led manufacturing
       (c)   export-led manufacturing; resource extraction
       (d)   agriculture; export-led manufacturing

       ANSWER: (c) Refer to p. 335 [647] for more details. ■

BRAIN TEASER SOLUTION: Growth can occur if the quality and/or quantity of resources improve or if technology improves. The arrival of Friday increases the resource base. In itself this does not represent growth—Friday had to apply his abilities to increase production. Growth in a primitive economy may be slower, perhaps due to obstacles imposed by a tradition-minded society, or, if the economy is at subsistence level, because of a lack of opportunity to "invest" in the future. Otherwise, however, the growth process is similar for both developing and developed countries.

PRACTICE TEST

I.   MULTIPLE-CHOICE QUESTIONS

Select the option that provides the single best answer.

_____   1.   Modern economic growth refers to a period of rapid growth in
              (a)   nominal GDP.
              (b)   per capita real GDP.
              (c)   nominal per capita GDP.
              (d)   real GDP.

_____   2.   The law of diminishing returns suggests that increases in the _____ , *ceteris paribus*, may not lead to increased _____ .
              (a)   stock of capital; employment
              (b)   number of workers; output per capita
              (c)   number of workers; efficiency of capital
              (d)   stock of capital; money supply

_____ 3.   The ability of technological change to affect productivity depends on both
    (a)   the discovery and implementation of new technology.
    (b)   the stock of capital and the acceptance of new technology.
    (c)   the number of new patents and the quality of the workforce.
    (d)   the willingness of the workforce to accept change and the overall level of macroeconomic activity.

_____ 4.   _____ generally enhances labor productivity. An increase in _____ can increase _____ .
    (a)   Competition; output, income
    (b)   Competition; population, output
    (c)   Training; capital, income
    (d)   Capital; capital, output

_____ 5.   Ultimately, the amount of capital accumulation is limited by
    (a)   the interest rate.
    (b)   marginal tax rates.
    (c)   disposable (after-tax) income.
    (d)   the saving rate.

_____ 6.   In general, economic growth will occur where there are additions to
    (a)   the labor force.
    (b)   per capita nominal income.
    (c)   the stock of money.
    (d)   import purchases.

_____ 7.   A public policy strategy designed to increase productivity might include which one of the following?
    (a)   Increased regulations on industrial pollution
    (b)   Tax breaks on interest income
    (c)   Tax incentives to increase consumption spending
    (d)   Increases in college tuition

_____ 8.   Each of the following has been suggested as a likely reason for the decline in the growth rate of labor productivity in the 1970s EXCEPT
    (a)   relatively low saving rates.
    (b)   increased government regulations.
    (c)   reductions in investment spending.
    (d)   reductions in educational standards.

_____ 9.   In 2005 a federal advisory panel on tax reform offered each of the following as a way to stimulate growth EXCEPT
    (a)   cutting tax rates in general.
    (b)   reducing tax rates on interest.
    (c)   allowing businesses to depreciate capital purchases over time instead of expensing them.
    (d)   lowering dividends capital gains to 15 percent.

_____ 10. Economic growth will occur in each of the following cases EXCEPT through
    (a)   an increase in the quantity of labor.
    (b)   an increase in the quality of labor.
    (c)   an increase in the quantity of money.
    (d)   an increase in the quantity of physical capital.

_____ 11. Jorgenson shows that, from 1973 to 2000, the contribution to overall growth of
    (a)   capital increased substantially.
    (b)   productivity declined over the period.
    (c)   information technology capital increased substantially.
    (d)   labor decreased significantly.

_____ 12. The introduction of robots is a
    (a)   labor-saving invention.
    (b)   labor-saving innovation.
    (c)   capital-saving invention.
    (d)   capital-saving innovation.

_____ 13. Malthus and Ricardo were concerned that there would be insufficient food because of the fixed supply of land. They failed to foresee the effect of _____ on agricultural production.
    (a)   additional labor supply
    (b)   technological improvements
    (c)   diminishing returns
    (d)   erosion

_____ 14. An increase in the capital/labor ratio will
    (a)   increase the productivity of capital.
    (b)   increase the productivity of labor.
    (c)   increase the productivity of labor and capital.
    (d)   decrease the productivity of labor and capital.

_____ 15. A hallmark of economies experiencing modern economic growth is
    (a)   a stable capital to labor (K/L) ratio.
    (b)   an increasing capital to labor (K/L) ratio.
    (c)   a decrease in public capital.
    (d)   a decreasing capital to labor (K/L) ratio.

_____ 16. Which of the following is not an investment in human capital?
    (a)   ABC Corp. establishes a wellness program for its employees.
    (b)   DEF Corp. trains its clerical staff to work with next-generation word processors.
    (c)   GHI Corp. introduces next-generation word processors for its clerical staff.
    (d)   the government introduces a free milk program for school-age children.

Use the following information for the next four questions. Formica's aggregate production function is $Y = 2K^5L^5$, where Y is total output, K is units of capital, and L is units of labor. Currently, Formica has 25 units of capital and 100 units of labor.

_____ 17.   Calculate Formica's total output.
(a)   50 units.
(b)   75 units.
(c)   100 units.
(d)   1250 units.

_____ 18.   What is the average productivity of a unit of Formican labor?
(a)   1 unit of output.
(b)   4 units of output.
(c)   10 units of output.
(d)   100 units of output.

_____ 19.   Now the quantity of labor increases from 100 to 121 units. What will happen to the average productivity of labor?
(a)   Labor productivity will increase to 1.10.
(b)   Labor productivity will increase to 1.21.
(c)   Labor productivity will decrease to 0.91.
(d)   Labor productivity will decrease to 0.75.

_____ 20.   Suppose, instead of the change in the quantity of labor, that the capital stock doubles to 50 units. What will happen to the average productivity of labor?
(a)   Labor productivity will increase to 1.41.
(b)   Labor productivity will increase to 1.21.
(c)   Labor productivity will decrease to 0.71.
(d)   Labor productivity will decrease to 0.91.

II.   APPLICATION QUESTIONS

1.   The following tables present data on three economies: Arbez, Arboc, and Aneyh. Complete the tables. What do the data tell you about the causes of growth?

Arbez Period	L	K	Y	Y/L	Growth Rate of Output
1	100	300	520.00	_____	—
2	110	304	546.00	_____	_____
3	119	307	578.76	_____	_____
4	123	312	596.12	_____	_____

Arboc Period	L	K	Y	Y/L	Growth Rate of Output
1	100	300	520.00		—
2	105	309	551.20		
3	111	317	589.78		
4	114	327	619.27		

Aneyh Period	L	K	Y	Y/L	Growth Rate of Output
1	100	300	520.00		—
2	105	304	540.80		
3	111	307	567.84		
4	114	312	579.20		

2. Which countries do you think provide the most (nonmilitary) development assistance per capita? You'll need to guess here. Rank the following eight *alphabetized* countries, ("1" being the most generous and "8" being the least generous), then check the *Practice Test Solutions* section to see if your intuition is correct. As a guide, the percentage of GDP given recently as aid by the eight countries is included *in ascending order* in the third column. It is not meant to suggest that Canada contributes 0.14% of its GDP, for instance.

Country	Ranking	Percentage of GDP
Canada		0.18
Denmark		0.28
France		0.40
Netherlands		0.52
Norway		0.77
Sweden		0.82
United Kingdom		0.89
United States		0.91

3. Ethiopia is one of the world's very poorest nations, with a GDI (Gross National Income) per capita of only $110 in 2006. By contrast, GDI per capita for the United States was $41,400 in the same year. In other words, the average U.S. citizen earns 376.73 times as much as the average Ethiopian. Use your intuition to pair the "multiplier" from the "Selection" column with the appropriate country, then check the *Practice Test Solutions* section. (The multiplier for Nation A is derived by dividing $41,440 by the GNI per capita of Nation A.)

Country	Multiplier	Selection
Ethiopia	376.36	376.36
Nepal		159.23
Canada		66.77
India		32.09
South Korea		6.12
Japan		2.96
Mexico		1.46
Norway		1.22
China		1.11
Switzerland		0.86
United Kingdom		0.80

4.   How will each of the following affect the long-run measured growth rate in the nation of Noil?

(a)   Noil's Ministry of the Environment imposes more stringent environmental regulations on businesses.

(b)   The government increases spending on education. The additional spending is financed by a tax on consumers.

(c)   The government pledges to trim the deficit by reducing the size of the Noilian army.

(d)   The government pledges to trim the deficit by cutting expenditures on education.

(e)   Noil opens its borders to migrant workers from Regit.

5.   There are two neighboring economies—Formica and Klorofill. Each economy has an identical production possibility frontier (ppf), as shown below. Currently at F_1, Formica prefers to produce investment goods while Klorofill, currently at K_1, prefers a relatively high rate of consumption.

Note: The ppfs are drawn as (constant-cost) straight lines merely for simplicity.

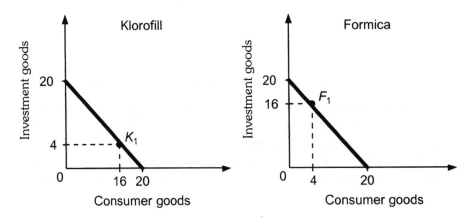

Suppose that each economy was in a recession last time period. In fact, each economy produced 4 units of consumer goods and 4 investment goods.

(a)   In Klorofill's case, the economy has moved to K_1. How would you represent this change on an *AS/AD* diagram? In Formica's case, the economy has moved to F_1. How would you represent this change on an *AS/AD* diagram?

Let us assume that the depreciation rate in each economy is four machines per year.

(b)   What is happening to the capital stock in Klorofill this year? In Formica?

(c)   Describe the effect on the Klorofillian ppf. Describe the effect on the Formican ppf.

(d)   Describe how Klorofill's *AS/AD* diagram will differ from that of Formica, as time passes.

Let us assume that the depreciation rate in each economy is five machines per year.

(e)   What is happening to the capital stock in Klorofill this year? In Formica?

(f)   Describe the effect on the Klorofillian ppf. Describe the effect on the Formican ppf.

(g)   Describe the differences in choices faced by Klorofillians and Formicans as time passes.

6.   Write down the six factors that cause growth in the following table and match each with one of the following examples.

Letter	Factor

Examples

(a)   The construction of a new, larger, factory

(b)   Improvements in health

(c)   The implementation of a newly discovered production process

(d)   Decreasing production costs as plant size increases

(e)   Managerial skills

(f)   Immigration

PRACTICE TEST SOLUTIONS

I.   Solutions to Multiple-Choice Questions

1.   (b)   Refer to the marginal definition of modern economic growth on p. 319 [631].

2.   (b)   If, as extra workers are added to productive activity, diminishing returns set in, output will still rise, but less rapidly. Five percent more workers might increase output by four percent. Accordingly, the average output of workers will decrease.

3.   (a)   New technology must be discovered, but this on its own will not increase productivity. The new ideas must be incorporated into the productive process.

4.   (d)   Capital is usually a complement for labor. Additional capital increases the productivity of each worker.

5.   (d)   Refer to p. 331 [643].

6.   (a)   Growth occurs when inputs increase or improve, or technology changes.

7.   (b)   If the rate of saving (non-consumption) is the ultimate constraint on growth, measures to encourage saving will encourage growth. Option (c) clearly moves in the opposite direction. Option (a) makes production more difficult while Option (d) reduces inputs in the future (i.e., human capital).

8.   (d)   Lower research and development spending has been offered as a reason. The issue is that the amount of R&D is too small, not low quality. Refer to p. 330 [642].

9.   (c)   It was proposed that businesses be allowed to expense capital purchases immediately rather than depreciating them over time. Refer to p. 331 [643].

10.   (c)   Money, by itself, is not a productive resource. Robinson Crusoe, on his island, would have had little use for dollar bills except, perhaps, to kindle a fire.

11.   (c)   The portion of overall growth contributed by information technology capital rose from 9% to 17%. Refer to Table 17.8 (32.8) for more details.

12.   (b)   Refer to p. 326 [638] regarding other advances in knowledge.

13.   (b)   Improved technology (better planting and harvesting techniques, improved fertilizers, more hardy and better-yielding hybrids) has allowed farmers to increase production while reducing the amount of land under cultivation.

14.   (b)   An increase in the capital/labor ratio means that each worker has more equipment with which to work. Labor productivity will increase. The productivity of capital will decrease because additional capital is being added to a given stock of labor. Refer to Table 17.4 (32.4) in the textbook.

15.   (b)   Refer to p. 323 [635].

16.   (c)   Each of the other options improves the quality of the labor force (or the potential labor force).

17.   (c) $Y = 2K^{.5}L^{.5}$, so total output is $2(25^{.5})(100^{.5})$.

18.   (a)   Average productivity of labor is determined by Y/L, so 100/100.

19.   (c)   With no increase in capital stock, workers will experience diminishing returns. Average productivity of labor (Y/L) is 110/121.

20.   (a)   The increase in capital stock causes output to increase to 141.42. With 100 units of labor, average productivity will be 1.41.

II.   *Solutions to Application Questions*

1.   Refer to the following tables.

Arbez Period	L	K	Y	Y/L	Growth Rate of Output
1	100	300	520.00	5.20	—
2	110	304	546.00	4.96	5.00%
3	119	307	578.76	4.86	6.00%
4	123	312	596.12	4.85	3.00%

Arboc Period	L	K	Y	Y/L	Growth Rate of Output
1	100	300	520.00	5.20	—
2	105	309	551.20	5.25	6.00%
3	111	317	589.78	5.31	7.00%
4	114	327	619.27	5.43	5.00%

Aneyh Period	L	K	Y	Y/L	Growth Rate of Output
1	100	300	520.00	5.20	—
2	105	304	540.80	5.15	4.00%
3	111	307	567.84	5.12	5.00%
4	114	312	579.20	5.08	2.00%

The growth rate is greatest in Arboc. Compared with Aneyh, whose rate of growth in labor resources is identical, Arboc is superior in output/labor ratio. Compared with Arbez, Arboc's *Y/L* ratio is increasing, while that of Arbez is *decreasing*. However, Arbez is growing more rapidly than Aneyh because Arbez's labor force is expanding more rapidly.

2.   The donor countries are ranked from most generous (1) to least generous (8). Perhaps the low position of the United States, in terms of GDP *per capita*, is remarkable—Danes contribute more than five times as much, as a percentage of GDP. In fact, the Scandinavian countries are consistently generous.

Country	Ranking	Percentage of GDP
Canada	7	0.28
Denmark	1	0.91
France	5	0.52
Netherlands	4	0.77
Norway	2	0.89
Sweden	3	0.82
United Kingdom	6	0.40
United States	8	0.18

3.   It is worthy of note that, although the United States citizen is still among the very highest income earners in the world, a few countries have leap-frogged ahead (those with multipliers having a value of less than one).

Country	Multiplier	GDI per Capita (U.S. Dollars)
Ethiopia	376.36	110
Nepal	159.23	260
Canada	1.46	28,390
India	66.77	620
South Korea	2.96	13,980
Japan	1.11	37,180
Mexico	6.12	6,770
Norway	0.80	52,030
China	32.09	1,290
Switzerland	0.86	48,230
United Kingdom	1.22	33,940

4.   (a)   More stringent environmental regulations on businesses will reduce the measured growth rate. Profits will be reduced and less investment will occur.

(b)   The growth rate will rise because of additional investment in human capital and because the tax on consumption will encourage households to save more.

(c)   The growth rate will increase because, with a reduced deficit, national saving will be greater and interest rates will be lower. Private investment will be encouraged.

(d)   The effect on the growth rate is uncertain. A reduced deficit will encourage investment (refer to part c, above), but lower educational expenditure represents a reduction in human capital investment (refer to part (b), above). The growth rate will increase if there is a greater return on private investment or on education.

(e)   Immigration increases the labor force and may reduce the capital to labor ratio. If so, productivity will decrease. However, the Regitani workers may be highly skilled (human capital) which will increase the capital to labor ratio. In addition, the migrants may be more highly motivated to succeed. If so, productivity would increase and Noil would benefit from the influx.

5.   (a)   The AD curve has moved to the right by the same amount in each case. Because of the additional investment, the AS curve will also shift to the right.

(b)   The capital stock in Klorofill is stationary, with four new machines being produced and four existing machines wearing out. In Formica, the capital stock is increasing by twelve (i.e., 16 – 4).

(c)   Klorofill's production possibility frontier is stationary; Formica's production possibility frontier is shifting outward as its productive resources increase.

(d)   Klorofill's AD curve will remain stationary with consumption at sixteen units and investment at four units. Productive capacity is not increasing, therefore the aggregate supply curve will not shift. In Formica, aggregate supply will increase to match expansions in aggregate demand because of the expanding resource base.

(e)   The capital stock in Klorofill is declining, with four new machines being produced and five existing machines wearing out. In Formica, the capital stock is increasing by eleven (i.e., 16 – 5).

(f)   Klorofill's production possibility frontier is shifting inward; Formica's production possibility frontier is shifting outward as its productive resources increase.

(g)   As time passes, the Klorofillians will be forced to cut back their standard of living. Currently, their resource base is shrinking. To prevent this they will have to increase investment good production at the expense of consumer good production. The Formicans face no such hard choice—their production possibility frontier is shifting outward so they can increase consumption and investment levels.

6.   (a)   An increase in physical capital.
      (b)   An increase in human capital.
      (c)   Technological change.
      (d)   Economies of scale.
      (e)   An advance in knowledge
      (f)   An increase in the supply of labor.

18 [33]

Debates in Macroeconomics: Monetarism, New Classical Theory, and Supply-Side Economics

C hapter objectives:

1. Outline the assumptions of the quantity theory and discuss the rationale for policy actions advised by monetarists that distinguish them from Keynesians.

2. State the assumptions of the new classical macroeconomic theory, especially the role of expectations, and describe the model's policy conclusions. Outline the reasoning behind the real business cycle theory.

3. Outline the reasoning behind (and summarize the evidence about) the supply-side policies that found prominence in the 1980s.

This chapter exposes some of the controversies that have boiled up within macroeconomics. It should alert you to the fact that no single model is accepted by all economists. Economics, unlike the physical sciences, is not governed by a set of undeniable laws. The model that is preferred often has as much to do with the prevailing philosophical attitude as it does with tested theories. A political dimension may be detected too. The activist "demand-side" Keynesian view is fairly liberal; Milton Friedman, the most famous monetarist, attracted the attention of Presidents Nixon and Ford; the supply-side theory was a major plank of Ronald Reagan's presidential campaign in 1980; and the new classical economics advocates a "hands-off" approach to government intervention in the economy.

BRAIN TEASER: The Lucas supply function, which is discussed in this chapter, argues that if inflation is higher than expected, the economy's output will increase. You expect 5% inflation and negotiate a 5% wage increase. What happens to your real wage if inflation actually runs at 10%? What happens to your employer's real wage bill? What would firms have an incentive to do in such a case? How would output be affected?

 OBJECTIVE 1:
Outline the assumptions of the quantity theory and discuss the rationale for policy actions advised by monetarists that distinguish them from Keynesians.

The short-run *AS/AD* model is essentially Keynesian. Keynesians believe that the money market and goods market are linked—cyclical unemployment can persist; government policy can influence economic activity (in the short-run). Eventually, "Keynesianism" became associated with both "activist" fiscal policy and "activist" monetary policy.

The *quantity theory (monetarist)* view of the economy relates the money supply (*M*) to nominal GDP (*PY*). On average, each dollar must be used a given number of times to buy all the goods produced; this given number is the velocity of money (*V*) and it is assumed to be (practically) constant. The central idea of the quantity theory is captured in the equation of exchange:

$$MV = PY$$

Given *V*, any change in *M* must cause a change in *PY*. If the economy tends to remain close to full employment and potential GDP (another part of the monetarist view), then sustained changes in *M* must show up as changes in the price level rather than as changes in output—inflation is caused solely by excessive growth in the money supply. To the extent that velocity is not constant—and there is, in fact, a positive relationship between velocity and the interest rate—the monetarist view is weakened. However, most modern economists do now agree with the view that sustained inflation is a purely monetary phenomenon, occurring on if the money supply is permitted to expand. (page 340 [652])

Many Keynesians support coordinated fiscal and monetary policy actions to stabilize the economy; monetarists argue for a "money growth rule"—the money supply should grow at a steady rate, equal to the long-term growth rate of the economy. If this is done, inflation is avoided. Monetarists claim that activist policies are doomed to fail, at the very least because of time lags. (page 342 [654])

▶▶   LEARNING TIP: As you study monetarism, focus on the "*MV = PY*" formula, which is sometimes called the "equation of exchange."

▶▶   LEARNING TIP: The effect on policy of time lags is covered in Chapter 15 (30).

▶▶   LEARNING TIP: Much of the difference between the Keynesian and monetarist schools can be seen as a difference in time horizons. Keynesians focus on the short run—sticky wages and cyclical unemployment are to be expected. Monetarists take a longer view—the *AS* curve is vertical and changes in aggregate demand have no effect on output (*Y*), changing only the price level (*P*). ◀

━━━━━━━━━━━━━━━━━━━━━━━━━ **Practice** ━━━━━━━━━━━━━━━━━━━

1.   In 2007, nominal GDP was $13,841.3 billion. The money supply (M_t) was about $1,360.5 billion. Velocity was approximately
      (a)   0.098.
      (b)   1.116.
      (c)   7.624.
      (d)   10.174.
      ANSWER: (d)   *V* = nominal *GDP* (*PY*)/*M*.

2.   The money stock is $400 million, the price level is $2, and velocity is 5.
      (a)   Real GDP is 2,000 million.
      (b)   Real GDP is 1,000 million.
      (c)   Nominal GDP is 160 million.
      (d)   Nominal GDP is 1,000 million.

      ANSWER: (b) In the equation $MV = PY$, Y stands for real GDP.

3.   Monetarists advocate
      (a)   a coordinated fiscal and monetary policy.
      (b)   a coordinated demand-side and supply-side policy.
      (c)   a policy of steady, slow growth in the money supply.
      (d)   an activist stabilization policy to control inflation and a passive stabilization policy to control unemployment.

      ANSWER: (c) Refer to p. 342 [654] for more on monetarism.

4.   Which of the following statements is false?
      (a)   Velocity can be affected by institutional factors, such as the frequency of payments to workers.
      (b)   Velocity can be affected by the development of new methods of payment of bills.
      (c)   The quantity theory is strengthened if the demand for money is dependent on the interest rate.
      (d)   A 10% increase in M, coupled with a reduction in V, will result in a less than 10% increase in nominal GDP.

      ANSWER: (c) The quantity theory is weakened if V is not constant. V will vary if the demand for money is interest sensitive.

5.   Each of the following is a valid argument suggesting that velocity may not be constant EXCEPT
      (a)   Velocity increases as the interest rate increases.
      (b)   Velocity will change if there is a change in the frequency with which workers are paid.
      (c)   Velocity increases as the supply of money increases.
      (d)   Velocity will change if the banking system becomes more efficient.

      ANSWER: (c) As the money supply increases, the interest rates decreases. As the opportunity cost of holding money decreases, there is an increase in the quantity of money demanded. For the same level of transactions, velocity will decrease. Note that institutional factors affect the demand for money (Options (b) and (d)).

6.   "Strict" monetarists claim that most of the inflation experienced in the U.S. economy over the past 25 years could have been avoided if
      (a)   the federal government deficit had been reduced.
      (b)   the Fed had not expanded the money supply so rapidly.
      (c)   income taxes had not been reduced to stimulate labor supply.
      (d)   the banking industry had not been deregulated, because deregulation has increased velocity.

      ANSWER: (b) For monetarists, inflation is purely a monetary phenomenon.

7.   Monetarists believe that the demand for money depends primarily on
       (a)   the interest rate.
       (b)   the level of nominal GDP.
       (c)   consumption expenditures.
       (d)   the overall price level.
       ANSWER: (b) Nominal GDP is *PY*. Option (d) is covered by the more general Option (b).

8.   In general, evidence since 1960 suggests that velocity
       (a)   has been fairly constant.
       (b)   has been increasing.
       (c)   has been decreasing.
       (d)   decreased in the first part of the period and increased in the second part of the period.
       ANSWER: (b) Refer to the Figure 18.1 (33.1) on p. 342 [654]. ■

✔OBJECTIVE 2:
State the assumptions of the new classical macroeconomic theory, especially the role of expectations, and describe the model's policy conclusions. Outline the reasoning behind the real business cycle theory.

The *new classical macroeconomics* is a newer challenge to the supremacy of the Keynesian model, partly because of the latter's unsatisfactory explanation of how expectations are formed. It combines the assumption of *rational expectations* (an hypothesis that states that the individual forms expectations by incorporating all available information into a "true model" of the economy) with the *Lucas supply function*.

Having rational expectations doesn't guarantee that one will be perfectly correct in one's predictions, but it does mean that individuals will adjust for expected changes and, on average, be correct. In other words, individuals will not make systematic over- or under-estimates of inflation and markets will clear. In the case of the labor market, there will be no (cyclical) unemployment. The conclusion is that anticipated changes in government policy won't be a surprise, won't affect output, and won't affect employment. The issue boils down to one question—do individuals have a true model of the economy and are they well informed? (page 343 [655])

The Lucas supply function tells us that price "surprises" (mismatches between the actual price level and the expected price level) can occur and that these surprises will affect output. Combined with the assumption of rational expectations, the Lucas supply function leads us to conclude that any announced policy change will have no effect on real output—policy only works if it surprises people.

Although the rational-expectations assumption is consistent with microeconomic behavior such as profit maximization and satisfaction maximization, opponents argue that it requires an unrealistic amount of information (and a true model) to be known by households and firms.

Real business cycle theory asks whether business cycles will occur if expectations are rational, wages and prices are perfectly flexible and markets (including the labor market) clear? Because these assumptions lead to a vertical *AS* curve, even in the short run, demand-side changes fail to have any impact on production. Fluctuations observed in the real-world economy must be due, therefore, to supply-side factors. Real business cycle theory investigates which factors might be significant, concluding that output fluctuations can be caused only by unexpected shocks to the *AS* curve (such as technological change). A positive technological shock will boost labor productivity, increase real wages, and encourage households to supply more labor. This, in turn, will lead to increased production.

ECONOMICS IN PRACTICE: On page 346 [658], the textbook raises the issue of how we form our expectations. The original Keynesian view was that expectations are "backward-looking" rather than rational, and the textbook offers some evidence to support that view. Further, the survey referred to in the text indicates that our economic expectations are based on one or two pieces of information.

First, consider flipping a coin that you are sure is unbiased. Suppose, the first 10 times, the result is "heads." Would that result influence your prediction of "heads" occurring on the next flip and, if so, how and why?

ANSWER: You may well be affected by a sequence of ten "heads" in a row. If so, you're expectations are not rational, but backward-looking. If it is an unbiased coin, the chance of "heads" occurring on the eleventh flip is still 50:50. Favoring either "heads" ("It's done it so many times, it'll continue") or "tails" ("The sequence can't possibly continue") is irrational. Past behavior in this case does not predict future behavior.

ECONOMICS IN PRACTICE (CONTINUED):

Now suppose that you're considering buying a new car. This is a significant and long-lasting purchase—you will make some estimate of how long you will keep your car (unless you trade in after a set length of time). Which factors do you take into account when estimating the life of your car? Are you looking backward or forward?

ANSWER: Probably, you'll be guessing about gas prices and your future transportation needs—a single person today and that same person in some years (married with children) will have different requirements. Also, you'll be concerned about the reliability of the car you choose. Does past performance affect your expectations of future performance? Clearly, for just this one purchase, a lot of information must be painstakingly gathered and evaluated.

ECONOMICS IN PRACTICE (CONTINUED):

The rational-expectations hypothesis looks specifically at expectations regarding inflation. Given that you are in an economics class (and currently learning about inflation), your ability to form expectations should be quite strong. First, do you know the most recently reported inflation and unemployment rates? How do the current rates compare with previous rates?

Can you determine why inflation has been behaving as it has over the past twelve months—which factors were important determinants of inflation?

ANSWER: If you are like most people (even those enrolled in a macroeconomics class), you will not have clear knowledge of the actual inflation and unemployment rates or how those rates compare with previous rates. Subjectively, many individuals think that inflation is "really high" and unemployment is "the worst it's ever been," opinions that are incorrect.

Assuming that you know the current inflation rate, and how it has been changing, you need still a lot of information to determine which factors are influential in shaping inflation—this entire course is an introduction to that process!

━━━━━━━━━━━━━━━━━━━━━━━━━━━━━━ **Practice** ━━━━━━━━━━━━━━━━━━━━━

9.   According to the Lucas supply function, when the _____ price level is greater than the expected price level, production will _____ .

   (a)   actual; increase
   (b)   actual; decrease
   (c)   previous; increase
   (d)   previous; decrease

   ANSWER: (a)   Firms and workers find their own price (or wage) to be higher than expected and produce more. Refer to p. 346 [658].

10.   When there is a mismatch between the expected price level and the actual price level, the difference is called a(n)
(a)   rational expectation.
(b)   irrational expectation.
(c)   price surprise.
(d)   untrue model.
ANSWER: (c)   Refer to p. 345 [657] for a discussion of this topic.

11.   According to the new classical economists, which of the following will affect output?
(a)   An expansionary and anticipated fiscal policy
(b)   An expansionary and anticipated monetary policy
(c)   A contractionary and unanticipated fiscal policy
(d)   A contractionary and anticipated monetary policy
ANSWER: (c)   Only unanticipated policy actions will be effective.

12.   The Lucas supply function states that real output depends on the difference between
(a)   the actual output level and the potential output level.
(b)   the actual price level and the expected price level.
(c)   the actual price level and the equilibrium price level.
(d)   the actual output level and the expected output level.
ANSWER: (b)   Refer to p. 345 [657] for a discussion of the Lucas supply function.

13.   Given rational expectations, unemployment is due to
(a)   announced expansionary policies, whether fiscal or monetary.
(b)   announced contractionary policies, whether fiscal or monetary.
(c)   deficient aggregate demand within the private sector.
(d)   unpredictable shocks.
ANSWER: (d)   If an event can be predicted, it will have no impact on the real economy.

14.   Which of the following statements about expectations is false?
(a)   The traditional treatment of expectations is flawed in that it is inconsistent with the microeconomic assumption that individuals are forward looking.
(b)   The traditional treatment of expectations is flawed in that it is inconsistent with the microeconomic assumption that individuals are rational.
(c)   The rational-expectations hypothesis assumes that errors in forecasting future inflation are systematic.
(d)   The rational-expectations hypothesis assumes that errors in forecasting future inflation are random.
ANSWER: (c)   If individuals use all available information with the true model, overestimates and underestimates will be randomly distributed, sometimes too large, sometimes too small.

15.   The major argument against the rational-expectations hypothesis is that
(a)   it requires households and firms to know too much.
(b)   it is inconsistent with the assumptions of microeconomics.
(c)   it assumes that expectations are formed rather naively.
(d)   it assumes that information collection is costless.
ANSWER: (a)   Refer to p. 347 [659] for an evaluation of the rational-expectations theory.

16.   According to the real business cycle theory, which of the following could not cause business cycles?
      (a)   A change in labor productivity
      (b)   A change in the money supply
      (c)   A change in the size of the labor force
      (d)   A change in the real quantity of the capital stock

      ANSWER: (b)   A change in money supply will affect aggregate demand; the other options will affect the supply side of the economy.

17.   According to the real business cycle theory, a technological advance will _____ the marginal product of labor, causing real wages to _____ .
      (a)   increase; increase
      (b)   increase; decrease
      (c)   decrease; increase
      (d)   decrease; decrease

      ANSWER: (a)   With better technology, workers will become more productive. Real wages will increase. ∎

OBJECTIVE 3:
Outline the reasoning behind (and summarize the evidence about) the supply-side policies that found prominence in the 1980s.

Supply-side economics came to prominence in the early 1980s and, in opposition to the traditional Keynesian "demand-side" policies, advocated policies designed to stimulate aggregate supply. Policies were intended to increase the incentives to supply labor, to save, and to invest. Personal tax rates were reduced and tax credits were given for investment—measures designed to boost production. Additionally, government regulation of the private sector was lessened. Such measures attempt to shift the aggregate supply curve to the right, which would combat inflation and unemployment simultaneously. (page 348 [660])

      The *Laffer Curve*, which relates tax rates and tax revenues, was a key element of this strategy. Its shape suggests that, if taxes are prohibitive, cuts in tax rates will *increase* tax collections and boost incentives to work. (This was an attractive theory for a president committed to reducing the federal deficit while cutting tax rates.)

      Although an alluring theory, studies have yet to find significant evidence to support the supply-side view. The tax cuts taken in the name of supply-side policy, it is argued, actually stimulated the economy through demand-side effects as disposable income expanded. (page 349 [661])

      Comment: Changes in income tax rates are acceptable policy options for the demand-side Keynesians and for the supply-siders. The effect of the tax cut is viewed differently. A Keynesian economist would see the tax cut boosting consumption and, thus, aggregate demand, whereas a supply-side economist would emphasize the effect on labor supply.

      An investment tax credit should increase investment (demand-side) and productive capacity (supply-side)—again, the difference between the two views is one of emphasis. The Keynesian would believe that the stronger and more immediate effect would be felt through a change in aggregate demand, while the supply-side economist would argue that the most immediate effect would be felt in aggregate supply.

━━■━━━━━━━━━━━━━━━━━━━━━ **Practice** ━━━━━━━━━━━━━━━━━━━━━━

18.   Supply-side economists argued that the government should focus on policies designed
      (a)   to stimulate demand.
      (b)   to stimulate supply.
      (c)   to discourage demand.
      (d)   to discourage supply.

      ANSWER: (b) Refer to p. 348 [660] for supply-side policy recommendations.

19.   According to the Laffer Curve, as tax rates increase, tax revenues will
      (a)   increase.
      (b)   decrease.
      (c)   increase and then decrease.
      (d)   decrease and then increase.

      ANSWER: (c) Refer to Figure 18.2 [33.2] for the diagram.

20.   Which of the following is a potential supply-side policy?
      (a)   An increase in government spending
      (b)   An increase in depreciation allowances for businesses intended to encourage investment
      (c)   Increases in the employer contributions to the Social Security program
      (d)   Increases in welfare benefits

      ANSWER: (b) Greater depreciation allowances will stimulate additional investment and greater
              aggregate supply. Note that the increase in planned investment will also increase
              aggregate demand.

21.   Supply-side cuts in personal tax rates and increases in investment incentives would
      (a)   increase aggregate demand only.
      (b)   increase aggregate supply only.
      (c)   increase aggregate demand and aggregate supply.
      (d)   decrease aggregate demand and increase aggregate supply.

      ANSWER: (c) Cutting tax rates and providing investment incentives would increase labor
              supply and the capital stock, but would also increase consumption and planned
              investment spending. ■

BRAIN TEASER SOLUTION: If inflation is higher than expected, your real wage will decrease and your employer's real wage bill will decrease. As the price at which the firm can sell is increasing more rapidly than the real wage bill, the employer has a profit incentive to hire more workers and increase production. When the actual inflation rate exceeds the expected inflation rate, aggregate supply will increase.

ENDPOINT: COMPARISONS OF THE KEYNESIAN, MONETARIST, NEW CLASSICAL, AND SUPPLY-SIDE MODELS

Here are a few of the differences between the models that you've seen. Use these generalizations to help you sort out the different views and, perhaps, to find the one *you* feel is most accurate.

Factor	Keynesian	Monetarist	New Classical	Supply-Side
Prices	sticky	flexible	flexible	flexible
Do markets clear?	no	yes	yes	yes
Expectations	adaptive	adaptive	rational	adaptive
Policy preferences	demand-side	demand-side	"hands-off"—	supply-side
	fiscal and monetary	monetary policy	no anticipated	fiscal policy
	policy		policy will work	

Note: "Adaptive" expectations is the name given to the traditional view of how expectations are formed, as described on p. 344 [656] in the textbook. Individuals adapt their expectations based on what has gone before. Proponents of the forward-looking rational expectations hypothesis term such adaptive behavior "backward-looking."

The models in this chapter can all be interpreted in terms of the *AS/AD* diagram. Keynesianism focuses on the short-run diagram and manipulation of aggregate demand. Monetarism also focuses on movement of aggregate demand (ultimately through changes in the money supply), but the long run arrives more quickly. Supply-side economics also claims that policy actions can shift the economy—by moving the aggregate supply curve. Again, markets are competitive and responsive, and the long run arrives rapidly. New classical economists argue that government intervention is destabilizing. With rational expectations, the economy achieves potential output rapidly.

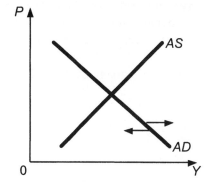

Keynesian: shift *AD*
(monetary and fiscal policy)

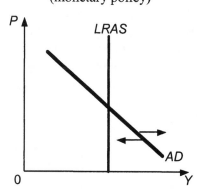

Monetarist: shift *AD*
(monetary policy)

Supply-Side: shift *AS*
(fiscal policy)

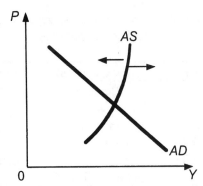

New Classical
(non-intervention)

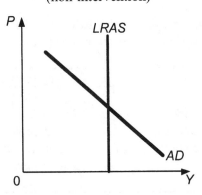

The debate about price surprises and employment can be quite difficult to follow. The following table will help you to grasp the main ideas.

| Price Level | Inflation | | Wage/Hour | Hours Worked | Reward/Hour | |
	Expected	Actual			Expected	Actual
1.00	0%	0%	10.00	8	10	10
1.00	0%	0%	11.00	9	11	11
1.10	0%	10%	11.00	9	11	10
1.10	10%	10%	11.00	8	10	10

Assume an economy that neither has nor expects inflation. The aggregate price level is $1.00.

The first two rows of numbers represent the supply of labor that will occur at two different wage levels. Given the price level, the worker will work 8 hours for a nominal wage of $10.00 per hour and 9 hours for $11.00 per hour. What is the real wage in each case?

The next row shows that, unexpectedly, prices have jumped 10%. Employers can now offer higher (nominal) wages. Employment increases because workers are "fooled" into thinking that their real wage has risen to 11 units/hour. Eventually, when workers discover that their real reward is only 10 units/hour, the quantity of labor supplied will decrease.

Conclusion: A price surprise can cause production and employment levels to change.

PRACTICE TEST

I.   MULTIPLE-CHOICE QUESTIONS

Select the option that provides the single best answer.

_____ 1.   The velocity of money is
         (a)   constant in the real world.
         (b)   the number of times an average dollar bill changes hands per year.
         (c)   equal to nominal GDP divided by the value of goods and services traded in a year.
         (d)   equal to nominal GDP divided by real GDP.

_____ 2.   The macroeconomic viewpoint that believes velocity is constant and that a direct relationship exists between growth of the money stock and the rate of inflation is
    (a)   new classical economics.
    (b)   classical economics.
    (c)   the quantity theory.
    (d)   the Keynesian theory.

_____ 3.   Under which of the following assumptions could we state that inflation is a purely monetary phenomenon?
    (a)   Velocity is constant.
    (b)   Real output is constant.
    (c)   Both velocity and real output are constant.
    (d)   The money supply is constant.

_____ 4.   The rational-expectations hypothesis assumes that
    (a)   full employment always occurs because rational individuals always realize that they should adjust to wage changes.
    (b)   there is no unanticipated inflation.
    (c)   decision-makers have a theoretical model of how the economy works.
    (d)   individuals are able to predict future inflation rates accurately.

_____ 5.   According to supply-side economic theory, the most important effect of a cut in personal income tax rates would be
    (a)   increased consumption spending.
    (b)   increased personal saving.
    (c)   increased number of hours worked.
    (d)   decreased tax revenues.

_____ 6.   The Laffer Curve shows the relationship between tax rates and
    (a)   inflation.
    (b)   tax revenues.
    (c)   the federal deficit.
    (d)   national income.

_____ 7.   Lucas hypothesized that aggregate _____ is reduced when the expected price level is _____ the actual price level.
    (a)   demand; greater than
    (b)   demand; less than
    (c)   supply; greater than
    (d)   supply; less than

_____ 8.   According to monetarists, inflation has persisted because
    (a)   the Fed has accommodated the federal deficit by cutting the rate of growth of the money supply.
    (b)   aggregate supply has failed to expand adequately because of regulation and tax laws.
    (c)   aggregate supply has risen quite sharply despite government regulation and tax laws.
    (d)   the Fed has accommodated the federal deficit through expansionary monetary policy actions.

_____ 9.   The new classical macroeconomic view developed because traditional economics
    (a)   unrealistically assumed that individuals have perfect knowledge of the future.
    (b)   failed to assume that, on average, individuals can accurately predict future events.
    (c)   assumed that individuals do not learn from errors in forecasts.
    (d)   assumed that consumers have less information than producers.

_____ 10.   According to the Lucas supply function,
    (a)   anticipated expansionary fiscal policy actions can increase production.
    (b)   unanticipated expansionary fiscal policy actions can increase production.
    (c)   anticipated expansionary monetary policy actions can increase production.
    (d)   anticipated contractionary fiscal policy actions can increase production.

_____ 11.   The Fed increases the money supply. Evidence suggests that, as the interest rate decreases, the quantity of money demanded _____ and the velocity of money _____ .
    (a)   increases; increases
    (b)   increases; decreases
    (c)   decreases; increases
    (d)   decreases; decreases

_____ 12.   The Fed increases the money supply by 10%; the interest rate decreases. Because velocity decreases, the _____ in nominal GDP will be _____ .
    (a)   increase; more than 10%
    (b)   increase; less than 10%
    (c)   decrease; more than 10%
    (d)   decrease; less than 10%

_____ 13.   M2 is _____ than M1; the measure of velocity based on M2 will be _____ than the measure of velocity based on M1.
    (a)   larger; larger
    (b)   larger; smaller
    (c)   smaller; larger
    (d)   smaller; small

_____ 14.   Which of the following schools of thought is not directly opposed to use of fiscal policy to manipulate the macroeconomy?
    (a)   Keynesian
    (b)   Monetarism
    (c)   Rational expectations
    (d)   New classical

_____ 15.   The velocity of money is the ratio of
    (a)   nominal GDP to the stock of money.
    (b)   real GDP to the stock of money.
    (c)   stock of money to real GDP.
    (d)   the stock of money to nominal GDP.

_____ 16.   When inflation is increasing and expectations are formed rationally, individuals will
   (a)   consistently overestimate inflation.
   (b)   consistently underestimate inflation.
   (c)   estimate inflation correctly every time.
   (d)   estimate inflation correctly on average, with randomly distributed errors.

_____ 17.   Supply-siders argued that a cut in tax rates would _____ the amount of taxable income and _____ tax revenues.
   (a)   increase; increase
   (b)   increase; decrease
   (c)   decrease; increase
   (d)   decrease; decrease

_____ 18.   According to the real business cycle theory, a beneficial productivity shock would _____ the real interest rate and _____ the price level.
   (a)   increase; increase
   (b)   increase; decrease
   (c)   decrease; increase
   (d)   decrease; decrease

_____ 19.   New classical economists conclude that
   (a)   neither anticipated nor unanticipated policy changes can have an impact on real output.
   (b)   either anticipated or unanticipated policy changes can have an impact on real output.
   (c)   only anticipated policy changes can have an impact on real output.
   (d)   only unanticipated policy changes can have an impact on real output.

_____ 20.   The notion that "short-run stabilization policies can't work because you can't fool all of the people all of the time" is most readily identified with
   (a)   the new classical economists.
   (b)   the Keynesians.
   (c)   the monetarists.
   (d)   the supply-siders.

II.   APPLICATION QUESTIONS

1.   In Arbez a simple proportional tax is imposed on wages. Tax revenues (T) are:

$$T = t \times W \times L$$

where t is the tax rate, W is the gross hourly wage rate, and L is the total supply of labor in hours.
   The after-tax (net) wage is

$$W_n = (1 - t)W$$

Suppose that $W = \$6$, $L = 10,000$, and $t = 0.3$.

(a)   Calculate tax revenues.

(b)   What is the net hourly wage?

(c)   Now suppose that the tax rate is reduced to 0.25. For tax revenues to remain unchanged, how much must the labor supply increase (assuming that the gross hourly wage rate doesn't change)?

(d)   Calculate the new net hourly wage.

(e)   Elasticity of labor supply is $\%\Delta L \div \%\Delta W_n$. Calculate the numerical value of the elasticity of labor supply.

(f)   Interpret the meaning of the elasticity number you've calculated with respect to the plausibility of reducing taxes while maintaining the same level of tax collections.

2.   (a)   Calculate the values for PY and write them in the following table. This is a short-run aggregate supply schedule.

P	Y	PY	$MV30$	$MV45$
$0.50	50			
$1.00	60			
$2.00	70			
$3.00	80			
$4.00	90			
$5.00	100			
$6.00	110			

(b)   Suppose that velocity (V) is constant and equal to 8, and that the money supply is equal to $30. Complete the $MV30$ column of the table.

(c)   In equilibrium, calculate the nominal GDP level, the price level, and the real output level.

(d)   Now the Fed increases the money supply to $45 (a 50% increase). Velocity remains constant. Complete the $MV45$ column of the table.

(e)   In equilibrium, calculate the nominal GDP level, the price level, and the real output level is.

Can you see that the $MV30$ and $MV45$ columns represent the dollar value of expenditures at different levels of the money supply? For a monetarist, this is the same thing as an aggregate demand curve!

Our supply schedule is short-run—monetary policy actions have an effect on output. In the long run, however, a monetarist would claim that a ten percent increase in money supply would result in a ten percent increase in prices and in wages; real wage and output level would be unaffected by price changes. Aggregate supply is vertical in the long run!

3.   Rational expectations theorists claim that the traditional (Keynesian) view of the formation of expectations about inflation leads to systematic mistakes. If formed rationally, these mistakes will not be systematic—they will be neither too large nor too small in a predictable way. Let

EP_t = Expected price level (this time period)
P_t = Price level (this time period)
EP_{t+1} = Expected price level (next time period)

Suppose that individuals are backward-looking, following the formula $EP_{t+1} = EP_t + 0.5(EP_t - P_t)$ when they form their expectations.

Calculate the expected price level in the following table.

Time Period (*t*)	0	1	2	3	4	5	6	7	8	9
Price level	100	100	110	121	131	142	126	115	107	100
Expected price level	100	___	___	___	___	___	___	___	___	___

Graph the values for the expected price level and the price level on the graph.

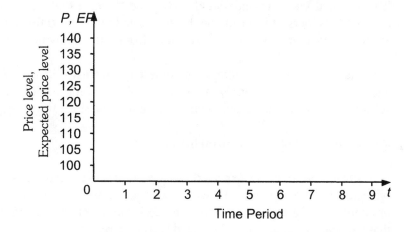

4.   (a)   In the following diagram, why are tax collections zero at Point *A*?

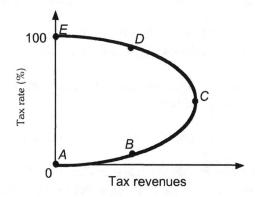

(b)   Why are tax collections zero at Point *E*?
(c)   At which point on the curve did Laffer believe the economy was in the early 1980s?
(d)   What policy action was called for?

(e)   Assuming spending programs remained unchanged, what effect would this have had on the budget deficit?

(f)   What effect did Laffer believe this sort of move would have on the supply of labor?

(g)   If the tax rate was at Point *B*, and the same policy was pursued, what would have happened to the deficit and the supply of labor?

PRACTICE TEST SOLUTIONS

I.   Solutions to Multiple-Choice Questions

1.   (b)   This is a good, easy-to-understand definition of velocity. Note that it does not require velocity to be constant.

2.   (c)   The "quantity" in the quantity theory refers to the quantity of money in the economy. Refer to p. 341 [653].

3.   (c)   In the equation $MV = PY$, if V and Y are both constant, then an increase in P (inflation) can be caused only by an increase in M.

4.   (c)   It is assumed that each individual knows the "true model" that generates inflation. We may not have perfect information, however, and our expectations may not be completely accurate. Given price surprises, deviations from full employment will occur.

5.   (c)   If the tax rate is cut, after-tax take-home pay increases. The substitution effect would encourage workers to supply more labor. The income effect would partly offset the substitution effect, but supply-siders believe that the substitution effect would dominate.

6.   (b)   Refer to p. 348 [660] for more on the Laffer Curve.

7.   (c)   A mismatch between the expected and the actual price level affects supply. If the actual price level is greater than the expected price level, each firm believes that the actual price it is able to charge is "high," and so it increases production. Each worker believes that the wage s/he earns is "high," and works more.

8.   (d)   Monetarists believe that inflation is a purely monetary phenomenon.

9.   (b)   Refer to p. 343 [655]. Note that individuals do learn from errors but, because consumers remain backward-looking, errors can persist.

10.   (b)   Anticipated changes will have no effect on the economy, according to the rational-expectations hypothesis.

11.   (b)   Refer to p. 341 [653] for more on this contentious issue.

12.   (b)   Given $MV = PY$, the decrease in V partly offsets the 10% increase in M. The right-hand side of the equation will increase, but by less than the full 10%.

13.   (b)   M2 includes M1 and other assets, such as savings accounts. Given the value of GDP, if we define V as PY/M, V will decrease the larger the value of M.

14. (a) Refer to p. 340 [652] for more on monetarism.

15. (a) Refer to p. 340 [652] for a discussion of velocity.

16. (d) The rational-expectations hypothesis does not claim that expectations will always be correct. It does claim that no systematic error will be made.

17. (a) According to the Laffer Curve, a reduction in tax rates will encourage more labor supply and, therefore, more income that can be taxed. Despite lower tax rates, tax revenues will increase, if the economy is initially at a point such as A in Figure 18.2 [33.2] on p. 349 [661].

18. (d) The AS curve will shift right.

19. (d) Only a discrepancy between the actual price level and the expected price level will affect output. Only unanticipated events will produce such a mismatch.

20. (a) Policy can only work, according to the new classical economists, if it systematically upsets expectations.

II. *Solutions to Application Questions*

1. (a) Tax revenue $= t \times W \times L = 0.3 \times \$6 \times 10,000 = \$18,000$.
   (b) The net wage (after tax) $= (1 - t)W = 0.7 \times \$6 = \$4.20$.
   (c) It must change from 10,000 to 12,000.
       Tax revenue $= t \times W \times L = 0.25 \times \$6 \times 12,000 = \$18,000$.
   (d) The net wage (after tax) $= (1 - t)W = 0.75 \times \$6 = \$4.50$.
   (e) $\%\Delta L = 2,000/(10,000 + 12,000) = 0.09091$.
       $\%\Delta Wn = 0.30/(4.20 + 4.50) = 0.03448$.
       $\%\Delta L/\%\Delta Wn = 0.09091/0.03448 = 2.6363$.

   (f) This elasticity coefficient indicates that labor supply would have to be very elastic for the government to undertake the tax cut and hope to avoid having tax revenues decrease. Essentially, the after-tax wage has increased by 3.448%. To accomplish its goal of maintaining tax revenues, the government must encourage a 9.091% increase in hours worked.

2. (a) Refer to the following table.

P	Y	PY	$MV30$	$MV45$
$0.50	50	$25	$240	$360
$1.00	60	$60	$240	$360
$2.00	70	$140	$240	$360
$3.00	80	$240	$240	$360
$4.00	90	$360	$240	$360
$5.00	100	$500	$240	$360
$6.00	110	$660	$240	$360

   (b) Refer to the preceding table. In each case, $M \times V = 30 \times 8 = 240$.

(c)   Nominal *GDP* = $240, price level = $3.00, output = 80. Recall that, in equilibrium, *MV* = *PY*.

(d)   Refer to the preceding table. In each case, $M \times V = 45 \times 8 = 360$.

(e)   Nominal GDP = $360, price level = $4.00, output = 90.

3.   Example of calculations:

$$\text{Year 2: } EP_{t+1} = EP_t + 0.5(P_t - EP_t) = 100 + 0.5(100 - 100) = 100$$
$$\text{Year 3: } EP_{t+1} = EP_t + 0.5(P_t - EP_t) = 100 + 0.5(110 - 100) = 105$$
$$\text{Year 4: } EP_{t+1} = EP_t + 0.5(P_t - EP_t) = 105 + 0.5(121 - 105) = 113$$
$$\text{Year 5: } EP_{t+1} = EP_t + 0.5(P_t - EP_t) = 113 + 0.5(131 - 113) = 122$$
$$\text{Year 6: } EP_{t+1} = EP_t + 0.5(P_t - EP_t) = 122 + 0.5(142 - 122) = 132$$
$$\text{Year 7: } EP_{t+1} = EP_t + 0.5(P_t - EP_t) = 132 + 0.5(126 - 132) = 129$$

Time Period (*t*)	0	1	2	3	4	5	6	7	8	9
Price level	100	100	110	121	131	142	126	115	107	100
Expected price level	100	100	100	105	113	122	132	129	122	114.5

In the following graph, note that individuals systematically underestimate increases in the price level and then overestimate them when the price level decreases.

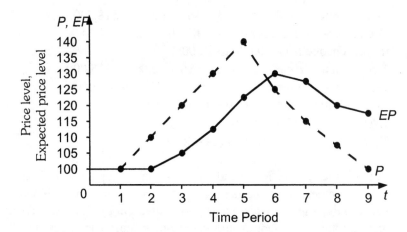

4.   (a)   Tax collections are zero because the tax rate is zero.

(b)   If all income were taxed away, there would be no incentive to earn income. Income (and tax collections) would fall to zero.

(c)   Point *D*. Laffer felt that tax rates were acting as a disincentive to work.

(d)   Reduce tax rates, moving from Point *D* toward Point *C*.

(e)   The deficit would have fallen because tax revenues would have increased.

(f)   Because after-tax pay was rising, labor supply would have risen, according to Laffer.

(g)   If the tax rate were reduced from Point *B*, the supply of labor should still have risen, but, because of shrinking tax revenues, the deficit would have increased.

Comprehensive
Review Test

The following questions provide a wide-ranging review of the material covered in Part IV (VI)—Chapters 15–18 (30–33) of the textbook. Each question deals with a topic or technique important for your understanding of economic principles. If you miss a question you should return to the relevant section of the chapter in the textbook and fine-tune your understanding.

I.   MULTIPLE-CHOICE QUESTIONS

Select the option that provides the single best answer.

_____ 1.   According to supply-siders, when tax rates are too high but are then decreased, labor supply will increase. This suggests that
       (a)   there is no income effect from a tax rate change.
       (b)   there is no substitution effect from a tax rate change.
       (c)   the income effect from a tax rate change dominates the substitution effect.
       (d)   the substitution effect from a tax rate change dominates the income effect.

_____ 2.   The household _____ control its constrained labor supply and _____ control its unconstrained labor supply.
       (a)   can; can
       (b)   can; can not
       (c)   can not; can
       (d)   can; can not

_____ 3.   Workers in Arboc have experienced rising inflation, and expect this trend to continue next year. The government, however, holds down the growth of the money supply so that the inflation rate actually falls. In the short run, we would expect unemployment to
       (a)   fall, but stay above the natural rate.
       (b)   rise, and be above the natural rate.
       (c)   rise, but stay below its natural rate.
       (d)   fall, and be below the natural rate.

_____ 4.   Which of the following is the least likely to be proposed as a supply-side policy action?
    (a)   Accelerations in depreciation write-offs
    (b)   Reductions in personal income tax rates
    (c)   Autonomous increases in government spending
    (d)   Reductions in capital gains taxes

_____ 5.   Short-run stabilization policies may be doomed to failure for each of the following reasons EXCEPT
    (a)   because workers will learn to anticipate policy actions, according the rational expectations theorists, and so expectations will change immediately (no short run).
    (b)   because in the short-run, any time the Administration reduces unemployment, inflation will rise.
    (c)   because it may take so long to decide which policy action to make that inappropriate policies may be enacted.
    (d)   because policy actions come from a variety of bodies (Congress, the Fed) and the actions may be uncoordinated.

_____ 6.   Jenny claims that, if her wage rate were cut, she would work more hours. This behavior
    (a)   is irrational.
    (b)   indicates that Jenny's substitution effect dominates her income effect.
    (c)   indicates that Jenny's income effect dominates her substitution effect.
    (d)   Jenny's substitution effect and her income effect operate in the same direction.

_____ 7.   Ultimately, inflation can be sustained from year to year only if
    (a)   the government runs larger and larger deficits each year.
    (b)   government spending increases each year.
    (c)   the money supply is increased each year.
    (d)   private spending increases faster than aggregate supply.

_____ 8.   Following the double-digit inflation of the 1970s, a growing proportion of American workers negotiated automatic cost-of-living adjustments (COLAs) in their wage contracts. This would make the short-run aggregate supply curve
    (a)   vertical.
    (b)   horizontal.
    (c)   steeper.
    (d)   flatter.

_____ 9.   Given the interest rate, firms are likely to be _____ optimistic and planned investment is likely to be _____ when output is expanding relatively rapidly.
    (a)   more; higher
    (b)   more; lower
    (c)   less; higher
    (d)   less; lower

_____   10.   A firm's inventories unexpectedly increase. We would expect the firm to _____ future production and to _____ labor hiring.
(a)   increase; increase
(b)   increase; decrease
(c)   decrease; increase
(d)   decrease; decrease

_____   11.   Over the business cycle, employment tends to fluctuate _____ than output, causing labor productivity to _____ during an expansion.
(a)   more; increase
(b)   more; decrease
(c)   less; increase
(d)   less; decrease

_____   12.   According to the real business cycle theory, economic growth is due to
(a)   rightward shifts of the aggregate demand curve.
(b)   expansionary fiscal or monetary policies that are fully anticipated.
(c)   expansionary fiscal or monetary policies that are not fully anticipated.
(d)   rightward shifts of the aggregate supply curve.

_____   13.   Lower income tax rates will _____ consumption and _____ labor supply if the substitution effect is dominant.
(a)   increase; increase
(b)   increase; decrease
(c)   decrease; increase
(d)   decrease; decrease

_____   14.   The greater the crowding-out effect, the _____ the multiplier; the smaller the percentage of imports, the _____ the multiplier.
(a)   larger; larger
(b)   larger; smaller
(c)   smaller; larger
(d)   smaller; smaller

_____   15.   Which of the following is NOT a "slippage" between an increase in output and a decrease in the unemployment rate?
(a)   The relationship between the change in output and the utilization by firms of their excess capacity
(b)   The relationship between the change in output and the increase in overtime work
(c)   The relationship between the change in the number of jobs and the change in the number of workers employed
(d)   The relationship between the change in output and amount of frictional unemployment

_____   16.   Mr. Micawber is in debt. The interest rate increases. The substitution effect will _____ his consumption level, and the income effect will _____ his consumption level.
(a)   increase; increase
(b)   increase; decrease
(c)   decrease; increase
(d)   decrease; decrease

_____ 17. Ebenezer Scrooge receives unexpected wealth. As a result, his consumption will _____ and his labor supply will _____ .
(a)   increase; increase
(b)   increase; decrease
(c)   decrease; increase
(d)   decrease; decrease

_____ 18. According to the Lucas supply function, workers who experience a positive price surprise will work more hours
(a)   if the substitution effect dominates the income effect.
(b)   if the income effect dominates the substitution effect
(c)   because there is no income effect in the presence of a price surprise.
(d)   because there is no substitution effect in the presence of a price surprise.

_____ 19. Rational expectations theorists claim that individuals
(a)   tend to underestimate inflation.
(b)   predict future events accurately.
(c)   tend to overestimate inflation.
(d)   neither persistently underestimate nor overestimate inflation.

_____ 20. In the long run, an increase in money supply would make aggregate demand increase and the price level increase according to
(a)   only the Keynesian model.
(b)   the Keynesian model and the monetarist model, but not the new classical model.
(c)   the Keynesian model, the monetarist model, and the new classical model.
(d)   the monetarist model and the new classical model, but not the Keynesian model.

_____ 21. Real business cycle theorists believe that involuntary unemployment
(a)   is due to flexible wages and prices.
(b)   can be alleviated by demand-side fiscal policy.
(c)   can be alleviated by demand-side monetary policy.
(d)   None of the above.

_____ 22. Consider a production possibility frontier. Which of the following represents long-run growth?
(a)   a movement from a point inside the production possibility frontier to a point on the production possibility frontier.
(b)   a movement from a point inside the production possibility frontier to a point beyond the production possibility frontier.
(c)   a movement along the production possibility frontier to where more capital is produced.
(d)   a movement of the production possibility frontier outwards.

_____ 23. There is a decrease in the supply of labor. This will cause the production possibility frontier to
(a)   become flatter.
(b)   become steeper.
(c)   shift outwards.
(d)   shift inwards.

_____ 24.   Real business cycle theory assumes that wages and prices _____ perfectly flexible, expectations are rational. The short-run aggregate supply curve is _____ .
   (a)   are; upward-sloping
   (b)   are; vertical
   (c)   are not; upward-sloping
   (d)   are not; vertical

_____ 25.   Today, most economists believe that _____ is purely a _____ phenomenon.
   (a)   cyclical unemployment; monetary
   (b)   cyclical unemployment; fiscal
   (c)   inflation; monetary
   (d)   inflation; fiscal

_____ 26.   In the 1970s, American labor productivity declined. Which of the following was not a likely cause of the productivity problem?
   (a)   Increasing energy prices
   (b)   Reductions in government regulation
   (c)   Low saving rates
   (d)   High rates of capital accumulation

_____ 27.   In the short run, an unanticipated reduction in the rate of inflation would
   (a)   increase unemployment.
   (b)   certainly increase the "discomfort index."
   (c)   decrease unemployment.
   (d)   lower the natural rate of unemployment.

_____ 28.   The actual multiplier is smaller than the theoretical multiplier because of all of the following reasons EXCEPT that, as spending increases,
   (a)   the interest rate rises and reduces investment spending.
   (b)   producers may increase prices instead of output.
   (c)   transfer payments tend to increase.
   (d)   excess labor may be pressed into service, with no change in employment.

_____ 29.   According to the concept of permanent income, most of a decrease in income taxes will be _____ , if perceived as a temporary change, and most of a decrease in income taxes will be _____ , if perceived as a permanent change.
   (a)   spent; spent
   (b)   spent; saved
   (c)   saved; spent
   (d)   saved; saved

_____ 30.   The optimal level of inventories will
   (a)   increase if the interest rate faced by the firm increases.
   (b)   increase if storage costs faced by the firm decrease.
   (c)   increase if the price of the good involved decreases.
   (d)   aggregate demand increases.

II.   APPLICATION QUESTIONS

1.   In each of the following cases, determine whether the factor will make the size of the Arbezani government spending multiplier higher or lower than would otherwise be the case. Assume an expansionary fiscal policy in a Keynesian economy.

(a)   Households become more sensitive to interest rate changes because of a high burden of credit card debt.

(b)   A new Arbezani law is passed requiring all wage contracts to include automatic cost of living adjustments.

2.   If consumption decreases as a result of a decrease in stock wealth, predict how different sectors of the economy will be affected by a stock market slump.

3.   Three small economies—Noil, Regit, and Aneyh—have asked you to be their economic consultant. Noil is an orthodox Keynesian economy, Regit is a monetarist economy, and Aneyh is a supply-side economy. Some higher-than-normal unemployment currently exists in each economy and you know that it has been caused by a supply shock.

(a)   The Noilian (Keynesian) Finance Minister asks you how to alleviate the unemployment that exists in the economy. How would you reply?

(b)   The Regitani (monetarist) Finance Minister asks you how to alleviate the unemployment that exists in the economy. How would you reply?

(c)   The Aneyhani (supply-side) Finance Minister asks you for recommendations to alleviate the unemployment. How would you reply?

REVIEW TEST SOLUTIONS

I.   Solutions to Multiple-Choice Questions

1.   (d)   As the tax rate falls, the opportunity cost of not working increases. Labor will be substituted for leisure. As the tax rate falls, after-tax income increases, encouraging workers to enjoy more leisure time. If labor supply increases, the substitution effect must dominate.

2.   (c)   The household can decide how much labor it would like to supply but the amount that it does supply is determined by the workings of the economy.

3.   (b)   If workers underestimate the inflation rate, they overestimate the rise in their real wage and work too much—unemployment is below the natural rate. If the inflation rate is overestimated, the reverse is true. Workers will work less and unemployment will rise above the natural rate.

4.   (c)   An autonomous increase in government spending certainly affects aggregate demand while each of the other proposals affects the economy's willingness to produce.

5.   (b)   A trade-off between inflation and unemployment does not mean that a stabilization policy will not success, although it does mean that the price tag of success may be high.

6.   (c)   Jenny's behavior indicates that her income effect dominates her substitution effect. The substitution effect of a lower wage would lead her to supply less labor but the income effect would encourage her to work more hours which, on balance, she claims she would do.

7.   (c)   To have sustained inflation, the money supply must expand. Option (a) is only possible, ultimately, if the Treasury prints money to cover the government's debts.

8.   (c)   The more rapidly input costs can respond to price changes, the less the impact of a price change on output.

9.   (a)   During periods of relatively rapid growth or optimism, firms tend to increase planned investment levels.

10.   (d)   If inventories unexpectedly increase, the firm is selling less than it planned to sell. Accordingly, it will scale back production.

11.   (c)   Firms often hold excess labor so that, when the economy expands, employment increases, but less vigorously. With output growing more rapidly than employment, labor productivity increases.

12.   (d)   Real business cycle theory assumes that the aggregate supply curve is vertical, so no change in aggregate demand can influence output level.

13.   (a)   As the tax rate decreases, after-tax income increases, increasing consumption. As after-tax income increases, the opportunity cost of not working increases—the substitution effect would lead us to work more. Note that the income effect would lead us to work less, but the question assumes that the substitution effect is stronger.

14.   (c)   Given an increase in government spending, the effect on aggregate expenditure will be less, the more significant the crowding-out effect. The smaller the leakage of spending power abroad, the greater the amount retained for recycling through the economy's circular flow.

15.   (d)   Okun's Law looks at the effect of changes in output on the unemployment rate through the business cycle—i.e., cyclical unemployment.

16.   (d)   The opportunity cost of consumption has increased—Micawber will substitute saving for consumption. As a debtor, a higher interest rate makes Micawber poorer; poorer individuals consume less.

17.   (b)   Scrooge is richer; richer individuals consume more. Richer individuals also wish to have more leisure time.

18.   (a)   Standard assumptions regarding the substitution effect and the income effect hold in the Lucas supply function. Refer to the discussion in Chapter 16 (31).

19.   (d)   Rational expectations theorists do not claim that humans are infallible, merely that we do not keep repeating the same errors.

20.   (c)   An increase in money supply is an expansionary demand-side policy. All three models indicate that the price level will increase.

21.   (d)   Real business cycle theorists believe that wages and prices are flexible but not that this causes unemployment. Demand-side policies have no effect if the aggregate supply curve is vertical even in the short run.

22.   (d)   Growth is represented by an outward shift of the production possibility frontier.

23.   (d)   The position of the production possibility frontier is determined by the quantity and quality of resources and the technology to combine them.

24.   (b)   Real business cycle theory assumes that wages and prices are perfectly flexible and markets clear. Because of this, changes in the price level do not influence the economy's level of production.

25.   (c)   Most modern economic models agree that inflation is caused by over-enthusiastic monetary policy.

26.   (b)   Critics suggested that U.S. productivity was being stifled by excessive government interference in business.

27.   (c)   Consider the long-run aggregate supply curve—all changes in the price level are fully accounted for. Now consider the short-run aggregate supply curve. Higher prices prompt greater labor supply and greater production, because the price change is not fully anticipated. Reverse this logic for an unanticipated decrease in the inflation rate. For your information, the "discomfort index" is the sum of the inflation rate and the unemployment rate.

28.   (c)   Transfers, such as welfare payments, decrease as workers leave the unemployment rolls and are hired.

29.   (c)   Households will respond to a permanent increase in income by spending more, but will save temporary windfalls.

30.   (b)   If storage costs faced by the firm decrease firms will be able to hold more items in stock for the same cost.

II.   Solutions to Application Questions

1.   (a)   The multiplier will be lower. An expansion in government spending increases the interest rate. If households are concerned about debt repayments, they will reduce their current purchases.
       (b)   The multiplier will be lower. The more rapidly input prices respond to changes in output prices, the less firms will be willing to expand employment opportunities and production.

2.   The consumer durable goods industries (cars, furniture, computers, electronics) will be hit hard. The service sector will be affected less, but discretionary services, such as dentists, beauty salons, whose work can be delayed, will be affected more severely. Housing starts will decrease. Nondurable goods (food, gasoline) will be affected least by a stock market downturn.

3.   (a)   The standard Keynesian response to cyclical unemployment is to increase aggregate demand—either through an expansionary fiscal policy (increased government spending or decreased taxes) or through an expansionary monetary policy (open market bond purchases, reduction of the discount rates, or reduction of the reserve requirement). Note that either policy would be inflationary, however.

(b)   As a monetarist, demand-side fiscal policy manipulations do not have a long-run effect and should be avoided. In this case, policymakers, preferably, should allow the self-correcting mechanism to take effect or, if a short-run cure is deemed necessary, increase the money supply to stimulate aggregate demand.

(c)   Supply-side economists would call for policies to boost short-run aggregate supply (reducing government regulation and increasing work incentives).   As with the Keynesians, fiscal policy could be used. However, the emphasis would be on cuts in tax rates to encourage productive resources. Lower tax rates on profits and income from saving should increase investment and the *AS* curve will begin to move to the right.

Part V

The World Economy

19 [34]

International Trade, Comparative Advantage, and Protectionism

Chapter objectives:

1. Distinguish between an open and a closed economy. Distinguish between a trade surplus and a trade deficit.

2. Distinguish between absolute advantage and comparative advantage and explain the logic behind the theory of comparative advantage. Given a particular two-country, two-good situation, calculate which country will trade which good and indicate the feasible range for the terms of trade.

3. Calculate the limiting values of the exchange rate in a given example and relate the exchange rate to the notion of comparative advantage. Describe how changes in the exchange rate can affect trade flows.

4. Provide an intuitive explanation of the Heckscher-Ohlin theorem.

5. Define a tariff, an export subsidy, and a quota. Outline, using a demand and supply analysis, the costs involved in the imposition of a tariff.

6. Give the arguments advanced for and against protection. Describe the costs involved in permitting free trade.

BRAIN TEASER: Choose some locally produced goods or, if nothing appropriate is available, beer, cigarettes, paper clips, and chewing gum. Suppose that the government has announced that it will protect only goods that are essential for national defense. What arguments can you come up with that would support each industry's claim for protection? Be creative! Remember that arguments that sound plausible may be difficult to refute.

OBJECTIVE 1:

Distinguish between an open and a closed economy. Distinguish between a trade surplus and a trade deficit.

In open economies such as the United States, aggregate expenditures are affected by the presence of exports and imports. We have seen international trade steadily increase in importance throughout the last several decades, as goods and services have moved across borders. If exports exceed imports, the country runs a *trade surplus*. In the oil-expensive years of the 1970s and 1980s, the value of imports into the United States swelled to over 12% of GDP (gross domestic product), and the United States began to experience *trade deficits*—that is, its imports exceeded its exports. Deficits have been recorded annually ever since. (page 354 [666])

▶▶▶   LEARNING TIP: Learn the difference between exports and imports. Imports are foreign-produced goods consumed here. Exports are domestically produced goods sold to customers overseas. Imports and exports are not opposites; they are determined by different factors.◀

Comment: The two terms, "balance of payments" and "balance of trade," are not synonymous. The balance of trade refers only to exports and imports of goods, while the balance of payments includes all international transactions.

────────■──────────────────────── **Practice** ─────────────────────────

1.   If the value of U.S. exports exceeds the value of U.S. imports, the United States has a
        (a)   balance of trade surplus.
        (b)   balance of trade deficit.
        (c)   balance of payments surplus.
        (d)   balance of payments deficit.

        ANSWER: (a)   There may be a balance of payments surplus or deficit—it depends on U.S. performance on all of its international transactions. ■

OBJECTIVE 2:

Distinguish between absolute advantage and comparative advantage and explain the logic behind the theory of comparative advantage. Given a particular two-country, two-good situation, calculate which country will trade which good and indicate the feasible range for the terms of trade.

The *theory of comparative advantage* provides the rationale for free trade. Given a two-country, two-good world, and assuming that the countries have relative cost advantages in the production of different goods, Ricardo showed that both trading partners could benefit from specialization in the production of the good in which they have the comparative advantage. Each country should specialize in the production of that good in which it has a comparative advantage and trade its surplus for the good that it is weaker at producing. Production and welfare will be maximized. Country A is said to have an *absolute advantage* if it can produce a unit of output with fewer resources than Country B. Comparative advantage, though, is a relative concept. Country A will have a *comparative advantage* in whichever good it can produce comparatively cheaper. Specialization and trade allow a country to consume more of a good than it can produce by itself. (page 354 [666])

▶▶▶   LEARNING TIP: If you're like most individuals, you'll need several numerical examples to strengthen your grasp of pure trade theory. The Applications below take you through all the steps included in the text.

Comparative advantage hinges on the concept of *opportunity cost*. (Take a little time to go back and review the material you learned in Chapter 2, especially Application questions 2, 7, and 10 of this Guide. They will lead you through the opportunity cost concept that underlies the theory of comparative advantage.) The producer (person, firm, or country) with the lower opportunity cost will hold the comparative advantage in that product. Don't be misled—absolute advantage is irrelevant.

Using the production possibility frontier (ppf) diagram, trade will be advantageous if the ppf's have differing slopes. The slope depicts opportunity cost. Differing slopes means that a comparative advantage exists—i.e., that the relative costs of production differ. Even though Country A may be more efficient in producing both goods—an absolute advantage—it is the *comparative* advantage of Country A that will establish the preferred pattern of specialization and trade. The country with the flatter ppf has an advantage in the good on the horizontal axis.◀

Given that specialization occurs, the *terms of trade* (the "price" at which one good trades for the other) must be negotiated. For trade to be beneficial for the exporter, the "price" of the exported good (in terms of the imported good) must be greater than its cost of production. A range of potential terms of trade will exist. The deal cut within this range will depend on the relative negotiating strengths of the two partners. (page 359 [671])

───────────────■────────────────── **Practice** ──────────────────────────

Refer to the following table to answer the next four questions. The table shows the possible output levels from one day of labor input.

	Arbez	Arboc
Wheat	12 bushels	6 bushels
Cloth	12 yards	12 yards

2.   Arbez
   (a)   has an absolute advantage in the production of cloth.
   (b)   has an absolute advantage in the production of wheat.
   (c)   has a comparative advantage in the production of cloth.
   (d)   should export cloth to Arboc.

   ANSWER: (b) Arbez can produce absolutely more wheat per worker than Arboc can.

3.   The opportunity cost of one bushel of wheat in Arboc is
   (a)   1/2 yard of cloth.
   (b)   2 yards of cloth.
   (c)   6 yards of cloth.
   (d)   12 yards of cloth.

   ANSWER: (b) Six bushels take the inputs that could have produced 12 yards of cloth, therefore 1 bushel costs 2 yards of cloth.

4.   Which of the following statements is false?
   (a)   Arboc has an absolute advantage in the production of wheat.
   (b)   Arbez should export wheat to Arboc and import cloth from Arboc.
   (c)   The opportunity cost of wheat is twice as high in Arboc as in Arbez.
   (d)   The opportunity cost of a yard of cloth in Arbez is one bushel of wheat.

   ANSWER: (a) Arboc is half as productive per worker as Arbez in wheat production.

5.   Arboc and Arbez decide to specialize according to the law of comparative advantage and trade with one another. We would expect that
   (a)   the trade agreement will be somewhere between 1 bushel of wheat for 1 yard of cloth and 1 bushel of wheat for 2 yards of cloth.
   (b)   the trade agreement will be somewhere between 1/2 bushel of wheat for 1 yard of cloth and 2 bushels of wheat for 1 yard of cloth.
   (c)   Arboc will benefit from trading with Arbez, but Arbez will not benefit from trading with Arboc.
   (d)   Arboc will specialize in the production of wheat and Arbez will specialize in the production of cloth.

   ANSWER: (a)   The Arbezani opportunity cost of 1 bushel of wheat is 1 yard of cloth. Arboc's opportunity cost of 1 bushel of wheat is 2 yards of cloth.

6.   The ratio at which exports are traded for imports is known as
   (a)   the exchange rate.
   (b)   the trade balance.
   (c)   the balance of exchange.
   (d)   the terms of trade.

   ANSWER: (d)   Refer to p. 359 [671] for the definition.

Use the following diagrams, which show the production possibility frontiers (ppf's) for Malaysia and Sri Lanka, to answer the next nine questions. Each country has an equal quantity of resources.

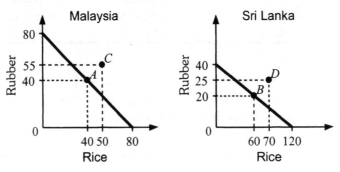

7.   Which of the following statements is true?
   (a)   Malaysia has an absolute advantage in the production of rubber; Sri Lanka has an absolute advantage in the production of rice.
   (b)   Sri Lanka has an absolute advantage in the production of rubber; Malaysia has an absolute advantage in the production of rice.
   (c)   Malaysia has an absolute advantage in the production of both goods.
   (d)   Sri Lanka has an absolute advantage in the production of both goods.

   ANSWER: (a)   Refer to p. 355 [667] for the definition of absolute advantage.

8.   Which statement is false?
   (a)   In Malaysia, the opportunity cost of one unit of rubber is one unit of rice.
   (b)   In Malaysia, the opportunity cost of one unit of rice is one unit of rubber.
   (c)   In Sri Lanka, the opportunity cost of one unit of rubber is three units of rice.
   (d)   In Sri Lanka, the opportunity cost of one unit of rice is three units of rubber.

   ANSWER: (d)   The Sri Lankan opportunity cost of one unit of rice is a third of a unit of rubber.

9.   Which of the following statements is true?
      (a)   Malaysia has a comparative advantage in the production of rubber; Sri Lanka has a comparative advantage in the production of rice.
      (b)   Sri Lanka has a comparative advantage in the production of rubber; Malaysia has a comparative advantage in the production of rice.
      (c)   Malaysia has a comparative advantage in both goods.
      (d)   Sri Lanka has a comparative advantage in both goods.

      ANSWER: (a) Refer to p. 355 [667]. A country can *never* have a comparative advantage in both goods.

10.   Given that Malaysia and Sri Lanka decide to trade,
      (a)   Malaysia should specialize in the production of rubber; Sri Lanka should specialize in the production of rice.
      (b)   Malaysia should specialize in the production of rice; Sri Lanka should specialize in the production of rubber.
      (c)   Malaysia and Sri Lanka should each devote half their resources to the production of each commodity.
      (d)   Malaysia should specialize in the production of rubber; Sri Lanka should produce some rice but continue to produce some rubber.

      ANSWER: (a) Malaysia's comparative advantage lies in rubber production; Sri Lanka's lies in rice. Each should play to their strength and specialize.

11.   Before trade, Malaysia produced at Point A on its production possibility frontier and Sri Lanka produced at Point B. Given complete specialization based on comparative advantage, total rubber production has risen by _____ and total rice production has risen by _____ .
      (a)   80; 120
      (b)   120; 80
      (c)   40; 60
      (d)   20; 20

      ANSWER: (d) Total rubber production was 60 (40 + 20); now it is 80. Total rice production was 100 (40 + 60); now it is 120.

12.   After trade, Malaysia is consuming at Point C and Sri Lanka is consuming at Point D. Malaysia is exporting _____ units of rubber and Sri Lanka is exporting _____ units of rice.
      (a)   80; 100
      (b)   55; 70
      (c)   25; 50
      (d)   15; 10

      ANSWER: (c) Malaysian rubber production is 80, and domestic consumption is 55, leaving 25 for export. Sri Lankan rice production is 120, and domestic consumption is 70, leaving 50 for export.

13.   After trade, Malaysia is consuming at Point C and Sri Lanka is consuming at Point D. Malaysia is importing _____ units of rice and Sri Lanka is importing _____ units of rubber.
       (a)   80; 100
       (b)   50; 25
       (c)   25; 50
       (d)   15; 10

       ANSWER: (b) Refer to the answer to the previous question. In a two-country world, Country A's exports are Country B's imports.

14.   Which statement is true?
       (a)   Only Sri Lanka will benefit if the terms of trade are set at 1:2, rubber to rice.
       (b)   Only Malaysia will benefit if the terms of trade are set at 1:2, rubber to rice.
       (c)   Both countries will gain if the terms of trade lie between 3:1 and 1:1, rubber to rice.
       (d)   Both countries will gain if the terms of trade lie between 1:1 and 1:3, rubber to rice.

       ANSWER: (d) Check these values against the opportunity cost values you calculated in Question 8. Also note the correct value of the rubber : rice ratio in Question 12.

15.   Which statement is false? If the terms of trade are set at
       (a)   1:1, rubber to rice, only Sri Lanka will gain.
       (b)   1:2, rubber to rice, both countries will gain.
       (c)   1:3, rubber to rice, only Malaysia will gain.
       (d)   1:4, rubber to rice, both countries will wish to produce rice.

       ANSWER: (d) If the terms of trade are set at 1:4, rubber to rice, then rubber is relatively valuable and can cover its opportunity cost in both countries. Both will wish to produce rubber. ■

OBJECTIVE 3:
Calculate the limiting values of the exchange rate in a given example and relate the exchange rate to the notion of comparative advantage. Describe how changes in the exchange rate can affect trade flows.

Trade flows are affected by comparative advantage but also by the exchange rate (the "price" of the domestic currency in terms of a foreign currency). There will be some range of exchange rates that will permit mutually beneficial specialization and trade. (page 360 [672])

The distribution of benefits from trade depends on the exchange rate. To buy foreign goods one must hold foreign currency, which is bought and sold in the foreign exchange market. If the value of the dollar changes, the relative attractiveness of the foreign goods will be affected. A strengthening dollar will decrease the price tag of an imported Toyota for a U.S. buyer, but the price tag of the domestically produced Ford will not change—the relative attractiveness of the Toyota will increase. Tourists watch exchange rates keenly—a stronger dollar is good news because each dollar will buy more foreign currency and, therefore, more foreign goods and services (which have, in that sense, become cheaper).

The previous comparative advantage material (in Chapter 2) was based on production capabilities only—supply is important; demand is absent. By incorporating prices, the demand side of the market can be represented.

▶▶▶   LEARNING TIP: An increase in the value of the dollar means that foreign goods cost U.S. citizens less (imports increase), but U.S. goods cost foreigners more (exports fall). Choose a foreign country and currency and make up your own example. ◀

―――――■――――――――――――――――――――――― **Practice** ――――――――――――――

16.   The exchange rate is one British pound equals $1.75. If the exchange rate changes to one British pound equals $1.50, we can conclude that, for a British buyer, a pair of American-made moccasins have become _____ expensive and, for a U.S. buyer, a British cashmere sweater has become _____ expensive.
    (a)   more; more
    (b)   more; less
    (c)   less; more
    (d)   less; less

    ANSWER: (b) Each pound is worth less U.S. currency—British buyers are becoming poorer. The opposite is true for U.S. buyers of British goods.

17.   As the exchange rate changes from one British pound equals $1.50 to one British pound equals $2.00, British traders will gain _____ from trade with the United States, and American traders will gain _____ from trade with the United Kingdom.
    (a)   more; more
    (b)   more; less
    (c)   less; more
    (d)   less; less

    ANSWER: (b) Each pound is worth more U.S. currency. British producers, selling the same amount of exports, will be able to claim more U.S. goods than before.

Use the following table, which shows the domestic prices per unit of steel and corn in Slovakia and Austria, to answer the next three questions.

	Slovakia	Austria
Steel	20 koruna	48 schillings
Corn	30 koruna	87 schillings

18.   If the exchange rate is 1 koruna = 1 schilling, then
    (a)   Slovakia will import both steel and corn.
    (b)   Austria will import both steel and corn.
    (c)   Slovakia will import steel and Austria will import corn.
    (d)   Slovakia will import corn and Austria will import steel.

    ANSWER: (b) In Austria, the domestic prices of steel and corn are 48 schillings and 87 schillings, respectively. The imported prices are 20 schillings and 30 schillings, respectively.

19.   If the exchange rate is 1 koruna = 3 schillings, then
    (a)   Slovakia will import both steel and corn.
    (b)   Austria will import both steel and corn.
    (c)   Slovakia will import steel and Austria will import corn.
    (d)   Slovakia will import corn and Austria will import steel.

    ANSWER: (a) In Slovakia, the domestic prices of steel and corn are 20 koruna and 30 koruna, respectively. The imported prices are 16 koruna and 29 koruna, respectively.

20.   Two-way trade will occur only if the price of the koruna is between
    (a)   1.0 schillings and 3.0 schillings.
    (b)   1.5 schillings and 2.4 schillings.
    (c)   2.4 schillings and 2.9 schillings.
    (d)   1.5 schillings and 3.0 schillings.

    ANSWER: (c) If the exchange rate is 1 koruna = 2.4 schillings, no trade in steel will occur. If the exchange rate is 1 koruna = 2.9 schillings, no trade in corn will occur. Between these rates, Slovakia will import steel and Austria will import corn. ■

OBJECTIVE 4:
Provide an intuitive explanation of the Heckscher-Ohlin theorem.

The *Heckscher-Ohlin theorem* builds on the theory of comparative advantage by focusing on the differing factor endowments of countries. Some countries seem more labor-abundant (India, China) whereas others are more capital abundant (United States, Japan). The Heckscher-Ohlin theorem states that a country will specialize in and export that good whose production calls for a relatively intensive use of the input that the country has in abundance. If India has an abundance of labor and little capital then India should export labor-intensive goods and import capital-intensive goods, for example. (page 362 [674])

    The assembly of T-shirts requires a large stock of semiskilled cheap labor with little capital. This favors Indonesia. Research into the capabilities of fiber optics requires a large stock of expensive capital. This favors the United States. The production of timber requires an abundant stock of forest land—a requirement that Canada meets.

    In practice, the United States exports Californian wine and imports Italian wine. Germany ships BMWs to Sweden and imports Volvos. There is product differentiation and a range of consumer preferences. Foreign goods may be more exclusive or thought of as "better".

Practice

21.   The Heckscher-Ohlin theorem explains that a country's comparative advantage stems from
    (a)   acquired comparative advantage
    (b)   relative factor endowments
    (c)   product differentiation
    (d)   differences in consumer preferences

    ANSWER: (b) The Heckscher-Ohlin theorem explain the presence of a country's comparative advantage by its relative factor endowments. A country with an abundance of labor will specialize in goods requiring labor-intensive production.

22.   We observe that Arbez produces wooden ornaments (a labor-intensive activity), and that Arboc produces plastic containers (a capital-intensive activity). Which of the following statements is true?
    (a)   Arbez has more labor than Arboc; Arboc has more capital than Arbez.
    (b)   Arboc has more labor than Arbez; Arbez has more capital than Arboc.
    (c)   Labor is relatively abundant in Arbez.
    (d)   Labor is relatively abundant in Arboc.

    ANSWER: (c) Assuming that the two countries are being rational, Arbez is producing the good in which it has a comparative advantage. ■

OBJECTIVE 5:
Define a tariff, an export subsidy, and a quota. Outline, using a demand and supply analysis, the costs involved in the imposition of a tariff.

Tariffs, export subsidies, and quotas are examples of trade barriers. *Tariffs* are taxes on imports (usually), designed to force up their price; *export subsidies* are government payments to U.S. exporters, intended to make them more competitive overseas; *quotas* are limits on the quantity of imports. *Dumping* is meant to price competitors out of the market; having achieved market domination, the firm can then raise prices. (page 362 [674])

ECONOMICS IN PRACTICE: On page 366 [678], the textbook reports that trade barriers on agricultural products were being reduced in 2008. Most trade barriers (but not export tariffs) tend to wax during economic slowdowns and wane during boom periods and 2008 was a boom period for agriculture. Note that the article refers to export tariffs as well as import tariffs. What is the effect of an export tariff? Why would a country impose such a tariff? Note, on page 365 [677], the reference to a U.S. tariff on sugar-based ethanol (a substitute for corn-based ethanol). In 2008, ethanol absorbed about 25% of the U.S. corn crop. Given rising global food demand, what do you think will be the fate of this tariff?
ANSWER: An export tariff is a tax on a country's exports (rather than on its imports). It seems counterintuitive for a nation *not* to want to export but that is the effect of such a tariff. Several reasons are given for the imposition of an export tax in the article. As another instance, in Argentina, in 2008, the government hiked the tax on beef exports from 5% to 15% in order to reduce export profitability, increase domestic supplies and reduce inflation. A reasonable prediction is that the tariff on sugar-based ethanol will be reduced or removed as corn prices increase and sugar becomes a more attractive input.

———■——————————————————— **Practice** ————————————————————

Use the following diagram to answer the next three questions. The diagram shows the American demand for and supply of T-shirts. The world price is $8 per shirt.

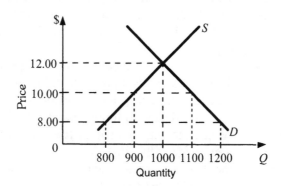

23.   In an unrestricted open market, the U.S. will
    (a)   export 400 T-shirts.
    (b)   export 200 T-shirts.
    (c)   import 400 T-shirts.
    (d)   import 200 T-shirts.

    ANSWER: (c) At a price of $8, there is an excess U.S. demand of 400.

24.   The garment industry successfully lobbies Congress to impose a $2 per shirt tax on imports. Now the U.S. will

(a)   export 400 T-shirts.

(b)   export 200 T-shirts.

(c)   import 400 T-shirts.

(d)   import 200 T-shirts.

ANSWER: (d)   An excess demand remains that must be met from overseas.

25.   The government will collect _____ in tariff revenues.

(a) $100

(b) $200

(c) $400

(d) $800

ANSWER: (c)   The government collects $2 per shirt on each of the 200 imported shirts. ∎

OBJECTIVE 6:
Give the arguments advanced for and against protection. Describe the costs involved in permitting free trade.

Historically, the United States has imposed high tariffs, particularly during the Great Depression of the 1930s. After the Second World War, there was increased pressure to liberalize trade, leading to the General Agreement on Trade and Tariffs (GATT) in 1947. In 1995, the World Trade Organization (WTO) was established to facilitate freer trade among nations. (page 363 [675])

There have been ongoing moves towards economic integration, with the European Community forming the world's largest free-trade area in 1991. NAFTA (a free-trade agreement involving the United States, Canada, and Mexico) went into effect in 1994.

The case for free trade is based on the theory of comparative advantage. Voluntary trade benefits the participants. Welfare increases if trade flows are allowed to follow their "natural" pattern; obstacles, such as tariffs and quotas, reduce that efficiency and result in a deadweight loss of welfare. Higher-cost production results. (page 366 [678])

The argument in favor of protection is based on the observation that efficient foreign competition will result in job loss for domestic workers and lost production. Individual arguments for protection from foreign competition may include claims that cheap foreign labor is "unfair," that national security must be protected, that trade encourages dependency on foreigners, that trade may encourage environmentally unsound production, and that we need to let infant industries develop. Some of these arguments are simply false, and others are misused. (page 368 [680])

Whatever the merits of the debate, most economists favor free trade and, increasingly, evidence shows that governments across the world have been reducing tariffs.

▶▶▶   LEARNING TIP: When trying to make sense of Figure 19.4 (34.4) and the effects of a tariff, recall that the concept of deadweight loss is dealt with in Chapter 4.◀

ECONOMICS IN PRACTICE: On page 369 [681], the textbook reproduces "A Petition," a famous article from the nineteenth century French satirist Frederic Bastiat. Bastiat, it should be noted, favored an import quota over a tariff. Now consider the case of softwood imports from Canada into the United States. From 2002 until 2006, the United States imposed an average tariff of 29% on Canadian softwoods harvested in forests owned by the provinces (in response to alleged dumping). Privately-owned Canadian lumber was not subject to the tariff. First, what do you think happened to the balance of production in Canada between privately- and publicly-owned lumber? More importantly, from the U.S. point of view, can you predict what happened to the relative efficiency of U.S. and Canadian lumber mills and to the size of the U.S. lumber industry? Why would a quota have been a better option from the point of view of the U.S. lumber industry?

ANSWER: The production of privately-owned lumber grew while publicly-owned timber production slumped. There was also a geographical shift in production—because the maritime provinces (Nova Scotia, New Brunswick) feature private ownership, they were big gainers from the U.S. measure. British Columbia's lumber industry lost 15,000 jobs. Protected American mills remained relatively high cost while Canadian mills were forced to become more efficient. In fact, many American mills closed down. A quota, rather than a tax, would have preserved a portion of the market for less efficient U.S. mills—a market that was eroded by Canadian competitiveness even in the face of a tariff. As a footnote, after the tariff had been scrapped, the WTO found the U.S. position on dumping "inconsistent."

—————————————————————— **Practice** ——————————————————————

26.   Which of the following is not an argument used by protectionists?
  (a)   Infant industries need support until they are strong enough to compete.
  (b)   Restricting trade builds up dependency on other counties.
  (c)   Protection is needed in the light of unfair foreign practices, in order to ensure a level playing field.
  (d)   Cheap foreign labor makes competition unfair.

  ANSWER: (b) Refer to p. 368 [680] for more on protectionist views. ∎

BRAIN TEASER SOLUTION: Almost any appeal can be made if one is sufficiently creative! Refer to Bastiat's "Petition" on p. 369 [681].

PRACTICE TEST

I.   MULTIPLE-CHOICE QUESTIONS

Select the option that provides the single best answer.

_____ 1.   According to the textbook, _____ of all cars and _____ of all consumer electronics bought in the United States are produced abroad.
  (a)   50%; 50%
  (b)   50%; 80%
  (c)   80%; 50%
  (d)   80%; 80%

_____ 2.   A country imports less than it exports. It has
  (a)   an export subsidy.
  (b)   a tariff quota.
  (c)   a trade surplus.
  (d)   a trade deficit.

_____ 3.   Relative to Arboc, Arbez has a comparative advantage in the production of goat milk. We can say that Arbez
(a)   uses fewer resources to produce goat milk than does Arboc.
(b)   must also have an absolute advantage in the production of goat milk.
(c)   is the producer with the lower opportunity cost of producing goat milk.
(d)   should diversify into other products rather than trade with the high-cost, inefficient Arbocalis.

_____ 4.   In trade between Arboc and Arbez, an increase in the exchange rate of the Arbezani currency (the bandu) relative to that of the Arbocali currency (the opek) means that
(a)   Arbezani goods will appear to be relatively cheaper to the Arbocalis.
(b)   Arbocali goods will appear to be relatively cheaper to the Arbezanis.
(c)   Arbez will lose any comparative advantage that it had.
(d)   Arbez will experience a decreasing trade deficit.

_____ 5.   The Heckscher-Ohlin theorem states that Arbez will have a(n) _____ advantage in the production of a good that uses its relatively _____ .
(a)   absolute; scarce input intensively
(b)   absolute; abundant input intensively
(c)   comparative; abundant input intensively
(d)   comparative; scarce input intensively

_____ 6.   Two goods are produced, pins and needles. Jill has a comparative advantage in the production of pins. Relative to Jack, and with the same resources,
(a)   Jill is better at producing pins than at producing needles.
(b)   Jill is better at producing both pins and needles.
(c)   Jill can produce pins more efficiently than Jack.
(d)   Jill can produce more pins than Jack.

_____ 7.   Jill chooses to trade pins for needles with Jack. It is likely that
(a)   Jill's gains equal Jack's losses.
(b)   pins are more expensive than needles.
(c)   each trader receives goods that he or she values more highly than those he or she gives up.
(d)   neither trader can gain more than the other.

For questions 8–10, assume that Arbez and Arboc have the same amount of resources and similar preferences for goat milk and bananas. The table shows the number of labor hours needed to produce 1 liter of goat milk and 1 kilo of bananas.

	Arbez	Arboc
Goat Milk	0.3	0.6
Bananas	0.5	0.2

_____ 8.   According to the preceding table,
  (a)   Arbez has a comparative advantage in the production of both goods.
  (b)   Arbez has a comparative advantage in the production of bananas, and
         Arboc has a comparative advantage in the production of goat milk.
  (c)   Arbez has a comparative advantage in the production of goat milk, and
         Arboc has a comparative advantage in the production of bananas.
  (d)   Arboc has a comparative advantage in the production of both goods.

_____ 9.   According to the table, one hour of labor produces
  (a)   3 liters of goat milk in Arbez and 6 liters in Arboc.
  (b)   5 kilos of bananas in Arbez and 2 kilos in Arboc.
  (c)   2 kilos of bananas in Arbez and 5 kilos in Arboc.
  (d)   6 liters of goat milk in Arboc and 2 kilos of bananas in Arboc.

_____ 10.   For trade to occur, the terms of trade might be
  (a)   2 liters of goat milk for 1 kilo of bananas.
  (b)   1 liter of goat milk for 4 kilos of bananas.
  (c)   1 liter of goat milk for 0.7 of a kilo of bananas.
  (d)   3 liters of goat milk for 1 kilo of bananas.

_____ 11.   Tariffs and quotas are economically inefficient because
  (a)   the government does not collect any revenues under a tariff.
  (b)   imports rise and this reduces the welfare of consumers.
  (c)   producers are saved from the pressure of foreign competition.
  (d)   domestic prices must be reduced.

_____ 12.   Which of the following is an argument in favor of increased protection?
  (a)   U.S. consumers have become too dependent on foreign countries for their
         luxury goods.
  (b)   National defense can be jeopardized if strategic supplies are produced by
         foreigners.
  (c)   Running a persistent trade deficit is unhealthy and must be avoided.
  (d)   Higher tariffs increase the welfare of U.S. consumers.

_____ 13.   Each of the following is a trade barrier EXCEPT
  (a)   a flexible exchange rate.
  (b)   a quota.
  (c)   an export subsidy.
  (d)   a tariff.

_____ 14.   Statement 1: A country with an absolute advantage in the production of a good will also
         have a comparative advantage.
         Statement 2: A country with a comparative advantage in the production of a good will
         also have an absolute advantage.
         Statement 1 is _____ ; Statement 2 is _____ .
  (a)   true; true
  (b)   true; false
  (c)   false; true
  (d)   false; false

_____ 15.   A tariff _____ increase the government's tax receipts; a quota _____ increase the government's tax receipts.
    (a)   does; does
    (b)   does; does not
    (c)   does not; does
    (d)   does not; does not

_____ 16.   In Tokyo, a Big Mac sells for 500 yen. The dollar : yen exchange rate is one dollar per 125 yen. The price of the Big Mac in dollars is
    (a) $500.00.
    (b) $0.25.
    (c) $4.00.
    (d) $5.00.

_____ 17.   In Tokyo, a Big Mac sells for 500 yen. The exchange rate changes from one dollar for 125 yen, to one dollar for 250 yen. The price of the Big Mac in dollars
    (a)   has increased.
    (b)   has decreased.
    (c)   has not changed.
    (d)   has doubled.

_____ 18.   The Heckscher-Ohlin theorem explains the pattern of trade by focusing on
    (a)   comparative advantage.
    (b)   absolute advantage.
    (c)   relative factor endowments.
    (d)   exchange rate variations.

_____ 19.   As the exchange rate changes from one British pound equals $1.50 to one British pound equals $1.00, the terms of trade shift _____ the United States. American traders will gain _____ from trade with the United Kingdom.
    (a)   in favor of; more
    (b)   in favor of; less
    (c)   against; more
    (d)   against; less

_____ 20.   We would expect a tariff imposed on an import to _____ the price of the import and to _____ the price of domestic substitutes for the import.
    (a)   increase; increase
    (b)   increase; not affect
    (c)   decrease; decrease
    (d)   decrease; not affect

II.   APPLICATION QUESTIONS

1.   The Arbezani Minister of Trade, a firm believer in the Heckscher-Ohlin theorem, asks your advice regarding some recent changes within the Arbezani economy. In each of the following cases, he wishes to know whether or not the Heckscher-Ohlin explanation of trade flows will be strengthened. Arbez has established a free-trade region with its sole trading partner, Arboc.

    (a)   Arbezani unions in a substantial number of industries lobby successfully for increased restrictions on movement between industries, e.g., longer apprenticeships, work permits, drug testing of new entrants into an industry.

    (b)   It has been discovered that Arbez and its trading partner, Arboc, have identical endowments of all resources.

    (c)   Nationalistic Arbezani politicians, concerned about the loss of sovereignty caused by a free-trade area, have successfully passed restrictions on the flow of labor and other inputs between Arbez and Arboc.

2.   The nations of Noil and Regit produce loaves and fishes. The labor supply is 12,000 labor units per year in Noil, whereas in Regit, the labor supply is 72,000 labor units per year. Assume that labor is the only input and that costs are constant within each economy.

The costs of producing loaves and fishes, in labor units, are given in the following table.

Units of Labor Supply Needed to Produce 1 Unit of:	Noil	Regit
Loaves	2	3
Fishes	1	3

    (a)   Calculate the maximum output levels of loaves and fishes for each economy and enter your results in the following table.

Maximum Units Produced:	Noil	Regit
Loaves		
Fishes		

    (b)   Draw the production possibility frontiers for each nation.

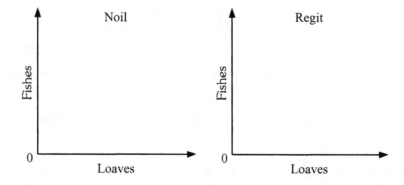

    (c)   When questioned about the possibility of establishing trade between the two nations, the Regitani Minister of Trade states his government's official line—the proposal is ludicrous because Regit has an advantage in the production of each good. Is the Regitani view correct?

In both nations, the custom is to consume two loaves with each fish.

(d)   Assume that no trade takes place. Calculate the annual production of loaves and fishes that will most satisfactorily meet demand in each country separately. Also determine the total production of loaves and fishes for the two countries without trade.

Maximum Units Produced:	Noil	Regit	Total
Loaves			
Fishes			

(e)   Yielding to pressure, the Regitani government opens its borders to trade with Noil. Based on comparative advantage, which good should Noil specialize in producing? Explain.

(f)   Assuming that specialization and trade flows are dictated by comparative advantage, determine the quantity of loaves and fishes that can be produced.

(g)   Suppose that the terms of trade are established at 1 fish = 2 loaves. Determine the consumption of loaves and fishes in each country.

Units Consumed:	Noil	Regit
Loaves		
Fishes		

(h)   Has trade been mutually beneficial in this case?

(i)   Suppose that the terms of trade are established at 1 fish = 1 loaf. Determine the consumption of loaves and fishes in each country.

Units Consumed:	Noil	Regit
Loaves		
Fishes		

(j)   Has trade been mutually beneficial in this case?

(k)   Suppose that the terms of trade are established at 2 fishes = 1 loaf. Determine the consumption of loaves and fishes in each country.

Units Consumed:	Noil	Regit
Loaves		
Fishes		

(l)   Has trade been mutually beneficial in this case?

(m)   Determine the "price" of a loaf (in terms of fish) necessary to have mutually beneficial two-way trade.

3.   The domestic price of Arbocali cloth is 4 opeks per yard. The domestic price of Arbezani leather is 12 bandu per hide. Arboc sells cloth to Arbez and Arbez sells hides to Arboc. The opek : bandu exchange rate is 2 opeks per bandu. The exchange rate is flexible.

Ignoring transportation and other such costs, calculate the price in Arbez of a yard of imported Arbocali cloth and the price in Arboc of an imported Arbezani hide.

4.   Use the diagrams below to answer this question.

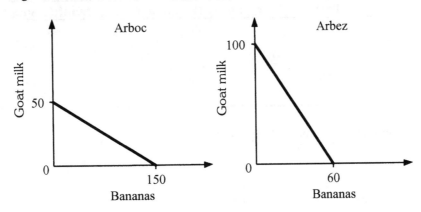

(a)   What is the opportunity cost of 1 kilo of bananas in Arboc?
(b)   What is the opportunity cost of 1 kilo of bananas in Arbez?
(c)   Which country has a comparative advantage in the production of bananas?
(d)   What is the opportunity cost of 1 liter of goat milk in Arboc?
(e)   What is the opportunity cost of 1 liter of goat milk in Arbez?
(f)   Which country has a comparative advantage in the production of goat milk?
(g)   If the terms of trade were 1 liter of goat milk/kilo of bananas, which country would want to export goat milk?
(h)   If the terms of trade were 3 liters of goat milk/kilo of bananas, Arboc should produce _____ and Arbez should produce _____ .
(i)   Suppose that the terms of trade were 1 kilo of bananas/1.5 liters of goat milk. _____ would export bananas and _____ would export goat milk.

5.   Arboc and Arbez produce wine and cheese, and each has constant costs of production. The domestic prices for the two goods are given in the following table. At the moment 1 Arbocali opek is traded for 1 Arbezani bandu.

	Arboc	Arbez
Wine	40 opeks	120 bandu
Cheese	20 opeks	30 bandu

(a)   Which country has a comparative advantage in cheese production?
(b)   Which country has a comparative advantage in wine production?
(c)   At the present exchange rate (1 opek = 1 bandu), will two-way trade occur? Explain.
(d)   Which country will have a balance of trade deficit?
(e)   What should happen to the value of the opek, relative to the bandu?
(f)   If the exchange rate is 1 opek = 2 bandu, what would happen to trade?
(g)   Cheese making is capital intensive, and wine making is labor intensive. Which country should have the relatively abundant supplies of labor, if the Heckscher-Ohlin theory is correct?
(h)   If the exchange rate is 1 opek = 4 bandu, what would happen to trade?

6.   Here are the domestic demand and supply schedules for diapers.

Price	Quantity Demanded	Quantity Supplied
$6	800	1,100
$5	1,000	1,000
$4	1,200	900
$3	1,400	800
$2	1,600	700

(a)   Graph the demand and supply curves.

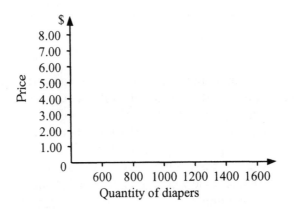

(b)   The equilibrium price is $_____ and quantity is _____ .

(c)   The world price for diapers is $3. Show this on the diagram as *Pw*. What will be the levels of domestic consumption and domestic production?

In order to preserve employment, diaper manufacturers contend successfully that theirs is an "infant industry" and should be protected.

(d)   A tariff is imposed that raises the price of imported diapers to $4. Show this on the diagram as *Pt*.

(e)   The tariff causes an increase in price and an increase in domestic production of _____ units. Consumption will fall to _____ units.

(f)   Imports will be _____ units. The tariff will yield $_____ in tax revenues.

(g)   Shade in the areas representing the net welfare loss caused by the tariff.

(h)   The loss in welfare is $_____ .

PRACTICE TEST SOLUTIONS

I.   *Solutions to Multiple-Choice Questions*

1.   (b)   Refer to p. 353 [665] for this information.

2.   (c)   Refer to p. 354 [666] for the definition.

3.   (c)   Arbez might be relatively inefficient in producing both goods but relatively less inefficient in producing goat milk. Because Arbez has a comparative advantage in producing goat milk, its opportunity cost of producing goat milk must be less.

4. (b) As the Arbezani currency becomes more powerful, Arbocali goods will become cheaper when calculated in terms of the Arbezani currency.

5. (c) Refer to p. 362 [674] for a statement of the Heckscher-Ohlin theorem.

6. (a) Remember that comparative advantage is a relative concept. It requires that we compare two producers and two goods.

7. (c) In voluntary trade, we expect each trader to gain something more than s/he traded.

8. (c) Goat milk is relatively cheap to produce in Arbez and bananas require relatively few resources in Arboc. In a two-good, two-country situation, one party can never have a comparative advantage in both goods.

9. (c) 0.5 labor hour gives 1 kilo of bananas in Arbez—1 hour gives 2 kilos. 0.2 labor hour gives 1 liter of milk in Arboc—1 hour gives 5 liters.

10. (c) The terms of trade must lie in the range from 1 liter of goat milk : 3/5 kilo of bananas to 1 liter of goat milk : 3 kilos of bananas. If Arbez has 6 hours of labor, it could produce 20 liters of goat milk or 12 kilos of bananas—a ratio of 1: 3/5. If Arboc has 6 hours of labor, it could produce 10 liters of goat milk or 30 kilos of bananas—a ratio of 1:3.

11. (c) Tariffs impose welfare losses in two ways. Consumers pay a higher price and, as mentioned in this question, marginal producers are allowed to survive. Option (b) is incorrect—imports don't increase, they decrease. Refer to p. 367 [679].

12. (b) The national security argument is persistent.

13. (a) Refer to p. 363 [675] for a discussion of trade barriers.

14. (d) A country may have an absolute advantage in the production of Good A and Good B; it may have a comparative advantage in the production of Good A and, therefore, a comparative disadvantage in Good B. Similarly, a country with a comparative advantage in the production of Good A might be less efficient than its partner in producing either good.

15. (b) A tariff is a tax that provides revenues; a quota merely restricts the number of units that may be imported.

16. (c) 125 yen equal $1.00, therefore, 500 yen equal $4.00

17. (b) 125 yen equal $1.00, therefore 500 yen equal $4.00; 250 yen equal $1.00; 500 yen equal $2.00.

18. (c) Refer to p. 362 [674] for more on the Heckscher-Ohlin Theorem.

19. (a) Dollars are becoming relatively more valuable.

20.   (a)   A tariff will drive up the price of the import, increasing demand for domestic substitutes whose price will then increase.

II.   Solutions to Application Questions

1.   (a)   Heckscher-Ohlin assumes that inputs are mobile within an economy. Such restrictions will work against Heckscher-Ohlin because, as an economy begins to specialize and trade, it will wish to reallocate inputs.
      (b)   According to Heckscher-Ohlin, comparative advantage is dependent on differences in factor endowments. No differences in factor endowments, no comparative advantage: no comparative advantage, no trade. Arbez and Arboc should have no basis for trade.
      (c)   The new restrictions should not affect the pattern of trade. The Heckscher-Ohlin theorem assumes that inputs are not mobile between countries.

2.   (a)   Refer to the following table.

Maximum Units Produced:	Noil	Regit
Loaves	6,000	24,000
Fishes	12,000	24,000

      (b)   Refer to the following diagrams.

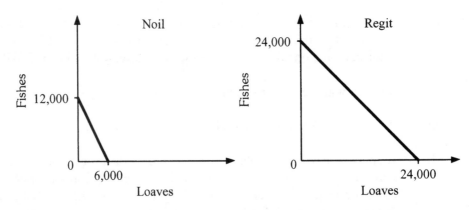

      (c)   The Regitani view is mainly incorrect. Regit does have an absolute advantage in the production of both loaves and fishes, but it does not have a comparative advantage in both, and it is comparative advantage that determines whether or not trade is advantageous.
      (d)   Refer to the following table.

Maximum Units Produced:	Noil	Regit	Total
Loaves	4,800	16,000	20,800
Fishes	2,400	8,000	10,400

Draw a line from the origin with a slope of 1/2 (corresponding to one fish for every two loaves). The solution is where the line intersects the production possibility frontier.
      (e)   Noil should produce fishes. In Noil, the cost of producing 1 loaf is 2 fishes whereas the cost of producing 1 loaf in Regit is 1 fish. Loaves are less costly in Regit. Regit has a comparative advantage in loaves; Noil has a comparative advantage in fishes.

(f)   Noil can produce 12,000 fishes and Regit can produce 24,000 loaves.

(g)   Refer to the following table.

Units Consumed:	Noil	Regit
Loaves	12,000	12,000
Fishes	6,000	6,000

Noil can produce 12,000 fishes and export 6,000, earning 12,000 loaves in return. Regit can produce 24,000 loaves and export 12,000, earning 6,000 fishes in return.

(h)   Trade has benefited Noil, but Regit has a lower standard of living than it had before trade!

(i)   Refer to the following table.

Units Consumed:	Noil	Regit
Loaves	8,000	16,000
Fishes	4,000	8,000

Noil can produce 12,000 fishes and export 8,000, earning 8,000 loaves in return. Regit can produce 24,000 loaves and export 8,000, earning 8,000 fishes in return.

(j)   Trade has benefited Noil, but Regit's standard of living is unchanged.

(k)   Refer to the following table.

Units Consumed:	Noil	Regit
Loaves	4,800	16,000
Fishes	2,400	8,000

Noil can produce 12,000 fishes and export 9,600, earning 4,800 loaves in return. Regit can produce 24,000 loaves and export 4,800, earning 9,600 fishes in return.

(l)   Trade has benefited Regit, but Noil's standard of living is unchanged.

(m)   The terms of trade need to be between 1 loaf = 1 fish and 1 loaf = 2 fish.

3.   A yard of imported Arbocali cloth will cost 2 bandu in Arbez. An imported Arbezani hide will cost 24 opeks in Arboc.

4.   (a)   1/3 of a liter of goat milk

(b)   5/3 liters of goat milk

(c)   Arboc

(d)   3 kilos of bananas

(e)   6/10 of a kilo of bananas

(f)   Arbez

(g)   Arbez, because it can produce a liter of goat milk at a cost of less than one kilo of bananas and, therefore, can gain through this specialization.

(h)   bananas; bananas. One kilo of bananas can be sold for 2 liters of goat milk. Both Arboc and Arbez can produce bananas more cheaply than this (1/3 of a liter of goat milk and 5/3 liters of goat milk, respectively).

(i)   Arboc; Arbez. One kilo of bananas can be sold for 1.5 liters of goat milk. Arboc can produce bananas more cheaply than this (1/3 of a liter of goat milk) and so will produce bananas. One liter of goat milk can be sold for 2/3 kilo of bananas. Arbez can produce goat milk more cheaply than this (6/10 of a kilo of bananas) and so will produce goat milk.

(ii)

5.   (a)   Arbez. Wine is four times as expensive as cheese in Arbez, but only twice as expensive in Arboc.

(b)   Arboc. Each country must have a comparative advantage in one of the goods.

(c)   No. Because Arboc can produce both goods more cheaply, the Arbezanis will import both. The Arbocalis will not wish to buy either Arbezani product.

(d)   Arbez, because it has some imports and zero exports.

(e)   The Arbocali currency (the opek) should be heavily demanded (by Arbezanis seeking to buy Arbocali goods). The demand for the bandu will be low. The opek will rise in value; the bandu will fall in value.

(f)   At a price of 30 bandu (15 opeks), Arbezani cheese will now be cheaper than Arbocali cheese (at a price of 20 opeks). Arboc will import cheese. Arbez will continue to import Arbocali wine. At a price of 40 opeks (80 bandu), Arbocali wine is still cheaper than that produced in Arbez (at a price of 120 bandu).

(g)   Arboc

(h)   At a price of 30 bandu (7.50 opeks), Arbezani cheese will be cheaper than Arbocali cheese (at a price of 20 opeks). Arboc will import cheese.
At a price of 40 opeks (160 bandu), Arbocali wine will be more expensive than that produced in Arbez (at a price of 120 bandu). Arboc will import wine.
Arboc will have a trade deficit and Arbez a surplus.

6.   (a)   Refer to the following diagram.

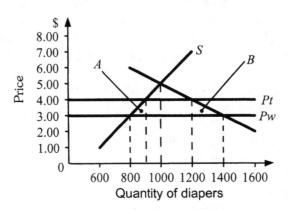

(b) $5, 1,000.

(c)   Refer to the preceding diagram; 1,400, 800.

(d)   Refer to the preceding diagram.

(e)   100; 1,200

(f)   300; $300

(g)   Refer to the preceding diagram. The net welfare loss is shown by triangular areas *A* and *B*.

(h) $(50 + 100)

20 [35]

Open-Economy Macroeconomics: The Balance of Payments and Exchange Rates

Chapter objectives:

1. Outline the components comprising the balance of payments and distinguish between the current account and the capital account.
2. Incorporate imports and exports into the *AE* diagram. Derive the expenditure multiplier and explain how imports affect the size of the multiplier.
3. List the variables that influence exports and imports. Outline how the trade feedback effect and the price feedback effect operate.
4. Explain why the demand for foreign exchange has a negative slope and the supply of foreign exchange has a positive slope. Use the demand and supply framework to describe the determination of the exchange rate in the foreign exchange market. Explain how each determinant plays a role in the process.
5. Explain the reasoning behind the purchasing-power-parity theory.
6. Describe the "J-curve effect" of exchange rate movements on imports, exports, GDP, prices, and the balance of payments.
7. Outline the effects of the exchange rate on the effectiveness of monetary and fiscal policy.

BRAIN TEASER: Is it better to have a "strong" dollar or a "weak" dollar? Suppose that the dollar experiences a substantial appreciation in value. Who will gain?

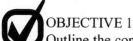OBJECTIVE 1:
Outline the components comprising the balance of payments and distinguish between the current account and the capital account.

When goods, services, or assets are bought and sold or transfer payments are made internationally, currencies flow between nations. These flows of foreign exchange (that is, all currencies other than that of the home country) are recorded in the *balance of payments*. (page 378 [690])

The balance of payments, which must "balance" (equal zero) is split into two parts:

(a)   the *current account*, which includes imports and exports of goods and services, net investment income, and net transfer payments) and

(b)   the *capital account*, which includes the "export" and "import" of U.S. and foreign assets—i.e., capital inflows and capital outflows.

If, on the current account, total credits are greater than (less than) total debits, the economy has a current account surplus (deficit). Funds from a current account surplus can be used to buy foreign assets, such as foreign government bonds or real estate. A current account deficit must be financed by attracting funds from overseas (capital inflows) by selling American assets (capital). The current and capital accounts must sum to zero.

▶▶▶   LEARNING TIP: Any transaction that brings in foreign exchange is a credit item; any transaction causing a loss of foreign exchange is a debit.

▶▶▶   LEARNING TIP: The capital account is difficult to conceptualize. The easy way into this topic is to imagine a nation (Japan) with a current account surplus. What happens to the extra foreign earnings? The Japanese can use the funds to buy U.S. assets and companies. A nation (the United States) that runs a current account deficit is overspending. To raise the foreign currency needed to buy imports, the United States must sell off some of its assets. Counterintuitively perhaps, capital inflows are rather like exports (in the sense that we're "exporting" IOUs), and capital outflows can be thought of as similar to imports (funds flow out to "import" foreign securities). A large capital account surplus (the same thing as a large current account deficit) may be a concern, as it may mean a country is borrowing too much or selling off too many domestic assets—although it may not be a problem if the borrowing is supporting investment that will yield future returns.

▶▶▶   LEARNING TIP: A Japanese purchase of an American factory in Texas is a capital *inflow* for the United States (funds flow in). An American purchase of a Brazilian coffee plantation is a capital *outflow* for the United States (funds flow out). Focus on which country receives payment, not which receives the asset.◀

Practice

1.   Imports account for _____ of U.S. GDP.
    (a)   less than 5%
    (b)   about 10%
    (c)   about 15%
    (d)   more than 20%
    ANSWER: (c) The proportion is approximately 15%, in fact. Refer to p. 377 [689].

2.   The price of Arboc's currency in terms of that of Arbez is the
    (a)   foreign exchange.
    (b)   exchange rate.
    (c)   balance of payments.
    (d)   currency ratio.
    ANSWER: (b) Refer to p. 377 [689] for the definition the exchange rate.

3.   The balance of payments is split into the
    (a)   current account and the merchandise trade account.
    (b)   capital account and the foreign exchange account.
    (c)   capital account and the current account.
    (d)   current account and foreign exchange account.
    ANSWER: (c) Refer to p. 379 [691] for more on this issue.

4.   Which of the following would be included in the current account?
        (a)   The purchase by an American citizen of stock in the Japanese company Sony
        (b)   The sale by an American citizen of a British government security
        (c)   The sale of an American-built computer to Germany
        (d)   The sale of IBM stock to a German citizen

        ANSWER: (c) This is an export.

5.   An increase in "foreign private assets in the United States" means that
        (a)   American citizens have increased their holdings of foreign private assets.
        (b)   American citizens have decreased their holdings of foreign private assets.
        (c)   citizens of foreign countries have increased their holdings of American private assets.
        (d)   citizens of foreign countries have decreased their holdings of American private assets.

        ANSWER: (c) The phrase "foreign private assets" means assets of the U.S. private sector (e.g.,
                an American company like IBM) held by foreigners.

6.   Which of the following is not an item in the capital account?
        (a)   Change in private U.S. assets abroad
        (b)   Change in U.S. government assets abroad
        (c)   Net investment income
        (d)   Change in foreign private investment in the United States

        ANSWER: (c) Refer to Table 20.1 (35.1). Items in the current account show income from
                earnings (on exports, investments abroad), expenditures (on imports), transfers,
                and investment income—no financial or real productive assets change hands. It
                is the capital account that shows the effects of the purchase or sale of financial
                and real productive assets. ■

OBJECTIVE 2:
Incorporate imports and exports into the *AE* diagram. Derive the expenditure multiplier and
explain how imports affect the size of the multiplier.

When exports and imports are incorporated into the macroeconomic model, exports represent an increase
in the amount of expenditures on domestically produced goods and services whereas imports reduce the
amount of expenditures on domestically produced goods and services.

In the open economy, $AE = C + I + G + EX - IM$. Foreign demand for American goods is
influenced mainly by foreign factors—the demand for exports is assumed to be constant as domestic
(U.S.) output changes. The demand for imports, however, increases as U.S. income increases, i.e., the
marginal propensity to import (*MPM*) is positive. The expenditure multiplier is smaller in an open
economy than it is in a closed economy because imports represent a leakage of spending power away
from domestically produced goods.

In the open economy, the multiplier formula is $1/[1 - (MPC - MPM)]$.

—■——————————————————————————— **Practice** —————————————————————

Use the basic Keynesian cross model and the following information to answer the next three questions. In the closed economy of Arbez, the marginal propensity to consume is 0.75. Arbez opens its borders to trade and finds that its marginal propensity to import is 0.15.

7.   The Arbezani multiplier was _____ for the closed economy and is _____ for the open economy.
    (a)   4; 2.5
    (b)   4; 10
    (c)   5; 2.5
    (d)   5; 10
    ANSWER: (a) In the closed economy, the multiplier is $1/[1 - MPC]$. In this case, $1/[1 - MPC] =$ $1/[1 - 0.75] = 4$. In the open economy, the multiplier is $1/[1 - (MPC - MPM)]$. In this case, $1/[1 - (MPC - MPM)] = 1/[1 - (0.75 - 0.15)] = 1/0.4 = 2.5$. In general, the open-economy multiplier is smaller than the closed economy multiplier, so Options (b) and (d) must be incorrect.

8.   Arbez finds that net exports are zero. As a result of world trade, the Arbezani economy has become _____ stable. If the economy expands, Arbez will experience a trade _____ .
    (a)   more; surplus
    (b)   more; deficit
    (c)   less; surplus
    (d)   less; deficit
    ANSWER: (b) In the open economy, the multiplier is smaller. Shifts in the components of planned aggregate expenditure will result in smaller changes in equilibrium income level—the economy is more stable. Currently, exports and imports are equal. An economic expansion will increase imports (MPM is 0.15), but exports, which depend on foreign demand, will not change and a trade deficit will occur. Note: This is a very difficult question.

9.   The Arbezani government increases government spending by 100. Equilibrium output will _____ and net exports will _____ . (Hint: Use the open-economy multiplier.)
    (a)   increase by 100; increase by 15
    (b)   increase by 100; decrease by 15
    (c)   increase by 250; increase by 37.5
    (d)   increase by 250; decrease by 37.5
    ANSWER: (d) As G increases, the economy will expand by 250 because the multiplier is 2.5. Refer to Question 9. Exports do not change, but imports will increase. MPM is 0.15, so imports will increase by 250×0.15, or 37.5, and net exports ($EX - IM$) will decrease.

10.   The quantity of U.S. exports depends directly on
    (a)   the output level in the United States.
    (b)   the output level in the other countries.
    (c)   the size of the multiplier in the United States.
    (d)   the size of the multiplier in other countries.
    ANSWER: (b) The demand for our exports depends on output (income) level of foreign purchasers. A *change* in their income will affect our exports through the marginal propensity to import of foreigners and their multiplier.

11.   Arboc opens its economy to world trade. Its net exports are negative. Compared with its *AE* function before world trade, the function now will be
   (a)   higher and steeper.
   (b)   higher and flatter.
   (c)   lower and steeper.
   (d)   lower and flatter.

   ANSWER: (d) Net exports are negative, so the level of expenditure on domestic goods is lower than before. Because the marginal propensity to import is a positive value, some part of any increase in income will be spent abroad, so the rise in domestic expenditures will be less—a flatter function. ∎

OBJECTIVE 3:
List the variables that influence exports and imports. Outline how the trade feedback effect and the price feedback effect operate.

American imports depend on income but also on the other factors that influence domestic demand, such as wealth of American consumers and interest rates. Both imports and exports are sensitive to the relative price of goods—we would buy more Volvos if they became cheaper. American net exports, then, depend on the relative price of American goods and services compared to foreign goods and services. Note that relative prices are affected by the exchange rate. Trade barriers also affect net exports.

   In the European Union, it has been said that Germany is the "engine of European growth." When Germany prospers, so do its trading partners; when Germany falters, the rest of Europe falters too because German income buys the goods produced by its trading partners. Some Canadians and Mexicans worried that, with the implementation of the North American Free Trade Agreement (NAFTA), the Canadian and Mexican economies would become "prisoners" of the United States. Clearly, events in one economy can have international repercussions (feedback effects).

   Two feedback effects operate in the open economy.

(a)   The *trade feedback effect*. Increased U.S. imports cause expansion in the export sectors of foreign economies. More prosperity abroad will stimulate increased imports from the United States. Similarly, increases in U.S. exports will expand the U.S. economy, causing more foreign goods to be imported and, ultimately, will result in increased prosperity overseas and at home. (page 384 [696])

   ▶▶▶   LEARNING TIP: Frequently, the media and our own intuition present trade as a "you-win-so-I-lose" situation. The trade feedback effect shows that, on a level playing field, trade benefits both participants. ◀

(b)   The *price feedback effect*. Higher import prices cause aggregate demand and/or aggregate supply to shift, causing higher prices for domestically produced goods, including exports. Accordingly, the price increase is passed on when exports occur. Changes in the price of imports cause changes in the price of exports, and vice versa. (page 384 [696])

   ▶▶▶   LEARNING TIP: Notice that a one-dollar increase in exports will cause imports to increase, but by *less* than a dollar. Although some of the export earnings will be used to buy imports, some will be used to buy domestically produced goods and some will be saved.
        To remember the price feedback effect, consider the impact of high oil prices in the 1970s. High import prices affected aggregate supply and forced U.S. companies to sell their exports at high prices. A worldwide stagflation (recession and higher prices) developed. ◀

——————————————————————————————— **Practice** ———————————————————————

12.   The trade feedback effect shows that
   (a)   an increase in economic activity in the United States results in an increase in the U.S. net exports.
   (b)   an increase in U.S. imports results in an increase in U.S. exports.
   (c)   an increase in U.S. imports reduces the imports of other countries.
   (d)   an increase in U.S. exports reduces the imports of other countries.

   ANSWER: (b) Refer to p. 384 [696] for a discussion of this effect.

13.   U.S. exports tend to increase when
   (a)   economic activity abroad is relatively low.
   (b)   U.S. prices are relatively low.
   (c)   U.S. prices are relatively high.
   (d)   U.S. inflation is relatively high.

   ANSWER: (b) When U.S. prices are relatively low, U.S. goods become more competitive overseas.

14.   The price feedback effect occurs because, when there is an increase in the prices of U.S. imported final goods and services, relative to domestic prices, households and firms will tend to substitute _____, shifting the U.S. aggregate demand curve to the _____ .
   (a)   domestically produced output for imports; right
   (b)   domestically produced output for imports; left
   (c)   imports for domestically produced output; right
   (d)   imports for domestically produced output; left

   ANSWER: (a) Higher prices for foreign goods and services will encourage U.S. buyers to demand more domestically-made output, shifting the AD curve to the right (and increasing prices). ■

OBJECTIVE 4:
Explain why the demand for foreign exchange has a negative slope and the supply of foreign exchange has a positive slope. Use the demand and supply framework to describe the determination of the exchange rate in the foreign exchange market. Explain how each determinant plays a role in the process.

In the foreign exchange market, U.S. dollars are traded for other currencies. The demand for foreign exchange is negatively sloped because as the price of a unit of foreign currency rises (costs more dollars to buy), foreign goods, services, and assets become more expensive and less attractive. The supply of foreign exchange is positively sloped because as the price of a unit of foreign currency rises (can be exchanged for more dollars), U.S. goods, services, and assets become cheaper and more attractive.

In a market-determined flexible exchange-rate system, an increase in the supply of a foreign currency or a decrease in the demand for it will cause that currency to depreciate in value and the dollar to appreciate. Demanders and suppliers of foreign currency include those who need foreign funds to import goods and services, those who wish to invest in overseas assets, and speculators. Accordingly, the major determinants of the exchange rate are relative price levels and relative interest rates. (page 386 [698])

▶▶▶   LEARNING TIP: The foreign exchange market is easier to understand if you remember that, when foreign exchange is supplied (by foreigners), it is because dollars are demanded. When foreign exchange is demanded (by U.S. residents), dollars are being supplied.

Any transaction resulting in an outflow of goods and services from the United States (exports) shows up as an increase in the supply of foreign exchange. (An increase in supply forces down the "price" of foreign exchange and increases the value of the dollar.) Any transaction that results in an inflow of goods and services (imports) shows up as an increase in the demand for foreign exchange. Example: A Japanese purchase of U.S. government bonds will increase the demand for dollars (and increase the *supply* of yen), whereas a U.S. purchase of a Japanese car will increase the *demand* for yen.

The easiest example is tourism. If the dollar strengthens relative to the Brazilian real, Americans will buy the bargain-priced reals so that they can vacation in Rio. There will be fewer tourists from Brazil, however, because dollars (and the American goods bought with them) are expensive. Note, though, that the strongest short-run influence on exchange rates comes from relative interest rates.◀

▶▶▶   LEARNING TIP: When graphing the foreign exchange market (for British pounds, for example), remember DIM SEX. Pounds are demanded (D) when we wish to buy British imports and securities—DIM. Pounds are supplied (S) when the British wish to buy our exports and securities—SEX. An increase in imports from Britain is mirrored by an increase in the demand for pounds. Add these subscripts to your demand and supply diagram for foreign exchange. An increase in imports from Britain raises the demand for pounds and raises the "price" of the pound, an appreciation. A decrease in British interest rates reduces the demand for British securities—demand for pounds decreases—and we can "export" more U.S. securities—the supply of pounds rises.

In terms of the foreign exchange market graph, a northward movement along the "price" axis is a pound appreciation *and* a dollar *depreciation*.

It is confusing and imprecise to talk of the "exchange rate" rising or falling—far better to refer to "the value of the dollar," and better still to utilize the terms *appreciating* and *depreciating*. The dollar is appreciating when its value is rising relative to another currency such as the pound (£). A pound appreciation is the same thing as a dollar depreciation.◀

■──────────────────────────────   **Practice** ──────────────────────────────

15.   A nation whose aggregate price level is rising relatively fast will see its exports become _____ attractive. Its currency will _____ .
   (a)   more; appreciate
   (b)   more; depreciate
   (c)   less; appreciate
   (d)   less; depreciate.

   ANSWER: (d)   As our price level rises, our exports become more expensive (less attractive). As the demand for a nation's exports falls, so does the demand for its currency. Refer to p. 388 [700].

16.   Swedish companies invest more intensively in the United States. This will
   (a)   increase the demand for dollars and increase the supply of euros.
   (b)   decrease the demand of dollars and increase the demand for euros.
   (c)   increase the demand for dollars and decrease the supply of euros.
   (d)   increase the supply of dollars and decrease the demand for euros.

   ANSWER: (a)   Holders of euros will place this currency on the foreign exchange market (increasing the supply of euros) to demand more dollars.

17.   The demand for dollars in the foreign exchange market is downward sloping because, when the price of a dollar (the exchange rate) decreases, _____ because they have become relatively _____ .
   (a)   Americans demand more foreign goods; less expensive
   (b)   Americans demand fewer foreign goods; more expensive
   (c)   foreigners demand more American goods; less expensive
   (d)   foreigners demand fewer American goods; more expensive

ANSWER: (c) A good that previously cost $2.00 (£1.00) becomes less expensive to a British buyer if the dollar weakens (and the pound strengthens). Each pound can buy more dollars, so the demand for American goods (and American currency) increases.

18.   A nation whose interest rate is rising relatively fast will see its securities become _____ attractive. Its currency will _____ .
(a)   more; appreciate
(b)   more; depreciate
(c)   less; appreciate
(d)   less; depreciate

ANSWER: (a) As our interest rate rises, our assets become more attractive. As the demand for our securities increases, so does the demand for our currency. ■

OBJECTIVE 5:
Explain the reasoning behind the purchasing-power-parity theory.

The law of one price (purchasing power parity) suggests that, with minimal transportation costs, similar goods in different countries should have similar prices, and that the exchange rate should reflect this. If U.S. prices rise, the exchange rate should compensate (the dollar would depreciate in value). Similarly, on assets with equally attractive features, if interest rates diverge, changes in the demand for and supply of foreign exchange should cause the exchange rate to adjust to make the assets equally attractive once more. (page 389 [701])

Comment: Just as competition in the goods market will tend to bring about purchasing power parity, competition in the financial markets will cause a similar phenomenon— interest rate parity—to arise. Interest parity suggests that the U.S. interest rate can be less than, say, the Japanese interest rate if the dollar is expected to appreciate and, therefore, compensate holders of U.S. bonds.

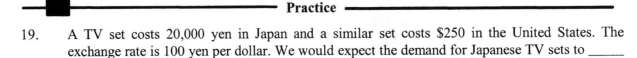

Practice

19.   A TV set costs 20,000 yen in Japan and a similar set costs $250 in the United States. The exchange rate is 100 yen per dollar. We would expect the demand for Japanese TV sets to _____ and the yen to _____ .
(a)   increase; appreciate
(b)   increase; depreciate
(c)   decrease; appreciate
(d)   decrease; depreciate

ANSWER: (a) In yen, the American TV costs 25,000 yen. It is more expensive than the Japanese set; therefore the demand for American TV sets and American currency will decrease. Looked at from the other side, in dollars, the Japanese TV set costs $200, which is cheaper than the American TV set. American buyers will demand more Japanese TV sets and more yen with which to buy them.

20.   The foreign exchange market is in equilibrium, with each British pound trading for $1.50. Now the overall U.S. price level increases. We would expect an excess demand for
(a)   pounds. The pound will appreciate.
(b)   pounds. The pound will depreciate.
(c)   dollars. The pound will appreciate.
(d)   dollars. The pound will depreciate.

ANSWER: (a) The British will wish to buy fewer American goods; Americans will demand more pounds in order to buy the relatively cheaper British goods. ■

OBJECTIVE 6:
Describe the "J-curve effect" of exchange rate movements on imports, exports, GDP, prices, and the balance of payments.

A depreciating dollar makes exports more competitive abroad (less expensive to foreigners) and imports less attractive domestically (more expensive to Americans). A depreciation should increase GDP. The balance of trade should improve but the *J-curve effect* indicates that the trade balance may worsen before it improves, if the short-term demand for imports is relatively unresponsive. In the longer term a depreciation, which makes imports more expensive and increases the demand for exports (net exports increase), will boost production and income, but it will also cause the price level to increase. (page 391 [703])

■————————————————— **Practice** —————————————————

21.   The J-curve effect suggests that a depreciation in the value of the dollar may
(a)   lead to an appreciation in the value of the dollar.
(b)   increase American imports and decrease American exports.
(c)   decrease American imports and increase American exports.
(d)   cause the balance of trade to worsen before it improves.

ANSWER: (d) Refer to p. 391 [703] for a discussion of the J-curve effect.

22.   A depreciation in the value of the dollar tends to increase the price level because
(a)   the depreciation makes imported inputs more expensive.
(b)   domestic buyers tend to demand more imports instead of domestically produced goods.
(c)   the depreciation makes imported consumer goods less expensive.
(d)   exports become less competitive in world markets, making demand decrease.

ANSWER: (a) It takes more dollars to buy the same number of barrels of imported oil, causing production costs to increase. Note that exports will increase, increasing aggregate demand.

23.   A depreciation in the value of the dollar is more likely to improve the U.S. balance of trade if the demand for U.S. exports is _____ and the U.S. demand for imports is _____ .
(a)   elastic; elastic
(b)   elastic; inelastic
(c)   inelastic; elastic
(d)   inelastic; inelastic

ANSWER: (a) If the United States reduces the price of its exports, the effect will be stronger if the demand for exports is elastic. A currency depreciation increases the price of U.S. imports—the effect will be stronger if the demand for imports is elastic (responsive). ■

OBJECTIVE 7:
Outline the effects of the exchange rate on the effectiveness of monetary and fiscal policy.

Monetary policy is strengthened but fiscal policy is weakened in an "open" economy. An expansionary monetary policy, for example, will depress the interest rate relative to that of other countries, causing the U.S. financial market to be less attractive. The dollar will depreciate. Because a falling dollar encourages exports and discourages imports, the impact of the monetary policy is stronger than in a closed economy—the expenditure multiplier is bigger. Monetary policy cannot be used with fixed exchange rates, because it would require a change in that fixed rate. The only exception is if the economy imposes capital controls that restrict the movement of currency across its borders.

In an open economy, the effectiveness of a fiscal policy is reduced unless the Fed cooperates by stabilizing the interest rate. An expansionary fiscal policy, say an increase in government spending, will increase the demand for money and the domestic interest rate and, as U.S. financial instruments become more attractive, the dollar will appreciate. Higher interest rates crowd out investment. A stronger dollar encourages imports and discourages exports—net exports are reduced. This decrease in spending power offsets the increase in expenditures on domestic production—the multiplier is smaller. (page 392 [704])

━━━■━━━━━━━━━━━━━━━━━━━━━━━ **Practice** ━━━━━━━━━━━━━━━━━━━━━━━━━

24.   In an open economy, an increase in U.S. government spending will _____ the interest rate and cause the dollar to _____ .
   (a)   increase; appreciate
   (b)   increase; depreciate
   (c)   decrease; appreciate
   (d)   decrease; depreciate

   ANSWER: (a)   Higher government spending increases transactions, the demand for money, and the interest rate. A higher U.S. interest rate draws funds from abroad, increasing the demand for dollars and leading to an appreciation.

25.   In an open economy, the effectiveness of an increase in U.S. government spending is reduced because the dollar
   (a)   appreciates, increasing net exports and increasing aggregate demand.
   (b)   appreciates, decreasing net exports and decreasing aggregate demand.
   (c)   depreciates, increasing net exports and increasing aggregate demand.
   (d)   depreciates, decreasing net exports and decreasing aggregate demand.

   ANSWER: (b)   An increase in government spending results in an appreciation in the value of the dollar. Exports are relatively more expensive and imports are less expensive in the United States.

26.   In an open economy, an increase in the U.S. money supply will _____ the interest rate and cause the dollar to _____ .
   (a)   increase; appreciate
   (b)   increase; depreciate
   (c)   decrease; appreciate
   (d)   decrease; depreciate

   ANSWER: (d)   An increased money supply will decrease the interest rate and stimulate aggregate demand. A lower U.S. interest rate will cause U.S. investors to buy foreign securities, decreasing the demand for dollars and leading to a depreciation. ■

BRAIN TEASER SOLUTION: You might think that a strong dollar must be an "improvement," but it depends on your viewpoint. Consumers will gain, because foreign goods will now be cheaper. But will anyone lose? Exporters (and their employees) will lose, because they will find it tougher to compete overseas; producers of domestic substitutes (Detroit car makers, for instance) for imported goods will also be hurt.

   Moral: An appreciation (or depreciation) has different effects on different groups in the economy. It makes sense to inquire into the special interests of any individual who is calling for an exchange rate change "in the national interest."

PRACTICE TEST

I.   MULTIPLE-CHOICE QUESTIONS

Select the option that provides the single best answer.

Use the following information to answer the next two questions. Arboc and Arbez are economies of similar sizes. Arboc's growth rate is 3% whereas Arbez is growing at a rate of 7%. The marginal propensity to import is the same positive value for both economies.

_____   1.   It is likely that Arbocali exports will _____ and that Arbocali imports will _____ .
      (a)   increase; increase
      (b)   increase; decrease
      (c)   decrease; increase
      (d)   decrease; decrease

_____   2.   *Ceteris paribus*, we would expect to see the _____ currency depreciating. The new exchange rate will _____ Arbocali consumers.
      (a)   Arbocali; hurt
      (b)   Arbocali; benefit
      (c)   Arbezani; hurt
      (d)   Arbezani; benefit

_____   3.   We have a flexible exchange rate system. It is in equilibrium and exports equal imports. Relative to Japan, the U.S. price level rises. The United States can expect to see a _____ on its balance of trade and a(n) _____ in the value of the dollar.
      (a)   surplus; depreciation
      (b)   surplus; appreciation
      (c)   deficit; appreciation
      (d)   deficit; depreciation

_____   4.   The current account includes all of the following EXCEPT
      (a)   merchandise exports.
      (b)   capital investment.
      (c)   tourism overseas by U.S. citizens.
      (d)   shipping.

_____ 5.   The balance on current account
   (a)   will be zero when merchandise exports equal merchandise imports.
   (b)   shows the direction and amount of gold flows between the nation and its trading partners.
   (c)   includes capital inflows but not capital outflows.
   (d)   equals net exports plus net investment income plus net transfer payments from abroad.

_____ 6.   Three of the following statements can be true at the same time. Which statement is the odd one out?
   (a)   Arbez has neither capital inflows nor outflows.
   (b)   The Arbezani capital account is equal to zero.
   (c)   The Arbezani current account is equal to zero.
   (d)   The current account and capital account sum to one.

_____ 7.   The multiplier in an open economy is _____ than in a closed economy because, as income level increases, _____ .
   (a)   greater; there is a wider market available
   (b)   smaller; some of the increase will be used to buy imports
   (c)   greater; exports become more attractive to foreigners
   (d)   smaller; consumers buy goods that had previously been sent abroad

_____ 8.   The United States has a trade deficit of $5 billion with Japan. To settle the debt, the United States can
   (a)   buy $5 billion worth of Japanese government securities.
   (b)   sell $5 billion worth of previously purchased private Japanese securities—e.g., those issued by Sony or Honda.
   (c)   lend $5 billion to the Japanese government.
   (d)   buy $5 billion worth of Japanese goods on credit next month.

_____ 9.   The marginal propensity to consume is 0.75 and the marginal propensity to import is 0.15. *Ceteris paribus*, the value of the multiplier is
   (a)   10.
   (b)   2.5.
   (c)   5.
   (d)   0.9.

_____ 10.   The British pound depreciates relative to the dollar. We should expect
   (a)   an increase in the number of British tourists visiting the United States.
   (b)   an increase in the U.S. demand for British goods.
   (c)   an increase in the British demand for U.S. goods.
   (d)   a decrease in the number of U.S. tourists visiting Britain.

_____ 11.   The trade feedback effect shows that an increase in U.S. _____ will result in a subsequent _____ .
   (a)   exports; depreciation in exchange rates
   (b)   imports; appreciation in the exchange rate
   (c)   income; increase in imports and increase in exports
   (d)   trade; reduction in income in the United States

_____ 12.   A one-dollar increase in export income will _____ imports by _____ than one dollar.
   (a)   increase; more.
   (b)   increase; less
   (c)   decrease; more
   (d)   decrease; less

_____ 13.   The U.S. interest rate rises relative to that of the United Kingdom. We would expect to see the demand for
   (a)   U.S. securities rising, and the dollar appreciating in value.
   (b)   U.S. securities falling, and the dollar appreciating in value.
   (c)   British securities rising, and the dollar depreciating in value.
   (d)   British securities falling, and the dollar depreciating in value.

_____ 14.   There is an increase in "foreign private assets in the United States," such as the borrowing of $10 million by Microsoft from a Swiss bank. This would show up as
   (a)   a credit on the current account.
   (b)   a debit on the current account.
   (c)   a credit on the capital account.
   (d)   a debit on the capital account.

_____ 15.   A transaction brings foreign exchange into the United States. This will be recorded as
   (a)   a debit on the balance of trade.
   (b)   a debit on the balance of payments.
   (c)   a credit on the balance of trade.
   (d)   a credit on the balance of payments.

_____ 16.   Ukraine increases its purchases of U.S. machine tools by $20 million. As a result the U.S. economy has _____ and its net exports have _____ .
   (a)   expanded; grown by $20 million
   (b)   expanded; grown by less than $20 million
   (c)   contracted; grown by $20 million
   (d)   contracted; grown by less than $20 million

_____ 17.   The _____ the marginal propensity to consume and the _____ the marginal propensity to import, the larger the multiplier.
   (a)   larger; larger
   (b)   larger; smaller
   (c)   smaller; larger
   (d)   smaller; smaller

Use the following information to answer the next three questions. The exchange rate is flexible. Assume that the two economies are similar in size. The marginal propensity to import is the same in both economies. The current equilibrium exchange rate is $1.00 = 1.25 euros (1 euro = $0.80).

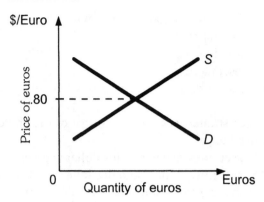

_____ 18.   If the United States grows at a rate of 2% per year and the European Union grows at 5% per year, we would expect the demand curve for euros to shift to the _____ and the supply curve for euros to shift to the _____ .
(a)   right; right
(b)   right; left
(c)   left; right
(d)   left; left

_____ 19.   If the United States grows at a rate of 2% per year and the European Union grows at 5% per year, we would expect the euro to _____ . The exchange rate would be _____ .
(a)   appreciate; $1.00 exceeds 1.25 euros
(b)   appreciate; $1.00 is less than 1.25 euros
(c)   depreciate; $1.00 exceeds 1.25 euros
(d)   depreciate; $1.00 is less than 1.25 euros

_____ 20.   If there is an increase in the interest rate on U.S. government bonds, we would expect the demand curve for euros to shift to the _____ and the supply curve for euros to shift to the

_____ .
(a)   right; right
(b)   right; left
(c)   left; right
(d)   left; left

II.   APPLICATION QUESTIONS

1.   Suppose that the price of a Big Mac is $1.50 in the United States and £1.00 in the United Kingdom (and that the United States and the United Kingdom are close neighbors with minimal transportation costs). The $/£ exchange rate is $1 = £1.
(a)   Calculate how much (in pounds) a Big Mac would cost a British tourist in the United States.
(b)   Is this more or less expensive than the price in the United Kingdom?
(c)   Calculate how much (in dollars) a Big Mac would cost an American tourist in the United Kingdom.
(d)   Is this more or less expensive than the price in the United States?
(e)   Assuming that Big Mac prices reflect overall price levels, what will happen to the demand for pounds (to buy British goods)? What will happen to the demand for dollars to buy American goods? When the demand for a commodity increases, what happens to its price?
(f)   Which currency will appreciate in value?

Suppose the $/£ exchange rate moves to $2 = £1. (Confirm that this is a dollar depreciation!)

- (g)   Calculate how much (in dollars) a Big Mac would cost an American tourist in the United Kingdom.
- (h)   Is this more or less expensive than the price in the United States?
- (i)   Calculate how much (in pounds) a Big Mac would cost a British tourist in the United States.
- (j)   Is this more or less expensive than the price in the United Kingdom?
- (k)   If British Big Macs are more expensive than American Big Macs, what should happen to the demand for pounds (to buy British goods)? What should happen to the demand for dollars to buy American goods?
- (l)   Which currency will appreciate in value?
- (m)   Somewhere between $1 = £1 and $2 = £1 an equilibrium exchange rate will occur. Where does purchasing power parity suggests that it will be?

2. (a)   "An expansionary monetary policy by the Fed will cause the dollar to appreciate against other currencies." Is this true or false? Explain.

-    (b)   "Short-term interest rates fall in European Union. The dollar should appreciate against the euro." Is this true or false? Explain.

3. The domestic price of Arbocali cloth is 4 opeks per yard. The domestic price of Arbezani leather is 12 bandu per hide. Arboc sells cloth to Arbez; Arbez sells hides to Arboc. The exchange rate is 2 opeks per bandu. The exchange rate is flexible.

-    (a)   Ignoring transportation and other such costs, calculate the price in Arbez of a yard of imported Arbocali cloth.
-    (b)   Calculate the price in Arboc of an imported Arbez hide.
-    (c)   Calculate the number of units of the domestic currency per unit of foreign currency from the Arbocali perspective.
-    (d)   Now the exchange rate changes to 4 opeks per bandu. For Arboc, does the exchange rate change represent an appreciation or a depreciation?

4. The exchange rate between Regit and Noil is 4 Regitani sponduliks per Noilian bonga.

-    (a)   A bottle of Regitani sherry sells at home for 50 sponduliks. Calculate its price in Noil.
-    (b)   A bottle of Noilian honey wine sells at home for 20 bonga. Calculate its price in Regit.
-    (c)   Find the price of a bottle of honey wine relative to a bottle of sherry in Regit.

Suppose that costs rise in the Noilian honey wine industry. The domestic price of honey wine rises from 20 bonga to 25 bonga. The exchange rate remains at 4 Regitani sponduliks per Noilian bonga.

-    (d)   Calculate the Regitani price of imported honey wine.
-    (e)   Find the relative price of wine to sherry in Regit.
-    (f)   Is honey wine now relatively more or less expensive in Regit?
-    (g)   Predict what will happen to Regitani imports and exports.
-    (h)   What will happen to the trade balance for Noil?
-    (i)   What will happen to Regit's aggregate demand curve?

5.   In each of the following cases, should the Arbezanis expect an appreciation or a depreciation in the value of their currency (the bandu)?

(a)   Because of financial uncertainty at home, Arbezani citizens find it more attractive to buy stock in the neighboring economy of Arboc.

(b)   Arbezani income levels increase.

(c)   The Arbezani central bank, ArbeFed, increases the money supply.

6.   Suppose the economy is described by the following model.

$$C = 30 + 0.8Y_d$$
$$I = 50$$
$$G = 100$$
$$EX = 60$$
$$IM = 0.3Y_d$$
$$T = 80$$
$$Y_d = Y - T$$

(a)   Calculate the equilibrium level of income (where $Y = C + I + G + EX - IM$).

(b)   Calculate the value of expenditure multiplier.

(c)   Calculate the value of imports.

(d)   The current account balance is a _____ (surplus/deficit) of _____ .

(e)   The government has a _____ (surplus/deficit) of _____ .

Suppose that government spending is increased by 25.

(f)   What will happen to the equilibrium income level?

(g)   What will happen to imports?

(h)   *Ceteris paribus*, what effect will this import change have on (1) the current account and (2) the capital account?

Suppose imports are fixed at their new level (through the use of quotas). Now the government increases spending again, by 25.

(i)   What will happen to the equilibrium income level?

Go back to the original economy (no quotas, G is at 100).

(j)   If exports were to increase by 36, indicate the effect this will have on:

(i)   income level _____

(ii)   imports _____

(iii)   the current account deficit _____

(k)   Given the original current account deficit, how much would exports have to rise to achieve balance on the current account? _____

(l)   Suppose a tariff is placed on imports, causing them to fall from their original level to 60. Indicate effect this will have on:

(i)   income level _____

(ii)   imports _____

(iii)   the current account deficit _____

(m)   To remove the original current account deficit, by how much would imports have to be reduced initially? _____

(n)   Explain this result.

7.   Two goods, U.S. blue jeans and Mexican tequila, are traded between the United States and Mexico: the exchange rate is 20¢ = 1 peso (exchange rate 1).

    (a)   If the exchange rate moves to exchange rate 2, $1.00 = 10 pesos (10¢ = 1 peso), with which rate is the dollar stronger?

    (b)   In their home countries, blue jeans sell at $10 a pair and tequila sells at 40 pesos a bottle. Calculate the price of tequila, in dollars, at the two exchange rates.
Exchange rate 1 _____ Exchange rate 2 _____

    (c)   At which exchange rate will Mexican tequila be more attractive to U.S. consumers?

    (d)   As the exchange rate moves from $1.00 = 5 pesos (20¢ = 1 peso) to $1.00 = 10 pesos (10¢ = 1 peso), what will happen to the quantity demanded of pesos?

    (e)   Show this demand curve on a graph, with vertical axis as "dollars/peso" and horizontal axis as "quantity of pesos."

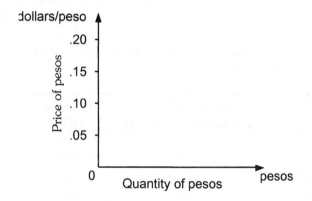

    (f)   Calculate the price of blue jeans, in pesos, at the two exchange rates.
Exchange rate 1 _____ Exchange rate 2 _____

    (g)   At which exchange rate will U.S. blue jeans be more attractive to Mexican consumers?

    (h)   As the exchange rate moves from $1.00 = 5 pesos (20¢ = 1 peso) to $1.00 = 10 pesos (10¢ = 1 peso), what will happen to the quantity supplied of pesos?

    (i)   Show this supply curve on the graph.

    (j)   Assume that the diagram is a fair representation of the demand and supply of pesos for purchases of exports and imports. If the exchange rate were fixed at $1.00 = 5 pesos (20¢ = 1 peso), would Mexico have a current account surplus or deficit?

    (k)   What can you say about the balance on capital account?

    (l)   *Ceteris paribus*, will Mexico have net capital inflows or capital outflows?

8.   Indicate whether each of the following transactions should be included in the current account or the capital account. Indicate whether it is a credit (+) or a debit (−).

	Account	+ / −	Transaction
(a)	____	____	U.S. citizens buy stock in Sony Corporation.
(b)	____	____	Sony Corporation sells an mp3 player to a U.S. audiophile.
(c)	____	____	Joe, who works in Japan, sends some money home to his mother in Tennessee.
(d)	____	____	A U.S. insurance company sells a policy to a Japanese resident.
(e)	____	____	Joe's mother goes to visit him in Japan for six months.
(f)	____	____	A drug dealer smuggles some cocaine into Florida.
(g)	____	____	A Japanese purchases some U.S. Treasury bills.
(h)	____	____	A Saudi oil sheik buys a chunk of California real estate.
(i)	____	____	Ford sells a consignment of cars to the Japanese.

9.   Use the following table to answer the questions. Government spending, investment, and exports do not change as output level changes.

GDP (Y)	Domestic Aggregate Expenditure (C + I + G)	Exports (EX)	Imports (IM)	Total Aggregate Expenditure
5,000	5,500	400	300	_____
6,000	6,400	400	400	_____
7,000	7,300	400	500	_____
8,000	8,200	400	600	_____
9,000	9,100	400	700	_____
10,000	10,000	400	800	_____

(a)   Calculate the marginal propensity to consume _____ and the marginal propensity to import _____ .

(b)   Calculate the expenditure multiplier.

(c)   Complete the table.

(d)   The equilibrium income level is _____ .

10.   When the dollar is relatively weak foreign companies, such as Volkswagen, become more keen to establish plants inside the United States. Can you explain why this makes sense?

11.   In 2008, after the dollar had lost over 30% of its value relative to the euro, effects were being felt in the National Basketball Association. Several players, such as Josh Childress, had left the league, or were threatening to leave, to go and play in Europe for salaries designated in euros. Suppose a basketball contract lasts for five years. What were these players expecting to happen to the value of the dollar?

12.   You are living in Europe and, over several months, are auctioning some of your large collection of Bazooka Joe bubble gum wrappers on an online auction such as eBay. Suppose that all potential buyers of such desirable and classic 1950s ephemera live in the United States but, because you live in Europe, you must designate your auction in euros (not dollars). With the euro appreciating relative to the dollar, what will happen to the proceeds from your auctions as time goes by?

PRACTICE TEST SOLUTIONS

I.   Solutions to Multiple-Choice Questions

1.   (a)   Because Arbez is growing, it will increase its imports from Arboc. Similarly, because Arboc is growing, it will import more.

2.   (d)   Because Arboc and Arbez are about the same size, Arbezani imports are growing more quickly than its exports. This imbalance will make the Arbezani currency depreciate or, at least, not appreciate as rapidly. As the Arbezani currency loses its value, the Arbocali currency increases in value. Arbocali consumers will benefit from the greater purchasing power of their currency overseas.

3.   (d)   If U.S. prices increase, exports will decrease and imports will increase because foreign goods are relatively cheaper. The balance of trade will slip into a deficit, and the dollar will decrease in value.

4.   (b)   Capital investment is included in the capital account. Refer to p. 380 [692].

5.   (d)   The balance on current account looks at merchandise exports and imports (Option (a)) but other items too. Capital inflows and outflows are reflected in the capital account (Option (c)).

6.   (d)   The current account and the capital account must sum to zero.

7.   (b)   The multiplier is smaller. Refer to p. 393 [705].

8.   (b)   If an economy spends more than it takes in, it must sell off some assets to make up the difference.

9.   (b)   Multiplier = $1/[1 - (MPC - MPM)] = 1/[1 - (0.75 - 0.15)] = 2.5$. Refer to p. 393 [705] for a discussion of the formula.

10.   (b)   A depreciation of the pound is the equivalent of an appreciation of the dollar. Because the dollar can now buy more pounds, British goods become cheaper to U.S. buyers.

11.   (c)   As U.S. economic activity increases, the positive marginal propensity to import will cause greater U.S. imports. The economic activity of exporting countries will be stimulated and, as a consequence, their imports of U.S. goods will increase.

12.   (b)   An increase in exports will cause an increase in economic activity. Given a positive marginal propensity to import, imports will increase.

13.   (a)   U.S. securities are offering a higher reward, relative to British securities. The demand for U.S. securities, and the dollars to buy them, will increase. As the demand for pounds decreases and the supply of pounds (to buy dollars) increases, the pound will depreciate and the dollar will appreciate.

14.   (c)   An increase in "foreign private assets in the United States" means that foreigners have purchased U.S. assets. This requires that foreign exchange flow into the United States.

15.   (d)   If foreign currency flows in, the transaction is a credit. If the transaction involved is an export, it is recorded on the balance of trade. However, the transaction could be the sale of a government security, which would be recorded on the capital account. In either case, however, the credit would show up on the balance of payments.

16.   (b)   The increase in exports increases net exports by $20 million, and increases U.S. output. As output increases, imports increase and net exports are reduced.

17.   (b)   The multiplier formula is $1/[1 - (MPC - MPM)]$. The greater the proportion of income being consumed rather than saved or lost overseas, the larger the multiplier.

18.   (a)   Both economies are growing, so the imports of both economies will increase.

19.   (c)   In Question 18, the demand curve and the supply curve both shifted right. Assuming that the economies are similar in size, the increase in European Union exports (demand for euros) will be less than the increase in European Union imports (supply of euros). A depreciating euro will now be worth less than $0.80.

20.   (c)   More European investors will wish to buy U.S. securities and will supply more euros to buy dollars. Fewer U.S. investors will wish to buy European securities and will demand fewer euros.

II.   *Solutions to Application Questions*

1.   (a) $1.50 × £1 = £1.50
      (b)   It is more expensive. A Big Mac in Britain costs £1.00.
      (c)   £1.00 × $1 = $1.00
      (d)   It is less expensive.
      (e)   The demand for pounds will increase. The demand for dollars will decrease. When the demand for a commodity increases, its price increases.
      (f)   The pound will appreciate.
      (g)   £1.00 × $2 = $2.00
      (h)   more. A Big Mac in the United States costs $1.50.
      (i) $1.50 × £0.50 = £0.75
      (j)   This is less expensive than in the United States.
      (k)   The demand for pounds will decrease. The demand for dollars will increase.
      (l)   The dollar will appreciate.
      (m) $1.50 = £1

2.   (a)   False. You can use a number of methods to prove the statement false. The purchasing-power-parity theory would explain the depreciation by noting that more units of U.S. currency have been printed. Similarly, a monetarist would note that an increased money supply increases U.S. prices, making each dollar worth less. Alternatively, an increased money supply will decrease the domestic interest rate, making foreign currency (needed to buy foreign securities) more demanded.

(b)   True. If interest rates fall in the European Union, investment in Europe will be less attractive. The demand for euros will decrease and, as Europeans seek to invest in other economies, the supply of euros will increase. These changes will cause the euro to decrease in value (depreciate) and the value of the dollar to increase in value (appreciate).

3. (a)   A yard of imported Arbocali cloth will cost 2 bandu in Arbez.
    (b)   An imported Arbezani hide will cost 24 opeks in Arboc.
    (c)   In Arboc, the number of units of the domestic currency per unit of foreign currency is 2 opeks per bandu.
    (d)   Arboc has experienced a depreciation and Arbez has experienced an appreciation.

4. (a)   Regitani sherry sells for 12.5 (50/4) bonga in Noil.
    (b)   Noilian honey wine sells for 80 (20 × 4) sponduliks in Regit.
    (c)   The price of a bottle of honey wine relative to a bottle of sherry in Regit is 1.6 (80/50).
    (d)   With the new costs in Noil, honey wine will cost 100 sponduliks in Regit.
    (e)   The price of a bottle of wine relative to a bottle of sherry in Regit is 2.0 (100/50).
    (f)   Noilian wine is now relatively more expensive in Regit.
    (g)   Regitani imports of wine will decrease because they are relatively more expensive whereas sherry exports to Noil will increase.
    (h)   The Noilian trade balance will worsen: Noil will see its exports become less competitive, and (relatively) cheaper imports will enter the country in greater numbers.
    (i)   Regit's aggregate demand curve will shift to the right as its exports increase and its imports decrease.

5. (a)   The bandu will depreciate as the demand for foreign currency increases and the supply of bandu increases.
    (b)   The bandu will depreciate. Arbezanis, wishing to buy more imports, will increase the supply of bandu.
    (c)   The bandu will depreciate. An increase in the money supply will depress domestic interest rates. Lower interest rates will lead to a lower demand for bandu by foreign investors and an increased supply of bandu by domestic investors who wish to seek higher interest rates abroad.

6. (a)   In equilibrium,

$$
\begin{aligned}
Y &= C + I + G + EX - IM \\
  &= 30 + 0.8Y_d + 50 + 100 + 60 - 0.3Y_d \\
  &= 240 + 0.8(Y - T) - 0.3(Y - T) \\
  &= 240 + 0.5Y - 0.5T \qquad T = 80 \\
  &= 200 + 0.5Y \\
Y &= 400
\end{aligned}
$$

    (b)   Multiplier $= 1/[1 - (MPC - MPM)] = 1/[1 - (0.8 - 0.3)] = 2.00$
    (c) $IM = 60 - 0.3(Y - T) = 0.3(400 - 80) = 96$
    (d) $EX - IM = 60 - 96 =$ deficit of 36. We have no information about net investment income or transfer payments.
    (e) $G - T = 100 - 80 =$ deficit of 20
    (f)   Income will increase by 50 because the multiplier is 2.00.
    (g)   Imports will increase by 15, from 96 to 111. $IM = 0.3(450 - 80) = 111$.

(h)   The current account ($EX - IM$) deficit will increase by 15. The capital account surplus will decrease by 15. Recall that the two accounts must balance.

(i)   The marginal propensity to import is zero (because of the quotas). The multiplier will be 5.00. Income will increase by 125.

(j)   (i)   Income will increase by $36 \times 2 = 72$.
       (ii)   Imports will increase by $0.3 \times 72 = 21.6$.
       (iii) The current account ($EX - IM$) deficit will fall by 14.4 to 21.6.

(k)   Exports would have to rise by 90.

(l)   (i)   Income would rise by 72 to 472.
       (ii)   Imports would fall by 14.4 ($-36 + 21.6$) to 81.6.
       (iii) The current account would have a deficit of 21.6 ($60 - 81.6$).

(m)   90

(n)   An initial fall in imports of 90 will make aggregate expenditure rise by an initial 90. The multiplier effect will cause income to expand by 180. As a result, imports will increase by 54. Net effect on imports: they fall by 36.

7.   (a)   Exchange rate 2. $1.00 = 10$ pesos ($10¢ = 1$ peso) shows a dollar appreciation

      (b)   Exchange rate 1: $8, that is $40 \times 20¢$
             Exchange rate 2: $4, that is $40 \times 10¢$

      (c)   Exchange rate 2 ($10¢ = 1$ peso)

      (d)   Quantity demanded will increase because Americans will wish to buy more of the (cheaper) Mexican tequila.

      (e)   Refer to the following diagram.

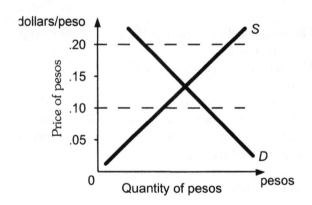

      (f)   Exchange rate 1: 50 pesos, i.e., 10×5 pesos. If $20¢ = 1$ peso, 5 pesos = $1
             Exchange rate 2: 100 pesos, i.e., 10×10 pesos. If $10¢ = 1$ peso, 10 pesos = $1

      (g)   Exchange rate 1 ($20¢ = 1$ peso)

      (h)   Quantity supplied will decrease because the Mexicans will be less keen on U.S. purchases. (It's assumed that Mexican demand for blue jeans is fairly responsive to price changes.)

      (i)   Refer to the preceding diagram.

      (j)   It depends on how you have drawn the diagram—i.e., where the curves intersect. As shown above, Mexico would have a deficit on its current account because Mexican exports are less than Mexican imports—the peso is overvalued.

      (k)   The balance on capital account will be showing a surplus equal in size to the current account deficit.

      (l)   Mexico will have a net capital outflow.

8.   Refer to the following table.

	Account	+ / –	Transaction
(a)	capital	debit	U.S. purchase of foreign assets
(b)	current	debit	import of merchandise
(c)	current	credit	private transfer
(d)	current	credit	export of a service
(e)	current	debit	tourism
(f)	capital	debit	statistical discrepancy
(g)	capital	credit	foreign purchase of U.S. assets
(h)	capital	credit	foreign purchase of U.S. assets
(i)	current	credit	export of merchandise

9.   (a) $MPC = \Delta C/\Delta Y = 900/1{,}000 = 0.9$. $MPM = \Delta IM/\Delta Y = 100/1{,}000 = 0.1$.
      (b)   Multiplier $= 1/[1 - (MPC - MPM)] = 1/[1 - (0.9 - 0.1)] = 5.00$.

GDP (Y)	Domestic Aggregate Expenditure $(C + I + G)$	Exports (EX)	Imports (IM)	Total Aggregate Expenditure
5,000	5,500	400	300	5,600
6,000	6,400	400	400	6,400
7,000	7,300	400	500	7,200
8,000	8,200	400	600	8,000
9,000	9,100	400	700	8,800
10,000	10,000	400	800	9,600

      (d)   8,000. Equilibrium occurs where $Y = C + I + G + EX - IM$.

10.   With the euro strong and the dollar weak, foreign workers (paid in euros) become relatively more expensive, as do other resources. Relatively, the costs of production decrease if cars are produced and sold in the United States. Note, too, that, by setting up plants in the United States, foreign car companies can avoid tariffs, appeals to patriotism, and rising prices as the dollar weakens.

11.   Some of the departing players were Europeans so, if they intended to stay in Europe after their playing days were over, it could make sense for them to have contracts denominated in euros—there was less exchange-rate risk. For American players, however, the issue was more complex. If they intended to relocate to the United States after their years playing in Europe, they were assuming that, at that time, the euro would still have retained its value relative to the dollar. If, relative to the dollar, the euro had lost value then, on conversion, the players would lose. At the time of writing (August 2008), 1 euro is worth $1.55. Was their gamble justified?

12.   Your proceeds will decrease. If an American bidder is willing to offer $10 (10 euros when the exchange rate is $1 = 1 euro), he will still be willing to offer only $10 when the exchange rate is $2 = 1 euro. From your point of view, the bid has decreased from 10 euros to 5 euros.

21 [36]

Economic Growth in Developing and Transitional Economies

Chapter objectives:

1. Describe the relationship between economic development and economic growth. Distinguish among conditions in the so-called First, Second, Third, and Fourth World countries.
2. List the factors that influence economic development. Explain why capital infrastructure is important for economic development.
3. Describe three trade-offs affecting strategies for economic development.
4. Distinguish between economic growth and economic development.
5. Outline the problems caused by rapid population growth and policies that have been instituted to deal with them.
6. Summarize the economic measures taken by former planned economies to transform themselves into viable market-based economies.

BRAIN TEASER: During the Soviet era, almost all agricultural land was collectively owned. However, peasants were permitted to own small plots that amounted to about 1% of the total acreage under cultivation. Economist Milton Friedman pointed out that this small portion of land was responsible for about 33% of the total value of agricultural production in the Soviet Union. Can you explain thisituation?

OBJECTIVE 1:
Describe the relationship between economic development and economic growth. Distinguish among conditions in the so-called First, Second, Third, and Fourth World countries.

In the past, the nations of the world have been roughly divided into three groups: the First World (Western, industrialized), the Second World (ex-Socialist, whose future is now uncertain), and the Third World (poor, largely agricultural). Nowadays, though, it is less clear cut. There is more mobility—China and India are almost in a class by themselves while others, such as Argentina and Korea, are breaking away from the Third World category and are being termed "newly industrialized countries." A number of nations are lagging so far behind that they have been called the "Fourth World" group. The main characteristic of a Third World country is that the great majority of its inhabitants are poor. Other dimensions that distinguish the "haves" from the "have nots" are: health care, educational facilities, and the percentage of the population engaged in agriculture. (page 401 [713])

> **Comment:** There's no single unambiguous term that distinguishes the "developing nations" as the textbook deals with them. After all, in one sense, the United States is a developing economy too. "Third World" tends to have some political undertones. Remember that these nations are a pretty varied group, including South American, Asian, and African countries as diverse as Mexico and Mali, Taiwan, and Togo. Don't allow yourself to overgeneralize!

Practice

1.   The poorest of the developing nations are sometimes known as the
    (a)   First World.
    (b)   Second World.
    (c)   Third World.
    (d)   Fourth World.

ANSWER: (d) Refer to p. 402 [714].

2.   Most of the Fourth World nations are to be found in
    (a)   Latin America.
    (b)   sub-Saharan Africa.
    (c)   Southeast Asia.
    (d)   the former republics of the Soviet Union and its satellites.

ANSWER: (b) Most of the very poorest nations are found to the south of the Sahara desert in Africa.

3.   Per capita Gross Domestic Income (GDI) is _____ in developed countries, and infant mortality is _____ than in other countries.
    (a)   higher; higher
    (b)   higher; lower
    (c)   lower; higher
    (d)   lower; lower

ANSWER: (b) Refer to Table 21.1 (36.1) in the textbook for this information. ∎

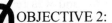

OBJECTIVE 2:
List the factors that influence economic development. Explain why capital infrastructure is important for economic development.

No single theory has emerged to explain the development process, but various factors have been identified as potential constraints on development. These include a low rate of accumulation of physical capital, a lack of human capital, a lack of social overhead capital (infrastructure), and a lack of entrepreneurial ability. These factors limit productivity and economic growth. Also, a lack of basic infrastructure (access to water, electricity, health services, and education facilities, for instance) can diminish the quality of life. (page 403 [715])

> ▶▶▶   LEARNING TIP: Pay attention to what is happening in your own state and locality. Many of the sources and strategies discussed in this chapter are not limited to poor foreign regions. Debates on economic development are also frequent at the state and local government level. ◀

——————————————————————— **Practice** ———————————————————————

4.   The brain drain refers to
       (a)   the movement of talented personnel from a developing country to a developed country.
       (b)   the absence of skilled entrepreneurs in the developing countries.
       (c)   declining literacy rates.
       (d)   the loss of human capital through the ravages of malnutrition.

       ANSWER: (a) Refer to p. 405 [717] for the definition.

5.   Each of the following has been advanced as a plausible constraint on development EXCEPT
       (a)   the quantity of available capital.
       (b)   the quantity of available labor.
       (c)   the quantity of infrastructure.
       (d)   the quantity of entrepreneurial ability.

       ANSWER: (b) The typical developing country has adequate numbers of workers, although
                    specific skills may be limited.

6.   Capital shortages are a typical problem for developing countries. Each of the following is a
       plausible cause of capital shortages EXCEPT
       (a)   lack of incentives leading to low saving rates.
       (b)   the inherent riskiness of investment in a developing nation.
       (c)   government policies, such as price ceilings and appropriation of private property.
       (d)   widespread poverty resulting in little surplus after consumption needs are met.

       ANSWER: (d) The vicious-circle-of-poverty hypothesis fails to account for the success of
                    previously poor nations like Japan. Refer to p. 404 [716]. ∎

OBJECTIVE 3:
Describe three trade-offs affecting strategies for economic development.

Many, often conflicting, development strategies have been attempted over the years.

(a)   Agriculture or industrialization? Development used to be equated with industrialization; many
       Third World nations sought to move away from agriculture and toward industrial production.
       However, merely trying to replicate the structure of the developed nations does not guarantee
       development. Opinion now favors a balanced growth in both agricultural and industrial sectors—
       "walking on two legs."
(b)   Export promotion or import substitution? Import substitution calls for the encouragement of
       homegrown substitutes for imported goods. This strategy has failed in almost every case; it
       results in high-cost production protected by trade barriers. Export promotion calls for producing
       goods for the export market and has seen some measure of success, although it depends on the
       willingness of the developed nations to import Third World production.
(c)   Central planning or free enterprise? The economy must choose the appropriate balance between
       free enterprise and central planning. Planning permits coordination of economic activities that
       private individuals or firms might not undertake (disease and pest control, or literacy training, for
       instance) and the channeling of funds into efficient projects, but may be difficult for a Third
       World nation to administer. (page 407 [719])

Following the Second World War, the initial emphasis was largely on rapid growth. The 1970s, however, saw increasing concern about how the benefits of growth were (or were not) being distributed. Despite growth, poverty persisted for a large percentage of those living in the developing countries, and aid was often tied to programs to satisfy basic needs. More recently, income redistribution has lost its prominence to market efficiency. One recent innovation is microfinance, where borrowers receive small loans with no collateral required. Such funding of emerging businesses is impractical for large financial institutions but community-based financing has had considerable success.

--- **Practice** ---

7. Experience suggests that, of the following, the development approach most likely to succeed is
   (a) rapid industrial mechanization coupled with labor migration to the industrial centers.
   (b) intensive training of human capital to occupy technologically advanced positions in import-substitution industries.
   (c) a balanced promotion of both the agricultural sector and the manufacturing sector.
   (d) slow, careful industrial growth combined with rapid expansion in food provision to improve human capital.

   ANSWER: (c) This is the "walking on two legs" strategy. Refer to p. 408 [720].

8. Noil is a small sub-Saharan nation with few sophisticated resources. However, it constructs an airport and hotel with lavish Western facilities and offers safari trips into its beautiful mountain ranges to groups from the developed countries. Noil is best described as having opted for a(n) _____ development strategy.
   (a) import substitution
   (b) export promotion
   (c) rural exploitation
   (d) balanced growth

   ANSWER: (b) Tourism is an export.

9. Generally, import substitution policies have
   (a) failed in almost every case.
   (b) succeeded, but only while the cost of imported oil was held down.
   (c) not been an unqualified success, but have had a better track record than export promotion policies.
   (d) succeeded in Latin America, but failed in Africa and had mixed results in Asia.

   ANSWER: (a) Import substitution policies reduce exports and foster inefficient, inappropriate (i.e., capital-intensive) production methods. ∎

ECONOMICS IN PRACTICE: On page 406 [718], the textbook looks at the extent of corruption and how it might retard economic development. Government agencies and red tape may impede entrepreneurs. Consider the potential problems involved in getting permission to open a small business given the presence of corrupt officials. What options might you explore and what might be the effects on the optimal allocation of resources?

ANSWER: In one study, researchers in Peru, paying bribes only when essential, reportedly took the best part of a year to open a small factory. In such a situation, entrepreneurs may give up, pay bribes or, perhaps, choose to operate as part of the "underground economy," i.e., businesses that are not officially recognized. In the first case, the result is a less efficient allocation of resources. If bribes are paid, there is a redistribution of income. If the business goes underground, the state may lose tax revenues, health and safety regulations may be ignored, and workers may be exploited. Finally, when corruption is present, international funds that are intended for development projects may be siphoned off for private gain rather than public benefit.

OBJECTIVE 4:
Distinguish between economic growth and economic development.

Economic growth and economic development should be treated as separate processes. Economic growth, as measured by higher levels of per capita income, may be taking place while indicators of economic development, such as nutrition, health, and education, may not be changing. Growth may occur without development. Whereas the World Bank had initially emphasized policies that would eliminate poverty, by the 1990s the focus had reversed to stress "structural adjustment" programs that stimulated growth. (page 410 [722])

Despite differences, China and India are good examples of rapid economic development accomplished by differing strategies. China's growth has been led by the manufacturing sector while India's is driven by a flourishing service sector. Both economies, however, share an emphasis on adopting free market economics.

ECONOMICS IN PRACTICE: On page 411 [723], the textbook examines how an innovation—cell phones—has improved the efficiency of fish markets in India, increasing profits, and reducing waste. The cell phones improved information about market conditions and allowed a better matching-up of buyers and sellers. Internet sales operate on a similar principle—reducing transactions costs through the application of a new technology. Your textbook refers to another example of the same principle— microfinancing, on pages 409-410 [721-722]. Review that material and confirm that a similar process— reducing the cost of information—is present and that growth possibilities are being enhanced by its application.

ANSWER: Peer lending solves many of the problems associated with conventional financing in developing countries. Most projects are too small to justify the expense of information collecting. By simplifying the loan process and by incentivizing the community's collection of information about creditworthiness (who gets loans first), funds are allocated more efficiently. This innovation, like the use of cell phones by the fishermen, reduces waste and fosters a more climate that permits development opportunities to be exploited.

━━━━■━━━━━━━━━━━━━━━━━━━━━━ **Practice** ━━━━━━━━━━━━━━━━━━━━━━━

10.   Structural adjustment programs could include each of the following EXCEPT
    (a)   reduction of public sector deficits.
    (b)   control of inflation.
    (c)   increases in the size of the public sector through nationalization initiatives.
    (d)   the encouragement of private saving and investment through tax reform. ■

    ANSWER: (c) Refer to p. 410 [722] for more on this issue.

OBJECTIVE 5:
Outline the problems caused by rapid population growth and policies that have been instituted to deal with them.

The Third World death rate has tumbled sharply because of better medical treatment, but the birthrate has declined much more slowly. Although large families may provide a cheap labor pool today and support in old age tomorrow, rapid expansion in the population places burdens on public services and may be undesirable from the viewpoint of society. In some nations, economic incentives have been applied successfully to encourage smaller families. (page 412 [724])

──────■────────────────── **Practice** ──────────────────────

11.   Birthrate minus death rate equals the
       (a)   fertility rate.
       (b)   mortality rate.
       (c)   natural rate of population increase.
       (d)   development rate.
       ANSWER: (c) Refer to p. 413 [725].

12.   Malthus predicted that the world population would grow at a(n) _____ growth rate, and the production of food would increase more _____ .
       (a)   increasing; rapidly
       (b)   increasing; slowly
       (c)   constant; rapidly
       (d)   constant; slowly
       ANSWER: (d) Refer to p. 412 [724]. Note that a constant rate of growth means rapid absolute growth in the population—10% of 100 is only 10; 10% of 10,000 is 1,000.

13.   High fertility rates may cause all of the following EXCEPT
       (a)   falling saving rates.
       (b)   reduced availability of social programs for each individual.
       (c)   labor shortages.
       (d)   food shortages.
       ANSWER: (c) As the population expands, there should be no labor constraint. ■

✓ OBJECTIVE 6:
Summarize the economic measures taken by former planned economies to transform themselves into viable market-based economies.

Beginning in the 1990s, the centrally economies of the former Soviet bloc began moves towards liberalization of markets. There were increased incentives, and the removal of price controls, with countries moving at different rates. There has been much debate whether the reform requirements should be introduced rapidly by "shock therapy" or phased in gradually. In fact, in the Russian case, due to the crippled state of the state-owned enterprises, shock therapy was not a feasible option, even if it had been the preferred alternative. Poland's shock therapy, on the other hand, was a success. China, India, and Vietnam are notable additions to the list of economies seeking to inject more competition into their economic practices. (page 414 [726])

Six requirements for a successful transition from a planned economy to a market-based one have been identified:

1.   Macroeconomic stabilization
2.   Deregulation of prices and trade liberalization
3.   Privatization of the means of production
4.   The establishment of a "support system" for the market
5.   A social safety net to lessen the distress of unemployment and poverty
6.   External assistance

Comment: The economic reforms within the former Soviet republics, China, India and other states are ongoing. You should be able to flesh out the material in this chapter by keeping your ears and eyes open to the news reports. Have the economic reforms been identical in each country? How much success/resistance are they experiencing? From the mid-1990s, Cuba began shifting position on economic matters, and more so in the past few years. The Vietnamese (and Vietnamese businesspersons in the United States) argued successfully for the relaxation of U.S.-imposed commercial barriers. Both of these economies are well worth watching.

Tragedy of Commons: Property owned communally, such as the bison, the dodo, or the grasslands of sub-Saharan Africa, is usually rapidly depleted. Taking the example of common grazing land, there is little incentive for the individual farmer to conserve pasture, and indeed the opposite may be true. Self-interest dictates that one would make the most of the "free" resources, although such thinking by each farmer would lead to a depletion of resources. At this point you might note the old saying that "Good fences make good neighbors." Capitalism, then, relies on the emergence of self-interest and the rewards of private property because the former without the latter would result in the tragedy of commons.

─────────────────────────── **Practice** ───────────────────────────

14.   Each of the following is seen as a requirement for a successful transition from socialism to a market-based economy EXCEPT
    (a)   price regulation.
    (b)   provision of a commercial infrastructure—i.e., market-supporting institutions.
    (c)   removal of trade barriers.
    (d)   a freely operating labor market.
    ANSWER: (a) To ration scarce resources efficiently, prices should be free to adjust.

15.   The notion that collective ownership of resources may be inefficient because individuals do not bear the full cost of their own decisions is called
    (a)   exploitation.
    (b)   the tragedy of commons.
    (c)   surplus value.
    (d)   the externality effect.
    ANSWER: (b) Refer to p. 416 [728] for a discussion of this topic.

16.   Each of the following is an example of the tragedy of commons EXCEPT
    (a)   pollution in the Great Lakes.
    (b)   overgrazing of shared tribal land.
    (c)   the decimation of the American bison by nineteenth-century settlers.
    (d)   the slaughtering of his entire herd by a Texan rancher.
    ANSWER: (d) The herd is private property. ■

BRAIN TEASER SOLUTION: Peasants had more incentive to work their own plots intensively—anything they produced, they could keep or sell. On the collective land, there were far fewer incentives for the individual to work hard because output was owned by the state. In addition, peasants often "borrowed" state resources to help them with their private plots. Furthermore, peasants were motivated to produce desirable produce that they could trade.

PRACTICE TEST

I.   MULTIPLE-CHOICE QUESTIONS

Select the option that provides the single best answer.

_____ 1.   Which of the following are characteristics of the average developing country?
    (a)   Large populations and high savings rates
    (b)   Low levels of human capital and low per capita GDP
    (c)   High infant mortality and high pollution indexes
    (d)   Low health standards and high literacy rates

_____ 2.   Import substitution occurs when a country
    (a)   becomes developed.
    (b)   erects trade barriers.
    (c)   no longer has sufficient foreign exchange to buy imports.
    (d)   strives to produce goods that were previously imported.

_____ 3.   Economic development occurs when there is an increase in the
    (a)   per capita nominal GDP.
    (b)   per capita real GDP.
    (c)   material well-being of the nation's citizens.
    (d)   labor force.

_____ 4.   Lack of economic development might be caused by
    (a)   a low marginal propensity to consume.
    (b)   an excess supply of private overhead capital.
    (c)   a high literacy rate.
    (d)   inadequate amounts of social overhead capital.

_____ 5.   Which of the following is an example of an improvement in social overhead capital?
    (a)   A multinational corporation opens a new plant.
    (b)   The workers at the local textile mill establish a credit union.
    (c)   There is an increase in the rate of growth of per capita real GDP.
    (d)   A national adult literacy program is established by the government.

_____ 6.   Labor is relatively abundant in Arboc. Arboc might best be able to develop by
     (a)   using production techniques that are capital-intensive.
     (b)   using production techniques that employ labor and capital in fixed and equal proportions.
     (c)   specializing in the production of labor-intensive commodities that should therefore be relatively cheaper to produce.
     (d)   specializing in the production of capital-intensive commodities, which should therefore be marketable at relatively higher prices.

_____ 7.   Local firms in Arboc are unlikely to undertake large investment projects such as highway construction because
     (a)   the government is unlikely to share the cost.
     (b)   interest rates are higher for the borrowed funds necessary for such projects.
     (c)   the "free-rider" problem will result in a low (or zero) rate of return.
     (d)   international agencies such as the World Bank and the IMF prefer short-term projects.

_____ 8.   Adopting the strategy of "walking on two legs" means that
     (a)   men and women should be treated equally in the workplace.
     (b)   import substitution and export promotion should be attempted simultaneously.
     (c)   attention must be paid to developing both the industrial sector and the agricultural sector.
     (d)   the dependent links with old colonial nations should be severed.

_____ 9.   Import substitution might fail to promote economic development if
     (a)   producers use domestic inputs that are lower in cost than imported inputs.
     (b)   firms make use of capital-intensive production methods that fail to reduce unemployment.
     (c)   such goods require labor-intensive methods of production.
     (d)   after establishment, these industries are subsidized by the state.

_____ 10. The "export promotion" strategy calls for
     (a)   the running of a balance of trade deficit.
     (b)   the production of goods that are demanded by consumers in the developed countries.
     (c)   the production of export goods for domestic consumers.
     (d)   the domestic production of goods that previously had been imported.

_____ 11. Sending savings from the Third World nation of Arboc to the United States _____ to growth in Arboc's physical capital. New Arbocali import controls will tend to _____ investment in Arboc.
     (a)   leads; increase
     (b)   leads; decrease
     (c)   does not lead; increase
     (d)   does not lead; decrease

_____ 12.   Deregulating prices is likely to cause _____ ; removing subsidies will cause _____ in the short term.
(a)   higher prices for staple items; unemployment
(b)   higher prices for staple items; increased employment
(c)   lower prices for staple items; unemployment
(d)   lower prices for staple items; increased employment

_____ 13.   China's recent economic growth has been led by the _____ sector; India's has been led by the _____ sector.
(a)   export; manufacturing
(b)   manufacturing; service
(c)   service; manufacturing
(d)   export; export

_____ 14.   In Arboc, the state provides goods such as education, national defense, universal health care, and roads. Other industries, which are privately owned, face government regulations on pollution and worker safety. Minimum wage legislation is present and wage earners are taxed on their income. Arboc is best described as
(a)   socialist.
(b)   communist.
(c)   capitalist.
(d)   totalitarian.

_____ 15.   "Shock therapy" refers to
(a)   the sudden change experienced by the Soviet Union following Gorbachev's economic reforms.
(b)   the overthrow of the Soviet Union's economic system.
(c)   Stalin's goal of electrification of collective farms.
(d)   rapid deregulation of prices, liberalization of trade, and privatization.

_____ 16.   _____ Poland, China has favored a _____ approach to development.
(a)   Like; rapid
(b)   Like; gradual
(c)   Unlike; rapid
(d)   Unlike; gradual

_____ 17.   All of the following discourage Third World development EXCEPT
(a)   the lack of skilled entrepreneurs.
(b)   insufficient social overhead capital.
(c)   insufficient labor-saving technological innovation.
(d)   inadequate amounts of human capital.

_____ 18.   _____ is a development strategy that is designed to encourage sales abroad.
(a)   Import substitution
(b)   Export promotion
(c)   "Walking on two legs"
(d)   Dependency

_____ 19. Rapid population growth rates may cause all of the following EXCEPT
   (a)   an eventual increase in the proportion of working-age adults in the population.
   (b)   an increase in the number of dependents.
   (c)   decreases in the rate of capital formation.
   (d)   decreases in saving rates.

_____ 20. The "tragedy of commons" exemplifies the problem of _____ in the case of resources that are owned _____ .
   (a)   inefficiency; privately
   (b)   inequity; privately
   (c)   inefficiency; publicly
   (d)   inequity; publicly

II.   APPLICATION QUESTIONS

1.   Compare and contrast the economic conditions in the "First World" and the Third World. Take a "typical" country from each group, for example, France and Peru. Examine such issues as life expectancy, number of doctors per thousand persons, educational level, rate of inflation, unemployment, and so forth. (A good source is the *World Development Report*, published annually by the World Bank—it will be in your library.   The Bank's website is at www.worldbank.org.) Compare the figures for an NIC (newly industrialized country), such as Taiwan or Korea with those of a sub-Saharan African nation. Is there really such a thing as a "typical" Third World nation?

2.   Suppose that 10 units of food are required per person per year in the developing nation of Arboc. Due to improved crops and farming techniques, food production will increase by a fixed amount every 10 years—suppose this amount is 1,000 units of food so that, in 2010, food production will be 11,000 units. Arboc currently exports its surplus food production. Imports run at a constant 2,000 units. Because of high birth rates and decreasing death rates, Arboc's population increases by 50% every 10 years.
   (a)   Given the conditions specified, complete the following table.

Year	Food Production	Population	Food Requirements	Food Surplus/Deficit
2000	10,000	400	4,000	+6,000
2010	11,000	_____	_____	_____
2020	_____	_____	_____	_____
2030	_____	_____	_____	_____
2040	_____	_____	_____	_____

   (b)   What happens in or about the year 2030?
   (c)   Other things unchanged, what will happen to Arboc's balance of trade?
   (d)   Given the situation in 2040, what do you think will happen to Arboc?

3.   Choose any developing country for comparison against the United States. Profile your country by doing research into the following characteristics. You can do this by reading, for example, the World Bank's most recent annual *World Development Indicators* or by visiting its website www.worldbank.org.

The characteristics you collect will require numbers. The numbers in parentheses are the values for the United States from the 2007 Report.

(a)	Life expectancy at birth	_____	(77.4 years)
(b)	Adult illiteracy rate	_____	(1%)
(c)	Population with access to safe water (%)	_____	(100%)
(d)	GNI per capita	_____	($41,400)
(e)	Agriculture as percentage of output	_____	(2%)
(f)	Infant mortality rate (per 1,000 live births)	_____	(6.43)
(g)	Percentage of population living on less than $1 per day	_____	(0%)

4.   List the following countries from most market-based to least market-based: Russia, United States, France, Cuba, Japan, China.

5.   Underline the correct answer found in parenthesis.

Russia's economic reform package included:
(a)   price controls: (increased/decreased/removed)
(b)   market-supporting institutions: (increased/decreased/ removed)
(c)   ownership of resources: more (centralized/privatized)
(d)   external aid: (increased/decreased/removed)
(e)   job security: (increased/decreased/removed)
(f)   trade: (restricted/liberalized)
(g)   money supply growth: (increased/curtailed)

6.   Why do birth rates tend to decrease as economies develop?

PRACTICE TEST SOLUTIONS

I.   *Solutions to Multiple-Choice Questions*

1.   (b)   Refer to p. 402 [714] for a full discussion of the characteristics of developing nations.

2.   (d)   Import substitution is a strategy that attempts to establish a domestic industry that can provide goods to replace imports. Refer to p. 408 [720].

3.   (c)   Improvements in per capita GDP do not guarantee development.

4.   (d)   To grow, an economy needs an adequate quantity and quality of resources, including socially provided resources.

5.   (d)   Social overhead capital includes projects that cannot be undertaken privately.

6.   (c)   This is an application of the Heckscher-Ohlin theorem from Chapter 19 (34).

7.   (c)   Unless a toll is charged, use of this public good will be free.

8.   (c)   The Chinese phrase "walking on two legs" describes the need to have both agricultural and industrial sectors developing together.

9.   (b)   To be effective, the strategy must play to the strengths of its own economy—typically labor-intensive production.

10.   (b)   Refer to p. 408 [720] for a discussion of this development strategy.

11.   (d)   Refer to the discussion of capital flight on p. 404 [716].

12.   (a)   Staple items were underpriced; inefficient firms will be driven out of business without subsidies.

13.   (b)   Manufacturing has been most important in China whereas the service sector has fueled India's expansion.

14.   (c)   With the exception of the health care, Arboc is quite like the United States.

15.   (d)   Refer to p. 418 [730].

16.   (d)   China's approach to development (*moshi guohe*) has been gradual whereas Poland successfully employed "shock therapy."

17.   (c)   The quantity of labor is not a significant constraint in the Third World. Labor-saving technology, then, is not critical to successful development.

18.   (b)   Refer to p. 408 [720] for a discussion of this development strategy.

19.   (a)   As more children are born, even as the population ages, the proportion of adults will decrease.

20.   (c)   "Commons" are commonly owned land. Typically, this resource is treated inefficiently.

II.   *Solutions to Application Questions*

1.   Although there is no single model for a developing nation, certain common characteristics emerge—high birthrates, improving life expectancy, improvements in literacy rates, better/more nutrition and shelter, and so on.

2.   (a)   Refer to the following table.

Year	Food Production	Population	Food Requirements	Food Surplus/Deficit
2000	10,000	400	4,000	+6,000
2010	11,000	600	6,000	+5,000
2020	12,000	900	9,000	+3,000
2030	13,000	1,350	13,500	−500
2040	14,000	2,025	20,250	−6,250

        (b)   Food requirements outstrip food production.

(c)   As the food surplus decreases, less will be available for export and the balance of trade will become less favorable. Somewhere around 2028, the trade surplus in food will become a deficit.

(d)   This is an open question. Arboc will be heavily in debt and will need to import food to feed its population. Imports of industrial goods would slacken. Reduced health care (per person) might cause famine and disease, reducing the population. Arboc might borrow to finance its overseas spending and might have to receive ongoing foreign aid. Population control policies would have to be considered or individuals might emigrate.

3.   Answers will depend on the country chosen.

4.   There can be some dispute here—systems evolve and emphases change—but a plausible ranking would be: Japan, United States, France, Russia, China, Cuba.

5.   removed; increased; privatized; increased; decreased; liberalized; curtailed

6.   Birth rates may decrease for several reasons in the face of economic development. Development usually involves a movement away from agriculture, where large families provide a valuable labor force. With the growth of government agencies, there is diminished need for an extended family to provide support. With women entering the labor force, the opportunity cost of child-bearing increases.

Comprehensive Review Test

The following questions provide a wide-ranging review of the material covered in Part V (VII)—Chapters 19–21 (34–36) of the textbook. Each question deals with a topic or technique important for your understanding of economic principles. If you miss a question you should return to the relevant section of the chapter in the textbook and fine-tune your understanding.

I.   MULTIPLE-CHOICE QUESTIONS

Select the option that provides the single best answer.

_____ 1.   A tariff imposed on imported French wine will cause the U.S. price of French wine to _____ and U.S. production of wine to _____.
(a)   increase; increase
(b)   increase; decrease
(c)   decrease; increase
(d)   decrease; decrease

_____ 2.   Trade barriers _____ welfare. Trade barriers _____ domestic employment in industries that lack a comparative advantage.
(a)   increase; increase
(b)   increase; decrease
(c)   decrease; increase
(d)   decrease; decrease

_____ 3.   A U.S. tariff imposed on goods that can be produced more cheaply overseas would tend to
(a)   benefit American consumers by making these goods cheaper.
(b)   make the goods more expensive in other (overseas) markets.
(c)   equalize the costs of production between U.S. producers and foreign producers.
(d)   make U.S. producers artificially more competitive relative to foreigners.

Refer to the following table to answer the next nine questions.

	England	**Portugal**
Wine	9 bottles	6 bottles
Cloth	18 yards	9 yards

_____ 4.   England has an absolute advantage in the production of
   (a)   cloth.
   (b)   wine.
   (c)   both goods.
   (d)   neither good.

_____ 5.   The opportunity cost of one bottle of wine in Portugal is
   (a)   2/3 of a yard of cloth.
   (b)   1 1/3 yards of cloth.
   (c)   1 1/2 yards of cloth.
   (d)   9 yards of cloth.

_____ 6.   England and Portugal decide to specialize according to the law of comparative advantage and trade with one another. We would expect that the terms of trade will be somewhere between
   (a)   1 bottle of wine for 1 yard of cloth and 1/2 of a bottle of wine for 1 yard of cloth.
   (b)   2/3 of a bottle of wine for 1 yard of cloth and 1 1/2 bottles of wine for 1 yard of cloth.
   (c)   1/2 of a bottle of wine for 1 yard of cloth and 1 1/2 bottles of wine for 1 yard of cloth.
   (d)   1/2 of a bottle of wine for 1 yard of cloth and 2/3 of a bottle of wine for 1 yard of cloth.

_____ 7.   Which of the following statements is true?
   (a)   England has a comparative advantage in the production of wine; Portugal has a comparative advantage in the production of cloth.
   (b)   England has a comparative advantage in the production of cloth; Portugal has a comparative advantage in the production of wine.
   (c)   England has a comparative advantage in both goods.
   (d)   Portugal has a comparative advantage in both goods.

_____ 8.   Suppose the terms of trade are that 1 bottle of wine trades for 1 yard of cloth. England should specialize in _____ production; Portugal should specialize in _____ production.
   (a)   cloth; cloth
   (b)   cloth; wine
   (c)   wine; cloth
   (d)   wine; wine

_____ 9. Suppose the terms of trade are that 1 bottle of wine trades for 13/4 yard of cloth. England should specialize in _____ production; Portugal should specialize in _____ production.
   (a)   cloth; cloth
   (b)   cloth; wine
   (c)   wine; cloth
   (d)   wine; wine

_____ 10. According to the theory of comparative advantage trade between the two countries
   (a)   will equalize their consumption levels.
   (b)   will benefit all industries in each country.
   (c)   will permit each partner to use its resources in the most efficient way.
   (d)   will permit each partner to achieve a consumption mix at some point on its production possibility frontier.

_____ 11. In terms of production possibility frontiers, if England's maximum production of cloth is 1,800 yards, its maximum production of wine is _____ bottles. If Portugal's maximum production of wine is 1,200 bottles, its maximum production of cloth is _____ yards.
   (a)   0; 0
   (b)   900; 900
   (c)   900; 1,800
   (d)   1,800; 900

_____ 12. Based on the information in the previous question, we should now conclude that
   (a)   England has an absolute advantage in the production of both goods.
   (b)   England has an absolute advantage in the production of cloth only.
   (c)   Portugal has an absolute advantage in the production of wine.
   (d)   England has an absolute advantage in the production of neither good.

_____ 13. The United States and the United Kingdom both produce cashmere sweaters and leather vests. In the United States, sweaters sell for $150 and vests sell for $150. In the United Kingdom, sweaters sell for £60 and vests sell for £100. Suppose the pound/dollar exchange rate is £1 = $2.
   (a)   The United States will import both sweaters and vests from the United Kingdom.
   (b)   The United States will import sweaters from the United Kingdom; the United Kingdom will import vests from the United States.
   (c)   The United States will import sweaters from the United Kingdom; the United Kingdom will import sweaters from the United States.
   (d)   The United Kingdom will import both sweaters and vest from the United States.

_____ 14. The small Asian nation of Regit chooses to follow an import substitution strategy and builds a fertilizer plant to serve its rice farmers. Based on similar experiments elsewhere, we would expect to see all of the following EXCEPT
   (a)   high fertilizer production costs.
   (b)   the imposition of tariffs to protect domestic fertilizer production.
   (c)   capital-intensive fertilizer production techniques.
   (d)   a rise in the international competitiveness of the nation's rice farmers.

_____ 15.   Each of the following is a tactic typical of the export promotion strategy EXCEPT
(a)   reducing the value of the domestic currency relative to other currencies.
(b)   increasing the nation's ability to compete domestically with the exports of other nations.
(c)   the provision of subsidies to exporters.
(d)   the provision of preferential investment tax breaks to exporting firms.

_____ 16.   Each of the following is a basic requirement for a successful transition from socialism to a market-based economy EXCEPT
(a)   a social safety net to deal with unemployment and poverty.
(b)   free and fair democratic elections.
(c)   deregulation of prices and liberalization of trade.
(d)   macroeconomic stabilization.

_____ 17.   Capitalism and socialism are distinguished primarily by
(a)   the ownership of labor.
(b)   the number of political parties.
(c)   the ownership of capital.
(d)   the distribution of income throughout society.

_____ 18.   The Russian transition to a market economy required all of the following EXCEPT
(a)   deregulation of prices.
(b)   privatization of the means of production.
(c)   the institution of controls over wages.
(d)   the removal of trade barriers.

_____ 19.   In the early transitional phase to a free labor market and liberalization of prices we would most likely see all of the following EXCEPT
(a)   increased risk of unemployment.
(b)   increased instability in prices.
(c)   increased instability in wages.
(d)   reduced incentives to work.

_____ 20.   Each of the following is seen as a requirement for a successful transition from socialism to a market-based economy EXCEPT
(a)   macroeconomic stabilization.
(b)   privatization.
(c)   price regulation.
(d)   a freely operating labor market.

_____ 21.   In the closed economy of Arbez, the marginal propensity to consume is 0.75. Arbez opens its borders to trade and finds that its marginal propensity to import is 0.15. The Arbezani *AE* curve will become _____ and the *AD* curve will become _____ for the open economy.
(a)   steeper; steeper
(b)   steeper; flatter
(c)   flatter; steeper
(d)   flatter; flatter

_____ 22. If the dollar depreciates, we would expect all of the following EXCEPT
- (a)   a rightward shift of the aggregate demand curve.
- (b)   a leftward shift of the aggregate supply curve.
- (c)   an increase in the price level.
- (d)   a decrease in economic activity in the United States.

_____ 23. A nation whose interest rate is rising relatively fast will see its securities become _____ attractive. Its currency will _____ .
- (a)   more; appreciate
- (b)   more; depreciate
- (c)   less; appreciate
- (d)   less; depreciate

_____ 24. The current equilibrium exchange rate is $1.00 = 110 yen. If there is an increase in the interest rate on U.S. government bonds, we would expect the yen to _____ . The exchange rate would be _____ .
- (a)   appreciate; $1.00 exceeds 110 yen
- (b)   appreciate; $1.00 is less than 110 yen
- (c)   depreciate; $1.00 exceeds 110 yen
- (d)   depreciate; $1.00 is less than 110 yen

_____ 25. The supply of dollars in the foreign exchange market is upward sloping because, when the price of a dollar (the exchange rate) decreases, _____ because they have become relatively _____ .
- (a)   Americans demand more foreign goods; less expensive
- (b)   Americans demand fewer foreign goods; more expensive
- (c)   foreigners demand more American goods; less expensive
- (d)   foreigners demand fewer American goods; more expensive

II.   APPLICATION QUESTIONS

The nations of Arboc and Arbez each produce shirts (S) and potatoes (P). The production possibility frontier for Arboc is described by the equation $S = 60 - 2P$. The production possibility frontier for Arbez is described by the equation $S = 60 - 4P$.

1. Draw a production possibility frontier graph that shows all the points that are feasible for Arboc. Put "shirts" on the vertical axis and "potatoes" on the horizontal axis. Draw a separate ppf diagram for Arbez. Include the values at the end-points of the ppf in each case.

2. Arboc has a constant-cost production possibility frontier. How do you know?

3. Is the product mix of 20 shirts and 20 units of potatoes on Arboc's ppf? If not, is it a feasible output mix?

4. On the Arbocali ppf, what is the opportunity cost of each shirt?

5. On the Arbezani ppf, what is the opportunity cost of each shirt?

6. Which country has a comparative advantage in the production of shirts? Which country has a comparative advantage in the production of potatoes?

7. If the terms of trade were one unit of potatoes traded for one shirt, what would be the pattern of trade?

8. If the terms of trade were one unit of potatoes traded for three shirts, what would be the pattern of trade?

9. Now assume Arboc becomes more efficient and can double its output of both shirts and potatoes. Which good(s) should Arboc now produce and trade? Explain your answer.

10. Explain what will happen to the opportunity cost of shirts in Arbez if a new high-yielding hybrid potato is introduced into Arbez.

REVIEW TEST SOLUTIONS

I.   *Solutions to Multiple-Choice Questions*

1. (a) The tax will push up the price of the import. This will increase the demand for substitutes.

2. (c) Refer to pages 366-368 [678-680] for the statement of the case for free trade.

3. (d) Typically, tariffs are for the protection of producers, not for the benefit of consumers. A tariff doesn't increase costs of production, as such, for a foreign producer, but rather the costs of marketing the good.

4. (c) England can produce absolutely more cloth and more wine per worker than Portugal can.

5. (c) Six bottles take the inputs that could have produced 9 yards of cloth, therefore 1 bottle costs 1 1/2 yard of cloth.

6. (d) The English opportunity cost of 1 bottle of wine is 2 yards of cloth. Portugal's opportunity cost of 1 bottle of wine is 1 1/2 yards of cloth.

7. (b) The English opportunity cost of 1 bottle of wine is 2 yards of cloth. Portugal's opportunity cost of 1 bottle of wine is 1 1/2 yards of cloth.

8. (a) The English opportunity cost of 1 bottle of wine is 2 yards of cloth—it doesn't pay to produce wine. Similarly for Portugal, because 1 bottle of wine costs 1 1/2 yards of cloth.

9. (b) The English opportunity cost of 1 bottle of wine is 2 yards of cloth—it pays to produce cloth and trade it for wine. For Portugal, because 1 bottle of wine costs 1 1/2 yards of cloth, it pays to produce wine and trade it for cloth.

10. (c) Each country will able to consume a combination of goods beyond its production possibility frontier and use its resources in the least costly (more efficient) manner.

11. (c) England can produce twice as many units of cloth as units of wine. Portugal can produce 3 units of cloth for every 2 units of wine.

12. (a) The maximum production levels for cloth are equal, and wine production is greater in Portugal, but those considerations do not get to the heart of absolute advantage. England uses fewer resources per yard of cloth and per bottle of wine—just as we concluded in Question 4.

13. (b) In Britain, imported sweaters cost $120 and vests cost $200—sweaters are cheaper in Britain; vests are cheaper in the United States.

14. (d) High-cost fertilizer will reduce the ability of the rice farmers to compete with foreign rice.

15. (b) This is typical of import substitution.

16. (b) Free and fair democratic elections (a political issue) are not part of the list of basic requirements.

17. (c) In a capitalist system, ownership of the means of production (capital and land) is in the hands of capitalists and in the hands of the state under a communist system.

18. (c) For the market economy to function correctly, both wages and prices must be free to adjust.

19. (d) The move from a planned economy to a market economy involves risk.

20. (c) To achieve efficiency, prices must be permitted to adjust to changes in demand and supply.

21. (d) With foreign substitutes available, the quantity of domestic goods demanded will decrease as the aggregate price level increases.

22. (d) If aggregate demand increases and aggregate supply decreases, the price level will increase, but the effect on the output level is ambiguous. Generally, the demand shift is stronger, in fact.

23. (a) As our interest rate rises, our assets become more attractive. As the demand for U.S. securities increases, so does the demand for dollars.

24. (c) As demand decreases and supply increases for the Japanese currency, its "price" will decrease—a depreciation. An appreciating dollar will now be worth more than 110 yen..

25. (b) A British good that previously cost £1.00 ($2.00) becomes less expensive to an American buyer if the dollar strengthens (and the pound weakens). Each dollar can buy more pounds, so the demand for British goods and currency increases, as does the supply of American currency.

II.   Solutions to Application Questions

1.   See the following diagram.

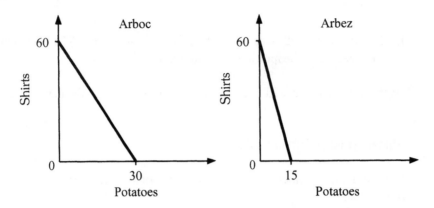

2.   Arboc's production possibility frontier graphs as a straight line—the trade-off is constant as resources are switched between goods.

3.   The product mix of 20 shirts and 20 units of potatoes is feasible. If 20 shirts are produced (using one-third of Arboc's resources), the other two-thirds can be employed producing potatoes.

4.   In Arboc, each shirt costs 1/2 of a unit of potatoes.

5.   In Arbez, each shirt costs 1/4 of a unit of potatoes.

6.   Arbez has a comparative advantage in the production of shirts whereas Arboc country has a comparative advantage in the production of potatoes.

7.   If the terms of trade were one unit of potatoes traded for one shirt, both countries would wish to produce and trade shirts.

8.   If the terms of trade were one unit of potatoes traded for three shirts, Arboc would gain by producing potatoes and Arbez would gain by specializing in shirt production.

9.   The opportunity cost of shirts and potatoes has not changed in Arboc, therefore Arbez retains its comparative advantage in the production of shirts.

10.   The opportunity cost of shirts will increase, possibly to the point that the comparative advantage will switch over from shirt production to potato production.